W9-BZW-846

DELIVERING CARRIER ETHERNET

EXTENDING ETHERNET BEYOND THE LAN

Abdul Kasim

Prasanna Adhikari
Nan Chen
Norman Finn
Nasir Ghani
Marek Hajduczenia
Paul Havala
Giles Heron
Michael Howard
Luca Martini
Mannix O'Connor
Matt Squire
William Szeto
Greg White

New York   Chicago   San Francisco
Lisbon   London   Madrid   Mexico City
Milan   New Delhi   San Juan   Seoul
Singapore   Sydney   Toronto

The McGraw·Hill Companies

Cataloging-in-Publication Data is on file with the Library of Congress

McGraw-Hill books are available at special quantity discounts to use as premiums and sales promotions, or for use in corporate training programs. For more information, please write to the Director of Special Sales, Professional Publishing, McGraw-Hill, Two Penn Plaza, New York, NY 10121-2298. Or contact your local bookstore.

Delivering Carrier Ethernet: Extending Ethernet Beyond the LAN

Copyright © 2008 by The McGraw-Hill Companies. All rights reserved. Printed in the United States of America. Except as permitted under the Copyright Act of 1976, no part of this publication may be reproduced or distributed in any form or by any means, or stored in a database or retrieval system, without the prior written permission of publisher, with the exception that the program listings may be entered, stored, and executed in a computer system, but they may not be reproduced for publication.

1234567890   DOC DOC   01987

ISBN: 978-0-07-148747-4
MHID: 0-07-148747-6

Sponsoring Editor Jane K. Brownlow	**Copy Editor** LeeAnn Pickrell	**Illustration** International Typesetting and Composition
Editorial Supervisor Jody McKenzie	**Proofreader** Ragini Pandey (International Typesetting and Composition)	**Art Director, Cover** Jeff Weeks
Project Manager Sam RC (International Typesetting and Composition)	**Indexer** Valerie Perry	**Cover Designer** Brian Boucher
Acquisitions Coordinator Jennifer Housh	**Production Supervisor** James Kussow	**Cover Designer** 12E Design
Technical Editor Paul Amsden	**Composition** International Typesetting and Composition	

Information has been obtained by McGraw-Hill from sources believed to be reliable. However, because of the possibility of human or mechanical error by our sources, McGraw-Hill, or others, McGraw-Hill does not guarantee the accuracy, adequacy, or completeness of any information and is not responsible for any errors or omissions or the results obtained from the use of such information.

About the Author

Abdul Kasim is the Vice President for Ethernet Business Development at ADVA Optical Networking, a global provider of Optical and Ethernet solutions for metropolitan networks. Mr. Kasim has over 16 years of experience in the US telecommunications industry. In his current position, he is responsible for developing and executing the business development strategy for an Ethernet access portfolio. Previously, he worked in several roles at Sprint, in areas spanning from product planning and service architecture to software development and equipment engineering. Most substantially, he led the engineering and implementation of some of the nation's earliest and largest SONET and WDM deployments. Mr. Kasim holds a Bachelor of Engineering degree in Computer Science and Engineering frm the University College of Engineering, Bangalore University, India; a Masters degree in Computer Science from Kansas State University. He also holds a Masters degree in the Management of Technology from the Massachusetts Institute of Technology (MIT). He has also undertaken graduate study at the University of Kansas and Harvard University. He is a member of the Hybrid Optical Packet Infrastructure (HOPI) corporate advisory board that supports the development of new technologies for Internet2, the next-generation Internet.

About the Contributing Authors

Prasanna Adhikari was most recently the Vice President of Networking at ClearMesh Networks. Mr. Adhikari has been involved in wireless optical technology since 1994 when he joined AstroTerra Corporation to participate in the development of satellite-to-ground laser-based communication systems. Later, as Director of Advanced Technology at Optical Access (MRV Communications), he developed technologies including a Gigabit Ethernet free-space optics product. At ClearMesh, he has been responsible for developing mesh networking technologies. He holds a BS with Honors in Electrical Engineering from the California Institute of Technology.

Nan Chen is well known in the telecommunications industry worldwide for his role as Co-Founder and President of the Metro Ethernet Forum (MEF). The MEF (www .MetroEthernetForum.org), a global standards organization, was founded in 2001 with the mission to accelerate the worldwide adoption of Carrier Ethernet networks and services. As such, it became one of the major success stories of the 21st century in the new Internet age, starting in 2003 with a surge of standards that lead to the announcements of Carrier Ethernet definition and certification programs in 2005. Nan Chen's drive to combine standardization and certification with dynamic, global marketing campaigns and educational programs, helped make Carrier Ethernet the fastest growth area in telecoms.

Having helped to raise $100+ million dollars in funding, Mr. Chen has successfully driven multiple networking equipment companies becoming the industry recognized technology and market leaders. While receiving thousands of quotations in worldwide media, Mr. Chen and his companies have garnered more than 30 significant industry awards.

Mr. Chen holds two MS degrees and a BS degree. In his past life, he was a record holder in pole vault at Beijing University.

Norman Finn is a Cisco Fellow at Cisco Systems. Mr. Finn is an industry expert on L2 protocols/switching and metro Ethernet. In the IEEE, he is known for editing a number of standards, such as 802.1s Multiple Spanning Tree Protocol and 802.1ag Connectivity Fault Management, as well as for initiating work in many areas, such as 802.1ad Provider Bridges, 802.1aj Two-Port MAC Relay, 802.1ak Multiple Registration Protocol, and 802.1ae MAC Security. In the ITU, Mr. Finn contributed greatly to the development of ITU-T Y.1731 Ethernet OAM. Prior to joining the IEEE, he was an active member of the ATM Forum where he authored much of the LANE UNI specification and contributed to MPOA, LANE v2, and LANE NNI.

Mr. Finn joined Cisco in 1993. In addition to his standards activity, he invented and/or influenced many of the Catalyst switching concepts/protocols including, but not limited to, Port Aggregation Protocol (PAgP), compact GVRP, shortest path bridging, MSTP, VTP, CDP, L2/L3 forwarding interactions in EARLs, port ASIC features, VLAN mapping, spanning tree improvements, and MAC security.

Mr. Finn is a graduate of the California Institute of Technology. Throughout his engineering career, he has enjoyed singing in barbershop quartets and choruses. He is also an avid traveler.

Dr. Nasir Ghani has gained a wide range of industrial and academic experience in the telecommunications area, and in the past, he has held senior positions at Nokia, IBM, Motorola, Sorrento Networks, and Tennessee Tech University. Currently, he is an associate professor in the Department of Electrical and Computer Engineering at the University of New Mexico, where he is actively involved in a wide range of funded research projects in the area of optical networks and cyber-infrastructures. Dr. Ghani has published over 80 journal and conference papers, several book chapters, various standardization proposals, and has been granted two patents. He recently served as a co-chair for the optical networking symposia for *IEEE ICC 2006* and *IEEE GLOBECOM 2006* and is a program committee member for *OFC 2007* and *OFC 2008*. Furthermore, he has been a program committee member for numerous IEEE, SPIE, ACM, and IEC conferences and has served regularly on NSF, DOE, and other international panels. He is an associate editor of the *IEEE Communications Letters* journal and has guest-edited special issues of *IEEE Network, IEEE Communications Magazine,* and *Cluster Computing*. Dr. Ghani is a recipient of the prestigious NSF CAREER Award and is a senior member of the IEEE. He received a bachelor's degree in Computer Engineering from the University of Waterloo, Canada, in 1991; a master's degree in Electrical Engineering from McMaster University, Canada, in 1992; and a PhD in Electrical and Computer Engineering from the University of Waterloo, Canada, in 1997.

Dr. Ashwin Gumaste is currently a faculty member in the Department of Computer Science and Engineering at the Indian Institute of Technology, Bombay (2005–07). He was previously with Fujitsu Laboratories (USA), Inc., as a member of the research staff in the Photonics Networking Laboratory (2001–05). Prior to this, he worked in Fujitsu Network Communications R&D and prior to that with Cisco Systems in the Optical Networking Group (ONG). He has over 40 pending U.S. and EU patents and has published close to 60 papers in referred conferences and journals. He has authored three books on broadband networks, namely *DWDM Network Designs and Engineering Solutions* (a networking bestseller), *First-Mile Access Networks and Enabling Technologies* (Pearson Education/Cisco Press), and *Broadband Services: User Needs, Business Models and Technologies* (John Wiley). Dr. Gumaste is also an active consultant to industry and has worked with both service providers and vendors. In addition, he has served as program chair, co-chair, publicity chair, and workshop chair for various IEEE conferences and has been a technical program committee member for *IEEE ICC, IEEE Globecom, IEEE Broadnets, IEEE ICCCN, Gridnets,* among others. Dr. Gumaste is also a guest editor for *IEEE Communications Magazine* and is the general chair of the *1st International Symposium on Advanced Networks and Telecommunication Systems (ANTS 2007)* to be held in Bombay, India. He can be reached via www.ashwin.name.

Dr. Marek Hajduczenia was born in Bialystok, Poland, in 1979. He received his MSc and Engineering diplomas in Electronics and Telecommunications, with a specialization in optical transmission systems, from Technical University in Bialystok in 2003. In 2004, he was accepted for PhD studies at the University of Coimbra, Portugal, and is currently working toward his degree in the field of Ethernet Passive Optical Networks (EPONs), specifically in designing second-generation EPON systems, Dynamic Bandwidth Allocation (DBA) mechanisms and Operation and Maintenance (OAM), EPON security, and generic Ethernet networking.

He is currently working at Nokia Siemens Networks S.A., Portugal, on projects connected with PONs systems (both EPON and GPON), data security, and optical networking. His main research interests include self-similar stochastic processes, control management layer and security for optical access networks, IPv4/IPv6 transition problems, optical burst switching, and many more.

He is involved in the IEEE 802.3 projects and is currently participating in the formation of the IEEE 802.3 10 G EPON Workgroup.

Paul Havala is Director of Data Product Planning at Fujitsu Network Communications. In this position, he leads data product planning and product marketing for Fujitsu, and is responsible for Fujitsu's overall data strategy. Prior to this role, Mr. Havala was responsible for technical marketing for Fujitsu's FASST data initiative, which he helped to create. In Mr. Havala's 16 years in the telecom industry, he has served in technical marketing, business development, product planning and management, and senior technical roles at companies such as Bellcore (Telcordia), DSC (Alcatel), White Rock Networks, and Fujitsu. Mr. Havala received BSEE and MSEE degrees from Michigan State University.

Giles Heron is a senior network architect at British Telecom, working in the 21st Century Network Converged Core team. He was previously senior technology specialist at Tellabs, focusing on deploying MPLS-based backhaul networks for mobile carriers. Prior to Tellabs he was the principal network architect for PacketExchange, a start-up carrier offering Ethernet services over a pan-European MPLS backbone—and the first carrier to have deployed draft-martini Ethernet Private Lines. Before co-founding PacketExchange Heron was a member of the global network architecture team at Level(3) communications.

Heron is an active participant in the Internet Engineering Task Force (IETF) and has contributed to various RFCs and Internet drafts in the PWE3 and L2VPN working groups—including the "LDP VPLS" specification for emulating multipoint Ethernet LANs over MPLS.

Michael Howard is Principal Analyst at Infonetics, a market research company that he founded. With over 35 years of network industry experience, Mr. Howard is recognized worldwide as one of the industry's leading experts in emerging markets, service provider network market trends, and user buying patterns. After graduating from UC Berkeley with a BS in Mathematics, he worked on operating systems and programming language compilers for Arpanet, which later became the Internet. He was the IT Director at Tymshare/Tymnet in the 1970s, where he created network accounting, and in 1978, he led the First Interstate Bank project that developed the world's first pre-Internet in-home banking system. He founded several data networking research firms in the 1980s and co-founded Infonetics Research in 1990. Mr. Howard focuses on optical technologies from the service provider edge to the core, metro Ethernet, and access networks, including FTTx, DSLAMs, next gen DLCs, and cable aggregation. He chairs program committees and speaks at industry events around the world, including the Broadband World Forum in Europe and Asia, Light Reading Webinars, NetEvents, N+I, and SUPERCOMM, and is frequently quoted in trade and business publications such as *Business Week, Forbes, InformationWeek, Investor's Business Daily, Light Reading, Network World, New York Times, San Francisco Chronicle,* and *The Wall Street Journal.* He is a consultant to startups, service providers, manufacturers, and the investment community, identifying new market opportunities, providing due diligence, and advising on positioning, product development, business plans, and M&A activity.

Dr. Glen Kramer is Chief Scientist for Teknovus, Inc. He received his PhD in Computer Science at UC Davis, where he remains a research associate in the Networks Research Lab.

Dr. Kramer is a member of the IEEE Standards Association and past editor of the EPON Protocol Clause in the "Ethernet in the First Mile" standard. Author of *Ethernet Passive Optical Networks* (McGraw Hill 2005), he has done extensive research in areas of traffic management, Quality of Service, and fairness in EPON networks. Dr. Kramer is the founder of the EPON Forum and teaches EPON tutorials and workshops at conferences around the world.

Dr. Lowell Lamb is the Vice President of Marketing at Teknovus. He has more than ten years of experience in the telecommunications industry. Prior to joining Teknovus, Dr.Lamb was the Director of PON Networks for Terawave Communications, where he focused on the architectural issues associated with integrating PON systems into end-to-end networks.

Before joining Terawave, Dr. Lamb worked on optical-transport, high-bandwidth wireless, NGDLC, FITL, aDSL, vDSL, network management, and FTTP for Telesis Technologies Laboratory/SBCTechnology Resources, Inc. Earlier in his career, Dr. Lamb was Assistant Director of the Arizona Fullerene Consortium at The University of Arizona and was a staff member in the Analytical Computer Division of the Federal Reserve Bank of New York. Dr. Lamb holds a PhD in Experimental Physics and is the author of 18 publications and patents.

Luca Martini joined Cisco in October of 2003 and has since been primarily involved with L2VPN technology that evolved from his original draft-martini design. This technology, which is now an IETF standard track RFC, has been accepted as the de-facto industry standard transport for Layer 2 protocols over MPLS.

Mr. Martini is the author of the so called draft-martini documents that became RFC4447, RFC4448, RFC4619, RFC4618, which are the standard IETF documents describing the IETF pseudowire technology. He previously worked at Level3 Communications. He has been involved in the Internet Engineering Task Force (IETF) for the past four years and contributed enhancements to the RFC2547 mpls-vpn design. He is the author of the draft-martini design for transporting Layer 2 protocols over the MPLS core network. In this position, he designed, planned, and chose the next-generation technology and equipment for Level 3 Communication Network.

Mr. Martini has worked as a network consultant (Storage Technology Corporation), network engineer (Sykes Enterprises), digital design engineer (Thought Technology), computer consultant (Wayin Corporation), computer programmer (HHS Canada Trading), and computer hardware consultant (Larken Electronics). His specialties include knowledge on routing and switching technology for large scale networks, from IP, Ethernet, ATM, to SNA. Over the years, he has worked with all types of IBM/Cisco networking technology, as well as ATM switching technology. Luca Martini graduated from McGill University, Montreal, Canada, (1992) with a BA in Electrical and Computer Engineering.

Mannix O'Connor was the founding Secretary of the IEEE 802.17 Resilient Packet Ring Working Group. He was also a founding member of the Resilient Packet Ring Alliance whose mission was to educate the marketplace about the new IEEE protocol. In addition, he served as co-chair of the Technical Marketing Committee of the Metro Ethernet Forum.

His executive positions include Director of Marketing for Corrigent Systems a 10 Gbps packet transport company serving carriers with Triple Play, Carrier Ethernet and Multiservice applications. Prior to that, he was a founding member of Lantern Communications, a company designing 10 Gbps RPR equipment for carrier network applications. C-Cor purchased Lantern in 2003 for $20m.

Mr. O'Connor held positions at MRV Communications (NASDAQ:MRVC) including, VP of Product Marketing where he created the Fiber Driver line of managed Ethernet access devices for public networks and also developed some of the first commercially available Ethernet switches sold under OEM agreement to Intel, Fujitsu, DEC, Ungermann Bass and others. At MRV, he served as VP of Sales for the Americas where he managed teams that sold Ethernet transport equipment to UUNet, SNET and Bell South among others. Prior to MRV he was Channel Sales Director for Synoptics and it successor company Bay Networks which was acquired by Nortel.

Mr. O'Connor also produces training, sales, promotional, investor and marketing videos for networking companies. Examples of his work are available at the leading telecommunications networking site, OpticalKeyhole.com. In addition, he contributed to and edited portions of the book series Guerrilla Selling, Guerrilla Marketing, Guerrilla Teleselling, etc., published by Houghton Miffllin.

He has spoken at Supercomm, ComNet, N&I, Comdex Argentina, Congreso Internacional de Telefonía IP Mexico, Convergence India and other networking and telecommunications conferences around the world. When not writing, speaking or promoting and selling networking equipment you will find him playing music in the SF bay area with his original music group, the Brunos Band. Mr. O'Connor holds an MBA in International Finance from George Washington University in Washington, DC.

Dr. Matt Squire is Chief Technology Officer for Hatteras Networks, a North Carolina startup focused on leveraging the existing copper infrastructure for new Ethernet service opportunities. Hatteras Networks is leading the Ethernet evolution of the access network—from ATM and TDM to Ethernet and IP.

During his career, Dr. Squire has proven to be a technical innovator. A recognized expert on Ethernet, switching, MPLS, IP, ATM, and voice, he already holds more than 15 patents with more than 10 in the pipeline. He has held leadership positions at a number of data telecommunications firms, including IBM, Bay Networks, Nortel Networks, and Extreme Networks. Dr. Squire focuses on product and network architectures, leveraging the simplicity and scalability of next-generation packet infrastructures.

Dr. Squire has also served in leadership roles in a number of standards committees. He serves on the board of directors of the Metro Ethernet Forum and has chaired the OAM sub-taskforce in the IEEE 802.3ah Ethernet in the First Mile working group. He also chaired the LAN Emulation and MPOA work at the ATM Forum, the pre-cursors to VPLS and MPLS. Additionally, he has performed editorial roles in the Metro Ethernet Forum and ANSI T1, serving to advance new standards in OAM and copper-based Ethernet access.

William Szeto is Founder, Chief Technology Officer of Ceterus Networks. He was Founder, President, and CEO of Ceterus until December 2003. Before founding Ceterus Networks, Mr. Szeto was Founder, President, and CEO of Iris Labs. From January 2000 to May 2000, he was an Entrepreneur In Residence (EIR) with Mayfield Fund, focusing on the review and development of opportunities in telecommunications technology and services. Mr. Szeto is a 28-year veteran of Sprint, where he was a senior manager focusing on the company's optical networking direction. He was instrumental in the development and implementation of Sprint's DWDM system and was responsible for the development of the technology needed to interface IP routers directly over wavelengths. He was Chief Technology Officer for Monterey Networks and Principal Technologist for the Core Optical Transport Business Unit for Cisco Systems. He was also a member of the board of directors for the Optical Internetworking Forum (OIF). Mr. Szeto holds a BSEE and an MBA from The Ohio State University and is a registered professional engineer in the state of Ohio and Kansas.

Greg White is Lead Architect for Broadband Access at CableLabs, currently working on the development of communication protocols for the DOCSIS and CableHome family of cable modem and residential gateway specifications. He has been with CableLabs since 1999 and has been directly involved in leading a number of specification development initiatives, including DOCSIS 1.1, DOCSIS 2.0, DSG, M-CMTS, and DOCSIS 3.0. Previously, he was with Motorola Labs in Schaumburg, Illinois, where he worked on forward error-correction, error concealment algorithms, and MAC protocols for 2.5G and 3G digital cellular systems.

He received a BS degree in Electrical Engineering from Carnegie Mellon University, Pittsburgh, Pennsylvania, in 1992, and an MS degree in Electrical Engineering from the University of Wisconsin-Madison, Madison, Wisconsin, in 1994. He has published several papers and holds two U.S. patents.

About the Technical Editor

Paul Amsden is an independent consultant with over 30 years experience in the networking and telecommunications industry. He has worked in the roles of architect and system engineer at Metrobility Optical Systems, Cabletron, and Digital Equipment. He has been involved in the hardware/software design and development of products based on Ethernet, ATM, SONET, and T1 using switching and routing technology. His most recent products have been Carrier Ethernet–compliant customer demarcation devices that incorporate Ethernet switching technology and his patent pending technology. He has been involved in standards development as part of the IEEE, MEF, IETF, and ATM Forum, and most recently has been involved with 802.1ad, 802.1ag, 802.1ah, and 802.1aj. He holds a Bachelor of Science Degree in Mathematics from Plymouth State University.

I dedicate this book to my family – for making life so meaningful.

– Abdul

Contents

Part I Background

Chapter 1   Ethernet: From LAN to the WAN   3
by Abdul Kasim

Chapter 2   Carrier Ethernet   45
by Abdul Kasim

Chapter 3   The Ethernet Market Opportunity 105

by Michael Howard

Part II   Solutions

Chapter 4   The Solution Framework 123

by Abdul Kasim

Chapter 5   Copper 131

by Dr. Matt Squire

Chapter 6   Hybrid Fiber-Coax 147

by Greg White

Chapter 9   Optical Wireless Mesh Networks 235

by Prasanna Adhikari

Chapter 10   TDM: Circuit Bonding 265

by William Szeto

by Giles Heron and Luca Martini

Chapter 15   WiMAX 469

by Prasanna Adhikari

Part III   A Look into the Future

Acknowledgments

When I originally conceived the idea of this book in the fall of 2005, several people encouraged and convinced me that this was a useful and a doable endeavor; but for this it would have never progressed. I am especially grateful to Dr. Bob Metcalfe for so graciously—and promptly—offering to write the foreword. That he, the inventor of Ethernet, thought it worthwhile despite his hectic schedule and probably numerous such requests definitely propelled this effort. I am also thankful to Manu Kaycee for his support, especially during the initial stages of this undertaking.

I am enormously grateful to each of my co-authors for sharing my vision and more importantly, for transforming it into reality. It took considerable effort, often at the cost of pressing personal and other professional obligations, to contribute to this book. To use a borrowed phrase, this book was possible because I stood on the shoulders of the giants in our industry.

Jane Brownlow, my editor at McGraw Hill patiently guided me through the process of this, my first publishing venture. I thank her and Jennifer Housh, the acquisitions coordinator, for making it all much simpler—and decidedly more pleasant—than it probably is. I am also very thankful to Paul Amsden, the external technical editor, for so diligently and cheerfully reviewing the material. Sam RC, the project manager, was a pleasure to work with as well.

I appreciate the support, encouragement and feedback that I received throughout the process, most notably from Shailesh Shukla at Juniper Networks, who has been a mentor and a great friend for the last 16 years, Stan Hubbard from Heavy Reading, as well as my colleagues Dr. Mehmet Toy, Bernie McElroy, Michael Mahoney and Dr. Per Hansen.

I thank my sisters Tasmia, Salma & Najma, brother Razak and my brother-in-law, Zia, for the love and support that one can only hope for.

I am ever grateful to Ammi and Abbi (my parents) for their unconditional love, support and best wishes that I have always been always assured of, in this and all other endeavors.

Most importantly, I would like to acknowledge my darling daughter Sophia Eeman. For her abundant love, inspiration, and for giving me a glimpse of the wondrous, I remain eternally thankful. This is for you my "jaan"

Ultimately, of course, all human endeavors are possible only because they are blessed by God. This is no exception. I remain grateful for His love.

—**Abdul Kasim**
September 25, 2007
New Jersey, U.S.A.
kasim@alum.mit.edu

Thanks for the dedicated efforts of the Infonetics Research team, who all contribute to each delivery of our research.

Michael Howard (Chapter 3)

I'd like to acknowledge all of the participants of the IEEE 8023.ah EFM working group who worked diligently to make this technology possible and all of the efforts of ITU SG15 to further expand the EFM market with continued improvements to the underlying technology.

Matt Squire (Chapter 5)

Many thanks to Charles Bergren, Michelle Kuska, and Ralph Brown for their comments and their support of this work.

Greg White (Chapter 6)

We would like to acknowledge Nuno Borges (Nokia Siemens Networks S.A., Portugal) for being open to all questions related to EPONs as well as financial support from Fundação para a Ciência e a Tecnologia, Portugal, through the grant contract SFRH/BDE/15524/2004 and from Nokia Siemens Networks S.A., Portugal.

Marek Hajduczenia, Glen Kramer, Lowell Lamb (Chapter 7)

We are very grateful to Mr. Abdul Kasim for his constant encouragement, patience, and invaluable insight into the preparation of this chapter. In addition, we are indebted to Mr. Qing (Gary) Liu for his tireless assistance with many parts of the survey, diagrams, tables, typesetting, and overall proofreading.

Nasir Ghani, Ashwin Gumaste (Chapter 8)

I wish to acknowledge the support of our investors and members of Ceterus Networks; without them, none of this would be possible. I also want to acknowledge the support of my family, my wife Liz and my sons Jonathan, Alex, and Stephen.

Bill Szeto (Chapter 9)

I would like to thank Leon Bruckman, CTO, Corrigent Systems, and editor of the EEE 802.17 standard for his contributions to this chapter.

Mannix O'Connor (Chapter 10)

First things first—thank you, Abdul, for inviting me to participate in this exciting project. Special thanks also go to Rodney Boehm, Bill Erickson, and Doug Saylor for your insightful comments, which helped shape this chapter. Joan, this is for you. Thanks for your encouragement and support.

Paul Havala (Chapter 11)

Thanks to Latha Vishnubhotla for preparing lists of vendors and equipment costs.

Norman Finn (Chapter 13)

Luca thanks Melissa for her patience during the writing of Chapter 14. Luca and Giles also thank MariaJose, Chris, and George for their review of the content.

Giles Heron, Luca Martini (Chapter 14)

Foreword

Ethernet was invented as a local area network (LAN) and named in a memo I wrote at the Xerox Palo Alto Research Center (Parc) on May 22, 1973. Dave Boggs and I never imagined that the Ethernets we started building in 1973 would proliferate and evolve as they have over these past 30 some years and certainly not as an access technology.

I now often quote IDC, which has published the amazing fact that over a quarter of a billion new Ethernet switch ports were shipped worldwide in 2006.

And I explain to puzzled family members that Ethernet is the plumbing that underlies the Internet (TCP/IP), which is the plumbing that underlies the World Wide Web (WWW), which in turn is the plumbing that underlies Google.

And now "Carrier Ethernet" is finally bridging what George Gilder calls the Telechasm, the last-mile carrier access gap between high-speed Ethernet LANs and high-speed wide area networks (WANs), which are also increasingly based on Ethernet technology. The Internet will soon be carrying packets from end to end in native Ethernet mode.

The most important reason why Ethernets have been winning for three decades is the six-part Ethernet business model. Carriers had better beware of at least two of these parts.

The six parts of the Ethernet business model are (1) de jure standards, (2) owned implementations, (3) fierce competition, (4) market demand for multi-vendor interoperability, (5) evolving standards based on market engagement, and (6) both backward and forward compatibility for leveraging the growing installed base.

Carriers had better note parts #3 and #6 especially. Ethernets have been winning because they are driven by fierce competition (#3), which is something new to most carriers. And Ethernets have been winning because they are based on rapidly evolving standards, which can be a problem when carriers are making massive infrastructure investments, which is why backward and forward compatibility (#6) is so important.

I highly recommend Abdul Kasim's helpful book on delivering Carrier Ethernet services. Even if I do say so myself, Carrier Ethernet is the next big thing.

—Bob Metcalfe, Inventor of Ethernet

Bob Metcalfe is a general partner at Polaris Ventures. Dr. Metcalfe had three careers before becoming a venture capitalist:

While an engineer-scientist (1965–1979), Dr. Metcalfe helped build the early Internet. In 1973, at the Xerox Palo Alto Research Center, he invented Ethernet, the local area networking (LAN) standard on which he shares four patents. In 2003, Ethernet's 30th year, 184 million new Ethernet connections were shipped for $12.5 billion.

While an entrepreneur-executive (1979–1990), Dr. Metcalfe founded 3Com Corporation, the billion-dollar networking company where at various times he was Chairman, CEO, Division General Manager, and Vice President of Engineering, Sales, and Marketing.

While a publisher-pundit (1990–2000), Dr. Metcalfe was CEO of IDG's InfoWorld Publishing Company (1992–1995). For eight years, he wrote an Internet column read weekly by over 500,000 information technologists. He spoke often; appeared on radio, television, and the Web; and produced conferences including ACM97, ACM1, Agenda, Pop!Tech, and Vortex.

Dr. Metcalfe's book credits include *Packet Communication* (Thomson), *Internet Collapses and Other InfoWorld Punditry* (IDG Books), and *Beyond Calculation: The Next Fifty Years of Computing* (co-edited for Springer Verlag).

He graduated from the Massachusetts Institute of Technology in 1969 with bachelor degrees in Electrical Engineering and in Management. He received an MS in Applied Mathematics from Harvard University in 1970. In 1973, he received his PhD in Computer Science from Harvard, where his doctoral dissertation was titled, "Packet Communication".

Among numerous awards, Dr. Metcalfe received the Grace Murray Hopper Award from the Association for Computing Machinery (ACM) in 1980. In 1988, he received the Alexander Graham Bell Medal from the Institute of Electrical and Electronics Engineers (IEEE). In 1995, he was elected to the American Academy of Arts and Sciences. In 1996, he received the IEEE's Medal of Honor. In 1997, he was elected to the National Academy of Engineering. In 1999, he was elected to the International Engineering Consortium. In 2003, he won the Marconi International Fellowship and was inducted into the prestigious Bay Shore High School Hall of Fame. He also has been awarded three honorary doctorates.

Introduction

How This Book Came About...

Even as the value of Ethernet beyond the LAN was being widely recognized, the major challenge was the lack of clarity as to what this "Carrier Ethernet" entailed, and more generally, a lack of understanding of the delivery solutions over the diverse network infrastructures used by Service Providers. This was to a large extent understandable given a) the infancy of the field, b) the numerous network solutions that could be used, and c) the fact that these solutions are generally very different from each other in terms of the technology, focus, relevance, and extent of optimization needed to deliver Ethernet services.

This book attempts to mitigate that hurdle—and in its own small way, accelerate the deployment of Carrier Ethernet services—by providing a comprehensive, practical, and insightful description of Carrier Ethernet and the different network solutions that can, and are, being employed currently. Furthermore, using a common template across the various commercial solutions focusing on the vital strategic and field issues, the book attempts to provide a meaningful relative assessment of the different solutions. In so doing, the book strives to provide both Service Providers and end users alike with a solid and holistic understanding to aid in making an informed choice in the delivery and usage of Carrier Ethernet services, respectively.

The absence of a reasonably comparable book on this subject of delivering Carrier Ethernet added to the urgency of this endeavor; although there is a lot of material on this topic available on the World Wide Web, it is largely fragmented, often with contradictory versions, and would take a substantial effort to distill the necessary information. The value of this book, therefore, became compelling; it is the first and, currently, the only book that addresses this very timely topic and one where the stakes are high, in the billions of dollars.

Given the substantial number of very different technologies/solutions that had to be covered in the context of delivering Carrier Ethernet, it was felt that the most effective and authoritative approach would be to leverage world-class experts who not only understood the technology in depth but also offered the wisdom acquired from substantial real-life field experience. It was enormous good fortune that exactly such a panel of leaders could be assembled and contribute to this book.

Distinctive Features of the Book

Some of the distinctive features of the book are as follows.

- **Comprehensive/Breadth**   This book deals with almost all the key Carrier Ethernet solutions delivered across both wired and wireless infrastructures, including ones only recently introduced such as WiMax. It also offers a holistic perspective on delivering Carrier Ethernet and encompasses both technology details and practical insights.

- **Easily readable**   This book presents a gamut of highly technical material spanning numerous very distinct technologies in a straight-forward manner. However, this simplicity does not preclude dealing with important questions in reasonable depth and capturing the essence of a solution.

- **Practical focus**   This book is not a regurgitation of material available elsewhere. Rather, it is a compilation of insights derived from substantial field experience deploying the different Carrier Ethernet solutions. It has a singular focus on a set of key technology and business considerations that inevitably come up in any decision making in the deployment and use of Carrier Ethernet services.

- **World-class authorship**   Each of the chapters on the solutions is authored by a world-renowned expert with considerable field experience deploying the respective solution(s).

- **Unique**   This is the first book published on Carrier Ethernet and how it is being offered today; there is no similar book currently available on this rapidly growing segment of the industry.

The Specifics: What the Book Provides

This book attempts to provide:

- An understanding of the transformation of Ethernet from primarily a connectivity protocol in the LAN to a carrier-class technology in the metro, access, and wide area networks.

- Insights into what is triggering this transformation, specifically the underpinning business drivers that have instilled urgency to Ethernet's new emerging role.

- A quick overview of what is meant by Carrier Ethernet and the efforts of standards bodies and the industry to enable Carrier Ethernet deployment.

- A comprehensive look at the various solutions, both wire-line and wireless, employed in Service Provider networks to deliver Carrier Ethernet and how each of these are evolving to deliver carrier-class Ethernet.

- Insights into considerations of real-life implementations of these different transport mechanisms.

- How these solutions stack up to each other relatively across a set of multiple considerations.

■ A brief discussion into the plausible future of Carrier Ethernet services and how they may be delivered.

Intended Audience

This book is intended for a fairly broad audience engaged in a range of technology and business roles. It assumes a fairly rudimentary knowledge of telecommunications networks and services but attempts to simplify and elaborate wherever possible.

Scope and Limitations

While the book attempts to cover a rather broad and diverse topic with reasonable depth, it is consciously restricted in scope to avoid becoming unwieldy, difficult to follow and consequently, less effective. The specific constraints are noted below.

■ **Enterprises only** This book focuses on the delivery of Carrier Ethernet primarily to enterprise end users. It does not consider the delivery of such services to residential end users, who are also increasingly employing Carrier Ethernet for triple-play (voice, video, data/Internet). The challenges of delivering Carrier Ethernet to business customers are more significant than those associated with offering it to residential customers. And while there is definitely some overlap across the business and residential segments, there are also significant differences, for instance, in the type of services, whether SLAs are required, pricing, etc.

■ **North American focus** Although, wherever possible, we attempt to maintain a global perspective in the discussions, the default is largely based on the North American experience.

■ **Technology/Solution depth** The focus of this book is not a detailed technical treatise of the technologies or solutions by themselves; there is considerable literature available that should be consulted for this purpose (and each of the chapters in the book identifies a list of useful references about the respective technology solutions). It is more concerned with answering, in some depth and based on practical experience, the vital questions when considering Carrier Ethernet solutions.

■ **Time-sensitive** The content and solution developments are current as of this publishing; given the dynamic nature of this field, it is anticipated that some content, notably on developments in standards, may need to be updated with time.

■ **Impact of style** Although some uniformity is enforced through a common template across the discussion of the various solutions to enable a relative comparison, it must be noted that, to some extent, it is very much a "comparing apples to oranges" exercise and as such, there are inherent differences between the solution chapters. Furthermore, despite best efforts to provide consistency, individual authors' styles will invariably introduce some differences; however, substantial care has been taken to minimize this and ensure that each chapter indeed serves as a solid source of practical and insightful information on a specific solution.

How the Book Is Organized

The sections and chapters of the book are organized in a logical fashion to bring some clarity and depth into what is a fairly complex and often confusing topic. There are three distinct parts to the book:

- **Part I: Background**   Provides the background and rationale for Carrier Ethernet; also illustrates the market opportunity for Carrier Ethernet.
- **Part II: Solutions**   Covers the specific solutions employed for providing Carrier Ethernet using a standardized template.
- **Part III: A Look into the Future**   Summarizes the available solutions relative to each other and attempts to briefly explore the evolution of Carrier Ethernet delivery solutions.

The first part of the book provides some useful background and detail about Carrier Ethernet. In Chapter 1, Ethernet, its origins, and eventually its dominance in the LAN and how it evolved into Carrier Ethernet, is described. Chapter 2 introduces Carrier Ethernet and its enablers formally, and Chapter 3 provides market data from both the standpoint of Ethernet services and the underlying vendor solutions to demonstrate the significance of Carrier Ethernet.

The second part of the book covers the various commercial solutions that are presently employed to deliver carrier-class Ethernet. It discusses all the major solutions available for Service Providers and highlights the technology underpinning the solution, the benefits of the solution, and how it is evolving. A balanced treatment in the technical and business realities of each of the solutions is offered. Each of the solutions is covered in its own chapter that is authored by an industry renowned expert and can be read independently of any other chapter without impacting its understanding.

The final part of the book summarizes and puts into context the landscape of the many, very different solutions discussed in the previous section. This is meant to provide the reader with a good understanding of the different solutions and their fit in relation to each other.

Finally, we share our opinion on how the world of Carrier Ethernet will evolve in the next few years. In so doing, the book attempts to provide practical and reasonably detailed insights into the landscape of available solutions in a burgeoning field and how they may evolve.

Any feedback is welcome and can be sent to kasim@alum.mit.edu.

Background

Ethernet: From LAN to the WAN

by Abdul Kasim

This first section provides only a cursory and informal introduction to Ethernet for the sake of completeness to the rest of the book. Ethernet has been around for several decades now and, as is to be expected, there is a good deal of literature available. Some of this literature [1–6] is noted in the reference section at the end of this chapter and should be consulted for more comprehensive information on Ethernet.

What Is Ethernet?

Ethernet, commonly, refers to the dominant[1] networking technology being used in Local Area Networks (LANs) for the *connection, communication, and inter-working* of personal computers, printers, servers, and other devices. A LAN typically operates within a geographically confined area (such as an office building or a small cluster of buildings within a range of few kilometers and is usually owned and managed by a single enterprise entity).

Ethernet specifically encompasses the following:

- The physical interface that interconnects a device over a coax/fiber (or some other) media ("the Ether").

- The frames being used as containers for transmitting and receiving the data between the physical interfaces on devices in the LAN.

- The underlying protocol employed to communicate between these devices. This includes building the frames and transmitting as well as receiving them, processing these frames for errors; it is also addresses all the associated signaling for enabling communication.

---

[1] Globally, well over 90 percent of LANs are based on Ethernet.

NOTE The associated control/signaling and management functions also normally employ Ethernet frames.

Ethernet typically manifests both in hardware and software to collectively provide the physical connectivity and processing capabilities just noted (more specific details are in the next section).

More formally, Ethernet is defined by the IEEE 802.3[2] standard and enables half-duplex (transmitting in one direction at a time over a shared physical medium) as well as full-duplex (simultaneously transmitting in both directions) data communication, and provides the underlying capabilities across three architectural layers: Physical, Media Access Control (MAC) and the Logical Link Control (LLC) these are discussed in some detail next. These capabilities correspond to those provided by the first two layers in the OSI Reference Model[3]: Physical and Data-Link Layers, or Layer 1 and 2, respectively. This is shown in Figure 1.1 and it should be clear that the MAC and LLC sub layers in the IEEE model are intended to have the same function as the Data-Link Layer alone, in the OSI model.

Physical layer The Physical layer, at the bottom of the OSI/IEEE stack, is concerned with the actual physical transmission of raw bits[4] over the (physical[5]) media.

This layer specifies the physical interface on a device connected to a LAN and also the associated cabling. Typically, the physical connectivity manifests in a transceiver, the Network Interface Card (NIC), that physically plugs into a device's (could be a computer or for that matter any device requiring Ethernet connectivity) motherboard. A NIC is identified by a three-part nomenclature based on the attributes of the physical connection: transmission rate, transmission method, and media type or signaling. For example, 10Base-T indicates a 10 Mbps baseband[6] over two twisted-pair cables, while a 1000Base-LX refers to 1000 Mbps, based band, long wavelength over fiber.

Each of the NICs has a unique static address (assigned by the manufacturer from a block of addresses purchased from the IEEE); this address is referred to as its MAC or Ethernet address, and it is based on a flat-addressing space[7] and uses 6 bytes written in a hexadecimal format.

Data-Link layer (DLL) layer The Data-Link layer provides the functionality to transfer data bits between entities in a network (basically between the numerous computers that are inter-connected) and detects and corrects, if necessary, any errors that occur at the Physical layer. In effect, its role is to ensure transmission free of errors.

---

[2] The IEEE 802.3 defines Ethernet in the LAN (and since 2005, also in the MAN)

[3] The Open Systems Initiative (OSI) defined by the International Standards Organization as the standard 7498-1, in 1984. This is the primary architectural model employed in networking.

[4] Binary digits (i.e., Os and 1s using which data is communicated)

[5] It could be over a non-'physical', i.e., a wireless medium as well (such as is the case with Wireless Fidelity or WiFi).

[6] Ethernet implementations typically use baseband transmission not broadband transmissions.

[7] As opposed to a hierarchical addressing space (e.g., used in regular mailing addresses, where there are many subgroups (addresses) based on an element, say, City Name; and from the networking realm, IP address assignment is another example of hierarchical addressing.

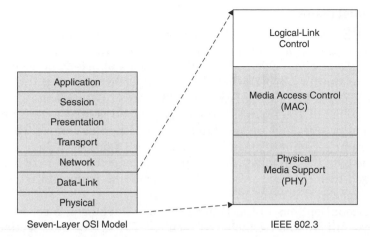

Figure 1.1   Ethernet as defined by IEEE-layered model (vis-à-vis the OSI model)

In the IEEE 802.3 standard, the Data-Link Layer (DLL) of the OSI model is essentially split into two sublayers: Media Access Control (MAC) and the Logical-link control (which resides on top of the MAC sublayer).

Media Access Control (MAC) sublayer   This sublayer defines medium-independent capabilities that are built upon the Physical layer and encompasses two main functions:

- **Data encapsulation**   Includes assembling and right-sizing[8], if necessary, the Ethernet frame prior to transmitting and also detecting any errors at receipt of an Ethernet frame.

- **Media Access Management**   This includes any collision avoidance and handling when a shared medium is used (i.e., multiple entities are using the same physical medium to communicate; see section on CDMA later in the chapter for more detail).

   An optional MAC Control sublayer, architecturally positioned between the Logical Link Control (LLC) or the MAC sublayer, may also be present (and is transparent to both the MAC and the LLC).

- **MAC Control Sublayer**   Initiates the transmission of the frames and the recovery from any transmission errors employing an algorithm such as CSMA/CD over a shared medium (see the next section for more detail)

Logical Link Control (LLC) sublayer   This sublayer corresponds to the upper part of the OSI Data-Link layer and provides the interface between the Ethernet MAC and the upper layers of the device/application. The LLC sublayer is primarily concerned with multiplexing and demultiplexing of frames transported over the MAC sublayer and also provides flow control, acknowledgement, and recovery, if necessary.

---

[8] If the frame is too large, for instance; see next section on framing for more detail

The Basic Ethernet Frame

The IEEE 802.3[9] has defined a basic Ethernet frame format, as shown in Figure 1.2. The fields that comprise the basic Ethernet frame (which is also referred to as the *Protocol Data Unit* or *PDU*[10]) are also shown and briefly described in the figure.

The maximum size of the Ethernet frame, referred to as the *Maximum Transmission Unit (MTU),* in the standard case is 1526 Bytes (1 Byte = 8 bits), including the maximum data payload of 1500 Bytes. If the data payload is larger than this, it is broken down into smaller sizes and encapsulated within Ethernet frames. The maximum and minimum frame size limits listed in the IEEE 802.3 do not include the preamble and start of frame bytes. This makes the maximum untagged frame 1518 bytes and the minimum untagged frame 64 bytes. Protocol analyzers and frame statistics probes normally report frames in this manner.

Additional options to the Ethernet frame have been incorporated to accommodate new capabilities and technologies such as VLANs (see next section), MPLS, and so on. To also accommodate a more efficient transmission of latency sensitive application data (such as video), larger MTU sizes called *Jumbo frames*—typically greater than 9000 Bytes—are being supported in commercial solutions.

VLAN Tagging Option   A Virtual LAN (VLAN) tag was introduced between the SA and the Length/Type fields of an Ethernet frame. This VLAN is defined in IEEE 802.1Q and provides these key capabilities:

- Allows data traffic to be prioritized.
- Allows data traffic to be categorized for more efficient handling; for instance, traffic can be separated or categorized and each of these categories treated differently. Traffic in an enterprise, for example, may be split by which department it belongs to, so that traffic belonging to the accounting department, the marketing department, and so on, may be separated using a corresponding VLAN identifier and treated accordingly. As will be evident shortly, this creates a lot of efficiency in the operation of LANs and also introduces additional flexibility as far as handling data within an enterprise is concerned.
- Simplifies the management of the LAN because, in effect, a large LAN is broken down to smaller, usually more easily managed LANs (i.e., the logical LANs).

The IEEE 802.3ac standard allows for the Ethernet frame extension required to accommodate a 4-Byte VLAN tag. The 4-Byte VLAN header comprises a 2-Byte VLAN type (i.e., the inserted frame should be interpreted as a VLAN frame) and a 2-Byte control field that, in turn, is made up of a 3-bit Priority field (called *P bits*), and a 12-bit

---

[9] IEEE 802.3 frame defined in 1997. There is a slight variation between frames from the traditional and DIX standards.

[10] A PDU specifies a unit used to communicate between the same layers on different devices. It is comprised of a header and a payload.

	7	1	6	6	2	46–1500	4	Bytes
	Preamble	SOF	DA	SA	Length/Type	Data	FCS	

Field	Bytes	Description
Preamble	7	Indicates a frame is coming
Start-of-Frame Delimiter	1	Tells where the frame begins
Destination Address (DA)	6	Identifies the devices (stations) to receive the frame
Source Address (SA)	6	Identifies the sending device (station)
Length/Type	2	Identifies number of data bytes or Frame ID (type of frame)
Data	46–1500	Actual data being carried
Frame Check Sequence (FCS)	4	Consists a cyclic redundancy check value that is used to validate that the frames were not damaged
	< 1526	

Figure 1.2   Ethernet frame as defined by IEEE 802.3 standard

VLAN ID (VID). There are 4096 (2^{12}) unique VIDs.[11] While this appears to be a fairly large number and is sufficient in most LAN environments, it could present a bottleneck (to scale) in larger and more complex enterprise environments and also when Ethernet extends beyond the LAN, into Service Provider networks.[12] The P bits are used to prioritize the handling of incoming Ethernet frames.

Elements of a LAN

Ethernet-based LANs make up the heart of enterprise[13] networks. A sample LAN is depicted in Figure 1.3. LANs are often shown using a bus topology but star topologies are frequently used in modern day LANs.

- **Data Terminating Equipment (DTE)**   These devices are either the source or destinations for the data and include PCs, servers, printers, and so on.
- **Data Communication Equipment (DCE)**   These are the intermediate devices that receive and forward Ethernet frames and include devices such as Ethernet switches and routers as well as the NIC (integrated into the PCs and other devices).

---

[11] Actually 4094 VIDs are usable; a VID of 0 identifies a priority frame and a VID of 4095 is reserved.

[12] A technique called Q-in-Q, defined in IEEE 802. 1Q, allows the stacking of two VLAN tags (an enterprise VLAN tag and a Service Provider–added VLAN tag) to overcome this scaling limitation, so multiple VLAN tags belonging to a specific customer can be mapped to one Service Provider tag.

[13] *Enterprise* is used broadly to refer to the host of entities—whether businesses, academia, or nonprofits—that have computer (or information technology) infrastructures.

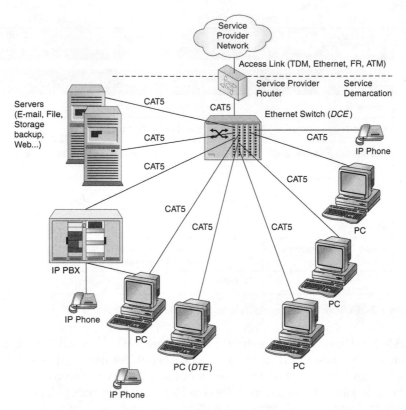

Figure 1.3 A typical enterprise Local Area Network (LAN)

- **Connectivity mechanism**   Different media are employed for connectivity (the "Ether," in the Ethernet). This medium physically connects the DCEs and the DTEs; Unshielded Twisted Pair (UTP) or (multimode) fiber optic cables are commonly used in enterprise LANs.

As depicted in the Figure 1.3, the devices in the LAN are usually connected in a star topology with a switch or router acting as a hub and the DTEs connected using a physical media (CAT 5, as shown in Figure 1.3, is commonly used).

How It All Works: A Simple Overview of LAN Operation   Briefly, if a device (say a PC) wants to communicate with another device (let's say a printer) on a LAN requesting a service (printing, in this case), then the sending device's print application request will be essentially converted into an appropriate Ethernet frame. The Ethernet frame will have the PC's MAC address as the source address (SA) and the printer's MAC address as the destination address (DA). Other parameters in the frame will be filled in appropriately.

The frame is then transmitted using the CSMA/CD protocol (described in section on CSMA/CD) if the device MAC is operating in a half-duplex mode (i.e., it can either send or receive but not send and receive simultaneously). This protocol was developed to more efficiently send and receive messages between multiple sets of devices (without having a large number of collisions). Alternatively, if the device is employing a full-duplex mode (i.e., it can transmit and receive simultaneously—the most common scenario in today's networks), there is no such protocol employed and transmission is fairly straightforward (just successive frames are sent after an Inter Frame Gap (IFG) to ensure no collisions).

The receiving device (the printer, in this case) will observe the incoming frame, identify the destination address on the frame as being the same as its own MAC address, and make sure the frame has not been corrupted. If everything is fine, the receiving device accepts the frame and sends it to the upper layer. This process is the same independent of whether the device's MAC is half-duplex or full-duplex.

If a frame has to be broadcast to all devices on the network, then an address of all 1s is inserted in the DA. The transmission is the same, however, and every receiving device will receive a frame as if it is the destination device.

An Ethernet LAN typically operates in its own domain or segment. Every DTE in a segment shares the same physical medium and receives all transmitted frames (but, as mentioned, will accept only those destined for it). When the number of devices on a LAN becomes large (there is no fixed definition of precisely what large means), it is more efficient to divide the LAN into multiple segments. This segmentation can be done using a device called an Ethernet Bridge.

Ethernet Bridges and Switches   An Ethernet Bridge is a LAN interconnection device that operates at the Data-Link layer (Layer 2 of the OSI model). It may be used to join two (or more) LAN segments to construct a larger LAN. It also regulates the traffic between these segments by filtering traffic based on (source and destination) MAC addresses in the traversing Ethernet frames; the bridge basically "learns" which MAC addresses can be reached through each of its ports and constructs a table that maps a list of (MAC) addresses to a port. It then parses incoming frames and forwards them based on the content of this table. Broadcast frames (with all 1s in their DA field) will be forwarded to all ports except the port they arrived on. A Bridge may also enforce a security policy separating different workgroups located on each of the LANs. Bridges were first specified in IEEE 802.1D.[14]

A Switch is essentially a bridge where the bridging—examining the packet and forwarding it—is done using hardware (so forwarding frames is done very quickly). A Switch also has multiple physical ports and can be used to interconnect multiple LANs. Another way to look at it is that a Switch has a node/device on its own segment. Broadcast and multicast (forwarding an incoming frame to a set of select destinations) are also supported.

---

[14] A note on IEEE nomenclature: In the IEEE, if a standard is a standalone document that will not be incorporated into another document, then the letter(s) following the period is an uppercase letter. The documents using lowercase letters are changes that will be incorporated into the main document. For example, 802.3ah includes changes to many of the sections of the 802.3 document; it also adds an additional section. At some point in the future, 802.3 will be republished with the 802.3ah reference and changes incorporated. At that point, 802.3ah will no longer be available.

Connecting Bridges and Switches   Bridges and switches can be connected to string together multiple LANs, in effect building a bigger LAN, thus leveraging and sharing the resources on all the subtending LANs. This approach is commonly employed in campus networks and even in smaller metro networks.

Switches must be connected in a tree topology and not connected in such a way as to form a ring. In other words, there must be only one path between any two devices (connected to any of the switches). If more than one path exists between any two devices, a loop is formed; this is unacceptable because frames can endlessly circulate over that loop, resulting in network overload. Bridges and Switches employ Bridge Protocol Data Units (BPDUs) to exchange information with each other regarding their individual status.

Because interconnecting multiple LANs usually means, in effect, interconnecting hundreds of devices, identifying such loops between every combination of devices is not done manually. The IEEE 802.1D defined an algorithm called the *Spanning Tree Protocol (STP)* that will, using the appropriate BPDUs, automatically detect such loops and disable the physical ports that enable the duplicate paths.

The STP is essentially the "Control Plane" of an Ethernet switch solution and is also used to recover from failures. On detecting a failure on a path between two devices, the STP figures out (or converges to) an alternative path and enables it for communication. The time taken to accomplish this is, however, unacceptable—especially with a large number of devices interconnected; a more efficient variant, Rapid STP (RSTP), is used to address this problem. As will be discussed in Chapter 2, when Ethernet moves beyond the LAN, there are an exponentially higher number of customer endpoints and services; even this approach is frequently insufficient and newer techniques need to be developed.

Ethernet—The Beginning

As soon as the power of interconnecting several computers and other ancillary devices became evident, numerous efforts were undertaken to enable this capability within an enterprise. One such effort was led by Dr. Robert Metcalfe, whose work at Xerox's Palo Alto Research Center (PARC) over several years culminated in Ethernet. "Ether"[15] in the word *Ethernet* referred to the single low-loss coaxial cable used in the original version of Ethernet. Figure 1.4 shows Dr. Metcalfe's hand-drawn schematic illustrating Ethernet.[16]

At that time (1973), Xerox was looking for a way to efficiently interconnect over 100 Alto computers and also drive their new high-speed laser printers, which were all physically connected over a shared 1-km coaxial cable (or "bus"). Dr. Metcalfe's first Ethernet design allowed this configuration to operate at a speed of 2.94 Mbps,[17] using a new algorithm known as *Carrier Sensing Multiple Access/Collision Detection*

---

[15] Ether is actually derived from the lumeniferous *ether* that, at one time, supposedly surrounded the Earth and served as the medium for electromagnetic radiation. It also signifies that Ethernet can be used to connect any computer, not just the Alto brand computers used.

[16] This figure was drawn by Dr. Metcalfe at the National Computer Conference in 1976.

[17] This speed was apparently chosen because it was derived from the system clock of the Alto computers that were being interconnected.

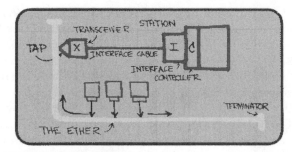

Figure 1.4   The original Ethernet schematic

(CSMA/CD).[18] This protocol not only enabled the relatively high speed of communication but also dramatically improved the transmission efficiency over the shared media in the LAN by up to 80 percent when compared to the existing methods[19] and hence, was deemed a great success.

The CSMA/CD Ethernet

At the time, the big challenge was to minimize the number of collisions that occurred when several computers interconnected over a shared coaxial cable tried to communicate with each other. The CSMA/CD algorithm mitigated this problem significantly.

Briefly, using the CSMA/CD approach, when a computer on a LAN wants to transmit, it listens to the cable (i.e., "senses" the cable); if the cable is busy, the computer waits until it goes idle; otherwise, it transmits immediately. If other computers on the cable simultaneously begin transmission as well (since they all sensed the cable was idle), collisions will occur. When a computer detects a collision, it stops transmission immediately for a random amount of time, after which it starts the process of listening to the cable again. The amount of time that a computer waits before listening again is determined by a "binary exponential backoff" algorithm, which dynamically adjusts the random interval before which a computer can attempt to retransmit. When two colliding computers back off using this algorithm, the chance of their respective transmissions colliding yet again when they both attempt to retransmit is negligible.[20] If a collision reoccurs, however, then a new backoff time is computed before a retransmission attempt is scheduled, so the possibility of colliding on this second retransmission is reduced exponentially again. Thus, either the transmission is successful or a new backoff interval is computed before a retransmit attempt. With each collision and back off, the chance of a subsequent collision is reduced. In this fashion, the CSMA/CD reduces collisions and improves transmission efficiency quite dramatically—an 80 percent improvement when compared to the prevailing solutions.

---

[18] When we refer to Ethernet, we usually mean the CSMA/CD Ethernet.

[19] At the time, existing protocols such as the ALOHA system developed at the University of Hawaii, had distinctly limited efficiency, mainly due to a higher collision rate.

[20] In essence, each computer waits for a different amount of time prior before attempting to retransmit.

In 1976, Dr. Metcalfe, along with David Boggs, published this research in a landmark paper entitled, "Ethernet: Distributed Packet Switching for Local Computer Networks" in the *Communications of the Association for Computing Machinery (ACM) [8]*. And on December 13, 1977, U.S. Patent number 4,063,220, "Multipoint Data Communications System with Collision Detection," was issued to Xerox Corporation, Dr. Metcalfe's employer, formalizing the advent of Ethernet.

The benefits of CSMA/CD Ethernet soon became obvious, and in 1979, Digital Equipment Corporation (DEC) and Intel partnered with Xerox to commercialize the technology—with DEC building the hardware (the Network Interface Cards) and Intel providing the semiconductor chips. They were, however, persuaded by Dr. Metcalfe and his associates, to make the technology publicly available and, therefore, avoid an Ethernet monopoly. To their credit, the three companies agreed to this enlightened[21] proposal and published the DIX standard,[22] the first Ethernet specifications for 10 Mbps transmission based on the CSMA/CD protocol; a second version of this specification was published in 1982. In the meantime, Dr. Metcalfe and others were also working with the nonprofit Institute of Electrical and Electronic Engineers (IEEE) to develop an open industry standard.

In 1983, the IEEE released the first truly open industry standard for Ethernet, "IEEE 802.3 Carrier Sense Multiple Access with Collision Detection (CSMA/CD) Access Method and Physical Layer Specifications." Developed by the 802.3 working group of the 802 committee, the standard was pretty much the same as the DIX standard[23] except for a few changes. Subsequently, the International Standards Organization (ISO) also approved the Ethernet standard as the 8802.3, catapulting it into use worldwide.

NOTE Any reference to Ethernet today usually means the IEEE 802.3 standards-based Ethernet [1]. The CSMA/CD is hardly used anymore, except in half-duplex, shared media environments; instead sophisticated switches and other equipment are used in a full-duplex fashion in star-topologies where the issue of collisions is moot.[24]

The Development of Ethernet

Several advances were made to the initial IEEE 802.3 standard. Over the past twenty-odd years Ethernet has, in fact, seen considerable innovation and subsequent standardization. The Ethernet standard has thus far focused on improvements across several dimensions:

- **Distance** Extended the physical distance more than 100 and up to approximately 2000 miles

---

[21] Enlightened because the companies forewent the short-term revenue prospects in favor of something that would ultimately be good for the entire industry.

[22] DIX stood for *D*igital Equipment Corportion, *I*ntel, and *X*erox.

[23] Hardware based on either standard can, in fact, interoperate.

[24] In typical enterprise LAN Ethernets these days, each workstation is connected over a dedicated point-to-point link to a switch in a hub/star topology and communicates (usually in a full-duplex manner) over this link. Hence, the issue of colliding with frames from another workstation on theLAN simply does not arise.

- **Speed/Bandwidth**   Increased line speed to 10 Gb/s and higher (a thousand-fold increase from the initial 10M bandwidth)
- **Media**   Enabled transmission over a host of wired and wireless media
- **Processing**   Added new capabilities to identify, separate, prioritize, and secure data
- **Scale**   Continually made it more robust and operationally efficient to deploy and manage large Ethernets

These and other key developments in the Ethernet standard are listed in Table 1.1 and illustrate the continuous improvements that Ethernet continues to undergo. Two IEEE[25] working groups, 802.3 and 802.1, were particularly active in extending Ethernet to operate beyond the LAN. A detailed discussion of these standards is beyond the scope of this book, but they are actively referenced wherever necessary.

NOTE   All standards are available from the IEEE website at www.ieee.org/getieee802

Other LAN Technologies: Token Bus, Token Ring, and FDDI

In addition to Ethernet, other LAN technologies were also developed during the 1980s. Three of them—Token Bus, Token Ring, and Fiber Distributed Data Interface (FDDI)—were notably prominent. They have even been standardized as IEEE 802.4 for Token Bus and IEEE 802.5 for Token Ring, whereas FDDI was standardized by the American National Standards Institute (ANSI), as the X3T9.5.

The discussion of these technologies in any detail is outside the scope of this book, but briefly, all these technologies employ a special control frame called a *token*. Only the workstation on the LAN that possess the token (and there is only one token per LAN) can transmit. Because there is only a single token and hence only one token holder, collisions are not possible.

Each of these LAN technologies was developed for different reasons and has its benefits and shortcomings. Token Bus was primarily driven by General Motors and others that were interested in factory automation and wanted a reliable, efficient, predictable, and high-throughput system at heavy loads that aligned well with their assembly lines. However, Token Bus was not particularly well suited for fiber transmission and experienced latency even at small loads.

Token Ring, mainly adopted by IBM, also had similarly attractive features. In addition, it could also be deployed in a ring topology and supported arbitrarily long frames efficiently (unlike the Token Bus), but like the Token Bus, Token Ring suffered from latency (as do all token passing schemes).

As more powerful workstations began to proliferate on LANs, these technologies became inadequate from the standpoint of scale, reliability, and bandwidth; FDDI

---

[25] Other standards bodies such as the IETF have also been active but most of the work on LAN Ethernet was done in the IEEE whose focus has been on the PHY and Data Link-layer

TABLE 1.1   Development of Ethernet: A Look at the (IEEE) Standardization Efforts

Year	Standard	Brief Description
1973	Ethernet Invented	2.94 Mb over coax
1982	DIX Standard	10M over thin coax
1983	IEEE 802.3	10Base5 (10 M over thick coax)
1985	802.3a	10Base2 (10M over thin coax)
1985	802.3b	10Base36 (10M over CATV cable)
1985	802.3c	10 M Repeater Specifications
1987	802.3d	Fiber Optic inter-repeater link
1990	802.3i	10BaseT (10M over twisted pair)
1993	802.3j	10Base F (10M over fiber)
1995	802.3u	100BaseT (100M with auto-negotiation)
1997	802.3x	Full-Duplex and Flow control
1998	802.3y	100Base over low quality twisted pair
1998	802.3z	1000BaseX (1000 M/1 G over fiber)
	802.1D	MAC Bridges
	802.1Q	Virtual LANs
1999	802.3ab	1000Base-T Ethernet over twisted pair
	802.3ac	Increased frame size to allow VLAN and priority
2000	802.3ad	Link Aggregation
2003	802.3ae	10GBASE (10000M or 10G over fiber)
2003	802.3af	Power over Ethernet
2004	802.3ah	Ethernet in First Mile (EFM) over Copper, Fiber and Passive
2006	802.3an	10GBase-T (1250M) Ethernet over UTP
2006	802.3aq	10GBase-LRM (10 G Ethernet over Multi-mode fiber)
In Progress	802.3ap	1G and 10G Backplane Ethernet (over a PCB)
In Progress	802.1ad	Provider Bridges
In Progress	802.1ag	Connectivity Fault Management (CFM); note ITU Y.1731 uses this as a basis and also added Performance Management (ratified in 2007)
In Progress	802.1ah	Provider Backbone Bridges (PBB)
In Progress	802.1Qay	Provider Backbone Bridges – Traffic Engineering (PBB-TE). Also referred to as Provider Backbone Trunking (PBT)
In Progress	802.1aj	2 port Relay and Demarcation

Source: IEEE, Wikepedia

was developed in the mid-1980s as a response to these shortcomings. *FDDI* was also token-based (in fact, it uses Token Ring as its basis) and supported 100-Mbps bandwidth using fiber optic cable deployed in a dual ring configuration. Traffic on each of the rings, referred to as the primary and secondary, flowed in opposite directions.

The primary ring was used for data transmission during normal operation, while the secondary ring remained idle; if the primary ring failed, the secondary ring took over. The primary purpose of the dual rings was to provide superior reliability and robustness.

FDDI was used mainly because it supported higher bandwidth at greater distances than usually possible over copper.[26] It also supported hundreds of users, and its dual ring architecture afforded reliability and fault-tolerance at distances greater than 100 miles. These capabilities made FDDI an attractive technology to build backbones for networks that extended beyond traditional enterprise LANs.

Table 1.2 offers a brief comparison of these standardized LAN technologies as of the mid-1980s and early 1990s, when they had been standardized with similar feature sets. As should be evident, there was no one overwhelmingly superior technology. The numerous studies conducted [7, 9, 10] on these LAN technologies were not conclusive on the superiority of one over the other per se, at least from a technology and performance standpoint; rather it appeared that any one of these could be made to look particularly appealing when modeled with the right combination of parameters. For instance, the token-based technologies performed better at higher loads than did Ethernet.

Despite not having any overwhelming technological superiority, or any significant time to market advantage (all the IEEE standards were developed around the same time and General Motors/IBM, having considerable market clout, actively backed the token technologies), Ethernet has gone on to become, by far, the most successful and widely deployed LAN technology in the world today. While Token Bus and Token Ring have become nearly obsolete, Ethernet has had more than 2 billion ports deployed (estimates from Dell'Oro and other analysts), making it the standard interface for most network-capable devices in the LAN today.

Domination in the Enterprise LAN

Ethernet has established itself as the overwhelmingly dominant technology in the LAN market. As shown in Figure 1.5, Ethernet LAN ports, even in the year 2000, made up well over 90 percent of total LAN ports and were growing almost linearly, while the port growth for Token Ring, minuscule as it was, was further declining. Token Bus registered even less than Token Ring and did not even merit further consideration. While the dominance of Ethernet has led market analysts to forgo such comparative studies in the recent past, it is reasonable to assume that the small base of Token Ring users will largely (or will in a short timeframe) inevitably migrate to Ethernet—they will simply have no other reasonable choice.[27] FDDI's small base is in much the same position as Token Ring's, although its use in some very niche applications may prolong the inevitable. Ethernet has indeed come to dominate the LAN.

Figure 1.6 tracks Ethernet from its inception to its dominance. Roughly, it underwent three stages[28]—what can be termed as "Beginnings," "Growth and Challenges," and

---

[26] A FDDI version using copper as the media was also introduced; this is referred to as CDDI.

[27] Because FDDI cannot simply compete against the Ethernet's price and performance, which will only further improve with time. Once the current token-based infrastructure is depreciated or new application support becomes necessary, it is reasonable to assume that these networks will transition to Ethernet.

[28] Based on the observations by Dr. Bob Metcalfe, founder of Ethernet

)

TABLE 1.2   Comparison of Key LAN Technologies During the Late 1980s and Early 1990s)

Factors of Comparison	Ethernet (IEEE 802.3)	Token Bus (IEEE 802.4)	Token Ring (IEEE 802.5)	FDDI (ANSI X3T9.5)
Service Connectivity	Connectionless	Connectionless	Connectionless	Connectionless
Bandwidth	10M	10M	4M/16M	100M
Engineering	Simple	Complex	Easy	Complex
Reliability	High	High	High	Very high
Performance Low Load Heavy Load	Good Poor	Poor Excellent	Poor Excellent	Good Excellent
Priorities Supported	No	Yes	Yes	Yes
Deterministic	No	More than 802.3	Yes	Yes
Suitability for fiber based implementation	Average	Poor	Good	Excellent

ultimately, "Domination." During the first stage, which lasted from the mid-1970s to the mid-1980s, Ethernet was a new entrant in a small market (comprising mostly research and development initiatives), where it competed against the likes of the Aloha protocol. During the second stage, lasting approximately from the mid-1980s to the mid-1990s, Ethernet faced some stiff competition in a fairly impressive growth market, stimulated

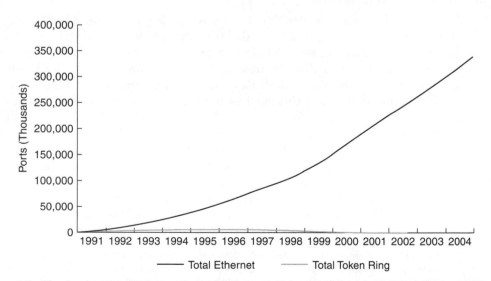

Figure 1.5   The domination of Ethernet in the LAN versus Token Ring (source: Dell'Oro Group, 2005)

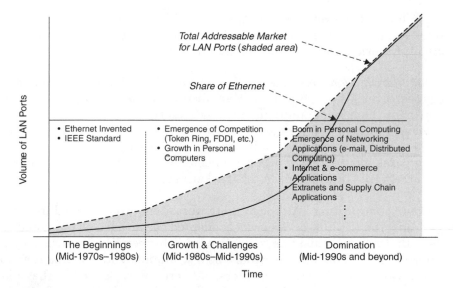

Figure 1.6   Tracking the dominance of Ethernet in the LAN

mostly by the growing popularity of the personal computer. Technologies such as Token ring and FDDI especially were taking a big share of the market. However, the fortunes of Token ring and others waned with the declining fortunes of its sponsors (IBM), while Ethernet with its unique business model and open standards continued to appeal. And so when the third stage came about, sometime after the mid-1990s when the proliferation of PCs continued unabated (thanks to Moore's law) and networking applications such as e-mail emerged along with the introduction and growth of the Internet, Ethernet had already begun to establish its dominance. And by 2000, as Figure 1.4 shows, it was the solution employed by nearly the entire addressable market.

This overwhelming adoption of Ethernet in the enterprise LAN was largely due to the *reasonable superiority of a combination of factors—notably simplicity and continual improvements in price and features, rather than a substantial competitive advantage in any one facet*. It is instructive to understand how Ethernet ascended to this dominant position in the LAN. Dr. Metcalfe identified [11] the main enablers for Ethernet's dominance in the LAN and these are briefly discussed next.

Continual Market-driven Innovation   As noted in the previous section, Ethernet did not initially have any overwhelming technical advantages over the other LAN technologies but that status quo changed quickly as higher speeds (from 2.94M in 1973 to 10G currently), new media (copper, coax, fiber, and even wireless), and increased functionality (such as switching, priority, and so on) were incorporated into Ethernet. With every new generation, the speed increased tenfold (10M to 100M to 1000M to 10000M), a phenomenon that was not (and has not been) replicated with any other LAN technology. In contrast, the other LAN technologies were decidedly slow and did not maintain the same level of improvement as Ethernet. Ethernet's capabilities thus became much more formidable than the other LAN technologies in a relatively short time, and to its credit, Ethernet has continued to maintain this pace of innovation.

Standardization   As shown previously in Table 1.1, innovations in Ethernet technology were quickly standardized. Manufacturers could incorporate these new features and bring them to market relatively quickly (see "Intense Competition"). The end users obviously wanted to leverage the benefits of these new features as well and being able to do so with the assurance of interoperability between devices from different vendors (as a consequence of standardization employed by these vendors) meant accelerating the acceptance of Ethernet in the marketplace.

Commercialization   Although there were standards for the different LAN technologies, only the IEEE 802.3 was widely adopted because it was promoted as an open standard that anyone could use to implement Ethernet NIC hardware by paying a small licensing fee.[29] This unique model was also aligned with the manufacturers' approach to the various devices (PCs, printers, etc.) present in the LAN; they did not integrate Ethernet itself into their devices but rather relied on NIC manufacturers (of Ethernet, Token Ring, etc.)—ostensibly, at least in the earlier days, because they wanted to have the option of employing the best possible solution in terms of cost and features. While this was meaningful initially, Ethernet with its growing customer base and product innovation soon became the obvious choice and was embraced by the manufacturers of LAN devices. In contrast, the other LAN technologies, with smaller, niche constituencies and not having the economies of scale, were not anywhere as successful as Ethernet.

Intense Competition   Because a large number of entities were developing Ethernet solutions, it led to fierce competition, a reduction in prices, and expectedly, by the law of economics, more customer demand. The intense competition meant that vendors sought to benefit from any differentiation that they could manage; as a result, the new capabilities being standardized were being brought to market as quickly as possible. This combination of advanced features and a competitive price accelerated Ethernet's adoption in the LAN marketplace.

Interoperability   Since there were many different (albeit standards-based) implementations of Ethernet from a multitude of vendors, interoperability became a key demand of enterprises. As a result, interoperability also became a prerequisite for Ethernet vendors. This ultimately enabled customers to deploy networking equipment (servers and other devices) from different vendors seamlessly and easily—hence lowering operating costs and consequently leading to even greater demand for Ethernet.

Backward/Forward Compatibility   This became a very important attribute of Ethernet, enabling customers to use new features without having to uproot their

---

[29] IEEE was given the Ethernet patents by Xerox and now officially licenses it to any manufacturer.

base infrastructure. The fundamental Ethernet frame largely remained the same[30] independent of, say Ethernet's speed.[31] This fact made it enormously easy to work with a mish-mash of Ethernet devices and applications and led to Ethernet being perceived as a future-proof investment that would not be obsolete in a short period.

The continual innovation and commercialization of Ethernet led to dramatic improvements in its performance that, along with the economies of scale, meant cost was correspondingly reduced while new demand was stimulated. Figure 1.7 generally reflects[32] the bandwidth/speed changes in Ethernet interfaces over time, with the corresponding price per bit. The bandwidth of Ethernet cards increased tenfold periodically for about 1/3rd increase in cost (or less with time). This led to a dramatic decrease (about 70 percent) in the cost per bit from a customer standpoint. In addition, other functionality (priority, traffic management, and so on) was continuously added as well, making the per-bit cost even more appealing. In comparison, the token-based competition, despite some initial appeal, was woefully left behind in a short while, as shown Figure 1.7.

As price and performance improved, Ethernet became even more popular in the enterprise, leading to further competition and improvements and thereby stimulating more demand. This increased-demand-leading-to-improved price/performance cycle—coupled with its inherent plug-and-play simplicity—was mutually reinforcing and clearly explains the near exponential demand growth in Ethernet LAN ports vis-à-vis Token Ring, for example. With such growth, the pool of IT professionals with expertise in Ethernet also grew; and this also contributed to furthering Ethernet's acceptance.

Thus, the decision to license Ethernet to anyone, continually improve its capabilities, standardize these capabilities, and enforce interoperability, definitely underpinned the success of Ethernet in the LAN. *A pervasive theme was the amazing responsiveness of Ethernet to market requirements, essentially leading to an Ethernet that is vastly different (improved) than the original 802.3 standard, so much so that it is sometimes asserted that the transformed version is simply being called Ethernet, even though it bears little resemblance to the original!*

The benefits of Ethernet should be obvious to anyone who manages a LAN today, whether in Beijing, Bangalore, or Boston, and even more vividly to anyone who is managing LANs in Beijing, Bangalore, *and* Boston simultaneously. The universal appeal of plug-and-play Ethernet in the LAN is unquestionable.

After Ethernet's astounding success in the LAN, it moved beyond the geographically limited, customer owned and operated LAN. Ethernet, in fact (refer to 802.1 standards in Table 1.1), had long been developing the capabilities to enable delivery at distances and

---

[30] There were actually enhancements made to the frame to provide more sophisticated features such as VLAN that allowed customers to separate, prioritize, and manage LAN traffic in a more optimal fashion. However, the Ethernet frame largely remained the same.

[31] The auto-negotiation capability of Ethernet interfaces, for example, allowed devices from different manufacturers to communicate with each other and set the appropriate speed without manual intervention.

[32] Note that actual pricing is a function of several variables including time, and it is infeasible to capture this without introducing complexity; a relative approximation meaningfully illustrates the price per bit changes that occurred.

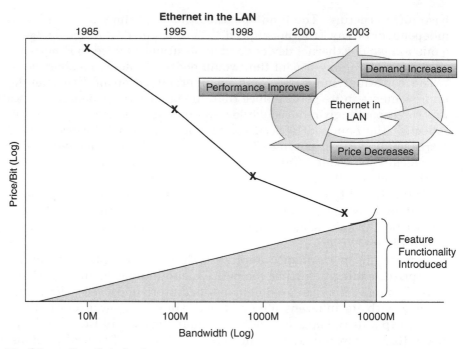

Figure 1.7 Ethernet's path to dominance

speeds more compatible with those required in inter-LAN networking (connecting LANs across a distance of tens of miles) and was well suited as a platform for the emerging data services. Service Providers were, to a limited extent, already offering Ethernet-based Point to Point (Ethernet extension) and Multipoint (transparent LAN) services.

The Failed Challenge of ATM and IP in the LAN

As a side note, it is important to mention two other technologies that also emerged as candidate LAN technologies. Unlike the ones discussed previously, however, these originated as technologies to be used in Service Provider networks but were later positioned as LAN technologies as well to compete with Ethernet. They were not successful.

Asynchronous Transfer Mode (ATM), a cell-based connection-oriented technology that successfully focused on enabling a converged infrastructure beyond the LAN (see "Ethernet: Evolution Beyond the LAN") and was positioned as a competitor to Ethernet in the LAN in the 1990s. It presented a very attractive option since it possessed several advantages over the traditional LAN Ethernet. It provided much more sophisticated traffic management and could support both packet-oriented and circuit-switched services (hence touted as the convergent platform); at that time, its speeds were also higher (OC-3 or 155M) than Fast Ethernet (100M). Given its success beyond the LAN (in metro networks), ATM in the LAN would have also meant a seamless connection to ATM networks beyond the LAN. And LAN Emulation (LANE), a mechanism to simulate the characteristics of a LAN (connectionless, multicast, etc.) over a switched ATM backbone was also developed.

However, it was significantly complex to engineer ATM LANs. This coupled with the fact that Ethernet continued to evolve mitigated—and even surpassed—the functional advantages of ATM in a short time, and that too at a much more attractive price,[33] ultimately resulting in Ethernet prevailing easily.

A similar argument held sway against the use of Layer 3/IP[34] routers in LANs. IP routers became commonplace beyond the LAN, mainly due to their scalability and resiliency benefits. In fact, most networking applications including the Internet were (and continue to be) built using IP routers. However, these advantages were not as significant in geographically smaller LANs. They were complex to set up, required the enterprise to relinquish some control,[35] and the Ethernet ports employed in routers were significantly more expensive (up to 10 times) than the corresponding ones in Layer 2 devices. Thus IP's appeal was significantly diminished against Ethernet.

Basically, these technologies (ATM/IP) had to be unnaturally forced-fit to LAN environments and consequently were less than optimal[36] in terms of the ever important criteria of price and simplicity.

Interestingly Ethernet's origins in the LAN actually better positioned it in (Service Provider) networks beyond the LAN vis-à-vis ATM/IP. This will be evident from the next section, "Ethernet: Evolution Beyond the LAN."

Ethernet: Evolution Beyond the LAN

The need to network[37] between distant locations in the same metropolitan area or to even more far-flung areas was a natural evolution. The benefits were significant for enterprises (actually for anyone who wanted to network) and included the following [7]:

- **Unprecedented means of remote communication** Now a user at a workstation in one office could communicate with a colleague or customer or supplier half way around the globe. With the advent of globalization, and communication applications such as e-mail, the importance of such communications became even more pronounced and productivity in the enterprise increased significantly.

---

[33] Due to the huge economies of scale it enjoyed

[34] IP refers to the Internet protocol in the network layer (which is Layer 3 in the OSI model).

[35] Because the enterprise is required to share its IP addressing with the Service, some control is given up in terms of how they manage their LANs.

[36] The underlying price-points and operational aspects of these technologies were simply untenable to those expected in the very cost sensitive and operationally simple LAN.

[37] For exchanging data; note that networking for voice preceded long before, and a well-developed infrastructure to support local and long distance (including international) calling has existed for years. Billions of dollars have been invested in this voice-optimized circuit-switching infrastructure.

- **Resource and information sharing**   Information located in different places could be acquired easily. Other resources whether files, processors, or storage could be shared remotely, meaning better optimization of resources and more efficient sharing of information across an enterprise.

- **Higher reliability**   Backing up vital information at a remote location, for instance, provided an extremely valuable and reliable service to the enterprise. Distributing other devices, such as computing servers, storage devices, and the like, at different physical locations also meant physical resources were available as backups in case of failures. In an era where information and data availability was increasingly becoming a strategic asset for enterprises, reliability was a necessity.

- **Increased productivity and efficiency**   With increased communication, exchange of information, and the distribution and maximizing of expensive resources, the efficiency of the enterprise has improved considerably. Such benefits underlie the development of the global Internet.

Thus there was significant value and motivation for enterprises to network beyond the LAN. As commercial networking applications became available, the need to network within Metropolitan Area Networks (MANs) became a business necessity. In fact, MAN interconnection soon became a vital part of an enterprise's communication infrastructure (for interconnecting LANs at different locations, for Internet access, for Intranets and Extranets, and a host of new applications).

Networking Beyond the LAN: Metropolitan Area Networks (MANs) and Wide Area Networks (WANs)

An enterprise needing to network beyond the LAN usually has to rely on a Service Provider for networking capability; this provider could be a telecommunications carrier, a cable Multi-Service Operator (MSO), or some other entity that usually owns and operates the underlying technology infrastructure and offers services over this infrastructure. The enterprise LAN physically connects to a Service Provider's network—this physical connection is referred to as the access, the last/first mile, or the local access loop. Specifically, a LAN device such as a router or switch is connected to a Service Provider's closest Point-Of-Presence (POP) or Central Office (CO) through some physical media via a Service Provider's equipment that is usually located at the customer's premises. The specific equipment depends on the solution employed by the Service Provider to offer the connectivity and will be discussed later in this chapter.

NOTE   Typically, the Access portion of the Service Provider network is considered to be a part of the Metropolitan (access) Area Network (although there are no standard definitions to this effect).

The network beyond the LAN is the Service Provider's network and is segmented in to the Access, MAN, and WAN. A Metropolitan Area Network (MAN), as the term suggests, refers to a network[38] that encompasses a metropolitan area, usually spanning a city and its surrounding areas and typically covering an area anywhere from tens of miles to a hundred miles in diameter. Like a LAN, a MAN is a high-speed network interconnecting many entities, albeit over a wider geographic location. As opposed to a LAN, which is usually a private, enterprise-owned network, Service Providers *typically* own and operate the MAN infrastructure. The networking capability in the MAN is provided as a service (or services) by the Service Providers for a recurring payment. A MAN may interconnect many LANs in the metropolitan area. Each of these LANs, however, operates as an entity independent of the MAN. A MAN generally encompasses the telecom access networks and its associated metro backbone. There is a lot of diversity in MANs in terms of the different types of customer applications, interfaces, and necessary bandwidth.

A Wide Area Network (WAN) refers to a network that covers a larger geographic area than that covered by a MAN. Again, there is no standard definition, but a WAN generally encompasses the network that extends beyond the typical distance of the MAN. In traditional telecommunications nomenclature, a WAN references the networks that include the metro core, regional, long haul, and ultra long-haul networks. A WAN connects multiple LANs/MANs and is usually owned and operated by multiple Service Providers (that may or may not, depending on local regulatory boundaries, also own and operate one or more MANs). A WAN typically uses optical fiber as the physical medium of transmission and usually has a much higher level of bandwidth capacity than the MAN (since in essence it aggregates and transports traffic from several MANs simultaneously).

Figure 1.8 illustrates the MAN (including the Access) and the WAN that encompass Service Provider networks.

Before exploring data networking in the MAN and WAN, it is instructive to note the fundamental differences between delivering communication services in a LAN versus doing so in the MAN and WAN. Table 1.3 highlights some of the key differences.

Basically, when enterprises require any connectivity in the MAN (to connect the local branch office to headquarters, for instance) or in the WAN (to connect another office in another region or even country to headquarters, for instance), they employ a Service Provider (or multiple Service Providers) to offer connectivity.

As Table 1.3 illustrates, delivering services in the MAN and WAN is substantially different than delivering them in the LAN. Apart from the exponentially higher number of customers and connections, there is a more attendant complexity and diversity introduced in the MAN and WAN, making manageability of services much more challenging.

The Solutions Available for Data Networking in the MAN and WAN   The natural approach to enabling data networking in the MAN and WAN was to use the existing telecommunications infrastructure. While the telecommunication infrastructure had evolved considerably[39] since its inception over a hundred years ago, it was (and still is) primarily

---

[38] Networks here and elsewhere in the book refer to a set of interconnected devices at physically diverse points. They do not indicate the specific technology used to interconnect.

[39] Telecommunications has evolved from analog to more efficient digital transmission, from being primarily circuit-switched to being a mixture of circuit-switched and packetized; from using exclusively copper to using some fiber, and so on.

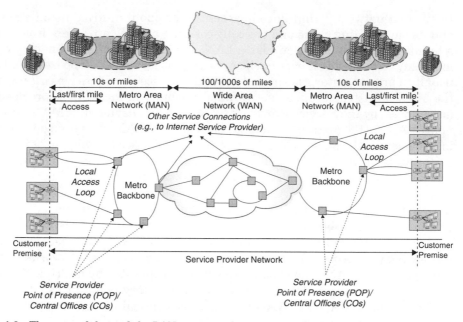

Figure 1.8 The network beyond the LAN, segmented into Access, MAN, and WAN

optimized to handle voice traffic (which almost always means telephony traffic—traffic originating and terminating on a telephone). Offering data solutions, therefore, meant transporting bursty, packet-based traffic over a voice-based infrastructure using Time Division Multiplexing (TDM) technologies (see chapter on TDM for an explanation of TDM) such as the T-carrier (T-1, T-3, etc.) on copper and fiber, and SONET (Synchronous Optical NETworking) rings over a fiber infrastructure. However, as traffic data (essentially non voice; could be anything like email, file transfers, etc.) began to reach a critical mass, alternative (and most often separate) packet-based network infrastructures were developed to carry data traffic (i.e., offer data services).

Initial packet services used a technology called X.25 quite extensively. X.25 was an ITU standard that enabled packet transmission at speeds between 2.4 and 4.8 Kbits/sec over traditional telecommunication networks; it was subsequently supplanted by other technologies, the more prominent being Frame Relay, Asynchronous Transfer Mode (ATM), and even traditional TDM (modified to be more efficient). And, as mentioned previously, Ethernet had also been used to offer data services as well. These services were delivered over a host of transport infrastructures or natively. Over the years, SONET-based TDM networks have the become dominant transport infrastructure, especially with the relatively increased deployment of fiber in metro and much more extensively in core networks. Table 1.4 provides a brief comparison among ATM, Frame Relay, traditional TDM, and Ethernet.

A typical (albeit partial) telecommunications transport infrastructure is shown in Figure 1.9. Although specific implementations vary across different telecommunication

TABLE 1.3   Comparing LANs to MANs/WANs

	Local Area Network (LAN)	Metro/Wide Area Network (MAN/WAN)
Geographic coverage	Usually a few hundred meters but typically less than a mile	10s, 100s, or even 1000s of miles
Service delivery model	Enterprise owns and operates the LAN and delivers applications over it. Usually does not rely on external entities for service within LAN	Service Provider (carrier, Cable Multi-Service Operator, and so on) owns the MAN/WAN infrastructure, which is comprised of transport/higher layer equipment). Service Providers deliver services/applications to end users—typically enterprises (and residential customers)—over this (shared) infrastructure for an initial and a recurring monthly price. The price, depending on the Service Provider and competitive factors, entails separate charges for the application/service, bandwidth, physical access, associated Service-Level Agreement guarantees, etc.
Scale	Tens of endpoints, usually PCs, servers, printers, and so on, owned by enterprise users	Usually tens of thousands of endpoints, each endpoint being an enterprise LAN physically connected by a variety of media and transport technologies.
Scope	Few services to meet a specific enterprise's needs	Numerous (voice, data, video, storage, etc.) services to address the needs of a broad range of customers in the serving area; further, the competitive element requires introduction of differentiation even amongst these services.
Bandwidth	Enterprise customer has dedicated use of bandwidth, typically 1GbE	Service Provider offers bandwidth on its infrastructure, typically anywhere from 64Kb and higher. Dedicated connections usually start from 1.544M (T-1 lines). The Service Provider charges for this bandwidth and aggregates different customers over a shared infrastructure—usually over 10G and higher.
Manageability	Relatively simple (fewer connections over a small area) and easily managed	Highly complex, managing thousands of remote users, each subscribed to a different set of services and its associated SLAs. Sophisticated mechanisms necessary to manage economically (i.e., keep the cost of delivery low)
Resiliency	Not very critical because problems can usually be fixed quickly	Critical, as unresolved failures will typically impact Service Provider revenues and long-term competitiveness (and hence, survival).
Service-level agreements (SLAs)	None usually necessary	Essential and often demanded by end users because their mission-critical applications increasingly employ Service Provider-offered services.

Carriers and across different regions of the world and to a large extent are dictated by local and national regulatory constraints, the figure represents a reasonable generalization.

As Figure 1.9 illustrates, enterprise customers are usually connected to the Service Provider infrastructure employing a TDM access circuit such as DS-0, T-1 (or DS-1), and OC-3 to connect to a Service Provider–owned SONET-based Multi-Service Provisioning Platform (MSPP) at its closest Point-Of-Presence/Central Office. The MSPPs are generally deployed in a ring topology (since this topology is physically supportive of a more resilient architecture) across a metro area and are used as collector rings. If traffic is

TABLE 1.4   Comparing Ethernet, Frame Relay, ATM, and TDM in the MAN/WAN

	ATM	Frame Relay	TDM	Ethernet
Technology	Cell-based, connection-oriented	Cell-based, connectionless	Not-packet, connection-oriented	Packet, connectionless
Bandwidth flexibility	Limited 155M or 622M Step function	Limited Steps: 1.544M or N × 1.544M (up to 45M), where N is usually an integer value	Limited Steps: 1.5M, 45M, 155M, 622M, 1250M, 2.48G, 10G	Highly flexible Granular bandwidth in increments of 1M or less
Scalability	Step function	Step function	Step function corresponding to traditional TDM hierarchy	Granular
Application support	Voice and data	Data	Voice	Data
Quality of service (QoS)	Very good; strong mechanisms to ensure QoS	Good	Excellent dedicated	Initially little to none, gradually incorporating new mechanisms
Management	Excellent	High	Very Good	Inadequate
Resiliency	Excellent		Excellent (SONET)	High
Cost	High	High	High	Low
Innovation	Limited	Limited	Reasonable	Continuous

dropped locally in the metro, the MSPP serves as a termination point for a service, or it is connected to a regional or long-haul ring that carries the traffic to a remote location. SONET/SDH Add Drop Multiplexers (ADMs) are usually used for transport, often times over a Wave Division Multiplexing (WDM) infrastructure to provide scale and transparency. (Of course, other equipment providing higher-level functions such as switching, routing, so on, is often present as well.) More information on SONET/SDH infrastructure for delivery of services is discussed in Part II of this book.

Ethernet in the MAN/WAN

In the decade following the 1990s, the trend of data traffic in Service Provider networks took a markedly upward turn. The emergence of the Internet, coupled with a whole host of other emerging data (multi-media) applications such as Napster and like resulted in a huge surge in data traffic.[40] In fact, it was factually estimated that (Internet) traffic was doubling at least every year (see Figure 1.10), which was indeed a disruptive—and unprecedented—phenomenon [13].

Around this time, regulatory constraints were also being eased with the Telecom Act of 1996 in the U.S. and similar competitive measures globally, and a new set of competitive

---

[40] Unfortunately the initial assessments on the rate of growth were somewhat exaggerated. "That [Internet] traffic was doubling every 90 days" was bandied about quite authoritatively! [12] and contributed, along with other factors, to the telecom boom—and the subsequent bust that followed. But it was indisputable that data traffic grew significantly.

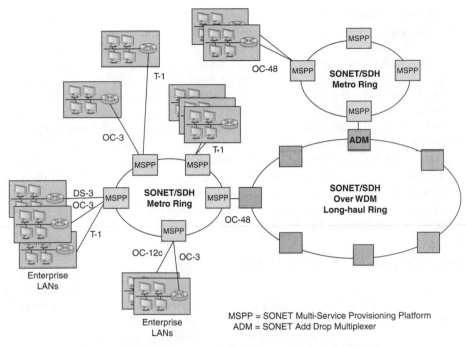

Figure 1.9 A typical Service Providers transport infrastructure in the MAN/WAN

Service Providers emerged—the Competitive Local Exchange Carriers (CLECs). These Service Providers, seeking to leverage the growth opportunity in data traffic, began to examine the most cost efficient and appealing solutions for end customers. Given the preponderance of data, they naturally explored the traditional data-oriented platforms, such as ATM, Frame Relay, and Ethernet. Since it was increasingly tenable to also packetize voice and carry it as a data service, the need for TDM solutions—at least with these Service Providers—was largely becoming moot.

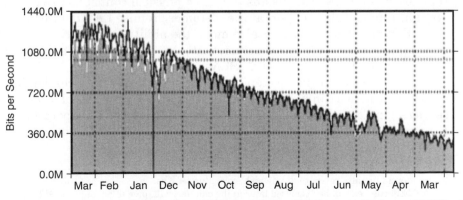

Figure 1.10 Graph of Internet traffic (1999 – 2000) from the London Internet Exchange (LINX), showing that traffic nearly doubled every 200 days! Source: LINX

Notwithstanding the reasonable maturity and fairly significant size of ATM and Frame Relay deployments in Service Provider networks, Ethernet came across as a very plausible candidate for delivering data services in the Access and MAN and also the WAN. As demand surged for bandwidth, ATM and frame-based networks were ill equipped to support the broadband[41] applications driving the bandwidth. Ethernet, with its periodic ten fold increase in bandwidth, began to seem like an attractive alternative to duplicating ATM equipment. Furthermore, most of the applications driving the bandwidth were based on the Internet Protocol (IP) and were especially well suited for Ethernet access and transport (IP devices such as routers typically have Ethernet interfaces). In addition, Ethernet, in line with its heritage in the LAN, continued to innovate and improve its capabilities, and consequently, as it had done so many times in the past (as noted previously, with token-based technologies in the LAN), Ethernet surpassed its competition on other aspects as well. The many key reasons for considering Ethernet beyond the LAN are discussed next.

Benefits of Ethernet Beyond the LAN

As noted previously, Ethernet had long ago begun in earnest to address distance, resiliency, and scaling issues that would be present in a MAN and beyond. In fact, it continually extended its functionality in each of these areas and standardized it as well as shown in Table 1.1. So there was already some appeal to Ethernet—as evidenced by the deployment of Ethernet-based Transport LAN Services (TLS) and Ethernet extension services in the metro. There were, however, numerous additional benefits as well.

A key distinction from the other competitive solutions such as SONET/TDM, ATM, and Frame Relay is the fact that there are significant benefits to *both* the end user enterprises seeking a cost-optimal connectivity solution for their networking applications and also to Service Providers typically offering such solutions (to enterprises) [14]. These are discussed next and are grouped in Figure 1.11; ultimately, the fact that Ethernet[42] offers extremely compelling benefits to both these constituencies is key to its increasing popularity beyond the LAN.

Note that beyond the LAN, Ethernet is delivered as a *service* to the end customer by the Service Provider. This means there is a physical connection so customers can plug straight into an Ethernet port at the customer premise LAN device (switch/router) and carry Ethernet frames; it may also mean the ability to subscribe to multiple services and applications (like Internet access, VoIP, etc.) over the same port, possibly with some sort of Service-Level Agreements (SLAs).

From a Service Provider's standpoint, these Ethernet services can be delivered over a host of transport infrastructures (much like the delivery of TDM or Frame Relay services) and technologies, including a native Ethernet transport as well. (Delivering Ethernet natively is the most optimal approach and does not entail any expensive

---

[41] Broadband usually refers to bandwidth exceeding 64 Kbs.
[42] LAN Ethernet, as will be discussed later in the chapter, will have to be augmented to serve beyond the LAN.

Why *Both* End Users and Service Providers Prefer Ethernet Services

	End Users	Service Providers
Attractive Economics	**Lowers IT cost and enables pay-as-you-use model** • Lowest per bit cost service • Potentially lowered bandwidth requirement • Only use and pay for the bandwidth required • Lower cost equipment at the premise • Lowered OPEX due to proficiency with Ethernet	**Higher Revenues and Improved Profitability** • New revenue potential from previously unaddressable bandwidth requirement. • Revenues ramp quicker • Lowered cost of delivering Ethernet (no truck rolls) • Multiple services on single interface reduces cost, improves profitability
Unparallel Flexibility and Simplicity	**No Trade-off between optimizing Spending and Flexibility** • No rigid bandwidth limitations • Rapid introduction of additional bandwidth/services possible • Single interface for all services means simplified premise equipment management. • Plug-and-play service aligned with LAN Ethernet	**Platform for Convergence** • Service and Network convergence • Wide array of services can be offered • Software provisioning allows rapid introduction of new services and revenues • Easier to manage one Interface
Strategic Appeal	**New Application Support and Lowered IT Spending** • New video, multimedia, and other enterprise applications will be packetized (including voice) running over a device with an Ethernet interface • Continued Innovation and standardization of Ethernet	**Strategic Competitiveness** • Meet customer demand • Potential to "capture customer" by delivering new services quickly • Long term profitability • Continued Innovation and standardization of Ethernet

Figure 1.11   Benefits of Ethernet Services in the MAN/WAN

protocol conversion.) The exact approach is, of course, likely to be decided based on several considerations such as the incumbent infrastructure technology being employed by the Service Provider, its strategy, the services offered, investment available, and so on.

Thus, from an end-user standpoint, the basic handoff of data is Ethernet, but how this is accomplished (behind the scenes) by the Service Provider is usually of less concern. We delve into the benefits of employing Ethernet as a service next.

Enterprises End Customer Benefits

End customers, already proficient with Ethernet, also find it as appealing as a service for three major reasons: simplicity, flexibility, and ultimately, economics. These not mutually exclusive benefits are expounded further here.

Ubiquity and Simplicity   Ethernet is ubiquitous in the LAN. Well over 90 percent of LANs employ Ethernet, so using Ethernet services in the MAN/WAN extends this ubiquity and enables the same plug-and-play operation that characterizes the LAN (from an end-user standpoint, all this means is connecting a LAN switch Ethernet port to a Service Provider-offered physical Ethernet connection).

Ethernet service also simplifies operational aspects significantly since, as per Metro Ethernet Forum (MEF) estimates, nearly 99 percent of the data traffic flowing through the MAN and WAN originates and terminates on an Ethernet LAN port. Carrying and delivering this Ethernet traffic without having to convert it into a host of intermediary services (like ATM, Frame Relay, TDM, etc.) makes for a preferred solution because it precludes the need for any overhead (in terms of hardware, expertise, management, etc.) that would otherwise be necessary.

Furthermore, when additional bandwidth is required or new services are introduced at the enterprise, these needs can be easily met with Ethernet in a very short period of time (since Service Providers can often remotely provision this) as opposed to TDM, Frame Relay, or ATM.

Single (converged) access for all services   In a typical enterprise, there are usually multiple discrete connections to the Service Provider, each of them delivering a different voice or data service. As shown in Figure 1.12, it is fairly common for a mid-size enterprise to employ different physical connections and transport technologies such as TDM, ATM, and Frame Relay, for its voice, storage, and other data traffic. The reason for this type of setup is largely historical evolution, and a function of how these different services were(are) delivered by Service Providers. This multiple-access approach presents several problems for the end user:

- There is additional cost and manageability associated with the expensive equipment.
- There is no opportunity to optimize bandwidth or the manageability of services internally.
- Each of these different connections requires truck-rolls[43], which translates in to delays for the enterprise

Often a SONET ADM node is used to support these multiple connections—an expensive proposition. These multiple discrete connections are inherently inefficient and cannot optimize the total bandwidth required by the enterprise: if a specific service on a discrete connection uses less bandwidth than provisioned, then the unused bandwidth cannot be used by any of the other services. Thus, the enterprise will waste bandwidth and pay more (than necessary).

As most of the applications, including increasingly voice (using Voice over IP or VoIP supported by IP PBX) are being packetized, then pretty much all applications/services an enterprise uses can be transported over an Ethernet access platform most (if not all) supporting equipment (for instance, a storage switch) now have an Ethernet interface.

Employing Ethernet as the common access interface not only simplifies the connectivity and the equipment necessary, but also enables the capability to optimize the bandwidth across multiple services. What this means is the likelihood of the enterprise reducing its recurring bandwidth cost. This when complemented with the typically lower cost of Ethernet makes it even more appealing reinforcing this appeal is the fact that new services can be added rapidly (this is a big advantage to Service Providers as well; see the following sections).

---

[43] Truck-roll is a common industry term used to indicate that service technician(s) are dispatched remotely (usually by truck/vehicle).

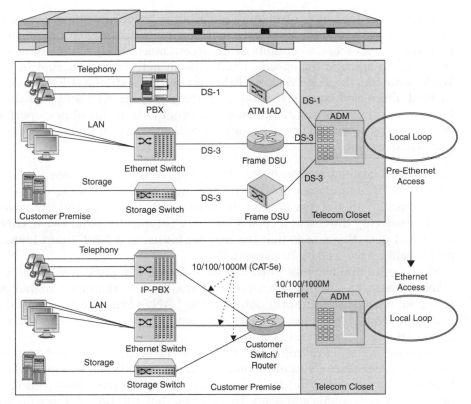

Figure 1.12 Ethernet enables converged—and simplified—access (Source: MEF)

The operational costs (OPEX) are also reduced due to simplified management of just a single (and familiar) connection, as opposed to managing several different types of connections. And, of course, the cost associated with the equipment for these connections is eliminated (as discussed in the next section).

Familiarity and In-house Expertise   The Ethernet LAN has been around for over three decades and has become an integral part of the IT infrastructure of any enterprise. As a result, there is usually considerable expertise within the IT group itself on how to manage an Ethernet LAN. Employing Ethernet as an access technology to the Service Provider infrastructure is, therefore, seen as a natural—and seamless—extension to the LAN and something that is comfortably manageable. Simple issues can be managed within the enterprise itself, often without having to involve a Service Provider and incurring the attendant cost and delays.

Contrast this with TDM or even a Frame Relay access; this usually imposes a different set of skills for the IT/networking group, resulting in additional operational overhead. And the Service Provider (offering the service) generally has to be involved with even relatively simple troubleshooting exercises, often making manageability a less than desirable experience.

So Ethernet (access[44]) ultimately contributes to lowering the operational expenditure for the enterprise. Further, Ethernet, true to its historical form, continues to evolve to make it even more acceptable as an access mechanism. Numerous standards are emerging to address the specific challenges of delivering Ethernet in the MAN and WAN; some like the IEEE 802.3ah Ethernet in the First Mile (EFM) have already been ratified (discussed later in chapter 2). Enterprises are well aware of the evolution of Ethernet in the LAN and the consequent benefits in terms of price/performance over the last three decades. They are comfortable that Ethernet in its new role in the MANs and WANs as well.

Bandwidth Scalability and Flexibility   Ethernet LANs commonly operate anywhere from 1M to 1000M, usually tending toward the higher speeds because of the relatively minor increase[45] in the cost of these interfaces and the substantially lowered cost per bit.(Considering the cost of a 1000M interface is typically about two to three times that of a 100M port, this means that the cost per bit using a 1000M port instead of a 100M port would be reduced by 70 percent.[46])

Multimedia applications (such as video conferencing and real-time backup) in the LAN are also bandwidth intensive and are, in fact, requiring higher speed LANs. However, when the traffic originating in the LAN is expected to terminate outside the LAN and across the Service Provider's telecommunications infrastructure, this usually means the traffic is severely throttled.

Consider a simple example, wherein some large files need to be transferred from one enterprise office location to another across the city; let's assume the LANs at either location are operating at 10M and the enterprise has subscribed to a T-1 private line (a very reasonable scenario). This means that the LAN file traffic is subjected to a significant (over 80 percent) reduction in speed, which is akin to traffic on a six-lane highway suddenly having to converge into one lane; naturally, one should expect a severe traffic-jam![47]

One obvious solution to the problem of using TDM, Frame Relay, or ATM infrastructure/ services is to use higher bandwidth, but this is not a highly efficient solution. Consider the bandwidth/speed hierarchy for SONET/TDM services that is typically available in the access. It is a step function, similar to that shown in the Figure 1.13, with a very inefficient profile. Let's assume a scenario wherein an enterprise customer who has subscribed to 155M of bandwidth (OC-3) realizes some time later (say, 48 months) that 500M of access bandwidth capacity is required to meet the growing needs of the enterprise. (It is also assumed that the enterprise will need 622M of capacity some

---

[44] Note—Ethernet access is the service here; just a connectivity service that entails a single physical Ethernet connection.

[45] In fact, most devices have a Network Interface Card operating at 10/100M, i.e., either at 10 or 100.

[46] If 100M costs $X, then 1000M costs cost roughly three times $X; cost per bit using 100M = $X/100M, using 1000M = 3 × $X/1000M = 0.3X (cost per bit using 100M)

[47] Admittedly, though, this may not be as severe because of the nature of data traffic, which typically has only some peaks interspersed with more modest traffic demands.

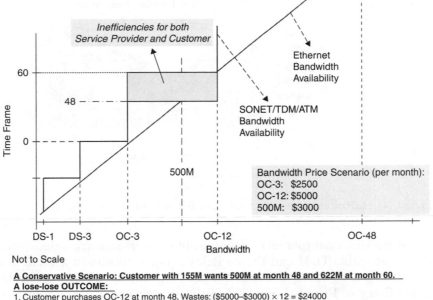

Figure 1.13   SONET/TDM versus Ethernet bandwidth availability

12 months later). At this point, however, the customer has two options to get to 500M in the case of SONET/TDM access:

- The customer can look at the next capacity available (i.e., OC-12 (622M)) but will then have to pay an extra amount for the additional 122M capacity that the customer will not use for another 12 months.

- The customer can defer until it needs the full 622M (12 months later); in this case, the customer is obviously making do with severely limited bandwidth capacity, which will inevitably have an adverse impact on the customer applications (at least for another 12 months). Of course, this also means the Service Provider will lose potential revenues for another 12 months.

Some sample (conservative) numbers are used in the Figure 1.14 and illustrate what is basically a lose-lose outcome for both Service Providers and end users.

Using Ethernet instead of SONET/TDM means that such scenarios can be avoided and furthermore, only the bandwidth required can be purchased. Ethernet ports on devices can be tuned to offer bandwidth, usually upward of 1M, in linear increments (of 1M or less). This flexibility means the ability to use the bandwidth optimally. Ethernet, therefore, enables a pay-as-you-use model that is naturally preferred over an inefficient and expensive TDM-based model.

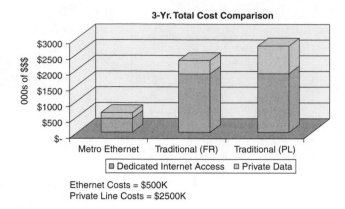

Figure 1.14   MEF commissioned study on total savings using Ethernet services

Lowest Service Cost (per bit)   Ethernet-based services are priced consistently lower than comparable TDM and Frame Relay services in almost all markets. Even though the actual pricing varies between markets, it is at least 20–30 percent lower than ATM, Frame Relay, or Private Lines. The fairly strong competition among Service Providers, coupled with the lower cost of delivering Ethernet services versus other traditional services (see the next section), has largely contributed to this situation.

Studies commissioned by the MEF used a scenario of a large enterprise with several sites, requiring Internet access and a point-to-point connection between multiple sites. These services could be delivered over a Frame Relay service, Private Line service, or an Ethernet service. It was found that the enterprise would save nearly 80 percent using an Ethernet service over a traditional Private Line. As important, in the scenario presented, this equated to a dramatically lower cost of nearly $500K using Ethernet services, as opposed to the $2.5 million of using the private line over a period of three years (see Figure 1.14). Thus, Ethernet services represent a significant savings in absolute terms as well, even when a nominally sized customer base is considered.

Simpler, Lower Cost Equipment at the Customer Premise   Employing a single Ethernet interface for all the services means simpler Ethernet equipment, such as a low-end switch or a router, suffices in lieu of complex multiport ADMs—and usually the associated demarcation devices like Integrated Access Devices (IADs), and CSU/DSUs, or similar devices.

A MEF-sponsored study using a sample configuration of just three services (ATM, Frame Relay, and Internet access) and replacing it with a single 10/100 Ethernet service showed a capital savings of nearly 95 percent! The initial cost of $2500–$7500 per WANside port was reduced to $300 for a 10/100 Ethernet port. In addition, there is an opportunity to optimize the total bandwidth required using Ethernet and potentially further reducing the port costs (so fewer ports may be required).

Lower Operational Expenditure (OPEX)   Using Ethernet (access) services, as mentioned previously, an enterprise reduces not only the amount (and cost) of equipment but also the attendant operational expenditure that would have been associated with the provisioning, operationalizing, and managing these multiple devices, each supporting a different technology.

Service Providers Benefits

Utilizing Ethernet in the access and beyond is also appealing to Service Providers primarily because it simplifies their infrastructure, reduces costs, and most importantly, offers a new source of potential revenues. Ethernet can be offered on a variety of infrastructures, and delivering over one infrastructure versus the others means the cost structure also varies (since some infrastructures are more optimized than others) and impacts profitability.

That enterprises are also demanding Ethernet for the reasons discussed previously further reinforces this appeal. The key benefits of Ethernet to Service Providers are summarized next.

Higher Revenue Potential Through More Granular Bandwidth Offering   Since more granular services are delivered using Ethernet, there is an opportunity to derive more revenues than with TDM services; for instance, if a customer has subscribed to a T-1 circuit, then if additional bandwidth, say 5M is required, the usual option is a T-3/DS-3 circuit, a 28 times increase in bandwidth at probably 15 times the price of a T-1, with over 80 percent wasted. This rather undesirable option may actually lead to the customer putting off purchasing the DS-3 until much later and consequently deferring Service Provider revenues. With a 5M offering over Ethernet, of course, revenues can be immediately realized.

Frequently, however, the market pricing is such that a customer will likely just purchase a 10 Mbps Ethernet circuit from the Service Provider for a nominally higher price (but still decidedly less than the price of a DS-3). Such a scenario is a win-win solution for both the Service Provider[48] and the customer. Almost all major Service Providers in the U.S. and elsewhere are providing granular Ethernet bandwidth in increments of 1M.

Delivering Multiple Services over a Single Interface   Using a single Ethernet interface, a Service Provider can offer a vast array of Ethernet-based services (such as Internet access, LAN extension, Transparent LAN) for low marginal costs. Employing Virtual LAN tagging, for instance, and with a bandwidth and performance profile, each of these services can be delivered on the same physical interface. With VoIP, voice applications, and the potential developments in the area of circuit emulation (see Chapter 3) of other TDM services, almost all current services can be offered over an Ethernet interface.

This scenario, which is not plausible with traditional TDM services, enables a Service Provider to leverage a single physical interface and derive the maximum revenue from that interface; more importantly, it positions a Service Provider to be able to deliver all

---

[48] Even though revenue per bit has possibly decreased, this could mean additional revenue from the customer.

services optimally—and hence maximize the potential revenue from customers. It also provides convenience and simpler management by using a single physical interface for multiple services (as noted in the end-user benefit discussion).

Rapid Delivery Through Software-defined Provisioning/Service Additions   Ethernet enables Service Providers to modify or upgrade the services offered to enterprise customers remotely. This capability offers the Service Providers two major benefits (apart from speedy delivery for the enterprise user): reduced cost of introducing additional bandwidth and an increase in revenue velocity.

For example, given the acceptably low marginal cost of deploying a 1000M versus a 100M connection, Service Providers can physically provision a 1000M port even when the customer initially requires much less bandwidth, say 25M. In this case, the Service Provider would only commission 25M of bandwidth (i.e., the customer can only use 25M even though the physical port can support up to a 1000M). Then, when there is a demand for higher bandwidth in the future (as will invariably be the case), the Service Provider can increase bandwidth remotely using software and without having to send a technician (truck roll) to the site and without having to bring down the service for any meaningful amount of time (perhaps for no more than a few minutes). Speedy delivery of additional bandwidth, unprecedented in the TDM world, is increasingly expected these days.

With TDM, this would simply not be possible; there would be significant downtime, change out in the physical ports on either end, and additional testing needed. An MEF commissioned study using a realistic scenario of 100 users receiving a host of services (private line and Internet access) over TDM (see Figure 1.15) showed that with Ethernet, the service provisioning cycle was reduced by 14 weeks and yielded revenues of $7.5 million in this period alone.

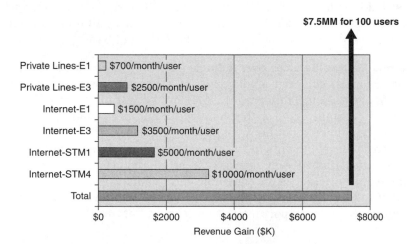

Figure 1.15   Revenue acceleration (velocity) by employing Ethernet services

Reduced Cost of Delivering Services Employing Ethernet in the Service Provider network to deliver traditional data services has a substantial economic advantage in terms of cost savings. A comprehensive study commissioned by the MEF compared capital and operational costs incurred by a Service Provider to deliver a host of data services to hundreds of small- and medium-sized enterprises over an (optical) Ethernet infrastructure[49] versus those incurred employing a traditional SONET infrastructure. Over a three-year period, there was a 39 percent savings in CAPital EXpenditure (CAPEX) and a 49 percent savings in OPerational EXpenditure (OPEX) when an Ethernet platform was used as opposed to the legacy SONET infrastructure.

Further, Service Providers employing an Ethernet platform can enable a comprehensive and sophisticated set of services; and with configurable software capability, most of this is done remotely and precludes truck rolls and the otherwise large overhead associated with TDM. Another study by the MEF (Figure 1.16) showed a 50 percent savings in truck rolls alone for provisioning a service using Ethernet versus the static approaches common when delivering TDM services.

Reduced OPEX Through Simple, Converged Access With voice increasingly transforming from a circuit-switched application to a packetized application delivered over an Ethernet interface, a key barrier to Ethernet becoming a platform for convergence is being overcome. Most, if not all, applications, whether simple data, storage, video, or multimedia, are already being delivered over Ethernet.

With a single physical connection supporting all voice and data applications, the Service Provider simplifies access to the customer; with the end-user enterprises also being generally proficient in Ethernet technology, this usually reduces overhead for commissioning and troubleshooting (as noted elsewhere in this section).

New (consumer and business) networking applications are almost exclusively being developed assuming an underlying IP infrastructure[50] and delivered over an Ethernet interface. As a result, Ethernet is also becoming further entrenched as the platform for convergent access.

Customer Retention By employing Ethernet, a Service Provider can reduce customer churn by offering

- Better pricing
- A pay-as-you-use flexibility
- A wider array of future services delivered over same interface

---

[49] Optical Ethernet infrastructure indicates transporting (and switching if necessary) Ethernet natively over a fiber-optic infrastructure.

[50] Almost all the popular networking applications presuppose working over the global Internet (in fact it is a necessary condition to gain mass market appeal), which of course is based on IP (Internet Protocol).

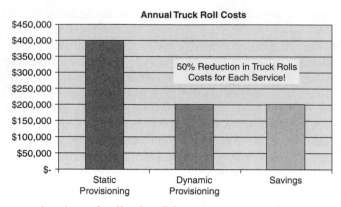

Figure 1.16 Total cost savings in truck rolls when Ethernet service is used

This ultimately leads to more profits for the Service Provider because they avoid the significant costs incurred during the acquisition of new customers to replace those who leave. Figure 1.17 shows a scenario illustrating the significant revenue benefits of delivering Ethernet services over traditional TDM services. Two Service Providers, A and B, start out delivering Internet access services and employing Ethernet and E-1, respectively. Assuming similar pricing and growth opportunities at both Service Providers and a better customer retention rate for Service Provider A (as noted previously, a Service Provider offering Ethernet service is better positioned to deliver almost all of a customer's service requests), we find that Service Provider A will, with time, receive higher revenues than Service Provider B. By the fifth year, Service Provider A will, in fact, receive 2.6 times more revenues than Service Provider B across a similar customer base of 100 customers.[51]

Meeting Customer Demand and New Growth Opportunities   Market assessments indicate a rapidly growing demand for Ethernet services for all the reasons discussed previously in this section.[52] According to Infonetics, over 86 percent of Service Providers indicated high customer demand for new Ethernet services with about 57 percent wanting to migrate from Frame Relay and ATM to Ethernet services.

Naturally, Service Providers find this demand appealing and are scurrying to provide Ethernet service; in the North American market alone, over 200 Carriers are providing some form of Ethernet service. In other global markets such as Asia, customer demand follows an even more aggressive trend. These different trends are discussed in detail in Chapter 3.

---

[51] When a user wants more bandwidth than the T-1 currently provisioned, the significant time and work required could lead to the customer switching to another Service Provider, especially in a competitive market. Thus, with TDM services, a customer will likely switch providers periodically.

[52] The relationship between Service Provider Ethernet offerings and customer demand is not only causal. Ethernet offers independent advantages to both customers and Service Providers.

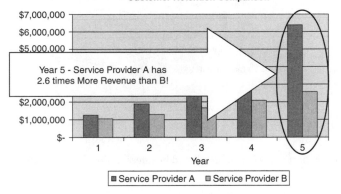

Figure 1.17 Reducing customer churn

Thus, Ethernet offers a compelling value proposition to both end users and Service Providers; this win-win proposition has led to significant growth in Ethernet services and positions Ethernet even more strongly in the MAN and the WAN.

The Current State of Ethernet Services Deployment

Revenues from Ethernet-based services worldwide are fairly significant and in the range of over $2 billion (based on 2005 figures from Infonetics). The market is expected to experience a Compounded Annual Growth Rate (CAGR[53]) of 40 percent between 2005 and 2009, reaching approximately $20+ billion. Some analysts have even more promising numbers; Vertical Systems Group, for instance, assesses that fiber-based business Ethernet services in the U.S. alone will be over $15 billion cumulative over the next five years (2007–2012). A more comprehensive discussion of the drivers of market growth is provided in Chapter 3, but it is clear that Ethernet in the MAN, and WAN is beginning to develop a critical mass and is growing at a very impressive pace. Ethernet is slowly beginning to dominate niche markets such as the metro access portion of Service Provider networks. Its ability to enable broadband access is without question beginning to extend to the MAN and WAN as well.

However, Ethernet beyond the LAN—especially deeper in the MAN and WAN—is still is a long way from dominating the market, notwithstanding the overwhelming advantages discussed earlier. Apart from its relatively late entry, at least in a substantial way, Ethernet's transition to becoming a serious contender as a Service Provider offering in the MAN, and WAN, requires it to support numerous other capabilities that are essential to competing with existing solutions such as ATM and Frame Relay. Figure 1.18 illustrates the spending of U.S. enterprises for broadband services today; Ethernet accounts for only a paltry 3 percent of spending. In order to achieve to LAN-like dominance in the MAN and WAN, Ethernet must grow at a near exponential rate

---

[53] CAGR is essentially the year over year growth over a period of time.

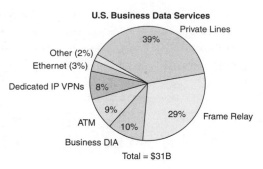

U.S. Business Data Services

- Private Lines 39%
- Other (2%)
- Ethernet (3%)
- Dedicated IP VPNs 8%
- ATM 9%
- Business DIA 10%
- Frame Relay 29%

Total = $31B

Figure 1.18   Ethernet portion of broadband business in the U.S. (Vertical Systems Group, 2006)

over the next several years. And it must address the challenges and shortcomings that it faces in that quest.

Barriers to Deployment of Ethernet Beyond the LAN

Notwithstanding the promise of Ethernet beyond the LAN, there are still quite a few challenges that need to be addressed before it can credibly become a dominant service. Seeing as it was originally conceived in the context of a LAN, some fundamental constraints have surfaced as Ethernet is transformed to a Service Provider–delivered service in a MAN or WAN. These are noted next.

Economic Barriers

Ethernet beyond the LAN is usually delivered as service by a Service Providers, and hence the economics associated with delivering this service should be attractive to the Service Providers. Put another way, delivering Ethernet services should entail both top-line (revenue) and bottom-line (profitability) growth.

Revenue per Bit Decreases Quite Dramatically   One of the key drivers for Ethernet services from an enterprise customer's standpoint is the significantly lower cost per bit—usually a tenfold increase in bandwidth is available for only a two- or threefold increase in cost. Conversely, however, for the Service Providers offering the service, this means that their revenues per bit are similarly reduced. Understandably, Service Providers can be reluctant to offer Ethernet-based services given that they can derive substantially higher revenues from incumbent legacy services like Frame Relay, Private Line, especially if customers are not demanding new services.

Cost of Delivering Ethernet Services   While Ethernet services are generally attractive to Service Providers from an OPEX standpoint, they are less compelling when you consider that a Service Provider's physical infrastructure is largely not optimized for Ethernet delivery. Most of it is based on SONET, so consequently delivering Ethernet often means force fitting these solutions for Ethernet delivery, which is inherently inefficient and increases costs.

Furthermore, a Service Provider's operational infrastructure (systems, personnel) are not yet optimized for delivering Ethernet services because most of this infrastructure was optimized for supporting the much larger revenue-yielding TDM services. While pockets of data expertise definitely exist (due to deployments of X.25, ATM, and other data technologies), it is still a limiting factor. Updating infrastructure is a time consuming and costly challenge.

Cannibalization A big challenge faced by Service Providers is that Ethernet is largely being used as a substitute for legacy services. As research from Vertical Systems Group (VSG) shows, at least in North America, such substitution accounts for a large portion, 86 percent, of the market.

And with considerably lower per bit revenues from offering Ethernet services, Service Providers face the very real prospect of declining revenues. Notwithstanding the benefits of Ethernet, the potential loss of revenues makes them, at best, reluctant to speed up the offering of Ethernet services.

However, to truly appreciate the extent of this problem, you have to put these factors in perspective. TDM applications still account for most of a typical carrier's revenue and so, arguably, Carriers are still investing in their SONET/TDM infrastructure, albeit at a lower rate than before. This opportunity cost impedes Ethernet services and infrastructure.

Operational and Technology Barriers

Offering Ethernet services beyond the LAN is quite a different proposition; there are inherent differences that necessitate additional capabilities to operate meaningfully in Service Provider networks, which make up the MANs and WANs.

Service Support and Traffic Management Ethernet as a service has largely covered a set of informally (and often ill) defined point-to-point services usually deployed over a fiber infrastructure. As Ethernet moves to the MAN and WAN as an increasingly serious contender for more sophisticated services based on multipoint architectures, there is an urgent need to formally define (and standardize) fundamental Ethernet services and their underlying features. This standardization would enable interoperability, clarifying what can be expected from such services and consequently encouraging wide-scale deployment.

In the MAN/WAN, traffic management is considerably more complex than in the LAN, where it is basically a best effort (and is often adequate). In the MAN and WAN, where the Service Providers invest significantly in transmission assets (for example, fiber and other transport equipment) and their manageability, a better return on investment is sought. This will require an ability to oversubscribe traffic and other related capabilities such as prioritization and service assurance.

Scalability While Ethernet has evolved impressively, it still largely remains a LAN-focused technology. Employing it in Service Provider networks is a different matter. There are many more endpoints that need to be connected in a typical MAN (thousands of connections) versus those in a typical LAN (tens of connections). Apart from the scalability to support so many more customers, failure mechanisms from the LAN such as the Spanning

Tree Protocol (STP) and its variants are ineffectual with such large deployments because of the long convergence time (the time taken to recover from a failure).

Quality of Service (QoS)   As previously mentioned, Ethernet is being considered as a platform for convergence so that all services are delivered by the carrier over an Ethernet connection. If this is done, then Ethernet should be able to support a variety of different applications, including latency sensitive voice and video applications. The Service Providers would have to ensure a Quality Of Service (QoS) for such services over Ethernet, something that is generally lacking because Ethernet was mainly confined to LANs, and in that context, a best effort has been largely acceptable.

Support for TDM Services   While Ethernet as a convergent platform makes for operational simplicity and reduced costs, it is somewhat naïve to assume that the billions-in-revenues that TDM services provide will be flash-cut over to packetized services. A snapshot of the current distribution of services by enterprise spending is shown in Figure 1.18 and vividly illustrates[54] that Ethernet currently forms a very small portion (3 percent) of the total. It is implausible to assume that the other 97 percent will migrate to Ethernet in a short period of time. For one thing, end users (and Service Providers) have spent a considerable amount of effort and cost stabilizing their TDM-based services, and there is invariably some real-and perceived risk involved in moving to an Ethernet-based service. For end users who have grown comfortable with TDM (or ATM or Frame Relay) services for their mission-critical applications, moving to Ethernet is, therefore, not compelling—particularly if there is no short-term growth in bandwidth or new packet-based applications being introduced.

It is realistic to assume that demand for TDM (and other incumbent) services will not dramatically reduce for a while longer. This offers a new challenge for Service Providers that, in an attempt to optimize their delivery infrastructure, are migrating to a packet-based (Ethernet) infrastructure; they should be able to support the delivery of TDM (and other packet and non-packet-based) services over an Ethernet infrastructure using some kind of emulation techniques

Operations, Administration, and Maintenance (OAM)   Finally, managing these Ethernet services in a MAN/WAN imposes significant new challenges. There are many more entities to manage, service-level issues that predominate, and new mechanisms for Operations, Administration, and Maintenance (OAM) required.

As Ethernet is moving down market, to small and medium businesses especially, significant cost overhead is introduced to manage these services. This cost is not particularly unique to Ethernet; earlier technologies such as TDM/Private Line, ATM, and Frame Relay faced similar challenges, i.e., how to keep operational expenditure low while delivering services. Ethernet will also have to introduce new "intelligent" edge devices to more economically enable wide-scale deployment. What all this suggests is

---

[54] Services for Ethernet, ATM, private line typically refer to all services that employ these technologies as a handoff.

that Ethernet requires additional "carrier-class" attributes before it's ready for larger scale deployments in Service Provider networks.

Overcoming The Barriers

As the value of Ethernet beyond the LAN is becoming increasingly accepted, there are numerous activities underway to overcome the shortcomings just identified and truly transform Ethernet into a mass market service. One such effort is to make it carrier-class. In its transformation to being a viable candidate beyond the LAN, this effort is a prerequisite, and although there has been considerable work done in this area, it still largely remains in its infancy.

The increasing competition, especially from newer players such as Cable/MSOs in North America, is making the cannibalization scenario moot; it is not simply about losing out on some of the existing revenue but rather losing out on customers (and hence, losing out on all revenue). The latter situation is obviously less acceptable to incumbent Service Providers, and they have no choice but to undertake Ethernet deployment more aggressively and seize the growing demand for Ethernet services. The fact that numerous up and coming services like Voice over IP (VOIP) are actually better suited to deployment over an Ethernet/IP infrastructure and that legacy services can be accommodated by circuit emulation techniques is actually negating the cannibalization argument.

The next chapter begins with a formal definition of Carrier Ethernet services and presents the broader framework that identifies the specific capabilities necessary to enable such services in Service Provider MANs and WANs. It also identifies all the various standards-based and commercial activities in the realm of Carrier Ethernet that are intent on positioning it for dominance, much like in the LAN. Not surprisingly, these enablers mirror, to some extent, the Ethernet story line in the LAN.

References

1. Charles E. Spurgeon, *Ethernet: The Definitive Guide* (City of Publication: O'Reilly: 2000).

2. Jan Harrington, *Ethernet Clearly Explained,* (City of Publication: Morgan Kaufmann, 1999).

3. Robert Breyer and Sean Riley, *Switching, Fast and Gigabit Ethernet* (City of Publication: Sams, 1998).

4. Philip Miller and Michael Cummins, *LAN Technologies Explained,* 2nd Ed. (City of Publication: Digital Press, 2000).

5. Rich Seifert, *The Switch Book: The Complete Guide to LAN Switching Technology,* 1st Ed. (city of Publication: Wiley, 2000).

6. Andrew Tannenbaum, *Computer Networks,* 2nd Ed. (City of Publication: Prentice Hall, 1988).

7. IEEE 802.3 standard, Institute of Electrical and Electronics Engineers, //standards.ieee.org/getieee802/802.3html.

8. Robert M. Metcalfe and David R. Boggs, "Ethernet: Distributed Packet Switching for Local Computer Networks," *Xerox Palo Alto Research Center, Communications of the ACM,* vol. 19, no. 5, (July 1976): 395–404.

9. J. L. Hammond and P. J. P. O'Reilly, *Performance Analysis of Local Computer Networks* (City of Publication: Addison-Wesley, 1986).

10. E. W. Fulp, "Comparison of LAN Technologies," CSC 343-643, Wake Forest University (Spring 2006): www.cs.wfu.edu/~fulp/CSC343/802.pdf.

11. Robert M. Metcalfe, Keynote Address at Light Reading Expo, New York City, October 2006.

12. Reed Hundt, *You Say You Want a Revolution* (New Haven: Yale University Press, 2000).

13. Andrew Odlyzko, *Internet Traffic Growth: A Gale or a Hurricane* RHK StarTrax conference, Palm Springs, CA, Nov. 2, 2000.

14. Anand Parikh, "The Benefits of Ethernet Services," IIR Deploying Metro Ethernet Services Conference, Metro Ethernet Forum, September 16, 2002.

Carrier Ethernet

by Abdul Kasim

In order to leverage the potential of Ethernet beyond the LAN, it had to be augmented with additional "carrier-class" characteristics; identifying and formalizing these detailed characteristics was, therefore, essential to enabling this role for Ethernet. This chapter focuses specifically on standardization and other efforts underway to develop a foundation for transforming LAN Ethernet into a Service Provider—based offering, henceforth referred to as *Carrier Ethernet (services)*. Carrier Ethernet delivered over Service Provider networks across the MAN and WAN optimally enables next-generation packet applications.

The first fundamental step is defining Carrier Ethernet, what it precisely means and understanding the rationale for this definition. Also as fundamental, is an established reference framework—the context in which this definition applies, and the necessary elements that make up this context. In so doing, a common and consistent understanding as well as a "language" to describe Carrier Ethernet services is provided; with this as the basis, the attributes are discussed in greater detail (note: in the context of this book, only a sufficient overview can be reasonably provided), with selective discussions in a few areas that are deemed especially critical to enabling Carrier Ethernet.

Most of the standardization effort, especially at the service-level, has been carried on by the Metro Ethernet Forum (MEF) and so expectedly, this chapter devotes a significant part to the MEF-initiated development; but efforts by other standards bodies are also identified. This chapter also attempts to incorporate some commercial developments enabling Carrier Ethernet. Often, forward-looking entities—whether Service Providers or equipment manufacturers—are ahead of the standards bodies in terms of recognizing and addressing the practical issues that usually emerge when offering new services. A look at these issues and their respective solutions in the marketplace serves, therefore, to provide a better understanding of the actual status quo in the field.

Defining Carrier Ethernet

Although numerous efforts, both informal and formal (standards-based), have been undertaken to make Ethernet more viable as a technology and service beyond the LAN, the MEF has been instrumental in initiating a substantial formal effort to define Carrier Ethernet services (delivered by Service Providers). This definition was a prerequisite to developing a common understanding and a common objective in the delivery of such services.

Among the first steps undertaken was to define more precisely what such Ethernet services would entail, since, as noted in the previous chapter and repeated in Table 2.1, there are fundamental differences in providing Ethernet in the Service Provider network (broadly referred to as Carrier Ethernet) as opposed to providing Ethernet in the LAN. The context in which Carrier Ethernet services are defined is, therefore, the Service Provider networks and the several types of services already being delivered over these

TABLE 2.1   Ethernet in the LAN Versus Ethernet in a Service Provide Network (Spanning the MAN and WAN)

Dimension	Local Area Network	Service Provider Network
Geography/Reach	Usually less than 1–2 km; deployed in building(s) and small campuses	10–100 km and longer; deployed in a metro area or even across distant metro areas
Service Provider	Enterprise (IT group); implemented by internal IT group.	Service Provider (Carrier typically); services offered commercially for an initial and recurring cost
User of service	Enterprise	Enterprise
Number of end users/points (Scale)	In the tens/hundreds	Thousands or tens/hundreds of thousands
Bandwidth	10M/100M/1000M	1M and greater—up to 10,000M; usually in granular increments of 1M Aggregation required
Services offered (scope)	Enterprise data applications	Voice/TDM and data connectivity applications such as Internet Access, intra-metro connectivity
Delivery of Ethernet services	Over coax (CAT 5) and fiber; Best effort	Over a host of media, incumbent transport technologies, and with an associated service-level agreement (SLA)
Tolerance to failures (resiliency)	Generally reasonable because network is usually intra-enterprise and over a smaller physical area so failures can be addressed relatively quickly	Very low tolerance because failures usually have a larger impact—often on revenues and competitiveness
Manageability	Manageability possible with fairly simple tools given fewer number of users and applications within a smaller physical area (typically a building or campus) and the relatively higher tolerance to failure issues	Scale and scope of the Service Provider network in terms of the number of users and the geographical footprint introduces significant complexity necessitating sophisticated management tools and capabilities

networks. In fact, *Carrier Ethernet essentially encompasses the deterministic and other service delivery aspects for standardized Ethernet services.* This point is key because it highlights the focus on standardized Ethernet services and the specific *characteristics* of such services and not necessarily the underlying transport infrastructure itself. So what is Carrier Ethernet?

Carrier Ethernet: A Formal Definition

The MEF[1] has defined Carrier Ethernet as the "ubiquitous, standardized, Carrier-class *service* defined by *five attributes* that distinguish Carrier Ethernet from the familiar LAN based Ethernet." As depicted in Figure 2.1, these five attributes, in no particular order, are

1. Standardized services
2. Scalability
3. Reliability
4. Quality of Service (QoS)
5. Service management

Carrier Ethernet essentially augments traditional Ethernet, optimized for LAN deployment, with Carrier-class capabilities which make it optimal for deployment in Service Provider Access/Metro Area Networks and beyond, to the Wide Area Network. And conversely, from an end-user (enterprise) standpoint, Carrier Ethernet is a service that not only provides a standard Ethernet (or for that matter, a standardized non-Ethernet[2]) handoff but also provides the robustness, deterministic performance, management, and flexibility expected of Carrier-class services.

Fundamental to both Carrier Ethernet and LAN Ethernet is the fact that data is carried in an *Ethernet frame.* What this means is, in effect, an Ethernet frame originating at a device in the LAN, now continues to traverse across one or more Service Provider networks,[3] largely unaltered, and terminates at a device in a remote LAN. *One way to look at this transformation is that it essentially creates one larger Ethernet, spanning LANs, MANs, and may be even the WAN, albeit delivered as a service to the customer.* This transformation is shown in Figure 2.2, courtesy of the MEF, and illustrates the remarkable potential of Carrier Ethernet. The terms *UNI* and *NNI* in the figure denote standardized interface hand-offs between the enterprise customer and

---

[1] MEF is the preeminent nonprofit industry body focused solely on enabling Carrier Ethernet. The "Metro" reference in MEF is now a misnomer, however, and does not accurately reflect its charter and focus, which has long extended beyond the metro.

[2] Because it can, as will be seen later, also support non-Ethernet services (albeit over an Ethernet layer).

[3] The Service Provider networks could encompass both the MAN and the WAN.

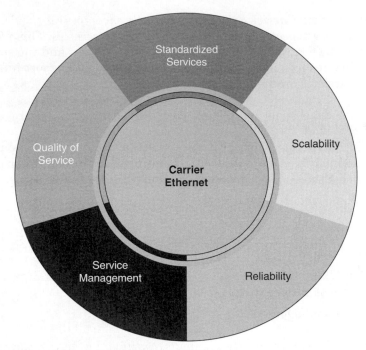

Figure 2.1   Attributes of Carrier Ethernet (Source: MEF)

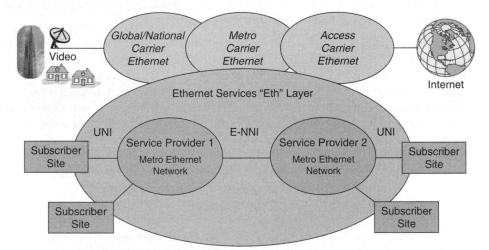

Figure 2.2   Carrier Ethernet spanning Access, Metro, and Wide Area Networks (Source: MEF)

the Service Provider network and between Service Providers (or Network Operators[4]), whose infrastructure is used to deliver the service, respectively, and are explained in more detail later in this chapter.

The Ethernet frame(s) may be transported as is, either natively and directly over a physical media or encapsulated and delivered over a variety of overlay networks built using different technologies. Each of these very different networking technology solutions, however, delivers[5] Carrier Ethernet services. It is critical to understand that the Carrier Ethernet attributes often manifest only partially in commercial solutions today because they exist at the network/transport/physical layers as opposed to the service layer[6]. This will become clear in rest of the Part II when the various commercial solutions currently employed to deliver Carrier Ethernet are discussed.

NOTE The focus in this book is primarily on delivering Carrier Ethernet services; the network and transport delivery infrastructure—the Carrier Ethernet solutions, provide the carrier-class attributes that enable commercial Carrier Ethernet services. Often, the term 'Carrier Ethernet' is interchangeably used to refer to both the Ethernet services and the underpinning enabling solution infrastructure.

The Carrier-class attributes are delivered differently by the various network solutions (for example, how reliability is offered in one solution versus another). This is largely a result of their respective geneses and subsequent evolution. It is important to also note that some of the Carrier Ethernet attributes in a solution existed pre-Carrier Ethernet (albeit at the transport layer and not at the service layer) and were, in fact, initial drivers for the use of respective solution. For example, SONET offered impressive resiliency to any failures in the fiber and/or equipment deployed in a ring topology, so it was adopted to support mission-critical voice services that required stringent SLAs.

Each of the Carrier Ethernet solutions and its respective evolution toward optimizing delivery in Service Provider networks is discussed in a fair amount of detail in Part II of the book.

Carrier Ethernet: The Attributes

The five attributes that define Carrier Ethernet essentially provide the additional capabilities necessary to use Ethernet in much the same way as the other preceding service provider technologies such as ATM and Frame Relay.[7] Each of these attributes is elaborated upon and its rationale highlighted in the sections that follow.

---

[4] A Network Operator is distinguished from a Service Provider by the fact that the former's infrastructure is employed in the delivery of Carrier Ethernet services; however, the service itself is commercially offered to the customers (usually on a subscription basis) by the Service Provider. Service Provider often lease infrastructure from network operators to deliver services.

[5] More accurately, as will be evident in Part II, the solutions strive to offer the attributes of Carrier Ethernet.

[6] Because at these lower layers inherently address only a subset of the higher-level service.

[7] Especially helpful today because Ethernet is largely being used as a substitute for Frame Relay and ATM.

Standardized Services   This attribute essentially enables a Service Provider to deliver a host of both Packet and traditional TDM (see chapter 10 for more information on TDM) multi-point services in an efficient and deterministic manner over standardized equipment platforms. These services underpin the multitude of customer applications that are emerging across voice, data, and video. Specific components that define this attribute comprehensively are defined next.

- **Ubiquity**   Carrier Ethernet enables ubiquitous Ethernet services provided via standardized equipment, independent of the underlying media and transport infrastructure. This is a critical prerequisite to extending Ethernet's appeal globally (similar to LAN Ethernet).

- **Ethernet Services**   Carrier Ethernet supports two types of services: Point-to-Point (also referred to as *Ethernet Line* or *E-LINE*) and multipoint-to-multipoint Ethernet LAN (referred to as E-LAN) Ethernet services. These services are discussed in greater detail later in the chapter and are expected to provide the basis for all Ethernet services.

- **Circuit Emulation Services (CES)**   Carrier Ethernet supports not only Ethernet-based services delivered across different transport technologies but also other (TDM) services transported over Carrier Ethernet itself. As noted previously, TDM services still remain an overwhelming contributor to Service Provider revenues and realistically need to be supported (and delivered over a converged Ethernet-based infrastructure). TDM-based voice applications especially need to be accommodated and characteristics of such applications such as synchronization and signaling need to be emulated.

- **Granularity and Quality of Services (QoS)**   The services supported by Carrier Ethernet provide a wide choice and granularity of bandwidth and quality of service options. This flexibility is vital in Service Provider networks with its multitude of end users, each with slightly different application requirements and, typically, operating equipment from multiple vendors. QoS capability is crucial to enforcing the deterministic behavior of Carrier Ethernet.

- **Converged transport**   Supports convergence of voice, data, and video services over a unified (Ethernet) transport and greatly simplifies the delivery, management, and addition of such services. Basically, all enterprise services and applications are now supported over a single Ethernet "pipe".

Scalability   One fundamental difference between a LAN and a Service Provider network[8] is scale. In a Service Provider network, there are usually a hundredfold more end users and as a consequence, exponentially more connections for Ethernet-based

---

[8] Or multiple Service Provider or Network Operator networks, since several such entities could be involved in the delivery of an Ethernet service. A Network Operator owns the delivery infrastructure but may or may not be the one offering a service (or the Service Provider).

applications simply because it covers a larger geographic area. Carrier Ethernet solutions, therefore, scale across several dimensions simultaneously:

- **Users/endpoints** A Service Provider network supports hundreds of thousands of endpoints and millions of Ethernet users in an optimal fashion. Specifically, it supports the delivery of millions of Ethernet services with an appropriate level of performance or QoS.
- **Geographical reach** The services delivered can span access, metros, and beyond to encompass very large geographical distances and over a variety of infrastructures including Ethernet, WiFi, WiMax, TDM, SONET, and so on. As noted previously, the reach of such services can be augmented by employing multiple Service Providers' adjacent networks.
- **Applications** Current and emerging applications supporting a host of business, information, and entertainment applications and benefiting from the convergence of voice, data, and video. The landscape or breadth of application support is a vital driver for Carrier Ethernet.
- **Bandwidth** Bandwidth scales from 1M to 10G in granular increments of 1M, enabling a much more palatable solution to both the end user and Service Provider because end users only have to "pay for what is required" and Service Providers would possibly receive higher revenues.

As these dimensions scale collectively, they make for a formidable problem to deliver, isolate, troubleshoot, and in general, manage thousands of users and hundreds of thousands of services in a robust manner.

Reliability As Carrier Ethernet services are expected to support mission-critical applications on a wide scale, the ability to detect quickly and remotely any failures that may arise in the physical infrastructure or in the Ethernet services layer underlying these applications is essential. Specifically, the following aspects are addressed by Carrier Ethernet.

- **Service Resiliency** The impact of failures is localized and will not affect other customers and/or applications; Correlation among multiple errors will be quickly identified. Further, the process of troubleshooting and recovery from failures will be rapid and employ tools that will minimize operational expenditures for the Service Provider and any adverse impact on the end users.
- **Protection** Carrier Ethernet services provide an end-to-end service-level protection that encompasses protection against any failures in the underlying infrastructure employed in the delivery of the services. This means protection against failures in the end-to-end "path" of the service, as well as against any underlying physical link and node equipment failures.
- **Restoration** Carrier Ethernet provides similar or better recovery than SONET. The benchmark for resiliency in Service Provider networks has long been the

SONET sub-50 ms service restoration to support circuit-switched voice networks. As latency-sensitive voice and video applications are deployed over a Carrier Ethernet infrastructure, this SONET-like resiliency is a critical prerequisite. Techniques such as Spanning Tree Protocol (STP) and its variants, while feasible in the LAN, are simply not acceptable in large Service Provider networks because depending on the size and complexity of the network, recovery of failures employing these techniques takes in the range of several seconds to even minutes. Carrier Ethernet supports a host of latency-sensitive applications that are often critical to an enterprise (for instance, regular telephony services), and consequently offers better fault-tolerant and recovery mechanisms.

Quality of Service   Providing Quality of Service (QoS) is necessary for Carrier Ethernet to be embraced as a substitute to ATM and Frame Relay and ultimately as a converged mechanism to deliver all services. QoS essentially conforms to a predefined level of performance expected by an application. As Carrier Ethernet supports delivery of critical enterprise applications that are commonly expected to adhere to certain performance levels, this QoS capability becomes essential.

The challenge to a Service Provider is significant given the fact that it has to *simultaneously* support individual QoS to typically thousands of applications and end users, using a limited set of resources (bandwidth, switching, and so on) whose availability varies with time.

Carrier Ethernet services providing QoS, encompass the following:

- **Performance Service Level Agreement (SLA)**   There is the capability to provide the stringent end-to-end[9] SLAs necessary to provide a host of critical voice, video, and data services over a converged Ethernet infrastructure. Such SLAs are essential, and end users often demand them since they are already accustomed to such an assurance using the ATM, Frame Relay, or Private Line services, and it is only natural for them to expect the same of Ethernet services that support similar and next-generation applications.

- **SLA parameters**   A set of configurable parameters allows a Service Provider to actually define the specific SLAs associated with a particular commercial service. These parameters provide significant latitude for defining numerous levels of service premiums. Further, these parameters although associated with a service, are enforced across the underlying infrastructure delivering that service.

- **Provisioning SLA**   The QoS provides a hard performance guarantee based on the typical elements that define QoS in networks such as availability at a particular performance, packet loss, packet delay, and packet delay variation or jitter.

In a LAN with its abundant bandwidth and high performance, QoS is usually not an issue; the simple priority queuing capability using IEEE 802.1P/802.1D provides a "soft"

---

[9] End-to-end refers to the end points between which an Ethernet service is delivered.

QOS, but this is not sufficient in a Service Provider network, where with a multitude of users competing for shared resources (bandwidth, switching, and so on), complexity is at a totally different level. Different techniques, therefore, become necessary.

Service Management   Managing a large number of customers stretched over a wider geographical area requires Service Providers to have a sophisticated capability for installing, troubleshooting, and upgrading Ethernet services cost effectively and quickly; engaging in a truck-roll each time there is an issue is simply cost-prohibitive and makes it infeasible to deliver Ethernet on a wider scale. Carrier Ethernet, in an attempt to address these issues, provides.

- **Unified management**   This encompasses standardized vendor-independent capability to monitor, diagnose, and manage the delivery infrastructure. It is not unusual to deliver services across multiple Service Provider networks, each of which is often comprised of equipment from one or more manufacturers and is frequently subject to individual differences; hence, managing services across the different vendors' equipment using a common streamlined approach becomes paramount.

- **Carrier-class OAM**   Carrier-class Operational, Administration, and Maintenance (OAM) capability that will integrate with existing Service Provider operational models. This covers a wide array of capabilities that enables life-cycle management at the service level. With Carrier Ethernet—based networks reaching tens of kilometers and thousands of subscribers, the need for sophisticated OAM features is apparent. Carrier Ethernet incorporates cutting-edge service creation and management techniques that exceed those of both enterprise Ethernet and the legacy telecom infrastructure.

- **Rapid Provisioning**   The capability to provision new Ethernet services rapidly is a key departure from the long and protracted commissioning intervals for traditional TDM services. This capability translates into allowing granular increases in bandwidth to existing services; the addition of new services, each with a specific performance assurance (SLA); and the ability to enable these services remotely most of the time.

Carrier Ethernet leverages the established benefits of LAN Ethernet to the end users while simultaneously enabling Service Providers to offer a set of carrier-class attributes in a manner that is not only aligned with other services such as ATM, Frame Relay, and Private Line, but does so in a scalable, robust, and flexible manner that supports the next-generation of packet-based applications much more cost effectively . This ultimately translates into lower CAPital EXpenditures (CAPEX), lower OPerational EXpenditures (OPEX), and competitive positioning for Service Providers. Thus, Carrier Ethernet helps realize the compelling benefits to both end users and Service Providers as detailed in the Chapter 1.

Defining the attributes of Carrier Ethernet in greater detail and refining them further to be more relevant for next-generation applications is an ongoing effort; considerable progress has, however, been made.

Enabling Carrier Ethernet

Carrier Ethernet is increasingly being adopted by the Service Provider and enterprise end–user community not only as the default access solution (i.e., service connectivity is via Carrier Ethernet), but also one that is being employed end-to-end across the WAN. Service Provider networks are, in fact, evolving to deliver the consistent Carrier-class Ethernet services end users are coming to expect. Chapter 3 highlights the growing demand for Carrier Ethernet services worldwide.

Carrier Ethernet is, however, still a work in progress; in fact, it is still in its infancy and being more formally defined, refined, and continually augmented based on learning from real–life field deployments supporting emerging applications. If it is to achieve the success and dominance of its LAN variant, it has to not only incorporate these lessons rapidly in terms of new value-added features, but also standardize them.

Standardization of Carrier Ethernet is thus a key approach to enabling and, in fact, accelerating the deployment of Carrier Ethernet services.

Standards Bodies

There are several standard bodies that are involved, to varying degrees, in enabling Carrier Ethernet. These include the IEEE (primarily the 802 body), the Internet Engineering Task Force (IETF), the International Telecommunications Union (ITU), the Metro Ethernet Forum (MEF), and to a lesser degree, others such as the Tele Management Forum (TMF).

While the involvement of several bodies working in the same area may appear to be at cross purposes or at best, partially redundant and with the potential to introduce confusion, the reality has been different. These bodies have been—and are—working with a largely complementary focus, and where there has been some overlap, there has also been significant collaboration, with the net result actually expediting standardization efforts.

The IETF has traditionally had an IT orientation, while the ITU has focused on developing international standards to support the needs of national Service Providers (known as PTTs in most countries). The IEEE, of course, has focused on the 802 Ethernet standards at the physical and data-link layer. It is continuing its legacy work on Ethernet and extending it in two areas from the standpoint of Ethernet in the MAN and WAN: OAM and Architecture. The ITU is working across the spectrum, from service definition to service architecture to OAM and Ethernet interfaces.

These bodies were involved with LAN Ethernet and are now also focused on Carrier Ethernet given its role as a converged platform appealing to both Service Providers and end-user enterprises and spanning their traditional Service Provider and IT constituencies.

The Metro Ethernet Forum (MEF), unlike the others, was formed relatively recently (2001) and exclusively to advance the deployment of Carrier Ethernet. Consequently, it has been the most active body focused on enabling Carrier Ethernet as a well-defined service to support the next-generation of applications. And although the MEF's initial focus was the delivery of Carrier Ethernet in the metropolitan area (hence the "Metro" in MEF), it has now extended its charter well beyond and focuses on end-to-end Carrier Ethernet services spanning the MAN and the WAN. The MEF represents the first comprehensive effort to address all service delivery aspects as well as the testing necessary for confirmation. Figure 2.3 depicts the different MEF standards and their respective focus as of August 2007; these are continually being augmented as the MEF tackles new issues in its attempt to accelerate the deployment of Carrier Ethernet. While the MEF has a broader mandate than the other bodies (at least as far as Carrier Ethernet is concerned), it extensively builds and reuses the efforts of these bodies.

Figure 2.4 summarizes the different standards bodies' respective focus across four distinct areas with respect to Carrier Ethernet: Architecture, Services, Management, and Testing. The specific standards are identified in each of these areas; standards underway but not yet ratified are italicized.

It is clear that only the MEF is focused across the board in all four areas and is notably the only standards body testing and validating Carrier Ethernet. The IEEE 802 addresses some architectural aspects (in fact, it did so even pre-Carrier Ethernet) but has also added several new efforts. A key contribution has been in the area of Carrier Ethernet Management, especially link level and connectivity management. The ITU has been very active in the Architecture, Service, and Management areas; it has not only leveraged the efforts from the other standards bodies—for instance, the MEF for the Ethernet services definition, the IEEE for Management—but has also augmented it by, for instance, adding Performance Management to its Management standard to address the requirements of its constituency.

Specification	Scope
MEF 2	Requirements and Framework for Ethernet Service Protection
MEF 3	Circuit Emulation Service Definitions, Framework and Requirements in Metro Ethernet Networks
MEF 4	Metro Ethernet Network Architecture Framework Part 1: Generic framework
MEF 6	Metro Ethernet Services Definitions Phase 1
MEF 7	EMS-NMS Information Model
MEF 8	Implementation Agreement for the Emulation of PDH Circuits over Metro Ethernet Networks
MEF 9	Abstract Test Suite for Ethernet Services at the UNI
MEF 10.1	Ethernet Services Attributes Phase 2
MEF 11	User Network Interface (UNI) Requirements and Framework
MEF 12	Metro Ethernet Network Architecture Framework Part 2: Ethernet Services Layer
MEF 13	User Network Interface (UNI) Type 1 Implementation Agreement
MEF 14	Abstract Test Suite for Ethernet Services at the UNI
MEF 15	Requirements for Management of Metro Ethernet Phase 1 Network Elements
MEF 16	Ethernet Local Management Interface
MEF 17	Service OAM Framework and Requirement
MEF 18	Abstract Test Suit for Circuit Emulation Services
MEF 19	Abstract Test Suit for UNI Type 1

Figure 2.3 MEF Standards specifications (Source: MEF)

Ethernet Standards Summary

Standards Body	Ethernet Services	Architecture/Control	Ethernet OAM	Ethernet Interfaces
IEEE	-	• 802.3 – MAC • 802.3ar – Congestion Management • 802.1D/Q – Bridges/VLAN • 802.17 - RPR • 802.1ad – Provider Bridges • .1ah – Provider Backbone Bridges (PBB) • .1ak – Multiple Registration Protocol • .1aj – Two Port MAC Relay • .1AE/af – MAC / Key Security • .1aq – Shortest Path Bridging • .1Qay – PBB – Traffic Engineering	• 802.3ah – EFM OAM • 802.1ag – CFM • 802.1AB - Discovery • 802.1ap – VLAN MIB	• 802.3 – PHYs • 802.3as - Frame Expansion
MEF	• MEF 10 – Service Attributes • MEF 3 – Circuit Emulation • MEF 6 – Service Definition • MEF 8 – PDH Emulation • MEF 9 – Test Suites • MEF 14 – Test Suites • Services Phase 2	• MEF 4 – Generic Architecture • MEF 2 – Protection Req & Framework • MEF 11 – UNI Req & Framework • MEF 12 - Layer Architecture	• MEF 7– EMS-NMS Info Model • MEF 15– NE Management Req • OAM Req & Framework • OAM Protocol – Phase 1 • Performance Monitoring	• MEF 13 - UNI Type 1 • MEF 16 – ELMI • E-NNI
ITU	• G.8011 – Services Framework • G.8011.1 – EPL Service • G.8011.2 – EVPL Service • G.asm – Service Mgmt Arch • G.smc – Service Mgmt Chnl	• G.8010 – Layer Architecture • G.8021 – Equipment Model • G.8010v2 – Layer Architecture • G.8021v2 – Equipment Model • Y.17ethmpls - ETH-MPLS Interwork	• Y.1730 – Ethernet OAM Req • Y.1731 – OAM Mechanisms • G.8031 – Protection • Y.17ethqos – QoS • Y.ethperf - Performance	• G.8012 – UNI/NNI • G.8012v2 – UNI/NNI
TMF	-	-	• TMF814 – EMS to NMS Model	

Figure 2.4 Standards bodies and their respective areas of Carrier Ethernet focus (Source: MEF)

The detailed specifications are, of course, vastly outside the scope of this book but they are referenced in sufficient detail in the context of defining Carrier Ethernet services and its underlying five attributes. This represents the formalized (i.e., standardization) effort thus far toward enabling Carrier Ethernet. It must be noted that Carrier Ethernet standardization activity is relatively dynamic and frequently there continues to be new developments. It is, therefore, advisable to check the websites of the standards bodies (see bibliography) to get a sense of the latest progress.

A Service Architecture for Carrier Ethernet

Since Carrier Ethernet is essentially a commercial service offered by a Service Provider, it was vital to establish a clear and precise specification of what it entails. This was especially necessary because Ethernet in the LAN was not typically offered as a service but rather as a product/solution wherein the equipment was purchased, set up, and managed by the enterprise (IT group) itself. As such, there were generally no service-oriented expectations of the LAN Ethernet. Unfortunately, this was also largely the case with the Ethernet services that were initially (and to some extent are still being) offered by Service Providers. There were no formalized definitions and expectations of these services. The effort to change this only recently began in earnest and has been driven primarily by the MEF. Although still in the beginning stages, reasonably significant progress has been made.

Even before formalizing Carrier Ethernet services, however, it was necessary to establish a context for such services—a Service architecture—and to identify the necessary service components of such an architectural context. The MEF (and also the ITU) undertook this effort and developed a set of standard specifications for a generic Service Architecture that provides a common language for describing Ethernet services.

In MEF 6 and MEF 10.1, the MEF has established what an Ethernet service is, how a variety of subscriber services can be offered, and how these Ethernet services can be customized for certain performance and Service-Level Agreements (SLAs).

The MEF has also defined an overall framework to discuss Ethernet services—the Ethernet Service Model (ESM), which identifies the building blocks or service attributes of these services. (The Ethernet Service Model does not define the Ethernet service itself; this is done in an Ethernet Service Definition framework explained later.)

The Ethernet Service Model (ESM) The basic Service Provider architectural model defined by the MEF is shown in Figure 2.5. It has two main components:

- The Subscriber or customer equipment (CE)
- The Metro Ethernet Network (MEN) or more accurately, the Service Provider Ethernet Network (SEN)[10] This is owned/operated by a Service Provider.

Basically, the customer equipment is connected to the MEN [through a User Network Interface (UNI) which is explained in greater detail in the next section]. Any OSI layer 1 or 2 transport technology can be used as long as Ethernet frames are being handed off. The Subscriber or customer equipment is typically a router or a switch (an IEEE 802.1Q bridge).

A MEN itself consists of physical components (e.g., network elements, ports, etc.) and logical components (e.g., meters, policers, shapers, virtual switches, links, etc.). It can be owned and operated by multiple Service Providers and provides the underlying transport (SONET, WDM, RPR, etc.) to carry the Ethernet frames. It essentially connects geographically separated enterprise LANs across the MAN and WAN. The Carrier Ethernet service is actually provided by the Service Provider owning the MEN over an Ethernet Virtual Connection (or EVC, which is defined in a later section).

The MEF has more formally defined a three-layered model (also shown in Figure 2.5) for the MEN; the Application services (APP) layer supports end-user applications carried over Ethernet connectivity services provided at the Ethernet services (ETH) layer, and these connectivity services in turn are delivered over various transport/networking technologies in the Transport services (TRAN) layer. The key focus of the MEF and other standards bodies is the ETH layer; Carrier Ethernet is defined in this layer. The delivery of these Carrier Ethernet services can be over various media and the transport and networking technologies that make up the TRAN layer (the subject of Part II).

---

[10] Since the MEF has extended its focus beyond the metro and into the WAN, it is generally more accurate to label the Metro Ethernet Network (MEN) as the Service Provider Ethernet Network (SEN), which could support the MAN and/or WAN.

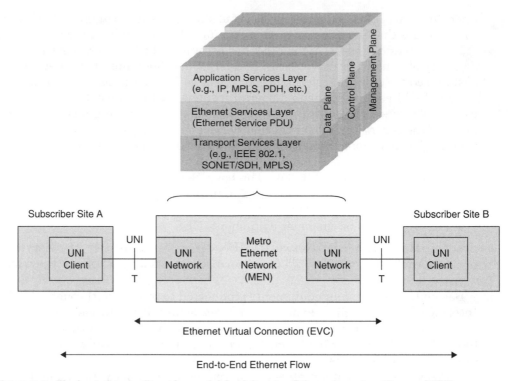

Figure 2.5 The basic Service Provider model for delivering Ethernet services (Source: MEF)

As will become evident in Part II, often the current—and evolving—attributes of Carrier Ethernet reside in the TRAN layer (depending on the specific technologies).

Each of the three layers has three associated operational planes: a Data plane, a Control plane, and a Management plane.

The Data plane, also referred to as the user/transport/forwarding plane, provides the functional elements required to steer the subscriber flow and supports the transport of subscriber traffic units among MEN Network Elements (NEs). The Control plane provides the functional elements that support distributed flow-management functions among NECs participating in the MEN data plane. The Control plane also provides the signaling mechanisms necessary to support distributed setup, supervision, and connection release operations, among other flow-control functions. The Management plane provides the functional elements that support Fault, Configuration (including flow and/ or connection configuration), Account, Performance, and Security (FCAPS) functions, as well as any related Operations, Administration, and Maintenance (OAM) tools.

The three operational planes are generally well defined for the TRAN layer (numerous standards bodies have addressed it, and these are identified in Part II). For the ETH layer, the effort was, for the most part (except in the data plane), begun only recently. As will become evident in the rest of the book, *the control and management functions of the TRAN layer are often employed in delivering Carrier Ethernet currently*.

Ethernet services delivered over the MEN invariably have two key service attributes associated with them: the User Network Interface (UNI) and the Ethernet Virtual Connection (EVC).

User-Network Interface (UNI)   The UNI is the interface used to interconnect a subscriber to an Ethernet Service Provider. The UNI also provides a reference point for demarcation between the MEN operator's (i.e., a Service Provider's) equipment that enables access to the MEN services and the subscriber access equipment. The demarcation point indicates the location where the responsibility of the Service Provider ends and where the responsibility of the subscriber begins. The UNI is a key Ethernet service attribute used to specify an Ethernet service.

Functionally, the UNI is an asymmetric, compound functional element that consists of a client side, referred to as the *UNI-C,* and a network side, referred to as the *UNI-N.* Thus, the term *UNI* is used to refer to these two functional elements and generically, to the data, management, and control plane functions associated with them.

UNI Client (UNI-C)   The UNI-C represents all of the functions required to connect a subscriber to a MEN. Individual functions in a UNI-C are entirely in the subscriber domain, and may or may not be managed by the Service Provider/Network Operator. From the perspective of the MEN, the UNI-C supports the set of functions required to exchange data, control, and management plane information with the MEN subscriber. As such, the UNI-C includes functions associated with the Ethernet services infrastructure, the transport network infrastructure, and if present, application-specific components.

UNI Network (UNI-N)   The UNI-N represents all of the functions required to connect a MEN to a MEN subscriber. The individual functions in a UNI-N are entirely in the Service Provider/Network Operator domain. From the perspective of the subscriber, the UNI-N supports the set of functions required to exchange data, control, and management plane information with the MEN. As such, the UNI-N includes functions associated with the Ethernet services infrastructure, the transport network infrastructure, and if present, application-specific components.

The MEF has defined a set of attributes to specify a UNI completely. These are listed at the end of the chapter (Figure 2.24).

Ethernet Virtual Connection (EVC)   The *Ethernet Virtual Connection (EVC)* is a construct that performs two functions: One, it indicates the association of two or more UNIs for the purpose of delivering an Ethernet flow[11] between subscriber sites across the MEN. Two, an EVC prevents data transfers between subscriber sites that are not part of the

---

[11] An Ethernet flow represents a particular and potentially noncontiguous (e.g., consecutive Ethernet frames may belong to different flows) unidirectional stream of Ethernet frames that share a common treatment for the purpose of transfer steering across the MEN.

same EVC. The attributes associated with an EVC are shown in Figure 2.24 (at the end of the chapter) and are employed when specifying an Ethernet service.

NOTE   There may be one or more subscriber flows mapped to a particular EVC. This capability enables an EVC to provide data privacy and security.

There are two basic rules that govern the delivery of Ethernet frames over an EVC. A service frame must never be delivered back to the UNI where it originated, and the Ethernet frame contents (including MAC addresses) must remain unchanged. The MEF has defined two types of EVCs: Point-to-Point or Multipoint-to-Multipoint. In a Point-to-Point EVC, exactly two UNIs must be associated with one another whereas in a Multipoint-to-Multipoint EVC, two or more UNIs must be associated with one another. Thus, an EVC can be used to construct a Layer 2 Private Line or a Layer 2 VPN[12] service.

Network to Network Interfaces (NNI)   As noted in the reference Service Architecture, one or more Service Providers can be used to deliver Carrier Ethernet services. The demarcation or handoff between the Service Providers is referred to as the Network-to-Network Interfaces (NNIs). The MEF has defined several NNIs:

- **External Network-to-Network Interface (E-NNI)**   An open interface used to interconnect two MEN Service Providers.

- **Internal Network-to-Network Interface (I-NNI)**   An open interface used to interconnect network elements from a given MEN Service Provider.

- **Network Interworking Network-to-Network Interface (NI-NNI)**   An open interface that supports the extension of transport facilities used to support Ethernet services and associated EVCs over an external transport network not directly involved in the end-to-end Ethernet service.

- **Service Interworking Network-to-Network Interface (SI-NNI)**   An interface that supports the interworking of an MEF service with services provided via other service enabling technologies (e.g., Frame Relay, ATM, IP, etc.).

Defining Carrier Ethernet Services

Carrier Ethernet services are essentially connectivity services that employ Ethernet frames transported over the MEN using a host of different technologies such as SONET, WDM, MPLS, and so on. As shown in Figure 2.5, Ethernet services are delivered over an EVC provided by a Service Provider over a MEN, which is connected to the customer equipment (CE) via a standardized UNI. Thus, all Ethernet services will invariably have associated with them, one or more UNIs and one or more EVCs. The specific UNI and EVC attributes differentiate the specific services.

---

[12] Virtual Private Network (VPN) is a connectivity service between multiple points to multiple points.

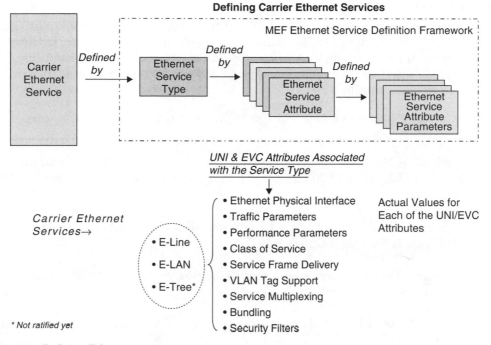

Figure 2.6   Defining Ethernet services

Carrier Ethernet services are defined from a subscriber perspective (and hence they're also referred to as "retail services"). As shown in Figure 2.6, the MEF has developed an Ethernet Services Definition Framework that defines any Carrier Ethernet service in terms of a predefined Ethernet service type. Each of these Ethernet service types (described next) are, in turn, defined by a set of Ethernet service attributes that define its capabilities. Some of these attributes apply to the UNI, others to the EVCs, and still others to both the UNI and EVCs associated with the service type. Specific parameters associated with each of these Ethernet service attributes ultimately define the Ethernet service fully.

This seemingly complicated approach is also illustrated in Figure 2.6, but it will become clearer when real-life examples are discussed later in the chapter. It is helpful to remember that every service is defined in terms of a service type and invariably has a set of UNI and EVC attributes[13] that will uniquely define it.

Before delving into the specific service types (which are defined in terms of the Ethernet service attributes), it is useful to understand these service attributes.

---

[13] Collectively referred to as the set of Ethernet service attributes.

Ethernet Service Attributes

The Ethernet service attributes are categorized into the following groups: Ethernet Physical interface, Traffic parameters, Performance parameters, Class of Service, Service frame delivery, VLAN tag support, Service Multiplexing, Bundling, and Security filters. Whether they apply to only the UNI or EVC or both is identified in the brief descriptions that follow.

Ethernet Physical Interface   At the UNI, the Ethernet physical interface has several service attributes.

Physical Medium   This UNI service attribute specifies the physical interface defined by the IEEE 802.3-2000 standard. Examples are 10BaseT, 100BaseSX, 1000BaseLX, and so on.

Speed   This UNI service attribute specifies the standard Ethernet speed—either 10 Mbps, 100 Mbps, 1 Gbps, or 10 Gbps.

Mode   This UNI service attribute specifies whether the UNI supports full or half duplex[14] and can provide auto-negotiation.

MAC Layer   This UNI service attribute specifies which MAC layer is supported, i.e., as specified in the IEEE 802.3-2002.

Traffic Parameters/Bandwidth Profile   The MEF has defined the Bandwidth Profile service attribute, which is associated with every Ethernet service and can be applied at the UNI or for an EVC. When there are multiple services associated with a UNI, there is a corresponding Bandwidth profile associated with each of these services.

A Bandwidth profile specifies a limit on the rate at which Ethernet frames can traverse the UNI associated with an Ethernet service. Bandwidth profiles enable both Service Providers and subscribers to optimize bandwidth and economics.

Service Providers have the ability to offer bandwidth in small increments and usually without having to add new physical interfaces. This means they can offer, engineer, and bill only the bandwidth needed by the subscriber for a specific service.

NOTE   Multiple services can be offered over a subscriber UNI, and each of these services can have its own bandwidth profile.

Subscribers can purchase and pay for only the bandwidth they need. Furthermore, subscribers can be assured of a "committed" amount of bandwidth that meets certain performance objectives (usually specified in an SLA) and "excess" bandwidth that may not meet the SLA.

---

[14] Half duplex means transmission in one direction at any one time. Full duplex means transmission in both directions simultaneously; these are briefly discussed in Chapter 1.

Bandwidth Profile Traffic Parameters   A Bandwidth profile associated with an Ethernet service consists of four traffic parameters: Committed Information Rate (CIR), Committed Burst Size (CBS), Excess Information Rate (EIR), and Excess Burst Size (EBS); in addition a service frame is associated with a Color Mode (CM). Together, these five parameters specify the bandwidth profile for a particular service:

Bandwidth Profile = <CIR, CBS, EIR, EBS, CM>

Committed Information Rate (CIR)   CIR is the *average rate* up to which service frames are delivered as per the performance objectives (such as delay, loss, etc.) associated with the service; these service frames are referred to as being *CIR-conformant.*

The CIR value is always less than or equal to the UNI speed[15] and basically guarantees that the specified amount of bandwidth (or service frames) will be delivered according to a predetermined performance level. A CIR of zero indicates the service has neither bandwidth nor performance guarantees.

NOTE   Independent of the CIR, the service frames are always sent at UNI speed.

Committed Burst Size (CBS)   CBS is the limit on the maximum number, or bursts, of service frames in bytes allowed for incoming service frames so they are still CIR-conformant.

Excess Information Rate (EIR)   The EIR specifies the average rate, greater or equal to the CIR, up to which service frames are admitted into the Service Provider network; these frames are said to be *EIR-conformant.* These frames are delivered without any performance guarantees and are not CIR-conformant; however, service frames that are not EIR-conformant are discarded.

Again, independent of the EIR, the service frames are always sent at the speed of the UNI (and hence, the EIR represents the average rate).

Excess Burst Size (EBS)   The EBS is the limit on the maximum number, or bursts, of service frames in bytes allowed for incoming service frames so they are still EIR-conformant

Color Mode and Color Marking   In addition to the bandwidth profile traffic parameters, there is also the concept of marking the service frames with a color. The color of a service frame is used to determine whether or not a particular service frame is in conformance with its bandwidth profile.

A service marked *green* is conformant with the CIR and CBS in the bandwidth profile. A green frame is always delivered per the performance SLA associated with the service.

---

[15] If multiple services are being delivered over a UNI, then the sum of the CIRs associated with individual services must be less than or equal to the UNI speed.

Yellow frames are out-of-bandwidth profile and will be delivered only if there are adequate bandwidth resources; if, on the other hand, the network is congested, then the frame is discarded. A *red* service frame is also out-of-bandwidth profile and is immediately discarded.

The Color Mode (CM) parameter specifies whether the UNI is operating in a color-aware or color-blind mode. When in a color-aware mode, the color associated with an incoming service frame is employed; in the color-blind mode, the color indication is ignored.

Bandwidth Profile Rate Enforcement   The Bandwidth profile is enforced through a two–rate (committed or excess), three-color marker (green, yellow, or red) algorithm, referred to as the *trTCM algorithm;* this algorithm is usually implemented using a token bucket concept and is shown in Figure 2.7.

Two buckets, one referred to as the "committed" or C-bucket and the other referred to as the "excess" or E-bucket, are used. Initially, each of these buckets is full of tokens; the C-bucket has green tokens and the E-bucket has yellow tokens. As service frames enter the Service Provider network UNI, the same number of tokens in the C-bucket are removed (decreased). If, after this, there are green tokens in the C-bucket, then the service frame is CIR-conformant, colored green, and allowed in the network.

If no green tokens remain, however, then the E-bucket is checked to determine if any yellow tokens remain. If there are yellow tokens, then the service frame is EIR-conformant, colored yellow, and allowed in the network. If no yellow tokens are available, then the service frame is colored red and discarded.

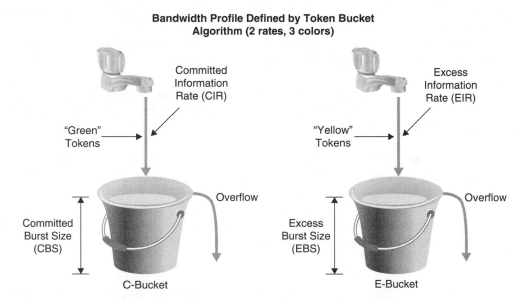

Figure 2.7   Enforcing a predefined bandwidth profile using the token bucket concept (Source: MEF)

The MEF has defined an additional capability whereby unused green tokens from the C-bucket may be added to the E-bucket as yellow tokens when checking EIR-conformance. If this capability is enabled, more yellow service frames are allowed in the Service Provider network.

Performance Parameters   The performance parameters affect the service quality experienced by the subscriber and consist of the following.

Availability   This is still being formalized by the MEF but essentially attempts to indicate the availability of a service at a predefined performance SLA.

Frame Delay   This critical parameter can have an impact on real-time applications such as VoIP and is defined as the maximum delay measured for a percentile of successfully delivered CIR-conformant (green) service frames over a time interval.
The frame delay parameter is used in the CoS service attribute described shortly.

Frame Jitter   This service attribute is also known as *delay variation* and is also critical in real-time applications such as VoIP or IP video. Such applications require a low and bounded delay variation to function seamlessly.

Frame Loss   Frame loss is defined as the percentage of CIR-conformant (green) fames not delivered between UNIs over a measured interval. At this point, frame loss has been defined for only Point-to-Point EVCs.

NOTE   The impact of frame loss depends on specific higher-layer applications. Usually such applications have the ability to recover from frame loss.

Class of Service (CoS)   Class of Service (CoS) refers to the performance enforced on a set of similar services. A CoS can be associated with each of the Ethernet services offered but it is usually associated with a group of services. This association becomes especially useful when there are numerous services offered over a resource (e.g., a physical port) that cannot simultaneously support all these services and also meet their respective bandwidth profiles; in such a case, a relative priority between these services becomes necessary. A CoS essentially provides this.

The CoS is also useful because it enables Service Providers to model service demands realistically; customers are increasingly subscribing to services with very different performance demands, for example, Internet access and VoIP require different treatments. With CoS, Service Providers can offer the required level of service and also charge accordingly. It also gives subscribers flexibility.

Each CoS has performance parameters associated with it, and typically the Service Provider will enforce the specified performance. These parameters include bandwidth profile and also jitter, delay, and so on, which will be in the next section.

A CoS is identified using a CoS ID. The various CoS IDs are described in the following sections.

Physical Port   Here a single CoS is provided per physical port. All traffic ingressing and egressing the port receives the same CoS. This is a very simple implementation of CoS, but it also affords the least flexibility; if a customer requires multiple CoSs for their traffic (VoIP and Internet access), then two separate ports would be required to enforce the appropriate CoS.

Customer Equipment VLAN (CE-VLAN or 802.1p)   This CoS ID refers to the CoS (802.1p) bits in the IEEE 802.1Q tag in a tagged Ethernet service frame. These are usually referred to as the *priority bits*. Using this MEF-defined approach, up to eight classes of service can be provided. A bandwidth profile and performance parameters, which can be enforced by the Service Provider,[16] are associated with each CoS. The user-defined CE-VLAN value(s) may be mapped by a service provider to its own CoS and acted on accordingly.

DiffServ Code Points (DSCP)/IP Type of Service (ToS)   The DSCP or IP ToS values in an IP header can be used to determine the CoS. IP ToS provides 8 CoS values, referred to as *IP precedence;* this is similar to the 802.1p bits in the VLAN tag of an Ethernet frame. DSCP, by contrast, specifies 64 different CoS values that correspond to a much more granular performance definition. In addition, DSCP provides a more robust capability that defines the performance over multiple hops in the network (referred to as *per-hop behaviors* or *PHBs*) and attempts to provide a QoS.

Types of Bandwidth Profiles   There are three types of bandwidth profiles defined by the MEF; the initial focus has been on the ingress traffic only. Figure 2.8 illustrates the profiles.

- **Ingress bandwidth profile per ingress UNI**   This profile provides rate enforcement for all Service Provider frames entering the UNI from subscriber to provider networks. This is useful when only a single service is supported at the UNI, i.e., the UNI is basically considered to be a pipe. The pipe's diameter (bandwidth profile) can be controlled by varying the CIR and EIR parameters. Rate enforcement is non discriminating and some frames may get more bandwidth than others.

- **Ingress bandwidth profile per EVC**   This bandwidth profile provides more granular rate enforcement for all service frames entering the UNI that are associated with each EVC. This is useful when multiple services are supported at the UNI; if each EVC is considered to be a pipe inside of a larger UNI pipe, then the bandwidth profile of the EVC—or diameter of the pipe—can be controlled by varying CIR and EIR values.

- **Ingress bandwidth profile per CoS (or CE-VLAN CoS)**   This bandwidth profile provides rate enforcement for all service frames belonging to each CoS associated with a particular EVC. The CoS is identified via a CoS identifier determined via the <EVC, CE-VLAN CoS> pair, so that this bandwidth profile applies to frames over a specific EVC with a particular CoS value or even a set of CoS values.

---

[16] Enforcement depends on whether the Service Provider is set up to handle the same CoS.

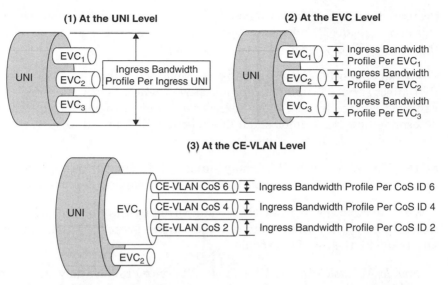

Figure 2.8 MEF-defined bandwidth profiles (Source: MEF)

Service Frame Delivery An EVC allows Ethernet service frames to be exchanged between UNIs that are connected via the same EVC. These may be data frames or control frames. A service provider can indicate what types of frames are supported and those that are not, and also the type of support provided, using four service frame delivery attributes. These are listed next.

Unicast Service Frame Delivery The unicast service frame is defined by the destination MAC address, which may be known (learnt by the network) or unknown. For each UNI pair, this EVC service attribute specifies whether unicast service frames are to be discarded, delivered conditionally (and the specific conditions), or unconditionally.

Multicast Service Frame Delivery In this EVC service attribute, a range of destination MAC addresses are specified, and for each UNI pair, whether multicast service frames are to be discarded, delivered conditionally (and the specific conditions), or unconditionally.

Broadcast Frame Delivery The IEEE 802.3 defines the broadcast address as a destination MAC address of all 1s. For each UNI pair, this EVC service attribute specifies whether broadcast frames are to be discarded, delivered conditionally (and the specific conditions), or unconditionally,.

In general, all Ethernet services support unicast, multicast, and broadcast service frames.

Layer 2 Control Protocol Processing This service attribute can be applied at the UNI or per EVC. There are many Layer 2 control protocols that can be employed (such as IEEE 802.3x MAC control frames, IEEE 802.1x Port Authentication, Spanning Tree

Protocol, Link Aggregation Control Protocol, and so on). The Service Provider can, using this attribute, decide whether to process or discard these protocols at the UNI or pass them to the EVC to discard or tunnel them.

VLAN Tag Support   VLAN tag support provides another important set of capabilities that affect service frame delivery and performance. This UNI service attribute allows Ethernet service frames to be 802.1Q tagged or untagged. They can also be used to determine how the frames should then be handled, and if tagged, whether the VLAN ID is used to determine frame delivery.

NOTE   UNI pairs for an EVC may support different VLAN tags (one may support it, the other may not; this is useful in service multiplexing described in the next section).

When VLAN tags at the UNI are supported by the Service Provider, then the subscriber needs to knows this and also the action—preserved or discarded or stacked—if any, taken by the Service Provider.

Provider Versus Customer VLAN tag   A Service Provider may add an additional VLAN tag to the incoming service frame header to separate from and preserve the customer's VLAN tag, using VLAN stacking (also referred to as *Q-in-Q*). The MEF has defined the term *Customer Edge VLAN ID (CE-VLAN ID)* to represents the customer's VLAN ID; this tag also contains the 802.1p field that the MEF has termed CE-VLAN CoS.

The MEF has defined two service attributes regarding CE-VLAN tag support: CE-VLAN ID preservation and CE-VLAN CoS preservation. The CE-VLAN tag consists of both the CE-VLAN ID and CE-VLAN CoS, so a service may preserve one, both, or neither.

The CE-VLAN ID preservation is an EVC service attribute that defines whether it is preserved across the EVC or not (if not, it is mapped to another value). This is useful for services such as LAN extension.

The CE-VLAN CoS preservation is an EVC service attribute that indicates whether the 802.1p bits are preserved across the EVC or not (if not, it is mapped to another value).

CE-VLAN IDs must be mapped when one UNI of a pair supports tagging whereas the other does not.

Service Multiplexing   Service multiplexing provides the ability for a UNI (a physical interface) to support multiple EVCs and precludes the need for a separate physical interface to support each EVC. As illustrated in Figure 2.9, there are multiple EVCs between UNI A and other UNIs in a network (assume that UNI A is at a higher bandwidth physical interface than the other UNIs). By service multiplexing at UNI A, multiple EVCs can be accommodated without needing multiple physical interfaces at UNI A.

Service multiplexing reduces the CAPEX associated with deploying services because it reduces the physical equipment costs. One or fewer physical interfaces are required instead of many; likewise, this reduces the amount of ancillary equipment needed, such as cables. It also reduces the OPEX by enabling quick and remote provisioning of new services.

Bundling   The bundling service attribute allows two or more CE VLAN IDs to be mapped to a single EVC at a UNI. These VLANs and the mapping specifics (i.e., which

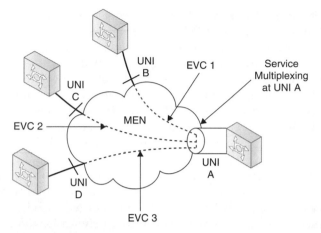

Figure 2.9 Service Multiplexing (Source: MEF)

VLANs map to which EVCs) should be agreed to by the end user and the service provider. A special case of bundling, *all to one bundling,* is enabled when all the VLAN IDs at a UNI are mapped to a single EVC.

Security Filters Security filters enable filtering of undesirable Ethernet frames to maintain security or traffic management. A very plausible case is one wherein a end-user subscriber wants only Ethernet frames originating from specific known sources (identified by the source MAC addresses) to be granted access; any other frames would be considered spurious and dropped, and the user alerted. This is akin to simple Access Control Lists (ACLs) at a UNI.

Ethernet Service Types

The Ethernet service type is essentially a generic Ethernet connectivity construct. The MEF has defined two basic service types:

- Ethernet Line (E-LINE)
- Ethernet LAN (E-LAN)

These two form umbrella categories, and any service can be created using these two categories, modifying only the specific attribute parameters. Therefore, any Ethernet service will be defined as an E-LINE or an E-LAN service, and it will have its own unique UNI and EVC attribute parameters. This should be clearer later in the chapter when we discuss common retail services.

NOTE A third service type called the *Ethernet Tree (E-Tree)* is also being considered by the MEF (possibly in MEF specification 6.1); since it is still in discussion, it is not presented here.

Ethernet Line (E-LINE) Service   Any Ethernet service that is based on a Point-to-point Ethernet Virtual Connection (EVC) is designated as an Ethernet Line (E-LINE) service type. The Ethernet Line service is illustrated in Figure 2.10. An E-LINE service type can be used to create a broad range of Point-to-Point Ethernet services between two UNIs.

In its simplest form, an E-LINE service type can provide symmetrical bandwidth for data sent in either direction with no performance assurances, for example, best effort service between two 10 Mbps UNIs. In more sophisticated forms, an E-LINE service type may be between two UNIs at different speeds and may be defined with performance assurances such as CIR with an associated CBS, EIR with an associated EBS, delay, delay variation, and loss.

Service multiplexing may occur at neither, one, or both UNIs in the EVC. For example, more than one Point-to-Point EVC can be offered on the same physical port at one or both of the UNIs. An E-LINE service without any service multiplexing, for example, is very much like the common TDM-based private leased line service (where a UNI physical interface is required for each EVC) except that with an E-LINE service, the range of bandwidth and connectivity options is much greater.

Ethernet LAN (E-LAN) Service   Any Ethernet service that is based upon a Multipoint-to-Multipoint Ethernet Virtual Connection (EVC) is designated as an Ethernet LAN (E-LAN) service type. The Ethernet LAN (E-LAN) service type is illustrated in Figure 2.11.

An E-LAN service connects two or more UNIs and service frames sent from one can be received at one or more of the other UNIs. In an E-LAN service, each UNI is connected to a multipoint EVC (even an E-LAN service connected to two UNIs is comprised of a multipoint EVC and hence, not an E-LINE service, which has a Point-to-Point EVC).

An E-LAN can be used to create a broad range of services. In its simplest form, an E-LAN service type can provide a best effort service with no performance assurances between the UNIs. In more sophisticated forms, an E-LAN service type may be defined with performance assurances such as CIR with an associated CBS and EIR with an associated EBS for a given CoS instance. The MEF has not defined service performance (delay, delay variation, and loss) attributes for the E-LAN service type.

For an E-LAN service type, Service multiplexing may occur at neither, one, or more of the UNIs in the EVC. For example, an E-LAN service type (Multipoint-to-Multipoint

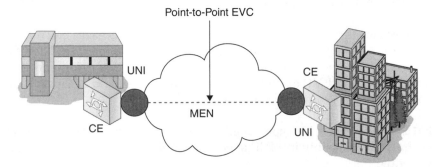

Figure 2.10   Ethernet Line (E-LINE) service type (Source: MEF)

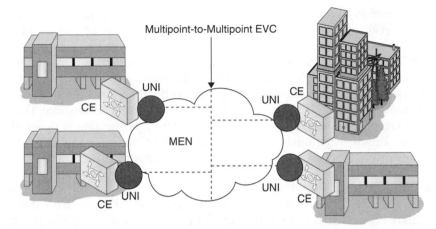

Figure 2.11   E-LAN service type using Multipoint-to-Multipoint EVC (Source: MEF)

EVC) and an E-LINE service type (Point-to-Point EVC) may be service multiplexed at the same UNI. In this example, the E-LAN service type may be used to interconnect other subscriber sites while the E-LINE service type is used to connect to the Internet with both services offered via EVC service multiplexing at the same UNI.

An E-LAN service may include a different bandwidth profile <CIR, CBS, EIR, EBS, CM> configured at each of the UNIs. An E-LAN service can also interconnect a large number of sites with much less complexity than legacy technologies such as Frame Relay and ATM. Furthermore, it can be used to create a broad range of services such as Private LAN and Virtual Private LAN service.

Ethernet Private and Virtual Connectivity Services   Using the E-LINE and E-LAN service types, the MEF has also defined simple connectivity services based on whether they are port-based or VLAN-based. The port-based service, where all-to-one bundling is employed, is essentially providing a private service with dedicated bandwidth, while the VLAN-based service allows service multiplexing at a UNI to enable a virtual service, in which bandwidth is shared among multiple EVCs. This is detailed in Figure 2.12.

Connectivity Services

Ethernet Service Type	Dedicated (All to One Bundling)	Shared (Service Multiplexed)
E-LINE	Ethernet Private Line (EPL)	Ethernet Virtual Private Line (EVPL)
E-LAN	Ethernet Private Line (EPLAN)	Ethernet Virtual Private LAN (EVPLAN)

Figure 2.12   E-LINE and E-LAN Connectivity Services

Ethernet Private Line (EPL) Using E-LINE Service Type   An Ethernet Private Line (EPL) service is specified using an E-LINE service type. EPL uses a Point-to-Point EVC between two UNIs and provides a high degree of transparency for service frames between the UNIs it interconnects, such that the service frame's header and payload are identical at both the source and destination UNI. The service also has an expectation of low frame delay, frame delay variation, and frame loss ratio. It does not allow for service multiplexing because a dedicated UNI (physical interface) is used for the service. Due to the amount of transparency in this service, there is no need for coordination between the subscriber and Service Provider on a detailed CE-VLAN ID/EVC map for each UNI because all service frames are mapped to a single EVC at the UNI. An EPL is depicted in Figure 2.13.

NOTE   MEF 6.1 might incorporate a further distinction in the Ethernet Private Line; specifically, there is consensus to define two EPL service variants: EPL-T (EPL-Transport) and EPL-P (EPL-Packet). EPL-T would essentially be the EPL defined here. EPL-T would be enhanced, adding features such as multiple CoS parameters as well as bandwidth profile parameters.

Ethernet Virtual Private Line (EVPL) Using E-LINE Service Type   An Ethernet Virtual Private Line (EVPL) is created using an E-LINE service type. An EVPL can be used to create services similar to the Ethernet Private Line (EPL) with some notable exceptions. First, an EVPL allows for service multiplexing at the UNI. This capability allows more than one EVC to be supported at the UNI whereas the EPL does not allow this. Second, an EVPL need not provide full transparency of service frames as with an EPL. Because service multiplexing is permitted, some service frames may be sent to one EVC while other service frames may be sent to other EVCs. An EVPL is also shown in Figure 2.13.

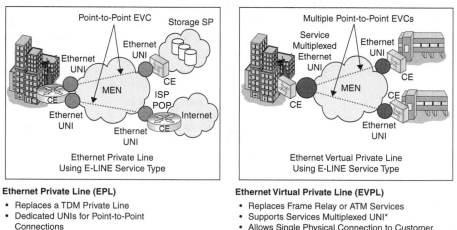

Example Services Using E-LINE Service Type

Ethernet Private Line (EPL)
- Replaces a TDM Private Line
- Dedicated UNIs for Point-to-Point Connections
- Single Ethernet Virtual Connection (EVC) per UNI

Ethernet Virtual Private Line (EVPL)
- Replaces Frame Relay or ATM Services
- Supports Services Multiplexed UNI*
- Allows Single Physical Connection to Customer Premise Equipment for Multiple Virtual Connections

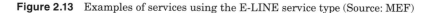

Figure 2.13   Examples of services using the E-LINE service type (Source: MEF)

Ethernet Private LAN (E-PLAN) Using E-LAN Service Type   E-PLAN enables a wide area LAN Ethernet in which service multiplexing is allowed at the UNI. There is full transparency of service frames within an E-PLAN. This essentially creates a transparent LAN service that makes the Service Provider network one large Ethernet, as shown in Figure 2.14.

Ethernet Virtual Private LAN (EVPLAN) Using E-LAN Service Type or Layer 2 VPN   Using an E-LAN service over a shared infrastructure, a transparent LAN service is created. This essentially makes the Service Provider network one large Ethernet and is typically used for applications such as intra-company connectivity services.

Sample Commercial Offerings Using Carrier Ethernet Services

Some common connectivity services delivered using Carrier Ethernet are briefly outlined next; higher level applications are increasingly employing Carrier Ethernet due to the many benefits that it affords.

LAN Extension   Subscribers with multiple sites in a metro area often want to interconnect them at high speeds so all sites appear to be on the same LAN and have equivalent performance and access to resources such as servers and storage. This is referred to as *LAN extension.*

In essence, the LANs at each site are connected; this is simpler and cheaper than routing, although it may not scale as well in large networks. To connect only two sites, a Point-to-Point E-LINE service can be used. To connect three or more sites, the subscriber has the choice of using either multiple E-LINE services or an E-LAN service.

Figure 2.15 shows a four-site LAN extension created using an E-LAN service. Each of the sites/UNIs support CE-VLAN ID and CE-VLAN preservation so the subscriber's

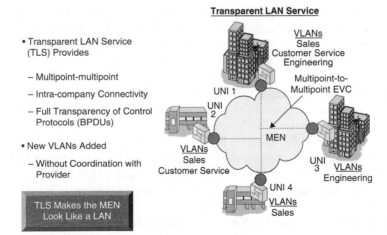

Figure 2.14   E-PLAN using E-LAN service type (Source: MEF)

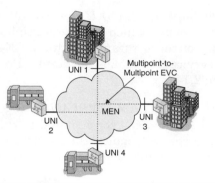

Figure 2.15 LAN extension service using E-LINE service type (Source: MEF)

UNI Service Attribute	Service Attribute Values and Parameters
Physical Medium	IEEE 802.3–2002 Physical Interface
Speed	10 Mbps (all UNIs)
Mode	FDX Fixed Speed (all UNIs)
MAC Layer	IEEE 802.3–2002
Service Multiplexing	No
CE–VLAN ID/EVC Map	All CE-VLAN IDs Map to the Single EVC
Bundling	No
All to One Bundling	Yes
Ingress Bandwidth Profile Per Ingress UNI	All UNIs: CIR = 5 Mbps, CBS = 256 KB, EIR = 10 Mbps, EBS = 512 KB
Layer 2 Control Protocol Processing	Process IEEE 802.3 x MAC control frames
	Process Link Aggregation Control Protocol (LACP)
	Process IEEE 802.1 x Port Authentication
	Pass to EVC Generic Attribute Registration Protocol (GARP)
	Pass to EVC Spanning Tree Protocol
	Pass to EVC a Protocol Multicasted to all Bridges in a Bridged LAN

EVC Service Attribute	Service Attribute Values and Parameters
EVC Type	Multipoint-to-Multipoint
UNI List	UNI 1, UNI 2, UNI 3, UNI 4
CE-VLAN ID Preservation	Yes
CE-VLAN CoS Preservation	Yes
Unicast Frame Delivery	Deliver Unconditionally for each UNI Pair
Multicast Frame Delivery	Deliver Unconditionally for each UNI Pair
Broadcast Frame Delivery	Deliver Unconditionally for each UNI Pair
Layer 2 Control Protocol Processing	N/A–IEEE 802.3 x MAC Control Frames
	N/A–Link Aggregation Control Protocol
	N/A–IEEE 802.1 x Port Authentication
	Tunnel Generic Attribute Registration Protocol (GARP)
	Tunnel Spanning Tree Protocol (STP)
	Tunnel a Protocol Multicasted to all Bridges in a Bridged LAN
Service Performance	One CoS for all UNIs Frame Delay < 30 ms, Frame Jitter: N/S, Frame Loss < 0.1%

VLAN tag is not modified. In this case, the MEN appears as a single Ethernet segment in which any site can be a member of any VLAN. The advantage here is the subscriber can configure new CE-VLANs across these sites without involving the Service Provider. The service attributes are also shown in the figure.

Dedicated Internet Access (DIA)   Dedicated Internet access enables subscribers to have a high-speed connection to the Internet to support their business objectives. An EVC can connect the subscriber's site to the local point-of presence (POP) of the Internet service provider (ISP) using a Point-to-Point E-LINE service.

If a customer is homed to multiple (say two) ISPs, as shown in the Figure 2.16, then a separate E-LINE would be used to connect each ISP. If the same UNI is expected to provide Internet access and other services, then a separate EVC would be used for each of the services.

At the ISP, service multiplexing is typically employed over a high-speed UNI to support multiple subscribers, so in effect, each subscriber appears to have a dedicated connection

UNI Service Attribute	Service Attribute Values and Parameters
Physical Medium	IEEE 802.3–2002 Physical Interface
Speed	UNIs 1 and 2: 100 Mbps UNI 3: 1 Gbps
Mode	UNIs 1 and 2: 100 Mbps FDX Fixed UNI 3: 1 Gbps FDX
MAC Layer	IEEE 802.3–2002
Service Multiplexing	No at UNIs 1 and 2 Yes at UNI 3
CE-VLAN ID/ EVC Map	N/A Since Only Untagged Frames Used Over the EVC
Bundling	No
All to One Bundling	No
Ingress Bandwidth Profile Per EVC	UNIs 1 and 2: CIR = 50 Mbps, CBS = 2 MB, EIR = 100 Mbps, EBS = 4 MB UNI 3: CIR = 500 Mbps, CBS = 20 MB, EIR = 1 Gbps, EBS = 40 MB
Layer 2 Control Protocol Processing	Discard 802.3 x MAC Control Frames Discard Link Aggregation Control Protocol (LACP) Discard 802.1 x port Authentication Discard Generic Attribute Registration Protocol (GARP) Discard Spanning Tree Protocol Discard a Protocol Multicasted to all Bridges in a Bridged LAN

EVC Service Attribute	Service Attribute Values and Parameters
EVC Type	Point-to-Point
UNI List	EVC 1: UNI 1, UNI 3 EVC 2: UNI 2, UNI 3
CE-VLAN ID Preservation	No. Mapped VLAN ID for Use with Multi-homed ISPs (if required)
CE-VLAN CoS Preservation	No
Unicast Frame Delivery	Deliver Unconditionally for each UNI Pair
Multicast Frame Delivery	Deliver Unconditionally for each UNI Pair
Broadcast Frame Delivery	Deliver Unconditionally for each UNI Pair
Layer 2 Control Protocol Processing	N/A[3] –IEEE 802.3 x MAC Control Frames N/A–Link Aggregation Control Protocol (LACP) N/A–IEEE 802.1 x Port Authentication N/A–Generic Attribute Registration Protocol (GARP) N/A–Spanning Tree Protocol (STP)
Service Performance	Only 1 CoS Supported. Frame Delay < 30 ms (95th percentile), Frame Jitter: N/S[10], Frame Loss < 0.1%

Figure 2.16 Dedicated Internet access using E-LAN service type (Source: MEF)

to the ISP. In Figure 2.16, the ISP may have a 1GbE UNI, while the subscribers' UNIs 1 and 2 may be 100 Mbps. There is no service multiplexing at the subscriber UNI. The service attributes are also shown in the figure.

Other Commercial Applications of Carrier Ethernet Services   Carrier Ethernet is increasingly being employed for several traditional and emerging applications that require carrier-class performance while minimizing the cost of delivery. A sample of some of the popular revenue-generating and value-added applications being enabled by Carrier Ethernet services includes packet video, VoIP and VoIP peering, Layer 2 VPNs, content peering, extranet connectivity, business continuity and disaster recovery, IP backbone expansion, and wireless backhaul.

Most of these are implemented over straightforward E-LINE services and, in some cases, over an E-LAN service. The simple but fairly encompassing nature of basic Ethernet services has enabled Service Providers to tailor a wide range of customized applications and generate new value-added and higher premium offerings literally every day. Currently, it is estimated that there are well over 500 different Ethernet services being offered by over 200 Carriers in the U.S. alone.

Carrier Ethernet: The Enablers

In this section, the developments of each of the attributes are presented. It is impractical to discuss these in any detail here, as several standards are involved, but they are highlighted with the progress to date. Some selective developments are, however, elaborated in reasonable depth given their importance in the enabling of Carrier Ethernet.

The MEF's prominent role in enabling Carrier Ethernet is shown in Figure 2.17, which highlights the specifications and specific attributes being addressed in the areas of Architecture, Management, Services, and Testing Measurement.

Standardized Services

The standardized services attribute requires support for Ethernet services and also for other prevailing services, notably TDM-based services over a Carrier Ethernet infrastructure (i.e., over an E-LINE/E-LAN service). There has been considerable effort spent on standardizing Ethernet services (as detailed in the previous section) in MEF 6 that encompassed setting up bandwidth profiles and traffic management. Major developments are outlined in Table 2.2.

Supporting other services, especially the TDM-based services, has also been addressed quite significantly by the MEF (and other bodies) and a reasonably detailed overview is provided next.

MEF Specs	Carrier Ethernet Attributes				
	Standardized Services	Service Management	Reliability	Quality of Service	Scalability
MEF 2			Architecture Area		
MEF 3	Service Area			Service Area	
MEF 4	Architecture Area				
MEF 6	Service Area			Service Area	Service Area
MEF 7		Management Area			
MEF 8	Service Area				
MEF 9	Test & Measurement Area		Test & Measurement Area		
MEF 10.1	Service Area			Service Area	Service Area
MEF 11	Architecture Area				
MEF 12	Architecture Area				Architecture Area
MEF 13	Architecture Area				
MEF 14	Test & Measurement Area		Test & Measurement Area	Test & Measurement Area	
MEF 15		Management Area			
MEF 16		Management Area			
MEF 17		Management Area			
MEF 18	Test & Measurement Area		Test & Measurement Area		
MEF 19	Test & Measurement Area		Test & Measurement Area		

Figure 2.17   The MEF specifications enabling Carrier Ethernet

TABLE 2.2   Standards Efforts Enabling Standardized Services

Key Components	Major Developments	Reference
Ubiquity	Standardization of UNI and traffic management for consistent delivery across different infrastructures	MEF 6, MEF 10.1, MEF 11
Ethernet services	Generic architecture and terminology developed; standardized Ethernet services defined in this context that form the basis for all Ethernet services	MEF 4, MEF 6, MEF 10.1
Circuit Emulation Services	Standardized circuit emulation services over Ethernet, along with performance requirements as well as practical implementation requirements	MEF 3, MEF 8, ITU-T, IETF PW3E
Granularity of bandwidth and QoS	A standard bandwidth profile for Ethernet services developed	MEF 6, MEF 10, MEF 11
Converged transport	A rich set of capabilities required for sophisticated implementation of converged enterprise and residential networks defined	MEF 12, ITU-8010

Circuit Emulation Services over Ethernet (CESoE)   As noted previously, non packet services such as PDH and SONET/SDH account for a significant amount of customer demand in the market today, and Service Providers expect to leverage this opportunity. As Service Providers move to a Carrier Ethernet–based packet-optimized network infrastructure, they should still be able to provide these services. This requirement translates into being able to transport these synchronous Time Division Multiplexing (TDM) digital signals over an asynchronous Ethernet infrastructure. Or put another way, a TDM circuit-switched network should be emulated over this packet infrastructure and provide what is referred to as circuit emulation services (CES). In effect, these services tunnel customers' TDM traffic over the Ethernet network, as shown in Figure 2.18. The customers' source and destination TDM equipment on either end is unaware of this circuit emulation. Such CES typically run over standard E-LINE service.

With CES over Ethernet (CESoE), service providers can leverage the inherent advantages of Carrier Ethernet—flexibility, simplicity, and lowered OPEX,[17] while delivering legacy applications such as TDM voice and private lines (which still account for a very large proportion of revenues for most Service Providers). Thus, with CESoE, Service Providers can cost effectively offer a complete portfolio of emerging Ethernet services along with the legacy services, obtaining an approximately 30 percent savings in infrastructure costs, and OPEX can be realized by migrating to an unified Ethernet infrastructure.

---

[17] Ironically, this also extends the longevity of these legacy applications.

T-LINE: *P2P TDM Connection b/w two Customer Premise locations*
TALS: *CES b/w Customer Premise and External Network (PSTN)*
Customer Operated CES: *IWF Owned and Operated by Customer*

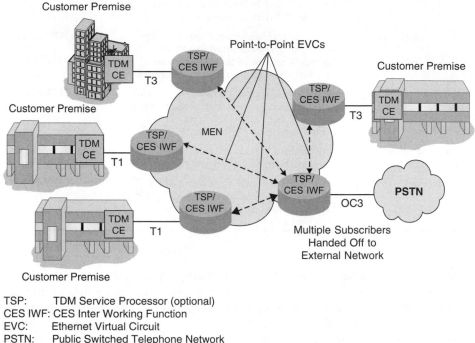

TSP: TDM Service Processor (optional)
CES IWF: CES Inter Working Function
EVC: Ethernet Virtual Circuit
PSTN: Public Switched Telephone Network
TDM CE: TDM Customer Edge

Figure 2.18   Circuit emulation over Ethernet (Source: MEF)

The MEF has provided the industry's first formal definition of CESoE that covers the ability to deliver both PDH services (e.g., N × 64 kbit/s, T1, E1, T3, and E3) and SONET/SDH services (STS-1, STS-3, STS-3c, STS-12, STS-12c, and European equivalents). The MEF 3 specifications address the types of CES that can be offered over a Service Provider–enabled Carrier Ethernet network (using EVCs) and also the requirements of these services. The specifications basically enable the support of traditional TDM handoffs to customer's voice equipment.

NOTE   Voice is by far the dominating application requiring underlying TDM circuit-switched services.

The MEF 8 addresses the practical aspects of CES and provides precise instructions for implementing interoperable CES equipment that will conform to the performance requirements outlined for CES in ITU-T and the ANSI TDM standards. The ITU-T recommendation Y.1413 is very similar to the MEF 8, except for MPLS networks, and employs identical frame formats for payload and encapsulation so that the equipment supporting Y.1413 should also be capable of supporting MEF 8. The IETF has several drafts, including PsuedoWire Edge to Edge Emulation (PWE3) and CES over Packet Switch Network, that are similar to the MEF 8 but focus on IP/MPLS networks. Because the payload and encapsulation formats are identical, any equipment supporting these drafts will also support MEF 8.

The MEF has essentially defined three types of CESoE that are generically portrayed in Figure 2.19. In each case, the CES is based on a Point-to-Point connection between two inter-working functions labelled CES IWF; this CES IWF essentially provides a translation function with a TDM application interface on one side (customer equipment facing) and an Ethernet interface (Service Provider network facing).

There is also an optional TDM service processor (TSP) that consists of any TDM grooming function that may be required to convert the TDM service offered to the customer into a form that the CES IWF can accept. For example, the TSP may be a framer device, converting a fractional DS1 service offered to the customer into a N×64 kbit/s service for transport over the MEN.

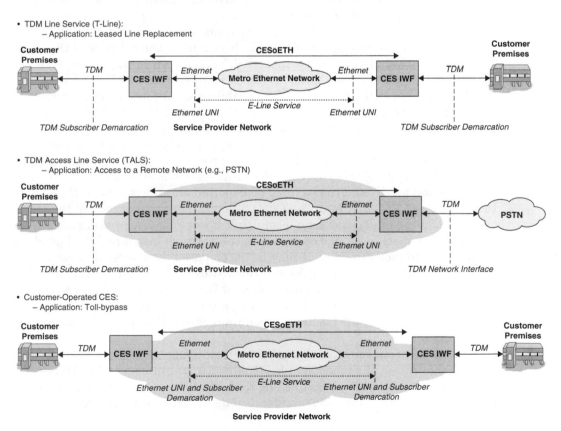

Figure 2.19 Types of CESoE defined by the MEF (Source: MEF)

The TSP and the CES IWF may physically reside in the Provider Edge (PE)[18] unit at the provider's nearest Point-Of-Presence or in a Service Provider–owned box in a customer location (e.g., a multi-tenant unit). From the architectural perspective, there is no difference between these alternatives.

TDM Line Service (T-Line)   The basic TDM Line (T-Line) service is a Point-to-Point, constant bit rate service, similar to the traditional leased-line type of TDM service. However, service multiplexing may occur ahead of the CES inter-working functions, (e.g., aggregation of multiple emulated T1 lines into a single T3 or OC-3 link), creating a Multipoint-to-Point or even a Multipoint-to-Multipoint configuration, as shown in Figure 2.19.

The service multiplexing is carried out using standard TDM multiplexing techniques and is considered part of the TSP block, rather than the CES inter-working function. The TDM interface at the input of the CES inter-working function is the same as the output from the CES IWF at the opposite end of the emulated link. It is the TSP that may be used to multiplex (or de-multiplex) that TDM service into the actual TDM service provided to the customer. This allows a TDM service to a customer to be provided as a collection of emulated services at lower rates.

There are, therefore, three modes of operation: unstructured emulation, structured emulation, and multiplexing mode; in all three modes, the delivery of the TDM service employs Ethernet Virtual Connections (EVCs) as shown in the Figure 2.19.

In unstructured emulation, the service is Point-to-Point and will have the identical TDM handoff on either end. The CES capability should maintain integrity across the network. In a structured mode, the service is also Point-to-Point and will have identical TDM service handoffs on either end, except that the overhead and payload entering on one end will terminate the overhead at the near endpoint and transport the payload transparently to the other end where it is mapped to the same type of overhead and terminated. Examples of this are typical OC-3 services where the SONET overhead (SOH) is terminated locally and the payload transported and the overhead then added before terminating at the other end. The CES will maintain the integrity of the transport.

Finally, in the multiplexed mode, multiple lower-rate transparent services are multiplexed at a specific service endpoint on the network into a higher digital hierarchy. Similarly, a higher rate service may be decomposed into several lower rate services. For example, a customer may have several sites—a head office with a full DS1 connection and several satellites with fractional DS1 connections, as shown previously in Figure 2.16. The same architecture can be used for multiplexing of other rate services, for example, several full DS1 services onto a single DS3 or multiplexing of VT-1.5s into an STS-1.

In order to attain some efficiency between mapping the TDM hierarchy signals into an Ethernet frame, the recommended bandwidth granularity is 100 kbits/s. TDM multiplexing of signals is also possible and a higher aggregated signal handed to the IWF for transport; at the other end, an identical de-multiplexing will occur.

---

[18] Provider Edge (PE) denotes the Carrier POP or CO.

TDM Access Line Service (TALS)   TALS is almost identical to the T-Line service except that it is a Multipoint-to-Point service, and one or more ends of the TDM service handoff is to an external network (such as a PSTN, as shown in Figure 2.19). A common example of such a service is when the Service Provider Ethernet network is an access to an external network. As with T-Line service, it can be operated in similar modes and should ensure that it maintains integrity of the signal on an end-to-end basis.

Customer-Operated CES   In this type of CESoE, the IWF is actually owned and/or provided by the customer and the customer only subscribes to a typical E-LINE service from the Service Provider. Usually in such a scenario, the Service Provider is expected to provide a stringent SLA with tighter definitions of parameters such as packet delay, variation in packet delay, and packet loss, to accommodate the TDM service.

NOTE   From a Service Provider's standpoint, the CESoE is actually just an Ethernet service.

The MEF 3 has also defined performance expectations for the Service Provider network delivering the CESoE to ensure that toll-grade voice quality is maintained. Specifically, it identifies the following four Class of Service (CoS) characteristics: Ethernet frame delay, Ethernet frame delay variation (jitter), Ethernet frame loss, and network availability. These parameters should conform to values consistent with those in a typical TDM environment (i.e., five 9s network availability, less than 10 ms jitter, and so on).

Implementation Support   MEF 8 provides further detail on implementing the requirements specified in MEF 3 when supporting PDH services over a MEN/Service Provider Ethernet Network (SEN). In so doing, the specification is attempting to address the inherent challenges of transporting TDM signals. The technical challenges faced by CESoE primarily stem from replicating constant bit rate TDM services over a variable bit rate Ethernet infrastructure. These challenges include packetization, frame delay variation, clock recovery, and synchronization and TDM performance monitoring.

In particular, five functions are specified to ensure interoperability: connectivity, timing, signaling, MEN performance criteria, and MEN services OAM. MEF 8 focuses especially on timing and signaling issues. The specification also augments the performance characteristics defined in MEF 3.

Timing/Synchronization   Synchronization is an important consideration in any circuit emulation scheme and the clock of the incoming signal (into the IWF) and outgoing signal (to the IWF) should be synchronized (i.e., the frequency should be the same). There are four options for this clock:

- **TDM line timing**   Use the clock from the incoming TDM line.
- **External timing**   Use an external reference clock source.
- **Free run timing**   Use a free-running oscillator.
- **Ethernet line timing**   Recover the clock from the Ethernet interface.

The last option, Ethernet line timing, covers all methods where information is extracted from the Ethernet, including *adaptive timing,* where the clock is recovered from data in the CESoE frames and the arrival time of the frames, and *differential timing,* where the clock is recovered from a combination of data contained in the CESoE frames and knowledge of a reference clock common to both the SEN-bound and TDM-bound IWFs.

For maximum applicability, it is recommended that CESoE implementations should support at least TDM line external and adaptive timing to enable the implementation to be used in the majority of timing scenarios. Synchronization (and jitter and wander) requirements are placed on a CESoE implementation by the MEF 8 and should conform to the ITU-T recommendations G.823 and G.824 for E1/E3 and DS-1/DS-3, respectively.

Signaling   CE applications interconnected over a CESoE service may exchange signaling in addition to TDM data. The typical example is telephony applications that exchange their state (e.g., off-hook/on-hook) in addition to TDM data carrying PCM-encoded voice.

With structure-agnostic emulation, signaling is not required to intercept or process CE signaling. Signaling is embedded in the TDM data stream, and hence it is carried end-to-end across the emulated circuit.

With structure-aware emulation, transport of Common Channel Signaling (CCS) may be achieved by carrying the signaling channel with the emulated service (e.g., channel 23 for DS1 or channel 16 for E1). However, Channel Associated Signaling (CAS), such as DS1 Robbed Bit Signaling or E1 CAS, requires knowing the relationship of the timeslot to the trunk multiframe structure. This is indicated by the framing bits, which may not be preserved by N×64 kbit/s basic service.

MEF 8 describes a generic method for extending the N×64 kbit/s basic service by carrying CE signaling (CAS or CCS) in separate signaling packets that are independent of the TDM circuit type. This method may be used in situations where the individual 64 kbit/s channels are selected from multiple TDM circuits or picked off a TDM bus rather than from a specific TDM circuit; it also saves SEN bandwidth.

Scalability

One of the major requirements of Carrier Ethernet is to scale to meet the needs of Service Provider offerings. The limitations imposed by the QinQ (IEEE 802.1ad, stacked VLANs) allow for only 4094 VLANs/service instances in a service area (based on the 12 bits used in the VLAN ID field for this purpose). However, this is inadequate to support the kind of scale required by the MEF. Key standards developments are noted in Table 2.3.

Provider Backbone Bridging   Provider Backbone Bridging (PBB) or IEEE 802.1ah addresses the service scaling limitations in native Ethernet networks by enabling millions of service instances in a serving area through the creative use of the MAC address.

TABLE 2.3   Standards Efforts Enabling Scalability

Key Components	Major Developments	Reference
Millions of users/endpoints	Extended the addressable space for users and architecture and framework for scaling services defined	IEEE 802.1ah, IEEE 802.1d, MEF 6, MEF 10.1
Geographic reach/applications	Provided for MAC encapsulation (MAC-in-MAC) to enable substantial Layer 2 scalability	IEEE 802.1ah, IEEE 802.1QAy
Bandwidth granularity	Defined how the bandwidth profile parameters can be set from 1M to 10G in granular increments	MEF 11

Essentially, PBB employs an additional Service Provider 16 bit MAC address[19] that corresponds to the ingress Ethernet ports of the Service Provider edge device and basically encapsulates the end user's MAC (this is also referred to as *MAC-in-MAC*). The outer MAC address is used to forward the Ethernet frames across the Service Provider network, and this much larger physical address space (approx 2^{16}) allows for a more scalable network than the traditional one with VLAN IDs—where even with the QinQ scheme, stacking a Service Provider VLAN tag over the customer VLAN tag, only 4094 service instances are supported.

The MAC-in-MAC significantly improves scalability and also provides some security by separating the customer and Service Provider address space. It also precludes a MAC address explosion and the need for learning substantially more end-user MAC addresses in the Service Provider's core infrastructure (switches and so on). Minimizing the number of MAC addresses that need to be learned also reduces the aging out and relearning of MAC addresses, enhancing end-to-end performance, and in general, making the network more stable as far as forwarding Ethernet frames is concerned.

The IEEE 802.1ah efforts to standardize PBB should be consulted for more updated information on PBB.

Provider Bridge Transport (PBT)/PBB with Traffic Engineering (PBB-TE)   While Carrier Ethernet can be delivered over numerous transport technologies, such as SONET and MPLS (see Part II for a compendium), one option is to deliver it over native Ethernet (see Chapter 13 on bridging and switching). However, native Ethernet itself has been limited as a plausible transport technology especially as Carrier Ethernet services were enabled on a wide area basis (beyond the access networks and stretching well into the core and beyond). One key hurdle is the inherent best-effort approach of LAN Ethernet, which is ill-suited in a service that supports time-sensitive applications.

With the emergence of a new standardization effort, namely the Provider Bridge Transport (PBT), a more deterministic Ethernet is being attempted. In fact, PBT

---

[19] The Ethernet frame size is now correspondingly augmented; the devices in the network should be able to support this.

aims to provide the connection-oriented features of TDM to the hitherto connection-less Ethernet. The IEEE has undertaken this effort—also referred to as the *Provider Backbone Bridge with Traffic Engineering (PBB-TE)*—since it is essentially a variation of the IEEE 802.1ah PBB standard. In fact, PBT also employs a MAC-in-MAC forwarding scheme from PBB and also distributes the bridging tables using the control plane. PBT, however, does not use some of the features defined in PBB such as broadcasting and MAC learning and does not support the Spanning Tree Protocol.

PBT basically provisions Point-to-Point Ethernet paths that are engineered across Service Provider Ethernet networks. These paths provide traffic engineering (and are referred to as *PBB-TE*) and allow for setting up QoS to meet predefined SLAs across the service provider WAN. PBT operates by adding configured routes to the standard PBB network.

In addition, 50 ms recovery can also be provided to meet the industry expectation of service provider networks. In conjunction with Ethernet OAM standards (discussed later in this chapter), proactive fault management can also be incorporated for these Ethernet paths. Because PBT transport can be independent of the service carried over this transport, it can be used to Carrier non-Ethernet services as well.

Given that existing technologies such as MPLS are more established (especially in the core of Service Provider networks), the need for PBT is being questioned in some quarters; while proponents claim compelling CAPEX and OPEX savings vis-à-vis MPLS, the incumbency of MPLS (i.e., already deployed and depreciating) may make it harder to displace, especially in existing networks. In green field networks, however, there may be a better opportunity for PBT.

More information on PBT can be obtained from the appropriately noted references.

Reliability

While MEF has defined service-level reliability and its components' service resiliency, protection, and less than 50 ms restoration, several of the underlying transport solutions employed to deliver Carrier Ethernet, particularly SONET and RPR, have established a high level of reliability in Service Provider networks. MEF 2 allows the MEN to leverage any underlying transport layer protection type if it can enable end-to-end service protection.

Table 2.4 identifies key standards based developments that are incorporating Reliability.

Two protection types, 1+1 and *M:N*, have been defined. In the 1+1 approach, duplicate traffic is the norm, and in the case of a failure/protection event, one stream of traffic is still available (unless the failure is catastrophic). In the case of *M:N*, *N* working resources are provided protection using *M* protection sources.

Four different protection mechanisms have also been defined: Aggregate Link and Node Protection (ALNP) to protect against local link/node failure; End-to-End Path Protection (EEPP), where redundancy is provided for the primary path on an end-to-end basis; MP2MP protection of E-LAN services including Rapid Spanning Tree Protocol (RSTP) and link redundancy; and finally, link protection based on link aggregation, where one or more Ethernet links connected between the same nodes can be aggregated.

TABLE 2.4 Standards Efforts Enabling Reliability

Key Components	Major Developments	Reference
Service resiliency	Less than 50 ms resiliency has been defined as a critical requirement	MEF 2, IEEE 802.1ag
Protection	Defined broad framework for hop by hop and end-to-end service-level protection Defined four protection mechanisms and also allowed leveraged end-to-end service protection available at the transport layer	MEF 2
Restoration	Different levels of restoration have been defined to afford a wide variety of application requirements	MEF 2, IEEE 802.1QAy (PBT/PBB-TE)

MEF 2 has provided for supporting a wide variety of restoration times, from less than 5 seconds to the less than 50 ms range, in order to support the wide variety of applications and their corresponding requirements. The MEF 2 also allows end users to choose a variety of protection parameters for a Carrier Ethernet service. These protection parameters must be applicable on a per service or a group level. Any of the ETH layer protection mechanisms in MEF 2 should be able to work in conjunction with the lower layer (transport) protection mechanisms.

Quality of Service

As mentioned earlier, Provide Bridge Transport (PBT) can provide deterministic transport of Ethernet services, and hence QoS much like other underlying transport used to deliver Carrier Ethernet. This is, in fact, a critical requirement of Carrier Ethernet, one that needs to be addressed well before the market begins to embrace it more wholeheartedly. At the ETH layer, MEF 10 has undertaken a significant amount of effort toward defining and implementing QoS to ensure rigorous SLAs.

Table 2.5 notes some of the key developments in the standards bodies' with regard to Carrier Ethernet QoS.

TABLE 2.5 Standards Efforts Enabling Quality of Service

Key Components	Major Developments	Reference
Wide choice of granularity and QoS options	Different levels of granular bandwidth defined; also bandwidth profile defined for providing different class of services	MEF 6, MEF 10.1
End-to-end performance SLAs	Defined how some traffic is delivered with strict SLAs while other traffic is delivered with best effort; traffic management algorithm to ensure SLA	MEF 3, MEF 7, MEF 10.1 IEEE 802.1Qay
Provisioning based on SLA components— CIR, frame loss, delay, and jitter	Defined bandwidth profile capability that enables provisioning traffic based on SLA attributes	MEF 3, MEF 10.1, IEEE 802.1ag, ITU Y.1731

Specifically, MEF 10.1 has defined a Bandwidth profile and also identified specific service-related performance parameters. It has also defined the algorithm to enforce QoS or performance by ensuring conformance to the bandwidth profile. This was discussed at some length earlier in the chapter.

Standardized Management

LAN Ethernet was most lacking in the area of standardized management; consequently, this has been the focus of considerable work in Ethernet's transformation to Carrier Ethernet. Specifically, Ethernet OAM has had to be developed from the ground up. The developments in this area are discussed at some length; Table 2.6 notes some of the developments in the standards bodies.

MEF 7 focuses on standardizing for Service Provider Element and Network Management Systems (EMS/NMS) to provision, configure, and fault manage Carrier Ethernet services. It also defines OAM at the Ethernet services layer; however, it does not define OAM at the transport link/network layers, and it complements the work done in the ITU, IEEE, and IETF at the transport data-link and network layers based on G.809.

MEF 7 also provides a framework and concepts for managing and monitoring flows across an end-to-end connectionless network, and it also provides mechanisms to perform node discovery, establish connectivity, monitor CoS, and detect service impairments.

Ethernet Operations, Administration, and Maintenance (OAM)   One of the key prerequisites to wide-scale Ethernet service deployment in Service Provider networks is a comprehensive Operations, Administration, and Maintenance (OAM) capability. The need to support hundreds of thousands of customers who are already accustomed to the fairly stringent SLAs for ATM, Frame Relay, and private line services means that significant new management capabilities are necessary for Carrier Ethernet; Ethernet has traditionally been weak in this respect and the relatively lower demands for OAM within an enterprise LAN (often within a building) were easily

TABLE 2.6   Standards Efforts Enabling Standardized Management

Key Components	Major Developments	Reference
Unified management	Defined a framework to monitor and manage flows across a connectionless network (at the Ethernet layer)	MEF 7, MEF 15, ITU G.809
Carrier-class OAM	Carrier-class link level management and end-to-end service-level management defined	MEF 7, IEEE 802.3ah, IEEE 802.1ag, Y.1731
Rapid services provisioning	Defined local management interface to enable rapid provisioning and management	MEF 16

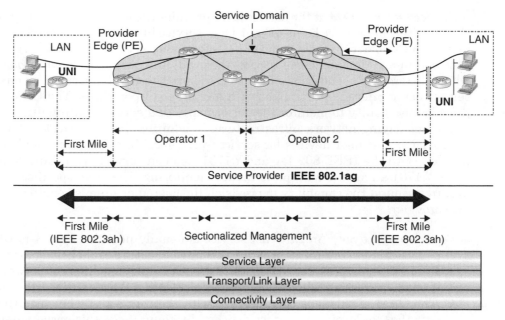

Figure 2.20   Ethernet OAM—a layered perspective

managed by the use of (less than efficient) Layer 3 protocols such as Simple Network Management Protocol (SNMP).[20]

As Carrier Ethernet is accelerating as a Carrier-class service delivered over multiple large and complex Service Provider networks, its OAM capabilities have to offer sophisticated tools to provision individual Ethernet services, monitor their performance, and identify and manage any issues quickly across such network topologies. Ultimately, this will lead to reducing the total cost of ownership, which is a prerequisite before Carrier Ethernet can meaningfully attempt to become a mass market service.

In attempting to define a comprehensive OAM capability for Carrier Ethernet, a layered approach is conceptually employed[21] to align with the layered nature of Service Provider networks used to deliver Carrier Ethernet. Each of the OAM layers delineate the different focus and functionality of the respective layer in the context of delivering Carrier Ethernet. This is shown in Figure 2.20. The three-layered OAM approach focuses on the service layer, the network/connectivity layer, and the transport/data-link layer. The OAM at each of the layers is independent of the other layers; however, they all employ standard Ethernet frames as the means of OAM-related communication.

---

[20] Ironically, these management protocols would not be usable without the Ethernet (layer 2) being operational. This scenario is somewhat ridiculous—when there is an issue in Layer 2, then the higher layer–based (i.e., Layer 3) management protocol is useless, defeating the very purpose of having a management capability.

[21] There is not yet a formally defined OAM-layered model available, but the ones employed are generally close.

Service Layer   OAM at the service layer provides the capability to manage the entire Carrier Ethernet *service* being offered, i.e., a service instance represented as a uniquely identified Ethernet Virtual Circuit (EVC) offered between two or more customer UNIs. This end-to-end domain of the service—basically the customer domain—is ultimately what matters to the end-user experience, so here the OAM is focused on ensuring the service being offered is compliant with any agreed upon SLAs. The OAM, therefore, provides the ability to monitor the performance of a service continually, independent of the underlying network infrastructure. In addition, it also provides the capability to provision customer devices for services with specific performance and operational profiles. Both the IEEE 802.1ag and Y.1731 focus on service layer fault management, while Y.1731 augments with performance monitoring. The MEF specification 16 standardizes around the capability to provision the customer premise equipment by a service provider.

Connectivity Layer   An Ethernet service is usually provided by a Service Provider over a physical network infrastructure; this infrastructure could belong to and be managed by one or more providers (or operators), each employing different network technologies to deliver Carrier Ethernet services (e.g., SONET, WDM, native Ethernet, MPLS, etc.). The OAM in this layer is concerned with the connectivity between the network elements that underpin the service delivery. In Figure 2.20, this encompasses the elements that exist between the boundaries of the Service Provider network (which, of course, could be comprised of networks belonging to multiple independent operators) and typically notated as being between the Provider Edge (PE) devices. Providing the capability to detect, troubleshoot, and *proactively* manage any issues emerging at this layer essentially means providing the ability to sectionalize any segment in the network quickly; thus an issue can be narrowed to a specific point in the infrastructure and quickly homed in on. Any issues at this layer will invariably have an impact on the higher service layer, and the specific impact (i.e., which service instances have been affected) on the management infrastructure needs to be identified. The IEEE 802.1ag and Y.1731 standards focus on this layer.

Transport / Data-Link Layer   At the Data-Link layer, the OAM is focused on providing the capability to manage a single physical data link between two Ethernet interfaces; such links, of course, make up the network infrastructure, but the OAM capabilities on this layer are restricted to only individual physical links and include the ability to troubleshoot any issues employing loopbacks and monitor performance effectively.

Any impact on this layer manifests in possible issues at the higher (connectivity and service) layers, and robust capabilities to monitor, troubleshoot, and identify any issues are vital. The key standard in this area, the IEEE 802.3ah, focuses on the access link (first/last mile) of native Ethernet access networks. Multiple transport solutions for Ethernet can be employed, such as SONET, WDM, etc., and there are well-established OAM standards for these respective solutions.

Standards Work   Key standard bodies such as the ITU, MEF, and IEEE and their respective standards/specifications are focused on developing OAM capabilities across

TABLE 2.7   Ethernet OAM Layers, Functionality, and Standards

Layer	Standards	Key Functions
Service	ITU Y.1731 IEEE 802.1ag MEF Spec 7, MEF Spec 16 (E-LMI)	Discovery Continuity check Loopback AIS/RDI (alarm indication signal/remote defect indicator) Traceroute Performance management
Connectivity	ITU-T Y.1731 IEEE 802.1ag	Discovery Continuity check Loopback AIS/RDI (alarm indication signal/remote defect indicator) Traceroute
Transport/ data-link	IEEE 802.3ah Misc. transport standards	Discovery Link monitoring Remote failure indication Remote, local loopback Fault isolation Performance monitoring

Source: ADVA Optical Networking

the three layers as shown in Table 2.7. Some of the key functions provided by the different standards at each of the layers are also briefly discussed.

Some of these functions and standards are focused beyond a single layer (IEEE 802.1ag/Y.1731, for example, is applicable to both the service and connectivity layers). Also, there are multiple standards in some of the layers. Generally, there is alignment between the respective standards efforts such that they mutually reinforce each other and do not conflict. Thus, both IEEE 802.1ag and ITU Y.1731 provide similar capabilities to monitor the service end-to-end.

- **Discovery**   This function enables auto discovery and exchange of information pertaining to OAM and other capabilities between peer entities in a network (or on a link in the transport layer).

- **Continuity check**   This function allows for continuous monitoring of a path (multiple hops) or a link between two endpoints using a periodic "I am alive" message exchange.

- **Loopback**   This common function provides the ability to test whether a physical/virtual circuit is operating correctly. It essentially sends and receives a set of Ethernet frames to a remote point in the Service Provider network. If the remote location is a physical Ethernet port/facility, then the loopback will be intrusive (i.e., will impact regular data flow); a nonintrusive loopback can be initiated on a per-service instance (i.e., a specific EVC) basis.

- **Alarm Indication Signal (AIS) and Remote Defect Indicator (RDI)**   This provides the capability of generating only one alarm message when an issue is detected and ensures that other devices that receive the same alarm suppress duplicate notifications (very much like what's available on SONET and ATM).

- **Traceroute**   This is a simple "ping-like" function that basically tests a specific multihop path across a Service Provider network (and likely across multiple operators' domains).

- **Performance monitoring**   This functionality allows measurement of specific SLA parameters relating to a particular service instance (EVC) such as delay encountered, loss packets, jitter (or differential delay), and availability over a period. These measurements are on an end-to-end basis and closely reflect the performance of an actual service.

At the data-link layer, performance monitoring is limited across a physical link. This section briefly introduces some of the key OAM standards and highlights their essential characteristics.

IEEE 802.1ag Connectivity Fault Management (CFM)   The IEEE 802.1ag is expected to be ratified in 2007 and enables Service Providers to manage individual EVCs, representing specific Ethernet services. Such management will be on an end-to-end basis across the network(s) over which the service is delivered. As such, this would require all the underlying equipment involved (and belonging to one or more operators) to also support the IEEE 802.1ag standard. The IEEE 802.1ag is closely aligned with the work on fault management from the Y.1731 standard.

The IEEE 802.1ag separates the Service Provider network—the one delivering the end-user service—into maintenance domains, which are each essentially managed/ administered independently. These domains are typically hierarchical and encompass the three distinct entities that are involved in delivering a service: the customers using the service, the Service Provider delivering the service, and the operators whose networks may be used to deliver the service. Such a framework is useful in quickly homing in on—and resolving an issue.

The IEEE 802.1ag uses normal Ethernet frames to communicate between the different devices, with the only distinction being the use of a special Ethernet MAC address identifying it as an 802.1ag message. There are fours categories of messages that are employed to troubleshoot and manage Ethernets:

- **Continuity check messages (CCMs)**   These are "I am alive" heartbeat messages that are issued periodically to identify any loss of service between two (equipment/devices) endpoints or intermediate points. Any erratic behavior in these messages could enable preemptively addressing any emerging issues.

- **Link trace messages**   These messages are used by a Service Provider to track a specific path between two pieces of equipment/devices traversing through the intervening devices. This hop-by-hop approach is useful in identifying whether a data path exists or not.

- **Loopback messages**   These allow a Service Provider to validate connectivity (either on a service or a circuit basis) to a particular maintenance point to determine whether it is reachable or not, without particularly worrying about the intermediate nodes.

- **Alarm indication signal (AIS) messages**   These messages are used to indicate that there is a fault in the network.

ITU Y.1731   The ITU Standards Group (SG) 13, in Recommendation Y.1731, identifies the OAM functions in an Ethernet network that are needed to allow fault management and performance monitoring. Fault management is closely aligned with the fault management capability of the IEEE 802.1ag (and hence includes capabilities such as discovery, continuity checks, loopbacks, link trace, etc.). However, the Y.1731 augments this with performance monitoring as well.

Performance monitoring allows the measurement of typical SLA parameters around error counts and delay measurements such as loss of Ethernet frames, delay between frames, variation between consecutive delays (also known as jitter), and other information such as link up or down, throughput, and so on.

Currently, the Y.1731 standard supports performance monitoring only for address Point-to-Point connectivity at this time (multipoint connectivity is expected in the next phase).

The ITU group is working closely with IEEE 802.1ag group to ensure alignment and preclude any conflicting approaches.

IEEE 802.3ah Ethernet over First Mile   The IEEE 802.3ah OAM is also known as Ethernet First Mile (EFM) OAM and provides OAM between the Ethernet ports at the CPE and the Provider Edge (the "first mile"), which is deployed over a physical IEEE 802.3 medium (copper, fiber, or PON). In fact, the IEEE 802.3ah also addresses the PHY (physical) layer characteristics for the different media in the first mile; the OAM part of the IEEE 802.3ah is, however, independent of the physical layer. EFM OAM is the first standards-based effort to ensure Ethernet devices in Service Provider networks have an inherent management capability.

The IEEE 802.3ah was ratified in 2004 and was expected to complement existing protocols such as SNMP that were otherwise being employed for management purposes.

The EFM OAM also uses Ethernet frames (albeit with a specific destination MAC address and the Ethernet type/length field to identify EFM-related frames uniquely (PDUs). It is also an in-band protocol (i.e., it uses the same bandwidth as the data frames) and is characterized as a slow protocol; it is not required for normal operation and typically uses about 10 frames per second.

The EFM OAM addresses some fundamental aspects necessary when deploying Ethernet over the first/last mile:

- **Link monitoring**   Gives the Service Provider visibility of the first mile physical connection through periodic heartbeat messages. In case of any issues on this link, the Service Provider is immediately notified with pertinent information.
- **Fault signaling**   Enables a device to convey to its peer at the remote location that severe conditions such as link failure (noted because it can no longer receive any signal) or a dying gasp (when the remote device is about to be powered down and operationally unavailable) have occurred.

■ **Remote loopback**   Enables a loopback to be initiated from one entity to a remote peer entity to ensure the quality of the intervening Ethernet circuit (specific tests for delay, jitter, and so on, can also be measured).

■ **MIB variable retrieval**   Provides a management information base (MIB), which is a database of management variables and typically includes all performance and error statistics maintained on an Ethernet link. The IEEE 802.3ah Ethernet OAM provides a read-only access remote MIB (and does not allow the variables to be set).

Organization Specific Extensions   The IEEE 802.3ah OAM also allows equipment vendors to extend Ethernet OAM capabilities through organizational-specific PDUs to support additional capabilities, such as extending OAM messages beyond one link and monitoring other equipment performance parameters, that will contribute to offering more robust Ethernet services.

Ethernet-Local Management Interface (E-LMI)   The E-LMI, specified in the MEF 16, defines the protocol to communicate service-level information to enable the automatic configuration of the Customer Premise Equipment (CPE). This ability allows the Service Provider to ensure, remotely, that the CPE is set up correctly to support a specific Ethernet service, rather than have the enterprise administrator configure it. Basically, the entire configuration for a specific service is downloaded into the CPE from the provider edge device using E-LMI. Specifically, the E-LMI provides the following capabilities to a Service Provider:

■ Add or delete an Ethernet Virtual Circuit (i.e., an Ethernet service instance) in the CPE.

■ Inform the status of an already configured EVC, specifically whether it is available or not.

■ Verify the integrity of the link between the Provider Edge (PE) and the CPE.

■ Ensure that the UNI and EVC attributes are correctly passed to the CPE.

Carrier Ethernet: Field Realities

While Carrier Ethernet is being embraced quite aggressively—evident by the number of Service Providers offering these services and also by the promising growth predicted, it is important to note that it (Carrier Ethernet) still accounts for a relatively small portion of the addressable market. In fact, a study by the Vertical Systems Group (VSG) indicates that it makes up less than 5 percent of business service spending on telecom services.

As Carrier Ethernet services are beginning to grow, they will invariably have to address the Small and Medium Enterprises (SME) that make up the larger part of the enterprise market opportunity and are represented graphically by the lower part of the pyramid in Figure 2.21. Essentially, this segment of the market is comprised of a much larger number of (relatively smaller) end customers as compared to the initially

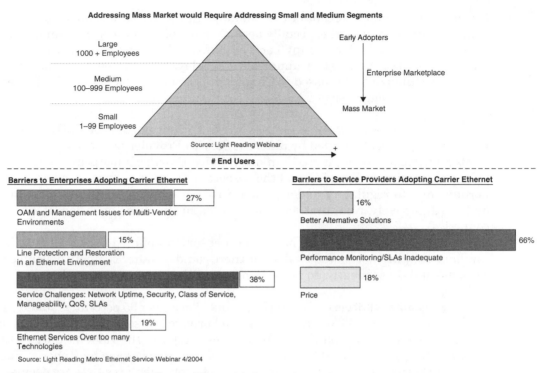

Figure 2.21 Key barriers to Carrier Ethernet today

addressed market represented by the top of the pyramid. Addressing the needs of this customer base economically is, therefore, a prerequisite to fueling Carrier Ethernet toward becoming a true mass market service. There are, however, several—some unique—challenges to addressing this segment of the market. These and other issues are discussed next, followed by an overview of the industry response.

Current Challenges in Delivering Carrier Ethernet

The challenges in delivering Carrier Ethernet, especially to the SMEs, are noted in the different studies depicted in Figure 2.21. The key issues are distilled in the sections that follow.

Availability of Carrier Ethernet Services   While SMEs are increasingly aware of the benefits of Ethernet services, a big issue is the availability of such services. Specifically, the following issues pose a barrier to subscribing to Carrier Ethernet services.

Fiber Availability   Carrier Ethernet services are being delivered significantly in a native fashion over a fiber infrastructure. Given that, according to Vertical Systems

Group, only about 11 percent of the buildings in the U.S. are connected to fiber. This definitely limits coverage, especially because most of the enterprises (and notably the SMEs) are the ones that occupy such buildings. The significant cost of laying fiber (actually the cost of regulatory approvals and delays) has slowed down the process considerably, although as discussed in Chapter 16, Service Providers are finally beginning to proceed fairly aggressively.

Lack of Availability at All Locations   It is not uncommon for SMEs to have multiple offices physically served by different Service Provider networks because they are located physically across more than one Service Provider's footprint (e.g., a SME has offices at location A, B, and C, and the respective telecom services are being delivered, perhaps due to regulatory and/or competitive constraints, by Service Providers 1, 2, and 3, respectively. Note that locations can be in the same or different cities and/or countries).

Such SMEs frequently do not have Ethernet services offered at each of their locations (perhaps they are not served by fiber or there could be other competitive and economic reasons) and consequently, do not subscribe to Ethernet services at all.

Lack of Key Carrier Attributes   The SME customer base (over 95 percent as stated earlier) is often served by legacy ATM, Frame Relay, and private line services today to support their voice, data, and video applications. While they recognize the value of Carrier Ethernet (see Chapter 1 for a detailed listing of the benefits), there is some hesitancy to migrate to Carrier Ethernet due to the (perceived[22]) lack of service features that are deemed important and that they're accustomed to with their legacy services. This feature deficiency is depicted in Figure 2.19 as well, the most important being the lack of service-level agreement (SLA) monitoring and, more generally, OAM capabilities.

SLA Monitoring   As SMEs are considering Carrier Ethernet as the convergent access, and hence relying on it for their mission-critical applications as well (storage backup, voice, etc.), it is imperative that SME customers have the assurance that the underlying Carrier Ethernet services are performing according to stringent SLA requirements. With private line and other technologies, they have that capability; with Carrier Ethernet, the absence of such SLA measurement capabilities precludes its adoption.

Lack of OAMs   As Service Providers are required to deliver Carrier Ethernet to a substantially greater number of individual customers (the SMEs), they have to make it an economically viable offering with adequate profitability margins. In order to provide Carrier Ethernet to a mass market, the capital expenditures (CAPEX) and, more importantly, their operational expenditures[23] (OPEX) need to be addressed. A significant contributor

---

[22] As will be evident in Part II, numerous Ethernet solutions do offer most of the Carrier-class attributes.

[23] It has been estimated that over 70 percent of the total cost of ownership of delivering a service is comprised of the OPEX. Hence, a reduction in OPEX has considerably higher impact on reducing cost.

to OPEX for Ethernet services currently is the largely manual and time-consuming effort required to manage these services—from provisioning to fault notification, troubleshooting to managing any issues that emerge. The key reason for this situation is the lack of sophisticated tools and features to manage Ethernet services, especially on an end-to-end service level; as noted in the previous section of this chapter, this Carrier Ethernet services' shortcoming has been the focus of the initial standards efforts.

Bandwidth Demand Curve   While newer bandwidth intensive applications such as video make Carrier Ethernet the natural solution for enterprises, it must be pointed out that a significant portion of the addressable market—nearly 95 percent according to Vertical Systems Group—is served by T1 (64 Kbps) connections. While bandwidth demand at these SMEs is indeed growing, it is not quite jumping to 10 Mbps—the typical Carrier Ethernet service offering. Even though Carrier Ethernet is designed to offer bandwidth anywhere from 1 Mbps in fine increments of 1M or even less (in fact, this is considered one of its big advantages as noted in Chapter 1), less than 10 M is not in reality being offered. This speaks to enforcing the Carrier Ethernet defined UNI to leverage the market opportunity.

Economics   One big advantage of carrier Ethernet services is the economics for both the Service Providers and enterprise end users. However, as these services are currently being delivered over numerous underlying technologies (refer to Part II for a discussion on these), the economics may be less attractive (as opposed to delivering native Ethernet). Further, because pricing of Carrier Ethernet services is combined with other application services such as Internet access, the true cost of Carrier Ethernet is hard to discern.

Interoperability   In a LAN Ethernet, enterprise customers have come to expect that any device, from any manufacturer with a standard Ethernet port, can be easily deployed in their LAN. A similar expectation is assumed by Service Providers when it comes to Carrier Ethernet; after all, their networks are akin to a LAN and any Carrier Ethernet equipment from multiple vendors deployed over these networks should inter-work and provide consistent services and, of course, offer the features and tools to provision and manage these services.

The Standardization Efforts   While the standardization efforts have made significant headway, this is a work in progress and still very much in the early stages. Functionalities such as Network to Network Interface (NNI)—which defines the handoff between two Service Providers and is a key requirement for wholesale Carrier Ethernet services or when the delivery infrastructure is leased from one or more network operators—needs to be formally defined before Carrier Ethernet will be deployed more aggressively in the WAN. This effort is still underway at the standards bodies.

Recent Industry Response to Challenges

Given the economic and competitive attractiveness of Carrier Ethernet services, the industry has naturally embarked on addressing some of the challenges noted above.

Two specific ones—Intelligent Demarcation and the MEF Certification Program, are discussed here, and illustrate the considerable and effective effort in this regard.

Intelligent Ethernet Demarcation

One industry response to enabling the acceleration of Carrier Ethernet has been to introduce a new class of intelligent *Ethernet demarcation devices (EDDs)*.[24] These are also referred to as *network termination units* or *network termination elements (NTEs)*.

NOTE   While these devices may be standalone, as is the case currently, this functionality may well be integrated into other edge devices (such as switches, routers, ADMs, etc.) as well.

These devices typically reside at the Customer Premise (CP) or Customer Edge (CE), and in addition to serving as a physical point of separation between the Service Provider and user networks (typically a LAN),[25] they provide three key functional capabilities:

- A standardized Ethernet UNI
- Ethernet OAM
- Media/protocol conversion

The standardized Ethernet UNI essentially provides the MEF-defined capabilities that include an IEEE 802.3 handoff (PHY), provisioning, and enforcing a bandwidth profile for any EVCs initiated there, along with the CoS, and any service multiplexing necessary.

The Ethernet OAM provides end-to-end visibility of the Ethernet service(s) and the associated performance SLAs. It also encompasses sophisticated and proactive fault notification so that any potential issues can be addressed remotely before they manifest more broadly. The OAM provides troubleshooting tools to enable such a capability. Most of this is based on the IEEE 802.1ag and ITU Y.1731 standards and can also measure typical SLA components (such as delay, jitter, frame loss, etc.) on a per-service (EVC).

The OAM capability, in addition to ensuring that the Ethernet services are being delivered per the SLAs, also reduces the Service Provider OPEX by providing the ability to address most of the typical service issues remotely (and thereby precluding expensive truck rolls).

Finally, the media conversion capability provides a standardized UNI to the customer while supporting a host of last/first mile transport technologies and media to

---

[24] This is not particularly unique; earlier technologies such as Private Line and ATM/Frame Relay addressed similar barriers to wide–scale deployment by introducing demarcation devices. It was almost natural that Carrier Ethernet followed suit.

[25] This physical demarcation between the Service Provider and the subscriber/customer also signifies where the responsibility of a Service Provider ends in terms of identifying and resolving any issues. Anything beyond the EDD (toward the customer) is the responsibility of the customer.

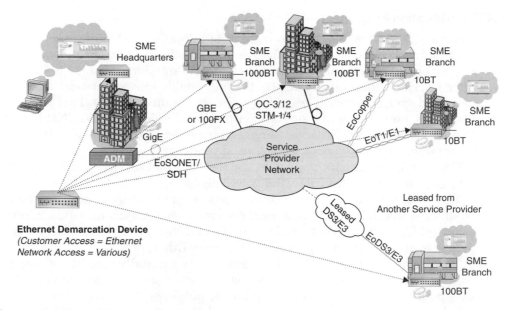

Figure 2.22 Use of Ethernet demarcation to provide Carrier Ethernet services to the mass market (Source: ADVA Optical Networking)

the Service Provider network (such as T1, DS-3, OC-3, OC-12, etc); thus, the Ethernet handoff is "converted" to whatever the last mile transport technology is.[26] What this means is that now a standardized Carrier Ethernet handoff can be provided to a customer independent of the last mile infrastructure.

Figure 2.22 depicts the use of Ethernet demarcation in a real-life scenario. In this example, a reasonably large enterprise customer with several physical locations, each of which are served by different last/first mile infrastructures, requires Carrier Ethernet services. Some of the locations are served by old SONET ADMs that have no Ethernet capability. By introducing Ethernet demarcation, such issues are addressed and the customer is provided a standardized Ethernet UNI, with the same look and feel at all locations.

Thus, Ethernet demarcation is enabling the delivery of Carrier Ethernet services despite the challenges of fiber shortage and the presence of a host of last mile infrastructures that may not always be amenable to delivery of such services (e.g., older SONET ADMs are usually not equipped with Ethernet interfaces). Further, it is important to note that Ethernet demarcation devices also enable Ethernet services quickly (i.e., speed to market), relatively easily (i.e., it is easy to augment current last mile technology solutions with a standalone EDD), and ultimately cost effectively. The IEEE 802.1aj (two-port relay) effort is considering standardizing such a functionality.

---

[26] Employing standard techniques such as encapsulating using GFP (Generic Frame Protocol) for carrying over SONET, etc.

The MEF Certification Program

Carrier Ethernet is designed to scale from a local to a ubiquitous worldwide service that could span thousands of offices and hundreds of countries and where everything works together harmoniously. It is therefore no small matter for Service Providers to offer Carrier Ethernet services that would enable mission critical applications, and delivered over a variety of transport technologies (discussed in Part II). Often Service Providers would have to cooperate with other Service Providers/Network Operators to offer these Carrier Ethernet services across the MAN/WAN and this would almost invariably entail equipment from several vendors.

Conversely, to the enterprise user, Carrier Ethernet services must work as simply as plugging in an Ethernet cable and powering up.

The MEF Certification Program was conceived explicitly to address the underlying challenges that inherently exist in simplifying the deployment, while ensuring consistency (of Carrier Ethernet services) in a multi-vendor environment. In so doing, the goal is to accelerate the deployment of Carrier Ethernet.

The program commenced in April 2005 and essentially consists of a series of thorough tests providing evidence for end-users, service providers and manufacturers alike, that products and services are compliant to published MEF specifications.

It initially certified equipment (systems) that it delivers MEF-compliant Ethernet services. This program subsequently also began certifying that Service Provider–delivered Ethernet services are also consistent with the MEF Carrier Ethernet specifications.

NOTE The MEF does not conduct the certification directly but rather works with an independent testing entity, Iometrix, for conducting the actual testing and validating compliance.

Thus, whether it is a Service Provider evaluating equipment for delivering Carrier Ethernet or end users assessing Carrier Ethernet services, knowing that the underlying equipment or service is MEF-compliant expedites deployment. Specifically, the MEF certification program offers the following benefits to the three main constituents that drive Carrier Ethernet:

Enterprises end users:

- Provides a common basis/terminology to meaningfully compare services from different Service Providers.

- Empowers informed decisions regarding equipment/CPE purchases and minimize risk.

- Assures that Ethernet services perform according to pre defined specifications and standards.

- Ultimately benefits from the efficiencies and cost savings to the Service Providers, which are usually passed on to the end users.

Service Providers:

■ Immediate assurance that vendor's equipment complies to MEF specifications.

■ Saves money and time on complex testing between vendors, especially on global accounts.

■ Establishes solid foundation for Carrier Ethernet ubiquity and interoperability.

■ Removes confusion caused by proprietary names and descriptions

■ Conformance to MEF 9 allows customers to specify their service requirements unambiguously using standards.

Equipment vendors/Manufacturers:

■ Globally recognized interoperability standard improves approval process

■ Increases tender opportunities and competitiveness.

■ Independent validation of function and conformance that their equipment is MEF compliant; this helps with positioning and deployment at Service Provider customers.

■ Dramatically reduces testing costs, time-to-market, as well as installation time.

■ Provides a performance and behaviour benchmark.

■ It forms the basis for RFP requests and helps manufacturers focus on their features that distinguish them from competition

The MEF certification program was rolled out in two phases and has focused on MEF 9 and MEF 14:

■ **Phase 1** The focus here was on equipment and systems that deliver Carrier Ethernet, specifically on whether they are compliant with the MEF-defined services. Thus far hundreds of systems from over 45 vendors have been certified for MEF 9 (Abstract Test Suite for Ethernet Services at the UNI; the Ethernet services are defined in MEF 6); certification for MEF 14 (Service Quality) is also now underway and numerous vendors — over 35, have already been certified as well.

■ **Phase 2** This is focused on ensuring that the Carrier Ethernet services offered by Service Providers are compliant with the MEF specifications. The first set of over 15 Service Providers was certified for MEF 9; this guarantees that the E-LINE and E-LAN from these Service Providers will be compliant with MEF. Eleven Service Providers have been certified for MEF 14 as well.

The certification program is extending to testing Traffic Management (MEF 10.1) according to the definitions in MEF 7.

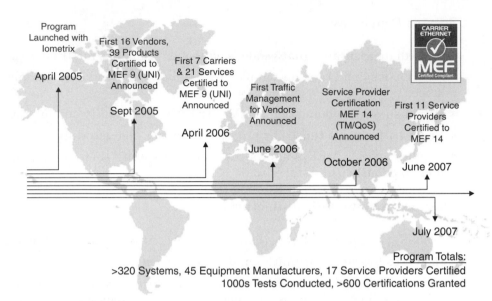

Figure 2.23   The MEF Certification Program—key milestones to date (Source: MEF)

Figure 2.23 depicts the extent of progress made in the MEF Certification Program, as of July 2007. To date 17 Service Providers and 45 equipment vendors with 320 systems have been certified.

MEF has also recently introduced two new technical test specifications, MEF 18 (Abstract test suite for CES over Ethernet services) and MEF 19 (Abstract test suite for UNI Type 1), and is working on developing potentially test suites for E-NNI and LMI.

Other Carrier Ethernet requirements—One Service Provider's perspective

While the MEF has made considerable strides in the realm of identifying and refining the Carrier Ethernet attributes, it is, of course, a work in progress. Emerging applications, field experience, and new network constraints/requirements continually push the boundary and need to be addressed if Carrier Ethernet is to dominate the market.

Here a brief overview of the requirements that Carrier Ethernet faces — or will face shortly, is provided and is based on the experience and insights of one of the foremost Carrier Ethernet Service Providers, Verizon[27]. That most of these requirements are already being actively addressed (or at least being considered) by the MEF vividly demonstrates the unprecedented participation—and influence, of Service Providers in MEF.

---

[27] Verizon identifies these requirements in the context of its four key drivers for Carrier Ethernet—Business Ethernet services, Broadband access, Residential video service transport, and wireless backhaul.

Standardized Services

- A common set of Class of Service (CoS) definitions and associated performance guarantees, bandwidth increments for each CoS and maximum frame service need to be developed (some work has already begun in MEF).

- Equipment (both customer and network) needs to incorporate configuration management as defined in the E-LMI specification (MEF 16). This would enable such equipment to automate, and hence simplify configuring the increasingly sophisticated services.

- Timing synchronization specifications have gained some urgency as carriers are beginning to migrate TDM services to converged Ethernet networks. (MEF has begun addressing in the mobile backhaul project).

Scalability

- A standard Carrier to Carrier interconnection specification is required (The E-NNI effort has commenced by the MEF)

- A standardized access interconnection for emerging access methods is required (MEF has begun developing the Service Node Interface, SNI)

- A dynamic control plane solution is required to enable automated provisioning.

- Overcome the VLAN/MAC limitations (actively being addressed by the PBB, MPLS etc as noted previously in the chapter)

- Efficiently forcing customer specific traffic only on some backbone links (Multiple Registration Protocol, MRP, per IEEE 802.1ak has begun focusing on this capability).

Reliability

- Standardized SNI required to provide an efficient method of introducing resilient access solutions in the metro. (MEF work underway)

- While fault management has been well defined, it is yet to be implemented in commercial equipment solutions.

Quality of Service

- Topology discovery tools in Network Management Systems to support Connection Admission Control (CAC) in an Ethernet network.

NOTE CAC is usually provided by Service Provider Provisioning systems, and so the Network Management systems should coordinate with Provisioning systems to ensure the delivery of stringent QoS.

- A distributed control plane is required to support large Carrier Ethernet networks.

- CoS awareness in Layer 1 transport devices in access networks is required to preclude any speed mismatches.

Standardized Management

- Standards available but need to be implemented in commercial solutions (most of them support pre-standard versions)
- Require enhanced version of Link Aggregation that distributes Ethernet frames based on VLAN ID (not just on MAC/IP addresses; this forces service-related and associated OAM frames are pinned to same links through out the network).

As should be clear, some challenges are already being identified by forward looking Service Providers such as Verizon; in most cases, it must be noted that proprietary solutions have been adopted in the interim to address the challenges, as to not impede the progress of Carrier Ethernet deployment.

The service attributes, their respective definition and parameters for the MEF-defined UNI and EVC, which were discussed earlier in this chapter, are shown in Figure 2-24.

EVC Attributes

Service Attribute	Service Attribute Parameters
EVC Type	Point-to-Point or Multipoint-to-Multipoint
UNI List	A list of UNIs (identified via the UNI Identifier service attribute) used with the EVC
CE-VLAN ID Preservation	Yes or No. Specifies whether customer VLAN ID is preserved or not.
CE-VLAN CoS Preservation	Yes or No. Specifies whether customer VLAN CoS (802.1p) is preserved or not.
Unicast Service Frame Delivery	Specifies whether unicast frames are Discarded, Delivered Unconditionally or Delivered Conditionally
Multicast Service Frame Delivery	Specifies whether multicast frames are Discarded, Delivered Unconditionally or Delivered Conditionally
Broadcast Service Frame Delivery	Specifies whether broadcast frames are Discarded, Delivered Unconditionally or Delivered Conditionally
Layer 2 Control Protocol Processing	Discard or Tunnel per Protocol
Service Performance	Specifies the Frame Delay, Frame Jitter and Frame Loss per EVC or frames within an EVC Identified via their CE-VLAN CoS (802.1p) value

UNI Attributes

Service Attribute	Service Attribute Parameters
UNI Identifier	A string used to identity of a UNI, e.g., NYCBldg12Rm102Slot22Port3
Physical Medium	Standard Ethernet PHY
Speed	10 Mbps, 100 Mbps, 1 Gbps or 10 Gbps
Mode	Full Duplex or Auto Negotiation
MAC Layer	IEEE 802.3-2002
Service Multiplexing	Yes or No. Defines whether multiple services can be on the UNI
UNI EVC ID	A string used identify an EVC, e.g., NYCBldg1Rm102Slot22Port3EVC3
CE-VLAN ID/EVC Map	Mapping table of customer VLAN IDs to EVC
Max. Number of EVCs	The maximum number of EVCs allowed per UNI
Bundling	No or Yes. Specifies that one or more customer VLAN IDs are mapped to an EVC at the UNI
All to One Bundling	No or Yes (all customer VLAN IDs are mapped to an EVC at the UNI).
Ingress Bandwidth Profile Per Ingress UNI	None or <CIR, CBS, EIR, EBS>. This Bandwidth profile applies to all frames across the UNI.
Ingress Bandwidth Profile Per EVC	None or <CIR, CBS, EIR, EBS>. This Bandwidth profile applies to all frames over particular EVC.
Ingress Bandwidth Profile Per CoS ID	None or <CIR, CBS, EIR, EBS>. This Bandwidth profile applies to all frames marked with a particular CoS ID over an EVC.
Layer 2 Control Protocol Processing	Discard, Peer or Pass to EVC per protocol

Figure 2.24   EVC and UNI service attributes and definitions (source: MEF)

They essentially represent how sophisticated the UNI and EVC can potentially be at the current time; of course, in time, one should expect these to evolve to accommodate new requirements imposed by forthcoming applications.

References

1. Extensively used MEF material in this chapter is reproduced with permission of the Metro Ethernet Forum.

2. MEF technical specifications 2, 3, 4, 6, 7, 8, 10.1, 11, 12, 13, 14, 15, 16, 17, 18, 19: www.metroethernetforum.org.

3. IEEE 802 specifications: www.getIEEE802.org.

4. ITU specifications: www.itu.int/publications/default.aspx.

5. IETF specifications: www.ietf.org

6. "Business Ethernet—The Game Plan for 2007," MEF, Vertical Systems Group, January 2007.

7. Provider Backbone Bridging (PBB) and Provider Backbone Transport, Nortel: www.nortel.com (http://www2.nortel.com/go/solution_assoc.jsp?segId=0&parId=0 &catId=0&rend_id=17102&contOid=100188013&prod_id=55120).

8. Carrier Ethernet: A Reality Check by Stuart Elby, Haidar Chamas, William Bjorkman, Vincent Alesi, Verizon, NFOEC, March 2007.

The Ethernet Market Opportunity

by Michael Howard

The main focus of this chapter is to present the trends and drivers that are shaping the robust opportunities for Ethernet equipment and services today and into the future. These opportunities comprise not only the Ethernet switches or routers that might first come to mind, but also Ethernet over SONET/SDH, Ethernet over WDM, Ethernet over DSL (VDSL especially), Ethernet over PON, and Ethernet FTTH. Worldwide service provider CAPEX and revenue trends favorably support these Ethernet opportunities. Finally, it is the undeniable service provider push to simplify their data networks toward an IP/Ethernet over optical model, coupled with user/corporate demand for the lower cost per bit with higher flexibility that Ethernet services offer, that propels these opportunities.

Ethernet, long supplied on personal computers for the home, business, government, and colleges and universities, is naturally the basis for nearly all LANs, including over 98 percent of business LANs. This ubiquity has pressured carriers to use Ethernet in their networks—it is cost effective to deploy, and carrier customers like it and want Ethernet services. Adopting Ethernet has substantial benefits for both sides.

Convenience is a driver: whereas upgrading the bandwidth of T1/E1/J1 connections requires upgraded hardware at both carrier and customer sites, with inevitable delays until everything is in place and tested, once a 10/100M or 10/100M and 1G connection is in place, no other interface needs to be installed for the foreseeable future. Bandwidth can be increased in hours or minutes through software, with many desirable outcomes of better provider, operations efficiency, quickly satisfied customers, customer retention, and lower equipment costs for everyone. Rather than forcing customers to jump from T1 (1.5M) to T3 (45M) or E1 (2.0M) to E3 (34M), nearly all service providers, alternatives, and incumbents are offering Ethernet at increments that make sense to customers and lowering the price per bit.

Despite the advantages, in the past carriers were reluctant to adopt Ethernet, as it was to them a relatively new technology, and their customers expected Ethernet to be less expensive. Demand and competitive pressures, however, were unrelenting, and Ethernet has now become an integral part of metro networks.

A particular measure of Ethernet in the metro networks is the investment in equipment used to support Ethernet services and connections in provider networks. By 2009, Infonetics Research forecasts Ethernet making major inroads into metro telecom equipment spending, as service providers have and will spend much, a cumulative total of over $49 billion for the five-year period 2005–2009. Over the next five to ten years, Ethernet will inexorably take over the metro—though there will never be a wholesale change because of the SONET/SDH installed base. Although total metro capital expenditures will hold steady or grow slowly, every year Ethernet will account for a greater portion of metro CAPEX, driving a 32 percent CAGR for 2005–2009.

Ethernet has moved out of the original LAN space and into the access and metro. With investments in Ethernet-enabled equipment and the expanding offerings of Ethernet services, service providers are now pushing manufacturers to develop the capabilities for Ethernet to be a viable transport for metro and long-haul networks. Many protocol efforts are underway to achieve this end, such as packet backbone transport (PBT) and transport MPLS (T-MPLS). With the development of a solid Ethernet transport, service providers will be able to design their next generation networks more simply, without a SONET/SDH layer, to reach the long-term goal of IP/Ethernet over optical networks.

Ethernet Service Providers and Their Offerings

Two major drivers have combined to propel the range of Ethernet service offerings and the provider's ability to offer them:

- Corporations and organizations are demanding Ethernet services, with the expectation of lower prices per bit to satisfy growing network capacity needs.

- In the face of fast growing data traffic, which has outstripped voice traffic, the old paradigm of transporting data traffic on networks designed for voice traffic is no longer valid; service providers are in the midst of adapting their often multiple data networks to a new generation data network designed to also handle voice, while supporting various forms of video traffic.

Corporate demand for Ethernet services is rising, an undeniable force as corporate traffic continues to grow unabated, still doubling in many carrier networks each year. Corporations are finding and exceeding the technology capacity limits of legacy frame relay, ATM, and private line networks. As these barriers are exceeded, corporations look for technology solutions with greater headroom that provide more bandwidth at a smaller price per bit, and the natural answer is Ethernet.

Corporate demand was satisfied early (circa 2000) by Asia competitive providers, city carriers in Europe, and alternative Ethernet LECs (ELECs) in North America, and slowly acknowledged by the embedded base of incumbents and PTTs. City Of London Telecom, now known simply as COLT, began by serving the single city of London, and helped establish the viable business model for city carriers elsewhere in Europe that established their entry into their markets riding on the back of Ethernet services on Ethernet networks.

In North America, YIPES was one of the earliest Ethernet focused pioneers, establishing its beachhead first in a few major metros and growing to 20–30 markets fairly quickly. In Asia, the largest city Ethernet network at the time was built in Seoul with over a 1000 Ethernet switches deployed across this major metropolitan area.

These early city carriers and Ethernet specialists deployed networks before carrier-class Ethernet equipment was available. They used what can be called enterprise-class Ethernet switches, which worked for some time in these networks as they never achieved the size or scale of an incumbent provider. They could use enterprise-class equipment by being smart about the design of their networks—overprovisioning bandwidth and using redundant hardware at critical network juncture nodes, and of course, not putting a huge number of customers on the network.

North America is the birthplace of ELECs, yet North American providers still have an installed base of millions of lines (T1/T3, Frame Relay, and ATM) from which the larger customers are cautious to move. Major carriers in North America have taken care of their large Ethernet-desiring customers by delivering highly reliable Ethernet service over SONET today, and many have rolled out services over an overlay Ethernet network to small medium enterprises (SMEs).

Ethernet currently makes up a small portion of the millions of WAN connections in the world. WAN connections are primarily T1/E1/J1 and T3/E3/J3 (including private lines, Frame Relay, and ATM), SONET/SDH, and WDM; these connections are moving to Ethernet rather rapidly, but remain the minority. Over the next five years, however, a growing portion will move to Ethernet-based services.

The second major driver is that service providers worldwide are moving to simplify their networks, while at the same time moving to the new model of a data services layer over an optical transport layer. Due to the gravitas of IP in the Internet, Ethernet in business buildings, and Ethernet built in to computers and installed in homes, Ethernet and IP are the *lingua franca* Layer 2 and Layer 3 service protocols of choice for the next generation access network, metro network, and eventually the long-haul network as well, with a companion choice of optical technology to serve as the underlying basic transport.

In short, service providers are deploying metro Ethernet to satisfy customer demand and to simplify their networks so they can carry fast growing data traffic while handling TDM traffic.

Service providers are also lowering the price per bit for Ethernet bandwidth and offering it at increments that make sense to customers, as opposed to jumping from T1 (1.5M) to $2 \times$ T1 (3.0M) to $3 \times$ T1 (4.5M) to T3 (45M) or similarly for E-carriers (E1 (2.0M) to E3 (34M). Examples include Time Warner Telecom, Cogent, XO, Level 3, KT (Korea Telecom), and large players such as BellSouth, British Telecom, France Telecom, NTT East, and AT&T.

Corporate, government, and other organizational customers are demanding Ethernet services, lower prices per bit, and the convenience of incremental bandwidth. Even with CAPEX pressures, service providers must respond to customers or lose them to competitors; this continues to drive Carrier Ethernet equipment sales.

More carriers are expanding their Ethernet services, for example:

- AT&T Ethernet Switched Service MAN provides high-speed bandwidth between customer locations in a metro area, with logical network configurations between locations (hub and spoke, partially meshed, and fully meshed) and speeds from 50M to 1G.

- AT&T Local Private Line Service offers point-to-point, fixed-bandwidth Ethernet transport (50M to 1G) between two locations within a metro area, transported over AT&T's Local Network Services SONET backbone network, with a latency rate of less than 10 ms and recovery in less than 50 ms.

- AT&T offers OPT-E-MAN switched carrier Ethernet service at speeds ranging from 10M to 1G, GigaMAN (a point-to-point Ethernet fiber service), and Ethernet-over-SONET at 100M or 1G.

- Deutsche Telekom and BT Netherlands offer Ethernet-over-optical services to corporate customers in Germany and the Netherlands, allowing companies to connect their Ethernet-based LANs directly to the optical backbone of either Deutsche Telekom or BT Netherlands without requiring WAN routers, with rates up to 100M.

- The UK ntl:Telewest offers a nationwide Ethernet service with a VPLS component that it is offering directly to retail customers and to other service providers as a wholesale offering.

- NTT Communications offers Arcstar Global e-VLAN network services, which extends a LAN environment to multiple offices at 10M, 100M, and 1G in 54 countries.

- Korea Telecom (KT) Ntopia delivers Ethernet-based services over fiber to serve over 5 million subscribers in roughly 80,000 dwelling units inside large apartment complexes, including multimedia applications (e.g., eLearning and online gaming), on-demand bandwidth provisioning, virtual private network (VPN) applications for home and office connectivity, and virtual leased lines (VLLs).

- Time Warner Telecom offers Point-to-Point Native LAN Service, MultiPoint Native LAN Service, Point-to-Multipoint Native LAN Service, and Native LAN Ethernet Internet Services at 10M, 100M, and 1G.

Worldwide during 2005, actual Ethernet services revenue was $5.9 billion, and the market will continue to grow 280% to $22.5 billion in 2009. The five-year CAGR from 2005 to 2009 is a healthy 40 percent.

Corporations and other end-user organizations have growing appetites for bandwidth and are looking for ways to connect their various sites with higher bandwidth at lower prices per bit. When faced with rising bandwidth needs, smaller organizations and sites are considering Internet connections on Ethernet as an upgrade from DSL or one or two T1/E1s. Medium and large organizations that have Frame Relay, ATM, and/or private line networks in place try to keep bandwidth use within the range of the technology limitations of these services, but when these limits are approached or exceeded, organizations must change technology, and at this point, they naturally consider Ethernet services.

Ethernet service growth is also driven by the fact that many organizations seek to reduce their WAN costs, and it's logical to evaluate Ethernet services, as they have a reputation for having lower prices per bit. Although pricing varies widely, Ethernet services are typically at least 20–30 percent lower than Frame Relay or private line services.

In 2005, 25 percent of Ethernet service revenue was for wholesale, representing $1.5 billion, much of which came from point-to-point GE (1 Gigabit per second Ethernet or Gigabit Ethernet) links. Wholesale Ethernet services will grow slowly to reach $3.8 billion in 2009, which will account for 17 percent of all Ethernet services—a five-year CAGR of 27 percent.

Just like corporations and other end-user organizations, service providers are looking for ways to connect their various sites with higher bandwidths at cheaper prices per bit, and GE point-to-point services meet this demand. Many carriers are quite comfortable using GE links, while others are just beginning to employ them, so the wholesale segment will continue to grow rapidly.

The other three-quarters of Ethernet service revenue is retail, comprising Internet, Ethernet Private Line (known as EPL, or also E-LINE), and Transparent LAN (known as TLAN, or also E-LAN) services. TLAN is growing strongly for two reasons: (1) many large providers are starting to introduce TLAN services, and (2) TLAN is a natural upgrade path from today's multisite networks connected with Frame Relay, ATM, or private lines (these networks are big ticket items).

Transparent LAN services are growing because they will become the mainstay of large corporate Ethernet services as the target of migration from legacy multisite services. TLAN services come in many shapes and sizes and include services known as E-LAN, Ethernet Private LAN (EPLAN), and Ethernet Virtual Private LAN (EVPLAN).

EPL is growing more quickly than Internet services, as many corporations that do not choose TLANs decide to replace their current private lines with EPL. Thus, EPL will be used by many organizations as a migration path to higher bandwidth from today's private line services.

Asia Pacific accounted for 43 percent of overall Ethernet service revenue in 2005, EMEA was next at 42 percent, North America at 21 percent, and CALA at 4 percent. By the close of 2009, Asia Pacific will drop just slightly to 42 percent, with most of the share growth in North America (26 percent). EMEA will drop slightly to 29 percent, and CALA will hold steady at 4 percent.

Asia Pacific is the largest market, and the EMEA market is strong, whereas the North American market was just gathering steam in 2006, as shown in Figure 3.1.

Carrier Plans for Ethernet

Infonetics Research regularly interviews service providers of all types around the world for detailed studies of their plans and strategies. In this section, I bring you some results that highlight current service provider trends.

As service providers shift their focus from legacy services (ATM, Frame Relay, leased lines) to ever-increasing optical and Ethernet traffic, they rely more heavily on new, innovative technologies and face the challenge of maintaining and upgrading their optical

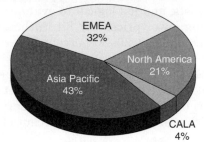

Worldwide Ethernet Services Revenue

Figure 3.1   Worldwide Ethernet services revenue in 2006

networks while defining and deploying new Ethernet services. In 2006, Infonetics published *Service Provider Plans for Metro Optical and Ethernet: North America, Europe, and Asia Pacific 2006*, a study conducted to determine the metro optical and Ethernet equipment requirements and network implementation plans of service providers over the next year. The study found that service providers are offering a surprising number of network-based services over Ethernet, including voice, video, and storage. Ethernet is used not only to collect and move Ethernet traffic, but also for IP and legacy services and to move data among customers and POPs and COs.

Service Providers have now made considerable investments in Carrier Ethernet and are considering what the most efficient approach for offering Ethernet services is. Most providers still use several types of networks to offer Ethernet. A majority of carriers leverage their installed infrastructure to offer Ethernet services over SONET/SDH rings; this is a staple in carrier networks, but Ethernet is growing in the access space to the detriment and displacement of SONET/SDH, which is beginning to lose favor as measured in many data points in this study. In fact, Ethernet over WDM will be offered by more respondents in and after 2007 (92 percent) than is Ethernet over SONET/SDH (80 percent). Building a separate Ethernet overlay network is the choice of over half of the Service Providers. Many large companies are willing to pay for the resiliency of SONET/SDH, but small and medium companies expect to pay lower prices for Ethernet services and need alternate paths. To reach small and medium businesses, Service Providers are using Ethernet over IP/MPLS and Ethernet overlay networks that have lower costs but with many hard SLA and resiliency options with carrier-class Ethernet products.

Infonetics asked respondents to name the Ethernet services they offered besides connectivity and bandwidth, in other words, what services are offered over their connections. The results are shown in Figure 3.2. By 2007, 84 percent of the respondents will offer packetized voice as an Ethernet service, and 84 percent will offer Ethernet Private Line. In 2007, several other popular offerings involve data storage and recovery: storage backup (72 percent) SAN extension (64 percent), and data-center mirroring (72 percent). Security services offered are also popular: stateful firewall (80 percent), encryption (68 percent), DoS prevention (72 percent), and URL filtering (48 percent).

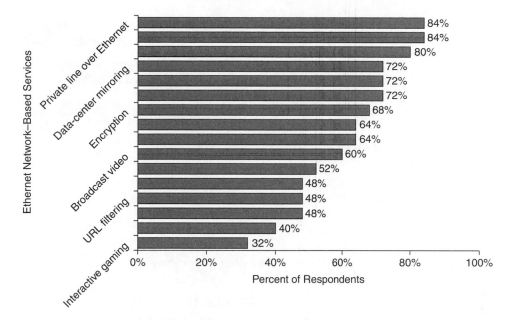

Figure 3.2 Services offered over Ethernet (besides connectivity and bandwidth)

Video services are popular, with triple play offered by 64 percent, broadcast video by 60 percent, video on demand by 52 percent, and video conferencing by 48 percent. The breadth and variety of service offerings exemplify one of the primary strengths of Ethernet: the ability to provision and deliver new services faster because Ethernet at Layer 2 is agnostic and impervious to services riding on Layer 3 IP or other protocols at Layer 4 and above.

All services in the list show increasing numbers of respondents using them between 2006 and 2007. This study has been performed three years running, and in general, these services are being adopted as predicted in the previous year's study.

Customers want Ethernet services, and service providers know it. When the study respondents estimated the level of demand they expect from their customers for technologies and applications, Ethernet for Internet connections came in first at 92 percent. Respondents rated the level of demand they expected for various technologies and applications in the next 12 months on a scale of 1 to 7, where 1 is *no demand* and 7 is *high demand*. The results are shown in Figure 3.3. Service Providers have discovered the limits of Frame Relay and ATM, as well as the costs, and they are anxious to move on.

In 2005, a major barrier for carriers to offer Ethernet services was the worry that they would cannibalize ATM, Frame Relay, and leased-line service revenue. Cannibalization was a major issue for most providers with these legacy services, but as of 2006, most carriers no longer worry about cannibalization, because they found that they had to go with Ethernet or lose customers to competitors. Most providers use two strategies to lead with Ethernet services: (1) overcome a legacy limitation (e.g., Frame Relay 45M) by

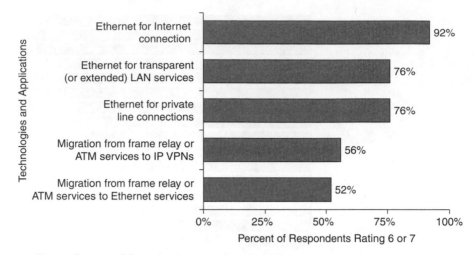

Figure 3.3 Demand expected for technologies and applications

using carrier Ethernet at higher speeds than those available to the legacy services, and 2) increase revenue by targeting competitors' customers.

Approximately 55–60 percent of major service providers have implemented Carrier Ethernet services on a new overlay optical Ethernet network somewhere in their territory. A majority offer Ethernet services over existing SONET/SDH rings. Increasing Ethernet traffic and the roughly 400,000 SONET and SDH rings worldwide means that Ethernet over SONET/SDH will not disappear quickly, but will die a long, slow death over the next 10 to 20 years.

Most ILECs offer a range of Ethernet services and want to carry TDM traffic— including video and voice—over their metro networks. Many products can now carry such traffic using Pseudowires (PWE3) technology.

The Effect of Worldwide CAPEX Patterns on Ethernet Adoption

Like the airline industry, the telecommunications industry is capital intensive, has low marginal costs, and is extremely competitive.

Capital intensive means a Service Provider that wants to provide services needs first to invest in significant assets prior to offering its services; in other words, it requires a large amount of network assets to finance a certain amount of sales, and automation leads to less and less labor to operate the networks.

Since the telecom industry is more capital- than labor-intensive, the marginal cost (the cost of turning on a new service) is low.

The deregulation and liberalization of the late 1990s created fierce competition all over the world as numerous new Service Providers entered regional, national, and international telecom markets, resulting in price pressures and consolidation among Service Providers. Competition also drives the price to the lowest marginal cost of production, which eliminates Service Providers that do not efficiently use economies of scale (e.g., minimization of the cost structure).

The need for service differentiation is fundamental. Those service providers that simply seek to offer *me too* services will not survive. A telling example of this was the pan-European wholesale market of the late 1990s post-liberalization, when numerous national and regional networks sprang up, all covering similar city-to-city routes (London-Paris-Frankfurt, etc.) with wholesale bandwidth offers. With no service differentiation, competition was in terms of price alone. The market as a whole suffered, resulting in the eventual demise of many players, such as Carrier 1, Unisource Carrier Services, Hermes Euro Railtel, Storm Telecom, and KPN Qwest. Service Providers have for the most part learned this tough lesson, as CAPEX strategies are now increasingly geared toward offering service differentiation. Carrier Ethernet equipment and the standards developed by the Metro Ethernet Forum (MEF) give Service Providers rich options for defining and deploying differentiated services.

Telecommunications has become a cyclical industry having four major phases: plateau, decline, recovery, and new investment. Infonetics Research's CAPEX analysis indicates that the industry is at the beginning of a new investment phase in 2006. This new investment phase, however, is not expected to reach the unsustainable levels of the late 1990s. The main reason lies in the fact that starting a Service Provider company, either cell phone- or VoIP-focused, does not require the build out of a costly network because startups can lease access to the networks of major carriers. This, in turn, is not helping the equipment makers, particularly as next generation networks use cheaper equipment, including Carrier Ethernet. This change in the Service Provider business model is forcing a change in the vendor business model—as Service Providers look to fixed mobile converged services, vendors are merging to offer strong product lines across fixed mobile networks (e.g., the Nokia-Siemens and Alcatel-Lucent mergers). A business founded on traditional telecommunications equipment (e.g., selling telephone switches for several millions of dollars) cannot survive against vendors selling next generation IP-based equipment (e.g., a Thomson-Cirpack softswitch for $100,000). Vendors have to adopt new models.

Table 3.1 shows capital expenditures for public wireline and mobile service providers headquartered in North America, Europe, and Asia Pacific (the data is from Infonetics'

TABLE 3.1   Public Service Provider Capital Expenditures

Capital Expenditures (in billion of dollars, U.S.)			
Region	2004 (A)	2005 (A)	2006 (E)
North America	$58	$63	$67
Percent change		8%	6%
Europe	$60 (€ 49)	$61 (€ 51)	$71 (€ 56)
Percent change		6%	9%
Asia Pacific	$61	$62	$65
Percent change		3%	5%
Total	$179	$180	$190
Percent change		0%	6%

Service Provider Capex Analysis series published in April 2006). Note that regional assignment is based on where each company is headquartered, and in many cases, revenue and CAPEX information includes data beyond the home region. Projections are based on Service Provider guidance and Infonetics Research estimates. Expenditures have been converted to U.S. dollars based on average exchange rates for each year.

Most readers will remember the great new investment phase in telecommunications in the second half of the 1990s, the relatively short, if not missing, plateau, and then the bubble bursting decline in 2000-2001. The recovery phase of the cycle was completed by the end of 2003. In 2004, the majority of Service Providers had cleaned up their balance sheets, cut their debt, solidified cash flow and profit margins, and for the largest incumbents, restored capital intensity to around 15 percent, which is considered sustainable. Since then, large service providers have consolidated (e.g., Sprint/Nextel, Verizon/MCI, AT&T/SBC/BellSouth), but local phone companies have yet to consolidate. In 2004, carriers in the three regions covered in this study saw a return to CAPEX growth due to network expansions and new technology rollouts. Going forward, CAPEX is expected to be fairly stable with marginal increases, but overall CAPEX-to-revenue ratios won't deviate much from 15 percent as Service Providers grow at a controlled pace. This is a positive capital spending environment for the fast-growing next-generation equipment market (including Carrier Ethernet), which will make up greater portions of overall CAPEX over the next five years. Most carriers say they are increasing CAPEX in growth areas tied to additional revenue, such as VoIP, broadband, IPTV, and mobile.

Nonetheless, carriers remain cost conscious and continue to need help improving their margins, particularly in an environment where it is difficult to identify new revenue streams. For further cost savings, Service Providers will focus on reducing operational expenditures, in part by shifting investments from legacy TDM equipment to products based on IP and Ethernet. Such new equipment enhances automation, consolidates functions, collapses the number of networks, increases performance per dollar, or introduces new functionality, all of which improve operational efficiency, reducing total cost of ownership. Ideally, these investments also lay the foundation for additional, margin-rich services. As operating expenditures are a bigger piece of a network's total cost of ownership, reducing these expenses has a longer-lasting effect on cash flow and improves pricing flexibility. A single converged IP/Ethernet-based network that supports multiple services is the goal.

The Carrier Ethernet Equipment Market

Ethernet permeates metro networks more thoroughly as each year passes. In the 1990s, Ethernet was first a cheaper interface to connect various types of network gear used in provider POPs and COs, basically carrying data traffic over Ethernet. These connections were between routers and Ethernet switches initially, but Ethernet interfaces were added to optical gear, both SONET/SDH and WDM, then to DSLAMs, and more recently to PON and Ethernet FTTH gear.

As Ethernet grew as a customer connection technology and network product to network product connection, Ethernet showed up in most types of metro equipment.

Manufacturers and providers started figuring out how to add more Ethernet capabilities to accommodate growing diversification of Ethernet services. Technologies, including VCAT/LCAS/GFP over SONET/SDH, RPR, VDSL, and especially MPLS, have paved the way for Ethernet to take its place as a respected telecom grade option for metro networks. Being part of Ethernet, these technologies naturally support data/packet traffic and add support for existing customer TDM and data traffic types by delivering resiliency, fast recovery, options for new services, rings, mesh, and marriage into existing carrier networks using SONET, SDH, DS1/DS3, and copper and fiber technologies.

Service Providers want to deploy Carrier Ethernet both to satisfy customer demand and to simplify their networks so they can carry fast growing data traffic while handling TDM traffic. As one measure of the young but growing market, Infonetics estimated there were over 350,000 Ethernet connections to buildings in North America at the end of 2005. Ethernet is beginning to be the preferred technology for fiber extension from already connected buildings to other nearby unconnected buildings; it began on a trial basis in 2003, with growth in 2005 and 2006, and it will be a fairly prevalent method in 2007.

In the Infonetics major study of Service Providers around the world (cited previously, *Service Provider Plans for Metro Optical and Ethernet, North America, Europe, Asia Pacific, 2006*), 72 percent of Service Providers were using Ethernet collector rings for customer access in 2006 and 84 percent were using them in 2007 somewhere in their networks. This growing use of Ethernet collector rings to connect customer buildings and to aggregate DSLAM and cable CMTS traffic is increasing the use of Ethernet to the detriment of SONET/SDH. In a telling trend, the number of providers that use Ethernet over WDM is increasing from 80 percent in 2006 to 92 percent after 2007, while similarly the number of providers using Ethernet over SONET/SDH decreases from 88 percent in 2006 to 60 percent after 2007. Many cable operators and some telcos are using GE channels on WDM for delivery of video on demand (VOD).

Service Providers mostly use 10/100M fiber for connecting customers, yet the use of 1G fiber is growing quickly, while 10G Ethernet is on the upswing from a small base. Many alternative Service Providers use less expensive copper 10/100M and 1G for short reach connections in POPs and COs. Growing bandwidth speeds for connection and aggregate traffic assure a long expanding market for Ethernet equipment.

Ethernet Runs on Many Technologies

The first use of Ethernet over DWDM is to connect customer LANs to POPs and COs for WAN and Internet and also to other metro locations, or for data center backup, typically using a 2.5G wavelength for a 1G or $2 \times 1G$ Ethernet connection. CWDM is growing as a less expensive alternative to DWDM for customer to provider access. CWDM (coarse wave division multiplexing) growth is slowed by decreasing prices in DWDM (dense WDM), which has narrowed the price difference between CWDM and DWDM.

Standards bodies, such as the EFMA, are driving the adoption of technologies like Ethernet over copper (VDSL, G.SHDSL), which are being deployed now for MTU/MDU in-building Ethernet connections; annual double-digit port growth is predicted from 2005–2009.

Ethernet over DSL is a fast growing technology, with VDSL now well suited for MTU/MDUs and G.SHDSL for longer connections. The MTU/MDU market is very strong in Asia Pacific and Europe, and looking good in North America. Carriers using VDSL extensively are Belgacom, Chungwha, KDDI, KT, NTT, and SoftbankBB.

A number of U.S. IOCs are deploying VDSL now, and ILECs are looking at VDSL technologies as the local loop vehicle for triple play (data, voice, and video) services to customers who might otherwise buy these services from a cable operator. AT&T's strategy is to use VDSL as soon as it is available for their FTTN plan to make IPTV services available to 18 million customers by end of 2007. ILEC/PTT selection of VDSL will be a boon to the technology, when the new VDSL2 products are delivered by manufacturers in 2007.

Ethernet over cable technology has been deployed by a few cable operators on a very limited basis. Most cable operators appear to be awaiting DOCSIS 3.0 solutions or plan to use fiber Ethernet or PON to address the approximately 6–8 million businesses passed by coaxial cable networks. Cable operators are already using Ethernet over WDM heavily.

Carrier Ethernet Switches and Routers

Carrier Ethernet switches and routers (CESR) represented the largest equipment type worldwide in 2005—43 percent of the total metro Ethernet equipment market. Carriers continue to invest in CESR equipment to the tune of a five-year CAGR of 21 percent. Carrier Ethernet switches and routers are a growing mainstay for providers to deliver Ethernet services, displacing enterprise-class Ethernet switches and enterprise routers with Ethernet interfaces, which waned quickly, as Carrier Ethernet products fully entered the market.

DSL

Ethernet services are offered over DSL, especially with the types of DSL covered here. DSL over copper (VDSL at 26M to 100M, G.SHDSL at 2.3M, ADSL2/ADSL2+, and bonding technologies) is deployed in the local loop by over half of the major Service Providers, and it will continue to grow strongly, as more manufacturers develop these products and customers in copper-fed buildings need higher bandwidth connections. VDSL2 products will stimulate this segment, with lynchpin customer plans by AT&T plus many Asian providers.

VDSL2 products will bring about a gradual shift from ADSL/ADSL2/ADSL2+ to Ethernet-based VDSL2; most DSLAM manufacturers will develop multimode VDSL2 ports for DSLAMs with the capability to deploy in ADSL2+ and ADSL modes; some manufacturers shipped these multimode VDSL2/VDSL1/ADSL2+/ADSL line cards in late 2005 for deployment in COs and RTs; several factors are at play in this transition to VDSL2:

- VDSL2 is a superset standard that combines ADSL2+ and VDSL1.

- Port densities of VDSL2 chipsets are already in 48–72 ports, which is the providers' sweet spot for ADSL2+; high-density and low-power consumption in the latest VDSL2 chipsets fosters the move to multimode DSLAM line cards.

- To offer video, voice, and data on DSL, Service Providers are pushing fiber deeper into their network in North America to take advantage of the higher bandwidths available only on shorter copper lengths. In Europe and Asia, the loops are generally shorter; the multirate ports allow providers to deploy VDSL2 for new premium services to some customers, while still offering interoperable ADSL2+ or ADSL modes of operation, so they do not have to swap out customer premises equipment (CPE) for existing customers.

- The year 2006 was generally seen as a year of testing, trials, and initial rollouts, with AT&T and Asia (especially Korea and Japan) leading the way; widespread adoption and ADSL displacement will begin in 2007.

- In 2004, 5 percent of total DSL ports shipped were VDSL or G.SHDSL used for Ethernet, increasing to 10 percent in 2005, 11 percent in 2006, and 46 percent in 2009 (from Infonetics's *DSL Aggregation Hardware*, a quarterly worldwide market share and forecast report, published in the second-quarter of 2007).

TABLE 3.2 Technologies Used for Ethernet Services

Ethernet Technology	Metro Applications
Ethernet switches and routers	Ethernet switches and routers are the basic tools of metro Ethernet networks, used in POPs and COs and the primary customer premises connection.
	10/100M fiber is currently deployed most frequently; the use of 1G fiber is increasing quickly and will close the gap over the next several years, and the use of 10G fiber is starting to rise as prices reach a comfortable buying level.
Ethernet over SONET/SDH (standard and RPR, including prestandard RPR)	Many carriers offer their large customers high-end Ethernet services that transit their very safe SONET/SDH networks.
	Carriers are using RPR, VCAT, LCAS, and GFP to efficiently pack packet traffic on their TDM rings.
RPR over Ethernet (including prestandard RPR)	RPR or resilient packet ring is standardized in 802.17; prestandard versions were developed mainly by Cisco, Nortel, and Extreme.
	RPR has gained traction among a minority of providers, and its demand is holding steady.
Ethernet over WDM	All major WDM suppliers offer Ethernet interfaces on their metro gear, and they are adding switching and other functions.
	Ethernet over CWDM/DWDM is used to connect a customer LAN to other metro locations, POPs or COs, or for data-center backup.
Ethernet over DSL	Industry bodies such as the EFMA have driven the adoption of Ethernet over copper (VDSL, G.SHDSL), which has been deployed for MTU/MDU in building Ethernet connections extensively in Asia.
	Ethernet over copper (VDSL (26M), G.SHDSL (2.3M), ADSL2/ADSL2+, bonding, etc.) is being used each year at an increasing rate in the local loop.

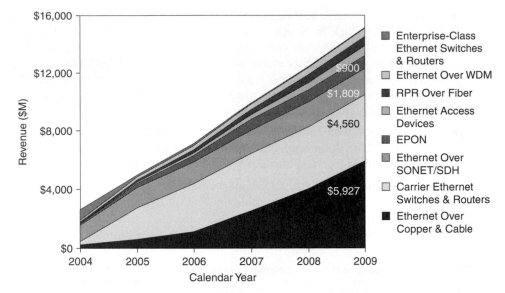

Figure 3.4   Worldwide metro Ethernet manufacturer revenue by technology

Metro Ethernet Manufacturer Revenue

The universal appeal of Ethernet is that it is less expensive than other technologies. Ethernet is becoming an increasingly integral part of metro networks; between 2005 and 2009, Ethernet is making major inroads into metro telecom equipment spending, accumulating $49.6 billion over this five-year period. Over the next ten years, Ethernet will inexorably take over the metro, though there will never be a wholesale change because of the SONET/SDH installed base. Metro CAPEX may hold steady or grow slowly, but every year Ethernet will account for a greater portion of metro CAPEX, driving a 32 percent CAGR growth rate for 2005–2009, led by Carrier Ethernet switches and routers with 43 percent of the market in 2005 (and 30 percent by 2009), Ethernet over SONET/SDH at 27 percent in 2005 (declining to 12 percent in 2009), and Ethernet over copper (VDSL/ G.SHDSL) with 12 percent in 2005, growing to 39 percent in 2009. Figure 3.4 details worldwide Ethernet revenue by technology.

Technologies and Trends

Service Providers use many technologies to deliver Ethernet services, mixing the old tried-and-true with new, hot off the lab bench services. The lack of carrier grade metro Ethernet products was an impediment to adoption of metro Ethernet in 2003, but MPLS and other technologies have made metro Ethernet products resilient and able to adapt to the rings that many large carriers strongly prefer (whether over SONET/ SDH or not). Products are being deployed by major carriers now, and the market will see constant growth.

The growing use of collector rings to aggregate DSLAM and cable CMTS traffic will increase the use of Ethernet in collector rings for packet traffic, while also carrying TDM traffic to the detriment of Ethernet over SONET/SDH. Ethernet is also beginning to be used as the preferred technology for fiber extension from connected buildings to other nearby unconnected buildings, and many MSOs and telco TV providers are using GE channels on WDM for delivery of video on demand (VOD).

Several Asian countries are outfitting their populations with high-speed (DSL, VDSL, Ethernet, PON) connections. The Japanese government established a goal of connecting 30 million consumers and SOHOs at 10M and 10 million at 100M by 2010. Growth continues in MTU/MDUs (a mix of VDSL and copper Ethernet).

According to a worldwide Service Provider study (*Service Provider Plans for IP, MPLS, and ATM: North America, Europe, and Asia Pacific 2005*), all types of data traffic grew between 2004 and 2006, but IP and metro Ethernet growth was the strongest, especially by 2006 when Ethernet grew an average of 162 percent. The movement from legacy protocols to IP/MPLS and metro Ethernet continues, as shown in Figure 3.5.

Frame Relay growth was small and declining such that it showed an absolute decline in traffic volume, not just a decline in growth in 2006. ATM was also winding down, but at a slower rate.

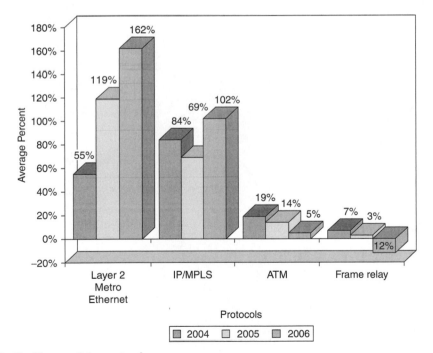

Figure 3.5 Traffic growth by protocol

As expected, incumbents showed stronger growth for ATM traffic than competitive carriers. Frame Relay was declining among European respondents while still gaining in North America. IP was growing faster in North America than in Europe or Asia Pacific.

To sum up, a major, large-scale trend is that Ethernet is everywhere: Ethernet services are offered by nearly all Service Providers around the globe. As discovered in the course of interviewing providers that were offering Ethernet services by 2006, every Service Provider queried already offered these services.

Ethernet is here to stay, but not only stay. Ethernet is here to dominate, especially in the access and metro for the foreseeable future.

Solutions

4

The Solution Framework

by Abdul Kasim

This chapter defines a simple framework that attempts to clarify and put into perspective, the different network solutions that are employed by Service Providers to deliver Carrier Ethernet services. Using this framework, the specific solutions themselves are described in the subsequent chapters.

Background

For the most part, the deployment of Service Provider networks in the metro (access) and wide area (or alternatively, the metro core, regional, and long haul[1]) pre-dates the emerging popularity of Carrier Ethernet. And as such, this infrastructure, which includes the physical media and the transport mechanisms as well as higher layer functionality such as switching and routing, is generally not optimized for the delivery of these carrier-class Ethernet services.

Carrier Ethernet is delivered across the gamut of physical media. In the First/Last-mile or Access portion of the network, an overwhelming majority (well over 80 percent is estimated in the U.S. according to a 2006 report by Vertical Systems Group) of the physical infrastructure is still based on copper; fiber makes up most of the rest and is increasingly being used in new deployments and wireless is also becoming a very viable option as its underpinning technologies mature. Deeper in the access networks–in the metro core and beyond, however, fiber begins to dominate because it is a natural fit for transmitting huge amounts of data over large distances.

---

[1] Metro access, metro core, regional, long, and ultra-long haul are terms often employed in the context of Service Provider transport networks; they do not identify precise physical boundaries but rather serve to delineate the geographic reach of a transport solution. These terms also signify different distances depending on the context; For example, in the U.S., a regional solution is usually in the several hundred mile range, but in Europe the range may be considerably shorter. They are discussed in Chapter 1.

The transport technologies that Service Providers overwhelmingly employed were mostly optimized for the delivery of voice services over the different physical media. Subsequently, as data services began to emerge, these services were still largely delivered over this voice-efficient infrastructure; the billions of dollars invested in these voice-optimized networks made it unrealistic to discard and replace them with data-optimized networks. As this infrastructure equipment depreciates[2] and competition intensifies, however, Service Providers are beginning to transition to next-generation packetized networks; a fair number of Service Providers have already begun this transition, but it will be a long while before this is complete. The pace is slow due to the amount of investment needed, fear of cannibalization of existing TDM services[3], and the changes required to the existing support infrastructure (methods and procedures and personnel skill sets, for instance). Furthermore, legacy solutions such as SONET are also evolving to be more accommodating to Ethernet services and consequently extending their appeal and longevity. Thus, it is anticipated that these voice-optimized solutions will exist in the foreseeable future.

Quite a few Service Providers also invested in new ATM and Frame Relay (often overlaid over fiber infrastructure and voice oriented transport platforms like SONET) networks to support data services exclusively. Of course, newer (green field) Service Providers that did not have to face the constraints of legacy infrastructures have already implemented transport networks that are more data and packet optimized.

The net result is that there are multiple solutions that can be employed to deliver Carrier Ethernet over Service Provider networks, each with its own specific genesis and focus, and consequently, different in how the Carrier Ethernet solution is offered. Some of these solutions are better suited than others in particular contexts. It is also not uncommon to have more than a single (delivery) solution deployed in a Service Provider network because of both legacy and practical considerations.

Understanding these different network solutions, their fit and limitations, is an extremely useful exercise to both Service Providers as well as end-user enterprises; after all, these solutions underpin the Ethernet services delivered or used, respectively. For a Service Provider, choosing the appropriate Carrier Ethernet delivery platform means improved profitability and a higher level of competitiveness, whereas for end-user enterprises, choosing the right delivery platform can mean minimizing their communication costs and taking advantage of the required flexibility, robustness, and scalability (the specific benefits of Carrier Ethernet are discussed fairly extensively in Chapter 1).

It is important to note that, in most cases, these delivery platforms provide "carrier-class" features independent of their capability to provide Ethernet services (e.g., SONET platforms offer resiliency to failures independent and, in fact, prior to optimizing their capability to deliver Carrier Ethernet services).

---

[2] i.e., its assessed value decreases (and hence, the taxes associated with it)

[3] TDM services still make up a large proportion of the revenue at most typical carrier Service Providers.

The Reference Model

Figure 4.1 depicts a simple model that is used to contextualize the discussion in Part II of the book. This model, based partly on the work done by the MEF [1], shows four distinct layers: Physical layer, Transport/Network layer, Ethernet layer, and Application layer.

- **Physical layer** This comprises the infrastructure that enables the physical transmission of data, and includes wired (coax, copper, fiber) and wireless media.

- **Transport/Network[4] layer** This layer provides the transport of Ethernet services (in terms of Ethernet frames) and employs a variety of different technologies operating over the Physical layer.

- **Ethernet layer** This layer enables the instantiation of the Ethernet connectivity services, whether E-LINE or E-LAN (as defined in Chapter 2). This layer is responsible for all the service-aware aspects of the Ethernet flow, including the Operations, Administration, and Maintenance and Provisioning (OAMP)necessary to support these connectivity services.

- **Applications layer** This layer supports the applications carried over the Ethernet services provided at the Ethernet layer. The Ethernet layer can also be used as a transport layer for some of the application layer connectivity services, such as T1, ATM, and so on.

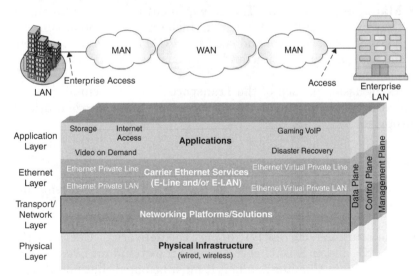

Figure 4.1   Reference model for delivering Carrier Ethernet

---

[4] We've combined network and transport into one layer to highlight that the solutions will provide transport and may also provide higher-order functions, such as switching and routing. Note, however, that this is strictly not aligned with the OSI model.

The primary focus of this book is on the Transport layer/Network layer that enables the delivery of Carrier Ethernet—specifically the MEF Carrier-class E-Line and E-LAN services, as defined in Chapter 2. The network technologies and solutions (these terms are used interchangeably throughout the book) that make up this layer are manifested in physical equipment—the hardware and software—generally offered commercially by several vendors. The physical equipment is usually made up of several discrete Network Elements (NEs) that are configured collectively to provide Carrier Ethernet services.

The Transport/Network technologies, encompassing transport and (or) higher-level functions such as switching and routing, employ a variety of physical media, both wired and wireless. Some of the technologies may, in fact, also use multiple physical media to deliver Ethernet services.

Each of the three layers—Application, Ethernet, and Transport/Network—can be further dissected into three key operational components or planes:

- **Data or User Plane**   This enables the flow of customer data between the network elements.

- **Control Plane**   The Control Plane provides the functional elements that support flow management functions among the NEs participating in the data plane. The Control Plane also provides the signaling mechanisms necessary to support setup, supervision, and connection release operations, among other flow control functions.

- **Management Plane**   The management plane provides the functional elements that support fault, configuration (including flow and/or connection configuration), account, performance, and security (FCAPS) functions, as well as any related operations, administration, and maintenance (OAM) tools.

The discussion of each of the Transport/Network technologies/solutions, in the subsequent chapters, will include a discussion of these three operational planes, wherever appropriate.

The Landscape of Solutions

In identifying the various (Transport/Network layer) solutions that will be discussed in this book, the following guidelines were used:

- The solutions (currently) support the delivery of Carrier Ethernet services (i.e., E-LINE and/or E-LAN services with the attendant five carrier-class attributes, as discussed in Chapter 2; albeit it must be noted that not all the carrier-class attributes may be provided just yet).

- They encompass the broadest range of solutions employed today by a host of different Service Providers (regulated Carriers, Inter exchange Carriers, Cable Multi Service Operators (MSOs), Local Loop Carriers, Competitive Carriers etc).

- They are delivered over different wired media such as copper, fiber, HFC, and also over wireless.
- They provide transport and/or higher-level networking functions such as switching and routing.
- They are delivered in the MAN and/or beyond, in the WAN.
- They are offered as commercial solutions by equipment vendors (although not necessarily for exclusively delivering Ethernet i.e., other services could also be delivered–and often are, using a particular solution).

Based on these criteria, the following solutions are considered in Part II:

- Carrier Ethernet over Copper—Chapter 5
- Carrier Ethernet over Hybrid Fiber Coax (HFC)—Chapter 6
- Carrier Ethernet over Passive Optical Networks (PONs)[5]—Chapter 7
- Carrier Ethernet over Fiber and Wave Division Multiplexing (WDM)—Chapter 8
- Carrier Ethernet over Optical wireless mesh/Free Space Optics (FSO)—Chapter 9
- Carrier Ethernet over Time Division Multiplexing (TDM)—Chapter 10
- Carrier Ethernet over SONET—Chapter 11
- Carrier Ethernet over Resilient Packet Ring (RPR)—Chapter 12
- Carrier Ethernet over Bridging/Switching—Chapter 13
- Carrier Ethernet over Multi Protocol Label Switching (MPLS)—Chapter 14
- Carrier Ethernet over WiMax—Chapter 15

This solution set is depicted in Figure 4.2, and represents well over 90 percent of the solutions being currently deployed. The corresponding chapters addressing the respective solution are also noted; the figure also attempts to capture the level of functionality typically present in a solution (i.e., transport, switching, routing etc.) as well as the underlying physical transmission media.

These solutions are not necessarily mutually exclusive, and in fact, it is not unusual to have multiple, complementary solutions deployed in a single Service Provider network. For example, a Service Provider offering E-LAN services in the MAN may use a Bridging/Switching solution, but they may also use a WDM solution to extend the distances covered. In some cases, of course, these individual solutions may be part of the same commercial solution, for example, a bridge/switch using WDM cards.

---

[5] Ethernet PONs only are discussed

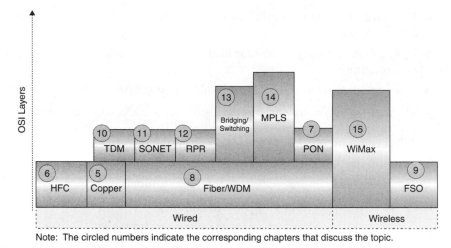

Figure 4.2   The landscape of solutions for delivering Carrier Ethernet

Service Providers can offer seamless Ethernet services to the end user across multiple underlying solutions primarily because of the common Carrier Ethernet layer. For example, a customer with an Ethernet Private Line (i.e., connecting two of its locations via an Ethernet Link) may be connected over a copper pair to a Service Provider Point-Of-Presence (POP) using a Ethernet over copper solution and beyond this, may employ an Ethernet over WDM solution to traverse over fiber to another POP and then terminate at the other location using an Ethernet over copper solution. Even though this Ethernet Private Line is being delivered employing two solutions, these underlying solutions (Ethernet over Copper and Ethernet over Fiber/WDM) would usually be hidden from the end customer (who may just want a seamless service with an associated Service Level Agreement).

Having said that, commercial solutions usually offer a different set of functionalities with respect to Carrier Ethernet; some may, for instance, only be able to provide E-LINE capabilities, while others may provide both but be distance-limited. Some may offer a limited amount of carrier-class attributes but this may be an acceptable solution in a specific context (e.g., the lack of a very robust fault-tolerant solution may be acceptable to a small Service Provider offering Ethernet-based Internet access at very low prices[6]).

Thus, the landscape of commercially deployed Carrier Ethernet solutions is fairly broad, fragmented, and ultimately a source of confusion as far as understanding how the specific solutions fit.

---

[6] This presupposes, realistically, that cheap Internet access service does not offer a 7×24 up time; and an occasional failure is tolerated by the end user.

A Solution Framework

In order to meaningfully assess the very different solutions discussed in this book, a common solution framework has been developed. This framework will be employed in the discussion of each of the solutions to ensure a holistic assessment of the solution that encompasses business, technology, and operational considerations, and also to provide a measure of uniformity across the various solutions. Using this framework, therefore, a meaningful and consistent evaluation is made possible.

The individual components of the solution framework and their respective objectives are described next.

Technology Description   This outlines the underlying technology solution and highlights its salient features. Any evolution that the technology solution underwent to support carrying Ethernet frames is discussed. We also look at how each of the Carrier Ethernet attributes are (or will be) addressed in this solution, and we identify other items necessary to delivery carrier-class Ethernet, if any. The discussion broadly details the three operational planes of the solution—data, control, and management.

Because the solution description is meant to be reasonably detailed but cannot be comprehensively detailed due to space constraints, all relevant standards are referenced.

Drivers for This Solution   Here, we provide insights into the original reason that this solution was developed (e.g., for introducing resiliency to voice connectivity). And we look at how this solution has evolved to accommodate Carrier Ethernet delivery.

Solution Fit   This discussion focuses on the scenarios where the solution is better suited (e.g., low competition, incumbency, specific architectures, demand for other non-Ethernet services); conversely, if necessary, we identify the scenarios where the solution does not make any business sense.

Benefits and Shortcomings   This discussion outlines the tangible benefits of employing this solution to deploy Carrier Ethernet services. For instance, a solution could inherently offer several of the carrier-class attributes or be optimal in certain scenarios or entail the lowest capital expenditure. Shortcomings, if any, are also similarly covered.

NOTE   Often this and the previous section overlap but this is meant to explicitly identify the specific advantages/disadvantages.

Typical Deployment Scenarios   This portion of the chapter helps illustrate how common Ethernet E-LINE and E-LAN services are offered over this solution. It also identifies any additional solutions that are required to provide these services (for example if a specific solution can only be used for E-LINE services, what would be required to offer E-LAN services).

Ongoing Developments   Here, we identify the areas where the standards bodies (such as IEEE, IETF, MEF, ITU et al.) and other forums are focused with respect to further optimizing the solution for delivering Carrier Ethernet. In general, the amount of focus on a particular solution in the standards bodies is proportional to its continued importance as a solution for delivering Carrier Ethernet.

Economic Assessment   This discussion gives a sense of the economic attractiveness of a particular solution. The goal is not necessarily to provide an exact cost (in fact, it is implausible to do so[7]), but rather to provide insights into the range of costs the solution entails.

Vendors Promoting This Solution   This section identifies the main vendors actively promoting the solution as of the time of this writing. It must be noted that the list of vendors is current but given the industry dynamics it would likely need to be revalidated often.

References

1. "Metro Ethernet Forum (MEF) Technical Specification 4," *Metro Ethernet Network Architecture Framework – Part I: Generic Framework,* May 2004. www.metroethernetforum.org

---

[7] By cost, we mean the cost to the Service Provider to deploy a particular solution; this is typically a function of several complex variables.

5

Copper

by Dr. Matt Squire

One of the more difficult aspects of delivering carrier Ethernet is the footprint problem—Ethernet simply does not reach every customer today. Certainly, that is changing as fiber deployments continue, but even with today's massive fiber builds for IPTV, it will still be decades before the majority of businesses and consumers have direct optical access. Alternatively, carriers can deploy Ethernet over low-bandwidth T1/E1 connections. These alternatives represent the "high" (optical) and "low" (T1/E1) bandwidth opportunity. But there is a huge need for a middle ground—a need for more bandwidth than with T1/E1 but less bandwidth than with optical services. This "middle" bandwidth opportunity, the Mid-Band Ethernet market, will be the prime service growth area for the next decade. Mid-Band Ethernet technologies use DSL physical layers and run Ethernet natively over one or more copper pairs to create highly reliable, high-bandwidth services.

Technology Description

In June 2004, IEEE 802.3 ratified a new amendment to the Ethernet standard, IEEE 802.3ah Ethernet in the First Mile (EFM) [1]. This standard adapted Ethernet—the best known and most widely used LAN technology in history—for widespread deployments in carrier access networks. With EFM, complex and costly ATM or SONET/SDH access networks can be migrated to simpler, more cost-effective Ethernet access networks, resulting in immediate savings in capital and operating expenditures, as well as increased bandwidth and service options to the subscriber.

As part of its sweeping potential in the access network, the EFM standards group defined two technologies for delivering Ethernet over plain-old telephone lines: 2BASE-TL and 10PASS-TS. These technologies offer higher bandwidth and higher quality services than existing T1/E1 and xDSL solutions, delivering the simplicity and flexibility of Ethernet, while still maintaining spectral compatibility within the existing access network.

Since these standards were created, their capabilities and benefits have been accepted and adopted by carriers and standards organizations around the globe.

These technologies have combined to create a whole new service market, the Mid-Band Ethernet market, that is poised to become the dominant access method for business and residential services. Mid-Band Ethernet services offer carriers a simple and natural way to extend their core and metro MPLS/Ethernet networks all the way to the customer, without the complexity and cost of TDM or ATM infrastructures.

Mid-Band Ethernet is revolutionizing and expanding the copper access network. For those carriers offering Ethernet services over optical or SONET/SDH infrastructures, Mid-Band Ethernet technologies make Ethernet services available to the vast majority of customers that do not have access to fiber. Instead of Ethernet services being limited by fiber availability to less than 10 percent of potential business sites and even fewer residential customers, these services are now available to almost any subscriber location. With distance potential beyond 20 Kft (6 km), 2BASE-TL can reach almost any subscriber, providing a universal multi-megabit on-ramp to any metro Ethernet network. And with rate potential in excess of 100 Mbps, 10PASS-TS can serve the highest bandwidth applications over shorter distances.

For those carriers already delivering services via ATM-based digital subscriber line (DSL) technology, Mid-Band Ethernet provides a path to simpler networks with lower operating expenses and to differentiated, higher-margin services currently out of reach using existing technologies. The simplicity and cost-effectiveness of Ethernet yields immediate savings in capital and operating expenditures. Subscribers connected to the network with 1000BASE-X Gigabit Ethernet and Mid-Band Ethernet experience the same service and are managed with the same paradigms and the same software—it's all Ethernet; the only difference is the access media and the available bandwidth.

The EFM copper standards leverage the best DSL layers, as defined by the International Telecommunications Union (ITU), as the physical layers for Mid-Band Ethernet. By utilizing these existing standards, IEEE 802.3ah benefits from the high volume of DSL chipsets while significantly improving upon the original silicon by defining new and efficient mechanisms for Ethernet transport. The advances include more efficient single-line transport as well as a novel multi-pair aggregation strategy that brings a new level of resiliency and bandwidth to the access network.

IEEE 802.3ah developed an encapsulation and loop aggregation technique for Ethernet, one optimized for the copper access network. As shown in the architecture diagram in Figure 5.1, the encapsulation and aggregation processes are transparent to higher layer applications—they sit below the Ethernet MAC. The switching and services layer of the device can be consistent across optical, CAT5, and EFM Ethernet interfaces, giving the provider the ability to offer a consistent service offering over any type of access media.

2BASE-TL

2BASE-TL offers a nominal symmetric bandwidth of at least 2 Mbps in a typical noise environment at reasonable distances. 2BASE-TL is based on the same physical layer

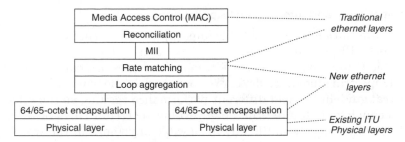

Figure 5.1   IEEE 802.3ah architecture diagram

as the enhanced SHDSL standards of ITU and ANSI T1 (also known as G.991.2.bis or E-SHDSL [2]). Whereas symmetric high-speed DSL (SHDSL, G.991.2) [3] has a maximum symmetric rate of 2.3 Mbps, enhanced SHDSL can run up to 5.7 Mbps on a single pair. With such high-speed symmetric access, subscribers can be offered a 10 Mbps Ethernet service on as little as two-pair of copper access lines (the same lines that are used for telephony services).

2BASE-TL and enhanced SHDSL increased the bandwidth over SHDSL in two key dimensions. First, a second constellation (or symbol encoding) is allowed that increases the throughput by 33 percent without affecting the spectral properties of SHDSL. This additional higher constellation cannot be used on the longest loops, but it does provide a "spectrally free" throughput increase on loops up to 10 Kft (3 km), depending on the noise environment. Second, 2BASE-TL and enhanced SHDSL increase the frequency (number of symbols per second) as compared to SHDSL, thus allowing even more throughput. This frequency addition increases the noise created by the technology, but it still falls within North American and international spectral guidelines such as ANSI T1.417.

10PASS-TS

The EFM short-reach solution is based on very high-speed DSL (VDSL) [4]. One of the major technical decisions of the EFM task force was to decide which VDSL technology was best suited for the short-reach Ethernet physical layer. At the time, there were two VDSL candidates. One candidate was based on Discrete Multitone Modulation (DMT), and the other was based on Quadrature Amplitude Modulation (QAM). Both technologies could yield similar performance results yet only one could be selected. Until EFM forced a decision, both technologies had progressed equally through ITU and ANSI T1 standards bodies, with no organization able to select a single solution.

After many months of debate, the EFM task force voted to use VDSL-DMT as the physical layer for 10PASS-TS instead of VDSL-QAM. The hope that VDSL-DMT could leverage the technology and volume of ADSL (which is also based on DMT technology) was a key factor in the selection process.

Spectral Compatibility and International Applications

As an international standard, it is important for Ethernet to be deployable anywhere in the world. EFM technologies are basis systems, which means they are universally deployable throughout the world. These technologies are capable of operating under different spectral guidelines depending on where in the world they are deployed. Different spectral guidelines yield different performance results, so the effective throughput of the technology is limited by the governing spectrum rules of the local country. EFM technologies are internationally deployable anywhere in the world, provided they are configured to conform to the regional guidelines.

Transporting Ethernet Packets over Copper

A long-standing tradition in Ethernet is that the method for carrying the actual frames over the wire must (1) have low overhead and (2) be incredibly resilient to false packet acceptance. False packet acceptance (FPA) is the probability of undetected corruption.

The EFM copper technologies use a novel encoding scheme called 64/65-octet encoding, where there is 1 overhead byte for every 64 bytes of data. This encoding scheme is incredibly efficient, which is vital in access technologies that must adapt to the environment and deliver the highest possible speed given existing outside plant conditions. Unlike traditional LAN Ethernet, the cable plant for Mid-Band Ethernet is old, uncontrolled, and irreplaceable (if it is going to be replaced, it will be replaced with optical fiber). Therefore, the technology must adapt to any cable plant quality and be very efficient to best utilize any environment.

Figure 5.2 illustrates 64/65-octet encoding. Using this encoding, the physical layer is partitioned into 65-octet blocks, and in each 65-octet block, up to 64-octets can hold data and 1 octet is used for synchronization purposes. This makes the encoding very efficient. Additionally, depending on the contents of the 64-octet block, the first byte of

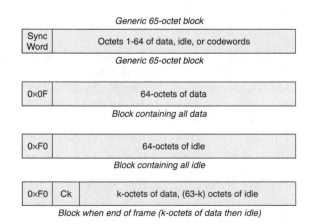

Figure 5.2   64/65-octet encoding examples

the data field may contain a special codeword that provides additional information on the contents of the block (whether it's the start of frame, end of frame, etc.).

Additionally, 64/65-octet encapsulation includes measures to improve the false packet acceptance results of traditional DSL encoding. DSL physical layers generally operate in modes that yield a bit-error rate of 10^{-7}. Traditionally, Ethernet technologies (and the IP layers above them) have been built upon an architecture where false packet acceptance cannot statistically occur. To achieve FPA performance acceptable for Ethernet and IP delivery, the 64/65-octet layer appends every frame (or fragment) with a CRC in addition to the Ethernet FCS. The combination of these two error-checking codes practically eliminates the possibility of FPA, thus maintaining the historically high reliability of Ethernet.

These changes result in a more efficient and more reliable access network. For example, carrying Ethernet over ATM results in 20–50 percent overhead, and carrying Ethernet natively via Mid-Band Ethernet results in less than 5 percent overhead. This allows carriers to squeeze more bandwidth (and more revenue) out of their existing infrastructure.

Multipair Aggregation

The loop aggregation techniques of IEE 802.3ah are simple and powerful. Frames are passed to the loop aggregation layer from the higher layer, where they are fragmented and distributed across the loops within the aggregate. When transmitted across the individual loops, a fragmentation header is prepended (see Figure 5.3), which includes a sequence number and frame markers. This header is used by the receiver to resequence the fragments and to reassemble them into complete frames.

To allow vendor differentiation, the algorithm for partitioning the frames over the loops is not specified. However, the partitioning algorithm must obey certain rules in that fragments must obey size constraints and that loops in an aggregate must obey rate and differential delay constraints. As long as the loop aggregation algorithms obey these constraints and restrictions, any fragmentation algorithm can be handled by the reassembly process, yielding a very flexible and interoperable solution.

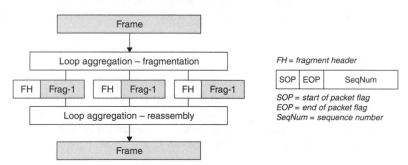

Figure 5.3   Multipair aggregation in IEEE 802.3ah

Not Link Aggregation   Although they may look similar, loop aggregation as defined in 802.3ah is *very different* than link aggregation as defined in 802.3ad. Loop aggregation fragments individual frames into variable-sized segments in order to minimize latency and maximize utilization of disparate speed links. Link aggregation load-balances frames over equal speed links in order to increase aggregate throughput.

One very key difference is that the loops in *loop* aggregation (802.3ah) can be running at very different speeds, which is not possible with 802.3ad link aggregation. Likewise, the ability to fragment large frames into smaller pieces is very important when trying to minimize latency. A 1500-byte Ethernet frame takes 12ms to transmit when lines are running at 1 Mbps. Breaking this frame up into N equal size fragments decreases transmit latency for this frame by a factor of N.

Automatic Resiliency   In addition to the efficiency and performance benefits of 802.3ah, loop aggregation has the added benefit that it's automatic and resilient. Pairs can come and go, and the Ethernet interface remains operational—only the available bandwidth is affected. New pairs can be wired up and automatically joined to the aggregate group with no additional configuration, realizing the plug-and-play potential of Ethernet. This makes IEEE 802.3ah the most suitable technology for business and residential services today, where unreliable, best effort delivery is simply not enough.

Drivers for This Solution

The growth of Mid-Band Ethernet is driven by multiple converging needs: the universal adoption of the Internet Protocol (IP), the economics of Ethernet, and the cost and complexity of real-world fiber deployments.

Ubiquity of IP

Enterprises continue to adopt more and more IP-based applications and dramatically grow their consumption of packet network capacity. Business applications such as file sharing, training, storage networks, and video conferencing are all growing in coverage and bandwidth requirements. Voice over IP (VoIP) is just starting to replace analog voice as the primary mechanism for telephony. All carriers are in the midst of rolling out more and more VoIP applications and removing their dependence on traditional voice services.

On the residential side, VoIP is also a driving application, as is IP television (IPTV). With IPTV, consumers can watch digital high-definition video over their broadband connection. This triple-play of services is the goal of every carrier.

All of these applications have similar requirements—high bandwidth, high reliability, and highly controlled QoS with low latency, loss, and jitter. Ethernet provides the technology that has enabled all of these applications in the LAN, and with Mid-Band Ethernet, across the WAN as well.

Economics of Ethernet

This drive toward higher bandwidth services is leading to fierce competition for customers. Wireline carriers are not the only suitors for residential and business service needs; cable companies and wireless providers are also vigorously pursuing the same market. Because these high-bandwidth pipes offer the potential for value-added service offerings, they prove to be very "sticky" and improve customer retention. It is often the case that the first carrier to deliver the service to the customer, wins that customer for a very long time. The fast time-to-market of Mid-Band Ethernet allows any wireline provider to reach the customers with a next-generation service alternative long before the competition by using their existing infrastructure, therefore locking in the customer's revenue stream.

Ethernet has long won the battle to become the natural link layer protocol for IP-based applications and services. IEEE 802.3 Ethernet standards have evolved to extend electrical and optical interface speeds from 10 Mbps to 10Gbps and beyond. Interface cards and Ethernet switches are ubiquitous and offer very high capacity at a very inexpensive cost per bit, resulting in Ethernet's near total domination of enterprise and campus area networks. Enterprises now wish to interconnect multiple sites and connect to the public Internet while maintaining the performance of their applications, and Mid-Band Ethernet allows this.

For years now, many carriers have been replacing and phasing out their ATM and SONET core infrastructure, migrating their customers to a less expensive, more reliable Ethernet/IP/MPLS infrastructure. The access network is really the final frontier—the last mile is the final barrier to cross in the carrier evolution from TDM to packet networking. Mid-Band Ethernet technologies erase that final barrier and permit a fully integrated packet network.

Cost and Complexity of Deploying Fiber

The market demand for these next-generation services is being met by the implementation of high capacity, metro area and/or intercity Ethernet services at attractive price points by all major service providers. Core packet networks have been rapidly built, and intensive capital spending programs have deployed fiber access to large buildings and major data centers. However, nearly 90 percent of business locations are not currently served by fiber, and even fewer residential subscribers have optical access. Although technologies such as optical Ethernet or Passive Optical Networks (PONs) offer maximum bandwidth potential, they require very expensive fiber builds. Using Mid-Band Ethernet allows providers to offer high-bandwidth services without deploying fiber all the way to the premise.

In some cases, the Mid-Band Ethernet copper access technologies are funding fiber build-outs. Because Mid-Band Ethernet has such a fast return on investment and can generate significant revenue very quickly, carriers can use it to pay for the fiber build. Suppose a couple of enterprise customers come online today with a 10 Mbps Ethernet service for $1000/month from the same business park. After a year or two, the carrier may very well have collected enough revenue to pay for a fiber drop to that business park.

So Mid-Band Ethernet is ideal for today's conservative, practical economic climate. It leverages the existing copper infrastructure and low-cost unbundled network loops to deliver high-bandwidth Ethernet services complementary to the optical network. Mid-Band Ethernet allows for "pay as you grow" deployment of electronics rather than up-front major capital and construction projects. And as part of a transparent Ethernet service, it operates in conjunction with the existing Ethernet services and management infrastructure. The footprint of the carrier Ethernet networks is extended tenfold to the 90 percent of customers who don't have fiber access, offering a high-margin revenue opportunity to any wireline service provider.

When Does This Solution Fit

Mid-Band Ethernet technologies are ideal for delivering high-speed, resilient connections to residential or business customers from any metro Ethernet network. Mid-Band Ethernet requires access to the in-place copper loops from a distribution site (for example, a central office or remote terminal) to business or residential locations. They are, therefore, mostly targeted at allowing incumbent or competitive telephony providers to deliver next-generation Ethernet services. However, Mid-Band Ethernet also has a very attractive multi-tenant application that can be used by any carrier to distribute services within existing buildings.

Triple Play with 10PASS-TS

10PASS-TS is an ideal technology for delivering triple-play services to residential customers. Or, more accurately, the "next-generation" 10PASS-TS (utilizing VDSL2 instead of VDSL) is ideal for triple-play services. The technology can be used in a highly asymmetric mode, allowing as much as 100 Mbps of bandwidth downstream. More realistically, it is likely to be deployed at rates of 20–30 Mbps downstream (because the reach is much longer). In the typical deployment, there will be fiber connecting a remote terminal (RT) to a central office, and copper-only connectivity from the RT to the subscriber. Gigabit Ethernet 1000BASE-X (or PON) is likely to be used from a central office to the RT, with 10PASS-TS from the RT to the subscriber. By deploying from an RT, copper loops are shorter and can provide higher bandwidth services.

Riser Extensions with 10PASS-TS

Similarly to the triple-play application, 10PASS-TS is ideally suited to in-building "up the riser" applications. Here, there is typically an Ethernet switch or add-drop multiplexer in the basement of an office or apartment building. 10PASS-TS can be used to deliver very high-bandwidth services to each tenant of the building using the phone lines that are already in place. The alternative, which is costly and time consuming, is to pull fiber from the basement to every tenant. 10-PASS-TS provides a much more practical and cost effective approach to high-bandwidth services to existing multi-tenant buildings.

Metro Ethernet Business Services with 2BASE-TL

The primary application of 2BASE-TL is to provide the next generation of business access, replacing the existing T1/E1 solutions that provide primary connectivity for the vast majority of enterprise locations. 2BASE-TL is generally not suited for residential applications because it is a baseband system (meaning traditional analog "POTS" cannot coexist with 2BASE-TL).

2BASE-TL can deliver over 45 Mbps of resilient, symmetric connectivity to any business location. The business service is highly resilient from multipair bonding. With multiple pairs, any one (or more) pair can fail, and the service remains operational over the surviving pairs. This enterprise service is much more reliable and has a much higher bandwidth than today's existing T1/E1 services. Carriers are already in widespread deployments of 2BASE-TL, using it as the standard next-generation access method for any business customer.

Wireless and DSLAM Backhaul with 2BASE-TL

Backhaul applications benefit tremendously from the higher bandwidth and unequaled resiliency of 2BASE-TL. These applications require a highly reliable access method because they are transporting traffic for multiple customers or multiple sites. And not only is reliability important, but high performance (bandwidth, latency, jitter) is equally vital. Cellular backhaul is a perfect example of such a service. Mobile operators are already deploying 2.5G and 3G data services using technologies such as HSDPA and EV-DO. These technologies allow cellular users to access the Internet, send and receive photos and e-mail, and download music and videos, in addition to traditional voice-calling capabilities.

2BASE-TL delivers these in a cost-effective manner because it can utilize the same copper running T1/E1s and deliver more than seven times the bandwidth of a T1—with better reliability and better performance. It is a perfect solution for WiFi, WiMax, cellular, and DSLAM backhaul.

When Does This Solution Not Fit

Mid-Band Ethernet based on the EFM technologies provide the perfect complement to optical Ethernet services. However, the carrier must understand the limitations of each technology as described next.

Target Carriers

Mid-Band Ethernet technologies target carriers that have access to outside copper plant loops, generally incumbent carriers and competitive carriers. Cable providers, because they generally have a fiber/coax plant and no outside plant copper, are not the intended targeted provider for most Mid-Band Ethernet services.

The exception to this is, of course, the in-building application of Mid-Band Ethernet, where Ethernet services are delivered up the riser to multiple tenants over the existing phone wiring. Any carrier with a building presence can benefit from a high-speed, existing distribution network.

Optical End-Game

In an ideal world, all services are delivered over all optical networks. Unfortunately, we don't live in an ideal world. Mid-Band Ethernet technologies are not meant to compete with fiber-based Ethernet deployments—optical connectivity will always deliver the highest amount of bandwidth possible. However, the Mid-Band Ethernet technologies can be used to complement fiber deployments and ensure that Ethernet services are delivered quickly and cost effectively today.

Given the relatively low-fiber penetration in the market (around 10 percent), and the tremendous cost to trench fiber to a customer (as much as $100,000 per mile of fiber), it is clear that fiber cannot and will not be economically deployed to a significant portion of the population for many years to come. The Mid-Band Ethernet technologies are capable of extending and complementing fiber builds so as many customers as possible can quickly and economically access the Ethernet network.

Mid-Band Ethernet's Dynamic Rate Adaptation

Mid-Band Ethernet technologies differ from traditional Ethernet technologies in that they are rate adaptive. One of the characteristics of xDSL technologies is that they run faster on shorter lines and slower on longer lines. Additionally, they can adapt to the length and quality of the line. The technology can basically determine the maximum rate that can be supported on a given line and initialize at that rate. Traditional Ethernet, such as 10/100BASE-T, has auto-negotiation features that can select a line rate based on peers and line quality, but Mid-Band Ethernet technologies are much more flexible and granular. 2BASE-TL, for example, can initialize at rates from 192Kbps thru 5696Kbps, in increments of 64Kbps, depending on the line length and quality. This speed is very beneficial in outside plant copper loops to homes and businesses where the quality and length of the cable vary greatly, and "replacing the cable" is not an option. But at the end of the day, the speed of the service depends on the quality and length of the cable. Deployment plans must utilize the rate-reach trade-off for Mid-Band Ethernet services.

Limitations of 10PASS-TS

10PASS-TS is a great technology for very short reach, asymmetric applications. Delivering residential triple-play data+voice+video services is a perfect application. Typical data and video services for residential users are highly asymmetric, with much more downstream bandwidth required. And with the advent of high-definition video signals, downstream bandwidth requirements are generally at least 20–30 Mbps.

Using a VDSL2-based implementation can deliver these speeds at a few thousand feet. Carriers are generally deploying this technology from an RT so the copper loops can be kept less than a few thousand feet and then feeding the RT with optical connectivity. If longer reach or more bandwidth is needed, multiple pairs can be aggregated to increase service potential.

VDSL2 is not particularly effective as a business service because it lacks a lot of upstream capacity at mid- and long-reach distances. Business users most often want high upstream, as well as downstream, bandwidth. Backup storage, e-mail, VoIP, and so on, all require high-quality upstream connectivity. Although 10PASS-TS can be configured to provide more upstream capacity, it is generally very distance limited.

Limitations of 2BASE-TL

Just as 10PASS-TS is targeted at residential applications, 2BASE-TL is targeted at business applications. It is not as effective a residential technology because it lacks triple-play asymmetric capabilities and also does not support simultaneous voice ("POTS") services. 2BASE-TL is targeted as a next-generation T1/E1 service replacement and can be used in an analogous manner to today's T1/E1 services—just with more bandwidth and higher resiliency!

Benefits and Shortcomings

The Mid-Band Ethernet Technologies discussed here can be applied to solve both business and residential applications. They offer next-generation Ethernet services without the cost and complexity of fiber deployments, but also without the unlimited bandwidth and unlimited reach of fiber deployments.

Copper-based technologies always have rate/reach limitations, meaning that customers farther from the serving office have less bandwidth potential than customers closer to the serving office; you have to trade rate to get reach and vice versa. This is a result of signal dissipation across the copper wires. VDSL2, for example, can deliver 100 Mbps on a single pair of copper, but only at very short distances (less than a 1000 ft). The higher the rates required, the smaller the service radius.

Mid-Band Ethernet has improved upon normal copper limitations by allowing multiple pairs of copper to be aggregated into a single connection. This improves the service radius, but doesn't remove it. Optical connections, on the other hand, have a relatively unlimited service radius—different optical transceivers can be used to cover hundreds and hundreds of miles. So the use of Mid-Band Ethernet services will always have distance and speed shortcomings when compared to optical services.

But Mid-Band Ethernet has the benefit of using the in-place copper plant—you don't have to dig, wait, or build new serving sites. It allows the carrier to leverage what is already in place to deliver better services and get more revenue today without heavy investment.

Typical Deployment Scenarios

The techniques for deploying Mid-Band Ethernet are pretty straightforward. Because the copper plant is already in place, deployments must fit the existing copper plant architecture.

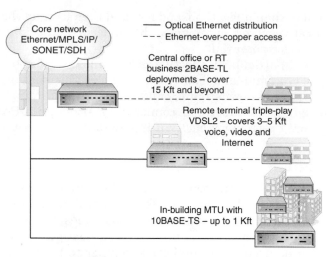

Figure 5.4 Typical deployments of Mid-Band Ethernet

There is generally a piece of equipment located at the customer site that terminates the copper pairs and translates the Mid-Band Ethernet to a more traditional LAN variety of Ethernet (e.g., a 10/100BASE-T port). There is also a piece of equipment that resides at the serving office, which aggregates multiple customers together and performs translation between the carrier Ethernet network and the Mid-Band Ethernet access network.

The variety in the deployments comes from where the serving office is located and where the customer demarcation is located. Figure 5.4 shows multiple scenarios. The serving office could be a carrier's central office equipment, a remote terminal, or a wiring closet in the basement of a building. The customer demarcation equipment could be at a termination at the customer's building, in the customer's building (for example, in a home office), or in a hut or other outside enclosure. All of these options are shown in the figure.

Ongoing Developments

In the time since IEEE 802.3ah developed the advanced mechanisms for Ethernet transport and bonding over outside plant copper, many other standards bodies around the world have recognized their work by incorporating those same techniques into other international standards.

Both ANSI T1 and the ITU have referenced the IEEE 802.3ah techniques for all forward-looking DSL technologies. The dependencies and relationships between the IEEE and ITU standards are depicted in Figure 5.5. The highly efficient IEEE 802.3ah 64/65-octet method for framing and transporting Ethernet packets on xDSL lines has been incorporated into ADSL2+ [5] and VDSL2 [6] as the preferred packet transport technique. Both of these standards reference IEEE 802.3ah as the technology source

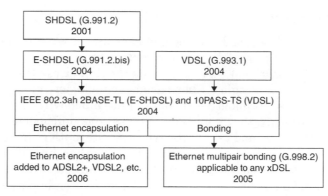

Figure 5.5 Evolution of IEEE 802.3 and ITU standards

for Ethernet transport. Likewise, the North American and European DSL standards bodies have incorporated the IEEE 802.3ah mechanisms into their standards via references to the ITU specifications.

The dynamic and flexible IEEE 802.3ah methods for bonding multiple pairs has been standardized by both groups as *the* method for delivering packet transport over more than one copper loop. In the ITU, Ethernet bonding is part of the G.bond (G.998.2) specification suite. In the ANSI T1 organization, it is known as the Ethernet bonding specification (ATIS T1.PP.427.02-2004). In all of these cases, the referencing standards use the IEEE 802.3ah bonding techniques and generalize them for any type of DSL.

Not only have these groups standardized on the IEEE 802.3ah methods, but also they have worked to improve those methods. For example, the IEEE 802.3ah framing mechanism has been extended by the ITU to allow transmission of small (less than 64-byte) frames. This simple adaptation of the IEEE method now allows for the use of the same technology for native IP transport (where frames may be very small).

Similarly, the ITU has added a preemption mechanism to the base 64/65-octet encapsulation method of EFM. With the preemption mechanism, a "low-priority" frame can be preempted by a "high-priority" frame, thus lowering the latency of high-priority traffic. This mechanism is intended to minimize the delay for latency sensitive applications such as VoIP.

With the ITU's VDSL2 standard being ratified in May 2005, it is likely that true 10PASS-TS implementations will never be deployed. Instead, VDSL2 leverages the technological advances of IEEE 802.3ah and provides additional physical layer flexibility. This "next-generation" 10PASS-TS, based on VDSL2 instead of VDSL, is already a key part of video deployments for a large number of carriers and would not have been possible without the work of IEEE 802.3ah; even though the 10PASS-TS standard is not technically being used.

The fast and widespread technical and market adoption of IEEE 802.3 ah, as well as the dedication to improving the technology, has cemented the IEEE 802.3ah techniques as the best way to deliver Ethernet services over the copper loop infrastructure.

Economic Assessment

The Mid-Band Ethernet EFM technologies are proving to be the most cost-effective on-ramp to the Ethernet/MPLS metro networks.

In general, traditional service providers can address the Ethernet access problem with wireless technologies, fiber-based technologies, or copper-based technologies. Although wireless technologies do not require much wired infrastructure and can thus be deployed quickly, they generally have serious deficiencies when targeted at high-value services—cost and reliability. Wireless alternatives have fairly high capital costs and offer solutions that can be affected by weather, line of sight, or other disturbers in the same wireless frequencies (in the unregulated wireless spectrum). For carriers trying to offer business services, or even reliable triple-play services, wireless access technologies are not a strong solution. They may be fine for simple best effort Internet access, but they are difficult to market as a high-margin reliable service offering.

Optical access, on the other hand, is ideal in that it provides almost unlimited bandwidth and very reliable services. The downside of optical access is its limited availability. Today, around 10–12 percent of business customers have access to optical connectivity. The percentage of residential customers with optical access is much lower. And unfortunately, although there are large-scale initiatives to push optical access to more and more subscribers, that penetration continues to grow at only 1–2% per year. Therefore, optical access will continue to serve only a minority of locations for the foreseeable future.

Copper-based access technologies, on the other hand, have almost universal reach—copper lines go to almost every building. Until recently, copper access suffered from unnecessary complexity, low performance, and uncertain reliability. The EFM standards changed all of that. By using Ethernet natively on the in-place copper plant, the access network became simpler and more efficient. The new EFM technologies also helped to increase the speeds of the access network, with 10PASS-TS speeds up to 100 Mbps and 2BASE-TL speeds over 5 Mbps per line. And finally, the flexible and dynamic bonding mechanisms of Mid-Band Ethernet can provide automatic resiliency against failures in the outside plant.

The Mid-Band Ethernet technologies can be economically compared to other access options such as fiber optics, more traditional T1/E1 architectures, and traditional xDSL. The primary drawback of fiber access is availability—to extend the fiber network requires a significant amount of capital and time. Trenching new fiber runs cost between $50,000 and $250,000 per mile and takes between 6 and 24 months. With this kind of up-front investment in time and money, it's easy to see why carriers aren't just deploying fiber everywhere; there has to be significant revenue opportunity in order to recoup the up-front costs.

Traditional T1/E1 technologies, on the other hand, are universally available but lack both the capability to deliver significant bandwidth and the resiliency necessary for highly reliable services. Mid-Band Ethernet technologies provide more than seven times the raw capacity of a traditional T1. Additionally, once the efficiencies of native Ethernet are included in the comparison, as compared to the overhead of frame relay, PPP, or ATM solutions of the T1, Mid-Band Ethernet can provide more than 13 times the user throughput experience—a significant bandwidth increase compared to the 1.5 Mbps provided from a T1 connection. This allows the deployment of 5, 10, 20, and even 40 Mbps services using the multi-pair capabilities of 2BASE-TL. And with the automatic resiliency provided by the EFM technologies, it's easy to see why so many carriers are looking to cap T1/E1 deployments and deploy Mid-Band Ethernet going forward.

Finally, Mid-Band Ethernet can also be compared with simply running xDSL from a traditional DSL Access Multiplexer (DSLAM). As with T1/E1s, two of the primary economic benefits are simplicity and efficiency. When compared with ATM DSLAMs, a Mid-Band Ethernet user can experience almost twice the throughput as an ATM/DSL user just from the ATM inefficiency alone. The capital expenditures of ATM/DSL architectures are also significantly higher than with Ethernet architectures. For example, an ATM/OC3 port can cost ten times as much as a Gigabit Ethernet port, and provide just a fraction of the capacity. Finally, there have been multiple studies that have compared the operating savings of Ethernet versus ATM/DSL architectures and have concluded that Ethernet can have an ongoing savings of 20–25 percent in operating costs. If you add up the capital and operational savings and throw in the simplicity and improved efficiency, EFM Ethernet becomes a significantly more cost effective technology then continuing ATM/DSL deployments.

One of the more interesting aspects of the economics of Mid-Band Ethernet services is that they are highly profitable for both incumbent and competitive carriers of almost any size. Access to copper loops is regulated and inexpensive. Any carrier that has access to the copper loops can deploy Mid-Band Ethernet services. With capital costs that are as low as traditional DSLAM prices, operational expenses that are significantly lower than any non-Ethernet technology, and no significant up-front deployment costs as with fiber builds, Mid-Band Ethernet is an attractive service offering for any carrier that wants to deploy high bandwidth next-generation services.

Vendors Promoting This Solution

The following vendors have Ethernet-over-copper solutions available on the market:

Vendor	Product(s)	Comments
Hatteras Networks	HN4000, HN400	Hatteras Networks provides state-of-the art Ethernet switching and QoS capabilities in a compact, scalable form factor, all utilizing Mid-Band Ethernet technologies for business services.
Actelis Networks	MetaLight 1300, 130, 50	Actelis Networks provides MetaLight EFM technologies in small and large chassis allowing delivery of 2BASE-TL business services.
Zhone	EtherXtend products: ETHX-SHDSL-4, ETHX-SHDSL-8, MALC	Zhone has integrated both copper and fiber access into a single access chassis, serving gigabit Ethernet and bonded copper in one platform for business access.
Aktino	AK5000	Aktino builds a proprietary physical layer that focuses on crosstalk mitigation. While not a standards-based EFM product, it does leverage some of the encapsulation techniques defined in Ethernet access standards.
DSLAM Vendor	Various	xDSL chipsets are migrating to pure Ethernet encapsulation. As this migration evolves, all DSLAMs will eventually support the EFM technologies discussed in this section for residential as well as business services.

References

1. "Part 3: Carrier Sense Multiple Access with Collision Detection (CSMA/CD) Access Method and Physical Layer Specifications - Amendment: Media Access Control Parameters, Physical Layers and Management Parameters for Subscriber Access Networks," Institute of Electrical and Electronic Engineers, IEEE Std 802.3ah-2004, October 2004.

2. "Single-Pair High-Speed Digital Subscriber Line (SHDSL) Transceivers," International Telecommunication Union, ITU-T G.991.2, December 2003.

3. "Single-Pair High-Speed Digital Subscriber Line (SHDSL) Transceivers," International Telecommunications Union, ITU-T G.991.2, March 2001.

4. "Very High Speed Digital Subscriber Line (VDSL) Transceiver," International Telecommunications Union, ITU-T G.993.1, June 2004.

5. "Asymmetric Digital Subscriber Line (ADSL) Transceivers," International Telecommunications Union, ITU-T G.992.5, April, 2004.

6. "Very High Speed Digital Subscriber Line (VDSL) Transceiver," International Telecommunications Union, ITU-T G.993.2, May 2006.

Hybrid Fiber-Coax

by Greg White

The predominant technology used to provide Ethernet service over the hybrid fiber-coax cable plant is the Data-Over-Cable Service Interface Specification, or DOCSIS, standard. The DOCSIS standard provides for a very cost-effective solution when overlaid on a cable system designed to carry analog and digital video signals. By design, a DOCSIS network coexists easily with native video services as well as with video set-top box return channels (used for addressability, pay-per-view, video-on-demand, and so on), and can provide quality of service guarantees that can be used to offer voice service or service to business customers. In addition, recent enhancements that allow the creation of Layer-2 virtual private networks will usher in a range of new services targeted at business customers.

Technology Description

The Data-Over-Cable Service Interface Specification (DOCSIS) is a Layer 1 and Layer 2 technology [1] standard that utilizes the IEEE 802.2 (Ethernet) Logical Link Control (LLC) and the IEEE 802.3 Media Access Control (MAC) addressing scheme and similar framing conventions. The remainder of the MAC layer functionality is markedly different from IEEE 802.3 Ethernet and is tailored for the particular demands and capabilities of the hybrid fiber-coax (HFC) cable plant.

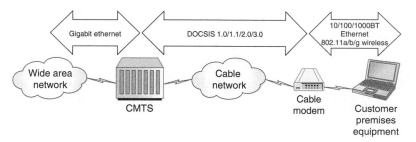

The first version of the DOCSIS standard, DOCSIS 1.0 [2], was created as a proof-of-concept for high-speed access over the North American HFC cable network. In creating the DOCSIS 1.0 standard, goals were kept fairly modest. Time-to-market and interoperability amongst multiple vendors were the primary concerns, so the complexities involved with implementing absolute state-of-the-art technology were purposefully avoided. For example, while the DOCSIS 1.0 protocols can support best-effort, non-real-time classes of service well, it cannot reliably support real-time or time-sensitive services. The tradeoff was a good one, and the DOCSIS 1.0 standard quickly became a success.

After realizing the tremendous success of the DOCSIS 1.0 standard, cable operators decided to pursue enhancements for delivering real-time services, such as voice and streaming video, over their networks. To enable those services, the second version of the DOCSIS standard, DOCSIS 1.1, was developed, which contained several improvements, including quality of service (QoS) capabilities. Those capabilities were put to use via a QoS provisioning and management architecture dubbed PacketCable. The first service offered via this framework was residential voice-over-IP telephony.

To significantly increase upstream capacity, a third version of the DOCSIS standard was developed that built on the success of the first two versions. Known as DOCSIS 2.0, this version enhanced the physical layer of the DOCSIS system by

- Significantly increasing upstream bandwidth
- Improving robustness to RF impairments
- Providing backward compatibility with DOCSIS 1.x
- Coexisting on the same channel as DOCSIS 1.x
- Including interoperable silicon from multiple suppliers

The latest revision of the DOCSIS standard, DOCSIS 3.0, also provided a number of enhancements, most notably

- Channel bonding (both downstream and upstream)
- Full support for IPv6
- Support for source-specific multicast and multicast QoS
- Enhanced encryption and authentication

Table 6.1 shows the data rates provided by the different versions of the DOCSIS standard.

DOCSIS Standards

The four successive versions of the DOCSIS cable modem specifications provide increasing capabilities and sophistication, while maintaining multi-vendor interoperability

TABLE 6.1   Maximum Data Rate for Each of the DOCSIS Versions

DOCSIS Version	Maximum Upstream Data Rate	Maximum Downstream Data Rate (6 MHz systems)	Maximum Downstream Data Rate (8 MHz systems)
DOCSIS 1.0	5.12 Mbps (10.24 Mbps in some systems)	38.8 Mbps	55.6 Mbps
DOCSIS 1.1	10.24 Mbps	38.8 Mbps	55.6 Mbps
DOCSIS 2.0	30.72 Mbps	38.8 Mbps	55.6 Mbps
DOCSIS 3.0	N*30.7 Mbps (N = 4 − 13)	M*38.8 Mbps (M = 4 − 100+)	M*55.6 Mbps (M = 4 − 80+)

Note: In the DOCSIS 3.0 specification, the multiplication factors N and M are equipment dependent, with the minimum for each being four and the maximums limited by the spectrum allocations.

and full backward and forward compatibility. As important enabling technologies for worldwide deployment of residential and commercial broadband data services, they have been standardized both in the U.S. and internationally.

Version	Standard
DOCSIS 1.0	ITU-T J.112-B (03/98), ANSI/SCTE-22
DOCSIS 1.1	ITU-T J.112-B (03/01), ANSI/SCTE-23
DOCSIS 2.0	ITU-T J.122 (12/02), ANSI/SCTE-79
DOCSIS 3.0	ITU-T J.222 (07/07)

All DOCSIS specification versions contain two technology options in order to comply with regional frequency planning practices. The first option, commonly known as *North American DOCSIS,* or simply *DOCSIS,* is intended for systems that use a 6 MHz downstream transmission channel and an upstream band in the 5–42 MHz range. The second option, commonly known as *EuroDOCSIS,* is intended for systems that use an 8 MHz downstream transmission channel and an upstream band in the 5–65 MHz range. Additionally, the ITU Recommendations include a third technology option developed for compatibility with certain systems in Japan that use a 6 MHz downstream transmission channel and an upstream band in the 10–55 MHz range.

The Hybrid Fiber-Coax Cable Infrastructure

The DOCSIS specification is designed to be deployed on a system developed to carry entertainment video programming and to coexist with that programming, leading to certain restrictions being imposed upon the network infrastructure.

Physical Plant The modern physical cable network is built upon a *hybrid fiber-coax (HFC)* architecture. At its simplest, this architecture is composed of optical fiber that connects the cable operator's "head-end" equipment to devices in the field (fiber nodes) that convert the signals from optical to electrical and vice-versa. Coaxial cable (coax) then connects the fiber nodes to the end devices located at the customers' premises.

Fiber nodes are typically not intelligent devices, in that they do not demodulate or process the signals that pass through them. They are physical layer devices that simply convert the signal from one form to the other.

The network topology is the "tree and branch" type, with the head-end at the base of the tree and the end devices at the leaves. In the coax portion of the plant, the cable is split at each branch using a passive device known as a *tap*. This plant topology was originally designed to handle one way communications from a Community Antenna Television (CATV) operator's head-end to subscriber residences, and for that purpose, it is an efficient and high-performance topology. Return signals, however, are not handled as efficiently, nor with as high a performance level. In particular, the branching structure of the cable network offers many points for noise and interference to enter the plant and be carried to the head-end. Each unterminated connector in a subscriber location is an opportunity for the ingress of noise and interference that affects all customers served by the same fiber node. This property has been termed *noise funneling* and results in a significantly lower signal-to-noise ratio in the return path relative to the forward path.

Spectrum Allocations A modern cable system is capable of fully bidirectional communication. The optical fibers between the head-end and the fiber nodes carry downstream (from the head-end to the customer) and upstream (from the customer to the head-end) signals on separate fibers, whereas the two signals are intermixed on the coax portion of the plant.

In order to allow bidirectional communications over the coax portion of the plant, and to maintain compatibility with the legacy downstream services (analog and digital video), the upstream communications operate at the low-frequency end of the spectrum (5–42 MHz in North America, 5–65 MHz in Europe), whereas the downstream transmissions operate in the normal video transmission band (typically 54–870 MHz in North America, 87.5–862 MHz in Europe).

Because cable networks were originally designed as one-way transmission media, the spectrum allocation for downstream (to the customer) and upstream (to the network) communication in cable networks is very asymmetric. The upstream radio frequency (RF) spectrum is fairly narrow compared to the amount of downstream spectrum. That, coupled with the highly robust modulation required for upstream transmissions, leaves a large asymmetry in capacity between the two channels. That capacity asymmetry has, fortunately, matched fairly well with the demand asymmetry historically seen in web-surfing traffic for residential broadband users and the predominantly downstream entertainment video services. Today, applications are increasingly making more use of the upstream transmission path, for example, peer-to-peer sharing of multimedia content and transmission of digital images. In addition, business customers may require a symmetric connection to the Internet in order to host a website or for virtual private network connections to remotely located employees. Furthermore, there are applications on the horizon that will absolutely require symmetric bandwidths (e.g., video telephony, video conferencing, and so on). All of these factors underscore the need for the higher capacity upstream technology introduced in DOCSIS 2.0 and the channel bonding introduced in DOCSIS 3.0.

Cable Modems

Digital data is transmitted over RF carrier signals on a cable system. For two-way communication, one carrier signal carries data in the downstream direction, and another carries data in the upstream direction. Cable modems (CMs) are devices at the subscriber premises that convert digital information into a modulated RF signal in the upstream direction and convert the RF signal to digital information in the downstream direction. A *cable modem termination system (CMTS)* performs the converse operation for multiple subscribers at the cable operator's head-end. Typically, a few hundred users can share a downstream channel and one or more upstream channels. The downstream channel occupies the space of a single television transmission channel in the cable operator's channel lineup; it can provide up to 38.8 Mbps (for 6 MHz channels) or 55.6 Mbps (for 8 MHz channels). In the DOCSIS 1.0 and 1.1 specification, the upstream channels can be up to 3.2 MHz wide and can deliver up to 10 Mbps per-channel (typically limited to 5 Mbps for DOCSIS 1.0). In the DOCSIS 2.0 specification, upstream channels can deliver up to 30 Mbps over channels as wide as 6.4 MHz. A Media Access Control (MAC) layer coordinates shared access to the upstream bandwidth. In the DOCSIS 3.0 specification, the MAC layer has been enhanced to support multiple physical channels in each direction simultaneously.

Although sometimes referred to as a "last-mile" (or "first-mile") access technology, a DOCSIS network can operate over much greater distances. In fact, the DOCSIS specifications are designed to operate up to a maximum optical-electrical distance of ~100 miles.

From a data-networking perspective, the cable modem is an IEEE 802.1d bridge (with some modifications), supporting an 802.3 (10BASE-T, 100BASE-T, or 1000BASE-T) Ethernet link on the customer side and the DOCSIS RF link on the operator side. The CMTS can simply be a bridge as well, but it often is implemented as a full IP router. A bridge is a Layer 2 device that operates on Ethernet frames, making forwarding decisions based on hardware (MAC) addresses and a bridging table (also known as a *forwarding database*), whereas a router is a Layer 3 device that operates on IP packets, making forwarding decisions based on IP addresses and a routing table.

Communications Protocols

At their core, the DOCSIS specifications define physical layer and Media Access Control layer protocols to provide Ethernet transport across the HFC plant.

The DOCSIS Physical Layer The downstream physical layer in the DOCSIS specifications uses the same MPEG-2 transport technology originally developed for carrying digital video programming. That technology is standardized as ITU-T J.83, and utilizes 64-QAM or 256-QAM as well as a concatenation of Reed-Solomon coding and trellis-coded modulation (TCM) for forward error correction (FEC). The downstream signal is a continuous stream of modulation symbols, so it can be received and demodulated with relatively low-cost hardware.

The upstream physical layer in the DOCSIS 1.0 and 1.1 specifications uses a combination of quadrature-phase shift keying (QPSK) and 16-QAM with Reed-Solomon FEC. Because the upstream consists of a series of transmission bursts from various CMs, each burst begins with a well-known preamble in order to aid acquisition by the burst demodulator at the CMTS. The upstream channel width is configurable from 200 kHz to 3.2 MHz in power-of-two increments.

In the DOCSIS 2.0 and 3.0 specifications, the upstream physical layer is extended in two ways. The first is by adding more choices for modulation, stronger FEC, and wider channels. The second is by adding a second, operator-selectable, physical layer technology based on synchronous code-division multiple access (S-CDMA) technology.

The upstream modulation choices in the DOCSIS 2.0 and 3.0 specifications are QPSK, 8-QAM, 16-QAM, 32-QAM, 64-QAM, and 128-QAM. The upstream FEC is enhanced by allowing a greater level of Reed-Solomon error correcting capability (up to 16 correctable symbols per codeword), as well as by allowing the inclusion of interleaving and TCM. The choice of upstream channel widths is also increased to include a 6.4 MHz setting. The use of both TCM and 128-QAM is limited to the S-CDMA mode of operation, and 128-QAM is only selectable when TCM is enabled, which effectively reduces its spectral efficiency to that of 64-QAM.

The S-CDMA physical layer technology partitions the upstream channel into (up to) 128 subchannels kept distinct by a set of orthogonal spreading codes. That structure is broken up in time into a series of equal-duration timeslots called *frames*. The CMTS then schedules upstream transmissions by codes and frames. Because any frame may see several CMs transmitting simultaneously (using different sets of codes), orthogonality of the transmissions is maintained by precisely synchronizing the CM transmitters to within 1 percent of the modulation period. At the highest symbol rate (5.12 Msps) that results in a synchronization accuracy of approximately 2 ns.

The DOCSIS MAC Layer Because the architecture of the cable system enforces a one-to-many topology for downstream transmissions and a many-to-one topology for upstream transmissions, the DOCSIS MAC layer protocol's primary task is to coordinate the upstream transmissions from all of the attached CMs. The basic mechanism by which this is achieved is via a reservation-based, time-division multiple access control system. When an Ethernet frame arrives at the 10/100/1000Base-T or USB port on a CM, the CM determines the size of the packet and then sends a request message to the CMTS to reserve an appropriately sized timeslot in which to send the packet. The request message itself is sent in contention using a slotted Aloha protocol with binary exponential backoff in the event of a collision. The CMTS prioritizes the request and then grants the CM the requested timeslot. The CMTS communicates the scheduling of upstream transmissions by periodically broadcasting a *map* message, which identifies contention request timeslots as well as timeslots that are granted to a particular CM.

Since the cabling distance, and hence propagation delay, between the CMTS and each individual CM may vary widely, all CMs are synchronized to a common time base using a periodic ranging mechanism. When triggered by an upstream ranging timeslot granted to it by the CMTS, the CM sends a ranging request message. The CMTS then calculates and sends a ranging response message that includes a timing adjustment as well as transmit power and frequency adjustments, if necessary. This ensures that each CM's transmissions stay within the timeslots allocated to it by the CMTS.

The DOCSIS 1.1 specifications and beyond include MAC layer extensions to support quality of service (QoS). For example, certain packet streams (service flows) can be given low latency by establishing an upstream scheduling type for the flow. By default, upstream service flows are of the "best-effort" scheduling type and so gain access to the upstream channel by the mechanism described previously. The alternative upstream scheduling types include a *real-time polling service* and an *unsolicited grant service.* Real-time polling service achieves lower latency for constant packet-rate but variable bit-rate streams (e.g., video telephony) by eliminating the contention request and back-off mechanism. The CM is instead given periodic, dedicated (i.e., contention-free) request opportunities in which to request timeslots to transmit its packets. Unsolicited grant service, on the other hand, achieves low latency and jitter for constant bit-rate streams (e.g., voice telephony) by eliminating the request mechanism entirely. The CM is given periodic, fixed-size timeslots (grants) in which to transmit its packets.

In addition to these tools that address latency requirements for certain upstream traffic types, the DOCSIS 1.1 specification and beyond provide support for data rate guarantees, bounds on data rates via a token-bucket rate-limiting algorithm, as well as priority levels for both downstream and upstream traffic. QoS capabilities can be managed dynamically in order to meet the particular needs of the traffic being actively transported, and multiple service flows with disparate QoS requirements can be supported simultaneously using a sophisticated packet classification mechanism.

Provisioning

CMs are provisioned and allowed service by the operator through the use of a binary configuration file. The configuration file contains settings to control the forwarding of data through the CM in accordance with the user's service-level agreement. For example, the configuration file defines rate limits and rate guarantees for data forwarding in both the upstream and downstream directions; the configuration file can also be used to limit the number of customer devices attached to the CM or to block traffic to or from certain IP addresses or traffic that uses certain protocols.

When a particular CM comes online, it requests an IP address from a Dynamic Host Configuration Protocol (DHCP) (RFC-2131) [3] server in the operator's data network. The response from the DHCP server includes information on the filename and server IP address for the configuration file that has been assigned to that particular CM.

The CM then downloads the configuration file using Trivial File Transfer Protocol (TFTP) (RFC-1350) and exchanges registration messaging with the CMTS in order to inform the CMTS of the file's contents and to enable bridging of user data.

Management

The DOCSIS specifications include sophisticated network management tools built upon the Simple Network Management Protocol (SNMP). A large number of required management information base (MIB) objects are used to instrument and control the various aspects of the network operation.

All DOCSIS devices support SNMPv1 and v2c, while DOCSIS 1.1–3.0 devices also support SNMPv3. The DOCSIS 1.1–3.0 specifications define two management modes, the NmAccess mode and the SNMPv3 Coexistence mode. Within the NmAccess mode, access is controlled via SNMP community strings and support is only provided for SNMPv1/v2c. Within the SNMPv3 Coexistence mode, access is controlled via the View-based Access Control Model (RFC-3415) and support is provided for SNMPv1/v2c/v3.

DOCSIS equipment also supports event reporting via SNMP traps, which are reported to the head-end SNMP manager and are logged both in the CM or CMTS and on a SYSLOG server in the head-end. Event messages are used to inform the operator of issues that may need to be addressed.

Security and Privacy

Although the physical layout and shared media of the cable plant mean that the data for each user passes by every other user on that section of the plant, the DOCSIS standards ensure that every user's data is kept private through the use of link-layer encryption technology. In DOCSIS 1.0–2.0, a 56-bit data encryption standard (DES) is provided. DOCSIS 3.0 equipment, on the other hand, supports the 128-bit advanced encryption standard (AES). During operation, each CM negotiates an encryption key with the CMTS that is used to encrypt the traffic in both directions on the HFC link. The encryption key is unique for each CM, known only to the CM and the CMTS, and updated periodically at a frequency set by the operator. Furthermore, DOCSIS 1.1–3.0 provide additional security tools, including

- A mechanism for the operator to prevent theft of service by requiring that each modem authenticate itself using a digital certificate
- A secure method to download new operational software to a modem
- A way to encrypt high-value "multicast" traffic and provide decryption keys only to those customers who are authorized for the service

Bandwidth Efficiency

Because the bandwidth on the upstream and downstream channels is distributed over a number of customers, bandwidth usage is much more efficient than the alternative of a point-to-point dedicated link. Since most communications links are idle for a significant portion of time, aggregating and distributing bandwidth allows users with data to send to take advantage of the otherwise unused capacity available from idle users. For packetized data services, the term *statistical multiplexing* is often used to describe the efficiency gains realized by distributing bandwidth. The advantages of statistical multiplexing increase as more bandwidth is aggregated. For example, doubling the raw channel capacity can increase the effective capacity by a factor of 2.5, according to one study [4]. Further, the distributed bandwidth provides a resource for the operator to provision a higher burst data rate for a customer than the nominal sustained data rate that the customer is allowed. This is controlled via the token-bucket rate-limiting algorithm, in which the operator can provision a customer with a burst size (in bytes) for which data can be sent and received at up to the line rate (e.g., 38 Mbps down, 30 Mbps up) and with a maximum sustained rate that applies to the long-term average for transmissions.

Layer 2 Virtual Private Networks

As part of the Business Services over DOCSIS family of specifications [2], CableLabs has developed a specification detailing a feature package that enables standardized configuration and management of Layer 2 virtual private networks (L2VPNs) that overlay the cable data network. These L2VPNs can coexist easily with other broadband data service offerings including residential broadband data service and VoIP telephony. This optional extension to standard DOCSIS equipment contains requirements on the CM and CMTS that ensure isolation of L2VPNs from one another as well as from the traditional (non-L2VPN) data customer traffic.

This specification defines point-to-point and point-to-multipoint L2VPN configurations that can be used to provide E-Line and E-LAN transparent LAN services. Data privacy is ensured by the underlying link-layer encryption technology provided by DOCSIS (56-bit DES or 128-bit AES).

Equipment built to support the L2VPN specification would be the most attractive to use in providing Carrier Ethernet services.

The L2VPN specification has also been standardized in the International Telecommunications Union as ITU-T Recommendation J.213.

TDM Emulation

To provide T1/E1 connectivity to customers over the DOCSIS network, a second Business Services over DOCSIS specification, the *TDM Emulation Interface* specification has been developed by CableLabs. Equipment built to support this optional specification can be used to provide a drop-in replacement for traditional telco T1 or E1 service.

Carrier Ethernet Attributes

The Metro Ethernet Forum (MEF) defines five attributes of Carrier Ethernet:

- Standardized services
- Scalability

- Reliability
- Quality of service
- Service management

The DOCSIS specifications define certain features that are directly applicable to these Carrier Ethernet attributes, while leaving significant room for vendor differentiation and innovation. Historically, these types of vendor-differentiation features have only been significantly developed on the CMTS. All current CMTS vendors have product offerings, which they consider "carrier-class, that provide varying levels of support for the attributes listed here. The following sections provide details on the features provided by the DOCSIS standards.

Standardized Services   From the outset, the DOCSIS specifications were developed as a multi-vendor standard for Ethernet transport across a hybrid fiber-coax wide area network. Equipment that supports the L2VPN Business Services over DOCSIS feature set can be used to provide seamless and secure Layer 2 virtual private network capabilities that enable a transparent LAN service in point-to-point and multipoint configurations connecting multiple customer locations. This is equivalent to the E-Line and E-LAN service definitions defined by the MEF. Further, T1 circuit emulation over Ethernet can be accomplished in a standard manner via equipment that supports the TDM Emulation Interface specification in order to provide connectivity to a customer's existing CSU/DSU equipment.

Scalability   The DOCSIS specifications provide a scalable Ethernet transport platform, with independently configured data rates currently ranging from 1 bps to 30 Mbps in the upstream direction and 1 bps to 38 Mbps in the downstream direction. The data rate in each direction can be configured with a granularity of 1bps in order to meet the demands of the application. In addition, data rates can be changed dynamically, without replacing equipment and without service outage. A service-level agreement can even be defined such that the configured data rate varies by time-of-day or by day-of-week in order to best meet the customer's needs.

As described previously, the DOCSIS 3.0 specification extends the bandwidth available to a cable modem in a scalable way, up to a maximum possible data rate of 176 Mbps in the upstream direction (384 Mbps in certain plant configurations) and 4.8 Gbps in the downstream direction, with initial DOCSIS 3.0 equipment expected to support data rates up to 120 Mbps upstream and 155 Mbps downstream.

Reliability   Reliability features, such as hitless failover and hot-swappable line cards, are available from all CMTS vendors in their carrier-class equipment offerings. The DOCSIS standard does not place any mandatory requirements on such features. The DOCSIS standard does specify the behavior of a cable modem when it detects that it has lost connectivity. Specifically, the cable modem will attempt to reestablish connectivity using the downstream and upstream channels it had been using previously, and if unsuccessful, after a time-out the CM will attempt to locate an alternative channel or channels. The CMTS is also required to report the status for each cable modem to which it is connected via standard network management tools.

Quality of Service   As described previously, DOCSIS specifications provide a very rich set of quality of service (QoS) features that can be used to customize the service offerings based on customer needs. A Service Provider can configure committed information rates, burst sizes, excess information rates, latency bounds, and so on, to match the QoS requirements of the customer. A mix of traffic with differing QoS requirements can be supported simultaneously, with each type of traffic, or even each session, getting the QoS guarantee needed to provide the customer with an acceptable quality of experience. QoS for aggregate traffic can be changed dynamically, and QoS for individual sessions can be provisioned on-demand to allow for a very efficient and customized service offering.

Service Management   The DOCSIS specifications specify the use of standardized network management tools, including Simple Network Management Protocol (SNMP) and Internet Protocol Detail Record (IPDR) streaming, and they define an extensive set of statistics and controllable parameters that are available to the network operator. The operator can make use of these parameters for administration and maintenance procedures.

Service provisioning involves entry of the cable modem hardware (MAC) address and service information into a provisioning server. The role of that server is to assign a management IP address and provide a configuration file to the CM during the cable modem initialization sequence. As discussed previously, the configuration file defines the service offering to the customer by setting up the QoS for the statically defined service flows that carry the majority of the customer traffic, installing filters to protect the customer from unwanted traffic, and potentially configuring Layer 2 VPN connections.

Drivers for This Solution

For several years, cable television operators have been transitioning from the traditional core business of entertainment programming to being full-service providers of video, voice, and data telecommunications services. DOCSIS cable modems, residential gateways based on CableHome [5], Voice over IP (VoIP) telephony devices based on PacketCable [6], and extensions to the DOCSIS specification such as L2VPN and TDM Emulation, are among the elements making this transition possible.

To date, one of the most successful and cost-effective means for providing residential broadband data services is via cable modems compliant with DOCSIS specifications. DOCSIS is a technology standard that was originally created to deliver high-speed data over the HFC cable network in North America. DOCSIS has since become a highly successful standards family comprised of four versions (1.0, 1.1, 2.0, and 3.0) that has gained significant worldwide popularity as a high-speed access technology and has become the foundation upon which a number of new services are being developed. As of the end of 2006, over 100 million DOCSIS-compliant cable modems have shipped worldwide [7].

When Does This Solution Fit?

The DOCSIS specification was originally designed to cost effectively offer broadband (1–10 Mbps) access-network connectivity to a large number of residential customers over the existing CATV plant, sharing the spectrum with analog and digital video services. While data rates have been extended with the latest versions of the DOCSIS specifications, and numerous extensions have been introduced in order to support business customers, the other aspects of this statement still ring true. DOCSIS technology is clearly a good solution as part of a voice+data+video service offering where channel capacity is shared by a large number of customers. Further, with the maximum CMTS-CM optical/electrical spacing of ~100 miles, DOCSIS technology works well in serving dense (urban) to moderately sparse (suburban) populations.

From the Carrier Ethernet customer's perspective, Ethernet services over a DOCSIS network are a clear fit where data rates in the range of 10s of Mbps to the low 100s of Mbps are required. A DOCSIS network may be a particularly cost-effective solution when a customer has low committed information rate requirements, but high burst data rate requirements (especially when the peak data rates occur outside of the typical residential data peak demand times).

When Does This Solution Not Fit?

From the Service Provider's perspective, a DOCSIS network might not make sense in a dedicated point-to-point link serving a single customer or in a link in which coexistence with video services is not necessary. This is due to the fact that current CMTS product offerings, as well as the DOCSIS MAC layer itself, are optimized for efficient sharing of the link (particularly the upstream link) by a number of users and would introduce unneeded overhead and complexity in the case of point-to-point communications. Further, if coexistence with video services is not required, then the adherence to legacy video spectrum allocations, channel formats, and coaxial cabling would be an unnecessary limitation.

From the Carrier Ethernet customer's perspective, DOCSIS technology might not currently make sense when data rates approaching or exceeding 1 Gbps are required.

Benefits and Shortcomings

Due to the volume deployment of DOCSIS equipment for residential broadband service, scale economics have made DOCSIS a very cost-effective solution for delivery of Ethernet service to a wide variety of customers. The rich quality of service controls and support for E-Line and E-LAN types of services make it well suited to providing Carrier Ethernet to business customers.

On the other hand, current DOCSIS equipment cannot achieve upstream data rates in excess of 38.8 Mbps downstream and 30 Mbps upstream. Equipment available in the near future will push those limits beyond 100 Mbps. While these data rates are sufficient for many customers, they are not sufficient for all of them.

Typical Deployment Scenarios

In a typical deployment scenario, shown in Figure 6.1, a single downstream channel with a data rate of 38.8 Mbps is split and shared over four fiber nodes, with each fiber node serving a population of approximately 500 households passed (HHP). Each fiber node has a dedicated upstream channel with a configured data rate of 10.24 Mbps. Assuming 20 percent penetration of high-speed data customers, the result is approximately 400 customers share the downstream channel and approximately 100 customers share each upstream channel. With interactive services, this type of deployment can typically support user data rates in the range of 5 Mbps downstream and 3 Mbps upstream. Operators generally offer different tiers of service with different configured data rates (controlled by the provisioning system).

The typical deployment is not a static configuration, however. As penetration rates increase, the data rates offered to customers increase and user behavior migrates to ever-higher bandwidth usage. Cable operators stay ahead of the demand by evolving their networks. Some tools available to the operator include node splits, node recombining, and multichannel load balancing. In a node split, the operator replaces a single fiber node with two, cutting in half the number of households passed per fiber node. With node recombining, the operator modifies the CMTS connectivity such that the downstream channel is split over a smaller number of fiber nodes (two or three rather than four). With multichannel load balancing, the operator adds a second (or third) downstream or upstream channel

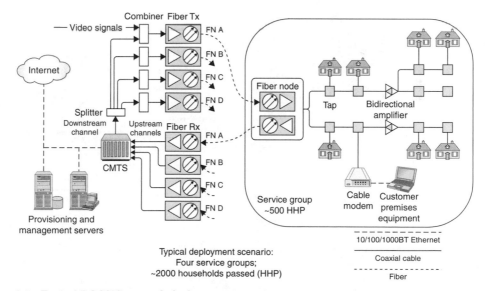

Figure 6.1   Typical DOCSIS network deployment scenario

that provides service to the service group(s). The CMTS then automatically (and dynamically) maintains a balance of modems on each channel. Additionally, to increase upstream capacity, the operator has the option of configuring the upstream channels with a higher data rate (20.48 Mbps or 30.72 Mbps rather than 10.24 Mbps), although these higher data rates require that the cable modems and CMTS be compliant with the DOCSIS 2.0 specification and that the upstream channel has sufficient signal-to-noise ratio to support higher-order modulations.

Ongoing Developments

CableLabs has recently released specifications for a DOCSIS Modular-CMTS. The M-CMTS architecture, shown in Figure 6.2, was designed as an extension to the DOCSIS specifications to allow for flexibility and independent scaling of certain CMTS functions and to allow operators to more efficiently use available network resources. One of the key elements of the M-CMTS architecture is the separation of the downstream physical layer QAM modulation and up-conversion functions from the CMTS and the placement of that functionality into an *edge-QAM (EQAM)* device. This separation allows for the development of EQAM products that support both video-on-demand services and DOCSIS services, which in turn allow operators to use the same network resources to support multiple types of services such as data, voice, and video.

DOCSIS 3.0 is the newest member of the DOCSIS standards family. The specifications have been published, and equipment is currently being developed by a number of vendors.

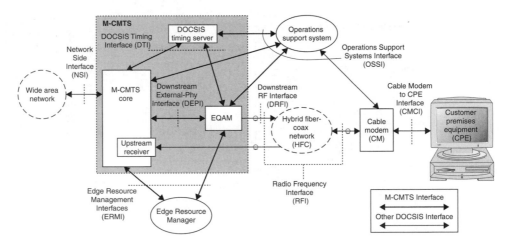

Figure 6.2   Modular CMTS architecture

The goals of the DOCSIS 3.0 specification are to increase the per-user and aggregate data rates significantly, to support IPv6 over Ethernet natively, and to provide tools for the operator to provision and manage IP multicast streams. The DOCSIS 3.0 specification utilizes *channel bonding* technology, where multiple physical layer channels are combined in the MAC layer to produce a higher capacity link. Conceptually, this is similar to other bonding schemes (e.g., 802.3ad Ethernet Link Aggregation or RFC 1990 Multilink PPP); however, because the DOCSIS link is a shared medium (one-to-many downstream and many-to-one upstream) rather than a point-to-point link, the similarity ends there. The DOCSIS 3.0 MAC layer has been enhanced to allow coordination of access to this multichannel link in an efficient, flexible, and scalable manner.

Economic Assessment

The incremental capital costs to provide broadband data service over an existing two-way HFC plant are fairly low. For a moderately sized cable system, the CMTS cost for a typical MAC domain (one downstream channel and four upstream channels) capable of serving four service groups (up to 500–600 residential customers at a data rate of 5 Mbps downstream and 1 Mbps upstream) in the typical deployment discussed in "Typical Deployment Scenarios" would be in the range of $30,000. That averages out to be $50–$60 per subscriber. Add to that approximately $50 per subscriber for a current DOCSIS 2.0 cable modem, and the result is a total capital cost on the order of $100 per subscriber for the two ends of the data connection. This obviously doesn't include other necessary capital expenses and the operational expenses of providing a data service offering to customers, but these costs would be present regardless of the access-network technology in use.

The costs to build and maintain the HFC plant are not as trivial. To build a modern HFC network costs on the order of $30,000 per mile of plant (including head-end equipment costs), and to maintain the network, costs are another $1000 per mile each year [8].

Vendors Promoting This Solution

Numerous vendors develop DOCSIS-compliant equipment. Compliance with the DOCSIS specifications is certified by CableLabs in the U.S. and EuroCableLabs in Europe.

Complete lists of certified DOCSIS- and EuroDOCSIS-compliant equipment can be found at the CableLabs and Excentis websites:

- www.cablelabs.com/certqual/lists/
- www.excentis.com/files/certified_qualifiedproducts.pdf

Some illustrative DOCSIS vendors/products are detailed here.

Vendor	Product(s)	Comments
Ambit (www.ambitbroadband.com)	CM: U10C018	Cable modems
ARRIS (www.arrisi.com)	CM: Touchstone CM550, Touchstone CM550 CMTS: Cadant C4, Cadant C3	Cable modems and Cable modem termination systems
BigBand Networks (www.bigbandnet.com)	CMTS: Cuda12000	Cable modem termination systems
Cisco Systems (www.cisco.com)	CM: Linksys BEFCMU10 CMTS: uBR 10012, uBR7200, uBR7100	Cable modems and cable modem termination systems
Motorola (www.motorola.com)	CM: SB5120, SB5101, SBG940, SBG900 CMTS: BSR 64000, BSR 2000, BSR 1000	Cable modems and cable modem termination systems
Scientific-Atlanta (www.scientificatlanta.com)	CM: WebSTAR DPC2100	Cable modems
Thomson (www.thomson.net)	CM: TCM425, DCM425	Cable modems

References

1. Information technology – Open Systems Interconnection – Basic Reference Model: The Basic Model, ISO/IEC 7498-1, 1994.

2. DOCSIS specifications may be found at the CableLabs website: www.cablemodem .com/specifications/.

3. The Internet Engineering Task Force RFCs and standards (including DHCP, TFTP, SNMP, SIP, MGCP, IntServ, DiffServ, RAP, COPS, IPSec, and IKE) may be found at the IETF website: www.ietf.org.

4. Lee and Bertorelle, "System-Level Capacity and QoS in DOCSIS 1.1 Upstream," SCTE Emerging Technology Conference, 2002.

5. CableHome specifications may be found at the CableLabs CableHome website: www.cablelabs.com/projects/cablehome/specifications/.

6. PacketCable specifications may be found at the CableLabs PacketCable website: www.packetcable.com/specifications/.

7. Various articles, *Cable Digital News* (February 2002, February 2003, May 2003, June 2006, October 2006, April 2007): www.cabledigitalnews.com.

8. John, Brouse, "Fiber Access Network: A Cable Operator's Perspective," ITU-T All Star Network Access Workshop, June 2004: www.itu.int/ITU-T/worksem/asna/ index.html.

Passive Optical Networks (PONs)

by Marek Hajduczenia, Glen Kramer, and Lowell Lamb

Passive optical networks (PONs) are poised to address the first mile in the telecommunication infrastructure, spanning between the service provider central office (CO)/point of presence (POP) and residential/business customers. Currently, the access network structure consists predominantly, in residential areas, of copper telephone wires or coaxial cable television (CATV) cables, whereas in metropolitan areas, where there is a high concentration of business customers, it also includes high-capacity synchronous optical network (SONET/ATM) rings, optical T3 lines, and copper-based T1s.

In order to alleviate the first mile bottleneck growing between high capacity LAN/enterprise networks and multi-wavelength (DWDM) MAN/WAN structures, the PON networks target the economic "sweet spot" between T1s and OC-3S links that other access network technologies do not adequately address. By promising high-speed Internet access at a reasonable price, PONs bring the vision of a fully digital home one step closer to becoming a reality. There are a number of available PON-based access network solutions, namely broadband PON (BPON), Gigabit capable PON (GPON), asynchronous transfer mode PON (APON), and Ethernet PON (EPON), to name the most important ones. Attempts have also been made to integrate SONET-based solutions with the PON technology, but so far this technology mix has not proven to be cost-effective and present any advantages over other available PON systems. Despite the number of existing technological options, there are only two main competitors for actual deployment, namely BPONs (and more precisely GPONs, which also support ATM transmission and are based on a more modern standard than BPON) and EPONs.

Asynchronous transfer mode PONs (APONs) were developed in the mid-1990s through the work of the full-service access network (FSAN) initiative, composed of 20 large carriers working together with their strategic equipment suppliers to agree upon a common broadband access system for the provisioning of both broadband and narrowband services and to develop standards for designing the cheapest, fastest way to extend emerging high-speed services, such as internet protocol (IP) data, video, and 10/100 Mbps Ethernet, over fiber to residential and business customers worldwide. At the time, ATM encapsulation was a logical choice because of a large number of ATM links in the backbone and metro networks at the time and its suitability for multiple protocols. The PON architecture was supposed to provide a cost-effective structure for service delivery. The APON format used by FSAN was accepted as an International Telecommunications Union (ITU) standard (ITU-T Rec. G.983). However, the APONs failed to meet original expectations since ATM-based cards and switches are far more expensive when compared with Ethernet equipment, and currently the manufacturing lots are decreasing.

Ethernet PONs (EPONs) were initiated and developed by start-up companies believing that the APON standard is an inappropriate solution for the local access loop because of its lack of inherent video broadcast capabilities, insufficient bandwidth, complexity and hardware costs. Adoption of first gigabit Ethernet in enterprise and local area networks (LANs), as well as the increasing pace of deployment of 10 Gbps Ethernet equipment first in wide area networks (WANs) and now also in LANs as the port costs decrease seem to confirm that EPON is the solution for linking the Ethernet-centric world of local networks with the transport layer of MANs/WANs. In November 2000, a group of Ethernet vendors initiated their own standardization effort, under the auspices of the Institute of Electrical and Electronics Engineers (IEEE), through the formation of the Ethernet in the first mile (EFM) study group, which resulted in approval of the IEEE 802.3ah standard at the end of 2004, providing a seamless connection between the environment of enterprise and community LANs based on Ethernet technology and emerging Carrier Ethernet equipment, thus minimizing the number of protocol conversions and allowing service providers to take advantages of very robust, effective, and inexpensive packet-based transmission technology.

Technology Description

In 1995, when the full-service access network (FSAN) initiative began to study PON systems for FTTB/C/H, asynchronous transfer mode (ATM) was envisioned as the base technology for the LAN, MAN, and WAN worlds. Since that time, Ethernet has eclipsed ATM, with over 320 million ports deployed worldwide (2000), offering staggering economies of scale [1] and with a deployment rate exceeding 100 million ports per year (2005). High-speed Gigabit Ethernet is in mass deployment, while 10 Gigabit Ethernet products are already beginning to replace 1 Gigabit ports providing significant increase in the available transmission bandwidth in a cost-effective manner. Due to the scalability and simplified management, Ethernet come thus to dominate the MAN and WAN areas.

Due to the increasing demand for bandwidth throughout the network, the FSAN consortium started a new effort to specify a PON system operating at bit rates exceeding 1 Gbps, with the new system targeting the generic framing procedure (G.7041) as a means to improve transport efficiency for variable length IP packets (including also Ethernet encapsulated IPdatagrams), while simultaneously allowing for a mix of variable-size frames and ATM cells. Based on FSAN recommendations, in 2003–2004 the Telecommunication Standardization Sector of the International Telecommunication Union (ITU-T) approved the new Gigabit-capable PON (GPON) series of specifications, known as ITU-T Recommendations G.984.1, G.984.2, and G.984.3. Although the GPON encapsulation method (GEM) was added to improve the efficiency of Ethernet transport, many artifacts of ATM and SONET/SDH remained in the GPON specification.

In January 2001, the Ethernet in the first mile (EFM) study group was formed by the IEEE community, targeting migration of existing Ethernet technology into the subscriber access area and focusing on both residential and business access networks. Keeping in touch with the very Ethernet tradition, the group set the goal of providing a significant increase in performance while minimizing equipment, operation, and maintenance costs, aiming in fact at the development of Ethernet PON system specifications.

Ethernet PON (EPON) is a PON-based network that carries subscriber data encapsulated in native Ethernet frames, as defined by the IEEE 802.3 standard [2], using 8B10B line coding (8 data bits of PCS layer data encoded into 10 line bits at the PHY layer) and operating at the standard Ethernet speed of 1 Gbps (PCS layer) / 1.25 Gbps (PHY layer). Where possible, EPON uses the existing IEEE 802.3 specification, including application of the existing 802.3 full-duplex media access control (MAC) as defined in 1000BASE-X specifications with PON specific extensions at the RS and PCS layers.

The IEEE 802 group has traditionally focused on enterprise data communication technologies. In EPONs, the main emphasis is on preserving the architectural model of Ethernet, and thus no explicit framing structure exists. Ethernet frames are transmitted in bursts, with a standard inter frame gap (IFG) inserted between individual frames. The burst sizes, as well as the physical layer overhead, are large in EPONs. As an example, let's consider the maximum automatic gain control (AGC) interval, which is set to 400 ns, thus providing enough time for the optical line terminal (OLT) to adjust gain without the need for optical network units (ONUs) to perform power-leveling. This simplicity enhances robustness and reduces cost. Additionally, because the laser on and off times are capped at 512 ns, a value significantly greater than that of GPON (16-bit times), lower quality, and thus much cheaper lasers, as well as receiver modules, can be used in EPON systems.

Moreover, EPON interfaces seamlessly with an IP core network, due to its inherent capability to carry variable sized datagrams, transparency for higher network layers, simplicity and OAM robustness. Newly adopted quality-of-service (QoS) techniques, including full-duplex transmission mode, prioritization (IEEE 802.1p), and virtual LAN (VLAN) tagging (IEEE 802.1Q), make Ethernet networks capable of supporting voice, data, and video. Not surprisingly, Ethernet is poised to become the architecture of choice for next-generation subscriber access networks.

Administration and Maintenance in EPONs

In the enterprise environment, local area Ethernet networks are typically managed via the so-called simple network management protocol (SNMP) [3]. In spite of being a flexible management solution, this protocol generally lacks efficiency and makes a number of assumptions about the underlying network structure, which are not necessarily valid in all possible cases, especially with the PON system architecture in mind. First, the standard operation of the SNMP protocol relies basically on the operability of the network structure and IP level connectivity (see RFC 1067 and RFC 1470), which may be impossible to sustain should the network suffer from a fatal, low-level failure. Second, the standard SNMP protocol implementation assumes the connected devices are accessible at IP-level at all times, which requires provision of public IP addresses from the ever shrinking pool of IPv4, its allocation and binding with the network equipment and then managing the complex IP-MAC associations for the local Ethernet links. This results therefore in deployment of a complete IP overlay on top of the Ethernet link, even when the provided services are as plain as Point To Point (P2P) Ethernet level connectivity, Which in the long run in an overkill for a carrier environment.

The Ethernet network layer provides no inherent management capabilities using any predefined OAM protocol, mainly due to short structure reach and limited area coverage. However, the IEEE 802.3 ah–compliant OAM protocol, targeting enhancement of the already existing SNMP in its management utilities rather than its replacement, seems to be a step in the right direction to provide link level, embedded administration and maintenance functionalities for Ethernet networks. Moreover, it is by definition compatible with all the Ethernet in the first mile (EFM) technologies, including Ethernet in the first mile over copper (EFMC), Ethernet in the first mile over fiber (EFMF) and Ethernet in the first mile using Passive Optical Networks (EPON). The underlying and shared OAM tools and procedures, common to all P2P and P2M Ethernet topologies currently defined in the IEEE 802.3 standard, provide network operators with the freedom to choose and mix any Ethernet link technologies, based on their business models, network architectures, and subscriber needs, without losing the underlying OAM functionality.

Additionally, EFM OAM is backward compatible with any already existing and deployed full-duplex P2P Ethernet links, dating back before the EFM ratification. Such a feature is available due to the decision to use standard Ethernet frames as the transport mechanism for OAM information and procedures.

SNMP over Ethernet   RFC 1089 defines SNMP protocol over Ethernet networks, describing an experimental method by which the SNMP as specified in Case et al [3] can be used over Ethernet MAC layer framing instead of the Internet UDP/IP protocol stack. This specification is critical for LAN-based network elements which contain no higher layer protocol functionality. This particular implementation allows for relaying SNMP frames in a pure Ethernet environment and thus is perfectly suited for deployment in a Carrier Ethernet environment. The original RFC 1089 will soon be replaced by the new RFC 4789 entitled "simple network management protocol (SNMP) over IEEE 802 Networks" (publication date November 2006, available online at http://www.ietf.org/rfc/rfc4789.txt), which defines the details of the SNMP over Ethernet implementation. In accordance with the current RFC draft specification, SNMP over IEEE 802 networks features a number of inherent restrictions. Using SNMP over IEEE 802 transport mapping restricts messages to a single logical IEEE 802 LAN, bridged LAN, or VLAN domain, while only a single SNMP engine can be addressed on a given IEEE 802 network interface, with all the command generators and notification receivers as well as command responders and notification originators sharing a single transport endpoint.

Serialized SNMP messages are sent in IEEE 802.3 frames with an Ethernet type field value of 33100 (hexadecimal $814C_{16}$). In IEEE 802 LAN networks using LLC mechanisms for link layer protocol identification, including IEEE 802.11 wireless LANs, the SNAP encapsulation method described in subclause 10.5, "Encapsulation of Ethernet Frames over LLC," of the respective IEEE 802 standard is used. When an SNMP entity uses this transport mapping, it must be capable of accepting SNMP messages up to 484 octets in size (inclusive). It is recommended that implementations be capable of accepting messages of up to 1472 octets in size. Implementation of greater values is encouraged whenever possible.

Main Ethernet OAM Features and Functionalities   Operation of the OAM protocol on a generic Ethernet interface (regardless of whether it is a legacy P2P full-duplex or EFM Ethernet link) does not affect standard data transmission in any substantial way. The OAM protocol relies on a "slow protocol" with very limited bandwidth consumption, generating at most 10 frames per second, and by definition, it is not required for normal link operation, but rather for its maintenance and fault detection. The OAM protocol can be implemented in hardware or software, thus providing the desired media independence and flexibility required—especially for legacy equipment where hardware changes are highly unwelcome and software alternations are limited in scope. OAM frames target the slow protocol MAC address (standard defined) and are intercepted by the MAC sublayer and thus do not propagate across multiple hops in an Ethernet network, assuring the OAM protocol data units (OAMPDUs) affect only the operation of the OAM protocol itself, while leaving the contents of the subscriber frames unaltered.

The main supported OAM features and functionalities include

- **Discovery process**   Defining the process in which OAM-enabled devices discover their peers on the link and notify each other of their OAM-related capabilities.

- **Link performance monitoring**   Defining attributes and status information for Ethernet links through exchange of specialized OAM link performance frames.

- **Remote fault detection**   Describing means of detecting and handling compromised links in any underlying Ethernet network infrastructure.

- **Remote loopback**   Providing means for the testing individual links and segments by sending test frames through them, based on a generic OAM protocol.

- **MIB variable retrieval**   Providing management information look-up from a remote database, delivering required OAM-specific information on the given network structure.

- **Organization-specific enhancements**   Enabling provision for vendor-specific enhancements to the protocol, adding any required functionalities that are out of scope of the respective IEEE standard.

Discovery   The OAM Discovery Process is the first phase of IEEE 802.3ah OAM protocol, and its basic functionality is limited to identifying the individual devices in the given network domain as well as their OAM capabilities. In the IEEE 802.3ah, upon powering up, a device enters a *discovery state* and attempts to send the Information OAMPDU to its link peer, thus establishing the local link information path, which will be used further on for exchange of more specialized OAM frames. In the case of standard Ethernet OAM, the discovery process relies on the Information OAMPDUs, which are propagated in the given network and trigger all connected OAM-enabled devices to issue their OAM capabilities information, which will be encapsulated in the appropriate frames and delivered to other link peer stations. During the discovery phase, the following information is announced in type-length-values (TLVs) carried within periodic Information OAMPDUs:

- **OAM configuration**   Also termed *OAM capabilities*, advertises OAM capabilities for the particular link entity, so that the peer station(s) can determine which functions are supported and accessible, for example, loopback capability, MIB access, and so on.

- **OAM mode**   This particular field conveys information defining whether the given link station has active/inactive OAM functionalities. Therefore, such information is typically used to determine the available functionality of the particular device.

- **OAMPDU configuration**   This particular field conveys the maximum OAMPDU size for reception and delivery processes and is typically used to limit OAM traffic bandwidth allocation, along with frame rate limitation.

- **Platform identity**   This particular field is a combination of an organization unique identifier (OUI) and 32-bits of vendor-specific information and is used to identify the given OAM protocol implementation version. OUI allocation is controlled by the IEEE, and OUIs are typically equal the first three bytes of a MAC address, the pool of which is allocated to each Ethernet MAC and equipment manufacturer.

The discovery phase includes an optional time period allowing for any local station to accept or reject the configuration of the link peer OAM entity; for example, a particular network node may require all its link peer stations to support the loopback capability. Selection and implementation of such policies are not covered by and specified in the respective IEEE standard and are left open for vendor-specific implementation. Such enhancements are typically developed on top of the standard OAM protocol.

Link Performance Monitoring   The OAM link monitoring administration tools target detection and identification of link faults, where the detection mechanism utilizes the Event Notification OAMPDU, sending link state–related events to a Link Partner OAM entity, relaying thus the information on the potential link problems. If the link partner happens to be SNMP enabled, a SNMP trap could pass the OAMPDU to a remote entity. There are a number of standard defined error events:

- **Errored symbol period (errored symbols per second)**   The total number of symbol errors that occur during a specified period exceed a certain predefined threshold, degrading link quality and impairing data transmission capabilities. The symbol errors typically include coding symbol errors, e.g., violation of 8B10B encoding rules.

- **Errored frame (errored frames per second)**   The total number of frame errors detected during a specified period exceeds a certain predefined threshold.

- **Errored frame period (errored frames per N frames)**   The total number of frame errors within the last N frames has exceeded a certain predefined threshold. Both detection threshold and observation window size are customizable.

- **Errored frame seconds summary (errored seconds per M seconds)**   The total number of errored seconds, defined in the standard as one second intervals with at least one frame error within the last M seconds, has exceeded some predefined threshold. Again, both detection threshold and observation window size are customizable.

Since the IEEE 802.3ah-compliant OAM mechanism does not include OAMPDU delivery guarantees and is a best-effort service, the Event Notification OAMPDU may need to be sent multiple times to increase the probability of detection of the particular event which is to be notified to the link partner. Such multiple events need to be recognized by all OAM-enabled stations and discarded, and thus each Event Notification OAMPDU is equipped with a serial number, providing thus the target link peer with the ability to detect and discard multiplied event notification frames. Recognizing the need for delivery guarantees for the SNMP protocol, newer specifications of the aforementioned mechanism include additional OAMPDUs, effectively creating an acknowledged transmission path, along with a keep-alive mechanism to ensure the given link is open and traversable at any time.

Remote Failure Indication   Any link faults in Ethernet networks are difficult to detect and isolate, especially when they are caused by slow decay of link quality rather than abrupt and typically catastrophic severance. A flag in the OAMPDU data frame allows any OAM-enabled unit to notify its peers on the link failure conditions, including during the following situations:

- Link fault event, occurring when the signal loss state is detected by the receiver. Such a notification flag is transmitted once per second (only the direct link peer is notified about this particular condition).

- Dying gasp event, occurring when an unpredictable external condition, such as a power failure, occurs, degrading the link transmission capabilities. Such a notification flag is transmitted immediately after the onset of the event and in a continuous manner (all link peers are notified about this event).

- Critical event notification, confirming the occurrence of an unspecified critical event, affecting the link quality and transmission capabilities of the particular link station. Such a notification flag is transmitted immediately after the onset of the event and in a continuous manner (all link peers are notified about this event).

Definitions of the dying gasp and critical events are left open for system vendor-specific implementation, thereby providing increased system design flexibility. Examples of the unrecoverable condition for dying include power failure, electrical power instabilities, and so on, causing the given piece of equipment to restart continuously and thus providing poor link quality or no service at all.

The link fault event, on the other hand, is applicable only to any particular situation when the physical sublayer is capable of independent transmission and reception, thus providing signaling even when the receiver is impaired or damaged. Providing the receiver fails to detect any data transmission from its peer at the PHY layer, due to, for example, laser malfunction in the peer station, the local entity can set this flag to let the peer know that its transmission interface is inoperable.

Remote Loopback   In the loopback mode, every Ethernet frame received is transmitted back on that same port except for OAMPDUs and pause frames, which provide flow control and OAM functionality. This particular functionality helps network administrators assure and measure link quality during installation or troubleshooting stages, when no standard data exchange occurs and the given links are subject to testing and quality evaluation. The remote loopback session requires a periodic exchange of OAMPDUs messages; otherwise, the OAM session is interrupted and all link peer stations transit into the standard transmission mode. It is interesting to note that any OAM-enabled station with a link in active mode (as opposed to passive mode) can force its link peer station into the remote loopback mode simply by sending a loopback control OAMPDU. The loopback command is acknowledged by responding with an Information OAMPDU, with the loopback state indicated in the state field.

OAM remote loopback sessions are, therefore, used to evaluate particular network segments in terms of their transmission quality, SLA compliance, end-to-end packet delay, jitter, and average/peak line throughputs. Test implementation during the remote loopback sessions is vendor specific and is not covered by the respective IEEE standard. Additionally, since the loopback information is dropped by the link partner initiating OAM exchange in accordance with the IEEE 802.3ah, measuring the two way end-to-end packet delay is not possible. Moreover, measuring the single-ended packet delay requires implementation of a timer and application at the looped site, which is not specified by 802.3ah, thus further complicating OAM-level transmission quality measurements.

MIB Variable Retrieval   The management information base (MIB) stores a network-level accessible database of so-called manageable variables, while the OAM protocol provides strictly *read-only* access to MIB variables describing a specific network branch. In this way, a network administrator may store a set of parameters describing any Ethernet network link, accessed remotely on-demand when link testing is underway. The on-demand character of the variable retrieval process may be easily interleaved with any OAM message exchange, resulting in flexible implementation of any measurement functions for estimating the link capability to support a SLA (similar to IP ping for measuring delay, jitter, and throughput).

Organization-Specific Extensions Any organization-specific extensions to the generic Ethernet OAM protocol are based on the allocation of specific TLVs carried in standard compliant OAMPDUs, as well as on the allocation of organization/task-specific OAMPDUs targeting other functionalities besides those originally defined in the respective IEEE standard. These OAM extensions carry an organization unique identifier (OUI) in the frame to indicate the designator of the extension and to facilitate interoperability testing.

System vendors have chosen to utilize organization-specific extensions to the standard Ethernet OAM protocol to implement additional and extended events, include additional information during the discovery phase, or even develop a completely proprietary OAM protocol, while maintaining the general framework compatibility with the standard IEEE-compliant OAM.

EFM OAM Even though the EFM OAM protocol is compatible with any legacy P2P full-duplex Ethernet technology and can be inherently used in even small local area networks, it was created mainly to reduce expenditures for first-mile service providers, based on IEEE 802.3ah-compatible EFM technology. The main functions provided by the EFM OAM include

- Link performance monitoring
- Fault detection and fault signaling
- Loopback testing

OAM is typically optionally implemented in the data-link layer between the MAC and LLC sublayers, and because it was termed *optional* in the IEEE 802.3ah standard, system vendors can use either proprietary or existing management solutions, depending on the required functions and supported extensions. The EFM OAM can be implemented in hardware (especially in stations where performance is the main issue, e.g., in OLTs) or in software (to provide extended flexibility and remote configuration, e.g., in ONUs). This means that only a certain group of network stations may support OAM features (e.g., ONUs providing service to premium customers). The OAM functionality can be implemented on any full-duplex point-to-point (P2P) link or emulated P2P link (EPON case), and the OAM protocol can be used simultaneously with the 802.3x MAC flow control PAUSE function, although when doing so, PAUSE inhibits all traffic, including the OAM protocol data units (OAMPDUs). The EPON OAM protocol is, therefore, a straightforward implementation of the generic Ethernet OAM protocol, with minor changes in the MIB targeting adjustment to the EPON environment conditions. The EPON MIB module is an extension for the generic Ethernet MIB, IF-MIB, and MAU-MIB devices, thus consisting of three distinct MIB groups:

- **MPCP MIBs** Containing objects used for configuration and status verification for the IEEE 802.3ah-compliant MPCP protocol. Additionally, the statistic table, termed *dot3MpcpStatTable* contains all metrics relevant to the operation of the multipoint access mechanism.

- **OMPEmulation MIB**   Containing objects required for configuration and status verification for all P2P emulation mechanisms present in EPONs, which are achieved by tagging each data frame traversing the EPON structure with the network unique Logical Link IDentifier (LLID) number, identifying the source/target entity in a unanimous manner. There are two distinct tables present, namely *dot3OmpEmulationTable* containing objects required for configuration and status polling and *dot3OmpEmulatio nStatTable* storing relevant mechanism statistics.

- **MAU MIBs**   Containing objects required for configuration and status verification for EPON MAU level interfaces. A MAU MIB is generally considered an extension of the generic Ethernet MAU MIB. It comprises a *dot3EponMauTable*, hosting the managed parameters of the EPON physical layer, and a *dot3EponMauType* type definition.

Additionally, there is a MIB module specific for EPON devices which contains objects that can be used to manage any Ethernet device, such as a bridge, with one or more EPON OLT interfaces. The MIB *eponDeviceRemoteMACAddressLLIDTable* contains a table mapping ONU MAC addresses to LLIDs addresses for the given EPON instance, thus storing the physical ONU port addresses—not the addresses of the end stations that may be attached to the subscriber ports of the device. The aforementioned ONU addresses are learned from incoming MultiPoint Control Protocol(MPCP) messages and are updated continuously during standard operation.

In an EPON-based bridge, a similar table must be present to store the associations between the MAC addresses of the end stations attached to the ONUs and the LLIDs, which need to be used to reach the particular Ethernet interfaces. A normal bridge learns associations between MAC addresses of the particular interfaces and given ports, though here the generic bridge ports are replaced by the LLID entities. The implementation details on this particular table are left open, allowing for greater flexibility and the addition of proprietary solutions.

Drivers for This Solution

In recent years, we have witnessed groundbreaking developments in the area of optical networking, especially with the emergence of such advanced transmission technologies as dense wavelength division multiplexing (DWDM), inline optical amplification in the form of erbium doped fiber amplifiers (EDFA), optical path routing (wavelength cross-connecting), wavelength add-drop multiplexers (WADM), high-speed switching, and so on—all of which were quickly adopted in core networks and WANs, boosting the transmission capacity of the telecommunications backbone and increasing its reliability. Simultaneously, LANs made a huge step forward by upgrading the existing infrastructure from 10 Mbps Ethernet lines to typically 100 Mbps or even 1 Gbps solutions, courtesy of a new Gigabit Ethernet standard recently adopted by the IEEE [2].

An increasing number of households are in possession of more than one personal computer, typically internetworked using home area networks (HANs) based on LAN solutions, with low-cost Ethernet switches and hubs being the devices of choice for such limited connectivity systems. New houses are commonly equipped with standard category 5/5+ cabling to facilitate deployment and interconnection of personal devices. Such HANs do represent a significant data source nowadays, mainly due to the increasing number of digital online services, such as online gaming, Video On Demand (VoD), and information searching, producing a steadily growing data flow that needs to be delivered to the WAN aggregation plane.

This transformation of backbone, enterprise, and home networks, coupled with the tremendous (virtually exponential) growth of Internet traffic volume observed for the last couple of years (see e.g., www.ieee802.org/3/hssg/public/mar07/bach_01_0307.pdf, www.ieee802.org/3/hssg/public/jan07/lee_01_0107.pdf, or www.ieee802.org/3/hssg/public/sep06/steenman_01_0906.pdf), only emphasizes the aggravating gap between the aforementioned network layers, resulting from the lack of well-developed access networks, where bandwidth is currently scarce, expensive, and commonly hard to obtain. With little investment and almost no plans for development, existing copper-based systems, including ISDN and DSL lines, as well as hybrid (mixed copper and fiber) solutions, deployed mainly by CATV companies, all exhibit signs of bandwidth shortage right now, with no advanced digital service available yet. This situation has occurred due to asymmetric channel characteristics as well as significant reach limitations, especially noticeable in the case of DSL technology, where deployment price grows almost exponentially as distance increases from the central office of the ISP.

The most widely deployed "broadband" solutions today are digital subscriber line (DSL) and cable modem (CM) networks. While they certainly represent a significant step forward from what used to be 56 kbps dial-up connections, they are still unable to provide sufficient bandwidth for such emerging digital services as VoD, online gaming, or multichannel video conferencing.

DSL technology uses the same copper twisted-pair cable as telephone lines and requires a special DSL modem located at the customer premises, as well as a digital subscriber line access multiplexer (DSLAM) terminating the given subscriber line in the CO of the ISP. DSL technology is mainly all about efficient spectrum division, providing a means of subdividing the available line spectrum into a number of transmission windows (one of which, located in the lower frequency region, is reserved for the standard telephone channel being used by the plain-old telephone service (POTS) equipment). The transmission windows are used to deliver data services to and from a subscriber modem. Several flavors of DSL lines have been developed over the years, such as basic digital subscriber line (bDSL), targeting backward compatibility with integrated services data network (ISDN) equipment; high-speed digital subscriber line (HDSL), compatible with the T1 rate of 1.544 Mbps; asymmetric digital subscriber line (ADSL), which is currently the most widely deployed flavor of DSL with short range transmissions reaching 16 Mbps in the downstream direction (toward the subscriber); and finally very high-speed digital subscriber line (VDSL), boasting 24 Mbps in the downstream direction, though with very short reach. Recent years brought also the development of VDSL2/2+ (specified in the framework of ITU G.993.2), which permits the transmission of asymmetric and symmetric (Full-Duplex) aggregate data rates up to 200 Mbit/s on twisted pairs using a bandwidth up to 30 MHz.

CATV networks were originally designed to deliver analog broadcast TV services to subscriber TV sets, thus adopting a standard tree-and-branch topology and allocating most of the transmission channel bandwidth for downstream analog channels. Typically, CATV networks are built as hybrid fiber-coax (HFC) structures with fiber spanning between a video head-end or a hub to a curb optical node, with the final drop section deployed using standard coaxial cable technology and repeaters (amplifiers) and tap couplers to split the signal among many subscribers. Faced with the growing competition from telecom operators in providing Internet services, cable television companies responded by integrating data services over their HFC cable networks, which, in turn, required replacing single direction (downstream) signal amplifiers with bidirectional amplifiers, in order to enable the upstream data path. An updated medium access protocol was also required to allow access of multiple subscribers to the same shared transmission channel, while avoiding collisions between individual data transmissions. However, since most of the usable transmission spectrum is tieddown with TV signal delivery, both downstream and upstream channels in such systems are very limited in bandwidth, thus providing decent access rates for only a limited number of subscribers.

It is interesting to note that, while the highly asymmetric nature of the traffic is observed in DSL and CATV systems, new and emerging applications tend to drive the bandwidth ratio toward unity. Applications such as video conferencing or data storage using storage area networks (SANs) require a symmetric transmission channel. File-sharing applications, as well as peer-to-peer traffic such as eDonkey, Kazaa, and Napster (to name just a few of them), increase traffic symmetry since each connected user simultaneously operates as network client and server, thus receiving and transmitting on average the same amount of data. It was recently reported that the current ratio of downstream to upstream traffic is approximately 1.4 to 1 [4]. The recent advent of IPVideo services and video file hosting services i.e. YouTube seems to skew this ratio again towards strong asymmetry (YouTube video sessions account for 20% of overall HTTP transactions and 10% of the overall traffic observed on the networks) [5]. As a result of streaming audio and video in Web downloads, HTTP traffic constitutes approximately 46% of all data transmitted over Internet, while the ratio itself has a strong positive increase factor. For comparison, symmetric P2P traffic constitutes in total roughly 37% of data being transmitted.

For some time, it has been expected that the traffic ratio would reach the full symmetry condition (1 to 1), with downstream and upstream data flows more or less balanced. The recent evolution of VoD applications, however, seems to bring the ratio into asymmetry again, with the downstream flow strongly dominating the upstream traffic (see: http://grouper.ieee.org/groups/802/3/cfi/0306_1/cfi_0306_1.pdf). Data traffic is increasing at an unprecedented rate, with a sustainable traffic growth rate of over 100 percent per year observed since 1990 (already quoted: www.ieee802.org/3/hssg/public/mar07/bach_01_0307.pdf, www.ieee802.org/3/hssg/public/jan07/lee_01_0107.pdf, or www.ieee802.org/3/hssg/public/sep06/steenman_01_0906.pdf). There were periods when a combination of economic and technological factors resulted in even greater growth rates, e.g., a 1000 percent increase per year in 1995 and 1996 [6]. This trend is likely to continue in the future, especially with the deployment of Voice over IP (VoIP) telephony and with the increasing role of online services, VoD, interactive gaming, and so on. Although the impact of these technologies is still very limited, they are very likely to spur currently unimaginable traffic growth in the near future.

Unsatisfied subscribers' demand for new services have attracted a new breed of market players. These players are namely smaller and very flexible companies, dealing mainly with data transfer services, that envision a global networking environment with fully converged digital services, including data, voice, and video, carried in digital format over a single network by a single protocol. To alleviate bandwidth bottlenecks, optical fibers, and thus optical nodes, are penetrating deeper into the first mile, promising to bring fiber all the way to offices (FTTB), apartment buildings (FTTC), or individual homes (FTTH). Unlike previous architectures, where fiber is used as a feeder to shorten the lengths of copper and coaxial networks, these new deployments use optical fiber throughout the access network and are capable of supporting Gbps data rates at costs comparable to those of DSL and HFC networks, while eliminating all active electronic devices from the signal pathway, thereby making the network structure passive, more robust, and less expensive. This is the environment in which passive optical networks (PONs) were born.

When Does This Solution Fit?

The main features of Ethernet PON systems can be summarized as follows:

- EPONs extend the reach of LAN/HAN systems, inherently using Ethernet equipment and allowing for native Ethernet frame transmission toward WAN systems, where an increasing amount of Ethernet equipment (mainly multi-wavelength 10 Gbps systems) will give rise to back-to-back Ethernet carrier networks in the future. In this way, Ethernet as a transport technology has entered an uncharted area where time division multiplexing (TDM)–based technologies used to dominate the market for many years, proving that optical access networks can be cost-efficient, while maintaining simple management, flexible architecture, and high efficiency.

- EPONs inherently carry Ethernet traffic, and thus no protocol conversion and additional operations in the electrical domain are required when forwarding subscriber-generated data streams (most of which are born natively in Ethernet ports) toward MAN/WAN and core networks for further transmission. This is a very important feature, since each protocol conversion adds complexity to the overall transmission system, along with hidden costs in the form of specific equipment (ATM, SONET, etc.), management problems, and conversion issues, as well as more complex monitoring, fault detection, and removal. EPONs are, therefore, perfectly suited for delivery of digital services from and toward subscriber equipment, in what seems to be a user friendly and fully plug-and-play architecture, as simple to set up as connecting your standard network cable to an ONU.

- EPONs are based on highly cost-effective components, where relaxed hardware requirements and increased guard-bands both in downstream and upstream channels allow for application of lower grade lasers and receiver modules with wider quality margins. A number of choices, in terms of EPON physical layer (PHY) parameters, have allowed this type of PON system to become one of the most promising solutions, as far as cost and service delivery are concerned. Native support for Ethernet framing and re-use of existing 1 Gbps Ethernet MAC chipsets, as well as the dramatically increasing number of deployed Ethernet ports, make EPONs a technology of choice for interconnecting Ethernet-based LANs, SANs, or other types of Ethernet-based networks.

- EPON systems are agnostic as far as transported data format is concerned. Recent add-ons to the generic Ethernet technology, in terms of pseudo-wire emulation, standard telecommunications quality of service (QoS) measures, VLAN tagging, and transmission system protection mechanisms, allow current EPONs to deliver any type of data (including digitized voice, video, etc.) with full QoS support, using a single framing format that perhaps has proven to be not the most efficient, as far as encapsulation overhead is concerned, but definitely the most robust among other existing data packet transmission protocols.

When Does This Solution Not Fit?

The use of IP over Ethernet in subscriber access applications eliminates unnecessary network layers. The elimination of network layers reduces the number of network elements in a network, and that reduces equipment costs, operational costs, and complexity. At the edge of the first mile, simpler architectures are always easier to manage. In the first mile, native Ethernet on copper or fiber will offer significant cost-performance advantage over competing technologies. These IP/Ethernet networks will, of course, co-exist with TDM and SONET/SDH services. For example, for business customers, T1 and fractional T1 might be provisioned over Ethernet on optical fiber. Also, in many cases, the service provider might backhaul data, voice, and video to a SONET/SDH network.

Metro access for business and residential subscribers with EFM technologies is one critical component of the larger metro solutions portfolio available currently on the market. The three EFM topologies being defined by IEEE 802.3ah will complement each other. Ethernet over VDSL on copper is the best fit for established neighborhoods, business parks, and MxUs because it can reuse the existing voice-grade, twisted-pair copper cable. For new residential developments and many business applications, Ethernet over PON will be the best fit because of its high bandwidth and long potential service life. For high-end commercial customers, Ethernet over point-to-point fiber may provide the best solution because it can scale to meet future bandwidth demands. Service providers will build hybrid networks, especially when the distance between the central office and the subscriber exceeds a mile. In FTTC applications, P2P optical fiber or EPON can be used as the interconnect technology to the central office, extending the reach of the Ethernet over VDSL solution. It is, therefore, very difficult to identify an application where EPONs do not serve their purpose in the best possible way.

Benefits and Shortcomings

The fundamental benefits of PON technology include flexibility, reliability, and simplicity. Their deployment eliminates active network components, such as amplifiers, switches, or regenerators from in-field locations, thus adding to the robustness, simplicity, and reliability of the structure. In EPON architecture, all active network components are placed at the ends of the fiber line and all in-field devices are completely passive, data rate transparent, and typically environmentally hardened, featuring mainly passive splitter combiners (PSCs). These splitters fit into standard splice enclosures and can be conveniently installed with the cable, providing little maintenance, if any. Environmentally controlled vaults (CEVs), required in DSL and other copper technology deployments are thus eliminated, thus no air conditioning systems, large pedestals, commercial powering, backup power systems as well as time-consuming technician dispatches are required.

EPON networks also employ bidirectional communications over a single fiber cable, thus reducing the amount of required fiber deployment by approximately 50 percent and providing a more cost-effective fiber structure for the network operator. In case of service providers with exhausted fiber capacity, EPON systems enable the reclamation of capacity through better fiber utilization, allowing for service provision for greater numbers of subscribers. A single fiber strand can, therefore, provide connectivity to as many as 16/32 customers at a distance of up to 20 km, in accordance with the IEEE 802.3ah standard. The smaller the network diameter, the greater the number of customers, thus typical upgrades from P2P Ethernet links to EPON systems result in a fiber structure capable of supporting more than 32 customers at a time.

The only shortcomings of the presented EPON system stem inherently from its advantages i.e., relaxed PHY requirements. Lower grade lasers and receiver modules as well as the application of 8B/10B channel encoding result in increased transmission overhead when compared with competitive ITU G.984 GPON systems. This fact has been recognized by the EPON proponents though it has been argued that the increased channel efficiency of GPONs comes with a much higher price tag, leading to less cost-effective solution. It is therefore difficult to identify whether the said relaxed PHY specifications are indeed disadvantageous for EPONs or whether they were originally the enabling factor for the wide adoption of the said system and its robustness.

Typical Deployment Scenarios

The EPON is a point-to-multipoint (P2M) network, with a single CO providing services to a number of residential/business customers. All transmissions in the EPON system are performed between the OLT and ONUs, where the OLT is typically a blade in a CO chassis, while the ONUs are more commonly deployed as stand-alone boxes, with their exact location depending on the deployment scenario (home for FTTH, curb in FTTC, business office in FTTB—see Figure 7.1 for details). Both active components also have other functions. The OLT connects the optical access network to the metropolitan area network (MAN) or wide area network (WAN),

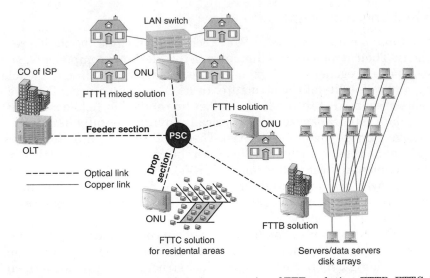

Figure 7.1 Standard EPON deployment with various scenarios of FTTx solution: FTTB, FTTC, FTTH, and mixed FTTH

typically termed backbone while ONUs typically aggregate traffic streams from individual subscribers and prepare them for transmission toward the OLT. ONUs additionally employ packet-prioritization mechanisms or scheduling, enabling full QoS support and enforcement of service-level agreements (SLAs) between the Internet service provider (ISP) and the end subscribers. The OLT typically employs complex mechanisms responsible for bandwidth allocation in the shared upstream channel as well as a number of agents dealing with registration of new subscriber units in the network, ranging, link control, and so on.

Several multipoint topologies have been suggested for the access network, including tree, tree-and-branch, ring, or bus (see Figure 7.2). Use of 1×2 optical tap couplers and $1 \times N$ optical splitters allows for virtually any deployment architecture, thus making EPONs a very flexible architecture capable of meeting any requirements in terms of providing connectivity for end subscribers.

Downstream Transmission in EPON Systems

In the downstream direction, Ethernet packets broadcast by the OLT pass through a $1 \times N$ PSC or a PSC cascade to reach the ONUs. Each ONU receives a copy of every downstream data packet. The number of connected ONUs can typically vary between 4 and 64, limited by the available optical power budget.

The downstream channel properties in this PON system make it a shared-medium network: packets broadcast by the OLT are selectively extracted by the destination ONU, which applies simple packet-filtering rules based on MAC and LLID addresses (see IEEE 802.3ah, Clause 64 [7] for details). The downstream channel operation is best depicted in Figure 7.3, where packets destined to different end subscribers are filtered out by the ONUs from the broadcast downstream data flow.

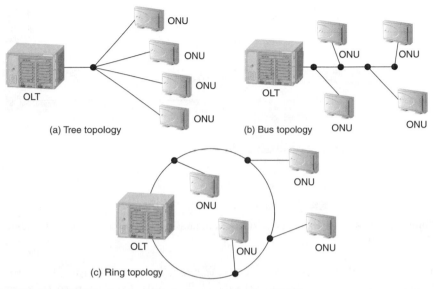

Figure 7.2 Standard PON deployment topologies supported by EPONs

Upstream Transmission

In the upstream direction, from the ONU toward the OLT (see Figure 7.4 and Figure 7.5), EPON operates in the multipoint-to-point mode (MP2P), where numerous ONUs transmit their data packets to a single receiver module located in the OLT. Moreover, since individual ONUs are not aware of other ONUs' transmissions (as the PSC is a directional device, an ONU cannot see the signal transmitted upstream by any other ONU), the resulting connectivity appears similar to the P2P architecture, where centrally managed access to the upstream channel allows for only a single ONU at a time to deliver pending packets. However, because all ONUs belong to a single collision domain, centrally managed channel access is required (typically via a dynamic bandwidth allocation algorithm or DBA for short), and ONUs in their default state are not allowed to transmit any data unless granted specifically by the OLT. In this way, data collisions are avoided because

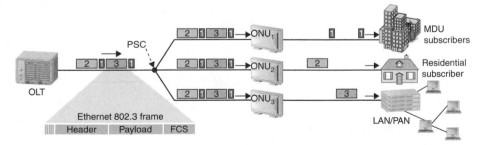

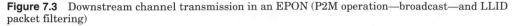

Figure 7.3 Downstream channel transmission in an EPON (P2M operation—broadcast—and LLID packet filtering)

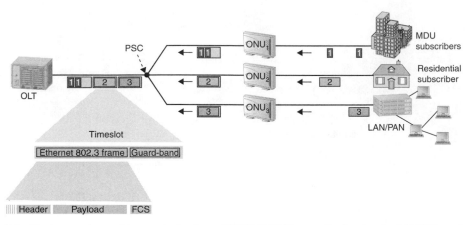

Figure 7.4 Upstream channel transmission in an EPON (MP2P operation)—standard TDM-based channel sharing

the central OLT controller at any and every moment of time is aware of the scheduled transmissions from individual ONUs. The only exception to this centrally managed upstream channel access scheme is the so-called discovery process [7], where new and not initialized ONUs are allowed to register in the EPON system.

A multiple access protocol is required in the upstream direction, since the EPON operates as a multipoint-to-point network and every single ONU talks directly to the OLT. A contention-based media access mechanism (similar to CSMA/CD [8, 9]) is difficult to implement; in the typical network deployment, ONUs cannot detect a collision at the OLT, and providing the architecture with a feedback loop leading to every single ONU is not feasible. Contention-based schemes also have the drawback of providing a nondeterministic service, i.e., node throughput and channel utilization may be described as statistical averages, and hence, there is no guarantee of an ONU getting access to the media in any small interval of time, which means this type of access protocol is ill-suited for delay-sensitive transmissions, such as video conferencing or VoIP. To introduce determinism in the frame delivery, different noncontention schemes based on request/grant mechanisms have been proposed [10-13].

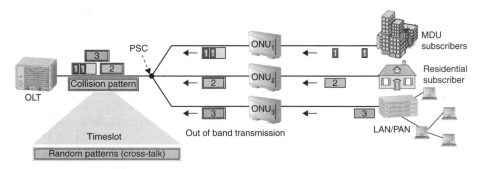

Figure 7.5 Upstream channel transmission in an EPON (M2P operation)—standard TDM-based channel sharing with ONU_3 transmitting out of assigned timeslot

Ongoing Developments

EPONs constitute a giant leap forward, when compared with DSL and cable modem technologies. With an effective data rate of 1 Gbps (1.25 Gbps line rate due to 8B10B encoding performed at the PHY layer) and 16+ subscribers typically served per single EPON system, each ONU is capable of receiving between 15 and 60 Mbps of usable bandwidth in a fully equipped EPON with all ONUs active. In most scenarios, a good fraction of the ONUs will be idle at any given time, and the excess bandwidth will be distributed to the active ONUs via the DBA mechanism, so on average, each customer receives more bandwidth. This performance far exceeds that of DSL and cable modem systems, while remaining highly cost effective. Even so, as more bandwidth-intensive services gain popularity, bandwidth capacity will be reached at some point in the future. Accordingly, it is crucial that EPON continues to evolve so that a smooth path for future upgrades is available. At least four upgrade paths for EPON can be envisioned: (1) increasing the number of individual transmission channels (wavelength upgrade), (2) increasing the data rate, (3) a mixture of (1) and (2), and (4) spatial upgrade.

Wavelength Upgrade

Providing that wavelength division multiplexing (WDM) technology reaches a significant level of maturity in the near future (i.e., achieves cost marks suitable for mass-market FTTH applications), the number of individual wavelength channels in a single EPON could be increased, adding a separate WDM overlay on top of existing burst mode–operated systems. In this scheme, some of the already deployed and active ONUs would be assigned, in a static manner, to a distinct wavelength domain for both upstream and downstream transmission lanes. While the effective data rate on each wavelength would remain the same, there would simply be fewer ONUs to share that raw bandwidth capacity, increasing the bandwidth available per subscriber. The extreme example of this approach would be a WDM PON system wherein each subscriber is allocated unique wavelengths for upstream and downstream transmission. It is still not clear when WDM components will be available at the appropriate prices to make this solution commercially viable. The price of the tuneable laser sources applicable for the ONUs is continuously dropping, allowing for development of colourless subscriber units, though the necessary control electronics, wavelength tracking systems and the need to employ the DWDM channel allocation to assure sufficient number of subscribers are still cost-prohibitive. The complexity of the OLT unit connected with the need for a dedicated receiver per subscriber port as well as highly complicated wavelength allocation plan and the requirement for a special wavelength allocation protocol make the management of WDM PON a real nightmare from the logistic point of view.

DWDM systems, which would be needed for the "λ-per customer" systems just described, operate over a narrow band of frequencies known as the C- and L-bands (between 1530 and 1620 nm). The wavelengths must be tightly bunched together, fitting from 32 to 128 channels in the C- and L-bands. Coarse WDM (CWDM), in contrast, operates on a much wider range of wavelengths (1270–1610 nm), with a maximum of 18 channels separated by 20 nm intervals. Figure 7.6 shows a mapping of the

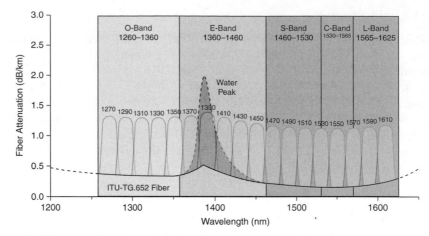

Figure 7.6   ITU-T G.694.2 CWDM wavelength grid

ITU-T G.694.2 CWDM wavelength grid against a standard ITU-T G.652 fiber attenuation curve. The wider spacing of the CWDM bands means that much more economical components can be used in these systems, and currently, there is active interest in adding CWDM to EPON systems to enhance their capacity.

Figure 7.7 presents three possible deployment scenarios for the tree-and-branch topology WDM PON systems. Obviously, other topologies are possible, though it has been proven already that this particular architecture minimizes both fiber deployment as well as splitter count in the PON network [11, 14-17].

Figure 7.7a depicts a tree-and-branch topology with cascaded AWG and PSC elements, where initial wavelength routing is performed in the AWG, multiplexing a number of incoming downstream channels, $\lambda_1 \ldots \lambda_n$, into n output ports. Each AWG output port is connected further on with a PSC performing the power-splitting operation for a single wavelength channel selected previously by the AWG component. This way, all ONUs connected to a given PSC module receive the same downstream channel, λ_3, thus making this scenario a simple CWDM overlay over the standard EPON structure, where ONUs are unaware of any existing multiple wavelength structure in the network. Such an approach has one huge advantage—namely a high degree of backward compatibility with existing PON equipment (no dynamic wavelength tuneability is required for ONUs operating at predefined downstream and upstream channels). Unfortunately, there are more drawbacks to such a system because static wavelength assignment through AWG routing operations causes stock problems for the network operator; ONUs cannot be switched between different domains without retuning the receiver filters and replacing the laser transmitter module. Additionally, the network operator must keep track of the wavelength domain ONU assignment by hand, since the system is unaware of this fact. There are also concerns with the dynamic allocation of resources because in this case, it is virtually impossible to effect this particular function. A particular PSC receives only a single wavelength and splits it into a number of output ports. All connected ONUs are, therefore, forced to operate at this wavelength

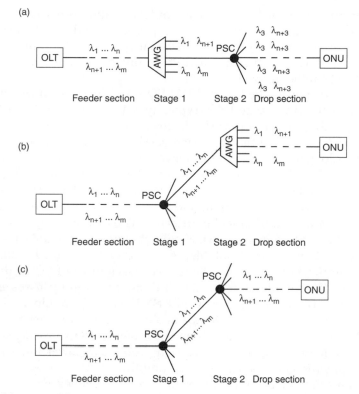

Figure 7.7 Possible tree-and-branch architectures for WDM PON networks

and cannot change the downstream/upstream channel—even if other wavelength channels in the WDM PON system have free resources to offer. It is anticipated that such a static wavelength assignment system is an intermediate solution for operators, with a number of individual PONs deployed in the field, striving to aggregate the system into a more compact form with higher management capabilities.

Figure 7.7b depicts a tree-and-branch topology with cascaded PSC and AWG elements, where the component order is opposite the one just described and depicted in Figure 7.7a. This time the first PSC performs simple power splitting, and assuming a broadband splitter operation, each output port of the PSC will have all the downstream channels, $\lambda_1 \ldots \lambda_n$, which are then subject to the AWG operation, performing wavelength routing from a single input port into n output ports. As such, each AWG output port features a single wavelength from the $\lambda_1 \ldots \lambda_n$ range. With this configuration, each ONU connected to a given AWG belongs to a completely different collision domain (PON instance). This solution has one important advantage: it is more dynamic in the sense that the ONUs in a given area might be assigned to various collision domains, depending on their traffic demand. Unfortunately, such assignment needs to be performed by a qualified technician and requires replacement of the ONU's hardware since the receiver must be tuned and the transmitter module replaced. In other words, the network operator again ends up with stock problems and wavelength quasi-static channel assignment. Additionally, this scenario features a greater number of AWG components, which are still more expensive than PSCs, unless polymer-based, temperature compensated AWG can be utilized.

Figure 7.7c depicts the target WDM PON architecture, in which a long feeder section ends up in the first stage PSC (typically a 1×16 or 1×32 port device), performing power-splitting operations with all downstream channels, $\lambda_1 \ldots \lambda_n$, present at each output port. A short interconnection section follows, terminated in the second-stage PSC module, performing another power-splitting operation. This time the port count depends on the subscriber population and ONU count demand. Typically, 1×16 or 1×32 are the expected splitting factors. In this system, all downstream wavelengths, $\lambda_1 \ldots \lambda_n$, reach each ONU in the system, and thus the ONU receiver must be broadband and must employ a form of tuneable filtering. The disadvantages of this scenario include a high splitting loss in the downstream channel; in a double 1×32 port PSC system, a total of 1024 ports are available, resulting in 10 log 1024 = 30.1 dB of splitting loss (ideal situation) increased by the excess losses in the PSC modules and coupling between the PSC modules and the fiber. Taking the coupling losses as well as fiber attenuation of 0.2 dB/km for standard G.652 SMF with 20 km physical reach (4 dB in total), a total power loss exceeding 35 dB is obtained. Such a power loss level is acceptable in the downstream and results from the inherent PON broadcast policy. It is, however, unacceptable in the upstream direction, where the power loss should be minimized to avoid application of expensive optical amplifiers.

A number of WDM PON proposals are also focused on the elimination of optical sources from the ONU module altogether, since it is expensive and risky (in terms of network security) to let the subscriber modules manage the upstream transmission wavelength. Assuming that for some reason (either deliberately or accidentally) one of the ONU transmitters deviates from the allocated channel, it can degrade not only its but also the adjacent channels. To prevent such a situation from occurring, it has been suggested that all optical sources should be placed in the OLT, so that the ONUs would only modulate the optical carrier delivered in the downstream direction. In certain solutions, the downstream and upstream channels operate at the same wavelength, where the downstream data stream is composed of the OLT data and unmodulated optical carrier slots, which are used by the ONU in accordance with the DBA mechanism to deliver the buffered data towards the OLT module. Such a solution constitutes therefore the so-called shared-source system. Two types of modulators are generally considered as fit for this particular system structure, either an external modulator or a reflective semiconductor optical amplifier (so-called R-SOA).

Raw Data-rate Upgrade

Migration to higher data rates to increase the available bandwidth is perhaps the most straightforward way to increase the supported subscriber population or provide more bandwidth per customer. Over the next few years, the EPON roadmap includes migration to a target data rate of 10 Gbps. With 10 Gbps Ethernet systems already standardized by the IEEE community and advanced research being carried out for 40 Gbps and 100 Gbps Ethernet solutions, increasing the data rate while maintaining the existing wavelength channel count seems to be a pragmatic and attractive solution. During the development of a 10 Gbps EPON [18], the key challenge will be to redefine the cost envelope for EPON system components (both electrical and optical), so that 10 Gbps EPON systems can enjoy the same economies of scale and price reduction trends that today's 1 Gbps EPON systems have enjoyed.

Mixed Upgrade Scenarios

The most interesting upgrade scenarios include both WDM overlay and raw data-rate upgrade, resulting in a significantly increased amount of subscriber accessible bandwidth, while using the best from both system capacity upgrade scenarios. We will briefly discuss two mixed upgrade scenarios here:

- A WDM scenario similar to the one employed in 10GBASE-LX4 systems, where four 2.5 Gbps transmission channels are multiplexed into a single transmission fiber, carrying a total of 10 Gbps of subscriber data and delivering four data streams to each ONU. This scenario allows for each ONU to use lower speed and lower cost electronic circuitry, although it also requires four times the number of receivers and requires data stream–recovery processing. Such a solution is, therefore, most attractive when deploying 10 Gbps EPON systems over older outside plant (OSP), where dispersion is significant and serial 10 Gbps operation is difficult.

- In another possible upgrade scenario, related to the one above, each ONU may contain a single transceiver module tuned to receive one of the four downstream wavelengths, thus providing 2.5 times the downstream capacity of today's EPON.

A simple spatial upgrade might be achieved simply by taking a subset of ONUs from one EPON and relocating this subset onto a new EPON. In this scenario, a new trunk fiber is deployed from the CO, spanning all the way to a new PSC, to which some branches are reattached. To avoid the construction costs associated with two fiber deployments, this upgrade fiber can be predeployed at the time of the original deployment.

Alternatively, some network operators deploy EPONs by placing the splitter in the central office. This EPON configuration will require as much fiber as in point-to-point all-fiber (AF) networks, but it will still require only one transceiver in the OLT. This allows much higher equipment densities, which is typically important in COs. In this scenario, moving ONUs from one PON to another to balance traffic loads is a simple matter of reconfiguring the access network at the fiber patch panel.

Initial Stages of Development of 10G EPONs

The effective data rate of 1 Gbps supported by the legacy IEEE 802.3ah compliant EPONs is already not considered sufficiently future proof to assure revenue growth within the next few years, mainly due to increased customer demand for bandwidth intensive applications and explosive utilization of HD-TV and online gaming, once available in the coverage area. Thus, development of higher capacity EPON systems was advocated in 2006 during one of the IEEE plenary meetings [18], resulting in the initial establishment of the 10G EPON Study Group. This Study Group quickly identified the market potential and evaluated the technical feasibility of the future 10G EPON systems, resulting in submission of the project authorization request (PAR) and its subsequent approval at the subsequent IEEE Plenary meeting. Effectively, the 10G EPON Study Group was officially transformed into 10G EPON task force (TF), identified as IEEE 802.3av, which is chartered with development and standardization of 10G EPON systems, providing increased channel capacity for both upstream and downstream channels, while maintaining the logical layer intact, taking advantage of the already existing specification of MPCP and DBA agent, which will remain compatible with legacy 1 Gbps EPONs.

The following system architecture evaluation process revealed that the future 10G EPON equipment must provide a gradual evolution path from the currently deployed 1 Gbps equipment, thus both symmetric and asymmetric data rates must be supported for both downstream and upstream channels. Since this evolution inherently assumes coexistence with legacy IEEE 802.3ah compliant equipment on the same PON plant, the 10G EPON TF must therefore resolve a number of technical issues, including the wavelength allocation issues for both data channels in a satisfactory manner, providing feasible technical solutions, especially in the upstream channel, as indicated below. As for this moment, no motions regarding the coexistence issues are officially approved by the TF. Nevertheless, a strong consensus exists in the group regarding the following issues:

- coexistence is mandatory to assure smooth transition path from 1 Gbps to 10 Gbps equipment and to avoid a significant one time investment into such a cost-sensitive market (CAPEX);

- wavelength allocation plan for 10 Gbps EPON systems must take into account existence of 1 Gbps equipment on the same PON plant for both downstream and upstream channels;

- the said wavelength allocation plan must also account for the existence of a downstream analog video delivery service, which will most likely be maintained in the future 10G EPON systems, mainly due to already existing equipment and significant CAPEX investment;

- due to incompatible data rates (1 Gbps EPONs use 8B/10B encoding increasing the data rate to 1.25 Gbps while 10 Gbps EPONs will most likely use 64B/66B encoding with PMD level data rate of 10.3125 Gbps), the downstream channels for the two EPON systems will be WDM multiplexed, with 1 Gbps using 1490 nm ± 10 nm window and the 10 Gbps using a currently undefined window, allocated between 1500 and 1600 nm, depending on the laser availability, power budget,

ONU triplexer design, filter requirements, and so on. The downstream channel cannot utilize dual rate transmission in a single wavelength channel due to lack of burst mode transmission i.e., the OLT sends towards the ONUs a continuous data stream, consisting of IDLE characters when there is no real data to send.

- the upstream channel coexistence will most likely be resolved via TDM multiplexing, where different data rate bursts will be received by the OLT, identified and then processed accordingly (the so-called dual rate burst mode transmission). The selected solution presents a number of technical hurdles which will have to be overcome, such as burst data rate detection, adjustment of trans-amplifier gain, and so on, and are currently under intensive study in the formed ad-hoc groups. The dual rate burst mode transmission in the upstream channel is considered a viable solution mainly due to the proximity of zero chromatic dispersion point for the G.652 SMF which is the most common type of optical fibre used in PON systems.

Since the transition process from legacy 1 Gbps equipment towards fully symmetric 10 Gbps network will be gradual in most cases and will require significant modifications of the active equipment in the deployed EPON, it is prudent to be aware of a number of technical hurdles which lie ahead in this process. The 1G and 10G EPON coexistence requirement will inherently result in the creation and deployment of a complex PON systems, where two partially independent transmission systems share a single PON plant, thus resulting in the need to share both downstream and upstream channels in a way which eliminates cross-talk and signal quality degradation. As indicated before, the downstream 1G and 10G data streams will be WDM multiplexed, resulting in two independent, continuous P2MP channels, separated by a sufficiently large bandwidth gap allowing for their uninterrupted operation under any temperature conditions accounted for in the IEEE standard. The 1G downstream link will therefore remain centered at 1490 nm with the 20 nm window size, while the new 10G downstream link will have to be allocated somewhere in the 1500–1600 nm window, where most of the group participants seem to agree that channel allocation above the current analog video service delivery band is a better option (above 1560 nm), mainly due to limited non-linear impairments and lower 10G signal degradation. The commercial availability of laser and receiver units was already proven by the TF members, indicating that such a channel allocation can be supported using existing technology.

Security Mechanisms for EPONs

EPONs have very specific security requirements due to the broadcast character of the transmission medium. The downstream broadcast channel is potentially available to any party interested in eavesdropping, since, in principle, this only requires disabling the LLID filtering rules at the ONU and operating the module in a so-called promiscuous mode with access to all downstream data flows. It is expected that service providers, using EPONs as a base for delivery of triple-play services, will ensure sufficient levels of subscriber data privacy. It is necessary, therefore, that EPON have effective countermeasures for eavesdropping (either global or local) and theft of service (ToS), wherein a malicious user impersonates another EPON subscriber and uses network resources (services, bandwidth, etc.) at the victim's expense.

Eavesdropping in EPONs   In EPONs, eavesdropping is always possible in the downstream direction simply by operating one of the registered ONUs in the so-called promiscuous mode. Since each ONU in the network receives a copy of every single downstream packet transmitted by the OLT (more correctly, broadcast by the OLT), no extensive modifications are required in the ONU hardware to enable its operation in a malicious mode. All that a network attacker has to do in this case is simply disable LLID filtering rules and enjoy unrestricted access to all information transmitted in the downstream channel. What makes the situation worse is that the employed eavesdropping method is completely passive, undetectable at the OLT level, and does not trigger any visible side-effects in network structure or behavior. Therefore, the attack might go unnoticed and even worse, continue undisturbed 24/7. This definitely violates all the provisions for data confidentiality and privacy.

In the upstream channel, subscriber data are more secure since, inherently, the network architecture prevents other subscribers from eavesdropping transmission contents from other stations at the hardware level. As such, the upstream channel is considered secure, as far as passive monitoring is concerned. Only the OLT receives ONU transmissions and is aware of the activity periods of individual ONUs.

Additionally, the PSC unit itself constitutes a significant security threat because this device is typically manufactured as a fully reciprocal device. Therefore, even though only one port of the device is connected to the trunk channel, many more ports are available but remain unconnected. A custom-designed device might be connected to such an unused port of the PSC and deliver an optical signal to a traffic analyzer, thereby providing access to subscriber and system sensitive data. However, progress in PSC packaging technology currently prevents this eavesdropping method by applying so-called secure packaging, where only one trunk port and a predefined number of drop section ports are available, while others are hidden in a hermetic casing. Access to other ports is disabled, and typically, device destruction is required to open the casing if attempting to gain unauthorized access to the upstream channel signal. Figure 7.8 presents an example of a modern PSC module in a secure casing, with one input and a predefined number of output ports.

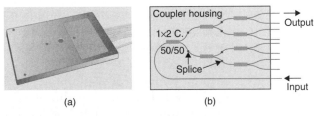

(a)   (b)

Figure 7.8   (a) Actual PSC unit with secure casing and (b) its internal structure

Denial-of-Service in EPONs   A denial-of-service (DoS) attack causes loss of standard services observed by all registered and active subscribers and potential loss of network connectivity if the network equipment is under attack, or severe service quality deterioration if only one local machine is subject to such an intrusion. Typically, the attack is carried out by consuming a significant share of the available bandwidth and network resources in the targeted system, overloading any existing pieces of hardware with strenuous and in many cases infinite tasks, resulting in denial of service for legitimate subscribers and/or deterioration in QoS, from a user's point of view. A standard DoS attack can be perpetrated in a number of ways, comprising three major types of security breaches:

- Consumption of computational resources, such as bandwidth, disk space, or CPU time.

- Disruption of system sensitive configuration information, such as routing information, LLIDs, MAC addresses, and VLAN tags.

- Disruption of network connectivity at the physical level, for example, by flooding the upstream channel with a strong laser signal, thereby preventing useful transmissions from any legitimate subscriber.

The simplest type of DoS attack that can be perpetrated in PONs, and more specifically in EPONs, is a simple network connectivity disruption, which, in this particular case, is limited to turning on a strong laser signal source transmitting in the upstream channel at the proper wavelength, coherent with the selected upstream transmission window.

Masquerading and Theft-of-Service in EPONs   A ToS attack occurs, in general, when one subscriber attempts to impersonate another legitimate network user by forging his digital signature and attempting to use network resources (bandwidth, access to specific premium services, etc.) that are not billed to the impersonator's account or are not available to the attacker in the first place. It must be noted here that the OLT provides a digital identity watermark for each ONU during its registration phase (LLID [7]), which is later used during bilateral transmissions (upstream/downstream channel) and is inserted by both ONU and OLT in transmitted data frames. However, transmission of such vital and security-sensitive data in plain-text format provides a perfect means for launching a masquerading attack, followed most typically by ToS, where the malicious subscriber simply forges his own LLID, substituting it with the legitimate LLID of another ONU, while transmitting upstream toward the OLT. Assuming the subscriber in question has sufficient knowledge of EPON hardware, this step is not any more difficult than disabling LLID filtering, which is required for passive traffic monitoring, as examined previously.

Of course, faking LLID and transmitting frames at a random moment in time is no good since the upstream channel is slotted and access time is strictly supervised by the central OLT controller. Thus, such an impersonator must also have the capability to passively monitor all downstream traffic, filter incoming data streams against LLIDs, and specifically, track and decode GATE MPCP DUs, which carry information on scheduled transmission windows, specifically their times and sizes. ToS and masquerading attacks are typically hard to detect once under way because a malicious user is perceived as a legitimate one, and the EPON system cannot properly identify a security breach in this case.

Proposed Security Mechanisms for EPONs   A number of security mechanisms have been proposed for EPONs, ranging from simple and straightforward subscriber payload protection using standard AES encryption (with either 128- or 256-bit long keys), to solutions based on periodic key churning [19, 20] to proposals to use complex authentication servers (RADIUS [19, 21]) and higher-level security mechanisms (IPSec [22], for example). It is clear that link-layer security should be provided for a number of reasons:

- Because most of the existing higher-level protocols assume, by default, that the link layer provides a secure transmission channel, it is expected that EPONs provide inherent subscriber security mechanisms at Layer 2, without the need to employ any solutions at Layer 3 and above.

- Because end subscribers are typically used to having inherent security provided by DSL lines, they cannot be expected to become security-aware IT experts overnight when switching from their legacy-leased copper-based lines to EPON connections; extra measures must be taken at the link level to assure a smooth transition for typical ISP customers, without privacy degradation and any security concerns for private and sensitive data.

- Huge enterprise LANs, which typically operate in the P2P mode providing inherent security (additionally supervised by experienced IT staff), can be open suddenly to all types of system-level security breaches once linked to the WAN level using insecure EPON connections. It is, therefore, imperative to provide inherent data privacy, authentication, and payload security; otherwise, business customers might stick with exiting leased lines.

Additionally, many opponents of link-level security mechanisms indicate that existing solutions such as secure socket layer (SSL) are more than sufficient to handle data transaction security, though again certain issues need to be emphasized at this point:

- Large servers using the SSL protocol need to handle a dramatically growing amount of data traffic. Because hardware resources (especially CPU processing power) are limited, a certain point might simply be saturated with a concurrent number of decryption requests (for incoming data streams) as well as encryption requests (for outgoing data streams), forcing the server to maintain huge lists of valid keys on a per flow basis. Additionally, such machines are typically very vulnerable to overflow attacks, where a malicious attacker attempts to overload the server key list by opening a great number of SSL connections, forcing the server to maintain an excessively long key list and forcing disk cashing, overall system performance degradation, and so on, and eventually system reset triggered by overflow errors.

Such a scenario does not need to be a result of a malicious activity, since, due to the number of concurrent SSL requests, the ever-growing data traffic capacity might eventually cause this situation on its own.

- A significant share of everyday rudimentary data transmissions protocols do not provide means for per-data transaction protection. Global keys and security mechanisms are typically utilized and can be easily compromised in, for example, DNS data transfers, PPP authentication messages, and instant messaging systems, leading to an increasing unwillingness to use them in the first place.

- Higher-level security protocols in internal EPON data transactions (between ONU and OLT) have also been proposed, though such a proposal has obvious shortcomings: in order to assure full system interoperability, a single security mechanism would have to be selected and agreed upon for implementation; additionally, ONUs and OLTs would need to inherently become IP packet routers, operating at protocol stack Layer 3 and above, and thus limiting Ethernet versatility while not preventing such simple forms of attacks as data mining, passive monitoring, and so on, which can be avoided if a strict link-layer security mechanism is employed.

In order to avoid most common problems with server overload, transition problems, system interoperability, security threats, and lack of data privacy, it is necessary to make PONs, and EPONs specifically, immune to most common types of security breaches, including passive monitoring, data mining, masquerading, ToS, and certain variants of DoS or distributed DoS (DDoS) attacks. Hardware-level attacks cannot be avoided without introducing a dynamic wavelength management system, which is currently both expensive and unwieldy. A lot of work is, therefore, required to provide viable and simultaneously efficient means for assuring subscriber data privacy and authentication, as well as antimonitoring measures, preventing any attempts at passive data-mining techniques, which typically constitute the first step in launching a more destructive attack on the EPON system.

Economic Assessment

Because of the wide variation in service requirements, costs, regulation, and degrees of modernization among service provider networks worldwide, it is not possible to construct a simple business case for EPON that would hold in all or perhaps even most instances. Instead, in this section, we will highlight some of the fundamental nontechnical issues surrounding a real EPON deployment. While it is safe to assume that a real business case would include most of these issues, we cannot predict how any one service provider might weigh the various factors.

Overall Installation Cost per Subscriber

A detailed cost model for an EPON deployment will include costs for central office equipment, fiber cable, splitters, supporting infrastructure (conduit and utility poles), construction costs at the subscriber's location, and customer premise equipment (CPE) costs.

Depending on the modeling assumptions, these itemized costs can vary dramatically. Let's take central office costs as an example: is an allocated share of the OLT the only cost included; or must the model also account for the costs of the PSTN gateway, the video distribution network, connections to ISPs, central office real estate and facilities, and so on? In other words, which elements of the network must be charged to the EPON deployment and which can be treated as sunk costs? Similar decisions must be made in modeling the costs of the outside plant, and it is worth noting that outside plant costs traditionally dominate such a deployment, with labor costs representing the largest component. Even though we cannot construct a generic bottom-up model here, we can get a top-down estimate for the magnitude of per-subscriber costs by using a 2005 published report on planned fiber-access spending by NTT, which stated that NTT foresaw investing $42 billion over a period of five years to provide fiber-based services to 30 million homes and businesses [23]. This leads to a simple estimate of $1410 per subscriber. Although this single number does not shed any light on the constituent costs or on what will be treated as sunk costs for this deployment, it is in line with typical estimates for EPON/FTTH per-subscriber costs.

Cost of the CPE

As with other mass-market broadband networks (e.g., xDSL or cable modem), one of the most closely watched costs in EPON deployments is the cost of the CPE, and some specific comments are warranted here. Early indications are that as EPON ramps into high volume, it is following a cost reduction curve very similar to that of DSL: approximately three years after the mid-2004 adoption of the IEEE 802.3ah standard, EPON equipment costs have decreased more than 50 percent. Concurrently, the cost of the most expensive ONU subsystem, namely the optical module, has fallen by 70 percent or more. There is good reason to believe that, as it matures, EPON CPE costs will be similar to those of other mass-market broadband-access devices.

EPON vs. Other PON Solutions

EPON is frequently compared with other PON solutions, most commonly with WDM PON and the ITU-T systems (APON, BPON, and GPON). Compared with the IEEE and ITU-T systems, WDM PON is in the earliest stages of development and commercialization (initial prototypes based on tuneable lasers, injection mode locked FP LDs and RSOAs are commercially available as for July 2007) and is not a single, well-defined solution. Rather, it is best thought of as a broad category of proprietary systems that vary markedly in terms of basic technology. As a rule, they are "λ-per-customer" systems, meaning there is a laser and a receiver in the OLT for every customer, instead of a single laser and a single receiver for the entire PON. This additional cost, along with the need for much more sophisticated WDM functionality in the system, leads to significantly higher per-subscriber costs when compared to either IEEE or ITU-T solutions.

The ITU-T systems, specified by the ITU-T G.983.x and G.984.x series, were originally designed as the access portion of an end-to-end multiservice ATM network, and this heritage permeates these platforms. At the physical layer, ITU-T PON systems use SONET/SDH requirements for timing, scrambling, and so on, which leads to intrinsically higher per-subscriber costs when compared to EPON. For example, the SONET scrambler must be able to tolerate up to 71 consecutive, identical digits, which presents a more difficult clock and data recovery (CDR) problem than that found in EPON, which uses 8B/10B. To deal with the jitter accumulation problems and tighter jitter transfer function requirements of GPON, large analog filters with low-time constants are needed, the system must deal with baseline wander due to an unbalanced line code, and more expensive DC-coupled optical receivers are needed. Additionally, the shorter upstream burst overhead of GPON requires faster CDR and gain adjustment than does EPON, which translates into a more expensive OLT receiver, while the ONUs must include much faster lasers with significantly decreased $laser_{on}/laser_{off}$ periods (approximately 50 times shorter than the ones adopted for EPON grade ONU equipment).

Lastly, the requirement for adjustable ONU laser power levels increases the relative cost and complexity of the GPON ONU. At the protocol layer, GPON uses fixed framing, and packets are fragmented at frame boundaries; hence, bidirectional SAR functions are needed for every flow. This adds considerable complexity and cost (in the form of buffering) to the system, especially at the OLT, which may need to support as many as 4000 flows simultaneously. In short, any business case that selects GPON must be able to tolerate significantly higher equipment prices than would be needed for an EPON deployment.

EPON vs. Alternate Architectures

Business cases for EPON often include comparisons with other broadband access architectures, usually either triple-play xDSL or HFC. As discussed previously, the majority of the cost for an EPON deployment is in construction of the outside plant, and this is true for xDSL and HFC networks also. For new construction, the costs for the three architectures are similar in some aspects because there is little difference in terms of trenching or cabling costs. For xDSL and HFC networks, however, there are additional significant costs associated with the placement of active electronics in the outside plant: right-of-ways for cabinets/enclosures must be secured; weatherproof cabinets/enclosures, slicing vaults, and so on, must be purchased and installed; and an overlay powering network must be constructed for the remote electronics. The additional cost for placing active electronics in the field will vary, depending directly on the average bandwidth requirement per subscriber, which in turn depends on the service model for the network.

Stated in another way, if a service provider intends to offer a rich and competitive spectrum of advanced services on either an xDSL or HFC network, more bandwidth per subscriber will be required, which means the active electronics must be placed deeper in the outside plant (smaller fiber-fed subnetworks). This will increase the number of fiber-fed powered terminals and the construction cost of the network. Partially offsetting the higher costs of network construction for xDSL and HFC is the fact that CPE costs currently are lower for these two mature technologies, when compared to EPON. However, as discussed previously, it is expected that differences in CPE price will narrow quickly as EPON volumes increase. Depending on the projected service mix and other cost-model details, side-by-side per-subscriber cost estimates for EPON vs. xDSL or HFC typically lie in a range from near-parity to a 50 percent premium for a network with active electronics in the outside plant.

Equally or more important than the initial construction costs just discussed, however, are the ongoing operational costs, and in this regard EPON possesses clear advantages. The fact that the remote electronics in xDSL and HFC networks, which are in high-stress environments, will require regular service and replacement, and that these ongoing operational costs are borne by xDSL and HFC networks and not by EPON networks, is obvious. What is perhaps less obvious is the significant cost associated with providing power to the remote active nodes, which can account for 30–40 percent of the total lifecycle cost of the access network, depending again on the service model, the bandwidth-per-customer requirements, and so on. In EPON, this high cost is taken from the network operator and assumed by the subscriber, thus providing a powerful, inherent advantage to EPON deployments when competing with xDSL or HFC network operators.

Evolving Service Models and Revenue-Stream Replacement

The current transition in telecommunications and cable services from narrow-band telephony and broadcast television to VoIP and video-on-demand and the emergence of new (or newly independent) players in broadband access, including, in particular, the entertainment industry, is rapidly driving existing service models and the underpinning networks into obsolescence. As income from payphones, traditional landline voice services, leased-line business services, and so on, erode, and as the price of Internet access declines, service providers are under enormous pressure to find new revenue streams. The focus has shifted naturally to advanced television and video services, which, as a class, will consume perhaps two orders of magnitude more sustained and dedicated bandwidth per customer, when compared to traditional services. Given that we do not yet know the point at which bandwidth demand will stop increasing, the strategic risks associated with deploying new xDSL or HFC access networks are apparent. These architectures have hard, upper limits on per-customer bandwidth, and if the per-customer bandwidth proves to be insufficient as the services evolve, the service provider must either upgrade the network (expensive and time consuming) or lose market share. In other words, in building a business case for an EPON deployment, the proper question may not be, "what is the cost of deploying an EPON-based access network?" but rather, "what is the cost of not deploying such a network?"

Vendors Promoting This Solution

The EPON market is a rich ecosystem with multiple system vendors focusing on various market segments, starting from chip vendors through system developers to network developers and planners. EPONs today are already under extensive deployment, with approximately 6+ million lines in operation, while the total deployed CO port capacity exceeds 16+ million units with the growth rate exceeding 300,000 ports per month. So far, the main EPON deployments are being carried out by Asian carriers, namely KDDI, K-Opticom, Korea Telecom, NTT, and Softbank BB. Other national carriers on the remaining continents, including the Americas and Europe, are mainly at the evaluation stage.

Following is a nonexhaustive list of EPON-specific component and hardware manufacturers, which is meant only to show the breadth of the manufacturing base (company names listed in alphabetic order):

Vendor	Solution/Product Name	Comments
Delta Electronics, ETRI, Fiberxon, Fujitsu, Furukawa, Hitachi/Lightron, NEC, Sumitomo, Vitesse, Zenko	Optics, transceivers, and PHY	
ETRI, Centillium, Conexant, Immenstar, GW, Passave, Teknovus	EPON ASIC vendors	Both OLT and ONU chipsets
Allied Telesyn, Alloptic, Corecess, Dasan/Siemens, Entrisphere, Fiberhome, Fujitsu, Furukawa, Hitachi, Huawei, Hyundai, Mitsubishi, OKI-Fujikura, Salira, Samsung, Sumitomo, UTStarcom, ZTE	System developers and integrators	
Agilent, Fujitsu	Test equipment	EPON-specific test equipment

References

1. S. Clavenna, "Metro Optical Ethernet," Lightreading (www.lightreading.com), 2000.

2. IEEE, "802.3," IEEE, Standard 2005.

3. J. Case, M. Fedor, M. Schoffstall, and J. Davin, "A Simple Network Management Protocol – RFC 1067," University of Tennessee at Knoxville, NYSERNet, Inc., Rensselaer Polytechnic Institute, Proteon, Inc. 1988.

4. D. Reed, "Copper Evolution," Federal Communications Commission, Technological Advisory Council III, Washington, DC, USA, report, available at http://www.fcc.gov/oet/tac/TAC_III_04_17_03/Copper_Evolution.ppt, 2003.

5. M. Burke, "Ellacoya Data Shows Web Traffic Overtakes Peer-to-Peer (P2P) as Largest Percentage of Bandwidth on the Network," online report, available at: http://www.ellacoya.com/news/pdf/2007/NXTcommEllacoyaMediaAlert.pdf 2007.

6. K. G. Coffman and A. M. Odlyzko, *Internet growth: Is there a "Moore's Law" for data traffic?*: Kluwer, 2001.

7. IEEE, "802.3ah – Clause 64 – Multi-Point MAC Control," IEEE, Standard 2004.

8. C. Chang-Joon, E. Wong, and R. S. Tucher, "Optical CSMA/CD Media Access Scheme for Ethernet Over Passive Optical Network," *IEEE Photonics Technology Letters*, vol. 14, pp. 711–713, 2002.

9. C. Chae, E. Wong, and R. Tuckker, "Ethernet over passive optical network based on optical CSMA/CD media access technique," *IEEE Photonics Technology Letters*, vol. 14, pp. 711–713, 2002.

10. G. Kramer, B. Mukherjee, and G. Pesavento, "IPACT: A Dynamic Protocol for an Ethernet PON (EPON)," *IEEE Communications Magazine*, vol. 40, pp. 74–80, 2002.

11. G. Kramer, B. Mukherjee, and G. Pesavento, "Interleaved Polling with Adaptive Cycle Time (IPACT): A Dynamic Bandwidth Distribution Scheme in an Optical Access Network," *Photonic Network Communications*, vol. 4, pp. 89–107, 2002.

12. G. Kramer, A. Banerjee, N. K. Singhal, B. Mukherjee, S. Dixit, and Y. Ye, "Fair Queueing With Service Envelopes (FQSE): A Cousin-Fair Hierarchical Scheduler for Subscriber Access Networks," *IEEE Journal on Selected Areas in Communications*, vol. 22, pp. 1497–1513, 2004.

13. M. Ma, Y. Zhu, and T. H. Cheng, "A bandwidth guaranteed polling MAC protocol for Ethernet passive optical networks," presented at IEEE Infocom 2003, San Francisco, CA, USA, 2003.

14. G. Kramer and B. Mukherjee, "Design and Analysis of an Access Network based on PON Technology," 2000.

15. G. Kramer, B. Mukherjee, and G. Pesavento, "Ethernet PON (ePON): Design and Analysis of an Optical Access Network," *Photonic Network Communications*, vol. 3, pp. 307–319, 2001.

16. G. Kramer and G. Pesavento, "Enabling Next Generation Ethernet Access with Ethernet Passive Optical Networks," presented at NFOEC, Orlando, 2003.

17. G. Kramer and G. Pesavento, "EPON: Challenges in Building a Next Generation Access Network," presented at 1st International Workshop on Community Networks and FTTH/P/x, Dallas, 2003.

18. IEEE 802.3, "Call For Interest: 10 Gbps PHY for EPON," online report, available at: http://www.ieee802.org/3/cfi/0306_1/cfi_0306_1.pdf, 2006.

19. J. Kim, "Authentication and Privacy in EPON," IEEE802.3ah Ethernet in the first mile, White Paper, 2002.

20. O. Haran, "Ethernet PON, Security Considerations," IEEE802.3ah Ethernet in the first mile, White Paper, 2001.

21. K. Murakami, Y. Fujimoto, and O. Yoshihara, "Authentication and Encryption in EPON," IEEE802.3ah Ethernet in the first mile, White Paper, 2002.

22. Y. L. Goff, Y. Fujimoto, K. Murakami, O. Haran, and O.-P. Hiironen, "Encryption layer comparison," IEEE802.3ah Ethernet in the first mile, White Paper, 2002.

23. H. Shinohara, "Broadband access in Japan: rapidly growing FTTH market," *IEEE Communications Magazine,* vol. 43, pp. 72–78, 2005.

Fiber and WDM

by Dr. Nasir Ghani and Dr. Ashwin Gumaste

Fiber-optic cable represents one of the best-known transmission mediums, offering unmatched bandwidth-distance scalability. In addition, this technology has excellent *electromagnetic/radio frequency interference (EMI/RFI)* immunity, very good protection against intrusion, and minimal long-term maintenance costs. As a result, fiber has become the solution of choice for large-scale, metro-regional, and backbone core infrastructures, where the prime focus is on achieving low-cost per bit. More recently, new build-outs are pushing this medium closer into the last-mile.

Concurrently, Ethernet has evolved over the last quarter century, becoming the preferred networking technology in the enterprise/campus local area network (LAN) space. Ethernet has proven low-costs, simplicity of installation and use, and minimal maintenance overheads. Today, this technology is widely used to interconnect a myriad of end-user devices—computers, servers, storage devices, and printers—and shipped ports now number in the hundreds of millions. In all, this gives Ethernet unmatched ubiquity and economies of scale. With growing end-user bandwidth demands, however, there is a strong desire to migrate Ethernet's reach across larger metropolitan and wide area network (MAN/WAN) domains. Traditionally, such Ethernet "extension" has been done by mapping over legacy "voice-centric" Time Division Multiplexing (TDM) infrastructures, for example, Synchronous Optical NETworking (SONET)/ Synchronous Digital Hierarchy (SDH) networks. Nevertheless, the operational and scalability limitations here are well-documented, and this has led to a renewed focus on improving fiber-Ethernet integration.

Over the past decade, there have been many crucial developments in fiber-based Ethernet transmission. Most notably, two key trends have been advances in optical networking, namely Wavelength Division Multiplexing (WDM) and the standardization of new "optical Ethernet" interfaces. These technologies now permit highly streamlined native-mode transmission of Ethernet frames across extensive carrier infrastructures. Specifically, two major approaches have evolved, namely direct

Ethernet over fiber (EoF) and *Ethernet over WDM (EoWDM)*. In light of this broad-based evolution, the very notion of Ethernet has been transformed from that of an interface/switching technology into a genuine *carrier service offering* spanning the full LAN-MAN-WAN geographic range.

This chapter looks at the delivery of Carrier Ethernet services over fiber-optic networks. Initially, the main technologies and standards in the area are reviewed. Subsequently the motivations behind the development of Carrier Ethernet are presented, and the EoF and EoWDM concepts introduced. In addition, the best-fit scenarios for these solutions are identified along with their benefits and shortcomings. Finally, ongoing and future developments are discussed along with economic assessments and a brief vendor survey. Note that there have been many recent developments in Ethernet over SONET (EoS), which also uses underlying fiber-based transmission. However, these avenues are more appropriately discussed in Chapter 11, and the focus herein is strictly upon native Ethernet transport over fiber cables.

Technology Description

EoF and EoWDM embody native Ethernet transmission over fiber and/or fiber-optic networks. These streamlined approaches can greatly reduce network complexity and lower overall service cost. In order to introduce these concepts, however, this section first reviews the latest advances in some crucial technology areas—WDM networks, fiber-optic Ethernet interfaces, and network control and management frameworks. The implementation of carrier services via EoF and EoWDM is then treated in the subsequent sections.

Advances in Optical Component Technologies

Commercial fiber optic transmission traces its origins to the 1970s when older *multi-mode fiber (MMF)* systems, as shown in Figure 8.1, were used to deliver interconnectivity between voice-switching exchanges. Here, associated bit-rates were tied to older *plesio-chronous digital hierarchy (PDH)* standards such as E1 (2.048 Mbps). Subsequently, the late 1980s and early 1990s saw concertive carrier efforts to standardize SONET/SDH technology, with interface speeds scaling from the low tens of megabits (STS-1, E3) to multigigabits (OC-192/STM-64). These advances were enabled by two key factors—high-speed electronic hardware and improved *single-mode fiber (SMF)* media, as shown in Figure 8.2. The telecom-bubble era of the late 1990s to early 2000s saw an even more profound evolution with the commercialization of WDM technology. This approach delivered unmatched terabits-per-fiber scalability by transmitting multiple channels (called *wavelengths*) of light in unused SMF spectral bands. Indeed, *dense WDM (DWDM)* now forms the foundation of modern optical networks, and key advances have come in crucial enabling component technologies, for example, passive elements (fibers, couplers, filters) and active elements (lasers, amplifiers, switches) [1]. Although the DWDM market has experienced severe realignment in the post-bubble era, it has since returned to normalcy and is now experiencing steady growth [2]. The key component advances are summarized in Table 8.1.

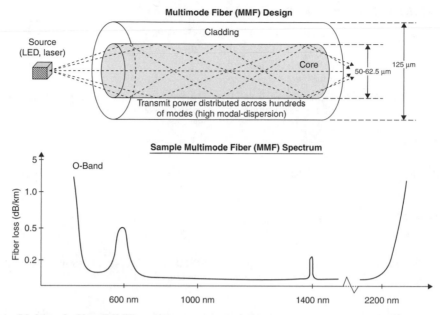

Figure 8.1   Multimode fiber (MMF) overview

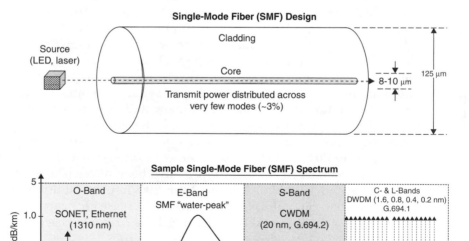

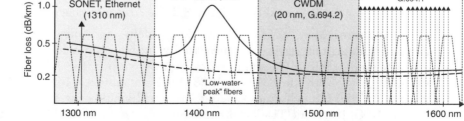

Figure 8.2   Single-mode fiber (SMF) overview

TABLE 8.1   **DWDM Enabling Component Technologies**

Component	Function	Technologies	Maturity	Cost
Fixed lasers	Transmitters, pump EDFA, and Raman amplifiers	DFB, external modulation	Very high	High
Tunable lasers	Transmitters, pump EDFA, and Raman amplifiers	External cavity laser, tunable VCSEL, two/three-section DBR, laser arrays	Medium	High
Amplifiers	Regenerate optical signals	Erbium doped fiber/waveguide amp (EDFA, EDWA), Raman	High	High
Fixed filters	Multiplex/demultiplex wavelengths, equalize gain, remove noise	Thin film, arrayed waveguide grating, Bragg grating	High	Low
Tunable filters	Multiplex/demultiplex wavelengths, equalize gain, remove noise	Fabry-Perot, Mach Zender interferometer, acousto-optic	Medium	Medium
Optical switches	Lightpath routing, protection switching	MEMS, liquid crystal, lithium niobate, SOA, bubble-jet	Medium-low	High

- **Optical fiber**   The main physical difference between SMF and MMF types is in their core thicknesses. Namely, MMF features much wider cores than SMF, e.g., 50–62.5 μm versus 8–10 μm, and this in turn induces multiple transmission modes (see Figures 8.1 and 8.2). Therefore, achieving high bit-rate transmission over MMF is very distance-limited owing to severe *differential mode delay (DMD)* effects. Hence, most MAN deployment networks use SMF (ITU-T G.652), which gives multiterahertz transmission windows. In particular, SMF is ideal for single channel transmission in the 1310 nm range since it has relatively low loss (0.5 dB/km) and zero chromatic dispersion [1]. As a result, many standalone SONET/SDH and Ethernet systems operate at this wavelength. Furthermore, SMF has even lower attenuation in the 1550 nm window (0.2–0.3 db/km), albeit with variable (wavelength-dependent) dispersion. The latter characteristic poses notable chromatic dispersion challenges for bit-rates over 10 Gbps and requires compensation for spans over 60 km. Hence, newer *non-zero dispersion shifted fiber (NZDSF)* and *negative dispersion fiber (NDF)* types have been developed, delivering extended uncompensated long-haul reaches over 200 km. In addition, various "metro-optimized" fibers have also been developed to increase fiber capacity by removing the 1350–1450 nm "water-peak" (see Figure 8.2), i.e., *low water-peak fiber (LWPF)* [3].

- **Laser transmitters**   SMF transmission is done using laser transmitters, and advanced integration techniques have yielded narrow line-width sources with very good thermal stability. To standardize channel values, the ITU-T has defined a wavelength grid for the SMF C (1525–1565 nm) and L (1570–1610 nm) bands using 100 or 50 GHz channel spacing. This grid yields over 100 wavelengths per fiber at 10 Gbps each (ITU-T G.694.1), and new "hyper-WDM" 25 GHz spacing is also available. Now a variety of laser types have been developed. Namely, directly modulated *distributed feedback lasers (DFB)* can deliver 2.5 Gbps speeds across metro domains up to 100 km. Meanwhile more powerful (costly) externally modulated variants can overcome dispersion issues at 10 Gbps speeds. After many years of development, tunable lasers have also come to market. These devices enable significant services automation by allowing carriers to select transmission wavelengths automatically. This effectively eliminates the need to stock/maintain fixed wavelength transponder (sparing) packs, lowering overall operations costs. This is a key point given that laser transponders tend to dominate DWDM economics. Moreover, market pressures and cost innovations have allowed full-band tunable lasers to be priced at nominal premiums over their fixed counterparts [2].

■ **Optical amplifiers** The development of wideband optical amplifiers has been another key driver of DWDM growth, most notably C- and L-band *erbium-doped fiber amplifiers (EDFA)* [1]. These devices deliver vast improvements in span lengths and curtail the need for costly per-channel electronic (SONET/SDH) regeneration. The net result has been a tremendous reduction in the cost-per-bit-per-mile. For example, commercial EDFA solutions offer very good noise/gain flatness across the C- and L-bands and increased 200–600 km reach. In addition some vendors also offer smaller, more cost-effective, subband EDFA devices to boost smaller wavelength groups, i.e., *amplets*. Moreover, many new designs also feature fully integrated *automatic gain control (AGC)* power balancing. Overall, the inherent transparency of optical amplification facilitates the coexistence of multiple protocol types over a single fiber-plant—a huge advantage. Note that many researchers today are also studying wider-band Raman amplification, albeit the costs are notably higher.

■ **Filters** Filtering plays a vital role in extracting individual DWDM wavelength channels from SMF cables, i.e., multiplex, demultiplex, and bypass operations. Currently, three key types of passive (or nonpowered) filtering technologies are in use—thin-film, planar waveguide, and fiber-gratings. Thin-film filters are ideal for wider channel spacings (100, 200 GHz) and exhibit good temperature stability and passband isolation. Meanwhile, increased C- and L-band densities and larger channel counts can be achieved using planar waveguide devices such as *arrayed waveguide gratings (AWG)* or fiber-grating filters. Examples include 40 channels at 100 GHz/0.8 nm or 80 channels at 50 GHz/0.4 nm.

■ **Optical switches** All-optical switches are crucial for implementing spatial interconnection in a dynamic manner, for example, for connection routing, protection, and so on. To date, numerous switching technologies have been developed including *micro electro-mechanical system (MEMS)*, lithium niobate, *semiconductor optical amplifier (SOA)* gate, beamsteering, liquid crystal, bubblejet, and so on [1]. In particular, two- and three-dimensional MEMS designs have gained the most attention, yielding submillisecond switching times and low crosstalk levels. However, port count scalability remains a key challenge (see also Mesh Switching) and future integration strategies are expected to provide much improvement here.

Optical Network Architectures

Component advances have led to major evolutions in *optical network element (ONE)* designs over the past decade. In turn, these have enabled much-improved service provisioning paradigms at the network layer, as shown in Figure 8.3. As a result, DWDM is now a multibillion dollar market that has seen tremendous growth in the metro/regional and long-haul networking sectors. In fact, this technology has largely usurped legacy SONET/SDH as the main underlying transport solution. Current ONE systems offer a wide range of capabilities and are becoming increasingly flexible and agile (see Table 8.2). Moreover, intense market competition continues to drive price reductions, about 20 percent per year [2], offering genuine prospects for capital (CAPEX) and operational (OPEX) expense reduction. These new paradigms are detailed in the following sections.

Point-to-Point DWDM Transport   The first commercial DWDM deployments took place in the mid-1990s and were primarily aimed at point-to-point "fiber-relief" on congested long-haul spans, i.e., first-generation DWDM (see Figure 8.3) [3]. These build-outs used optical terminal multiplexer (OTM) systems to improve cost-per-bit-per-mile by exploiting the multichannel transmission/amplification economics of DWDM. Although these systems were very costly at the time, they saw strong uptake due to the large amortization base of the long-haul sector. Over the years, more cost-optimized OTM renditions were also evolved for the metro/regional sectors in order to relieve congestion on heavily

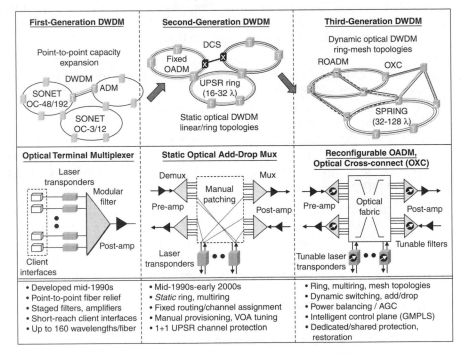

Figure 8.3   Optical network evolutions and optical network elements (ONE) designs

TABLE 8.2   Summary of DWDM Optical Network Element (ONE) Designs

ONE Type	Cost	Topologies	Survivability	Applications
Optical terminal multiplexer (OTM)	Low	Point-to-point, linear	1+1, 1:1, 1:N	Fiber-relief on congested spans
Static optical add-drop multiplexer (SOADM)	Medium	Linear, ring	1+1 UPSR, 1+1 span	Metro and access add-drop
Reconfigurable optical add-drop multiplexer (ROADM)	Medium	Linear, ring	1+1 UPSR, OCh/ OMS-SPRING	Metro-core/regional IOF add-drop
All-optical cross-connect switch (OXC)	High	Mesh, interconnected rings	Mesh protection, restoration	Long-haul backbone
Optical+digital cross-connect switch (OXC+DCS/MSTP)	High	Mesh, interconnected rings	Mesh, ring protection	Traffic add/drop, 3R regeneration

loaded *interoffice fiber (IOF)* spans. Current commercial OTM offerings can now scale to well over 100 wavelengths per fiber with 10 Gbps wavelength speeds, yielding unmatched terabit capacity.

The generic OTM design is shown in Figure 8.3 and consists of client interfaces, wavelength transponders, amplifiers, and multiplexing/demultiplexing filters. The transponders perform optical modulation for client signals, and new compact pluggable interfaces are widely available for most protocol interfaces, e.g., Fast Ethernet, Gigabit Ethernet, 10 Gigabit Ethernet, Fibre Channel, SONET/SDH OC-n/STM-n, and so on. These interfaces can be bypassed if the client gear directly supports ITU-T-compliant DWDM optics on their interface cards; for instance, many SONET/SDH and Ethernet/ IP platforms are equipped with 1550 nm lasers for direct interconnection purposes. Moreover commercial DWDM systems—particularly metro/regional—also offer staged filter designs to reduce up-front costs and facilitate "pay-as-you-grow" expansion, as shown in the parallel and serial designs depicted in Figure 8.4. In general, the latter can give low first cost but are more expensive to scale and tend to yield higher losses (2–3 dB per stage), see [3].

Many OTM systems also feature a wide range of laser and amplifier combinations to handle different span lengths and device losses. For example, DFB lasers are sufficient for SMF spans less than 60 km and bit rates up to OC-48/STM-16 (2.5 Gbps). However, for increased 10 Gbps speeds, more powerful externally modulated lasers and EDFA devices are necessary. In fact, larger spans may even mandate *dispersion compensation fiber (DCF)* coil placements. An alternate means for boosting reach for higher data rates is via *forward error correction (FEC)*, though this adds cost and compromises service transparency (see the ITU-T "digital wrappers" approach detailed in Optical Network Management).

Given the massive terabit capacity of a single fiber strand, most OTM systems implement some type of fiber/span protection. The most common scheme is dedicated 1+1 protection, which uses passive splitters to bridge/switch all client traffic onto separate working and protection fibers, as shown in Figure 8.5. This simple setup is purely hardware-based and precludes any "end-to-end" span signaling as it splits and sends

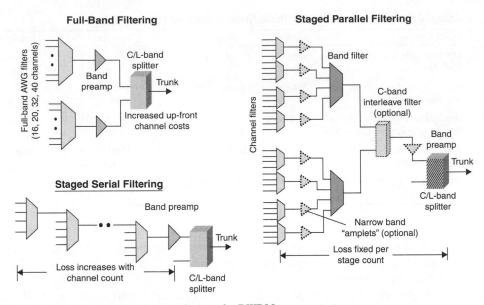

Figure 8.4 Serial and parallel filtering designs for DWDM transport stages

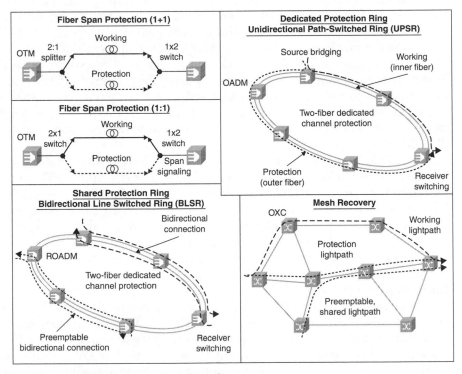

Figure 8.5 Fiber and WDM layer survivability schemes

two copies of each signal. As such, 1+1 protection doubles fiber requirements but halves power budgets (distance reach). Alternatively, 1:1 or 1:N shared protection can improve fiber efficiency and span reach. These setups use active switching and rapid protection signaling and allow for lower priority users to share idle protection fibers. However, there are no standards for optical fiber/span protection and most offerings are vendor-proprietary. Albeit nonselective at the service layer, fiber protection can significantly lower higher-layer protection costs.

Fixed Add-Drop Rings   As point-to-point DWDM systems proliferated, the next logical step for carriers was the extension of wavelength channels across fiber rings, i.e., second-generation DWDM [3]. In essence, the goal was to leverage entrenched ring-fiber plants in incumbent carrier networks. This evolution yielded transparent *optical add-drop multiplexer (OADM)* designs, as shown in Figure 8.3, which implemented all-optical wavelength bypass at intermediate ring sites, creating multihop lightpath connections. OADM designs proved much more cost-effective than back-to-back OTM configurations, as they obviated the need for service-specific electronics to retransmit bypass channels. With add-drop traffic averaging almost 25 percent per site these "transponderless" designs enable sizeable CAPEX reduction, particularly at higher 10 Gbps speeds.

Static OADM nodes augment basic OTM designs by adding wavelength/wavelength band *bypass-and-add-drop* filters (see Figure 8.3). These designs lower insertion losses for transit channels (by about 2 dB per node) and deliver commensurate increases in ring diameters. Most OADM designs are also complemented with pre- and post-amplifiers in order to handle transmission and nodal losses, respectively. Nevertheless, fixed OADM rings have sizeable manual overheads (OPEX) and require skilled technical staff. Careful preplanning is required to ensure wavelength connectivity for all node demands, i.e., static *routing and wavelength assignment (RWA)* [1]. In addition, complex amplifier preengineering is needed to maintain lightpath signal-to-noise ratios (SNR). Finally, careful power-balancing is also required between bypass and add-drop channels within an OADM to ensure proper EDFA operation. This is commonly done using advanced EDFA gain equalization features and placing a *variable optical attenuator (VOA)* along channel paths. In fact, many OADM filters directly incorporate manual or software-selectable VOA control.

In terms of survivability, fixed OADM rings are most amenable to *unidirectional path-switched ring (UPSR)* protection, also termed *dedicated protection ring (OCh-DPRING)* [3, 4]. This robust scheme is basically an optical adaptation of SONET/SDH UPSR [5] and features simplified and extremely fast per-wavelength recovery (under 10 ms). Nearly all OADM vendors support this capability, which uses two counter-propagating fibers (working, protection) to implement dedicated channel protection via head-end splitting and receive-end switching (see Figure 8.5). Again, this is a hardware-based, nonsignaled recovery approach in which the receiver simply selects the better of two bridged signals. Although more selective than span/fiber protection, associated per-channel hardware cost/complexities limit the scalability of UPSR in handling fiber cuts. Moreover, splitting the signal at the source also lowers achievable ring diameters. In general, UPSR rings have been widely deployed in many metro-area domains and can achieve very high "five nines" reliability.

Nevertheless, fixed OADM rings are generally best-suited for static, long-standing service profiles, e.g., weeks long or months long holding times. Moreover these setups mandate careful demand projections, and inaccurate estimates can result in significant stranded capacity. To mitigate operational complexity, many OADM vendors offer detailed software planning tools. These packages allow carriers to input their connection demands and fiber routes/characteristics and then compute the required system configurations at all nodes, for example, wavelength assignments, VOA settings, amplifier locations, and so on. Many such tools also provide automated order placement for required modules.

Reconfigurable Add-Drop Rings   As traffic dynamics increase, static rings become less efficient due to excessive preplanning and manual provisioning requirements. Moreover, larger IOF rings need improved scalability and dynamic on-demand provisioning, particularly for meshed demands. These contingencies, coupled with advances in "soft optics" switching/tunable technologies, have led to the emergence of third-generation DWDM systems [3]. A key example here is the *reconfigurable OADM (ROADM)* node, which allows carriers to add-drop wavelength circuits dynamically at a given node, in other words dynamic online RWA. This ONE design vastly accelerates service delivery times (from days/weeks to minutes/hours) and lowers manual operational costs. Akin to its static counterpart, a ROADM also features transport, amplification, and (dynamic) add-drop stages (see Figure 8.3).

Initial ROADM designs were "opaque" and used opto-electronic transponders and SONET/SDH fabrics to implement add-drop functions. Although these systems provided subrate TDM grooming and client-side hair-pinning capabilities, service transparency was eliminated. Overall, opaque ROADM nodes proved too expensive for most carriers, as large transponder arrays were needed to terminate/launch all wavelength channels. Additionally, related OPEX costs—footprint and power consumption—were also very significant. As a result, new advances have shifted carrier interests toward transparent all-optical ROADM designs. Today the ROADM market represents one of the fastest-growing and most promising sectors in DWDM space [2]. In fact, related price-points for ROADM systems are even becoming competitive with static OADM systems (owing to technological innovations, market competition, and intense pricing pressures from carriers).

Commercial ROADM systems can provide remote automated add-drop of up to 40 wavelengths (any-wavelength-any-node) and use various technologies [2]. For example, some vendors deploy *wavelength selective switch (WSS)* fabrics whereas others use broadcast and select designs. In addition, tunable filters can also be used on input trunks to drop selected channels, for example, fiber Bragg gratings. Nevertheless all-optical ring transmission is quite challenging and requires some very specialized provisions. Foremost is the need for rapid AGC to stabilize wavelength powers across all links [3]. This is a crucial requirement as individual lightpath connections can experience sizeable power fluctuations during transient events such as connection setup/takedown or faults. AGC is achieved by coupling EDFA amplifier designs with attenuators and modern subsystems to provide good gain flatness over wide input ranges with millisecond timings.

Another challenge in all-optical rings is optical-layer performance monitoring. Currently, there are no standards in this area, and most vendors provide their own proprietary schemes such as fiber/wavelength powers, optical SNR, and so on. However, it is well-understood that these offerings can only detect hard faults—not degenerative conditions—because they lack the bit-level resolution of SONET/SDH. Regardless, these features still suffice for ROADM applications [3]. For example, trunk power monitoring can rapidly isolate hard failures (fiber cuts and node faults) in order to support protection switching. Note that transparent ROADM rings use more specialized *outband* control setups with separated data and control planes; most vendors use the 1510 nm *optical supervisory channel (OSC)* wavelength for control signaling. Nevertheless, there are no standards for OSC signal formats and vendors either use SONET/SDH or Ethernet framing. In general, this yields lower levels of vendor interoperability.

ROADM rings can easily implement UPSR protection. In addition, these nodes can also facilitate more advanced *shared protection ring (SPRING)* schemes [4]. These concepts extend upon SONET *bidirectional line-switched ring (BLSR)* operation via the automatic protection switching (APS) protocol. In particular, SPRING achieves spatial reuse to improve wavelength efficiency and provides multiple protection levels; wavelength plans route bidirectional demands along the same set of nodes and allow working /protection traffic to travel in both directions. In contrast, UPSR cannot provide such reuse since connections traversing different ring segments are unable to use the same wavelength. Overall, SPRING architectures include two- and four-fiber variants that operate at the fiber and wavelength levels [3]. These designs also permit wavelength sharing (backup multiplexing) between multiple working paths and/or lower-priority traffic. Hence, operators can differentiate protection levels to meet a broader set of customer demands such as dedicated (platinum), shared (gold), unprotected (silver), and preemptable (bronze). A major drawback of SPRING, however, is again the lack of related standards. Therefore, this design is only supported by a few vendors, and interoperability is extremely low.

Finally, many commercial DWDM OADM nodes also blend in higher-layer TDM and Ethernet capabilities to boost wavelength efficiency. For example, various high-density "thin-mux" blades (muxponder) are available for subrate client tributary aggregation and output onto DWDM wavelengths. Key examples include TDM blades (4:1 OC-12 on OC-48, 4:1 OC-48 on OC-192) and Ethernet multiplexers (8:1/10:1 Gigabit Ethernet to 10 Gigabit Ethernet, etc). Some of these units can even provide decent levels of electronic-layer functionality, e.g., SONET/SDH APS and/or Ethernet switching/VLAN support. Overall, these "grooming" devices are blurring the boundaries between the optical and electronic layers. Alternatively, many higher-layer Ethernet/MPLS switches, IP routers, and SONET/SDH devices readily support powerful SMF or DWDM optics interfaces.

Today's ROADM technologies offer the very real prospect of dynamic "intelligent" optical networks. When combined with tunable laser transponders, these systems can essentially reduce provisioning times down to minutes with little to no manual configuration—a huge cost savings. Note, however, that static preengineering is still not eliminated altogether. For example, carriers will still have to design for all possible link budgets (e.g., EDFA per 80–120 km distances) and handle dispersion effects at higher 10 Gbps bit rates (e.g., DCF coils on selective spans).

Mesh Switching   Mesh fiber networks represent the next topological progression from OADM rings. For example, most long-haul backbones are of a mesh nature and large metro domains also comprise a meshed interconnection of rings. In order to provision wavelengths over these topologies, generalized *optical cross-connect switch (OXC)* nodes are needed to handle increased fiber connectivity (refer back to Figure 8.3, earlier in the chapter). Today, nearly all such designs use SONET/SDH digital cross-connect (DCS) [5] fabrics with full regeneration of all wavelengths, which is very costly. In order to increase scalability and transparency, all-optical fabrics have also been considered, such as two-dimensional MEMS. Nevertheless, these systems face a host of cost and complexity limitations and have seen very minimal traction with carriers. For example, current MEMS fabrics are limited to smaller 16×16 sizes and require costly multistaging to scale port counts, further increasing loss and crosstalk (Clos, Banyan, etc.). Although three-dimensional MEMS can support much larger port counts, the post-bubble market has curtailed most development efforts. Hence, only a few vendors offer all-optical OXC systems today, and future variants will likely use hybrid OXC + DCS designs. Ring interconnection will likely be the first application of such designs [3].

Optical mesh control frameworks have seen aggressive standardization over the last decade. Additionally, a wide range of RWA schemes—centralized and distributed—have been developed to provision and recover lightpath connections. Specifically, DWDM mesh networks can employ both *protection* and *restoration* strategies [4]. The former uses preassigned recovery routes (fiber or lightpath level), whereas the latter uses active, post-fault signaled recovery (lightpath level). Protection is generally much faster and offers high availability via dedicated and shared strategies. This enables mesh networks to support multiple service tiers, akin to SPRING. Meanwhile, restoration schemes are very wavelength efficient but have slower recovery times (hundreds of milliseconds).

Coarse WDM (CWDM)   *Coarse WDM (CWDM)* is a form of WDM that is targeted for cost-sensitive carriers with smaller metro-edge reach requirements. Specifically, CWDM uses much wider channel spacing, typically 20 nm, and precludes the need for costly EDFA amplifiers. In fact, the CWDM grid (ITU-T G.694.2) spans the entire SMF spectrum, as shown previously in Figure 8.2, and supports much smaller channel counts, typically about 16–32 per fiber. The main cost savings of this technology comes from its use of low-power/wider-line-width (uncooled) laser sources and lower-cost coarse filtering devices. These laser types mitigate center-wavelength temperature drift and allow unamplified transmissions up to 40 km.

In general, CWDM is very cost effective for client interface speeds under OC-48/STM-16 (2.5 Gbps), and hence this technology makes sense for Gigabit Ethernet services. Alternatively, faster 10 Gigabit CWDM transceivers are also available but offer less cost reduction than their DWDM counterparts. Moreover, the larger economies of scale in the DWDM market will, over time, erode the first-cost advantage of CWDM [3]. Finally,

TABLE 8.3   Fast Ethernet and Gigabit Ethernet Fiber-optic Interfaces

Interface	Fiber	Type	Freq.	Reach	Applications
100 Base-FX2	MMF	Serial	1310 nm	2 km	Data center
1000 Base-SX	MMF	Serial	850 nm	2–220 m	Intraoffice cabling, data center
1000 Base-LX	MMF	Serial	1310 nm	2–550 m	Intraoffice cabling, data center
1000 Base-LX	SMF	Serial	1310 nm	5–10 km	Data center, campus LAN

CWDM systems require opto-electronic conversion in order to interface with larger metro/regional DWDM networks, i.e., signal relaunch on DWDM. This technology is best suited for smaller isolated networks with simple point-to-point or static OADM setups such as low-cost interconnection routers/switches in large campus settings.

Optical Ethernet Interfaces

Another crucial area that has seen much progress is Ethernet interface designs. Here, the most remarkable outcome has been Ethernet's continual ability to adapt and expand over multiple *physical media dependent (PMD)* sublayers. Most notably, optical Ethernet interfaces have played a vital role in propelling the technology into a converged LAN-MAN-WAN solution. Current standards support a full range of speeds— 10 Mbps–10 Gbps—and retain crucial interoperability with a vast installed Ethernet base (the interfaces are summarized in Tables 8-3 and 8-4). More importantly, the recent specification of SMF- and DWDM-based interfaces has paved the way for genuine interoperability across DWDM optical networks.

TABLE 8.4   10 Gigabit Ethernet Fiber-optic Interfaces

Interface	Fiber	Type	Frequency	Reach	Applications
10G Base-SR	MMF	Serial	850 nm	26–300 m	Campus, data center
10G Base-SW	MMF	Serial, OC-192c	850 nm	26–300 m	Campus, data center
10G Base-LRM	MMF	Serial	850 nm	300 m	Campus, data center
10G Base-LR	SMF	Serial	1310 nm	2–10 km	Metro, storage networks
10G Base-LW	SMF	Serial, OC-192c	1310 nm	2–10 km	Metro, storage networks
10G Base-ER	SMF	Serial	1550 nm	2–40 km	Metro, storage networks
10G Base-EW	SMF	Serial, OC-192c	1550 nm	2–40 km	Metro, storage networks
10G Base-LX4	MMF	Parallel	1310 nm	30–300 m	LAN, data center
10G Base-LX4	SMF	Parallel	1310 nm	240 m–10 km	LAN, data center, metro
Nomenclature 10 G-Base xyz		x- S (short, 850 nm) y - R (LAN serial) z - # channels L (long, 1310 nm) W (WAN, OC-192c) E (extra long, 1550 nm) X (LAN)			

Early Renditions for Fast Ethernet and Gigabit Ethernet   The first 10 Mbps fiber-optic Ethernet interface was standardized in 1996 via the ISO/IEC 10 Base-F specification. This interface was defined over two MMF spans and supported distances up to 2 km (50 or 62.5 μm core). At about the same time, the IEEE introduced the first Fast Ethernet 100 Base-F standard for MMF by adapting proven transceiver and encoding schemes from Fiber Distributed Data Interface (FDDI) technology. Nevertheless, no formal standard has been developed for Fast Ethernet over SMF, although many vendors have proprietary solutions on the market (1310/1550 nm, 10–100 km reach).

Ethernet's entry into the gigabit-fiber realm came in 1998 with the approval of the IEEE 802.3z 1000 Base-F standard. This interface preserved the minimum/maximum Ethernet frame sizes and used 8b/10b encoding. Again, the interface leveraged transceiver design and 8b/10b encoding formats from existing 1.0 Gbps Fibre Channel technology. The only difference was a slightly higher clocking rate to support full gigabit data transfers (i.e., 1.25 Gbps versus 1.06 Gbps). Specifically, two interface types were defined. Namely, the 1000 Base-SX standard was targeted for intra-building/data-center MMF cabling (550 m reach), whereas the 1000 Base-LX standard was targeted for larger campus networks (MMF and 1310 nm SMF) with a range of 10 km (see Table 8.3). These were also the first Ethernet interfaces to use laser optics with associated low-loss frequencies of 850 nm (MMF) and 1310 nm (SMF). In addition, *mode condition path (MCP)* solutions were developed to overcome modal dispersion effects over MMF, yielding improved reach up to 2–3 km. Nevertheless, all official Gigabit Ethernet fiber interfaces were restricted to campus/enterprise applications such as aggregating Fast Ethernet ports. To resolve this limitation, many vendors have developed proprietary SMF interfaces with extended reach up to 150 km.

10 Gigabit Ethernet   Work on the 10 Gbps Ethernet interface started in late 1990s and was driven by improvements in high-speed electronics and lasers. A major goal of this effort was to scale to ten times the aggregation of Gigabit Ethernet for a small multiple of its price (two to three times). Another aim was to project Ethernet well out of the LAN as a genuine "carrier-grade" solution, i.e., LAN-MAN-WAN convergence. The first 10 Gigabit Ethernet specifications (IEEE 802.3ae) emerged in 2002 and defined full-duplex operation without carrier-sensing multiple-access with collision detection (CSMA/CD) operation. However, Ethernet frame formats were maintained to ensure interoperability and protect existing investments.

Given many potential applications, 10 Gigabit Ethernet interfaces support a wide range of distances and fiber types, as detailed in Table 8.4. In particular, the standards define two physical interface layers, one for LAN and the other for MAN/WAN. The former supports full 10 Gbps bit rates (10.3 Gbps clock rate) and runs over SMF (1300 nm) or DWDM (1550 nm). Meanwhile, the latter defines a new *WAN interface sublayer (WIS)*, i.e., *WAN PHY*, which is based on a simplified concatenated SONET STS-192c/SDH-4-64c frame with a 9.58464 Gbps data rate (10G-Base-SW/LW/EW) [6]. This facilitates seamless interconnection across extensive SONET/SDH infrastructures such as add-drop multiplexer (ADM) rings, DCS meshes, DWDM networks, regenerators, and so on. In order to reduce cost, however, full SONET functionality is not supported in the WAN PHY. Specifically, only minimal path/section/line overhead processing is done (enough to isolate faults), and stratum clock timing is eliminated along with stringent laser source requirements. As a result, 10 Gigabit Ethernet ports are significantly cheaper than comparable *packet-over-SONET (PoS)* interfaces (RFC 1619) [6]. In addition, the WAN PHY also supports additional 64b/66b encoding to handle faster 10 Gbps rates. Note that the actual distance reach of the 10 Gbps DWDM interfaces (e.g., 10G Base-ER/EW) are not of direct consequence since carrier DWDM networks usually provide amplification and/or regeneration to traverse hundreds or thousands of kilometers.

There has also been an ongoing miniaturization of optical transceiver modules and the move toward end-user pluggables. Notable examples of such form factors include *gigabit interface converters (GBIC), small factor pluggables (SFP)*, XENPAK, X2, and XFP. Specifically, the GBIC design was originally adopted from Fibre Channel and subsequent improvements (halving of size) led to the SFP transceiver. In terms of optical Ethernet interfaces, the GBIC and SFP modules support Gigabit Ethernet, whereas the others support 10 Gigabit Ethernet. In particular, hot-pluggable XENPAK modules are available for all 10 Gbps media types (MMF and SMF). Collectively, these interfaces allows carriers to couple ports seamlessly on DWDM systems (OTM, OADM, and OXC) with any type of client signal (Ethernet, SONET/SDH, Fibre Channel, and so on). In addition, these compact designs help reduce footprint density and associated co-location costs.

NOTE   10 Gigabit Ethernet is also being adapted for very short-reach data center and even intrasystem backplane applications. For example, the 10G Base-LX4 standard uses a four-wavelength parallel interface over a single fiber pair. Meanwhile others variants are even extending interconnectivity over non-fiber media types, such as twin-axial cables (10G Base-CX4) and unshielded twisted pair (UTP) copper (10G Base-T with 100 m reach).

Optical Network Control

Multi-wavelength optical network architecture and control standards have evolved significantly over the last decade, paving the way for improved vendor interoperability and "intelligent on-demand" provisioning [7]. From the ITU-T side, a comprehensive optical transport network (OTN) architecture has been defined based on a three-layer transport hierarchy comprising *optical channel (OCh), optical multiplex (OMS)*, and *optical transport (OTS)* sections. Associated frame structures and bit-rate hierarchies for mapping a host of client protocols (native formats) are also defined. Within this framework, G.8070 (formerly G.astn) defines the requirements for an *Automatic Switched Transport Network (ASTN)* via a set of functions for connection setup/takedown. Meanwhile, the reference architecture for supporting ASTN control is given in G.8080 (formerly G.ason), which details a distributed client-server setup along with its associated components and interactions. In particular, G.8080 identifies hierarchical distributed routing and signaling setups. However the ASON framework does not define specific control protocols for optical networks. Here, the major contribution has come from the IETF's *generalized multiprotocol label switching (GMPLS)* framework [7].

GMPLS extends packet-based *multiprotocol label switching (MPLS)* by abstracting labels to cover a range of Layer 1 entities—TDM timeslots, wavelengths, bands, and fibers. This solution defines key protocols for resource discovery, signaling, traffic engineering, and link management. For example, resource discovery is done via extensions to existing *interior gateway protocols (IGP)* such as *open-shortest path first-traffic engineering (OSPF-TE)* and *intermediate-system to intermediate-system (IS-IS)*. Namely, routing updates provide state on wavelength/timeslot usages, protection/diversity, and so on. Meanwhile GMPLS signaling extends the *resource reservation-traffic engineering (RSVP-TE)* protocol for setup/takedown of lightpath (or SONET/SDH) circuits. In turn RSVP-TE is driven by *constraint-based routing (CBR)*, which performs advanced resource engineering. Recently, there have also been many liaison efforts between the ITU-T and IETF to streamline GMPLS protocols to be ASON-compliant. Overall, GMPLS increases horizontal control plane integration (data-optical) and eliminates feature overlaps in traditional multilayered setups, for example, addressing, signaling, routing, and so on.

The Optical Internetworking Forum (OIF) has also defined an optical user network interface (UNI) [8] protocol that allows clients to request/release capacity without knowledge of network internals, i.e., an "optical dial-tone." In addition, the OIF external-network node interface (NNI) helps to automate connection establishment between domains [9]. Collectively, these standards facilitate a wide range of on-demand end-to-end network-level provisioning features, as demonstrated for EoS settings in Jones et al. [10].

Network and Services Management

Operations, administration, and maintenance (OAM) support is vital for carriers to provision, monitor, and protect client services. In fact, these very OAM features can be deciding factors in deploying a particular technology or vendor product. Now most incumbent operators have come to rely upon SONET/SDH for robust carrier-class OAM [5]. Clearly, similar capabilities are required at the DWDM and Ethernet layers, and there have been some notable developments herein.

Optical Network Management The *telecommunication network management (TMN)* framework defines a hierarchical management model in which *element management systems (EMS)* interface to vendor *network management systems (NMS)* or carrier *operational support systems (OSS)* [3]. Although most early DWDM, OTM, and OADM systems provided limited EMS/NMS support, newer offerings have much better capabilities. Here a key requirement is "end-to-end" wavelength channel management, which is generally complicated by the transparency of DWDM systems. Therefore, as an interim solution, many vendors have adapted some form of SONET/SDH overhead monitoring. Although this is usually only done at the edge or at select opaque (regeneration) points inside ROADM/OXC networks, it still forces TDM framing of all client data. Alternatively some vendors offer proprietary "BER-agnostic" optical-layer monitoring, for example, laser powers, link powers, amplifier gain, and so on.

To better address wavelength monitoring concerns, the ITU-T OTN (G.872) has standardized a "digital wrapper" solution for its optical payload unit (OPU) hierarchy.

This standard combines channel-level OAM bytes with client-protocol agnostic payload sections. These overhead features include performance monitoring, payload-independent FEC, and reserved ring protection/restoration bytes. For example, sample FEC solutions can deliver 2–3 dB gain with about 6 percent bandwidth overhead—a good improvement [3]. Nevertheless, protocols have not yet been defined for actual protection switching. Overall, the digital wrappers approach is not fully transparent but does extend carrier-grade BER-level monitoring to all formats (Ethernet included). In the longer-term, this may be acceptable as network regeneration will still be a necessity (albeit regeneration distances may increase with improving technology). In particular, this solution is most germane in long/ultra-long haul DWDM settings.

As DWDM platforms add more diverse capabilities and interconnect with multivendor nodes (Layers 1, 2, 3), advanced NMS/OSS solutions are required for end-to-end services management. Specifically, these tools must support a host of features such as remote configuration, performance monitoring, fault detection/alarming, failure isolation, diagnostics, and logging/reporting. Hence, many incumbent carriers have developed advanced embedded OSS solutions based upon the Telecordia *Operations Systems Modification for the Integration of Network Elements (OSMINE)* process. To assist with OSS integration, many DWDM vendors now provide associated northbound CORBA interfaces and/or direct TL1 (or SNMP) communication with the EMS/NMS solutions.

Ethernet Management   Enterprise Ethernet OAM has traditionally lagged far behind SONET/SDH [11]. Therefore, carriers wanting "carrier-grade" OAM support for their data services have had to choose EoS delivery—mandating a costly TDM layer. This deficiency has prompted much work in native Ethernet OAM and new standards are finally maturing and offering SONET-like capabilities. Broadly speaking, Ethernet OAM defines a multisegmented hierarchical model for end-to-end management across multiple domains, client and carrier. Here, multiple *Ethernet demarcation devices (EDD)* are defined along the end-to-end (data) connection path to assist with testing and monitoring. Specifically, client-side EDD entities reside on carrier-owned devices that connect to customer premise equipment (CPE) and implement the carrier-to-customer interface, or UNI. Meanwhile, core EDD entities reside at the carrier-to-carrier interface, or NNI.

Using this framework, three OAM layers are defined, including service, connectivity, and link. Service-layer OAM focuses on end-to-end Ethernet visibility (UNI-to-UNI) and implements a host of features such as continuity checks, service loopback, fault/defect indication (signaling), and SLA monitoring (ITU-T Y.1731EthOAM). In particular, the latter collects statistics based upon carrier-settable thresholds and compares against SLA metrics for packet delay, packet jitter, packet loss, and so on. Client service-specific OAM is also possible here. Meanwhile, the connectivity OAM layer is somewhat similar, but more focused on multipoint features between carrier edge devices (IEEE 802.1ag). Finally, transport/link-layer OAM (IEEE 802.3ah) handles localized (link-level) threshold alarms, remote failure indication, and loopback testing functions. Overall, multilayer OAM enables rapid segment-by-segment fault localization between the EDD elements, helping reduce management costs and minimize truck rolls.

As of today, however, only the Ethernet services layer OAM standard has been ratified, although the others are close to being approved. Broader vendor support and carrier adoption will also take time.

Drivers for This Solution

In light of the technologies and standards just described, the evolution of fiber-based Ethernet transmission is now taking shape. Today, the primary drivers for Ethernet services over fiber/WDM are the rapid growth in corporate data-center needs and much-improved end-user access technologies [2]. These developments have yielded substantial increases in data traffic volumes and forced carriers to look for improved services scalability and lower costs—both capital and operational. Consider some details briefly.

The residential sector has seen the adoption of many "last-mile" broadband access solutions with multimegabit speeds. For example, most cable operators have aggressively deployed high-speed data-over-cable solutions and migrated their infrastructures to highly scalable hybrid fiber-coax (HFC) setups. Meanwhile, competing incumbents have rolled out various DSL schemes to deliver improved data (and some video) services. Furthermore, many incumbents are even starting to deploy fiber-based Passive Optical Networks (PON), raising the bar to genuine gigabit-level scalability. Concurrently, various high-speed wireless technologies are maturing rapidly, including WiMAX (IEEE 802.16). All of these build-outs have shown a strong unifying trend toward low-cost packet-based delivery and bundled triple-play services, for example, voice, video, and data. These changes have propelled IP/Ethernet data volumes well beyond legacy voice levels, generating large back-haul requirements.

Meanwhile, the corporate space has also seen its share of transitions. In the last decade, more and more business activities have moved online, including sales, support, accounting, and training. As businesses have expanded their operations, the need for reliable data sharing and access across dispersed MAN/WAN regions has surged. In turn, these developments have driven up corporate bandwidth requirements—and stringencies—as embodied by applications such as LAN extension, storage area networks (SAN), and virtual private networks (VPN) (see also "Sections 8.5.1" and "8.5.2"). A noteworthy trend here is the reversal of the "80/20" traffic rule, where nearly 80 percent of traffic now heads into the network core. In the past, corporations have used separate technologies for their internal communication needs. For example, voice calls were supported by TDM branch exchanges whereas data services (e-mail, ftp, and Web) were heavily Ethernet-based. However businesses are now moving toward converged setups that leverage Ethernet's cost-effectiveness, port scalability, and ease-of-use/ maintenance. Some telling examples include the migration of TDM voice to Voice over IP (VoIP) and new packet video services. In light of this shift, there is a pressing need to extend Ethernet as a *service* beyond the enterprise in a manner that preserves its ubiquity and cost efficiency.

Ethernet extension has usually been done using traditional TDM-based leased line or direct dark fiber provisioning. In particular, leased line services run at slower T1 or OC-3 speeds and require costly intermediate protocol gears such as Frame Relay or asynchronous transfer mode (ATM). It is well known that these multilayered set-ups suffer from huge bandwidth inefficiency and are very costly from an operational perspective [6]. More importantly, they have failed to keep pace with today's gigabit-level Ethernet port speeds. Alternatively, enterprise Ethernet systems simply do not offer the high-end capabilities needed for true MAN/WAN operation, for example, high availability, QoS, management, and so on. In fact, a recent survey of IT managers indicated that high bandwidth, low latency, low loss, and security are some of their major requirements [12]. Along these lines, the Metro Ethernet Forum (MEF) has defined five attributes for a Carrier Ethernet service, namely QoS, scalability, reliability/protection, TDM support, and services management [13].

Indeed, fiber-optic and WDM technologies are very well-aligned to support these needs. In fact, the ongoing growth in Carrier Ethernet services is perhaps one of the main factors behind the post-bubble resurgence of the optical networking market. In all, this is leading to a very strong convergence between the data and optical networking layers. Consider the individual MEF attributes for Carrier Ethernet:

- **Quality of service (QoS)** The MEF defines various QoS attributes as part of a client's end-to-end SLA profile. These include the connection's committed information rate (CIR), excess information rate (EIR), committed burst size (CBS), and excess burst size (EBS). In general, these parameters are more germane for packet-switching implementations that tend to deliver relative "soft" QoS between competing services, such as MPLS, Ethernet switching, and resilient packet ring (RPR). Hence, the inherent circuit-based nature of WDM ensures its ability to provide "hard" QoS with full-rate guarantees, minimal delay, and near zero jitter and loss.

- **Scalability** This MEF requirement stresses the need to support large numbers (100,000 range) of Ethernet virtual connections (EVC) and high aggregate system/link scalability (tens of gigabits). Again, the former requirement is more tailored for higher packet-switching layers as it pertains to individual end-user counts. However, DWDM is very well-positioned with regards to the latter requirement since current OTM and OADM systems can readily scale to support hundreds of channels at gigabit-level speeds.

- **Reliability/protection** The MEF standards also call for rapid service protection at the end-to-end path level, with speeds matching 50 ms SONET/SDH timescales. Additionally, the need for line and node level protection is also stated. Today, many commercial WDM platforms are already fully network-equipment building systems (NEBS)–compliant and offer "five nines" (99.999 percent) availability—under five minutes annual downtime. Moreover, a full range of WDM survivability options are available, most of which can match SONET/SDH timescales (see "Optical Network Architectures"). In fact, some dedicated schemes such at 1+1 span or UPSR path protection can even achieve lower millisecond recovery (less than 10 ms).

- **TDM support** This requirement mandates legacy TDM voice support via circuit emulation ("pseudo-wire"). Again, this issue relates more to packet-switching technologies that use mechanisms such as scheduling, buffer management, and call admission control. Although these requirements are not directly applicable to DWDM, it is important to note that this technology can transparently host legacy TDM equipment (services) alongside Carrier Ethernet. Also, existing TDM management solutions can also be used, greatly facilitating interim service migrations for carriers with existing SONET/SDH architectures.

- **Services management** DWDM and Ethernet OAM standards have been steadily evolving to meet "carrier-class" OAM needs, as detailed in "Network & Services Management" Robust provisioning control at the DWDM layer is also becoming available via GMPLS (see "Optical Network Control"). As vendors start to integrate these offerings into their EMS/NMS systems, carriers will benefit from a full range of end-to-end service differentiation and SLA management capabilities.

When Does This Solution Fit?

This section introduces the EoF and EoWDM concepts for provisioning Carrier Ethernet services. Foremost, it is evident that *service definitions* will play a critical role in formalizing the overall client-carrier experience. Along these lines, the MEF has defined its own UNI setup [14] and standardized various Carrier Ethernet service categories for MAN/WAN operation. These include point-to-point Ethernet Private Line (EPL) and Ethernet Virtual Private Line (EVPL) services and multipoint-to-multipoint Ethernet Private LAN (EPLAN) and Ethernet Virtual Private LAN (EVPLAN) services [13]. This section introduces the EoF and EoWDM approaches for provisioning these new services.

NOTE It is assumed that readers have basic familiarity with these service models.

Ethernet Private Line (EPL) Services

EPL provides point-to-point connectivity using client data interfaces and has similar characteristics to legacy private lines. Namely, each connection has a standard set of attributes including traffic parameters such as CIR, EIR, CBS, and EBS. Furthermore, other attributes are also defined, including performance parameters (SLA packet delay, packet jitter, and packet loss), service priority, and security [13]. The EVPL service extends this definition via port-multiplexing; in other words, multiple virtual EPL connections can share an EPL connection.

A simple means of provisioning EPL services is to interconnect client-side optical Ethernet ports using (leased/purchased) dark fiber routes or Ethernet over fiber (EoF), as shown in Figure 8.6. This native solution is limited to the reach of associated SMF 1310 nm Ethernet interfaces (see Optical Ethernet Interfaces), proprietary versions of which can extend to 100 km. At the data-plane level, this setup obviously provides hard QoS at full-rate Ethernet tributary speeds, for example, CIR = 100 Mbps, 1.0 Gpbs, 10 Gbps. Nevertheless, obtaining dark fiber routes between all endpoints is generally very costly and gives reduced service velocity—from a range of days to weeks. Additionally EoF relegates all control and management to higher-layers, as shown in Figure 8.7.

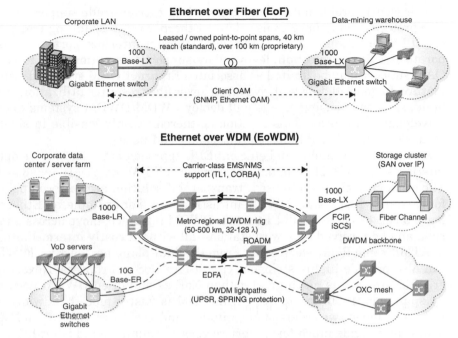

Figure 8.6 Ethernet private line services over fiber (EoF) and WDM (EoWDM)

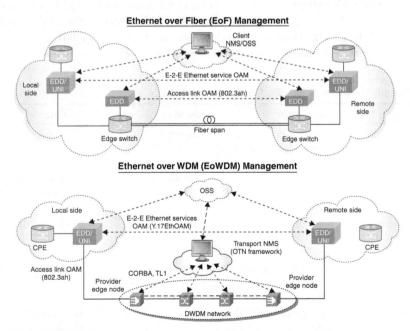

Figure 8.7 EoF and EoWDM service management scenarios

This is clearly problematic if client gears lack carrier-grade support. For example, service protection may have to use slower Ethernet rapid spanning tree protocol (RSTP) or MPLS rerouting protocols. Although Ethernet interface ports could possibly incorporate 1+1 fiber protection, few vendors support this option. Similarly, carrier-grade OAM support may be limited as associated Ethernet OAM standards will take time to mature. In general, EoF will give much lower fiber resource utilization and higher overbuild, since few leasing clients will deploy CWDM/DWDM systems to exploit unused wavelength capacities. This solution is, therefore, only feasible in smaller, fiber-rich scenarios with relaxed fault-tolerance and OAM needs.

A much more scalable and efficient EPL approach is to map native optical Ethernet interfaces onto WDM lightpaths—Ethernet over WDM (EoWDM)—as shown in Figure 8.6. The economics of this collapsed "transparent" solution are very compelling, especially for carriers with existing DWDM infrastructures. For example, an Ethernet packet can leave a server via a Gigabit Ethernet DWDM interface, move across a metro ROADM ring, and be received on a workstation—all without costly intermediate SONET/SDH or ATM/Frame Relay electronics. From the data-plane perspective, EoWDM (like EoF) can also provide highly stringent circuit-like QoS guarantees. Nevertheless, its geographic coverage is much greater than EoF, as amplified DWDM networks can readily span over 1000 km. Moreover, EoWDM is vastly more bandwidth scalable than EoF—by almost two orders of magnitude—and new third-generation DWDM ROADM nodes can provide much faster service velocity (minutes and hours).

EoWDM can also leverage the full range of WDM survivability schemes (see Figure 8.5) to offer multiple tiered (i.e., differentiated and value-added) EPL packages. Some examples are shown in Table 8.5 and include high-end EPL services using dedicated protection (1+1 span, UPSR, and mesh protection) to more wavelength-efficient services using shared protection (SPRING, shared mesh protection, and mesh restoration). Also note that EoWDM

TABLE 8.5   Sample DWDM-enabled EPL Service Categories

EPL Type	Carrier Pricing	Data Rates	Recovery Timescales	Comments
Platinum	Very high	Fast Ethernet/Gigabit Ethernet/10 Gigabit Ethernet	< 10 ms	1+1 span, dedicated UPSR
Gold	High	Fast Ethernet/Gigabit Ethernet/10 Gigabit Ethernet	< 50 ms	1:1 span, dedicated SPRING or dedicated mesh protection
Silver	Medium	Fast Ethernet/Gigabit Ethernet/10 Gigabit Ethernet	~ 100 ms	Shared SPRING or mesh protection
Bronze	Low	Fast Ethernet/Gigabit Ethernet/10 Gigabit Ethernet	NA	Nonprotected SPRING or mesh
Copper	Very Low	Fast Ethernet/Gigabit Ethernet/10 Gigabit Ethernet	NA	Preemptable (1:1 span, SPRING, mesh protection/restoration)

recovery will generally be faster—but less selective and service aware—than higher-layer mechanisms such as MPLS fast-reroute, Ethernet RSTP, and RPR ring wrap-around. Hence, careful interlayer escalation strategies will be required to prevent recovery collisions [3]. The simplest strategy may be to disable protection at the higher layers.

Perhaps most important of all, the EoWDM approach provides definitive service control, OAM visibility, and protection features, as there is an actual optical networking layer per say. Here, the adoption of intelligent control plane standards (see "Optical Network Control") in advanced third-generation DWDM networks will notably accelerate EPL delivery and automation. Meanwhile the availability of carrier-grade DWDM OAM capabilities (proprietary or OTN-based) will ensure mission-critical EPL support. Carefully note, however, that emerging Ethernet OAM standards will inevitably have functional overlaps with DWDM OAM (see "Network & Services Management"), and this will complicate carrier OSS integration. In many cases, large carriers may prefer to use service-agnostic OTN OAM capabilities for the DWDM layer and run Ethernet service OAM via higher level OSS tools, as shown previously in Figure 8.7. Hence, an EPL lightpath will appear as a virtual link between two EDD entities. Either way, EoWDM is well-suited for implementing highly stringent large granularity EPL services across MAN/WAN domains ("Section 8.5" details some scenarios).

Many customers may request lower-priced fractional (subrate) EPL services with speeds ranging from 50 Mbps to 1.0 Gbps. This is particularly true of small and medium enterprises (SME) clients. This poses a clear fiber/wavelength efficiency problem for EoF and EoWDM, which can only provision full-rate channels. In a related concern, EVPL support (via EoF or EoWDM) is also difficult as port partitioning requires Ethernet switching functionality at the endpoints. Because many DWDM OADM nodes can come with Ethernet thin-mux blades (see "Reconfigurable Add-Drop Rings"), in the practical sense some form of fractional EPL and/or EVPL can be achieved. Alternatively, carriers can use point-to-point EoF/EoWDM to interconnect Layer 2 Ethernet/MPLS switching nodes that are equipped with 1310 nm or 1550 nm SFP interfaces. In this case, EoF/EoWDM basically serves as an underlying compliment to EVPL switching devices supporting full VLAN stacking and QoS.

Overall, many carriers are already offering EPL services today using a variety of technologies, see the comparison in "Benefits & Shortcomings" Within this market, EoF and EoWDM-based services currently comprise a decent portion, about 20 percent, with EoF being the more prevalent type [12]. Nevertheless, given the ongoing deployment and expansion of metro-area DWDM infrastructures, particularly ROADM, it is widely expected that EoWDM will emerge as the preferred native-mode EPL-over-fiber solution.

Ethernet Private LAN Services (EPLAN)

EPLAN is a multipoint-to-multipoint (any-to-any) service designed to support Ethernet transparent LAN and Ethernet virtual private networks (Layer 2 VPN) applications [14]. Similarly, EVPLAN is a further enhancement that allows for multiple EPLAN entities to share a single port. These services basically interconnect multiple customer sites, making them appear linked by a LAN segment. These services require some form of packet broadcasting over WAN/MAN domains, which is very difficult to achieve at the optical layer. Perhaps the only means of implementing EPLAN at the optical layer (e.g., via EoF or EoWDM) is to establish direct connectivity between all source-destination pairs (e.g., dark fiber or WDM lightpath mesh). In the EoF case, this approach is too exorbitant and will quickly lead to fiber-exhaust. Similarly, in the EoWDM case, it will lead to wavelength exhaust (unscalable). For example, an EPLAN service between 8 sites requires 56 lightpaths, which can easily lead to lightpath blocking even with 16 or 32 channel DWDM networks.

In summary, EPLAN services will mandate full Layer 2 switching functionality at the service endpoints. Although some OADM thin-mux blades may offer switching support, these units cannot generally match the features and price-points of "best-of-breed" Ethernet systems, forcing a difficult compromise. Carriers may also find it costly and time consuming to integrate these specialized subsystems into their embedded OSS systems. As a result, the most feasible alternative will be to furnish EPLAN at the Ethernet/MPLS switching layers and interconnect these devices using underlying point-to-point EoF or EoWDM EPL services.

Benefits and Shortcomings

Carriers can use a variety of technologies to deliver carrier-grade Ethernet services, including high-end Ethernet switching, EoS, *Ethernet over MPLS (EoMPLS), Ethernet over RPR (EoRPR)*, and of course EoF/EoWDM. The related data and control plane protocol stacks are shown in Figure 8.8 and further details can be found in other chapters

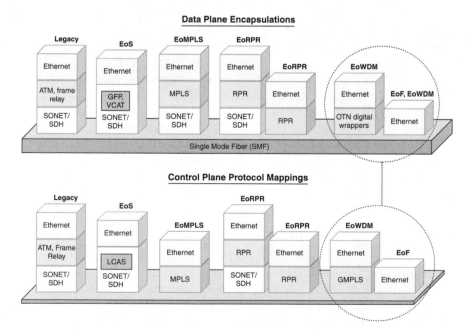

Figure 8.8   Carrier Ethernet data and control plane mappings

of this book. Clearly, the choice of a particular solution will depend upon various contingencies such as cost, existing infrastructures, projected demands, and competition. Moreover, these choices need not be mutually exclusive; in many cases, operators can selectively internetwork solutions to achieve maximum coverage. This section details some of the actual benefits and shortcomings of EoF and EoWDM vis a vis the competing alternatives (see Table 8.6).

Benefits

Fiber-optic transmission offers many inherent benefits for carrier-grade Ethernet services. Foremost, the unrivalled bandwidth capacity of DWDM transmission/switching systems makes EoWDM by far the most scalable approach for high-density/high-speed data port aggregation, for example, $n \times 10$ Gigabit Ethernet. By contrast, SONET/SDH or MPLS switching platforms are simply not cost-competitive at multiterabit switching rates. Moreover, EoWDM can enforce hard-QoS guarantees at all network loadings, and this capability is only matched by EoS—also a circuit-switching technology—albeit at much lower absolute loadings. Conversely, packet-switching solutions (such as EoMPLS, EoRPR, Ethernet switching) use more complex scheduler and priority mechanisms to enforce "relative" separation between coarse classes of service (CoS). At the carrier level, this requires a level of over-engineering as latency performance is very load-dependent [12], further increasing CAPEX and lowering amortization/payback periods. Also note that next-generation SONET (NGS)/multiservice provisioning platform (MSPP) technologies have become very popular with incumbents and can deliver very high efficiency and carrier-class OAM (see Chapter 11). Nevertheless,

TABLE 8.6   Comparison of Different Solutions for Carrier Ethernet Services

Feature	Ethernet Switching	Ethernet-SONET	Ethernet MPLS	Ethernet RPR	Ethernet-Fiber	Ethernet WDM
Topologies	Mesh	Linear, ring, mesh	Mesh	Dual ring	Point-to-point	Linear, ring, mesh
Service types	EPL/EVPL, ELAN/EVPLAN	EPL/EVPL	EPL/EVPL, ELAN/EVPLAN	EPL/EVPL, ELAN/EVPLAN	EPL	EPL
Scalability	Medium (Gbps)	Medium (Gbps)	Medium(Gbps)	Medium (Gbps)	Medium (Gbps)	High (Tbps)
Granularity	Very fine (kbps-Mbps)	Fine (VT1.5)	Very fine (kbps-Mbps)	Very fine (kbps-Mbps)	Coarse (Gbps)	Coarse (Gbps)
QoS Support	Soft/relative	Hard	Soft/relative	Soft/relative	Hard	Hard
Protection	100s ms to seconds	< 50 ms	100s ms	< 50 ms	Per higher layers	< 10 ms to 100s ms
OAM support	Ethernet OAM (maturing)	SONET/SDH OAM (excellent)	Ethernet OAM with MPLS LSP ping/ trace route (maturing)	Ethernet OAM with RPR ping (maturing)	Ethernet OAM (maturing)	DWDM OAM (excellent)

these technologies still face many challenges in transitioning to the next TDM carrier rate, 40 Gbps OC-768/STM-256. As such, NGS/MSPP is most germane as a grooming solution and fundamentally cannot scale capacity—this is only possible via multichannel DWDM.

The native format transparency of EoWDM (and EoF) provides vital cost savings for carriers—particularly at 10 Gbps rates. Namely, ROADM and EDFA-based networks can transparently move packets across large MAN domains without any intermediate electronic packet/bit-level processing and regeneration. This allows EoF/EoWDM to concurrently support all Ethernet line rates and keep pace with any future rate increases, future-proofing it. Specifically, EPL rate changes will only require edge interface (transponder) upgrades and possibly selected changes to amplifier and dispersion module placements. This contrasts with EoS or EoMPLS, which require comprehensive node upgrades throughout the network to run increased interface speeds. Optical transparency also enables full-rate EoWDM services to co-exist with other network implementations over the same fiber-plant (EoS, EoMPLS, and even legacy TDM private line). This is of crucial importance to incumbents since it allows them to complement subrate EoS systems and achieve staged, timely migrations. Finally, the physical-layer separation of WDM channels ensures high-security/confidentiality between clients.

As mentioned earlier, EoWDM replicates "five nines" resiliency and sub-50ms recovery. Although EoS and EoRPR can also achieve these bounds, their switchover capacities are much more limited. For example, DWDM-layer protection can restore well over a hundred 10 Gbps EPL connections in one span switch. However, EoWDM recovery is very coarse, and hence, carriers may have to perform some form of higher-layer grooming to achieve service selectivity. Namely, traffic flows with similar QoS profiles or price points will have to be combined over the same lightpath. Also note that the decoupled nature of data and control planes in transparent DWDM networks (see Optical Network Control) can improve overall EoWDM service resiliency, giving them a measure of immunity to control plane faults.

Finally, optical networking technology offers various other cost savings for EPL services. From an operational perspective, DWDM systems have smaller footprints and lower power consumption than equivalent-rate SONET/SDH systems. This provides very sizeable OPEX reduction at dense co-location sites. Moreover, EoWDM is very attractive for carriers with existing fiber infrastructures. For example, incumbents can migrate their entrenched fiber rings by slowly replacing legacy SONET/SDH nodes with modularized ROADM nodes. These upgrades can be done in a timely, cost-sensitive manner, where DWDM ports (e.g., filters, ROADM) are initially put in place and later populated with pluggable Ethernet transceiver modules as demands increase. This accelerates service delivery and minimizes equipment costs as transponders/transceivers form the bulk of optical network expenditures.

Shortcomings

As detailed in earlier, EoF and EoWDM can only furnish full-rate connections and cannot (in isolation at least) support subrate or switched Ethernet services. leaving a substantial service gap, particularly since fractional Gigabit Ethernet demands from SME outfits will form a large portion of overall demand. Hence, carriers must incur added capital and operational expenditures to deploy higher-layer devices to fill this void. At current market price-points, EoWDM transponders are best-suited for EPL speeds exceeding 1.0 Gbps [2]. As a result NGS/MSPP solutions will be more cost-effective for "fractional" service rates in the lower ten-hundreds of megabits range, particularly if SONET/SDH infrastructures are already in place. As a compromise, some carriers can use CWDM transport in these slower-rate settings.

Another area of concern for EoF and EoWDM is the lack of fully matured standards. For example, EoF is generally incapable of supporting full-spectrum management, at least until switch vendors offer full Ethernet OAM functionality on their ports (see Ethernet Management). Meanwhile, even though EoWDM provides much better OAM capabilities, most offerings are still vendor proprietary. In addition, there are no standardized protocols for optical layer protection. Although many vendors provide good solutions, these are proprietary and borrow heavily from SONET/SDH schemes. In all, these factors give increased OSS integration costs, low interoperability, and impose complexities for operations staff. By contrast, EoS can extend established carrier-class OAM coverage to full *and* fractional-rate EPL/EVPL services via new standards such as *generic framing procedure (GFP)*, ITU-T G.7041, and *link capacity adjustment scheme (LCAS)*, ITU-T G.7042 (see Figure 8.8).

Finally, DWDM is a relatively new and highly specialized technology with complex underlying physical-layer concerns. Hence, most DWDM networks require a sizeable amount of preplanning design and continual fine-tuning to maintain BER performance. Some of the key issues here include span loss budgets, amplifier placements, dispersion compensation, and wavelength assignment. Although third-generation soft-optics DWDM technologies (see Optical Network Architectures) are helping automate many manual provisioning tasks, it will still take time and money for carriers to master these technologies. As a result, skilled technical staff will be required to run these networks, adding to operational overheads and inevitably impacting Carrier Ethernet (EoWDM) pricing.

Typical Deployment Scenarios

In light of the just described benefits and shortcomings, a consensus is emerging on some amenable scenarios for EoF and EoWDM. In general, EoF is good for shorter-distance fiber-rich settings and customers with relaxed fault tolerance and OAM needs. Alternatively, EoWDM is a more carrier-ready approach and has a "sweet-spot" for multigigabit users with genuine MAN/WAN coverage and robust QoS/OAM needs. As DWDM costs decline, the price-per-bit economics of EoDWM will also become increasingly compelling [12]. Some of the main deployment scenarios are now detailed.

Corporate Extension Scenarios

Businesses continue to scale and simplify their networks and are moving away from legacy private line services. In the corporate sector, Carrier Ethernet demand is coming from several key areas. A major application is data-center/back-office consolidation of server farms and data-warehousing operations to improve operational efficiencies. Another pressing scenario is LAN-over-MAN extension across inter-campus sites. For example, many operations are being moved from high-rent downtown areas to suburban regions to lower costs and facilitate worker access. This is driving the need for virtual LAN solutions via underlying point-to-point EPL or multipoint EPLAN services. Note that direct LAN extension at the Layer 2 level also reduces the need for costly Layer 3 devices because only a few routers or MPLS nodes are needed for *external* connectivity.

Now most corporate demands today are comprised of fractional EPL and represent a growing migration from legacy private lines. In general, these speeds are best provisioned by electronic-layer routing and switching solutions such as EoS or EoMPLS. EoS is particularly cost-effective in low demand incumbent networks, as it can augment existing legacy voice and leased line offerings. Alternatively, for carriers operating CWDM/DWDM infrastructures, thin-mux aggregation devices can be considered in conjunction with EoWDM. Regardless, a gradual shift toward gigabit-level EPL speeds is expected. For example, 10 Gbps Ethernet interfaces are now becoming standard on most servers and storage arrays. It is here that the economics of EoF/EoWDM will begin to dominate. Specifically, EoF will make sense for smaller service providers offering less-critical full-rate LAN extension at lower price-points, for example, competitive local exchange carriers (CLEC). Meanwhile larger operators—particularly those with built-out WDM infrastructures—can target high-density/longer distance EPL interconnections with robust OAM support.

Storage Area Networks (SAN) Scenarios

Many corporations are dispersing critical data over wide geographic areas using storage networking concepts (SAN). Again, there are various applications of interest here. Foremost is disaster recovery (via remote backup) to ensure mission-critical operation during natural disasters, power outages, and so on. Another requirement is for real-time, synchronized mirroring (replication) of data at different sites for load-balancing, business scaling/productivity, and so on. Finally, the storage-on-demand market is also being explored by some provider organizations. In all of these settings, geographic diameters are generally limited to 100 km, although these are expected to scale over the years.

Today, Fibre Channel is the most prevalent SAN technology, delivering extremely reliable transfers via a low-latency block transfer protocol. Related interface speeds range from 1.0 to 10 Gbps, and most setups are of a closed nature, implemented over dark fiber. Given its specialized nature, Fibre Channel requires skilled technical staff, yielding a high total cost of ownership (TCO). It is here that new "IP/Ethernet-based" standards are helping to open up this sector to improved economies of scale, namely, *Fibre Channel over IP (FCIP)*, which allows organizations to recoup their SAN investments and extend interfaces over ubiquitous IP domains. Meanwhile *Internet SCSCI (iSCSI)* and *remote direct memory access (RDMA)* move a step further by directly implementing SAN-type transfers at the IP/Ethernet layer.

IP/Ethernet-based storage will inevitably drive high-end EPL service growth. Namely, EoF and EoWDM are much better positioned (versus EoS, EoMPLS, or EoRPR) given the multigigabit speeds of most SAN interfaces. For example, many corporations may consider lower-cost EoF solutions using Gigabit Ethernet FCIP (iSCSI) interfaces to complement (replace) Fibre Channel in leased or owned-fiber scenarios. Alternatively, EoWDM is more compelling since corporations can preclude costly fiber infrastructure builds and instead purchase guaranteed hard-QoS EPL services for storage extension. This approach also gives much larger geographic coverage for SAN applications. Note that many SAN vendors also offer Fibre Channel DWDM interfaces (50–100 km reach) that will inevitably compete with EoWDM strategies. Nevertheless, carriers can leverage WDM technology to transparently host both types of storage networking solutions over metro/regional networks—a key advantage.

Residential and Backhaul Scenarios

The growing scalability and convergence in the access space (highlighted in "Solution Drivers for Ethernet over Fiber/WDM") is driving the need for bulk data backhaul. In particular packet-video services represent a primary growth area and residential providers are offering a very broad range of related services, for example, IP TV, video-on-demand (VoD), personal video recorder (PVR)/playback, and so on. Now typical broadcast quality video requires about 4 Mbps per stream, whereas higher-end DVD quality requires about 9–10 Mbps per stream. Aggregating these figures over large user populations gives genuine multigigabit requirements, and hence many VoD servers already support Gigabit and 10 Gigabit Ethernet interfaces.

In response to this growth, nearly all cable operators have moved to HFC setups, using fiber to interconnect master head-ends with dispersed local hubs. Meanwhile incumbents are actively pursuing the residential video market to offset declines in long-distance voice. Here video delivery architectures are being overlaid on top of entrenched metro/edge fiber-plants. Namely localized video switching offices (VSO) at smaller edge ring sites are being interconnected to video hub offices (VHO) at larger metro core/regional hubs. The former sites connect to DSL access multiplexers (DSLAM) or PON optical line terminals (OLT) units for last-mile delivery. Meanwhile, the latter sites house large VoD servers. Overall EoWDM is ideal for native packet-video backhaul over existing cable/incumbent fiber plants. Scalability is the paramount concern here, and only multi-channel DWDM can realistically provision large head-end flows with thousands of homes crossed. Moreover, because head-end/hub or VSO/VHO locations are largely fixed, lower-cost static OADM setups are also very feasible.

Additionally, the wireless sector is seeing very strong growth with the induction of 3.5G technologies and new service types. Most notably, web access and video streaming/casting are the key bandwidth drivers, and wireless operators are also converging to IP/Ethernet packet-switching architectures. However, most wireless access devices, such as base-station controllers, still use older T1/E1 private lines for data backhaul over SONET/SDH networks. Here, related legacy private line service costs can consume about 40–60 percent of a typical wireless operator's operational expenditures, and these costs are becoming a big bottleneck with increased content volumes. As a result, Gigabit Ethernet is now becoming the preferred interface for cellular backhaul and future evolutions to 4G may very well drive 10 Gigabit Ethernet rates. Clearly point-to-point EoF and EoWDM will provide a strong fit for low-latency/high-reliability data backhaul between wireless access and core sites.

Point-of-Presence (PoP) Scenarios

Many large ISPs and carrier backbones consist of IP routers and/or MPLS label switching routers (LSR) deployed at large point of presence (PoP) locations. These sites commonly hub last-mile traffic and interconnect to each other using dedicated high-speed links, commonly OC-192 PoS. However, many carriers are now scaling toward terabit-level router setups to support growing inter-PoP traffic requirements over public networks. Here EoF and EoWDM offer the most amenable strategies for high-density point-to-point PoP interconnection. Foremost, 10G Base-LW/EW (WAN) interfaces will provide good cost-effectiveness over more expensive OC-192 PoS router interfaces. Secondly, the use of underlying WDM transport (via EoWDM) can extend such peering setups over much larger domains.

Ongoing Developments

Future technology developments will continue to shape the EoF and EoWDM service sectors. In particular, major advances are expected in three areas: improved DWDM designs, higher-speed Ethernet interfaces, and evolutions in optical network control. These areas are highlighted briefly.

Advances in WDM Networking

Ongoing advances in soft-optics for ROADM and OXC devices will continue to drive improved DWDM-layer capabilities in the metro and long-haul space. In particular, *photonic integrated circuit (PIC)* technologies hold much promise in coalescing multiple discrete optical *and* electronic components onto a single substrate, for example, lasers, amplifiers, photo-detectors, filters, switches, and so on. PIC devices can drastically reduce opto-electronic transponder costs—which dominate carrier CAPEX—and help lower nodal losses. Indeed, this technology promises a true leap in capabilities by reducing footprints, increasing reach, and enabling more elaborate optical-layer monitoring. Recently, some PIC-based transport and OXC solutions have already come to market and future evolutions are expected.

There is a lot of ongoing research in *optical burst switching (OBS)* and *optical packet switching (OPS)* technologies [3]. These schemes introduce data-packet "visibility" at the optical layer by processing packet header routing information (and optically bypassing data segments). As such, OBS and OPS could conceivably support advanced EVPL and EPLAN/EVPLAN services. However, both of these technologies face many technical and "prove-in" hurdles, and despite many years of study, remain far from real-world deployments [2].

Ethernet Interface Evolutions

There is much ongoing debate in the data and optical networking communities about the next Ethernet rate—40 Gbps or 100 Gbps. (The TDM hierarchy already specifies 40 Gbps OC-768/STM-256 as the next increment.) Such extreme demands are being motivated by projections for massive data-center aggregation needs, i.e., large numbers of 10 Gigabit Ethernet ports. While some support maintaining Ethernet's traditional "10x" scaling factor, others are contemplating a break from tradition in light of technological and cost factors.

There have been some impressive achievements in 40 Gbps OC-768/STM-256 transport with vendors demonstrating ultra-long haul reach and many tens of channels per fiber. In fact, some OC-768/STM-256 products are even coming to market (e.g., DWDM transport and router interfaces), and various carriers are planning 40 Gbps backbones. Nevertheless, others are actively studying long-haul 100 Gbps transmission via either serial or parallel interfaces [15]. Expectedly, serial transmission is much more challenging as it poses extreme constraints on associated serializer/deserializer devices, optical modulators, detectors, and so on. Moreover, related SMF dispersion effects will mandate extensive compensation at much closer distances (10–20 km). Alternatively, parallel transmission ameliorates electronic barriers by streaming multiple data paths over separate DWDM wavelengths, for example, 10×10 Gbps or 4×25 Gbps. As DWDM transceiver costs decline and PIC component integration becomes more commonplace, this approach opens up the very real possibility of Ethernet scaling to unprecedented terabit rates. These issues will be closely studied in the relevant standards bodies in the coming decade.

New Control Protocol Frameworks

Although GMPLS optical control standards have been available for several years now, overall market traction has been slow. For example, very few equipment vendors fully support GMPLS in their product lines today, and most DWDM ROADM and DCS/MSPP systems still use centralized TL1 management (because of the strong SONET/SDH influence). A key reason here has been the lack of demand for highly dynamic wavelength-rate services. However, it is expected that continued growth in high-end EPL services will inevitably drive the adoption of this framework. In particular, GMPLS offers much promise in provisioning multiple service tiers for lightpath connections (see Optical Network Control).

Recently, there has also been some activity in the IETF to extend the GMPLS control plane for point-to-point Ethernet label switching [16]. By and large, this draft focuses on adapting GMPLS protocols for the Ethernet layer and details various Layer 2 issues, such as label encapsulation in Ethernet frames and data plane modifications. Although this work is in its early stages, it may lead to a very tight integration (cost savings) between the Ethernet packet-switching and SONET/SDH-DWDM circuit-switching layers. This is particularly germane for unified MSPP platforms that implement Layer 1 and 2 capabilities.

Finally, another noteworthy development is the *Layer 1 VPN (L1 VPN)* framework [17], which defines "infrastructure virtualization" at the SONET/SDH and DWDM layers.

Indeed, this standard is very well-aligned with various intra-carrier and carriers' carrier business models. For example L1 VPN technologies will allow organizations to purchase virtual DWDM networks and offer customized EPL or EPLAN services over them. This new paradigm has the potential to dramatically lower barriers to entry in the Carrier Ethernet market, as entrants will no longer have to deploy or lease their own physical fiber-optic infrastructures. L1 VPN remains an active focus area today within the IETF and ITU-T (Study Group 13).

Economic Assessment

This section presents a brief economic assessment of high-grade Ethernet services over fiber. Specifically, the EoWDM and EoS schemes are chosen for comparison, as they are best-suited for supporting genuine MAN/WAN carrier-grade EPL services and they are the most likely strategies for incumbents. Figure 8.9 shows the sample network used in this study, representing a ubiquitous ring topology with eight add-drop sites. Here, each add-drop location is either populated with ROAM nodes (EoWDM) or next-generation multiservice SONET/SDH MSPP platforms (EoS). Furthermore, the ring circumference is assumed to be 300 km to reflect larger MAN/WAN service settings, and all nodes are evenly spaced. This increased geographic span is chosen as it mandates the use of preline and inline EDFA devices in the ROADM solution to, for example, stress CAPEX costs.

This network has been evaluated for EoS and EoWDM provisioning for various full-rate EPL service scenarios. Owing to the larger regional nature of the ring, it is assumed that the traffic is evenly distributed and arrives from enterprise and other provider clients.

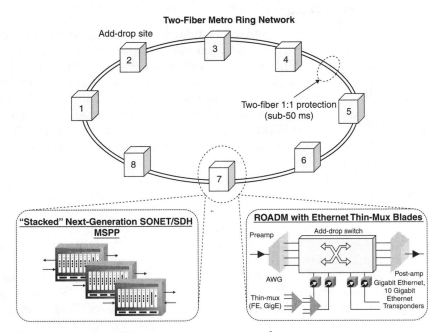

Figure 8.9 Sample network used in economic assessment study

TABLE 8.7   Overview of Traffic Scenarios (EPL Connection Requests)

Scenario	Fast Ethernet	Gigabit Ethernet	10 Gigabit Ethernet
Small	80	0	0
Medium	80	8	0
Large	80	12	8

This contrasts with smaller metro-edge rings that exhibit more hubbed traffic patterns [3]. In particular, three types of traffic loading scenarios have been studied: small, medium, and large (see Table 8.7). In the small loading case, the client demands only comprise 100 Mbps Fast Ethernet requests. The medium traffic case augments the above with a small amount of Gigabit Ethernet demands (about 10 percent). Finally, the large loading case adds a full range of demands from Fast Ethernet to Gigabit Ethernet and even full 10 Gigabit Ethernet. To assess the economic CAPEX costs of the two schemes, the required subsystems are briefly reviewed, as highlighted in Table 8.8.

NOTE   The prices stated here are bound to decline over time, and hence the listing is provided more for relative comparison purposes.

Consider the EoWDM solution first. Here, the overall ROADM systems are comprised of three main sections—multiplex, amplification, and local access. The multiplex section consists of two AWG filters that are used to multiplex/demultiplex composite DWDM signals. Meanwhile, the amplification section consists of preline and inline (i.e., post-line) EDFA devices for analog DWDM amplification. Finally, the local access section consists of an optical switch, for example, WSS, that allows for adding or dropping wavelength lightpaths. These units form the main ROADM node at an add-drop site and can handle anywhere from several to many tens of wavelengths. In addition, DWDM transponders are also needed to convert client-side signals to network-side ITU grid wavelengths and related costs vary per signal rate. Finally, two types of

TABLE 8.8   Sample Subsystem Costs

EoWDM Solution		EoS Solution	
Subsystem Type	Typical Cost	Subsystem Type	Typical Cost
Gigabit Ethernet transponder	$4,000	OC-48 transponder	$8,000
10 Gigabit Ethernet transponder	$7,500	OC-192 transponder	$12,000
8:1 Fast Ethernet to Gigabit Ethernet thin-mux muxponder	$4,000	8:1 Gigabit Ethernet to OC-192 muxponder thin-mux	$14,000
8:1 Gigabit Ethernet to 10 Gigabit Ethernet thin-mux muxponder	$8,000	OC-48 SONET add-drop multiplexer unit	$10,000
DWDM SPRING protection module	$4,000	OC-192 SONET add-drop multiplexer unit	$20,000
ROADM (40 channel multiplex, amp, local sections)	$30,000	SONET BLSR protection switching module	$4,000

thin-mux blades (*muxponders*) are also assumed for EoWDM to help aggregate slower (full-rate Fast Ethernet) clients.

Meanwhile, the EoS solution uses SONET ADM units to add/drop traffic from the TDM ring (either OC-48 or OC-192). Here, each ADM has the ability to *groom* traffic in multiples of STS-1 and comprises an STS cross-connect fabric. In addition, the EoS approach uses SONET-based transponders and thin-mux blades. The latter commonly support advanced features such as GFP and LCAS to optimize full/fractional rate EPL support. For the purposes of this study, the SONET thin-mux is assumed to be a simple blade for aggregating eight full-rate Fast Ethernet signals onto a OC-192c payload. Note that both EoWDM and SONET solutions also require protection modules. Namely, SONET APS is commonly done using the robust BLSR approach, whereas ROADM-based offerings can deliver (proprietary) path protection in a dedicated or shared manner (see Table 8.8).

The overall cost summary of the EoWDM and EoS approaches is given in Table 8.9 (presented for OC-192 rates only). Here, it is seen that EoWDM is generally more cost-effective for full-rate demands, particularly as the number of high-rate EPL demands increases. Namely, EoWDM provides an almost 40 percent lower cost for the large traffic scenario, and operational overheads are also expected to be much lower as no "box-stacking" is needed. Note, however, that EoWDM benefits tremendously from the use of Fast Ethernet thin-mux aggregation blades, without which the cost would spiral well over EoS. Overall, the declining costs of DWDM technology (20 percent per year) coupled with increasing gigabit-level demands present very good amortization/payback periods, for example, range of months to a few years. More importantly, most ROADM systems feature modularized designs that can grow to accommodate increased channel counts at moderate costs, providing lower cost-per-bit for higher-volume services.

Carefully note that dark fiber costs are not factored into this study. Instead, it is simply assumed there are multiple fiber pairs available on the ring. In practice, however, the lower scalability of EoS will require "stacking" multiple TDM rings to match increased demands, and hence, fiber costs may not be negligible (unless of course EoS is blended with DWDM transponders). This is of particular relevance to greenfield scenarios.

TABLE 8.9   Summary of Solution for OC-192 Transponders Case (all costs in thousands of dollars)

Solution	Laser Transponders (# / Cost)	Thin-mux or ADM (# / Cost)	AWG Filters (# / Cost)	WDM EDFA (# / Cost)	Protection Modules (# / Cost)	Total Cost
EoS (Small)	16 / 128	16 / 128	- / -	- / -	8 / 32	288
EoS (Medium)	20 / 196	20 / 160	- / -	- / -	8 / 32	388
EoS (Large)	28 / 296	28 / 300	- / -	- / -	8 / 32	628
EoWDM (Small)	12 / 48	12 / 48	8 / 64	8 / 32	8 / 32	224
EoWDM (Medium)	16 / 72	16 / 72	8 / 64	8 / 32	8 / 32	272
EoWDM (Large)	20 / 96	20 / 120	8 / 64	8 / 32	8 / 32	344

Vendors Promoting This Solution

At the time of this writing, many network equipment vendors are offering EoF and EoWDM solutions. These vendors range from optical vendors providing related transport, switching, and transponder solutions to Layer 2/3 switch vendors directly integrating optics onto their switching systems. Some of the key ONE vendor offerings are summarized in Table 8.10.

TABLE 8.10   Vendors Offering EoF and EoWDM Solutions

Vendor	Solution/Product Name	Comments
ADVA	FSP3000	Optical transport system, ROADM
	FSP500	MSPP
Alcatel	Alcatel 1660	MSPP
	Alcatel 7450	Metro Ethernet platform (core)
Atrica	A2000	Metro Ethernet platform (edge)
	A4000	Metro Ethernet platform (aggregation)
	A8000	Metro Ethernet platform (core)
Calient	DiamondWave PXC	Optical transport system
Ciena	CoreDirector	MSPP, DCS, optical transport system
Cisco	ONS 15327	MSPP
	ONS 15454	MSPP
	ONS 15600	MSPP
	ONS 15800	Optical transport systems
Extreme Networks	BlackDiamond Series(6800-12804)	Metro Ethernet platform (aggregation, core)
	Alpine 3800	Metro Ethernet platform (edge, aggregation)
Fujitsu	Flashwave 4500	MSPP
	Flashwave 5150	Metro Ethernet platform (edge, aggregation)
	Flashwave 7500	Optical transport system, ROADM
Infinera	DTN	Optical transport system
Lucent	LambdaUnite	MSPP
	Ethernet Router 15800	Metro Ethernet platform (edge, aggregation)
Nortel	Optical Metro 3500	MSPP
	Optical Multi-Service Edge 6110	MSPP
	Optical Multi-Service Edge 6500	MSPP
	Optical Packet Edge System	Resilient packet ring (RPR)
	Optical TN series	MSPP

(Continued)

TABLE 8.10   Vendors Offering EoF and EoWDM Solutions (*Continued*)

Vendor	Solution/Product Name	Comments
Sycamore Networks	OM1000	MSPP
	IAB-3000	MSPP
	OX8000	MSPP
	SN 3000	MSPP
	SN 16000, SN 16000 SC	MSPP, DCS
Tellabs	Tellabs 6315	Metro Ethernet platform (edge, aggregation)
	Tellabs 7110	Optical transport system
	Tellabs 7100	Optical transport system
	Tellabs 6370	Optical transport system, ROADM
Zhone	GigaMux 6400 DWDM	Optical transport system, static OADM
	GigaMux 1600/3200 CWDM	
	GigaMux 50	

References

1. B. Mukherjee, *Optical WDM Networks* (New York: Springer Publishers, 2006).

2. R. Ramaswami, "Optical Networking Technologies: What Worked and What Didn't," *IEEE Communications Magazine,* vol. 44, no. 9 (September 2006): 132–139.

3. N. Ghani, Y. Pan, and X. Cheng, "Metropolitan Optical Networks," *Optical Fiber Telecommunications (OFT) IV,* I. Kaminow and T. Li (eds.) (City: Academic Press, March 2002): 329–403.

4. D. Zhou and S. Subramaniam, "Survivability in Optical Networks," *IEEE Network,* vol. 14, no. 6 (November/December 2000): 16–23.

5. T. H. Wu, *Fiber Network Service Survivability* (Boston: Artech House, 1992).

6. P. Bonenfant, A. Moral, "Generic Framing Procedure (GFP): The Catalyst for Efficient Data Over Transport," *IEEE Communications Magazine,* vol. 40, no. 5 (May 2002): 72–79.

7. G. Bernstein, B. Rajagopalan, and D. Saha, *Optical Network Control: Architectures, Standards, Protocols* (Boston: Addison Wesley, 2003).

8. B. Rajagopalan, et al., "User Network Interface (UNI) 1.0 Signaling Specification," OIF Contribution OIF2000.125.7, October 2001.

9. "NNI 1.0: Inter-Domain Control Plane Requirements," OIF Contribution OIF2002.054.03, May 2002.

10. J. Jones, L. Ong, and M. Lazer, "Interoperability Update: Dynamic Ethernet Services Via Intelligent Optical Networks," *IEEE Communications Magazine,* vol. 42, no. 8 (August 2004): S4–S10.

11. A. Meddeb, "Why Ethernet WAN Transport?" *IEEE Communications Magazine,* vol. 43, no. 11 (November 2005): 136–141.

12. "Optical Ethernet's Role in Enabling Carrier-Class Ethernet Services," Heavy Reading White Paper, April 2005.

13. "Metro Ethernet Services Definitions Phase I," Technical Specification, Metro Ethernet Forum (MEF 6), June 2004.

14. "Metro Ethernet Network Architecture Framework Part 1: Generic Framework," Technical Specification, Metro Ethernet Forum (MEF 4), May 2004.

15. M. Duelk and M. Zirngibl, "100 Gigabit Ethernet—Applications, Features, Challenges," IEEE INFOCOM 2006 High-Speed Networking Workshop, Barcelona, Spain, April 2006.

16. L. Andersson, A. Acreo, and D. Papadimitriou, "Use of the GMPLS Control Plane for Point-to-Point Ethernet Label Switching," IETF Draft draft-andersson-gels-bof-prep-00.txt, August 2006.

17. T. Takeda, I. Inoue, R. Aubin, and M. Carugi, "Layer 1 Virtual Private Networks: Service Concepts, Architecture Requirements, and Related Advances in Standardization," *IEEE Communications Magazine,* vol. 42, no. 6 (June 2004):. 132–138.

Optical Wireless Mesh Networks

by Prasanna Adhikari

The optical wireless mesh network brings together two technologies: optical and mesh networking. Optical wireless technology uses a wireless infrared optical signal to transport high bandwidth data over distances in the range of tens of meters to hundreds of meters. It has the benefit of being able to deliver data rates comparable to that of fiber-optic cables with the added flexibility of wireless communication. Mesh networking technology, on the other hand, offers the benefit of high reliability and high capacity networking. It can also deliver the high-grade network services demanded by Carrier Ethernet services. Optical wireless mesh networks therefore bring together the benefits of three diverse technologies, optical, wireless and mesh, as illustrated in Figure 9.1, Because of these benefits, an optical wireless mesh network can provide an ideal platform for delivering carrier-class Ethernet services and other kinds of network services in a large number of applications.

In this chapter, we discuss the benefits and shortcomings of both these technologies and how they fit together as an emerging technology to deliver Carrier Ethernet services. We also discuss typical applications and deployment scenarios and end the chapter with a brief review of products available today from various vendors.

Technology/Solution Description

The term *optical wireless* captures two essential elements of the technology that makes it very appealing for networking applications. It is a technology that offers ultra-high bandwidth of optical communication along with the convenience of wireless communication. The technology uses optical signals to communicate wirelessly over a range of distances.

The first recorded use of an optical signal as a mean of communication goes as far back as the times of the Ancient Greeks when signals were transmitted over long distances by using shiny objects to reflect sunlight. Its first modern use, in the form of a device called a *heliograph,* was in 1935 when the U.S. and British armies sent Morse code over distances of tens of miles by using mirrors to create flashes of reflected sunlight.

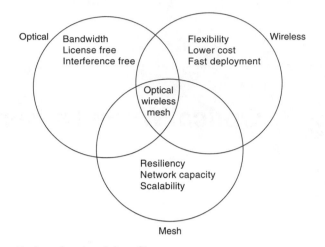

Figure 9.1   Wireless optical mesh network benefits

The early development of optical wireless as a wireless communication technology goes back to the time of the early development of radio frequency (RF) wireless communication technology. An optical wireless telephonic device called the *photophone* was invented by Alexander Graham Bell in 1880, at about the same time as Marconi and Edison were demonstrating wireless telephony using radio frequency. The photophone used lightbeams to transmit voice conversation over distances of a few hundred meters. Bell considered this invention to be one of his most important inventions. It, however, had the same limitation as heliograph. It used sunlight as the source of its optical beam, making it unreliable because of its susceptibility to weather conditions.

Despite early attempts to develop optical wireless, the technology was in no position to compete with RF wireless technology, which served the needs of the time with much more reliability. In fact, optical wireless technology remained mostly dormant until recently when the need for capacity grew significantly enough that its benefits over RF wireless could be brought to fruition.

There have been many forms of modern optical wireless communication technology, including signaling devices such as remote controls and communication technology such as IrDA. However, the optical wireless communication technology discussed in this chapter is a technology that can be used to transfer large volumes of data over extended periods of time as part of a reliable network infrastructure. This technology is also commonly referred to as *Free Space Optics (FSO)* technology. Throughout the remainder of this chapter, the terms *FSO* and *optical wireless* are used interchangeably.

The Technology

Optical wireless technology consists of a method for data transmission and reception using light signals over *free space*. Unlike fiber-optic communication, in which the medium is a fiber-optic cable, FSO uses free space as its medium. An FSO system consists of three key subsystems, each of which has achieved maturity as a technology in its own right.

Communication Channel (Transmitter and Receiver)   For the transmission and reception of data, FSO uses the same underlying technology as fiber-optic technology. Not only is this underlying technology a mature technology, but also it has the benefit of offering a significant potential to scale when it comes to delivering fiber-like bandwidth with the flexibility of being a wireless medium.

Most FSO systems use the infrared (IR) spectrum with wavelengths between 785 nm and 850 nm. Infrared signals are not visible to human eyes but are "visible" to silicon detectors. Some FSO systems also use 1550 nm wavelength IR beams, a spectrum popular in long-haul fiber-optic communication. The 1550 nm IR beam has the benefits of being slightly less susceptible to atmospheric effects and safer for the human eye than 850 nm IR beam. However, the current state of transmitter and receiver technology makes it less cost-effective.

Unlike RF wireless, FSO does not use sophisticated modulation techniques. FSO systems, in general, use the same modulation techniques as fiber-optic systems do, referred to as *On-Off Keying (OOK) modulation,* where the optical signal is turned ON or OFF to transmit the "1" or "0" state of a bit in a digital datastream.

One of the key differentiations between the transmission technique of FSO and fiber optics is the optical power transmitted. In fiber-optic systems, signals do not experience significant loss as they travel from the transmitter to the receiver, as they do in the case of FSO due to geometric spreading and atmospheric attenuation of the signals. In the case of fiber optics, only a very small fraction of the transmitted light gets lost over a comparable distance. On the contrary, in the case of FSO, only a very small fraction of the transmitted light actually makes it to the receiver. Therefore, the amount of transmitted power needed to achieve comparable distances is significantly higher in the case of FSO than in the case of fiber optics.

Based on the transmitter and receiver techniques, FSO systems can be divided into two broad categories: active systems and passive systems.

Active System   Active FSO systems consist of active electro-optic components to transmit and receive data. Electro-optical devices such as light-emitting diodes (LEDs) or laser diodes are used to generated modulated signals to be transmitted. Electro-optical devices such as PN diodes or avalanche photodiodes (APDs) are used to receive and demodulate the received optical signals.

LEDs used in FSO devices are close cousins of LEDs used widely as electronic displays and are even closer to LEDs used in remote controls and IrDA devices. In a typical FSO system, LEDs are modulated at a much higher rate than LEDs in IrDA. Besides being less expensive than laser diodes, LED also has the benefit of being a source of incoherent light. The incoherent light makes FSO systems based on LEDs safer (for eyes) than those based on laser diodes. Additionally, it also makes such systems less susceptible to effects of atmospheric scintillation, a topic to be discussed in more detail later.

Laser diodes offer their own sets of benefits. For one, laser generates a much narrower band of optical spectrum, making it easier to eliminate background light at the receiver by using a narrowband optical filter, a benefit that will be discussed in more detail in Section *Receive Field of View (FoV)*. In general, more optical power can be generated using laser diodes than can be done with LEDs. Lasers also have optical properties that make them more suitable for very long-range FSO systems.

Passive Fiber Coupled Systems   Unlike active systems, passive systems do not contain any active electro-optical components as part of the communication subsystem. Passive Fiber Coupled Systems (PFCS) are designed to directly couple optical signals coming out of a fiber-optic cable to its transmission optics without electrically regenerating the signals. Similarly, they are designed to collect and inject the received optical signal directly into the fiber-optic cable without electrically regenerating it. In its simplest comparative description, PFCS can be thought of as serving the same purpose as the directional antenna in RF wireless.

There are two key benefits of PFCS technology. First, such systems are independent of the underlying data transmission rate because they do not regenerate the signal electrically. They can truly serve as a means of wireless fiber extension. Second, such systems (when designed with the right kind of optical components) can support multiple wavelength transmission, making them viable for transmission of WDM signals. Both of these benefits can bring the virtually unbounded capacity of the fiber-optic world to the wireless world, something that will never be matched by RF wireless technology.

Such systems, even though proven in the field at data rates as high as 40 Gbps, have yet to find their way into mainstream FSO product offerings in a commercially viable way. However, as demand increases and technology advances, costs will continue to decrease, enabling such FSO technology to enter the mainstream communication world as an economically viable technology.

Optics   Optics is a key component of FSO technology, and this is where it differs most significantly from fiber-optic technology and draws closer to RF wireless technology. Optics in FSO systems play the same role as antennas in RF communications. They allow the creation of a narrow beam of light to be transmitted. They also allow for the collection of optical signals at the receiving end. The optics technology used in FSO systems are the same ones found in other optical systems such as telescopes and cameras. Therefore, the technology is very mature and well proven.

Transmit Optics   The transmit optics in an FSO system consist of optical components such as lenses and/or mirrors. The transmit optics serve the purpose of collecting the light from the transmit source such as the LED, laser, or fiber-optic cable and then transmitting it in the form of a narrow beam of light. Such beams are characterized by two parameters: beamwidth and divergence. A simple form of transmit optics is illustrated in Figure 9.2.

Transmit Beam Width   The beamwidth is the measure of the diameter of the transmit beam as it launches out of the system. The desirability for a larger beamwidth is in its ability to transmit more optical power while meeting the safety requirements mandated by government agencies. FSO system safety, as regulated by government agencies,

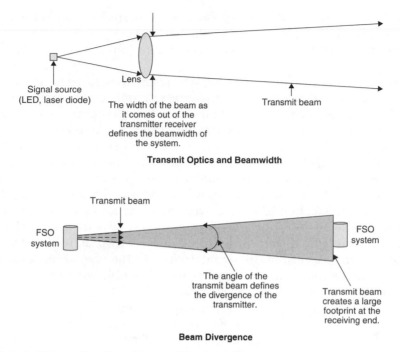

Transmit Optics and Beamwidth

Beam Divergence

Figure 9.2 A typical transmit optic and transmit beam profile

depends on the optical power per unit cross-sectional area of the beam. Therefore, systems with larger beamwidths can maintain the same level of eye safety while transmitting more total power than systems with smaller beamwidths. For example, an FSO system can transmit four times as much power as one with half its transmit beamwidth while maintaining the same level of eye safety.

Another benefit of using a wider beamwidth is in reducing the effect of atmospheric scintillation. *Scintillation* is an atmospheric phenomenon commonly observed as the twinkling of stars or distant light sources. Scintillation produces a similar effect on FSO systems, causing fluctuation in optical signals over long propagation distances. Wider beams can reduce the overall signal fluctuation caused by scintillation because of the averaging effect over a greater area. Scintillation will be discussed in more detail later in separate section on this subject.

Both of the benefits derived from larger transmit beamwidths can also be achieved by FSO systems using multiple transmitters. For example, an FSO system that uses four transmit beams of 1-in diameter can achieve the same transmit power level and the same safely level as a system using a single 2-in diameter transmit beam. In fact, a system with four separate transmit beams can achieve a better scintillation immunity.

The downside of a system with either wider transmit beams or multiple transmit beams is the size, weight, and cost of the system. The optical components required to create large beamwidths are not only bigger and heavier but can be significantly more costly than smaller optical components. Some of the benefits of the large transmit beam may not be of any significance for the particular application being considered. For example, for short-range links, the effect of scintillation is insignificant.

Transmit Beam Divergence   Transmit beam divergence measures the degree of beam spreading as it propagates away from the transmitter. Divergence is the property, measured in degrees or radian, that identifies the spreading factor of the transmit beam. The smaller the divergence, the less spread out the beam is.

In any wireless communication system, such spreading of the signal is one of the greatest sources of signal loss. To illustrate the point, consider Figure 9.2 where two FSO systems are located a half mile from each other. Let's assume the transmit beam divergence is about 1 degree, a typical value for an FSO system. By the time the signal arrives at the location of the receiver, the transmit beam would have spread enough to create a beam 46 ft in radius. Unless a receiver with a diameter of 46 ft is used to collect all the light, an impractical proposition, any practically sized receiver would not be able to collect most of the signal. In fact, in the case of this example, a typical FSO system with a 6-in diameter receiver would be able to collect only about 1/10000th of the total power arriving at the receiving end.

Significantly reducing divergence requires higher precision optics and a higher precision manufacturing process. For example, to recover 1/10th the transmitted signal by a 6-in receiver at a distance of 0.5 miles from a transmitter, the transmitted beam needs to have a divergence of about 0.034 degrees. Such a system requires much more precise components and manufacturing processes than a system with 1 degree of divergence. Though technically feasible, the cost of such high precision systems may not make them economically viable in all applications.

Systems with a narrower beam divergence also pose a significant challenge to the task of aligning FSO links and maintaining alignment during their operation. For example, for the system with 0.035 degrees divergence, a deflection of the transmit beam by as little as 0.035 degrees can mispoint the transmit signal away from the receiver. As explained later, such mispointing is quite common, but mechanisms to maintain alignment within such small angles, though technically feasible, can be very costly.

Receive Optics   The receiver optics serve purposes exactly complementary to those of the transmit optics. The receiver optics collect the light signal and focus it onto the detector (or into the fiber-optic cable in the case of a passive system). They are made out of combination of one or more lenses and/or mirrors. From all perspectives, the receive optics in FSO systems serve the same purpose as antennas do in RF wireless systems—they collect the signal. The receive optics are characterized by two key parameters: the receive aperture and the field of view (FoV). A simple form of receive optics is illustrated in Figure 9.3.

Receive Aperture   Receive aperture is the diameter of the receiver through which the received signal is collected. It is, therefore, a key factor in determining the amount of light collected by the receiver. A receiver with twice the receive aperture can collect

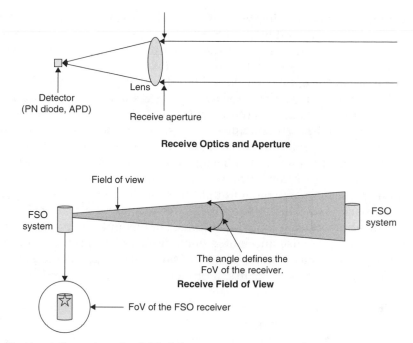

Figure 9.3   Receive optics and receive field of view

four times the amount of light. A larger aperture also has the benefit of mitigating the effect of atmospheric scintillation due to averaging over a greater area of the receiver. However, as in the case of transmitter optics, the downside of using a large aperture is the size, weight, and cost of the system.

Unlike transmitter optics where multiple transmit beams can be used to transmit more power, using multiple receive optics to increase the amount of received signal collected is not always efficient because of the challenges in combining the signals received from multiple receivers. This is unlike RF receivers, where multiple antennas are used at a great advantage to system performance. Such advantages in RF systems are derived mostly in cases of non-line-of-sight and point-to-multipoint communications systems; both of these scenarios do not apply to optical wireless systems as discussed in this chapter, however.

Receive Field of View (FoV)   Field of view (FoV) is the region within which the receiver can "see." It is the counterpart of beam divergence and is defined by the angle of the cone (measured in degrees) within which the transmitter has to be located in order for the receiver to receive the signal. As shown in Figure 9.3, the receiver can see the transmitter within its FoV, identified by the circle, and thus can receive the signal from the transmitter within the FoV.

The downside of having a larger FoV may not be apparent until the impact of background light is considered. By virtue of being able to "see" everything within its FoV, a receiver collects all the light it sees within its FoV. For the most part, the light consists of the signal transmitted by the FSO system at the other end of the link. However, the collected light also consists of all the background light that exists within the FoV. The background light thus collected acts as noise that, when sufficient, can degrade the performance of the optical wireless link. Therefore, a system with a larger FoV collects more background noise than a system with a smaller FoV, though it may collect the same amount of signal, thus reducing the overall signal-to-noise ratio.

The amount of background noise can also be reduced significantly by optically filtering the received signal. Narrowband optical filters are routinely used in optical wireless products to knockout unwanted background light from the receiver. However, the ratio of background light received by receivers with different FoVs remains the same. For example, regardless of the amount of filtering used, an FSO system collects four times as much background light as a similar system with half the FoV. Additionally, doing optical filtering poses its own limitations. For example, using too narrow a filter, which is often costly, may also knock off signals from wider spectrum sources such as LED.

Finally, making FoV smaller poses the same challenges as reducing beam divergence. It requires precision components, precision manufacturing, and complex alignment.

Active Tracking   As discussed in the preceding sections, it is often desirable to use FSO systems with narrow divergence and FoV. However, even a small scale mispointing of such a narrow beam can easily disrupt the FSO link established by the beam.

There are several reasons for such involuntary mispointing. FSO equipment is generally installed in open environments such as buildings and on poles that are likely to exhibit small movements. For example, buildings are subject to daily sway due to thermal expansion and contractions and poles exhibit oscillations under heavy winds. In other cases, FSO systems often get installed too close to sources of vibration such as large air conditioners causing the FSO systems to resonate along with the vibrating equipment. All of these involuntary movements can cause beam mispointing.

There are two common ways to compensate for mispointing due to involuntary movement for FSO links: (1) passively by means of a relatively large beam divergence and FoV and (2) actively by means of tracking. Larger beam divergence and FoV are not highly desirable, as discussed in the preceding sections. On the other hand, the complexity of tracking required to compensate for all types of mispointing may make it impractical for certain applications. The right solution is often a combination of both methods.

Movements that produce large magnitude mispointing, such as building expansion, happen at much slower speeds, in the order of several minutes to a few hours. Compensation for such a large mispointing solely by passive means would require a relatively large divergence and FoV. However, such slow movements are suited to being corrected by means of active tracking using much simpler mechanisms than would be required to compensate for fast movements. On the other hand, movements that are fast (in the order of milliseconds such as the ones produced by vibrations) cause much smaller magnitude mispointings. Compensation for such fast and small mispointings solely by means of active tracking may not be commercially viable for certain applications. However, they can be compensated for much more reliably by passive means without having to use too large a divergence and FoV. The key benefit of using a passive mean of compensation is that it can compensate for all small-scale vibrations no matter what their frequency and vibration characteristics are.

It is, therefore, often desirable to use FSO systems with sufficiently large divergence to compensate for fast movements, combined with simple automated tracking to compensate for large-scale mispointing. However, even though both passive and active means can compensate for mispointings, there is still a need for a solid foundation for installing an FSO system. Having solid foundations can only make the link more reliable.

Regardless of whether tracking is used to compensate for fast movements or slow movements, the underlying technology is a very mature technology. The limitation of tracking is not about developing a new technology but instead about making it commercially viable. Slow tracking systems are significantly more cost-effective than fast tracking systems.

Understanding Link Margin and Atmospheric Effects

Before considering FSO for deployment as a viable technology, it is important to understand how atmospheric effects affect FSO links and their impact on the link margin of FSO systems.

Link Margin   The link margin of an FSO system represents the margin on the amount of received optical power available for the system to perform to its specifications. It is expressed in terms of dB and is computed as 10 times the Log of the ratio of the available received power and the minimum required power. For example, a link with a 0 dB link margin has just enough optical power at its receiver to perform to its specifications. A link with a 3 dB link margin has twice as much optical power at its receiver as would be necessary for it to perform to its specifications.

Link margins for FSO systems are often specified for various weather conditions and link distances. However, the actual available link margin may be different as weather conditions or installation properties change. For example, a system specified to have 9 dB of margin in clear weather conditions when operating at a distance of 200 m would most likely have a margin of 8 dB during heavy rain. The same system would have only 3 dB of margin when operating at a distance of 400 m in a clear weather conditions.

Having a extra link margin allows a system to operate normally even in conditions that can reduce the amount of optical power received by the system. For example, with sufficient link margins, FSO systems are immune to weather conditions that are detrimental to signal propagation. The amount of link margin needed depends on the distance of the communication link and the weather condition against which immunity is sought.

Weather   The effect of weather on optical wireless is very well understood. Weather can produce conditions that can affect the propagation of the optical signal through the atmosphere. These weather conditions include fog, haze, rain, and snow. The net effect of any one of these weather conditions on an FSO link is the reduction (or loss) of the total amount of received optical power.

The loss in received optical power due to a weather condition is expressed in terms of dB and is computed as 10 times the Log of the factor by which the received optical power is reduced. The loss of an optical signal due to weather conditions has been well studied. Table 9.1 provides a list of various weather conditions and the loss caused per km on a typical optical wireless signal. Loss at other distances can be derived simply by multiplying the loss per km listed in the table by the desired distance in km. For example, heavy rain results in signal loss of about –4 dB/km, which means an FSO system operating at 0.5 km would experience an additional signal loss of –2 dB during heavy rain.

The dB loss/km for the IR signal of FSO is also correlated to visibility during these weather conditions. A sample data correlating visibility and weather conditions with dB/km attenuation of 850 nm signal is provided in Table 9.1. The data can be used to compute the link margin of a 850-nm FSO link in various weather conditions. For example, according to the table, a moderate fog, which has a visibility of 500 m, causes an attenuation of about –21 dB/km. This means an FSO link operating at 1 km would need 21 dB of link margin for it to be able to overcome atmospheric attenuation during conditions of moderate fog. An FSO link at 500 m would need half that amount, 10.5 dB of margin, for it to be able to overcome the same weather condition.

In order for an optical wireless system to be immune to all weather conditions, its link margin during the worst condition has to be at least 0 dB. From Table 9.1, it is evident that the worst weather condition, dense fog, can produce a loss of as much as –270 dB/km. In order for an FSO link at 1 km to be immune from all weather conditions, it needs to have a clear weather margin of 270 dB. Just to put this number in perspective, for a typical commercially available FSO system to have a margin of 270 dB at 1 km, it needs to be transmitting at least 10^{20} watts of optical power, a number that is not even a theoretical possibility. Therefore, such FSO systems at 1 km may never be immune from all weather conditions.

TABLE 9.1   Signal Loss Due to Various Weather Conditions [1]

Weather Condition	Precipitation		Amount (mm/hr)	Visibility	dB Loss/km
Dense fog				0 m–50 m	–271.65dB
Thick fog				200 m	–59.57dB
Mod. fog	Snow			500 m	–20.99
Light fog	Snow	Cloudburst	100	700 m–1 km	–12.65, –9.26
Thin fog	Snow	Heavy rain	25	1.9 m–2 km	–4.22, –3.96
Haze	Snow	Mod. rain	12.5	2.8 m–4 km	–2.58, –1.62
Light haze	Snow	Light rain	2.5	5.9 m–10 km	–0.96, –0.44
Clear	Snow	Drizzle	0.25	18.1 m–20 km	–0.24, –0.22
Very clear				23 m–50 km	–0.19, –0.06

Now consider a link at 100 m. The loss due to the worst weather condition at 100 m is –27 dB. Therefore, in order for the link to be immune from all weather conditions, it needs to have a link margin of 27 dB. For a typical FSO system, it means transmitted optical power of about 100 mW to 1 W, a much more realistic number. This example illustrates that FSO links can be immune from all weather conditions when they are deployed over short distances.

Another aspect of weather to consider is the probability of occurrence of a particular weather event. For example, in cities such as Phoenix, the probability of fog events denser than a thin fog may be negligible. In such environments, a link with 12 dB of margin at 250 m can also be immune from all *likely* weather conditions. Therefore, the viability of long-distance FSO links depends on local weather patterns.

Scintillation   Scintillation is a phenomenon experienced quite often in our daily life. It is an atmospheric effect commonly observed as the twinkling of stars or distant light sources. It is caused by variations of air density through the different parts of the atmosphere constantly changing over time. The variation is caused by the turbulent mixing of warmer and cooler air and is more pronounced during hotter days than cooler days.

The primary cause of scintillation in FSO is due to the constant changing of the course of a beam. As a light beam radiates from a source and propagates through the atmosphere, it passes through regions of air with varying density. The optical phenomenon of refraction causes the entire beam or parts of the beam to change its course slightly as the density of medium (the air) changes. As the beam propagates through more of the atmosphere, the variation accumulates such that the beam arrives at the receiving end with uneven power density distributed along its cross-section. Different part of the cross-sectional area of the beam end up with different optical power densities. Due to turbulence, uneven distribution of the power density also changes constantly over time, resulting in fluctuation of the received signal. Such fluctuation happens typically in the order of a few milliseconds.

The net effect of scintillation on an FSO system is in the fluctuation of the received signal. However, if a link has sufficient link margin to accommodate the fluctuation, scintillation would not adversely affect link performance. For a typical FSO system in a typical deployment, signal fluctuation due to scintillation is anywhere from 1 to 3 dB. Therefore, a typical installation with 3 dB clear weather link margin is usually immune from the adverse effects of scintillation. Since scintillation occurs during hot weather conditions, its effect is insignificant during weather conditions such as fog and rain. Therefore, the same link margin that provides immunity from the effects of these weather conditions can effectively provide immunity from the effects of scintillation.

The effects of scintillation can be minimized by using systems with large beamwidths and large receive apertures. Additionally, FSO systems using incoherent light sources such as LED are more immune to the effects of scintillation than those using coherent light sources such as laser. Distance also makes a difference in the amount of scintillation experienced, with shorter links experiencing less scintillation. Finally, good deployment practices can also minimize the effect of scintillation. For example, beam propagation over sources of air turbulence such as vents and air conditioners should be avoided. Similarly, installations that result in the optical beam propagating over the roof of a building can result in a lot of scintillation during hot sunny days and should be avoided. When installing on a building, the system should be closer to the roof's edge than toward its middle.

Wireless Mesh Networking Technology

A mesh network is a network of equipment, called *nodes,* where each node directly communicates with multitudes of other nodes to create a network. Each node in a mesh network serves as an ingress and egress point for network traffic, and the traffic flows through the network by hoping from one node to another node. The term *mesh* signifies a key defining characteristic of the network, namely the existence of independent redundant data paths from one node to the other. For example, a tree network is not considered a mesh network because it lacks redundant data paths between nodes. Mesh also implies a generic topological structure where most nodes communicate directly with more than two other nodes. A mesh network can be a *regular* mesh where nodes are interconnected to create a well-defined topological structure, such as a rectangular mesh network. A mesh network can also be an *irregular* mesh where nodes are interconnected without any topological rules and in a seemingly random fashion. Figure 9.4 illustrates regular and irregular mesh networks.

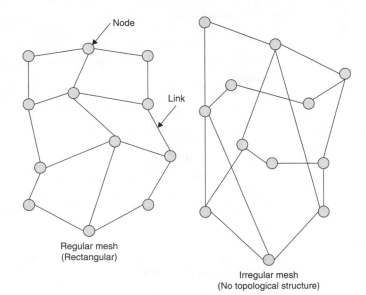

Figure 9.4   Regular and irregular mesh networks

A wireless mesh network is a mesh network in which the nodes are interconnected by means of wireless links such as RF or FSO. Wireless mesh network technology has received significant attention recently, primarily due to the suitability of wireless technology for mesh networks and due to the development and proliferation of wireless technologies such as WiFi. The benefits of wireless mesh networks have been widely appreciated, and several wireless mesh products are now offered by manufacturers. In this section, we will discuss the attributes of wireless mesh networks, especially when used with optical wireless technology.

There are generally two types of wireless mesh networks: (1) point-to-point (PtP) mesh networks that are made up of nodes interconnected by means of point-to-point wireless links, and (2) point-to-multipoint (PtM) mesh networks that consist of nodes interconnected by means of point-to-multipoint links. FSO being a PtP technology, the optical wireless mesh network discussed throughout the remainder of this chapter is a PtP mesh network. However, it is valuable to discuss PtM mesh networks briefly.

PtM is a mesh network of nodes that use point-to-multipoint RF wireless technology to communicate with other nodes. By virtue of having used a PtM RF wireless technology, the physical topology of a PtM mesh network does not have to be predefined and static. The nodes can be nomadic or even mobile in certain cases. This attribute makes PtM mesh networks ideally suited for ad-hoc networks where randomly distributed nodes communicate with each other to create a mesh network. Unlike PtP mesh networks where every connection between two nodes has to be predefined, PtM mesh networks have the benefit of being dynamic—in the sense that the number of neighboring nodes that a node can directly communicate with can be dynamic. This facilitates the creation of a dense mesh network, giving it more redundancy.

PtM mesh networks have several limitations compared to PtP mesh networks. Mostly, nodes in PtM mesh networks can communicate with only one other node at any given time, even though these nodes may be capable of communicating directly with multitudes of nodes at different times. This is in contrast to PtP mesh networks, where a node can simultaneously communicate directly with more than one node at any given time. This limitation results in the reduced capacity of a PtM network because not all direct communication links can be utilized at the same time. Data traffic in PtM mesh networks also experience higher end-to-end latency and jitter, due to the higher delay experienced by data traffic at each hop. Because PtM technology is a shared-medium technology, the underlying network capacity may also degrade beyond certain utilization. The density of nodes in a geographical area may also be limited, and a complex spectral planning and routing algorithm may be needed in such PtM mesh networks.

FSO being a point-to-point wireless technology, the optical wireless mesh network discussed in this chapter falls under the category of PtP mesh networks. Throughout the remainder of this chapter, the discussion of mesh networks is limited to PtP mesh networks. We start by discussing the key attributes of wireless mesh networks, which make the technology highly attractive.

- **Redundancy** Redundancy is one of the most valuable, if not *the* most valuable, attribute of a mesh network. As stated previously, a mesh network is a network of nodes with all or many nodes in the network having multiple connections to the other nodes. Consequently, there are multiple paths from each node to any other node in the network. The denser a mesh network, the more alternate paths there are in the network. In the event that a failure occurs in a path such that the traffic cannot be routed through the path, alternate paths may be used to route the traffic. In general, a mesh network does not have a single point of failure. Therefore, mesh networks provide a level of redundancy unmatched by most other types of networks.

■ **High end-to-end capacity**   For the same reason that a mesh network provides ample redundancy, it also provides a higher level of end-to-end capacity than could normally be realized. In a mesh network, each alternate path not only serves as a backup path to be used during failure, it also serves as an alternate path to be used to serve more capacity. For example, in Figure 9.5, traffic from node A to B can be routed along node C to the extent that the path through node C meets the capacity demand of the traffic. However, if more capacity is needed than what is offered by the path through C, the path through node D could also be used to meet the higher demand.

■ **High network capacity**   A mesh network allows for more efficient use of available network resources thereby maximizing network capacity. High end-to-end capacity, as discussed above, is one example of an efficient use of network resources. In a similar fashion, traffic between one set of nodes can be routed without

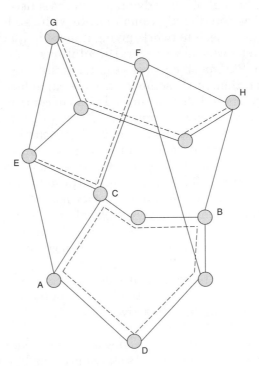

Figure 9.5   Higher capacity of mesh network

compromising the capacity available to route traffic between another set of nodes. For example, as illustrated in Figure 9.5, data traffic between node A and node B can be routed (along the dotted line connecting the two nodes) without affecting the data traffic between node E and F (which is routed along the dotted line connecting the two nodes). In the similar fashion, mesh networks can confine regional traffic to the region without compromising capacity throughout the rest of the network. For example, traffic between node G and H can be confined to the links shown by the dotted lines without affecting the traffic in other parts of the network. Another way to look at it is that mesh networks can be segmented into small clusters such that each cluster can serve to its full capacity potential without compromising the service capacity of all the other clusters.

- **More is better** In a mesh network, each node serves not only as an access point to the network but also as a part of the network's infrastructure. Each new node added to a mesh network provides an additional level of redundancy and capacity. In a mesh network, growing the size of the network mostly means strengthening the network by increasing the redundancy and capacity of the network. This is unlike many other types of networks where adding a new element means adding overall load to the network and perhaps weakening it as a consequence.

- **Gradual growth** Mesh architecture allows for gradually increasing the reach of the network, therefore obviating the need for large upfront investment in a network infrastructure. This benefit is derived from the fact that, in mesh networks, each node also serves as the core of the network from which the network can be further extended; the network can be extended either from the outer edge of the mesh or from somewhere deep within the mesh. This benefit facilitates deployment on a more "need-to-grow" basis.

Optical Wireless Mesh Network In the earlier sections, we discussed the attributes and shortcomings of optical wireless as well as the attributes and shortcomings of wireless mesh networks. When the attributes and shortcomings of the two technologies are put together, they are ideally matched in that an attribute of one complements a shortcoming of the other. We start by discussing the shortcomings of wireless mesh networks and how FSO complements them.

- **Latency and jitter** In a mesh network, data traffic has to hop through several nodes as it is routed through the network. At each node, the traffic experiences certain forwarding delays. Therefore, the total end-to-end delay experienced by the traffic within the mesh network may add up to be significant and unacceptable for certain applications. Additionally, if the forwarding delay is not constant at each hop (as in the case of PtM mesh networks), the traffic may also experience significant amounts of jitter. However, FSO links add virtually no delay, especially when compared with most other wireless solutions. On the contrary, most RF solutions incur delay when advanced modulation techniques or error recovery techniques are used. FSO systems generally do not use such techniques and thus add only negligible delay. FSO is, therefore, well suited for wireless mesh applications.

- **Density**   Higher density makes mesh networks more robust. However, creating a dense mesh network may pose a challenge when you consider the wireless links. If there are many links close to each other, the links may interfere with each other. When using RF wireless, the problem may be alleviated by using a larger amount of the RF spectrum in a mesh. However, this solution can be too costly due to the licensing fee for the spectrum. FSO systems overcome this because of its narrow beam and by using the unlicensed part of the spectrum. With divergence of about 1 degree for a typical system, links separated more than 2 degrees will not interfere with each other.

- **Cost**   A mesh network is created by interconnecting multitudes of equipment. If the cost of the underlying technology is fairly high, the overall cost of a mesh network may skyrocket. For example, if RF wireless technology is used and spectral licensing is required, the cost to deploy (and perhaps maintain) a wireless mesh network could be prohibitive. However, the cost of FSO systems that are targeted for short-range operations are fairly low. Such systems are built out of low-cost optical components and simple mechanical systems. Another significant cost savings, both upfront and recurring, also comes from the fact that FSO systems do not require any spectral licensing fees.

Based on the preceding points, it should be clear how using FSO technology helps wireless mesh networks overcome some of their limitations, making FSO ideally suited for wireless mesh networks. This complement does not flow in only one direction, however. Mesh networks also enable FSO to overcome some of its key limitations.

- **Distance**   FSO technology performs with exceptional reliability when used over comparatively short distances, something in the order of tens of meters to a few hundred meters. However, when used over longer distances, it becomes less reliable during atmospheric events such as fog and heavy rain. Therefore, in order to achieve fiber-like reliability, it is necessary for the lengths of FSO links to be fairly short. The multihop capability of a mesh network allows the lengths of FSO links to be maintained at less than a few hundred meters.

- **Point-to-multipoint**   FSO is a point-to-point technology and, therefore, cannot, by itself, provide point-to-multipoint services. This shortcoming of FSO is complemented by mesh networking technology, which can offer both point-to-multipoint and multipoint-to-multipoint services.

- **Line-of-sight**   FSO technology is a line-of-sight technology. Therefore, FSO by itself cannot be used to offer its high capacity network services to a location not in line-of-sight of a POP. However, mesh networks enable delivery of services to locations that are not in direct line-of-sight of the POP.

- **Failure resiliency**   All communications systems are prone to failure and FSO links are no exception. Because of its line-of-sight requirements, any event that could rob an FSO link of its line-of-sight would disrupt the link. This limitation is complemented by the redundancy inherent in mesh networks.

Optical wireless mesh technology is, therefore, a perfect marriage of two emerging technologies: wireless optics and mesh networking. Throughout the remainder of this chapter, we will discuss its applications, primarily in the context of Carrier Ethernet service delivery.

Carrier-Class Ethernet with Optical Wireless Mesh

In this section, we discuss how optical wireless mesh networking technology fares in terms of some of the key attributes required to deliver carrier-class Ethernet services.

Failure Resiliency   FSO technology is a simple physical layer transport technology that can surpass all other wireless technologies in its ability to offer high-quality data transport service. When deployed at short distances, it can offer immunity from all weather conditions. It uses the same underlying technology as fiber-optic communications, and it can provide link-level performance comparable to that of fiber optics. Due to its immunity from external RF interference, FSO can offer fiber-like performance with much more consistency than other wireless technologies that are susceptible to interference. Therefore, FSO technology, when deployed properly, can provide the kind of failure resiliency required to offer Carrier Ethernet services.

No physical layer technology is 100 percent immune from failure due to external events and FSO is no exception. The time-proven method of achieving resiliency in a network using any physical layer technology is by means of redundancy, and redundancy is one of the key attributes of a mesh network. Therefore, with the redundancy of a mesh network and the self-healing mesh operating system, an optical wireless mesh network can provide the kind of resiliency expected from Carrier Ethernet.

Scalability   Optical wireless technology offers network bandwidth comparable to that of fiber-optic technology and not easily matched by RF wireless technology. Systems commercially available today can operate between 100 Mbps and 1 Gbps, and the potential for higher data rates exists and will be available once industry demand makes them commercially viable. Additionally, mesh networks also offer higher end-to-end and network capacity. Therefore, optical wireless mesh technology can scale very well to meet future growing service demands.

Optical wireless mesh networks are also very scalable when it comes to network size. First of all, increasing the size of a mesh network only strengthens it due to added redundancy rather than weakening it. Additionally, as more nodes and links are added, the network's overall capacity grows rather than shrinks. And finally, because it uses noninterfering and unlicensed spectrum, the size of the network can be increased with impunity without compromising network performance. Therefore, optical wireless mesh is a very scalable technology.

Quality of Service   At the physical level, the quality of service (QoS) offered by optical mesh can come close to the quality of service offered by any other network technology. The optical wireless links in a mesh network provide reliability comparable to that of fiber-optic cable, ensuring end-to-end delivery of data traffic. Optical wireless networks also offer very low latency and jitter, also comparable to that of fiber-optic networks. And in the unlikely event of link failure, a mesh network's resiliency allows the traffic path to be reestablished, the expediency of which is comparable to that of any other wired network.

At the network level, each node of a mesh network can offer the full suite of QoS capabilities, making wireless optical mesh like virtually any other network. Each node can be a fully MEF-compliant Layer 2 switch, offering MEF-compliant QoS and SLA. Each node can even be an MPLS switch, enabling the mesh network to offer the type of traffic engineering required to offer Carrier Ethernet and matched only by wired networks.

Support for TDM Services   An optical wireless mesh network is no different from any other wired technology in its ability to offer Carrier Ethernet services. For all practical purpose, optical wireless mesh can be thought of as an interconnection of carrier-grade Ethernet service–capable switches interconnected by FSO links. To the extent that a mesh network of switches interconnected by means of fiber-optic cable can deliver Carrier Ethernet services, so can a mesh network of nodes interconnected by means of FSO links. Therefore, an optical wireless mesh network of MEF-compliant nodes can deliver MEF-compliant services.

Service Management   The same arguments for the support of TDM services also applies to the service management attributes of optical wireless mesh networks. Optical wireless links are virtually zero latency PtP physical layer links that behave no differently from fiber-optic links. These links do not have or need to have any notion of service. Therefore, the extent to which service management is supported by optical wireless mesh is determined by the switching equipment serving as the nodes of the mesh.

Applications

Throughout the rest of this section, we will discuss the wide varieties of applications for optical wireless mesh networks. Some applications relate directly to Carrier Ethernet services, whereas most of the applications are various derivates of such services where the optical wireless mesh network excels over other technologies in its suitability.

Ethernet Services in Urban Commercial Environment   Optical wireless mesh is ideally suited for offering carrier-grade Ethernet services in metro environments where only a small set of buildings have access to fiber backhaul. Such opportunities may be located in a downtown-like environment or in business parks where fiber reach at one of the buildings could be extended virtually to the regions by means of deploying optical wireless mesh. Such deployment can provide Carrier Ethernet services to tenants in each building lit by optical wireless. In such environments, the relative short distance between the buildings enables the offering services comparable to that of fiber-optic networks.

Surveillance Network   With security rising in importance and the deployment of surveillance video by property managers and security agencies growing, the need for surveillance networks capable of transporting broadband traffic has grown dramatically. Such security surveillance networks may include deployments such as intrusion detection in and around public places like open malls and airport perimeters. In addition, surveillance networks may include networks for monitoring traffic along freeways or large parking lots. In either case, such surveillance networks are used to capture live video from many locations and stream the live video to a central location.

Deployment of video surveillance and monitoring networks can be a costly proposition when a large deployment is considered. RF wireless technology may not be able to provide the kind of bandwidth required to aggregate all the traffic from a large number of surveillance cameras, each generating ~2 Mbps of traffic. The alternative of laying cable to each surveillance camera can be cost prohibitive, especially if it requires laying the cable under public infrastructure. Optical wireless mesh is very well suited for such applications, primarily due to the high bandwidth it can support.

Wireless Access Infrastructure   Over the past several years, there has been tremendous growth in the deployment of WiFi access networks. These networks may include public networks owned and operated by municipalities as well as hotspots provided by private enterprises. With the ubiquitous growth of WiFi networks, we have also seen significant activity in the arena of WiFi mesh networks, where WiFi access points are meshed by means of the RF wireless connections among them.

Even though such RF mesh technology can provide backhaul capability, it may not be the best use of the precious RF spectrum. The same purpose can also be served by optical wireless mesh networks, and it is perhaps one of their most promising applications. The use of optical wireless mesh for backhaul makes the RF spectrum that would have otherwise been used for backhaul available as much well-suited RF access medium. By repurposing a spectrum for access instead of backhaul, access point capacity can be increased several times. Additionally, optical wireless mesh offers the bandwidth necessary to accommodate traffic growth due to the increased network capacity.

Optical wireless mesh can also offer the advanced networking capabilities only expected from wired networks and unmatched by traditional WiFi mesh networks. It offers extremely low delay and jitter along with the QoS only expected in wired networks, enabling the wireless network operator to offer the advanced services used in wired networks.

Disaster Recovery   This application is where all wireless technologies standout, but optical wireless technology shines. Optical wireless mesh can be used during a disaster's aftermath to create a temporary network for search and rescue operations. However, it is in rapid response to restoring services in urban environments following a disaster event that optical wireless can be an extremely invaluable technology.

Following a major event such as earthquake or hurricane, network services in an urban area may be disrupted due to damage to infrastructure. Repairing the damaged infrastructure and restoring the service may take days if not weeks. However, services may be restored in a matter of hours by deploying optical wireless mesh networks. This may be achieved by creating backhaul from a remote location to a building in the area where the service has been disrupted and then distributing the service throughout the area by means of optical wireless mesh.

Internet Services in Urban MDU Environment   For an urban multi-dwelling unit (MDU) environment, where only a small number of buildings, if any, are lit by fiber-optic cable, optical mesh can be deployed to provide ultra-broadband Internet services to their tenants. Although Ethernet services may not be needed by the end customers, Carrier Ethernet services provided by a network can only facilitate the delivery of advanced network services such as VoIP and IPTV.

Drivers for This Solution

As stated in the prior section, the history of optical wireless communication is as long as the history of RF wireless communication. However, it didn't see significant growth as soon as RF communication did primarily due to limitations that were easily overcome by RF communication technology. In addition, its key attributes, such as high bandwidth and freedom from RF interference, didn't have any appeal until the modern days of information age and spectral shortage.

The genesis of modern day FSO technology was primarily driven by its appeal to military applications. With the use of optical transmission, FSO technology provided the potential to transfer large amounts of data at rates unmatched by RF technologies. It also provided a communication medium that was not only secure from eavesdropping but also "RF silent." Its immunity from external RF interference meant its immunity from jamming. With these benefits, the U.S. military saw opportunities for the application of this technology and funded several projects starting in the early 1980s for the development of the technology and its applications. These projects facilitated the understanding of the basic principles and limitations of FSO communications. These projects also resulted in the development of some of the underlying technologies, some of which were later adapted for FSO technology for commercial applications.

FSO technology didn't find much appeal in commercial applications until the mid 1990s. With the explosive growth of information technology, the need for a higher bandwidth communication medium was growing. Although much of the need was being met by cable-based technologies, such as Ethernet, Fibre Channel, DSL, and cable modems, FSO technology provided a unique opportunity to fill the gap where cable-based technologies were not viable. Additionally, earlier advances in fiber-optic technology provided low-cost components that could be used in FSO products, making them commercially viable. With the understanding of FSO technology, opportunities for niche applications, and the availability of the underlying components, several vendors started developing commercial FSO products in the 1990s.

When Does This Solution Fit?

In order to understand where this solution fits, we need to start by considering some of the benefits of this solution. One of the key benefits of FSO technology is that it is a wireless technology. Another benefit is its high bandwidth, which is difficult for other wireless technologies to match. Additionally, the license-exempt and interference-free nature of FSO technology sets it apart from other wireless technology. Mesh technology provides additional benefits such as resiliency and higher network capacity.

This solution fits very well in applications where creation of a wide area network using a wired infrastructure is prohibitively expensive. For example, in urban commercial environments where distributing new services by laying out new fiber or copper is cost prohibitive, this solution can provide a very competitive alternative.

This solution also fits very well in applications where wireless technology is required but RF technology does not serve the purpose: the capacity of RF is often insufficient; the latency due to RF wireless solutions is usually high; the recurring cost of RF licensing can be significant; and the use of license-exempt RF solutions can pose reliability issues due to potential interference issues. In any one of these cases, an optical wireless mesh solution fits better than most other alternative solutions.

When Does This Solution Not Fit?

Optical wireless technology is not without its limitations, and because of these limitations, there are applications where this solution does not make sense. One such limitation is the dependency of its performance on weather conditions. As was discussed, FSO links can experience severe attenuation during heavy fog conditions, and the degree of such attenuation is a function of link distance, with longer links experiencing more outage than shorter links. Therefore, FSO technology does not make sense in applications where link lengths are fairly long. For example, links that are shorter than 100 m can achieve 100 percent availability, whereas links that are more than 1 km cannot be guaranteed to achieve 100 percent link availability. Based on the type of FSO system and local weather conditions, such links can be expected to achieve availability between 95 percent and 99 percent. Therefore, optical wireless mesh technology is not well suited for applications requiring long-range reach.

FSO links also require direct line-of-sight (LOS). Therefore, FSO technology by itself is not well suited for applications that do not have direct LOS. This limitation, however, is overcome by the mesh technology whereby communication with locations that are not in LOS can be achieved by hopping through another location(s). However, this still requires "indirect" LOS between the two points. Optical wireless mesh cannot achieve true NLOS communication as some RF technologies can. Therefore, in applications requiring true NLOS, FSO and optical wireless mesh technologies do not make sense.

As discussed at the beginning of this chapter, FSO technology makes use of fairly narrow beams and has a very narrow field-of-view—a consequence of which is the need to keep the two ends of an FSO link pointed at each other very precisely. This precludes the use of optical wireless mesh technology for mobile or even nomadic applications.

Benefits and Shortcomings

Like all technologies, optical wireless mesh technology has its own benefits and shortcomings. As discussed previously, optical wireless mesh technology is a fusion of two distinct technologies, optical wireless and mesh networking, each of which has its own benefits and its own shortcomings. However, the key advantage of the combined solution is the way the benefits of one complement the shortcomings of the other, leaving the solution with a large set of benefits and a small set of shortcomings, as recounted here.

Benefits

- **Wireless flexibility** One of the key benefits of an optical wireless mesh network is the fact that it is a wireless technology that brings with it most of the benefits of wireless technologies. Such benefits include rapid deployment and the lower cost of creating an infrastructure.

- **Higher bandwidth** For a wireless technology, optical wireless technology excels in its ability to deliver much higher bandwidth and network capacity, comparable to that of fiber, than other wireless technologies.

- **Higher network capacity** Because of the mesh topology, optical wireless mesh networks can offer higher end-to-end capacity by utilizing multiple alternate paths between any two points that may exist in the network. Additionally, mesh networks also offer higher network capacity by simultaneously utilizing the capacity of two or more noninterfering regions of the network.

- **Network resiliency** Mesh networks find their strength in their ability to route traffic using alternate paths. This ability gives optical mesh networks a very high degree of resiliency.

- **Noninterfering and license-free** All RF wireless products have the limitation that they either require a license for exclusive use of an RF spectrum or are vulnerable to interference from other users of the license-free spectrum. Optical wireless technology does not use the RF spectrum and, therefore, does not require an FCC license to operate. Optical wireless is also not vulnerable to external interference because of its narrow field of view.

- **Low latency and small jitter** Optical wireless technology adds virtually no latency as compared to most other wireless technologies. Mesh architecture does have the potential to add delay at each hop of the mesh. However, with each node of a mesh providing traffic classification and prioritization functions, the delay experienced by data traffic at each hop can be minimized to be insignificant.

Therefore, the end-to-end latency and jitter experienced by data traffic in an optical wireless mesh network can meet or exceed the stringent requirements of even the most demanding applications.

Shortcomings

- **Weather dependency/link distance**   Weather is undoubtedly the most significant shortcoming of optical wireless technology. Severe weather conditions such as heavy fog can cause significant outage of FSO links. Moderate weather conditions such as light fog or rain can cause outages of most FSO links operating at distances over 1 km. The link distance can be traded off for better weather tolerance. However, the shorter link distance in itself becomes a shortcoming. Mesh architecture complements these limitations of optical wireless by allowing for the creation of reliable networks using short-range FSO links.

- **Line-of-sight requirement**   Optical wireless is a line-of-sight (LOS) technology, a shortcoming that limits the scope of its applications. The shortcoming is, however, somewhat complemented by the mesh networking technology that allows for connecting two points that are not in LOS of each other through an intermediate point, though this solution is not practical for all applications.

- **Lack of industry standard**   The lack of a coherent industry standard is one of the significant shortcomings of FSO solutions.

Typical Deployment Scenarios

In this section, we will concentrate on typical deployments of optical wireless solutions providing Carrier Ethernet services. Typical deployment of all other applications are usually very similar to the typical deployments providing carrier-grade Ethernet services and are beyond the scope of this chapter.

Deployment of Carrier Ethernet Services

In general, there are two possible ways of deploying a wireless optical mesh network. The first method is to deploy optical wireless mesh networking equipment products that are designed to be deployed as optical wireless mesh networks. Such products have optical wireless technology, carrier-grade Ethernet–capable switching engine and management capability integrated into one product. The second approach is to create an optical wireless mesh network by means of integrating optical wireless equipment from one supplier with a carrier-grade Ethernet switch from either the same or a different supplier(s). The benefit of the second method is the flexibility in identifying the networking equipment based on the specific need. The downside of the second method is the integration effort and manageability of the network. The first method has the benefit of using single equipment with all the essentials of an optical wireless mesh technology integrated. Additionally, because the equipment is designed exclusively for mesh architecture, performance can be expected to be better. However, regardless of whether mesh equipment is used or the equipment is from different manufacturers, the deployment scenario is not significantly different. Throughout the remainder of this section, we will assume a deployment using mesh equipment.

A typical deployment consists of a wireless service POP "lit" by a metro ring or some form of backhaul connection. The POP may consist of a Carrier Ethernet–grade networking service either as an aggregation point or a NNI interface. The POP would serve as a service injection point.

The roof of the POP building may be populated with one or more optical wireless mesh devices, referred to as *nodes*. Some of the buildings within the specified range that are in line-of-sight of the POP may also be populated with one or more of the nodes. Optical wireless connections among the nodes would create a mesh network.

Each of the buildings would consist of an indoor CLE device for the distribution of the services throughout the building, which may define the UNI interface. In the event that only a small number of UNIs are required, the node may also provide the UNI, obviating the need for a CLE switch.

From each building with a node, the mesh may be further extended to additional buildings that are within range and in LOS of one of the nodes. The expansion to additional buildings may be done on a need-to basis.

An optical mesh network thus created would be capable of serving various kinds of Carrier Ethernet services. Whether point-to-point E-Line services or point-to-multipoint E-LAN services, the optical mesh network would be able to deliver such solutions throughout the mesh network.

Deployment of Wireless Access Network

One of the most promising applications of optical wireless mesh with Carrier Ethernet services is as a backhaul to interconnect RF wireless access points such as WiFi access points.

A wireless access network may consist of several access points distributed throughout a region, as illustrated in Figure 9.6. Such access points may be installed on small buildings, cell towers, traffic light posts, or lampposts. Depending on the density of the service provided, they may be spaced at 50 m to a few hundred meters.

Located with each access point is an optical wireless mesh node, enabling each access point to be interconnected with one or more access points in its line-of-sight. The transport technology provided to each of the access points can be provided by one or more of the Ethernet services as defined by MEF. For example, all the access points may be served by a single E-LAN service. Alternately, each access point may be served by multiple E-LAN services, with each E-LAN service dedicated to a specific purpose. For example, each E-LAN service may be dedicated to a particular WISP provider, enabling multiple providers to share the same wireless infrastructure. In a different deployment scenario, each E-LAN may serve only a subset of access points, enabling segmentation of the network.

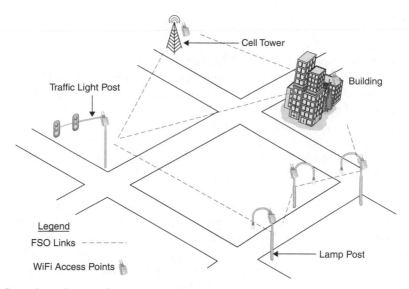

Figure 9.6   Optical wireless mesh interconnecting wireless access points

Ongoing Developments

The ongoing evolution of free space optics can be grouped in two fronts, those driven by prevailing commercial interests and those that are at the forefront of the cutting edge of the technology, driven by military interests.

The commercial front of FSO technology is primarily limited to a set of vendors introducing slightly higher-capacity and lower-cost products, each trying to differentiate from the other. Since commercially available technology already achieves gigabit per second and more bandwidth, meeting or exceeding bandwidth needs of most of the applications, developments in the commercial front have mostly been on cost reduction rather than performance enhancements. Perhaps the only deviation from this general trend has been the mesh networking approach where FSO technology is taken from being a point-to-point link technology to a mesh networking technology.

The dominant portion of development at the cutting edge of FSO technology has been occurring at military and university laboratories. There have been significant efforts and development on optical technologies to overcome atmospheric effects such as fog and clouds by means of techniques such as famto-second pulses. Efforts have also been made on developing highly sensitive detectors such as photon-counting detectors. University labs have also conducted research efforts on networking aspects of FSO technology. Some of these developments are likely to make their way to commercial applications soon, while the others, though they may take much longer time to become commercially viable, are bound to have a lasting impact on the wireless communication technology landscape.

Economic Assessment

In the absence of an optical wireless mesh solution, the only feasible method of providing more than 10 Mbps of Ethernet service in a metro environment is by means of extending the reach of fiber to every building to be served. The building of such fiber extension takes a few months of planning, permits, and actual deployment. Besides the time and the lost opportunity cost, the cost of laying fiber to each service point can range from $50,000 to $120,000. Therefore, in the absence of alternate solutions, the cost of trying to deliver Ethernet services can be staggering.

With the deployment of optical wireless mesh networking, the cost can be significantly lower. Consider an identical scenario of trying to deliver Ethernet services in a metro environment by means of "fiber extension"; the up-front capital expenditure incurred per service point can be lowered to close to $10,000. Provided the presence of a fiber at one location (POP), the cost of extending the service by one hop to a neighboring building can be achieved by means of an FSO link and Ethernet service–capable switching equipment located at the service point. The cost of such a switch can be less than $5,000 since the number of ports needed for such switches is fairly low. The cost of an FSO link can also be less than $10,000. (This assumes that the distance between the POP and service point is less than a few hundred meters so that FSO links designed for short-range operation can be used. FSO links deployed over more than a few hundred meters may not provide the kind of resiliency demanded by service providers. However, even if FSO systems capable of longer ranges were deployed, the overall cost per service point would not be significantly higher). Therefore, the upfront capital expenditure (CAPEX) of extending the fiber-like services to a new service point can be less than $15,000 per service point. From each service point, services can be further extended to more service points for additional upfront CAPEX of less than $15,000 for each added service point. This cost is almost an order of magnitude less than the cost of extending fiber-grade, as discussed previously.

The cost as well as the manageability of the network can be further improved by using optical wireless mesh equipment instead of integrating different equipment as discussed in the preceding section. Such mesh equipment consists of multiple FSO links and a switching engine integrated in a single package, reducing overall cost and simplifying manageability.

Vendors Promoting This Solution

There are two different scenarios for deploying optical wireless mesh networks. In the first scenario, optical wireless mesh could be deployed by means of integrating PtP FSO equipment with carrier grade networking equipment such as switches and routers. In the second scenario, an optical wireless mesh network could be deployed using optical wireless mesh equipment that already integrates optical wireless technology and mesh networking technology. In order to address both these scenarios, this section provides a brief overview of PtP FSO products and optical wireless mesh networking products currently being offered by various vendors. The discussion of the various networking equipment that may be deployed using the first scenario is beyond the scope of this chapter.

One of the challenges for FSO vendors is the lack of underlying interoperability of these devices. Even though one vendor's PtP FSO equipment may be replaced with another vendor's equipment, they are not designed to interoperate with each other.

Point-to-Point Optical Wireless (FSO) Vendors

There are several vendors that offer varieties of PtP FSO products. Most of these products are compatible with Ethernet standards and may be used to offer Carrier Ethernet services. Given the large number of vendors and their product offerings, a detailed discussion of each PtP FSO product is beyond the scope of this chapter. Instead, we have provided a list of various products along with their key characteristics. The range of each product is listed in terms of kilometers (km) and is specified for operation during clear weather conditions. Only the data rates compatible with the Ethernet standard are listed. The specification of these equipment may have changed since list was compiled.

Vendor	Model	Comments
Canon	DT-110	0.2 km , 100 Mbps, auto-tracking
	DT-120	2.0 km, 100 Mbps, auto-tracking
	DT-130	1.0 km, 1 Gbps, auto-tracking
fSONA	52-E	3.8 km, 10 Mbps, 1550 nm spectrum,
	155-E	3.3 km, 100 Mbps, 1550 nm spectrum
	155-S	4.4 km, 100 Mbps, 1550 nm spectrum
	155-M	6.4 km, 100 Mbps, 1550 nm spectrum
	622-S	3.8 km, 100 Mpbs, 1550 nm spectrum
	622-M	5.4 km, 100 Mbps, 1550 nm spectrum
	1250-S	3.6 km, 1 Gbps, 1550 nm spectrum
	1250-M	5.3 km, 1Gpbs, 1550 nm spectrum
LaserBit	PLUTOMobility	0.02 km, 100 Mbps, lightweight, PoE compatible
	PICO II	0.2 km, 100 Mbps, lightweight
	PICOPLUS	0.2 km, 100 Mbps, lightweight, PoE compatible
	PINTO	0.5 km, 100 Mbps
	PINTOPLUS	0.5 km, 100 Mbps, PoE compatible,
	PRONTO	1.0 km, 100 Mbps
	GigaPico	0.2 km, 1 Gbps
	GigaPinto	0.5 km, 1 Gbps,
	GigaPronto	1.0 km, 1 Gbps, 4 transmitters
	SuperGig	2.5 km, 1 Gbps, 8 transmitters
	LB-1500	1.5 km, 100 Mbps, modular
	LB-2500	2.5 km, 100 Mbps, modular
	LB-5000	5.0 km, 100 Mbps, modular

(Continued)

Vendor	Model	Comments
LightPointe	FlightLite-155E	2.9 km, 100 Mbps, lightweight
	FlightLite-155EW	1.7 km, 100 Mbps, lightweight
	FlightLite-G	1.3 km, 1 Gbps, lightweight
	FlightLite 100	0.5 km, 100 Mbps, lightweight, PoE powered
	FlightLite 100E	1.0 km, 100 Mbps, lightweight, PoE powered
	FlightStrata 155E	4.8 km, 100 Mbps, 4 receivers, 4 transmitters
	FlightStrata 155EW	2.4 km, 100 Mbps, 4 receivers, 4 transmitters
	FlightStrata G	2.0 km, 1 Gbps, 4 receivers, 4 transmitters
MRV Communication	TereScope 1(PAL)	0.5 km, 100 Mbps, lightweight
	TereScope 10	5.9 km, 10 Mbps, lightweight
	TereScope 155	4.2 km, 100 Mbps, lightweight
	TereScope 155 PI	4.0 km, 100 Mbps, multiple transmitter
	TereScope 5000	5.5 km, 100 Mbps, multiple transmitter
	TereScope 4000	4.0 km, 100 Mbps, multiple transmitter
	TereScope 700	0.75 km, 100 Mbps, lightweight
	TereScope 1000 P	0.3 km, 1 Gbps, lightweight

Optical Wireless Mesh Vendors

ClearMesh Networks is the only equipment vendor, as far as this author knows, that offers equipment designed specifically for optical wireless mesh networks. The equipment, CM 300, consists of three FSO transceivers, each operating at 100 Mbps full-duplex data rate and integrated with a Layer 2 switching engine.

FSO links for the CM 300 are based on LED, transmitting nominally 870 nm infrared light and are specified to be eye safe. The operating range of each FSO link is specified to be between 40 m and 250 m. Each transceiver, which consists of the transmitter and receiver, can be individually aligned remotely to facilitate easy installation. Each transceiver is actively auto- tracked to compensate for misalignment due to slow movements. Transmit divergence and the receive FoV is in the order of half a degree, wide enough to compensate for small scale involuntary movements.

From the networking perspective, CM 300 is a Layer 2 switch operating IEEE 802.1w (Rapid Spanning Tree Protocol). The equipment supports up to 256 VLANs and 802.1p classification with four levels of priority queues. In addition to the three FSO ports, CM 300 consists of four user ports, two of which are 10/100 Base-TX capable and the other two 10/100/1000 Base-TX capable. These user ports are located at the bottom of the CM 300. One of the 10/100 Base-TX ports can also be used as a serial port.

The equipment consists of active environmental controls and is qualified for outdoor operation in extreme weather conditions. Each CM 300 comes with its own separate indoor power supply (IPS) with 48 VDC. CM 300 nominally consumes about 30W, but may consume close to 300W when its internal heater is used during cold weather conditions.

CM 300 provides a full suite of industry standard management interfaces. It provides a command link interface (CLI) that can be accessed through serial, Telnet or SSH. It also provides a GUI that is accessible by means of HTTP/HTTPS. Complete configuration and management of the device can also be performed remotely by means of SNMP v2. Both industry standard and enterprise MIBs are supported along with a large set of SNMP traps for alarm generation by management systems. ClearMesh also offers a full-featured element management system, referred to as the ClearMesh Management System, tailored to manage the CM 300 remotely.

References

1. Dr. Heinz Willebrand and Baksheesh S. Ghuman, *Free Spare Optics: Enabling Optical Connectivity in Today's Networks* (City: Sams Publishing, 2002).

TDM: Circuit Bonding

by William Szeto

While Ethernet is the dominant protocol for the enterprise, its deployment by service providers in TDM-based networks has been limited. One reason for this limited deployment is that Ethernet fundamentally is a data transport technology and has difficulty "fitting" into a TDM-based network.

A service provider's legacy TDM network is designed to support voice services in a robust manner with only a small amount of signal overhead. By conforming to a TDM-centric hierarchy, low bit-rate signals are multiplexed neatly into timeslots for efficient transport, grooming, and switching. While in operation, TDM systems continuously transmit bits at a fixed rate. This regular transmission of bits aids in monitoring the health of the transmission system and in clock and data recovery circuitry. The embedded base of telecommunications equipment was developed with TDM payloads in mind. The fixed bit-rate signals traveling through the transmission channels are neatly carved into smaller TDM signals at the endpoints, efficiently supporting voice and other TDM payloads. Conversely, data networks, with inherently "bursty" characteristics, have developed much differently. The differences between voice-optimized and data-optimized networks have resulted in difficult interoperability between the two network types. A conversion, or mapping, is required to support data on the TDM links.

But mapping protocols onto other formats is neither simple nor efficient. If a signal with a different bit rate and protocol is mapped onto the next *higher* bit rate, the bandwidth difference between the lower and higher rate is lost. For example, when you map Gigabit Ethernet (1 Gbps) into OC-48 SONET (2.5 Gbps), you lose the difference between the two—1.5 Gbps, or over half the OC-48's capacity. This inefficiency represents a new cost for carriers.

This approach to mapping also assumes the data signal has a lower bit rate than the signal it is being mapped into. In a TDM-multiplexing hierarchy, this is always true. With data-networking interfaces such as Ethernet, however, this is much less likely to be the case—and this causes problems. While the service provider may have enough network bandwidth for large customer data payloads, the bandwidth is not likely to be in a single contiguous channel. In this case, the simple mapping approach just described will not work.

It is obvious that a more sophisticated approach—one that allows for the efficient mapping of *any* payload into existing TDM transmission capacity—must be created to handle fast-growing Ethernet transport needs. The technology must decouple the payload to be carried from the transmission system used to carry that payload. This technology must also apply to multiple bit rates, formats, or applications.

Some of the requirements include the following:

- Combine bandwidth across multiple, physically diverse transmission channels, independent of the data rate and transport protocol.

- Allow multiple clients, possibly of different formats, to share the concatenated bandwidth simultaneously regardless of client format and data rate.

- Provide consistent client protection against channel failures due to transmission impairments, such as arrival time variation excessive bit error rate.

- Provide a protection mechanism that is independent of client and transmission rate and format.

- Support prioritization of clients enforced during transmission channel failures.

In recent years, the International Telecommunications Union (ITU-T) has approved several standards that have allowed this evolution to occur. These standards are

- Generic Framing Procedure (GFP)
- Virtual Concatenation (VC)
- Link Capacity Adjustment Scheme (LCAS)

With the introduction of these standards, circuit bonding was created, providing an effective way to carry Ethernet traffic over the existing TDM network. circuit bonding extends the life of the current transport network by allowing carriers to introduce new services over legacy equipment. With the advent of circuit bonding, the TDM network has evolved and can now carry Ethernet traffic. The focus of this chapter is to highlight how circuit bonding provides effective, efficient, and transparent transport of multiple service formats. In essence, circuit bonding is able to transport TDM and data protocols via any line interface, whether optical or copper. In the access portion of the network, circuit-bonding systems can be used to efficiently transport Ethernet via DS1s, E1s, DS3s, or OC-ns.

Technology Description

In today's access and metro networks, delivering broadband services to businesses is both an attractive business opportunity and a technical challenge. Less than 20 percent of all businesses are serviced directly by fiber, and the copper plant, in some instances, can be over fifty years old. Additionally, even recent copper installations are inherently limited in bandwidth. Achieving true broadband speeds requires some means of combining multiple pairs into a common bandwidth pool. Once established, this bandwidth pool should be utilized in a way that maximizes the revenue potential for both individual services or customers and services delivered to multi-tenant unit (MTU) locations. Circuit bonding is a platform that addresses these network issues without adversely impacting the existing network infrastructure, and it can be used with both fiber and copper infrastructure.

Additionally, circuit bonding can support clients with higher rates than the individual transport facilities. This capability is realized due to circuit bonding's ability to create a large pool of bandwidth between locations by concatenating multiple parallel transmission channels. By creating a single pool of bandwidth, the boundaries normally encountered in each channel are replaced by a single boundary equal to the total bandwidth of all of the channels. As long as a payload can fit into this concatenated channel, it can be transported and protected. This capability is particularly beneficial when transporting signals that have bit rates greater than any individual line channel, transporting signals with formats that are not accepted neatly into the transmission channels, or mixing different types of signals in the same system.

Access Network Issues

The access infrastructure is the final frontier in broadband networking. The single most limiting factor in the current access network is the availability of fiber to any given building. Only by bonding or concatenating multiple channels can true broadband speed be achieved on wireline networks where there is no fiber connectivity.

While the standards bodies have recognized this bonding need with the development of virtual concatenation (VCAT) and link concatenation adjustment scheme (LCAS) for SONET, IMA for ATM, MLPPP for IP, and so on, each of these approaches is unique to the protocol or network supported. Circuit bonding is created by using the current GFP/VC/LCAS standards.

Even if a building has fiber access, Multi-Service Access (MSA) platforms are not optimal for providing Ethernet transport. A fundamental issue related to MSAs is that these platforms are either TDM- or IP-centric. A TDM-centric MSA strands bandwidth when transporting IP since this type of MSA must use static multiplexing based on SONET STS boundaries. Because the IP-centric MSA generally does not have the resiliency of SONET to transport TDM traffic, optimal transparent transport of Ethernet services has not been fully realized. In most circumstances, bandwidth and transparency are traded off for the proper connectivity.

Traditional Ethernet access solutions use transport bandwidth inefficiently; therefore, the following issues need to be addressed when providing Ethernet transport services in the access network:

- Transparent transport of FE/GbE over available copper/SONET infrastructure.
- Efficient concatenation of available bandwidth.

- Solutions must be payload agnostic—independent of data/TDM client formats.
- Solutions must be independent of fiber availability.

Circuit Bonding Technology

Circuit bonding solves all of the major problems (just noted) that are associated with the transmission of Ethernet service in the MAN environment. Ethernet frames are transported over the network using the ITU standard GFP/VC/LCAS scheme.

In many instances, it is desirable to concatenate or "bond" many different links—either physical or virtual—into a single virtual link or *pipe*. Doing so offers customers or service providers several advantages, including increased efficiency of the physical transport medium and potentially simplified management of one link versus complicated management of several. Let's examine the basic theory and standards utilized for circuit bonding.

SONET Multiplexing: Virtual Concatenation, LCAS, and Generic Framing Protocol   A SONET multiplexer combines STS-1s by interleaving bytes to create a "higher-order" STS-N. The protocol is designed to scale by increasing the size of the multiplexed channel. Figure 10.1

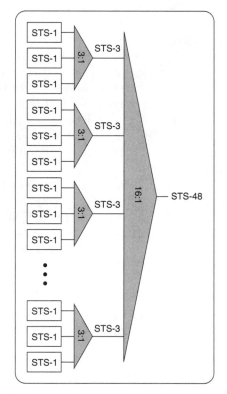

Figure 10.1   SONET multiplexing

is a block diagram showing a possible method to construct an STS-48 from 48 STS-1s. In Figure 10.1, the multiplexing occurs in stages as the STS-1s are first combined into STS-3s, and then the STS-3s are combined into an STS-48. The STS-48 can be converted directly into an OC-48 and transmitted through a fiber or passed to another SONET device.

Contiguous Concatenation   In SONET, for the transport of payloads that exceed the payload capacity of the standard set of Synchronous Payload Envelops (SPEs), contiguous concatenation can be used. As the name implies, the VTs or STSs used for the concatenation must be adjacent and free of other traffic.

When using SONET contiguous concatenation, contiguous bandwidth must be maintained throughout the whole transport network. Because of the need to keep the bandwidth contiguous throughout the network, the maximum bandwidth of the concatenated pipe is limited to that of the highest SONET rate commercially available today, OC-192/ STS-192. In the future, these rates could reach OC-768/STS-768 or higher. Additionally, SONET contiguous concatenation cannot be done across SPEs that are on different SONET line signals. These constraints can result in stranded bandwidth. Figure 10.2 is a block diagram of the SONET multiplexer supporting contiguous concatenated STS-3c and STS-12c payloads.

Virtual Concatenation and LCAS   Virtual concatenation allows an arbitrary number of STS-1s to be concatenated and transported across a SONET network. The STS-1s do

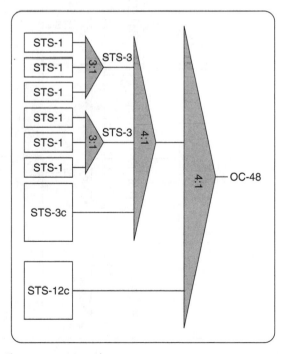

Figure 10.2   SONET contiguous concatenation

not need to be contiguous and can be transported independently across the network and recombined at the transmission endpoint. Only the source and destination are involved in the virtual concatenation process. virtual concatenation allows concatenation of up to 256 STS-1/STS-3c SPEs and up to 64 VT1.5/2/3/6 SPEs. Figure 10.3 is a block diagram illustrating the capabilities of virtual concatenation for STS rates.

Link Capacity Adjustment Scheme (LCAS) is a two-way handshake protocol designed to change the capacity of a virtual concatenated signal dynamically . LCAS must be used in conjunction with virtual concatenation and is not able to create or adjust the virtual concatenated circuit. Virtual Concatenation is used to build the pipe, and LCAS dynamically defines which of the concatenated group members is carrying traffic.

LCAS messages are continuously exchanged. Changes in the link capacity are sent in advance so that the receiver can switch to the new configuration as soon as it arrives. This allows for dynamic resizing of the concatenated channel or the temporary removal of a failed member link. LCAS utilizes the same H4 path overhead bytes that virtual concatenation uses. Because the H4 bytes are in the SONET path overhead, only the path terminating elements are involved in maintaining the circuit. In order to utilize this concatenated channel, a method to distribute client data across the STS-1s and recover them at the far end is required.

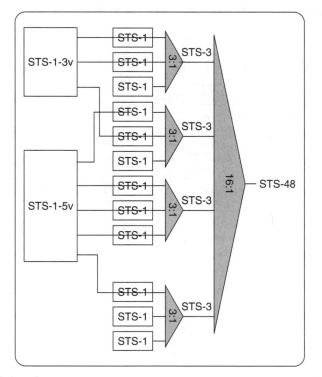

Figure 10.3   SONET virtual concatenation

Generic Framing Procedure (GFP)   The Generic Framing Procedure (GFP) standard was created by ITU to standardize framing capability for upper layer protocols to run over transmission systems. There are two favors of GFP: Frame-MappedMode and Transparent Mode.

A Frame-Mapped GFP is a Protocol Data Unit (PDU)- oriented adaptation mode. It is defined as a type of GFP mapping in which a client signal frame is received and mapped in its entirety into one GFP Frame.

A Transparent Mode is a block-code oriented adaptation mode. In this mode, a block-coded client characters are decoded and then mapped into a fixed length GFP frame and may be transmitted immediately without waiting for the receipt of a complete client data frame.

Circuit-Bonding Platform   The circuit-bonding platform is a combination of GFP, virtual concatenation, and Link Capacity Adjustment Scheme (LCAS). LCAS has the ability to increase or decrease the number of client connections or the size of a given pipe. Circuit bonding is engineered to utilize the entire capacity of the bonded pipe, making all the bandwidth available to users. Figure 10.4 shows the client and line side view of circuit bonding.

Circuit bonding allows

- Aggregated bandwidth across multiple physically diverse transmission channels, independent of line data rate and format.
- Multiple clients mapped simultaneously into the aggregated line-side bandwidth.
- Inherent compensation for variations in the arrival time of the aggregated channels.
- Protection of client channels against individual channel failures.
- Simple addition of transmission channels to the aggregated group.

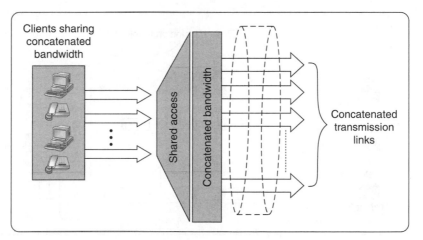

Figure 10.4   Client-and line-side view of circuit bonding

- Cross connection of transmission channels between transmit and receive ends.
- Ability to function as a stand-alone transport protocol.

Circuit bonding is independent of the transmission format or protocol. It can be used to provide transport over virtually any line transmission type and was not developed for a specific network type. Furthermore, the protection afforded by circuit bonding is available to all client signals regardless of their format.

Circuit bonding is also different from protocols that aggregate client-side interfaces. While a circuit bonding platform can carry those clients over either single or multiple facilities, it can carry mixed format signals equally well. As Figure 10.5 illustrates, those clients can be packet-based or TDM-based.

How Ethernet Frames Are Transported over Circuit-Bonded Networks   Circuit bonding can be used to carry Ethernet frames over bonded OCns, DS3s, and T1/E1s. Figure 10.6 shows how this can be achieved.

Figure 10.6 shows Ethernet connectivity using a circuit-bonding system over DS-1, DS-3 transport, or SONET transport. Because circuit bonding separates the client layer from the transport layer, Ethernet can be efficiently transported over a variety of parallel transport mechanisms with the following benefits:

- **Transparency**   Circuit bonding allows complete decoupling of the client interface and transport. A point-to-point Ethernet connection using a circuit-bonding system will transport Ethernet frames from multiple clients over a variety of intermediate transport mechanisms completely transparently.
- **Efficiency**   A circuit-bonding system can throttle Ethernet client speeds in small increments, depending on the size of the transport pipe and the Ethernet bit rate. This allows the service provider to offer "fractional rate" Ethernet services,

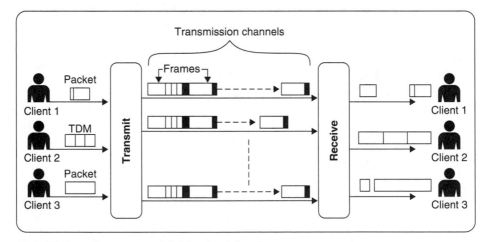

Figure 10.5   Various client types carried by circuit bonding

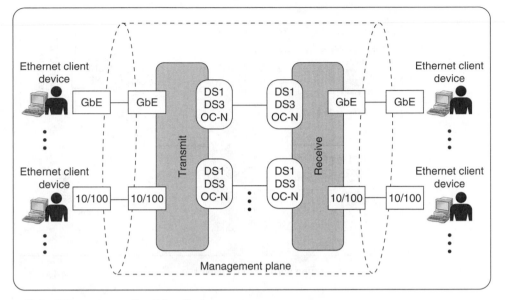

Figure 10.6 Ethernet over circuit bonding

instead of just 10, 100, or 1000 Mbps rates. In addition, the ability to multiplex the client signals efficiently on "just enough" line-side transport allows these fractional services to be offered at lower cost points, and the line service can grow as the client base grows. The amount of bandwidth used can be adjusted dynamically as Ethernet demand grows. For example, suppose additional Ethernet demand requires the addition of a DS-3 line in a bonded circuit that is carried over a SONET device. Because circuit bonding decouples the Ethernet layer from the SONET layer, the available bandwidth is dynamically increased in a transparent manner to the Ethernet layer. Simple SONET STS-1 transport is preserved with no need for complex virtual concatenation.

- **Adaptability** Circuit bonding can transport Ethernet frames over a variety of line-side transport types. These include optical transport, such as OC-3, OC-12, and OC-48, as well as DS-3 and DS-1. This allows the circuit bonding to be applied in a wide array of off-net and on-net situations. Circuit bonding can extend the usefulness of existing transport networks, eliminating the expense of deploying next-generation SONET systems.

Circuit bonding can be used for any type of DS-3 facility. Figure 10.7 shows the use of a circuit-bonding system with a variety of DS-3 facilities. These DS-3 facilities may be transmuxed into SONET or transported over copper or radio.

Circuit bonding can also be adapted to copper facilities even if the Ethernet client is using optical interfaces. Figure 10.8 shows the use of a circuit-bonding system over several existing and planned copper-line interfaces, including DS-3 (existing), DS-1, and E-1.

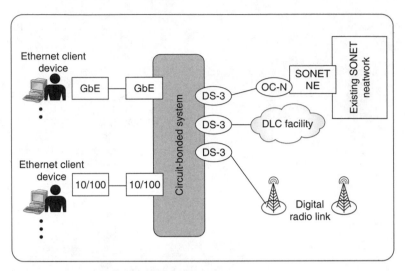

Figure 10.7   Using circuit bonding with DS-3 transport

- **Manageability**   Circuit bonding provides a complete transmission layer management system. This allows carrier-grade fault isolation and performance monitoring of a circuit bonded link, effectively extending carrier-class networking off-net to the Ethernet customer.

Figure 10.9 shows circuit bonding being used to extend Ethernet to an off-net customer. Transparency is maintained. And carrier class end-to-end transmission layer management is available.

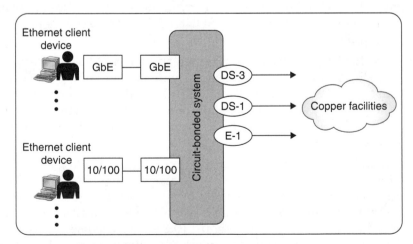

Figure 10.8   Using circuit bonding with copper facilities

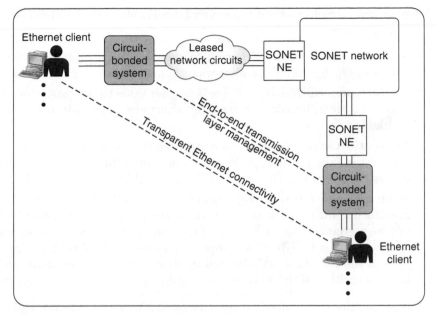

Figure 10.9 Using circuit bonding to extend Ethernet to an off-net client

Carrier Ethernet

Ethernet services in the MAN can take on a number of forms, and the service can be described by a number of parameters. From the perspective of providing Carrier Ethernet transport service in the MAN, the following is a list of the most important characteristics as defined by the Metro Ethernet Forum (MEF):

- Protection
- Hard QoS
- Backward compatibility
- Service management
- Scalability

These topics will be discussed in more detail in the following sections.

Protection   Ethernet networks are generally protected using the Spanning Tree Protocol per IEEE 802.1D. When a segment of the Ethernet network fails, a new spanning tree is calculated. If a redundant path around the failure is available, the network uses it instead of the failed segment. This protection scheme is robust from an interoperation point of view and has been implemented in the LAN environment for some time.

However, this simple method has several drawbacks, all of which are magnified in the MAN environment:

- **Segment protection**   Ethernet segments are not protected within the segment. For example, if a hub fails, all workstations on the hub can no longer communicate.

- **Protection availability**   There is no guarantee that a protection path is available. Ethernet reconfigures and uses an alternate path only if the alternate path is available.

- **Protection size**   There is no guarantee that a protection path will be the same size as the failed link. A gigabit path may only have access to a 100 Mbps path to use as an alternate. This may not be acceptable for mission-critical data.

- **Performance monitoring**   Ethernet does not offer sophisticated performance monitoring, making a geographically diverse Ethernet MAN difficult to manage in failure scenarios. The lack of good fault isolation mechanisms (such as SONET LOS alarms) makes it difficult to pinpoint failures in the network. This may be acceptable in the case of a LAN located in a controlled environment, but fault isolation becomes critical if the network is leased and extends across a metropolitan area.

Circuit bonding can be used to overcome some of these limitations. By using circuit bonding to transport Ethernet (either over SONET or copper facilities), the well-established, carrier-class standards of protection equivalent to those offered by SONET are available. While other solutions exist to carry Ethernet over SONET, only circuit bonding offers full transparency and efficient transport.

Circuit bonding supports line-side $M{:}N$ protection. This allows the clients to share the bandwidth of multiple parallel line-side connections and also use some of these lines as active, load-sharing "standby" facilities.

Circuit bonding can also provide redundant diverse path protection. It maps client information onto a set of line-side transmission paths. By using physically diverse routes, a circuit-bonded system can offer path protection. Circuit bonding reacts very quickly to failures and automatically performs "load sharing" across all available paths well within the MEF-required 50–ms timeframe. This capability allows a service provider to offer protected off-net or on-net Ethernet service without the cost of SONET transmission.

Hard QOS/Throughput   One of the primary strengths of packet networking, such as Ethernet, is that statistical multiplexing becomes possible. This greatly increases the bandwidth efficiency of networks. A typical customer requires the bandwidth to transmit data in minimal time. Because of expense, it is very difficult to provide customers with a full-time, fast end-to-end network. Fortunately, most customers do not require the maximum bandwidth be available all the time. Because of this, packet networks that allow some of the resources to be shared can be utilized. Each Ethernet segment is capable of a maximum bit-rate based on the physical layer transmission medium. For example, each client on a 100BaseT segment can transmit at 100 Mbps, but only one segment at a time. The same principle can be applied to switched or bridged Ethernet segments. A segment connecting a set of other segments to a server may have less bandwidth available than the sum of the segments connected to each workstation. This oversubscription is a useful tool for a network designer to control network costs while offering adequate performance.

Broadly defined, oversubscription is a state that allows more traffic to be switched or routed over a given transmission link than that link is normally capable of transmitting. In other words, the sum of the possible input to a given link is greater than the link itself. In general, all networks have some form of oversubscription. Although it is often associated with packet networks, even circuit networks are oversubscribed. In fact, you could argue that the whole purpose of switching and routing is to oversubscribe links purposely. For example, in a voice network, the entire capacity of voice circuits subtending from the switch is, in practice, always larger than the capacity of the Inter-Machine Trunks (IMTs) connecting the switch to other switches. If every caller on one switch tries to place a call to the same far-end switch at the same time, the IMT would not have enough capacity. Therefore, the IMT can be said to be oversubscribed.

Things are similar in the packet world of Ethernet switches. Take, for example, a simple Ethernet switch with five 10BaseT ports and one 100BaseT uplink. There is no way for the 10BaseT ports to overfill the 100BaseT uplink because it always has enough capacity. If instead the switch had fifteen 10BaseT ports and one 100BaseT uplink, it would be possible for the client ports to send more data than the uplink could carry, resulting in network congestion. With simple Ethernet, there is no management of the traffic. The Ethernet switches essentially work on a first-come, first-served basis. With the addition of IEEE 802.1q, Ethernet becomes capable of client prioritization. Although this standard is primarily a definition of VLAN, it also includes 3 bits that can be used to assign priority to individual Ethernet frames. An IEEE 802.1p-compliant switch uses these three bits to manage traffic in congestion situations.

The circuit-bonding platform is also capable of oversubscription. It differs from simple Ethernet in that it allows hard quality of service guarantees to individual client ports. Some of the QoS features are discussed next.

Guaranteed Bandwidth   If a client is provisioned with 20 Mbps of guaranteed bandwidth, it gets that amount as long as the line facilities are not reduced due to link failure or deprovisioning.

If a single Ethernet client is provisioned to have multiple priority bandwidth assignments (i.e., 10 Mbps of guaranteed, 10 Mbps of shared/burst, and 10 Mbps of best effort), it is up to the client source device to prioritize its own packet streams appropriately. The circuit-bonding device will always transport the guaranteed bandwidth first, followed by the shared/burst, and then the best effort as long as sufficient line bandwidth exists.

Priorities and Provisioning

- A circuit-bonded system can tag guaranteed, burst, and best effort per port (i.e., DS3/OC-n). A service provider can assign priorities on a per-client basis. This stands in contrast to traditional Multi-Service Provisioning Platforms (MSPPs), which cannot provide prioritization; this needs to be done at Layers 2 and 3.

- Each client gets bandwidth assigned; all three priorities can be assigned on a block of bandwidth. That bandwidth is weighted based on client provisioning. A round-robin approach allows the service provider to prioritize one customer over the next fairly. This means that clients will be degraded proportionally across customers on a weighted basis; all will be degraded by an equal percentage.

- Rate limiting is based on a "dual leaky bucket" because there are two priority levels (guaranteed and best-effort traffic). The circuit bonding system also allows burst traffic. Pause frames are used to slow down the transmitter if the client has surpassed its capacity. A pause frame is also passed on to the customer. Rate limiting on the circuit- bonding system is accomplished at the client I/O port by using IEEE 802.3 PAUSE frames (if supported by the client device, otherwise, it's accomplished by dropping packets).

- Flow control, based on client priority classes, is applied using PAUSE frames as well. Each client can be provisioned with guaranteed, shared, and/or best-effort bandwidth. This bandwidth can be provisioned in granularities of 1Mb for 10/100 Mbps Ethernet and 10Mb for Gigabit Ethernet. The flow control applies consistently to an entire client signal.

Service Management   Service management for circuit-bonding systems is well defined by the ITU. A recently approved ITU standard on service management includes both architecture and requirement definitions for circuit bonding optical- and copper-based systems. While additional capabilities are being defined in the standards, it is safe to say that service management for circuit bonding will provide full service management capabilities for the carriers.

Backward Compatibility   Circuit bonding can be used to carry TDM traffic as well as Ethernet traffic, making it backward compatible with various types of client traffic. It can be used to carry traditional voice as well as the modern VoIP traffic. Circuit bonding can also be used to carry Frame Relay traffic in addition to the Ethernet traffic for IP access.

Scalability   Circuit bonding can be used to bond multiple TDM pipes together, forming large pipes for Ethernet and TDM traffic. It can be scaled from bonding two T1s together to bonding two OC12s for a full-rate GbE requirement.

Drivers for This Solution

In the following section, we will look at the drivers that led to the development of this solution. The main driver obviously is the rapid growth of data traffic coupled with the current architecture of the current transport network. Ways must be developed to handle the current data traffic with the existing network infrastructure.

The Need for a New Transport Solution

It has been a very long time since fundamental changes were made to the transport systems utilized by service providers. The technology of copper-based systems predates that of fiber-based SONET systems developed in the 1980s. At the heart of these systems lie multiplexers and switch fabrics optimized for the Time Division Multiplexing (TDM) networks they were designed to create. What has changed is the mix of services required by customers as data has become the dominant payload. Superficial modifications in transport systems have been made, but no fundamental changes have occurred to reflect the changing needs of data payloads. Recently the introduction of Dense Wavelength-Division Multiplexing (DWDM) has dramatically lowered the cost of transporting bandwidth and facilitated the explosive growth in data traffic.

It is clear that a new generation of flexible transport equipment capable of supporting any type of payload is needed. It is also important to decouple the line-side interface from the client-side interface, allowing each of them to evolve independently. The immediate opportunity is to provide platforms that utilize the capability of the existing network and allow new data transport services to be offered. It is also important that the same technology can be used as the basis for an efficient and economical transport infrastructure for both voice and data.

Circuit Bonding Standards Development

The pre-standard circuit-bonding technology relies on a set of integrated processes to create a point-to-point connection. It combines the capacity of multiple links into a single concatenated pipe. This circuit/channel bonding provides several benefits. First, the large pipe is a single entity reducing the number of connections that must be managed. Next, payloads can be supported that require more capacity than is available in any of the individual channels, a gating issue for other systems. Last, there is the efficiency of packing multiple payloads into a single large pipe.

Bonding is accomplished with a protocol that resides within the payload of the existing links. Therefore, the links are not required to participate in any way and can be any bit rate or format, utilizing copper or fiber. Skew compensation is included so the individual channels are not required to travel the same path through the network.

Historically, different types of payloads are not combined by transport systems into a single channel. The ability to adapt payloads of any type is a differentiating factor for this new technology. Each payload in the channel may be a different format and have different performance and bandwidth requirements. Supporting requirements ranging from fixed bit rate (TDM) to burst data payloads are accomplished by mapping all clients into a common structure call a Payload Data Unit (PDU). Once in this common structure, the differences in the payloads are reflected in the amount of bandwidth and the priority assigned to each payload.

Another basic feature provided by circuit bonding is channel protection. Failures in the individual channels are recognized quickly and inoperable channels are removed from service. The payloads continue to be supported using the bandwidth available in the remaining operational channels. This channel protection feature along with the skew compensation can be used to create robustness in the connection by diversely routing channels. In this scenario, a single cable cut cannot disable the entire link.

The processes just described create a single large pipe with all the capacity available to the clients. Priorities assigned to each client dictate the distribution of capacity, and data clients provisioned to burst compete with each other for this bandwidth (statistical multiplexing). The implementation of these basic functions creates a simple platform that is easy to operate, manage, and deploy.

The deployment of point-to-point circuit-bonding solutions allows the service provider to create new revenue from data services utilizing existing infrastructure. These deployments are also the first step toward a modern full-featured transport platform.

The International Telecommunications Union (ITU) has passed several standards making circuit bonding an industry standard from the bonding of optical circuits (OC3 and OC12s) to DS3 and DS1s. Additional work is being done in standardizing the service management issues for services derived from bonded circuits.

Networked Solutions

Circuit-bonding-based products can be used to support networked data transport applications as well as point-to-point services. As service providers deploy high volumes of point-to-point systems, this creates a need for larger, more highly integrated devices with additional functionality. These devices aggregate multiple circuit-bonded transport links and incorporate a packet-based switch fabric instead of the TDM-based fabric typically used today. The circuit-bonding platform thus supports flexible provisioning, circuit switching, and network protection features that go beyond just handling point-to-point links.

Future Applications for Circuit Bonding

Current applications using circuit-bonding technology are very much limited to the access network. The process of aggregating the capacity of many channels together to achieve a single big pipe has been defined in a generic manner. This allows for the level of aggregation to change depending on the rates of the individual signals involved and the desired rate of the big pipe. This flexibility will allow the big pipe architecture to remain simple over time even as more and more capacity is created. The deployment of higher-speed transmission channels, higher-wavelength-count WDM systems or higher-speed ports on packet-processing devices does not change the fundamental process. As opposed to bandwidth management approaches that are focused on wavelengths, the big pipe architecture allows all of the independent technologies to be developed and deployed separately. Therefore, carriers are not forced to change several aspects of their network to capitalize on developments in any particular area.

Protection mechanisms for the big pipe solution are also fundamentally different from those considered by proponents of wavelength-switching solutions. In a wavelength-based solution, the only issue to consider in the event of failure is the restoration of the lost wavelength. Solutions ranging from path-level protection to mesh-based span protection have been proposed.

With the big pipe concept, the capacity of several transmission channels is combined to form a single large payload. In this scenario, many options exist for implementing protection. If a single transmission channel fails, for example, the failure may not affect the transmission of data if extra capacity exists in the big pipe. Alternatively, it may be desirable for the failure to result in a switch to a protection subchannel to replace the failed channel. The protection mechanisms are very similar to those of previous solutions that deal with aggregated signals.

Packet Network Benefits

Current IP routers can process 10Gb/s of packets. Each time port speeds have been increased in the short history of these devices, network builders have immediately adopted the faster technology. The benefits of high-speed ports are significant for data networks.

Several factors drive data network builders to implement higher-speed ports. The first is that the alternative, deploying several parallel links, leads to management and scalability issues. Each link in the data network is monitored and maintained by a link-layer protocol such as OSPF. The status of each link in the network must be monitored, maintained, and distributed to many of the elements in the network. As the number of links increase, even with parallel ports, the task of maintaining the link state tables is increased.

Another simplifying factor is that very large LSPs can be created in the superchannel and more effectively packed with data. Additionally, the large LSPs reduce network complexity since fewer are created. Instead of creating many LSPs on many physical connections, each large LSP in the superchannel contains a tremendous payload.

Another benefit of the superchannel in data networking is the creation of a new level of multiplexing. The high-speed ports allow for the aggregation of packets from many low-speed ports from various routers. Creating this layer eliminates the wasteful interconnections that exist between routers in current networks.

From a data-networking perspective, there are no benefits—only drawbacks—to maintaining many parallel links between network locations. Each physical link must be managed independently. A more scalable solution is to deploy high-speed interfaces. The big pipe concept supports this philosophy by transporting the high-speed superchannel signals generated at the routers.

Transmission Benefits

Today, wavelengths in WDM transmission networks are independent. No relationship exists between any two wavelengths, and no assumptions are made concerning where the payloads originate and terminate. Therefore, the current generation of WDM systems has been produced with full flexibility down to the wavelength level.

With the rapid growth of communication networks in recent years and with service devices being created using the big pipe concept, operating at the granularity of the individual wavelength loses appeal. Many wavelengths in the core of the network have the same origination and termination nodes. Therefore, it is not necessary to treat the individual wavelengths independently. Instead, groups of wavelengths or, more accurately, pieces of optical spectrum can be treated as a single entity.

Several benefits can be realized when transmission systems operate with the big pipe architecture. The transmission span budget is improved because a series of filters do not have to be in place at every network node to demultiplex the wavelengths. Instead, all signals are demultiplexed to the optical band granularity, and only those being added or dropped are demultiplexed to the wavelength granularity.

As with many aspects of the big pipe concept, network management of the transmission system is simplified. Instead of managing each wavelength in the network, the optical bands are managed, greatly reducing the scale of the problem. With the capacity of each WDM system reaching several Tb/s, and with many routes in the network relying on WDM, the increase in granularity is appropriate.

A major obstacle to the deployment of optical cross connects is the requirement of having very large port counts. The optical-band concept virtually eliminates this issue. An all-optical cross connect with a modest number of ports can provide a tremendous amount of throughput by operating at the level of the optical band.

The optical bands described fit neatly into the big pipe concept. In light of the rapid growth occurring in carrier networks, the scalability of the big pipe concept has great appeal. Carriers can continue to increase capacity while maintaining a manageable network.

The increasing amount of information carried over core networks is forcing service providers to continually upgrade their networks. The deployment of WDM equipment is providing the capacity, and service providers are searching for a means to manage the large number of wavelengths that will operate in the near future. Considering that the amount of information carried on each wavelength is relatively constant, however, deploying the hottest optical or electrical-switching technology in the form of wavelength-based optical cross-connects loses its appeal in the long term.

The scalable long-term solution for the network core has not changed. Signals in the core of the network must continue to be aggregated to produce high-speed connections. In today's long-haul networks, this means aggregating wavelengths. The number of wavelengths will continue to grow, but management complexity will not, as the focus shifts from managing wavelengths to managing large segments of capacity.

The circuit-bonding-based big pipe concept is ideally suited to the requirements of rapidly growing packet networks and high-capacity transmission. The ability to flexibly provide new service and capacity lies in the devices that provide the aggregation.

Where This Solution Fits?

Ethernet is the dominant LAN technology utilized in enterprise networks to interconnect virtually every type of office equipment and to interconnect LANs that are in close physical proximity. Ethernet is a simple and mature connection technology to transport IP data that combines low cost and ease of operation. Ethernet, as a LAN technology, was never intended as a service delivery platform. It does not contain features required by service providers to operate and support services. As such, Ethernet will not become a service delivery platform, but service delivery platforms must evolve to support the transport of Ethernet at any required bandwidth. Ethernet connectivity will expand as methods are developed to support efficient and economical transport. The key to expanding the size of LANs beyond a small geographic area is to enable existing service provider networks to support the transport of Ethernet. The introduction of carrier-grade Ethernet has changed this. Carrier Ethernet is rapidly becoming the technology of choice for both service and network convergence.

Ethernet Transport Applications

A few common applications for Ethernet transport are described here:

- **Enterprise LAN extension** Today, network nodes on a LAN must be in close physical proximity due to the distance limitations of the underlying Ethernet technology. The inability to add remote nodes to a LAN is strictly a matter of transmitting the Ethernet frames and is not an inherent limitation in the network protocols or other scaling issues. An enterprise with facilities in multiple locations may wish to share resources between the locations. A simple solution from the LAN manager's perspective may be to connect the LANs using an Ethernet port as though they were not in separate locations.

- **Enterprise to Internet service provider connection** A typical enterprise LAN network is comprised of nodes interconnected by Ethernet ports. Other technologies such as Fiber Distributed Data Interface (FDDI) and token ring are also in use, but Ethernet is by far the most widely deployed. Regardless of the LAN protocol in operation, the enterprise's connection to its ISP is typically of another variety. Because the ISP's router is located at a remote location, the ISP connection must use the existing TDM network to make the connection. Therefore, both the enterprise router and the ISP's router must use a more expensive TDM port. If it were possible to transmit Ethernet directly to the ISP's router, both of the routers could use a more economical Ethernet port, and the network managers would not have to deal with TDM ports.

- **ISP router interconnection** The any-to-any connectivity of the Internet is created by a vast network of interconnected routers. An ISP's routers are interconnected, and the ISP's network is interconnected, or peered, with other ISPs and service provider networks. When these routers are in close physical proximity, they can be interconnected with Ethernet ports. When they are not in close physical proximity, they must be interconnected with TDM ports such as Packet over SONET. This connection is more expensive and often at a relatively low data rate. A simple and economical solution from the perspective of the ISP is to utilize Ethernet ports for all connections regardless of physical distance.

Existing Ethernet Services

Today there are several options for services supporting Ethernet beyond the LAN. Three common options will be described. The first option is router-based; the service provider installs an Internet Protocol (IP) router with TDM ports in each location, as shown in Figure 10.10a. The TDM ports (DS1s or DS3s) use the copper infrastructure to connect to the nearest service provider Point of Presence (POP).

A service provider's router running many high-layer protocols must be installed and provisioned to deliver Ethernet frames from one point to another. The router provides the Ethernet port for the service connection and TDM ports to interface to the transport network. This gives the service provider a presence at the customer location and the ability to provide managed services. A protocol such as MultiLink Point-to-Point (MLPPP) may be required in order to utilize the bandwidth on multiple TDM ports. If the goal is simply to interconnect two LANs, this is an expensive and complicated solution for a very simple task.

The second option is fiber based. This simple option bypasses any existing infrastructure. An Ethernet extension device is installed at each enterprise location and an optical fiber is patched together between the locations, as shown in Figure 10.10b. Major issues include the fiber connectivity requirement and distance limitation.

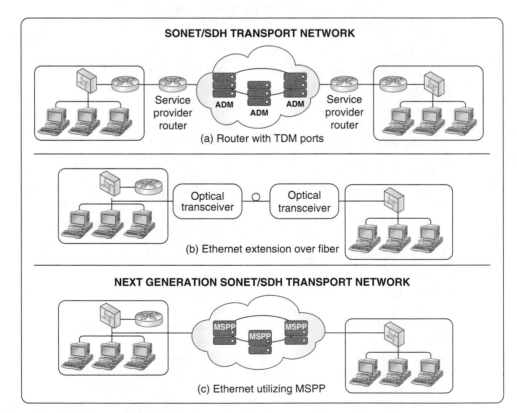

Figure 10.10   IP Router with TDM ports

A third option is based on a multi-service provisioning platform (MSPP). The MSPP is basically a Synchronous Optical Network (SONET) or Synchronous Digital Hierarchy (SDH) Add/Drop Multiplexer (ADM) designed to support standard TDM services as well as data services such as Ethernet. The MSPP is connected to the service provider network by optical fiber, which once again limits its deployment. MSPPs are typically deployed with SONET/SDH ring architectures, as shown in Figure 10.10c. New equipment build-outs by service providers will use MSPP devices. However, it is expensive to replace existing SONET/SDH equipment with MSPP devices. If the goal is to provide Ethernet connectivity, and capacity is available in the existing transport infrastructure, an overlay network of MSPPs will be very costly compared to using the existing network to support the service.

Each of the Ethernet connectivity solutions described here may be perfectly acceptable, or even ideal, for certain applications and deployments. In order for Ethernet transport to reach its full potential, however, service providers must be able to reach all customers, whether connected by copper or fiber, with the desired bandwidth. Solving this problem is the initial focus of a transport solution using circuit bonding.

Transport Solution Using Circuit Bonding

Although several types of Ethernet services have been described, circuit bonding provides reliable delivery of Ethernet frames across facilities where directly connecting Ethernet ports is not otherwise possible. In effect, the application requires the use of the service provider's infrastructure to remove the Ethernet distance limitation. This creates a virtual direct connection between Ethernet ports, with TDM-like Quality of Service (QoS) and service assurance and management capabilities. Circuit bonding is able to transport Ethernet over new or existing infrastructure by augmenting the transport network, allowing the interconnection of devices with Ethernet ports as though they were physically next to each other, regardless of their true location. Except for the transport delay caused by the added distance and the appearance of PAUSE frames, the distance extension is undetectable by the interconnected devices. The circuit-bonding solution for the case of an enterprise connecting a LAN at one location to its main corporate LAN is shown in Figure 10.11. Utilizing circuit bonding, this connection is made over the existing carrier infrastructure with any number of DS1s, DS3s, OC-3s, or OC-12s required to achieve the desired bandwidth.

Figure 10.12 shows an example where tenants in an office building are receiving service from an ISP. Without circuit bonding, the enterprise and ISP routers must use expensive TDM ports or the service provider must build-out a data transport network. With circuit bonding, the router can use more economical native Ethernet ports, and the circuit-bonding connection can be provisioned—and easily reprovisioned—to the desired bandwidth as needs change.

For the service provider, the economics governing the deployment of Ethernet service are often driven by the ability to use the existing infrastructure to reach a broad base of customers who could otherwise not be serviced. A single bonded circuit incorporates all of the features required to utilize the existing infrastructure to offer Ethernet services to any business. The functions performed by circuit bonding are described next.

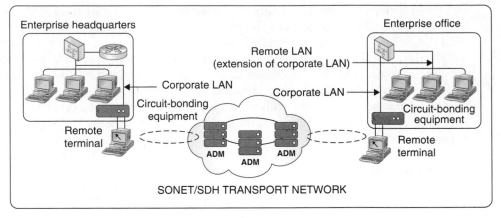

Figure 10.11   Circuit bonding solution for enterprise

Circuit Bonding Functions

In order to economically and efficiently transport Ethernet over new or existing infrastructure, circuit bonding has incorporated several transport functions in its platform. These functions, absent in current transport systems in most cases, establish circuit bonding as an extension to the transport system. circuit bonding should be used when appropriate performance, protection, operation, and reliability features are required for the transport of Ethernet over the existing TDM infrastructure.

For businesses with ISP connections, or those operating LANs in multiple physical locations, establishing Ethernet connectivity between LANs allows them to manage and share network resources economically. Additionally, utilizing Ethernet for their ISP

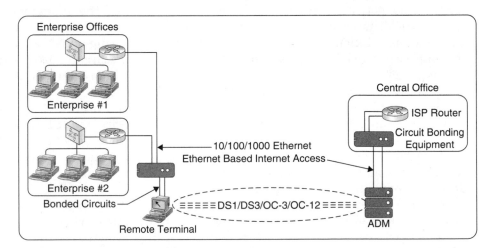

Figure 10.12   Tenants in an office building receiving service from an ISP

connection provides an economical and scalable solution eliminating the TDM interface on their router. Service providers are beginning to deploy solutions to meet this need, but the majority of their existing network is not capable of supporting Ethernet.

Today, all services, regardless of whether they are voice or data, are provided over the same TDM network. Emerging Ethernet services will be the same. Ethernet does not offer new challenges that cannot be met utilizing the existing TDM network with a few new functions incorporated at the edge of the network. Circuit bonding was developed to perform these functions.

Benefits and Shortcomings

The benefits of circuit bonding are realized when bandwidth aggregation is coupled with bandwidth sharing among multiplexed payloads and protection capabilities. Operating in concert with existing transport systems, these functions extend the capabilities of transport networks. Although there are several high-layer protocols with bonding features, circuit bonding is most efficient as a simple, low-layer transport function allowing any payload to be supported over any transport network.

The major benefits for deploying circuit bonding include

- **100 percent Ethernet reach**   Carriers deploying circuit bonding can serve all customer buildings with or without fiber access.

- **Highly efficient**   A higher bandwidth utilization percentage helps to improve the profit margin and reduce leased bandwidth cost. Carriers can offer Ethernet service in bandwidth increments that more closely match customer requirements, therefore increasing customer acceptance of services provided.

- **Ability to grow**   Circuit-bonded pipes can grow with customer needs without hardware replacement and truck roll. Bandwidth can be added remotely in small increments.

- **Quality of service and protection**   Ethernet services based on circuit bonding can provide carrier-grade services that are able to meet stringent SLA requirements similar to TDM services.

100 percent Ethernet Reach

Historically, businesses have been connected to their service provider's network by copper pairs, while fiber has been deployed slowly over time to meet increased bandwidth requirements. Figure 10.13 contains a prediction for the number of businesses requiring data connectivity at T1 or higher rates in the coming years. The graph shows the number of businesses in locations with copper connectivity only and those with fiber connectivity. Although fiber build-outs are occurring, the majority of businesses exist at locations served only by copper. This will not change in the near future.

This data must be interpreted carefully. Deployed fiber is generally intended for the service provider's use to interconnect facilities. Having fiber in place allows the service

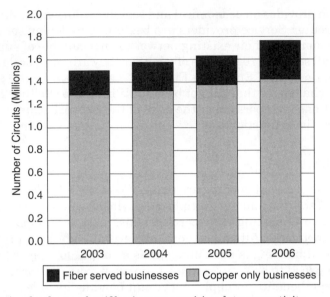

Figure 10.13 Prediction for the number if businesses requiring data connectivity

provider to efficiently support all of the customers in a large building. Fiber entering a building is generally not connected directly to the end customer, as a relatively small percentage of individual businesses have bandwidth requirements necessitating fiber. Fibers that reach the end customer's building are typically terminated on service provider equipment. The cost of utilizing fiber within a LAN is negligible, while the cost of using fiber in the MAN is high. Even after expensive fiber build-outs occur, the extension of fiber to a building does not necessarily mean fiber is available and economical for use by individual businesses, especially for point-to-point connectivity between geographically diverse locations.

Circuit bonding can be used to provide Ethernet services by bonding multiple T1s together to form a broadband pipe. Additionally, this pipe can then be used to support Ethernet services and other legacy traffic, such as TDM voice traffic.

Because fiber is expensive, scarce, and generally not needed from a bandwidth perspective, an Ethernet deployment requiring fiber to the customer location severely limits the market for the service. Fiber connectivity is typically provided to large businesses with high bandwidth requirements. The vast majority of the businesses, however, lack fiber connectivity and can make use of circuit-bonding solutions.

Highly Efficient

The current transport network is designed for TDM voice traffic. As demonstrated in Figure 10.14, it has very inflexible and rigid TDM increments. For example, from a T1

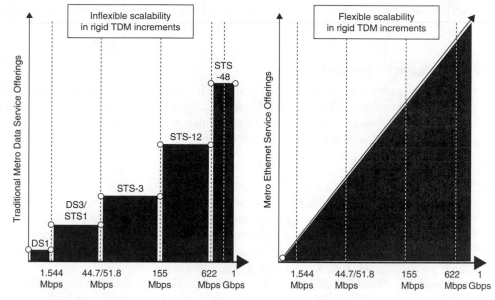

Figure 10.14 TDM bandwidth increments

(1.544 Mbps), the next bandwidth increment is a DS3 (45 Mbps). On the other hand, Ethernet has a much more flexible and granular bandwidth increments. Circuit bonding can help to bond smaller TDM pipes together so it will match the smaller Ethernet bandwidth granularity much better. In this way, circuit bonding helps reduce the cost of leased circuits and the cost of providing these services by matching customer requirements with the appropriate transport pipe.

The following table shows some examples of the efficiency gained by using bonded circuits.

Customer Requirements in Mbps	Current Provisioning Method	Circuit Bonded Pipe	Bandwidth Provisioned	Bandwidth Saved	Percentage Bandwidth Saved
10 Mbps	DS3–45 Mbps	$7 \times T1$	10.8 Mbps	34.2 Mbps	76%
90 Mbps	OC-3–155 Mbps	$2 \times DS3$	90 Mbps	65 Mbps	42%
450 Mbps	OC-12–622 Mbps	$3 \times OC3$	465 Mbps	157 Mbps	25%
1 Gbps	OC-48–2500 Mbps	$2 \times OC12$	1244 Mbps	1256 Mbps	50%

Ability to Grow

With the adaptation of the ITU standard on LCAS for virtual concatenated signals (ITU standard G.7042/Y.1305), circuit bonding has the ability to dynamically and hitlessly change (add and subtract) the capacity of a bonded transport pipe. This ability to add capacity seamlessly without a truck roll offers carriers the ability to sell additional bandwidth without adding more hardware and operational costs.

Quality of Service and Protection

One of the main features of circuit bonding is its ability to offer hard QoS and multiple levels of protection. Much like TDM/SONET-based services, carriers can offer SLAs on Ethernet services to their customers and deliver carrier-grade Ethernet services without building out a completely new overlay network.

Shortcomings

Circuit bonding is designed to provide Ethernet services to business customers where high levels of reliability and QoS are desired or required. It requires the bonding of TDM circuits to achieve the level of services required. When only best-effort traffic is sufficient for the application, the cost of circuit bonding may be higher than other solutions, such as copper bonding where only copper cables are required.

Secondly, the bandwidth of circuit bonding is still based on the hierarchy of the current TDM- and SONET-based network. The granularity, while much better than the TDM network, is still not as smooth and flexible as other solutions.

The other shortcoming of circuit bonding involves the additional overhead requirements beyond the overhead associated with TDM/SONET. While the overhead requirement for circuit bonding is relatively small, a portion will not be available for traffic transportation.

Typical Deployment Scenarios

Figure 10.15 provides an overview of how circuit bonding fits into carrier networks. Circuit-bonding equipment can also be deployed in several modes (see Figure 10.16):

- **Point-to-hub mode**   In this scenario, a circuit-bonding hub can be deployed in the network core and can be used as a hubbing device for multiple CPE devices at customer sites. These devices can be either circuit-bonding platforms, integrated access devices, or native Ethernet devices.

- **Point-to-point mode**   Circuit bonding can also be deployed in the "success-based" mode for Ethernet private line (E-Line) services. In this case, circuit-binding equipment can be deployed after the customer order is received, and it will be installed on a point-to-point basis. In this way, no advance investment will be required, and the system will only be installed after the circuit is sold.

Figures 10.17 to 10.21 illustrate various circuit-bonding architectures. It is also important to note that with the exception of the circuit-bonding equipment, no other complementary assets are needed to deliver Carrier Ethernet to customers.

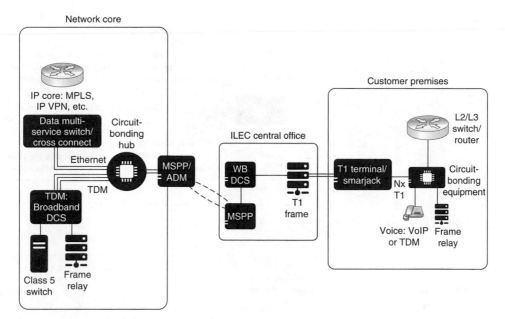

Figure 10.15   Circuit bonding in carrier networks

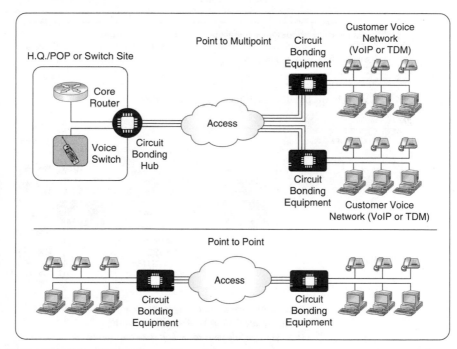

Figure 10.16   Circuit-bonding modes

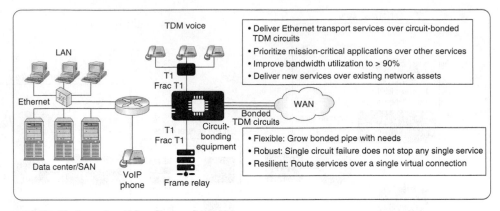

Figure 10.17   Various circuit bonding architecture

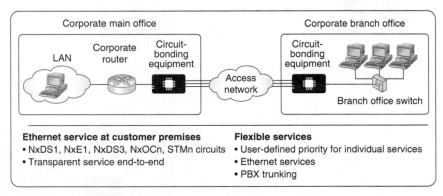

Figure 10.18   Using circuit bonding to link two corporate offices

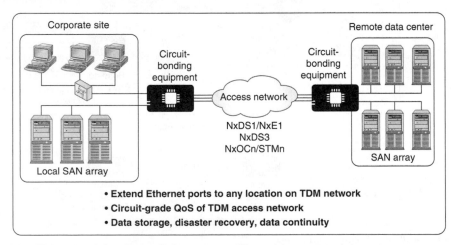

Figure 10.19   Using circuit bonding to link corporate offices with a remote data center

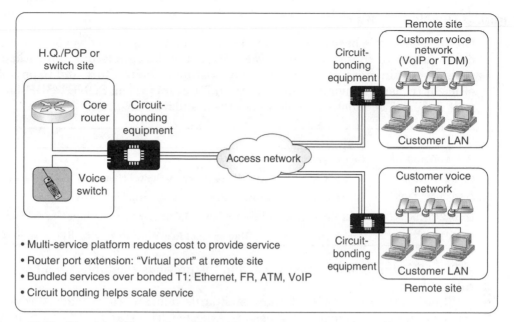

Figure 10.20   Circuit bonding used to offer multi-services in a corporate network

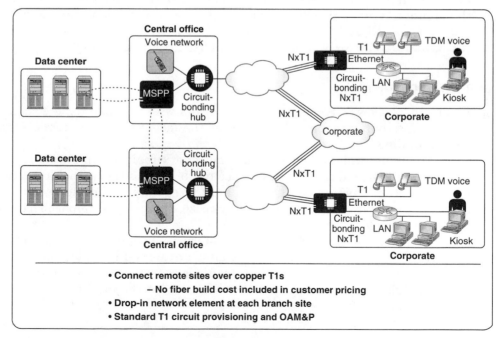

Figure 10.21   Large corporate network using circuit bonding

Ongoing Developments

Circuit bonding is based on a set of ITU-T standards approved several years ago. The development of these standards was initiated by large telecommunications carriers seeking to gain more benefits from their existing infrastructure and to provide a more efficient transport environment for data traffic over existing SONET/SDH-based transport system. The following table shows the standards involved:

ITU Standard	Description
G.7041/Y.1303	Generic framing procedure (GFP)
G.7043/Y.1343	Virtual Concatenation of Plesiochronous Digital Hierarchy (PDH) signals
G.8040/Y.1340	GFP frame mapping into Plesiochronous Digital Hierarchy (PDH)
G.7042/Y.1305	Link Capacity Adjustment Scheme (LCAS) for Virtual Concatenated Signals
G.8601/Y.1391	Architecture of Service Management in a Multi-Bearer, multi-carrier environment

The ITU standard documents listed in the previous the table are all approved and, released.

While small adjustments to these standards continue to be made through the contribution process, no major changes are expected. The standard for circuit bonding is likely to be very stable.

The only area where standards work is still continuing is in the network management areas for circuit-bonding services. Several contributions related to this are included in the approved standard G.8601. Additional work is being done especially with N×T1s and N×DS3s. Digital Communication Channel (DCC) standards for optical circuits (OC3s and OC12s) are well-defined and in use for circuit-bonded optical services.

Economic Assessment

Figure 10.22 shows a typical corporate network with multiple remote sites and a data center. This configuration will be used as the model for an economic assessment of circuit bonding.

This section evaluates the economic impact of circuit bonding from both the enterprise perspective and the carrier perspective. It is important to point out that the economic impact of any technical solution must be equally applicable to end users as well as to carriers for it to be acceptable. In this case, the economic impact of circuit bonding will be applicable to both parties.

In the example shown in Table 10.1, enterprise headquarters and the data center have fiber access. None of the remote sites are served by fiber, and they are being served by copper pairs only. All data traffic is considered to be mission-critical, and the enterprise requires a strict SLA to guarantee the quality and security of the connections.

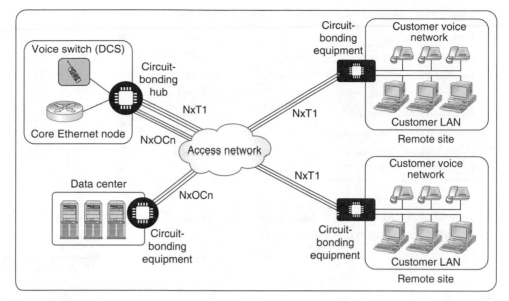

Figure 10.22 Typical corporate network with multiple remote sites and a data center

Table 10.2 illustrates the carrier's perspective on how services can be provided today.

In this example, the two 10 Mbps Ethernet circuits cannot be served without the expensive construction of fiber to the two remote sites. Optical equipment, such as SONET or SDH MSPPs, will also be required. The following table shows the inefficiency of bandwidth utilization for the present solution and the inefficient use of bandwidth

TABLE 10.1   Service Requirements from Enterprise's Perspective

From	To	Application	Bandwidth	Format
Headquarters	Remote site A	Voice	8 POTS lines	TDM
Headquarters	Remote site B	Voice	8 POTS lines	TDM
Headquarters	Data center	Voice	6 POTS lines	TDM
Headquarters	Remote site A	LAN	10 Mbps	Ethernet
Headquarters	Remote site B	LAN	10 Mbps	Ethernet
Headquarters	Data center	Data	500 Mbps	GbE Ethernet
Data center	ISP	Internet access	10 Mbps	Ethernet

TABLE 10.2 Service Requirements from Carrier's Perspective

From	To	Application	Bandwidth	Format	Bandwidth Provided
Headquarters	Remote site A	Voice	8 POTS Lines	TDM	1 T1
Headquarters	Remote site B	Voice	8 POTS lines	TDM	1 T1
Headquarters	Data center	Voice	6 POTS lines	TDM	1 T1
Headquarters	Remote site A	LAN	10 Mbps	Ethernet	DS3
Headquarters	Remote site B	LAN	10 Mbps	Ethernet	DS3
Headquarters	Data center	Data	500 Mbps	GbE Ethernet	OC48
Data center	ISP	Internet access	10 Mbps	Ethernet	DS3

provided to the end user. Any improvements in efficiency can help reduce cost for the carriers and improve profit margin.

From	To	Application	Bandwidth	Bandwidth Provided	Bandwidth Not Used	Inefficiency Percent
Headquarters	Remote Site A	Voice	8 POTS Lines	1 T1	16 DS0s	66%
Headquarters	Remote site B	Voice	8 POTS lines	1 T1	16 DS0s	66%
Headquarters	Data center	Voice	6 POTS lines	1 T1	18 DS0s	75%
Headquarters	Remote site A	LAN	10 Mbps	DS3	35 Mbps	78%
Headquarters	Remote site B	LAN	10 Mbps	DS3	35 Mbps	78%
Headquarters	Data center	Data	500 Mbps	OC48	1900 Mbps	79%
Data center	ISP	Internet access	10 Mbps	DS3	25 Mbps	78%

Circuit bonding can be used to help carriers improve profit and reduce cost and at the same time provide Ethernet services to all areas, including those not served by fiber. End users can also take advantage of circuit bonding to reduce their communication cost and improve service as well. The following table shows the connections for the enterprise using circuit bonding.

From	To	Bonded Service	Applications	Bandwidth Provided	Bandwidth Used	Percent Used
Headquarters	Remote site A	$7 \times$ T1s	Voice and Ethernet	10.8 Mbps	10.5 Mbps	97%
Headquarters	Remote site B	$7 \times$ T1s	Voice and Ethernet	10.8 Mbps	10.5 Mbps	97%
Headquarters	Data center	$3 \times$ OC3	Voice and GbE	465 Mbps	465 Mbps	100%
Data center	ISP	$6 \times$ T1s	Internet access	9.26 Mbps	9.26 Mbps	100%

In this example, the number and capacity of the circuits are greatly reduced, and the circuits are fully utilized. By using the multiplexing gain functions of circuit bonding, two of the circuits are not fully provisioned.

Vendors Promoting This Solution

To provide a list vendors promoting a circuit-bonding solution, it will be necessary to separate the list into three different categories:

- N × STSs
- N × DS3
- N × T1s

The vendors included in this list represent only a sample of vendors providing circuit-bonding solutions.

Vendors	Products
N × STSs	
Lucent	N × STSs, N × VT1.5
Alcatel	N × STSs, N × VT1.5
Fujitsu	N × STSs, N × VT1.5
Cisco	N × STSs, N × VT1.5
Tellabs	N × STSs, N × VT1.5
Ceterus Networks	N × STSs, N × VT1.5
N × DS3	
Ceterus Networks	N × DS3s
N × T1s	
Ceterus Networks	N × T1s
Zhone	N × T1s
ANDA	N × T1s

11

SONET/MSPP

by Paul Havala

Since its standardization nearly 20 years ago, SONET technology has grown into the predominant method of optical access for North American service providers. It is only natural that these providers would want to use their tremendous installed base of SONET equipment to deploy Ethernet services. This spurred the initial Ethernet over SONET (EoS) implementations nearly 10 years ago.

Since then, EoS has matured quite a bit. The late 1990s saw the birth of the multi-service provisioning platform (MSPP), a network element that combined SONET transport, SONET switching, and data capabilities such as EoS. Soon after, several key technologies, including the generic framing procedure (GFP), virtual concatenation (VCAT), and link capacity adjustment scheme (LCAS), helped to increase the bandwidth efficiency of EoS implementations and to lower their costs.

More recently, service providers have focused on the deployment of Carrier Ethernet services. This has heightened interest in EoS solutions because the underlying SONET technology enables these solutions to provide strong support for a number of the Carrier Ethernet attributes, most notably reliability, quality of service (QoS), and standardized services.

This chapter explores the technological innovations that have enabled EoS to support Carrier Ethernet services and looks at the unique and important role of the MSPP. It also explores many of the issues that service providers face as they deliver Carrier Ethernet services using EoS solutions—and the issues that equipment vendors face as they develop the EoS solutions to support these services.

Technology Description

EoS represents a marriage of two important technologies, one from the telephony world, and one from the enterprise data world. This section provides an overview of the key EoS technical concepts. It assumes that the reader has some familiarity with Ethernet, either through prior knowledge or from the material in the preceding chapters.

It, therefore, focuses on SONET, the EoS technology that enables SONET to carry Ethernet, and the application of EoS technology within multi-service provisioning platform (MSPP) systems.

SONET Overview

SONET has its roots in voice telephony. In the 1980s, many of the Regional Bell Operating Companies (RBOCs) began deploying fiber-optic transport systems, mainly to transport plesiochronous DS-1 signals (1.544Mbps); these DS1s typically carried 64kbps voice channels, either from a customer location to a digital switch or between digital switches. Because these fiber-optic transport systems were based mainly on vendor-proprietary technology, the RBOCs commissioned Bellcore (now Telcordia) to develop a uniform technology for fiber-optic transport. Bellcore dubbed this technology *Synchronous Optical Network (SONET),* and introduced it into ANSI committee T1X1 in 1985. ANSI ratified the SONET standard in 1988 [1]. In 1989, CCITT (now ITU-T) standardized the Synchronous Digital Hierarchy (SDH) [2], which is optimized to carry E1 signals (2.048Mbps), but is in most other ways identical to SONET.

Synchronous Transport Signal-1 (STS-1) is the fundamental signal structure for SONET. The bytes of the STS-1 may be represented by a 90-column×9-row structure; the first three columns (27 bytes) contain the transport overhead, whereas the remaining 87 columns (783 bytes) carry the STS payload. This structure is transmitted every 125 μs, resulting in a bit rate of 51.840Mbps.

The Synchronous Payload Envelope (SPE) is an 87×9-byte structure that occupies the STS payload. The SPE has its own overhead, the Path OverHead (POH). An STS-1 SPE carries a single DS3 (44.736Mbps) or up to 28 DS1s. Generally, the SPE will not align with STS-1 boundaries. A mechanism called a *pointer* (a byte in the STS-1 transport overhead) indicates where the SPE begins inside the STS payload. The pointer mechanism provides a simple, elegant way for SONET to map plesiochronous DS3 or DS1 signals into a synchronous SONET payload.[1] When small variations between the clock rates of the DS3 signal and the SONET network build up over time, the SONET network simply shifts the location of the SPE (and the DS3 it carries) inside the STS-1 payload and adjusts the pointer. Figure 11.1 illustrates the STS-1 frame and its relationship to the SPE.

The STS-1 frame structure represents the basic building block for SONET signals. Fixed multiples of STS-1 signals may be byte-interleaved to form higher-rate signals such as STS-3, STS-12, and STS-48, etc. (see Table 11.1). This increases the number of STS-1 payloads that a SONET interface can support. As a way to increase the payload size (not just the number of STS-1 payloads), the payloads of N STS-1 signals (N = 3, 12, 48, 192, and 768) may be concatenated into a single STS-Nc SPE. Most routers use some form of payload concatenation (e.g., STS-48c) on their Packet over SONET (PoS) interfaces.

---

[1] SONET systems carry DS1s within the STS-1 SPE by first mapping them within synchronous virtual tributaries (VTs); an STS-1 SPE carries up to 28 VT1.5 signals (and therefore up to 28 DS1s). As with STS-1 signals, each VT has a corresponding SPE and uses a pointer to locate the SPE within the VT payload capacity.

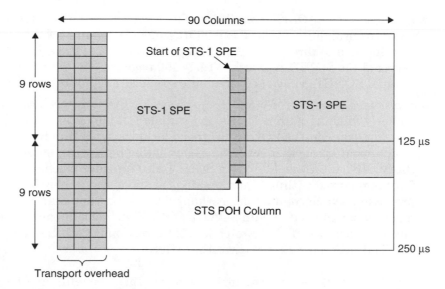

Figure 11.1   SPE inside two STS-1 frames

SONET (and SDH) technology features several key improvements over the proprietary technology it replaced:

■ *It is standard.* This enabled systems from multiple vendors to interoperate. It also allowed the RBOCs to develop uniform operating procedures for their new fiber deployments, which lowered operating costs dramatically.

■ *It provides a synchronous multiplexing hierarchy.* This radically simplified the functions of optical transport equipment, because it no longer needed to recover the original plesiochronous DS1 or DS3 signal to switch it; transport equipment could now synchronously switch DS1s and DS3s (or aggregates of them) carried within VTs or STSs. SONET's multiplexing hierarchy also enabled service providers to deploy a single fundamental technology that could scale from 155Mbps (OC-3) to 10Gbps (OC-192) and beyond.

TABLE 11.1   Signal Rates and Capacities for SONET and SDH

SONET Signal	Bit Rate (Mbps)	SDH Signal	SONET Capacity	SDH Capacity
STS–1, OC–1*	51.840	STM–0	28 DS–1s or 1 DS–3	21 E1s
STS–3, OC–3	155.520	STM–1	84 DS–1s or 3 DS–3s	63 E1s or 1 E4
STS–12, OC–12	622.080	STM–4	336 DS–1s or 12 DS–3s	252 E1s or 4 E4s
STS–48, OC–48	2,488.320	STM–16	1,344 DS–1s or 48 DS–3s	1,008 E1s or 16 E4s
STS–192, OC–192	9,953.280	STM–64	5,376 DS–1s or 192 DS–3s	4,032 E1s or 64 E4s
STS-768, OC-768	39,813.120	STM-256	21,504 DS-1s or 768 DS3s	16,128 E1s or 256 E4s

* The designation *OC-N* refers to the optical signal that corresponds to the *STS-N* electrical signal.

- *It supports strong OAM capabilities.* Over 5 percent of the SONET bandwidth is devoted to OAM. Fundamental capabilities include alarm surveillance, performance monitoring and thresholding, and loopback functions; these cover virtually every aspect of the SONET network. Nearly 150 pages of GR-253-CORE [3], Telcordia's seminal SONET generic requirements specification, address OAM capabilities.

- *It provides a rapid protection mechanism.* The SONET specifications require protection switching within 50 ms and include fundamental mechanisms to enable this. For example, the SONET overhead includes bytes (the K1 and K2 bytes) that communicate protection switching information between systems on either side of the SONET interface. Moreover, SONET also provides mechanisms that ensure a fault is reported within 10 ms, making the "60 ms" number (from time of fault to protection switch completion) perhaps more important than the well-known "50 ms" number associated with SONET. SONET includes linear (i.e., 1+1) protection and two varieties of ring protection: Unidirectional Path Switched Ring (UPSR) and Bidirectional Line Switched Ring (BLSR).

In the late 1980s, several vendors recognized these benefits and began developing SONET systems. In particular, SONET's synchronous multiplexing and ring protection capabilities enabled vendors to build very low cost multiplexers—systems that could sit on an optical fiber ring (the preferred deployment topology because of its low fiber cost and inherent route diversity) and add and drop traffic at each location on the ring. These multiplexers, called SONET Add Drop Multiplexers (ADMs), ushered in a new paradigm in optical access and transport. The ADM has served as the primary building block for optical transport networks for nearly 20 years. Figure 11.2 illustrates the SONET ADM.

The combination of SONET's benefits and the advent of the ADM has resulted in the widespread deployment of SONET technology in service provider networks over the past 20 years, with North American service providers deploying hundreds of thousands of SONET network elements (most of them ADMs) over that time. And, although SONET originally was designed to carry DS1 and DS3 signals, its tremendous base of installed equipment (and engineering know-how), as well as its strong operational and survivability characteristics, remain attractive to service providers who provide Ethernet services.

EoS Overview

The initial drive to carry Ethernet over SONET dates back to the mid-1990s and the first wave of telco Ethernet services.[2] Many of these services used dedicated, proprietary networks. At the same time, SONET deployment was in full swing. Service providers and equipment vendors saw a simple opportunity to lower costs by integrating the

---

[2] For example, Bell Atlantic's FDDI Network Service (FNS) and Ameritech LAN Interconnect Service (ALIS)

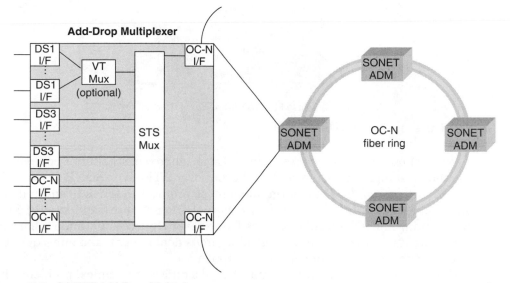

Figure 11.2   SONET Add Drop Multiplexer

delivery of Ethernet services with the delivery of circuit services over the burgeoning SONET infrastructure. This drove the need for network elements that could carry Ethernet over SONET.

The fundamental technical issue with EoS technology is the mapping of Ethernet frames, which ride on asynchronous interfaces, within synchronous SONET payloads. While there is nothing technically foreboding about this (recall that SONET was invented to carry plesiochronous signals within synchronous payloads), the industry first needed to define a standard set of protocols to map Ethernet frames into the SONET SPE.

Two methods of mapping Ethernet into SONET emerged in the mid-1990s. Ethernet over asynchronous transfer mode (ATM) proved a natural choice, since ATM's future looked bright at that time, and standards, including the ATM Forum's user network interface (UNI) 3.1 specification [4], already included a mapping of ATM cells into SONET payloads. If Ethernet frames could be mapped into ATM cells, then they could be carried over SONET. The Internet Engineering Task Force (IETF) defined the mapping of Ethernet into ATM in the well-known Request for Comments (RFC) specification, "RFC 1483" (now superseded by RFC 2684 [5]). Fujitsu's FASTLANE product, first introduced in 1997, featured one of the industry's first ATM-based EoS implementations. FASTLANE comprised a set of plug-in cards for Fujitsu's popular FLM 150 ADM system. Figure 11.3a illustrates the FLM 150 ADM.

Meanwhile, several router vendors were developing SONET-based router interfaces using the point-to-point protocol (PPP) and high-level data-link control (HDLC) protocol to map IP packets into the SONET payload [6, 7]. Some SONET ADM vendors adopted a variant of this method to map Ethernet frames into SONET. Positron's Osiris product (shown in Figure 11.3b) featured an early implementation of PPP/HDLC-based EoS.

(a) Fujitsu FLM 150 ADM   (b) Positron Osiris XTS

Figure 11.3   Early EoS implementations

While these mappings worked and had some degree of standards' compliance, technical shortcomings hampered both. Ethernet-over-ATM-over-SONET was saddled with the infamous *cell tax*—the large amount of protocol overhead required to segment variable-length datagrams (such as Ethernet frames) into fixed-length, 53-byte ATM cells. And, while ATM technology has found several successful (and rather large) niche deployments, it has not enjoyed the ubiquitous deployment, and subsequent reduction in costs, that many had hoped would happen.

HDLC-based implementations manifested a different technical problem—bandwidth expansion. HDLC uses a *flag* (a predefined pattern of eight bits) to delimit frames. When that same bit pattern appears within the frame (i.e., as part of the actual user data), an escape sequence (a different predefined pattern of eight bits) is added so the receiving equipment does not confuse the bit pattern within the frame with a flag. Every occurrence of the flag pattern within the frame results in an escape sequence—and the frame growing by one octet. When Ethernet is mapped into SONET using HDLC, the mapping overhead is nondeterministic and a function of the *contents* of the Ethernet frame. This subtle issue can adversely affect the performance of networks and can prove difficult to identify as the culprit when performance problems do arise.

The industry clearly needed a standard EoS mapping that addressed the shortcomings of both the ATM and HDLC-based approaches. In the late 1990s, several companies (led by Lucent Technologies) began working in ANSI T1X1 toward this end. These efforts brought the generic framing procedure (GFP), which was standardized first in ANSI and then in ITU-T [8].

GFP works much like a variable-length version of ATM. Each GFP frame (see Figure 11.4) carries an Ethernet medium access control (MAC) frame. GFP frames are transmitted continuously within the SONET SPE; idle GFP frames are transmitted when there is no Ethernet frame to carry. GFP delimits frames using the Header Error Check field, much like ATM, and therefore obviates the need for flag sequences (and the resulting bandwidth expansion). GFP also provides relatively little protocol overhead; in fact, GFP is more efficient than IEEE 802.3 Ethernet at mapping Ethernet frames into the physical layer.[3]

---

[3] IEEE 802.3 Ethernet requires a minimum of 20 bytes of protocol overhead (12 bytes for the interframe gap and 8 bytes for the preamble/start of frame delimiter) between successive MAC frames. Typical GFP implementations require only 12 bytes of protocol overhead (4 bytes for the core header, 4 bytes for the payload header, and 4 bytes for the payload FCS) to carry an Ethernet MAC frame (see Figure 11-4). Table 11-2 illustrates the reduced overhead of GFP.

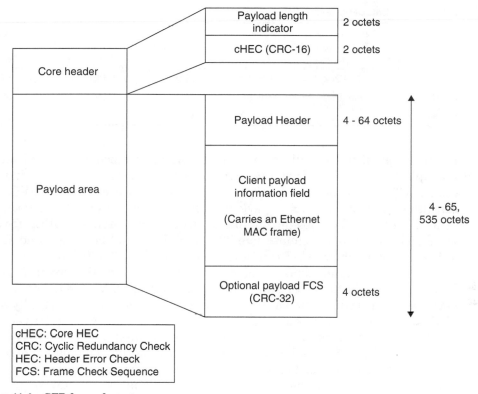

Figure 11.4 GFP frame format

ITU-T also standardized another EoS mapping, Link Access Protocol for SONET (LAPS) [9]. Some early router and CPE implementations still use X.86 for their EoS interfaces. However, this mapping uses the fundamentals of HDLC and, therefore, carries its technical disadvantages. Because of its technical superiority and broad basis in North American and international standards, GFP appears to be gaining momentum as the preferred EoS mapping.

While technologies such as GFP solve the most fundamental technical issue with EoS (i.e., how does SONET actually carry Ethernet?), they do not address an issue that is nearly as critical: How does SONET carry Ethernet *efficiently*?

SONET was designed to carry DS1 and DS3 signals. Its rate structure (see Table 11.1) is optimized for this. Beyond the STS-3 rate, SONET rates grow by factors of four. The fundamental Ethernet rates look nothing like DS1 or DS3 rates and grow in multiples of ten. This means that, while GFP is a very efficient protocol, the rate mismatch of SONET and Ethernet can still result in tremendous bandwidth inefficiencies, as Table 11.2 illustrates.

Virtual concatenation (VCAT) helps address these inefficiencies by allowing SONET payloads to combine into a single, virtual payload. VCAT provides a byte-wise inverse

TABLE 11.2   EoS Bandwidth Efficiency with VCAT

Ethernet Interface Rate	Required EoS Bandwidth (500-byte frames)	Minimum SONET Rate	Bandwidth Efficiency	Minimum SONET Rate with VCAT	Bandwidth Efficiency with VCAT
10Mbps	9.85Mbps	STS-1	19.9%	VT1.5-7v	87.9%
100Mbps	98.5Mbps	STS-3c	65.7%	STS-1-2v	99.4%
1Gbps	985Mbps	STS-48c	41.1%	STS-1-21v	94.6%

multiplexing of the overall payload (e.g., Ethernet frames mapped within GFP) over multiple SONET SPEs. Low order virtual concatenation (LOVCAT) virtually concatenates VT1.5 payloads, while high order virtual concatenation (HOVCAT) virtually concatenates STS-1 or STS-3c payloads. The notation for VCAT signals carries an additional tag that identifies the number of virtually concatenated SPEs; for example, an HOVCAT signal that combines five STS-3c SPEs would be designated an STS-3c-*5v*. Table 11.2 shows how VCAT can improve EoS bandwidth efficiency.

All the VCAT intelligence resides at the endpoints of the virtually concatenated SONET paths; the SONET network knows nothing of VCAT and treats the paths as independent (e.g., a different pointer identifies the location of each virtually concatenated STS signal, and each STS has its own POH). As a result, VCAT requires additional tools for the VCAT endpoints to control the grouping of links within a VCAT group (VCG). These tools allow VCAT to handle gracefully the addition and deletion of SONET paths within a VCG, due either to provisioning or to network failure or restoration. The link capacity adjustment scheme (LCAS), which ITU-T has standardized [10, 11] provides these tools. Figure 11.5 illustrates VCAT and LCAS.

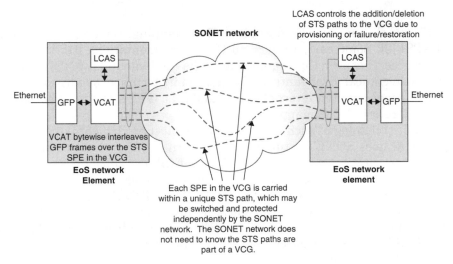

Figure 11.5   VCAT and LCAS

The Multi-Service Provisioning Platform (MSPP)

As EoS technology matures, it is finding its way into more service provider network equipment. Specifically, the integration of EoS into the SONET ADM has given birth to a new product category—*the multi-service provisioning platform (MSPP)*. While the definition of this term has broadened over the past five years, the original MSPP usage referred to a SONET ADM that added packet technology (Ethernet, most importantly), as well as more advanced SONET capabilities such as full SONET switching. Figure 11.6 illustrates an MSPP with Ethernet capabilities. The Cerent 454 (now the Cisco ONS 15454) and Fujitsu's FLASHWAVE 4300 represent two of the earliest MSPP systems.

The marriage of EoS and the ADM is a natural one. SONET ADMs are the fundamental building blocks for service providers' optical access networks. Most Ethernet services operate at high bandwidths that require optical access. The MSPP enables a single device to handle optical access for all services.

Moreover, the GFP/VCAT/LCAS mapping features technical properties that lower the costs of MSPP deployment. Not only do GFP/VCAT/LCAS provide a standard, efficient, and robust way to map Ethernet into SONET, they do so in a way that interoperates with legacy SONET equipment that is not EoS-enabled, such as traditional

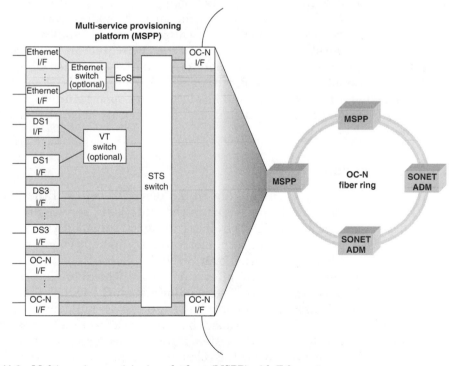

Figure 11.6 Multi-service provisioning platform (MSPP) with Ethernet

ADMs (see Figure 11.6). Service providers may, therefore, deploy MSPPs to provide multi-service access, while still making use of their multi-billion dollar investment in traditional SONET equipment.

How Much Ethernet Is in an MSPP?

Mapping Ethernet frames into SONET represents the initial and most fundamental issue with EoS. All Ethernet-enabled MSPPs perform this function. However, Ethernet means more than just a frame format; it also includes a switching technology—Ethernet Medium Access Control (MAC) bridging, more precisely. Historically, the integration of Ethernet switching into SONET systems has been met with mixed results.

The issue is only partly technical. While equipment vendors certainly can design new systems that feature high performance, low-cost combinations of Ethernet switching and full SONET ADM functionality, most implementations have grown from systems that were optimized for either Ethernet or SONET. These designs carry the burden of tradeoffs made early in the design process.

More limiting than that, however, are the current operating environments of the largest service providers. These providers have large embedded operations support systems (OSSs) that cover all aspects of their optical transport networks (e.g., TIRKS, NMA, and other systems from Telcordia). These systems are optimized to model point-to-point transport of circuits. Simple EoS mappings (e.g., point-to-point EoS "circuits" using GFP/VCAT/LCAS) fit well within the current models. However, more complex data functionality, such as Ethernet switching, is complex and expensive to model in these systems. Operational support for Ethernet switching, for instance, requires large investments from these service providers, either in the embedded OSSs or in new OSSs that handle the advanced data functions of MSPPs and other highly integrated systems. Investment has been slow and has focused on opportunities where revenues are relatively large and easily forecasted, e.g., in dedicated networks for large corporate customers.

Drivers for This Solution

As mentioned previously, cost was the initial driver to deliver Ethernet services over SONET. As Ethernet services emerged in the mid-1990s, service providers looked for ways to lower service delivery costs by integrating Ethernet with the rapidly expanding SONET infrastructure. This, in turn, motivated equipment vendors to build network elements that could carry Ethernet over SONET.

This driver subsided somewhat after a few years. The abundant capital (as well as some market hype) of the telecom bubble diminished the value of integration and favored a "green field" approach. Carriers had the money to build new separate networks, so they built them. In addition, because these networks were relatively small, they did not require large-scale operations systems, and so this "green field" approach allowed serviced providers to circumvent the costs and complexities of integrating these services into their existing OSS environment.

Recently, however, EoS has returned to favor for two reasons. The first reason is that the cost pendulum has swung back to favor EoS solutions. Post-telecom bubble capital budgets are looking to squeeze more revenue out of the existing infrastructure, and once again they value integration. While some professed the death of SONET during the telecom bubble, SONET technology instead emerged with new vigor—energized by a new set of data-aware standards (e.g., GFP, VCAT, and LCAS) and equipment vendors (both old and new) who packaged this technology in aggressive physical designs and at significantly lower price points. The second reason is the emergence of Carrier Ethernet, as described in Chapter 1. Service providers wishing to deliver Carrier Ethernet services require equipment that can support five key attributes: standardized services, scalability, reliability, quality of service (QoS), and service management. This has renewed interest in EoS solutions.

In any Carrier Ethernet equipment solution, Ethernet functionality plays the most critical role. Each of the five Carrier Ethernet attributes depends mainly on what the network equipment does with the Ethernet frames—how it forwards them (especially during periods of network congestion or failure), monitors them, reports them, and associates them with end user services.

However, the underlying transport technology can also play an important role in the delivery of Carrier Ethernet services. SONET technology features some fundamental characteristics that enhance the ability of EoS solutions to support some of the Carrier Ethernet attributes. Specifically, EoS solutions are particularly strong in the following areas:

- **Reliability** Reliability lies at the heart of SONET technology. SONET protection schemes—and all the operations and management capabilities required to support them—provide failure detection and reporting within 10 ms and restoration within 50 ms. For this reason, and because most SONET network element solutions come from vendors with years of experience delivering reliable products to service providers, SONET has become synonymous with survivable optical networking. EoS solutions can leverage the ability of SONET to provide underlying protection for reliable Carrier Ethernet services,[4] while service providers can sell Ethernet over SONET to their customers using the power of the SONET "brand" for reliable, survivable networks.

- **Quality of service** QoS is typically a packet-level function; it comprises the ability of a packet-based system to assign the right network resources to the right packets when there is contention for those resources (e.g., when the network is experiencing congestion due to the statistical nature of packet arrivals). SONET provides a

---

[4] Some have criticized SONET protection and its application to data services because it reserves half the network bandwidth for protection. However, any service (packet or circuit) that requires dedicated bandwidth under all network conditions (including link or node failure) must have that amount of dedicated bandwidth reserved on the protection path. So, while some Carrier Ethernet services are "best effort," some important customer applications (digital video delivery is one example) require Carrier Ethernet services where *all* the bandwidth is dedicated. For these dedicated-bandwidth Carrier Ethernet services, SONET protection is no more or less efficient than packet-based protection schemes.

complete optical networking layer beneath the packet layer—and one that, from the perspective of the packet layer, provides *perfect* QoS. Ethernet frames that are mapped within an STS path will traverse the SONET portion of the network with no contention for network resources—and therefore no packet loss, no packet jitter (delay variation), and only minimal additional latency (typically tens of microseconds per SONET node traversed, plus speed of light delays on transmission links). An EoS solution that combines robust Ethernet-level QoS control and judicious use of the underlying SONET network can provide unparalleled Carrier Ethernet QoS.

- **Standardized services**   This attribute, too, depends a great deal on the packet level functions of a Carrier Ethernet solution. However, the transport layer remains a large and integral component of service delivery. Standardized services depend on a predictable transport layer—one that operates consistently over different portions of the network and different vendors' implementations and transparently under a variety of packet-level implementations and a range of standardized service types. EoS solutions excel at providing predictable transport for standardized Carrier Ethernet services. Moreover, EoS solutions allow service providers to use the enormous installed based of SONET equipment, which helps make those services more ubiquitous—another key factor in the delivery of standardized Carrier Ethernet services.

While EoS networks can also meet the other two key attributes, scalability and service management, these attributes tend to depend almost exclusively on the functions at the packet layer, and very little on the functions of the underlying transport network.

When Does This Solution Fit?

At a high level, EoS enables service providers to leverage the strengths of SONET technology and its massive installed base to cost-effectively deliver Ethernet services. Specifically, EoS (and the MSPP) best fit in access networks where

- *Carrier Ethernet services must be supported.* As the previous section discusses, EoS technology can play a key role in enabling Carrier Ethernet services, especially those that require dedicated bandwidth.

- *The service bandwidth requires optical access.* Because many Ethernet services operate at rates up to 1Gbps, optical access is often necessary.

- *The customer location requires a mix of Ethernet and traditional circuit services.* This requires a multi-service access platform. Since SONET is the *de facto* method to deliver DS-n and OC-N services over optical access networks, the MSPP is an ideal tool here.

- *The Ethernet service requires highly fault-tolerant access.* The SONET standard supports ring topologies (i.e., physical diversity) and restoration in less than 60 ms following a fiber or node failure.

- *The access network requires a high degree of operational integrity.* Ethernet OAM capabilities are emerging (e.g., in standards such as IEEE 802.1ag [12]) and will provide valuable capabilities at the Ethernet layer. Meanwhile, SONET provides a set of underlying operational capabilities that no other transport technology can rival.

- *The SONET access network already exists.* One network typically costs less than two.

When Does This Solution Not Fit?

Clearly these criteria cover a wide range of service provider applications and deployment scenarios and make EoS-enabled MSPPs an excellent general-purpose solution for the delivery of Carrier Ethernet services over optical access networks. Still, EoS does not fit everywhere. Some scenarios where EoS and MSPPs may not provide the optimal solution include the following:

- **Access networks where none of the above criteria hold** The benefits of EoS show up in many—but not all—service provider applications. Some Ethernet access applications have no TDM component and require little or no redundancy. Some Ethernet services are "best-effort" and don't require Carrier Ethernet attributes. Some low-bandwidth access applications may be best served with other technologies, such as Ethernet over copper.

- **Access networks that require a high degree of Ethernet switching capability** For reasons discussed previously, most of today's MSPP implementations support Ethernet switching functionality, but typically at lower interface densities and higher cost points than "pure" Ethernet solutions, such as Native Ethernet or Virtual Private LAN Service (VPLS)–based solutions.

- **Limited OSS support** The strong operational capabilities of SONET forge a double-edged sword. As discussed previously, these capabilities are so strong and so entrenched in carriers' OSSs that adding new functionality, such as EoS, can be complex and expensive. Generally more Ethernet functionality means more cost and complexity. Equipment vendors and service providers must walk a fine line so that they integrate enough Ethernet functionality to lower network deployment costs, but not so much that the networks cannot be managed cost-effectively.

Table 11.3 summarizes where EoS and MSPP solutions best fit—and do not fit—in service provider access networks.

TABLE 11.3   Application Fits for EoS and MSPPs

Where EoS and MSPPs Best Fit	Where EoS and MSPPs Do Not Fit
Carrier Ethernet services are required. The service bandwidth requires optical access. The customer location requires a mix of Ethernet and traditional TDM services. The Ethernet service requires highly fault-tolerant access. The access network requires a high degree of operational integrity. The SONET access network already exists.	Access networks where none of the "best fit" criteria hold. Access networks that require a high degree of Ethernet switching capability. Access networks where OSS support for EoS is limited.

Benefits and Shortcomings

Given the market drivers for Ethernet over SONET and the key applications where this technology and MSPPs should (or should not) be used, this section summarizes its benefits and shortcomings from the perspective of a service provider.

Benefits

The main benefit of EoS lies in its ability to enable Carrier Ethernet services. Carrier Ethernet services represent new revenue potential for service providers who provide either rudimentary Ethernet services based on enterprise-grade network technology or no Ethernet services at all.

An example from the wireless world illustrates the benefits of Carrier Ethernet services and the potential role of EoS. Most wireless service providers lease traditional DS1 circuits from their cell tower or base station locations to their mobile telephony switching offices (MTSOs). The incumbent wireline carrier typically provides the wholesale leased DS1 services.

Wireless providers lease DS1s from ILECs for several reasons. First, their base stations and MTSO equipment, while featuring a mix of technologies including Time Division Multiple Access (TDMA), Global System for Mobile Communications (GSM), and Universal Telecommunications Mobile System (UMTS), typically provide DS1 network interfaces. DS1 wholesale services are also widely available. These services typically feature guarantees on important service-level parameters such as service availability (i.e., uptime) and end-to-end latency.

Wireless network equipment, however, is transitioning to Ethernet. The emerging generation of equipment (e.g., based on UMTS Release 5) will provide network interfaces based on IP/Ethernet, not DS1 technology. Wireless providers will look to incumbent wireless service providers to offer wholesale Ethernet leased-line services. When they do, they will want services that are consistent and widely available. They will also demand Ethernet services that provide guarantees for high service availability and low end-to-end latency. This provides an opportunity for wireline carriers to offer wholesale Carrier Ethernet services, especially those services that accentuate the key attributes of standardized services, reliability, and QoS. As discussed previously, these three Carrier Ethernet attributes fall into the "sweet spot" of EoS solutions.

Moreover, the transition to UMTS Release 5 and IP/Ethernet will take time, as will the growth of Carrier Ethernet services to match the near-ubiquity of DS1 leased-line services. During this transitional time, wireline providers need to provide solutions for wholesale Carrier Ethernet *and* DS1 leased-line services. EoS solutions offer the unique ability to deliver both services cost-effectively. Wireline carriers may leverage the Carrier Ethernet and traditional TDM capabilities of EoS solutions to provide both cell site access (where fiber is available) and interoffice transport services for their wireless provider customers.

Service providers may realize the additional EoS benefit of low Ethernet service delivery costs, especially in deployment scenarios where three conditions hold: First, the Ethernet service should require the key Carrier Ethernet attributes of standardized services, reliability, and QoS, and should not require the transport equipment to support a high degree of Ethernet switching (as in the previous wireless network example). Second, EoS solutions generally prove cost-effective when the service demand comprises a mixture of Carrier Ethernet and traditional TDM services (also in the wireless network example). Third, deployment costs are minimized when a SONET network, especially one featuring MSPPs, already exists. The economic analysis in "Economic Assessment," later in the chapter, will illustrate this further.

Shortcomings

EoS solutions can result in higher service deployment costs when the network architecture mandates that the transport network support a high degree or density of Ethernet switching functionality and when the conditions described in the benefits section (e.g., a mixture of Carrier Ethernet and traditional TDM services and an existing SONET network) do not apply.[5] Determining when all these criteria apply can be difficult to quantify; in some cases, the nature of the Ethernet service and the profile and distribution of its subscribers call for a high degree of switching content in the optical transport network; just as often, perhaps, this architectural decision is driven by history—by previous service delivery architectures and vendor selections.

When the transport network must support a high degree of Ethernet switching functionality, EoS solutions tend to cost more for two reasons. First, existing MSPP solutions often have advanced Ethernet functions, but typically not at the cost points and service densities of other technology solutions. This could result in more EoS equipment or in ancillary equipment (e.g., Ethernet switches or edge routers) to support the advanced Ethernet functions. This can be mitigated somewhat by the integration of more Ethernet functionality into SONET equipment. More integration is possible and is being pursued by equipment vendors, but this has technical and operational limits.

Service providers push against these operational limits when they try to integrate EoS equipment with complex Ethernet functionality into their existing OSSs. This process can be time-consuming (meaning deferred or lost revenues for service providers) and extremely expensive, and is perhaps the chief argument today against integrating significant amounts of complex Ethernet functionality into SONET transport equipment.

Typical Deployment/Scenarios

As service providers consider the strengths and weaknesses of EoS-enabled MSPPs, they have converged on several typical deployment scenarios for MSPPs in Ethernet

---

[5] Network element solutions using EoS, or any Ethernet technology, can support a low density of Ethernet switching capabilities and still provide MEF-compliant, Carrier Ethernet services.

service networks. This section investigates three key Ethernet service network applications where EoS-enabled MSPPs play a prominent role:

- Ethernet Private Line (E-Line) service delivery
- Ethernet access to Ethernet or IP services
- Dedicated EoS networks

E-Line Service Delivery

The MEF defines an Ethernet Private Line (E-Line) service to be a *point-to-point* service, one that uses a point-to-point Ethernet Virtual Connection (EVC) between two user network interfaces (UNIs) [13]. However, the term *private line* connotes not only point-to-point connectivity, but also the reliability attribute of Carrier Ethernet (to match the high availability of traditional DS-1 and DS-3 private line services). For fault tolerance alone, the MSPP proves an ideal vehicle for delivering E-Line services. In many cases, the service provider needs to provide DS-n private line and E-Line services to the same customer location—another key advantage for EoS. The OSS capabilities required to manage E-Line services match closely those for traditional private line services, so for those service providers who already deploy large-scale traditional private line service, the operational hurdle to deploy EoS on MSPPs is relatively low.

Figure 11.7 illustrates the role of the EoS-enabled MSPP in the delivery of E-Line services. In this scenario, the MSPP provides transport *and* delivers the service. It must, therefore, provide not only the functions of EoS transport (e.g., GFP/VCAT/LCAS), but also the capabilities necessary to provide MEF-compliant E-Line service. These service delivery functions include Ethernet frame classification, policing, QoS and traffic management support, and proper handling of Ethernet control protocol data units

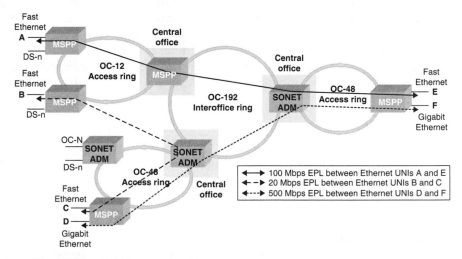

Figure 11.7 The MSPP and E-Line service delivery

(PDUs) [13]. Examples of E-Line services that use MSPPs include Verizon's Ethernet Private Line, Verizon's Optical Networking (VON) services, and Time Warner Telecom's Extended Native LAN (ENLAN) service.

Ethernet Access to Ethernet or IP Services

Figure 11.8 illustrates how the MSPP may provide Ethernet access to MEF-compliant E-Line or Emulated LAN (E-LAN) services or to IP-based services, such as Internet or IP Virtual Private Network (IP-VPN) services. In this scenario, the service provider sells the Ethernet or IP-based service to its customer and the EoS portion provides access from the customer to the E-Line, E-LAN, or IP-based service; this is similar to the way DS-1 or DS-3 circuits have historically provided dedicated access to Internet services.

In this scenario, the role of the EoS network differs from its role in the previous (E-Line delivery) scenario, where it delivers the service itself, not just access to the service. However, many of the attributes of the EoS network remain, including point-to-point EoS transport, the ability to deliver traditional DS-n private line service, high survivability, and operational commonality with traditional private line services. MEF compliance is not strictly required in the access MSPP (the equipment that provides the E-Line or E-LAN service must provide that), although the MSPP may not transport the EoS in a way that interferes with the ability of other equipment to deliver the Ethernet service.

Examples where MSPPs provide access to Ethernet or IP-based services include Qwest Internet Port, AT&T ACCU-Ring Network Access Service, and Verizon's Internet Dedicated Ethernet service.

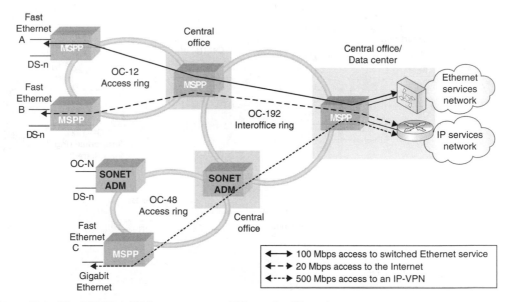

Figure 11.8 The MSPP and Ethernet access to Ethernet or IP services

Dedicated EoS Networks

In this scenario, a service provider deploys a network dedicated to a single customer—often a large corporation or an entity in one of the government, education, or medical (GEM) vertical markets. The customer often wants MEF-compliant E-LAN service to provide LAN-like connectivity among its sites, along with DS-n connectivity for PBXs and other traditional telephony equipment, as Figure 11.9 illustrates. Because these typically are high capacity, high functionality, and high dollar networks, survivability is essential. For these reasons, dedicated SONET networks with Ethernet capabilities provide a large and profitable business for many service providers. Examples include AT&T Ultravailable Managed OptEring Service and Verizon's Enhanced Dedicated SONET Ring (EDSR).

With dedicated networks, the network *is* the service. The network elements—most often MSPPs—must provide not only EoS transport, but also all the attributes of MEF-compliant E-LAN and E-Line services (as well as traditional DS-n private line services). For this reason, MSPPs in dedicated networks must often support a rich set of Ethernet functions, including Ethernet switching. Resilient packet ring (RPR) functions enable Ethernet bridging over SONET rings and often fit well in this application. The relative complexity of the Ethernet capabilities means that traditional transport OSSs often cannot manage all the functions of dedicated EoS networks. This places a higher burden on service providers' abilities to integrate these networks into new OSSs and on vendors' abilities to develop capable element management systems (EMSs). Table 11.4 summarizes the typical deployment scenarios for EoS and MSPPs.

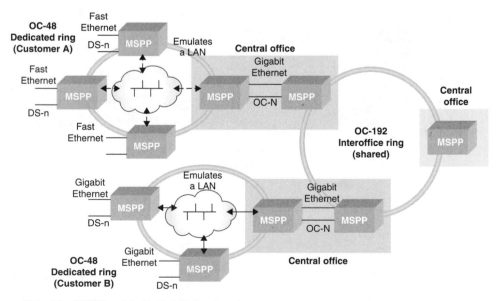

Figure 11.9   The MSPP and dedicated EoS networks

TABLE 11.4 Typical Deployment Scenarios for EoS and MSPPs

Attribute	E-Line Service Delivery	Ethernet Access to Ethernet or IP Service	Dedicated EoS Networks
Carrier Ethernet service	E-Line	E-Line, E-LAN, and/or IP service (e.g., Internet access or IP-VPN)	E-LAN, E-Line
MSPP Ethernet service support	E-Line	None required E-Line-like functions	E-LAN, E-Line
Point-to-point EoS transport in MSPP	Yes	Yes	Yes
Ethernet switching in MSPP	Not required	Not required	Yes Often with RPR
Mix of Ethernet and TDM services	Often	Often	Often
Survivability	High	High	High
OSS environment	Traditional transport OSSs	Traditional transport OSSs for EoS portion	New OSSs and vendor EMSs
Examples	Verizon's Ethernet Private Line; Verizon's Optical Networking (VON); Time Warner's Telecom ENLAN	Qwest Internet Port; AT&T ACCU-Ring Network Access Service; Verizon's Internet Dedicated Ethernet	AT&T Ultravailable Managed OptEring Service; Verizon's EDSR

Ongoing Developments

When compared with Ethernet or SONET, EoS (in particular the standard GFP/VCAT/LCAS mapping) is a relatively young technology. Several trends are emerging as this fundamental EoS technology matures, and its applications grow in breadth and depth.

Increasing EoS Integration

The first major trend is the integration of EoS into network elements other than MSPPs. Although the MSPP remains the primary vehicle for the deployment of EoS, the technology provides benefits that extend beyond MSPPs. Other network elements that have begun adopting EoS technology include the following:

- **Low-cost access devices** Compact, ultra-low cost systems that include EoS (possibly along with traditional DS-n over SONET), but without the full functionality of an MSPP. Examples include Fujitsu's FLASHWAVE 4020 and RAD's RIC series of Intelligent Converters.

- **Routers and MSSs** These network elements are beginning to feature EoS interfaces (e.g., channelized OC-48 interfaces with GFP/VCAT/LCAS) as a way to provide a high capacity, highly survivable interface with EoS-based access networks. Examples include Tellabs' MSR 8800 and Hammerhead Systems' HSX 6000.

■ **High-capacity multi-service transport systems** This catch-all includes high capacity Dense Wavelength Division Multiplexing (DWDM) systems such as Fujitsu's FLASHWAVE 7500, and new devices that combine Ethernet switching, SONET MSPP functionality (including EoS), and DWDM technology, such as Alcatel's 1850 TSS and Fujitsu's FLASHWAVE 9500.

EoS Protocol Enhancements

Another significant EoS technology trend comprises enhancements to the EoS mapping protocols. Implementations of GFP, VCAT, and LCAS continue to grow in quantity, quality, and interoperability. This technology triumvirate forms a solid technology foundation for the delivery of Carrier Ethernet services over SONET networks. However, beyond GFP/VCAT/LCAS are additional protocols that augment EoS to improve its ability to deliver Ethernet services in some cases.

Resilient packet ring (RPR) technology, based on the IEEE 802.17 standard [14], can improve SONET's ability to support E-LAN services in some scenarios. RPR provides a MAC layer on top of SONET that enables an RPR/SONET ring to act as a shared LAN (with built-in multipoint capabilities). This allows Ethernet bridging functions (required for E-LAN services) in MSPPs to view the SONET network not as a collection of point-to-point links, but as a shared LAN, which can improve significantly the efficiency of MSPP bridging implementations.[6] For this reason, some carriers have deployed MSPPs with Ethernet/RPR/SONET for dedicated ring applications. However, in North America the application of RPR has not gone far beyond this, due, in part, to some RPR limitations:

■ RPR is confined to a single ring, which limits its use as a general-purpose infrastructure technology.

■ For a number of reasons, including the complexity of the IEEE 802.17 standard, multi-vendor interoperability has been slow to develop.

Multi-protocol label switching (MPLS) technology represents an intriguing, if not obvious, complement to the GFP/VCAT/LCAS protocols. MPLS was born as a way to speed up forwarding of IP packets; later its connection-oriented properties helped to provide traffic engineering for IP networks. Now segments of the industry are beginning to view MPLS for what it fundamentally is—a switching and transport layer for IP, Ethernet, and other packet-based protocols.

---

[6] Broadcasting of frames is a regular part of an Ethernet learning bridge's operation. Consider a network of six learning bridges. If point-to-point links (e.g., using EoS transport) interconnect those bridges, then each bridge must have five bridge ports for the bridge interconnection and must replicate a broadcast frame five times to ensure that each of the other bridges receives the broadcast frame. If a shared LAN connects the six bridges (e.g., using Ethernet/RPR/SONET), then each bridge has only one bridge port for the bridge interconnection and must send only a single broadcast frame over that bridge port.

The pseudowire is the lens that has given clarity to this view. In standard terms, a pseudowire is a "mechanism that emulates the essential attributes of a service such as ATM, frame relay, or Ethernet over a packet switched network" [15]. In other words, it is an adaptation of a packet-based service that makes an IP/MPLS network appear to be a wire—a *pseudo*wire—for that service.

This process[7] is called *PseudoWire Emulation Edge-to-Edge (PWE3),* and for Ethernet transport, it is straightforward: An ingress provider edge (PE) device adapts an Ethernet frame into a pseudowire by adding additional header information (a pseudowire label or "shim" header). The pseudowire label contains enough information for the egress PE device to identify the pseudowire and handle the Ethernet frame appropriately. In between the ingress and egress PEs lies a "tunnel"—a way to get from one PE to the other without looking at either the original Ethernet frame or the pseudowire label. In most cases, the tunnel is an MPLS label switched path (LSP); this is commonly referred to as the "Martini" encapsulation, named after Luca Martini, the primary author of the original IETF submissions [16, 17]. In cases where the pseudowire traverses a non-IP network, many of the benefits of an MPLS-based tunnel are lost, and the pseudowire may, therefore, use an attribute of the underlying network, such as an ATM VC or SONET STS path, as the tunnel. This is the basis for "Dry Martini" encapsulation [18].

The marriage of MPLS, and in particular Ethernet-based PWE3, and SONET networks provides some unique benefits:

- MPLS provides a scalable packet-layer multiplexing technology for Ethernet. Because MPLS labels have 20 bits, MPLS-enabled EoS networks can aggregate and switch traffic from over one million PEs. This far exceeds the scalability of other multiplexing technologies such as VLANs (limited by a 12-bit field) and RPR (limited to the stations on a single ring). Moreover, MPLS provides a way to "stack" multiple MPLS labels, making MPLS scalability practically unlimited—and helping to enable another key attribute (scalability) of Carrier Ethernet.

- MPLS provides a connection-oriented packet transport layer in between the Ethernet and SONET layers. This layer provides the bandwidth efficiency and flexibility of a packet multiplexing layer, while enabling many features, for example hard QoS, rapid protection, and OAM features, that are difficult or even impossible with connectionless technologies such as Ethernet bridging. This allows EoS networks to use Ethernet bridging as a service-level function (usually near the edges of the network), with MPLS providing efficient, manageable, and resilient transport in between.

- Pseudowires enable MPLS to provide a common data transport for Ethernet and other data services, such as ATM, frame relay, and IP. This enables the SONET network to carry these services more cost-effectively.

---

[7] And the IETF working group that is defining it.

■ PWE3 and MPLS support an IP-based control plane, which governs the way the network sets up, maintains, and tears down pseudowires and MPLS tunnels. An MPLS-enabled EoS network that implements this control plane can interwork easily with the large installed based of IP/MPLS-based core networks.

Figure 11.10 illustrates the application of pseudowires and MPLS in EoS networks.

Control Plane Enhancements

The addition of an intelligent control plane represents a third trend for EoS networks. As stated previously, PWE3 and MPLS support an IP-based control plane that governs all aspects of connection management at the pseudowire and MPLS layers (e.g., routing of connections through the network, distribution of pseudowire and MPLS labels, resource allocation, and QoS support). This control plane places the resources for real-time connection (or *virtual* connection, for pseudowires and MPLS tunnels) management within the network itself, not in external systems such as element management systems (EMSs)—or human beings. This automates the connection management process, which can dramatically speed service provisioning times and reduce provisioning errors.

Generalized MPLS (GMPLS) extends the benefits of the MPLS control plane to physical layer connections such as SONET paths and DWDM lightpaths (i.e., wavelengths). While the GMPLS control plane is functionally similar to the MPLS control plane—it uses many of the same routing and label distribution protocols—the two control planes work at different network layers and often operate independently. Because an EoS

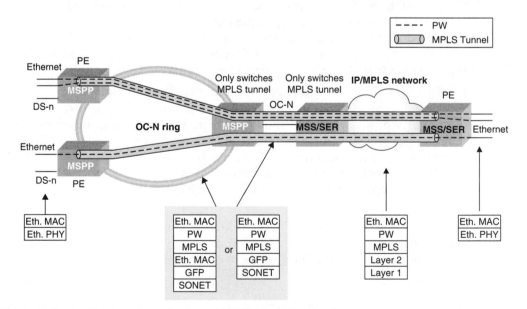

Figure 11.10   Application of pseudowires and MPLS in EoS networks

network element such as an MSPP can support Ethernet/MPLS/SONET, it is often the place where the MPLS control plane meets the GMPLS control plane. As the deployment of control plane functions grows, MSPPs will play an important role in tying together the MPLS and GMPLS control planes. This will help service providers to see a more unified view of Layer 1 and Layer 2 connection management and further speed provisioning times and reduce network operations costs.

Economic Assessment

This section examines a small network that highlights the economic benefits of EoS. Figure 11.11 illustrates this example network, which comprises five customer locations (A through E), two central offices (COs), and one data center. Two access rings connect the customer locations to the COs, and an interoffice facility (IOF) ring connects the COs and the data center.

In this example, the service provider uses two types of EoS-equipped network elements to build the network:

- MSPPs, which are capable of supporting OC-12, OC-48, and OC-192 SONET interfaces, Ethernet interface cards that support EoS transport (Ethernet/GFP/VCAT/LCAS), and Ethernet interface cards that support RPR/SONET.

- Small "micro-MSPPs" (μ-MSPPs) that support OC-12 SONET interfaces and EoS transport only.

Table 11.5 highlights the typical costs of these systems.

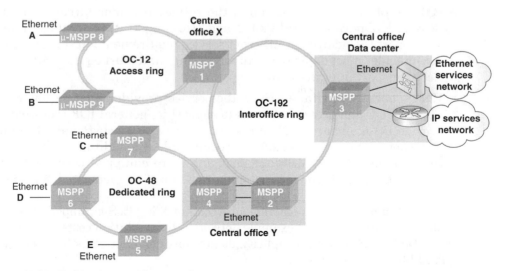

Figure 11.11   EoS in an example network

TABLE 11.5   EoS Network Elements in the Example Network

EoS Network Element	Typical Cost: Common Equipment + SONET and DS-n Interfaces	Typical Cost: EoS Transport Interface Card (GFP/VCAT/LCAS)	Typical Cost: EoS/RPR Card
MSPP (OC-12/48/192)	$40,000	$4000	$6000
μ-MSPP (OC-12)	$10,000	$1000	N/A

This network supports the three key applications of EoS (refer to Section "Typical Deployment/Scenarios"):

- **EPL service delivery**   In the example network, customer locations A and B have E-Line services to customer location D.

- **Ethernet access to Ethernet or IP services**   Customer locations C, D, and E have access to the Ethernet and IP services provided by the switch and router at the data center.

- **Dedicated EoS networks**   Customer locations C, D, and E (and the node at CO Y) form a dedicated Ethernet network with E-LAN connectivity among these three locations.

The economic analysis investigates three deployment scenarios:

- **Greenfield network**   In this scenario, none of the EoS network elements have been deployed. The service provider must build the entire access network.

- **IOF in place**   In this scenario, the service provider already has deployed a SONET IOF network (MSPPs 1, 2, and 3) to support its general IOF requirements. To support the additional Ethernet service requirements in this example, the service provider must deploy the two access rings and must equip MSPPs 2 and 3 with EoS transport interface cards.

- **IOF + access in place**   Here, the service provider already has deployed the SONET IOF and access networks to support its general IOF requirements and to provide DS-n and/or OC-N access and services to its customers. The incremental Ethernet services in this example require only the addition of Ethernet interface cards at the MSPPs. MSPPs 4, 5, 6, and 7 are equipped with EoS/RPR cards to support the E-LAN connectivity requirements of the dedicated network.

Table 11.6 summarizes the incremental costs of using EoS-equipped MSPPs to deliver the Ethernet services in this example network. These solution costs use the typical unit costs in Table 11.5 and, for simplicity, do not consider fiber costs (i.e., they assume the required fiber already exists).

TABLE 11.6   Example Network Solution Costs

Scenario	MSPPs	MSPP EoS Transport Cards	MSPP EoS/ RPR Cards	Micro- MSPPs	Micro-MSPP EoS Transport Cards	Solution Cost
Greenfield	7	2	4	2	2	$334,000
IOF in place	4	2	4	2	2	$214,000
IOF + access in place	0	2	4	0	2	$34,000

This simple example shows that EoS can be a cost-effective general-purpose access technology for a variety of Ethernet service profiles and deployment scenarios. However, as the "IOF in place" and "IOF + access in place" scenarios illustrate so clearly, its real power lies in its ability to leverage the investment of the enormous installed base of SONET network elements. Once a SONET network featuring MSPPs is in place to support IOF and access for circuit services—a commonplace scenario for many large service providers—the equipment cost to deliver Ethernet services using that infrastructure becomes marginal.

A look at the cost per subscriber further illustrates this point. The example network in Figure 11.11 shows five customer locations, A through E. The example assumes that each EoS transport interface card, EoS/RPR card, and μ-MSPP can support up to four subscribers (a conservative assumption based on the state of vendor implementations). The network equipment in Table 11.6 can, therefore, support up to four subscribers per location, or a total of twenty subscribers. Increasing the number of subscribers per location requires additional MSPP or μ-MSPP Ethernet cards.[8]

Figure 11.12 shows the cost per subscriber for one, four, and eight subscribers at each of the five customer locations for each of the three deployment scenarios. This example reinforces the cost benefit of using EoS to deliver Ethernet services when an MSPP-based SONET network already exists. It also shows that the per-subscriber cost of using EoS technology to deliver Ethernet services can be quite low, especially as the number of subscribers per location grows. At these per-subscriber costs, this solution delivers high-bandwidth, fully protected Carrier Ethernet services, along with the ability to deliver traditional DS-n and OC-N circuit services.

As this simple analysis shows, the MSPP provides a powerful tool for service providers to build networks that support a wide variety of services, including fast-growing Ethernet services and the large base of traditional TDM services.

---

[8] Increasing the number of subscribers also decreases the amount of service bandwidth that the carrier can allocate per subscriber. For example, when the OC-12 access ring delivers E-Line services to two subscribers, each of those E-Line subscribers may enjoy up to approximately 300Mbps of dedicated bandwidth (assuming for this illustration that the service provider evenly allocates the dedicated bandwidth among the subscribers on the ring). When that ring supports a total of eight subscribers, each of those subscribers may access up to roughly 75Mbps of dedicated bandwidth. For simplicity, and because many types of access networks share this tradeoff, the bandwidth per subscriber is not considered in the per-subscriber cost analysis.

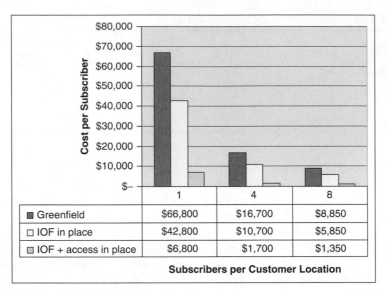

	1	4	8
■ Greenfield	$66,800	$16,700	$8,850
□ IOF in place	$42,800	$10,700	$5,850
▨ IOF + access in place	$6,800	$1,700	$1,350

Subscribers per Customer Location

Figure 11.12   Example network cost per subscriber

Vendors Promoting this Solution

Table 11.7 lists a sample of vendors with EoS solutions, along with the products that implement those solutions.

TABLE 11.7   Vendors Promoting EoS Solutions

Vendor	Solution/Product	Comments
ADVA Optical Networking	FSP-150-CCx	Ethernet access and demarcation
Alcatel-Lucent	Alcatel 1677 SONET Link	Next-generation SONET multi-services platform
	Alcatel 1850 TSS	Transport service switch
	LambdaUnite Multi-Service Switch	Multi-service optical switch
	Metropolis DMX Access	Access multiplexer
	Metropolis DMXplore	Access multiplexer
	Metropolis DMXtend	Access multiplexer
	Universal Packet Mux (UPM)	Multi-service platform
Cisco	ONS 15310-CL	SONET multi-service platform
	ONS 15327	SONET multi-service platform
	ONS 15454	MSPP

(Continued)

Vendor	Solution/Product	Comments
Fujitsu	FLASHWAVE 4020	Compact optical Ethernet module
	FLASHWAVE 4100	Multi-service optical access solution
	FLASHWAVE 4300	Multi-service optical loop aggregation solution
	FLASHWAVE 4500	Multi-aervice optical core transport solution
	FLASHWAVE 5150	Ethernet access platform
	FLASHWAVE 7500	ROADM
	FLASHWAVE 9500	Packet Optical Networking Platform
Hammerhead Systems	HSX 6000	Layer 2.5 Edge Platform
Nortel	Optical Metro 3100	Multi-service platform
	Optical Metro 3400	Multi-service platform
	Optical Metro 3500	Multi-service platform
	Optical Metro 5100	Multi-service platform
	Optical Metro 5200	Multi-service platform
	OME 6110	Optical multi-service edge
	OME 6500	Optical multi-service edge
RAD Data Communications	RIC-155	Network termination unit
	RIC-155GE	Network termination unit
	RIC-622GE	Network termination unit
Tellabs	Tellabs 5500 NGX-S	Transport switch
	Tellabs 5500 NGX-MX	Transport switch
	Tellabs 6315	Metro Ethernet node
	Tellabs 8820	Multi-service router
	Tellabs 8830	Multi-service router
	Tellabs 8840	Multi-service router
	Tellabs 8860	Multi-service router
Turin Networks	Traverse 600	Multi-service transport switch
	Traverse 1600	Multi-service transport switch
	Traverse 2000	Multi-service transport switch
	TraverseEdge 50	Multi-service edge platform
	TraverseEdge 100	Multi-service edge platform

Source: Vendor web sites

References

1. Synchronous Optical Network (SONET)—Basic Description including Multiplex Structure, Rates, and Formats. ANSI T1.105-2001.

2. Network Node Interface for the Synchronous Digital Hierarchy (SDH), Recommendation G.707/Y.1322, Amendment 2.

3. Transport System: Common Generic Criteria, GR-253-CORE SONET, Issue 3, September 2000.

4. ATM User-Network Interface Specification, Version 3.1, af-uni-0010-002, September 1994.

5. D. Grossman and J. Heinanen, Multiprotocol Encapsulation over ATM Adaptation Layer 5, RFC 2684, September 1999.

6. W. Simpson, The Point-to-Point Protocol (PPP), RFC 1661, July 1994.

7. W. Simpson, PPP in HDLC-like Framing, RFC 1662, July 1994.

8. Generic Framing Procedure (GFP), Recommendation ITU-T G.7041/Y.1303.

9. Ethernet over Link Access Protocol—SONET (LAPS), Recommendation X.86/Y.1323.

10. Link Capacity Adjustment Scheme (LCAS) for Virtual Concatenated Signals, Recommendation ITU-T G.7042/Y.1305.

11. Virtual Concatenation of PDH signals, Recommendation G.7043/Y.1343.

12. Connectivity Fault Management, IEEE 802.1ag, D5.2, December 2005.

13. Ethernet Services Definitions, Phase 1, MEF Technical Specification, MEF 6, June 2004.

14. Resilient Packet Ring (RPR) Access Method and Physical Layer Specifications, IEEE Std 802.17-2004, September 24, 2004.

15. X. Xiao et al., Requirements for Pseudo-Wire Emulation Edge-to-Edge (PWE3), September 2004.

16. L. Martini et al., Encapsulation Methods for Transport of Layer 2 Frames over MPLS, February 2001 (currently at version 17, January 2006): draft-martini-l2circuit-encap-mpls-01.txt.

17. L. Martini et al., Transport of Layer 2 Frames Over MPLS, May 2000 (currently at version 17, January 2006): draft-martini-l2circuit-trans-mpls-01.txt.

18. P. Pan, Dry-Martini: Supporting Pseudo-wires in Sub-IP Access Networks, July 2005: draft-pan-pwe3-over-sub-ip-01.txt.

12

Resilient Packet Ring (RPR)

by Mannix O'Connor

The IEEE 802.17 Resilient Packet Ring standard (RPR) defines a new media access control (MAC) to accesses ring topologies using the resilient packet ring (RPR) protocol. RPR is intended to be used in metropolitan/regional area networks (MAN) and wide are a networks (WAN) for efficient transfer of data packets at rates scalable to multiple Gigabits per second.

The main features of RPR include:

- Support for up to 255 stations per ring
  - Optimization for rings with a maximum circumference of 2000 Km
- Support for unicast, multicast, and broadcast traffic
- Multiple (three) classes of service
- Increase usable bandwidth beyond those of existing technologies
- Provide weighted fairness between all the stations on the ring
- Automatic topology and station discovery and capability for plug and play
- Robust frame transmission:
  - Service restoration in less than 50 ms
  - Lossless MAC
  - No single point of failure
  - Operation, Administration, and Maintenance (OAM) features

The services provided by the MAC sublayer allow the local MAC client to exchange data with peer client entities in other stations, and to exchange parameters to control the operation of the local MAC entity. The RPR standard contains the following features that simultaneously make the efficient support for TDM and data services possible.

Support for Four Classes of Service   RPR supports four classes of service over the shared packet ring. This allows service providers to match end-users' applications to the right CoS on its network. All classes-of-service are reclaimable and no bandwidth is ever stranded.

Flexible Classification of End-user Traffic   RPR provides four classes of service of packets labeled with 802.1p bits for VLAN segregated traffic or labeled by TOS or DSCP bits in the IP header. These capabilities allow classification of traffic according to the marking done by the customer CPE or according to the marking performed by the broadband access network element.

Strict Separation of Traffic   RPR Provides for a clear separation between control plane and forwarding plane functions guarantees maximum separation and resiliency.

Efficient Transport of Multicast—only one copy is carried over the ring   The use of the standard RPR MAC represents a scalable and efficient way to deliver large amounts of broadcast and multicast traffic on physical ring topologies. Alternative solutions require deployment of a logical hub-and-spoke architecture on the physical fiber ring, which preclude efficient transport of multicast traffic. Hub-and-spoke designs require more fiber, more virtual connections and multiple copies of multicast streams to be broadcast simultaneously. All recipients can get a multicast stream from an RPR ring with only one copy of the packet on the ring.

Efficient Bandwidth Management   RPR is designed to deliver packets over a shared ring using statistical multiplexing, spatial reuse, and efficient allocation of protection bandwidth to deliver more services and therefore more revenue per equivalent amount of bandwidth.

- **Statistical multiplexing**   The RPR-based shared media enables multiple nodes to share the same network resources and thus take advantage of effective statistical multiplexing. Bursty services share the same resource, and the allocation of bandwidth to support excess traffic becomes significantly more efficient.

- **Spatial reuse**   The RPR shared media natively provides the ability to spatially reuse unused spans on the shared ring. Spatial reuse allows reuse of bandwidth not only on different spans than the ones carrying a service, but also on asymmetrical services.

- **Efficient allocation of protection bandwidth**   RPR allows flexible allocation of protection bandwidth on a per service basis. This allows a carrier to provision protection for the committed-rate portion of any service.

- **Fairness**   The RPR MAC guarantees fair distribution of bandwidth across the ring. While Connection Admission Control (CAC) mechanisms guarantee that high-priority traffic is delivered with the appropriate SLA, the RPR fairness algorithm dynamically allocates free bandwidth in a fair manner to all excess and best effort traffic over the shared ring.

Complete Transparency to End-user Traffic   RPR can carry all services transparently, without any manipulation of end-user traffic. All end-user control traffic is also carried transparently, and all traffic management is done on a per-CoS basis, in a manner transparent to specific end-user traffic.

Support for Ethernet-based E-Line & E-LAN Services for Business Users   RPR supports the full range of Ethernet-based E-Line and E-LAN services and for metro networks it is an efficient solution for Ethernet-based traffic from business users.

Resiliency and No Single Point-of-Failure   The standard RPR MAC guarantees that all traffic provisioned over the shared packet ring, including point-to-point, broadcast and multicast traffic, is restored within less than 50 ms after a link or node failure. Unlike SONET/SDH five-nines availability can be guaranteed for all classes-of-service, including best-effort traffic. In addition services can be partially protected so that no user ever has to go unprotected or buy more protection bandwidth than is required.

Technology Description

Beginning in 2001 the Metro Ethernet Forum (MEF) began work on defining a common set of specifications for Ethernet services. These service definitions were intended to give service providers a common language and set of performance criteria that would allow them to offer Ethernet Service Level Agreements (SLAs) and provide common performance parameters for network-to-network interfaces between carriers. While the Technical committee received proposals and drafted specifications the Marketing committee developed a common framework to discuss these specifications for Ethernet services that could be used by service providers around the globe. As defined by the MEF Marketing committee the key characteristics of an Ethernet service include: (1) Support for multiple standardized services including TDM, (2) Quality of Service (QoS), (3) Reliability, (4)Management including Operations and Administration, (5) Scalability.

These were defined because carriers needed these qualities and they were, for the most part, absent from Ethernet equipment as it evolved in the Enterprise market. 100 years of evolution of service provider networks had proven the value of these qualities. However, the use of Ethernet in Enterprise LANs did not need the rigorous performance required of service providers. Many vendors began to label their equipment "carrier-class", yet this term had little meaning until the MEF began to define the meaning of Ethernet services.

Support for Multiple Standardized Services Including TDM   Enterprise Ethernet switches and routers had few requirements to interface with circuits or cross connect circuits. Occasionally, routers had a WAN port to pass packet traffic to a WAN circuit but that was the extent of their support. Ethernet switches and routers are designed for packet traffic. Support for circuits is practically unavailable.

However, for large service providers to build cost effective packet-based networks, support for circuits is required and the MEF's statement on multiple standardized services and TDM support indicates this as a requirement of Carrier Ethernet.

Quality of Service   Every switch or router can offer some form of Quality of Service. However, for the effective transport of voice and video the QoS performance must be quite rigorous. Video and voice lose significant quality and become almost impossible to transport unless the network can guarantee tight controls on delay and delay variation. Networks of Ethernet switched introduce queuing delay that makes accurate delivery of video and voice unpredictable.

Reliability   A legacy of the voice network is a standard restoration time of < 50ms. This evolved to ensure that a failure of a voice circuit could be correct in a time rapid enough to be undetectable to the human ear during a voice call. Ethernet switching and routing have restoration mechanisms including Spanning Tree and Rapid Spanning tree that restore in under a minute for large networks, which is fine for many data applications but not within the tolerance required for voice and video. However, when voice and video are transported on Ethernet networks it becomes a required characteristic of Carrier Ethernet.

Management   Ethernet has historically used Simple Network Management Protocol (SNMP) Management Information Bases (MIB) to communicate Ethernet network fault information. This protocol however, is insufficient for the detailed link-by-link and end-to-end fault detection and management required on large nationwide networks that may involve multiple service providers. The definition of new protocols and specifications to provide this type of visibility is important for Carrier Ethernet support.

Scalability   Historically, carriers had to offer bandwidth in very coarse increments. TDM jumps from 1.5 Mbps to 45 Mbps. This discontinuity in bandwidth introduced inefficiency into the WAN data network that Carrier Ethernet is designed to overcome. In addition, scalability implies a need to span large geographies and support millions of customers on the same network, all while potentially keeping each customer data separate.

All five of these characteristics indicate areas where definitions, specifications, standards, and new approaches are required to make Ethernet packets and Ethernet services efficient and effective on large public networks. The IEEE 802.17 working group created the RPR standard to address these service provider requirements.

RPR and Multiservice Support   As mentioned in point C above and discussed in greater detail later in this chapter, RPR provides 4 classes of service. It also contains a ring wide protocol that makes each switch aware of the state of every link on the ring. The practical result of these two mechanisms is that delay and delay variation on the RPR become irrelevant even for voice and video applications. Hence, RPR networks support any data or circuit application with whatever performance is required for the application.

RPR and Quality of Service   These same mechanisms ensure quality of service (see Table 12.1). An RPR ring is deterministic. The performance of services put on a ring is guaranteed. Along with classes of service and ring-wide awareness of the bandwidth state of each inter-switch link there is a transit buffer, described in greater detail later in the chapter, which passes any traffic through the switch without queuing. This eliminates delay variation from the RPR network. Ethernet switches, having no network-wide information about link-states on the network may require packets to queue at each node. This introduces potential delay and delay variation into the system and makes video and voice services unpredictable.

RPR and Reliability   A protocol called Resilient would obviously place a significant emphasis on availability. Indeed, one of the primary characteristics of the protocol is its ability to restore any service in less than 50 ms. The RPR protocol has two mechanisms to restore service; steer and wrap. Applications are either more sensitive to lost packets or delay. Steer and Wrap are mechanisms to minimize either packet loss or delay, depending on the requirements of the application.

RPR and Management   RPR has a sophisticated topology discovery protocol and a management protocol built into the standard. These features provide information that is useful for the management standards that are being defined in the ITU, the IEEE and the MEF. Taken together this group of protocols will create and end-to-end OAM that will provide the kind of visibility required for large service provider Carrier Ethernet Networks.

RPR and Scalability   RPR is defined for data rates from 155 Mbps up to 10 Gbps. It also does nothing to preclude the introduction of faster data rate RPR. The most likely candidates for higher speed RPR are 40 Gbps and 100 Gbps. In addition the standard defines rings of up to 255 nodes and 2000 km in circumference.

Layer Model

The RPR layer model and its relationship with the OSI reference model are illustrated in Figure 12.1. The RPR standard specifies the MAC control sublayer, the MAC datapath sublayer, the reconciliation sublayers, the MAC service interface and the PHY service interface.

The MAC service interface provides service primitives used by MAC clients to exchange data with one or more peer clients, or to transfer local control information between the MAC and MAC client. The MAC control sublayer controls the datapath sublayer, maintains the MAC state and coordination with the MAC control sublayer of other MACs, and controls the transfer of data between the MAC and its client. The MAC datapath sublayer provides data transfer functions for each ringlet.

The PHY service interface is used by the MAC to transmit and receive frames on the physical media. Distinct reconciliation sublayers specify mapping between specific PHYs and medium independent interfaces (MIIs). The standard includes the definition of a reconciliation sublayer for each of the most commonly used PHYs and permits other reconciliation sublayers.

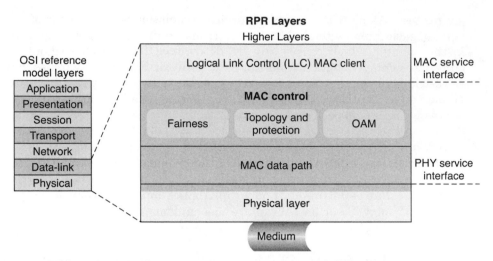

Figure 12.1   RPR service and reference model relationship to the ISO OSI reference model

Ring Structure

RPR employs a ring structure using unidirectional, counter-rotating ringlets. Each ringlet is made up of links with data flow in the same direction. The ringlets are identified as ringlet0 and ringlet1, as shown in Figure 12.2.

Stations on the ring are identified by an IEEE 802 48-bit MAC address. All links on the ring operate at the same data rate, but may exhibit different delay properties.

The RPR MAC Specification

The services provided by the MAC sublayer allow the local MAC client to exchange data with peer client entities in other stations, and to exchange parameters to control the operation of the local MAC entity. The client may omit some parameters, and leave their control to the discretion of the MAC sublayer; the MAC sublayer will set these parameters according to the standard definitions. Optionally the MAC operation can be fully controlled by the client, but in that case it is the client responsibility to use these parameters in a way that does not violate the standard behavior of the MAC.

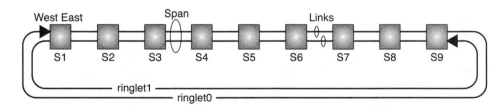

Figure 12.2   Dual ring structure and conventions

The MAC provides two types of frame transmission services: Strict and Relaxed

Strict   The Strict transmission service guarantees that all delivered data units are not duplicated nor reordered, at the expense of discarding more data frames than in the Relaxed mode.

Relaxed   The Relaxed transmission service has the same guarantees as the Strict service, except while recovering from failures in the ring in which case a negligible amount of reorder or duplication can occur.

Since Relaxed mode is more effective than Strict mode, its use is recommended when possible.

To support services with different quality of service demands, the MAC supports three classes of service (CoS) into which the services may be mapped by the MAC client according to their specific quality of service requirements.

ClassA   ClassA service provides an allocated, guaranteed data rate and a low end-to-end delay and jitter bound; as such classA can be used to support services such as TDM pseudo wire emulation. Within this class, the MAC uses two internal subclasses, subclassA0 for reserved bandwidth and subclassA1 for reclaimable bandwidth. The subclassA1partition is more efficient, but limited by the sizes of secondary transit queue.

ClassA traffic is not subject to the fairness algorithm at ingress to the ring or when transiting through the ring. ClassA traffic has precedence over classB and classC traffic at ingress to the ring, and during transit through the ring (for dual-queue stations). ClassA traffic moves through the primary transit path in each station as it propagates around the ring, as a result a classA frame in transit can be preempted only by a frame that started transmission into the ring before the classA arrived to the transit station.

Description and operation of the primary and secondary transit paths, and descriptions of single-queue and dual-queue models, are provided later on in this paper.

ClassB   ClassB service provides an allocated, guaranteed data rate, bounded end-to-end delay and jitter for the traffic within the allocated rate; and access to additional best effort data transmission that is not allocated, guaranteed, or bounded, and is subject to the fairness algorithm. Within this class, the MAC uses fairness eligibility markings to differentiate the committed information rate portion of classB (classB-CIR) and the excess information rate portion of classB (classB-EIR). ClassB is useful for services that require a guaranteed bandwidth component, but have also the ability to accesses more resources when available.

ClassC   ClassC service provides a best-effort traffic service with no allocated or guaranteed data rate and no bounds on end-to-end delay or jitter. ClassC traffic is always subject to the fairness algorithm. In a single-queue implementation, classC traffic moves through the primary transit path. In a dual-queue implementation, classC traffic moves through the secondary transit path.

TABLE 12.1   Quality of Service Options in RPR

| Class of Service | | | Quality of Service | | | |
Name	Use	Subclass	Guaranteed Bandwidth	Delay/Jill	Bandwidth Type	Bandwidth Subtype
ClassA	Real-time	subclassA0 SubclassA1	Yes	Low	Allocated	Reserved Reclaimable
ClassB	Guaranteed	classB-CIR classB-EIR	Yes No	Bounded Unbounded	Allocated Opportunistic	Reclaimable
ClassC	Best-effort		No	Unbounded	Opportunistic	Reclaimable

The MAC Reference Model

As illustrated in Figure 12.3, the MAC is comprised of the MAC control sublayer and the MAC datapath sublayer. The MAC datapath sublayer is comprised of the ringlet selection entity and the datapaths for the two ringlets. These components and their interconnections are illustrated in Figure 12.3 within the context of a single station view of the MAC architecture.

Figure 12.3 also shows the activities implemented by each block within the MAC. The main activities are further described in the following paragraphs.

Fairness   Bandwidth management is done to maintain fairness for fairness eligible frames (those without or beyond allocated bandwidth), with mechanisms to assure that all stations receive their fair share of ring capacity across the links being used by the stations, where the fair share is not necessarily the same for all stations. The fairness algorithm ensures weighted dynamic distribution of available link bandwidths to source stations using those links.

The fairness procedure has the following characteristics:

- Support independent fairness operation per ringlet.
- Carry control information on the ringlet opposing that of the associated data flow.
- Regulate only classC and classB-EIR (i.e., fairness eligible) traffic.
- Compute fair rates associated with a source station.
- Scale fair rates in proportion to an administrative weight assigned to each fairness instance.
- Allow ringlet capacity not explicitly allocated to be treated as available capacity.
- Allow ringlet capacity explicitly allocated to subclassA1 or classB-CIR, but not in use, to be treated as available capacity (i.e., bandwidth reclamation).
- Support either single transit queue or dual transit queue deployment.
  - Support either the aggressive or the conservative rate adjustment method.

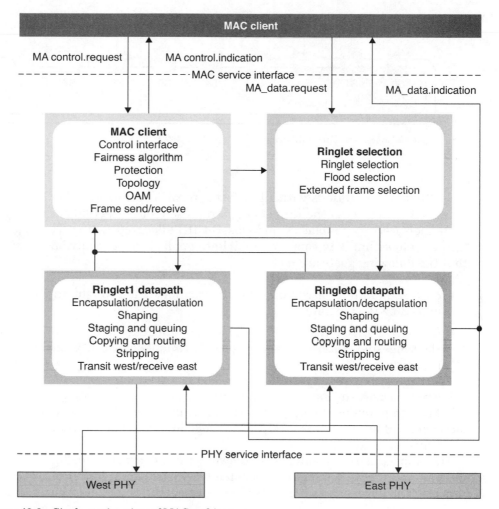

Figure 12.3 Single station view of MAC architecture

A station deploying a dual transit queue MAC is congested when occupancy of the secondary transit queue (STQ) is excessive. A station deploying a single transit queue MAC is congested when the rate of transmission is excessive relative to the capacity of the transmission link or traffic is delayed excessively while awaiting transmission.

Figure 12.4 shows a congested station (S6) and the set of contiguous stations (S1 to S6) contributing to the congestion at S6.

Each contributing station is associated with a rate (bi) at which it adds fairness eligible traffic crossing the outbound link of the congested station S6. The rate, b_i, is scaled by an administrative weight (w_i) that allows a station to add at a rate higher or

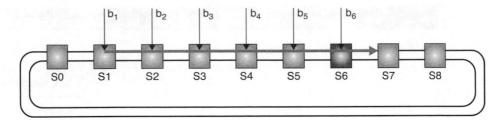

Figure 12.4   Congestion control in a ring

lower than other stations without violating fairness principles. The LINK_RATE represents the capacity of the ringlet and *fa* represents the fraction of capacity consumed by higher-precedence (classA and classB-CIR) allocated traffic. The objective of the fairness algorithm is to compute a fairRate applied to the contributing stations such that the following goals are met:

- $b_i/w_i \leq fairRate$: Contributing stations maximize their weight-adjusted rate without exceeding the fairRate.

- $b_1+\cdots+b_6 \leq$ LINK_RATE(1-*fa*): The sum of fairness eligible traffic transmitted by the congested station maximizes use of available capacity without exceeding that capacity.

In order to meet the condition $b_i/w_i \leq$ fairRate at each contributing station (S1–S6), the fairRate computed by the congested station is propagated hop by hop in the upstream direction, by fairness frames transmitted regularly, making the value known to each of the contributing stations.

The propagation of the fairRate is known as rate advertisement. Figure 12.5 illustrates the path of an advertisement propagated on ringlet1 in order to control congestion on ringlet0. The advertisement carries the identity of the ringlet on which it is transmitted (i.e., ringlet1).

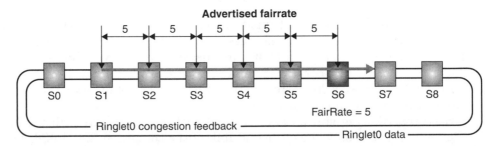

Figure 12.5   The fairRate advertisement

The advertisement allows each contributing station to limit its rate, to the current weight-adjusted fairRate, resulting in changes to rate statistics measured on the downstream link of the congested station. The rate statistics are used to ensure that the condition $b_1+\ldots+b_6 \leq \text{LINK\_RATE}(1\text{-}fa)$ is met when adjusting the fairRate. The adjusted fairRate is then advertised upstream. The feedback between the congested station and the contributing stations allows continuous adjustment of rates to meet the fairness objectives.

The fairness procedure is able to indicate a single congestion point, known as a choke point, to each station. Figure 12.6 provides an example in which multiple stations on the ringlet are congested. Each station independently computes a fairRate. Congested station S4 computes a fairRate of 10 units and receives an advertised fairRate of 5 units from downstream neighbor S5. The advertisement originated at downstream station S6. Comparing the fairRates, S4 determines that the fairRate of S6 is more restrictive (i.e., smaller) than its own fairRate. S4 propagates the advertised fairRate of S6 (5 units) instead of advertising its own fairRate (10 units). By advertising the more restricted fairRate of S6, it is ensured that the condition $b_i/w_i \leq$ fairRate is met for both sets of contributing stations (i.e., S1–S4, and S5–S6). The result is that stations S1–S3 are not aware of the less restrictive congestion being experienced by S4, and will not limit the traffic destined to S5; this will not create a problem because if the congestion at S4 becomes more restrictive than the congestion at S6 the result will be similar to the next example.

Figure 12.7 illustrates the case in which stations S4 and S6 are again congested but the fairRate computed by S4 is more restrictive (i.e., smaller) than the fairRate computed by S6. Station S4 computes a fairRate of 10 units and receives an advertised fairRate of 20 units originating from S6 and propagated by S5. Comparing the fairRates, S4 determines that its fairRate is smaller than that of S6. S4 advertises its own fairRate rather than propagating the advertised fairRate of S6. By advertising the more restrictive fairRate of S4 between S4 and S1, and the less restrictive fairRate of S6 between stations S6 and S4, it is ensured that the condition $b_i/w_i \leq$ fairRate is met for both sets of contributing stations (i.e., S1–S4 and S5–S6), while not unnecessarily restricting the rates of stations S5 and S6.

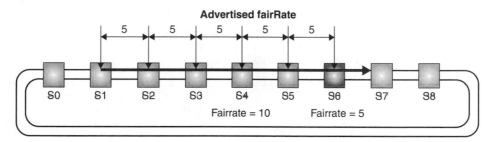

Figure 12.6 Received fairRate more restrictive than local fairRate

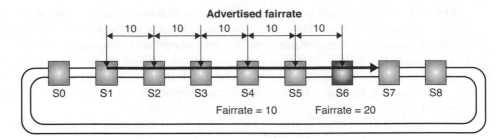

Figure 12.7   Local fairRate more restrictive than received fairRate

As illustrated in Figure 12.8, an exception to the rule of propagating the more restrictive fairRate is made when it is determined that no station upstream of S4 is adding traffic that passes through both S4 and S6 at a rate greater than the fairRate advertised by S6. In the example, the stations S1, S2, and S3 add fairness eligible traffic at rates of 1 unit, 2 units, and 1 unit, respectively. While S4 does not have knowledge of these individual rates, it does measure the rate of transiting traffic bound for destinations beyond S6; in this case, 4 units. It can be inferred that no single contributing station, S1, S2, or S3, is contributing (i.e., adding fairness eligible traffic transiting S6) at a rate greater than 4 units since it is known that the sum of this traffic is not greater than 4 units. Propagation of the fairRate of 5 units beyond station S4 would, therefore, not reduce the contributing rate of any station upstream of S4. S4 advertises the value FULL_RATE indicating to upstream stations that their contributing rates need not be restricted.

As illustrated in the preceding examples, a station can advertise one of three possible values to its upstream neighbor.

- Its locally computed fairRate.
- The fairRate advertised by its downstream neighbor.
- The value FULL_RATE indicating that upstream stations are not contributing to downstream congestion.

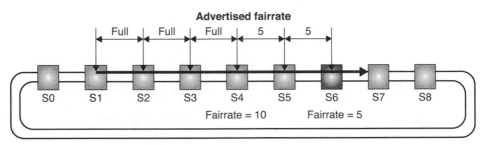

Figure 12.8   Advertising the FULL_RATE

An advertisement carries the identity of its station of origin. A station advertising the FULL_RATE always identifies itself as the origin. In all other cases, the origin is the station whose locally computed fairRate and source MAC address is carried by the advertisement. The advertisement also carries a time to live field that is assigned the value 255 by the originating station and is decremented by each station through which it passes. Stations receiving an advertisement can infer the originating station by examining the MAC address or the time to live fields.

Two methods of adjusting the fairRate are defined: Aggressive and Conservative.

Aggressive   The Aggressive method provides responsive adjustments that favor utilization of capacity over rate stability. The rates can be changed without significant delay and amounts of rate change are not highly damped. Stations transition immediately to the uncongested state after the congestion conditions are removed.

The aggressive method is the simpler of the two.

Conservative   The conservative method differs from the aggressive method in that a station can remain in a congested state after the congestion conditions are removed. This provides hysteresis in the transition between congested and uncongested states and prevents rate oscillation. In most cases, the conservative method requires that the fairRate not be adjusted until sufficient time has passed to ensure that the effect of any previous adjustment has been observed. This waiting period is known as the fairness round trip time (FRTT).

The FRTT is computed only by a station that performs conservative rate computation and is the head of a congestion domain (the station generating the advertisement). The FRTT value is recomputed when a valid pair of fairness differential delay (FDD) frames from the tail station (the last station advertising the fairRate generated by the head station) has been received by the head station. The FDD pair is sent by the tail at regular intervals.

The head station estimates the FRTT by referencing the FDD and the loop round trip time (LRTT). FRTT is the sum of FDD and LRTT.

$$FRTT = FDD + LRTT$$

FDD is a measure of the difference in delay between the classA and classC paths from the tail station to the head station, as shown in Figure 12.9. Stations are requested to generate the FDD frames only if they are a tail of a congestion domain whose head station is deploying the Conservative method.

LRTT is a measure of link delay experienced by classA frames from the head of the congestion domain to the tail of the congestion domain and back. A station implementing the Conservative method sends LRTT request frames to each station in the ring at regular intervals; each station in the ring (regardless of the fairness method being deployed by such station) returns a LRTT response frame for each LRTT request frame received. LRTT values are maintained in each station implementing the conservative method for each station in the ring.

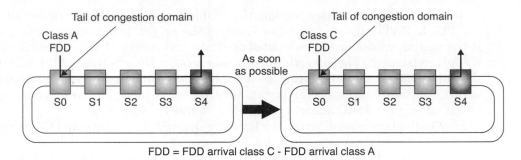

Figure 12.9 FDD calculation

Each station advertises its fairness method using the topology attribute discovery (ATD) frames defined later on in this document. Stations deploying the aggressive and conservative methods interoperate on the ringlet. Both methods converge to the fairRate value when the offered traffic at stations on the ringlet is constant.

Topology Discovery and Protection

Protection and topology discovery protocols are tightly related to each other. Protection information is used to update the topology data base, and a common frame carries information relevant to both functions.

Protection provides reliable mechanisms for fewer than 50 millisecond protection for all protected traffic on a ring. Each station receives all the span status change information required to make protection switching decisions reliably, and fast.

Topology discovery provides a reliable and accurate means for all stations on a ring to discover the topology of the stations on the ring, and any changes to that topology. It also provides a mechanism for rapid detection of topology changes, and a mechanism to convey additional station information to the ring.

The topology and protection protocol has the following features:

- Responsive
  - Restoration in less than 50 ms
  - Quick dissemination of changes in the protection state
- Robust
  - Support of a comprehensive protection hierarchy
  - Dynamic addition and removal of stations
  - Topology and protection frame loss tolerant
  - No need for a master or a management station

- Assurance of topology image conversion for all stations
- Context containment for strict order traffic
- Flexible
  - Support of revertive and non-revertive operation
  - Closed and open ring topologies
  - Scalable to 255 stations
  - Means to share additional information between stations
- Efficient
  - Requires insignificant ring traffic
  - Consumes minimal software execution time
  - Requires minimal hardware

The standard defines two protection mechanisms: Steer (mandatory) and Wrap (optional)

Steer Steering stations direct unicast traffic onto ringlet0 or ringlet1 on a per destination basis, to avoid failed spans. Multicast frames are sent in both directions, with the *ttl* set to the number of stations to the defective span, on each ringlet.

As illustrated in Figure 12.10, station S2 normally sends to station S6 via the ringlet0. After the fiber cut, S4 that detects the failure sends a protection message to all stations in the ring. Based on this message, station S2 updates its topology database and steers protected S6-destined traffic via the ringlet1. In flight frames, destined to stations beyond the point of failure, are dropped at the edge. Steer protection has the advantage that the traffic is routed through the optimal path even after a failure.

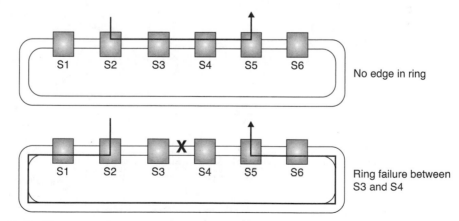

Figure 12.10 Steer protection

Wrap   In addition to steering, RPR stations may support wrapping. Wrapping stations direct traffic onto ringlet0 or ringlet1 on a per destination basis, regardless of failed spans. An edge station wraps eligible frames that would otherwise be transmitted across the edge.

As illustrated in Figure 12.11, station S2 normally sends to station S6 via the ringlet0. After the fiber cut, station S2 still sends the traffic via the ringlet0 path. Station S6 does not strip frames from the opposite ringlet of that indicated in the wrapped frame (ringlet1 in this case) to avoid frame mis-ordering during the protection event. In flight frames, destined to stations beyond the point of failure, are wrapped at the edge.

Wrap protection is usually faster that steer protection, because the protection decision (wrap traffic) is local to the stations detecting the failure (S3 and S4 in Figure 12.11). Another advantage of wrapping is that there is no need to duplicate multicast frames, since all stations remain reachable trough both ringlets.

Steer and wrap stations can not coexist in a ring, if a mismatch is detected an alarm condition is declared. On the other hand, by using a special bit in the RPR header, a ring that is configured for wrap protection can allow the client to steer specific packet flows using the Selective Wrap Independent Steer (SWIS) method.

SWIS   The RPR frame includes a wrap eligibility (*we*) bit. During a span failure, wrapping stations wrap frames only if *we* is set, if *we* is clear frames are discarded at the edge of the failure. In a wrapping ring, a client may specifically request that a frame be sent by the MAC with the *we* clear, and by manipulating the parameters provided by the client to the MAC for each transmit frame, the client can steer these frames during a failure condition.

SWIS allows the client to tailor the protection method to the service preferences: services that require minimum packet loss can be wrapped while services that require minimum delay can be steered.

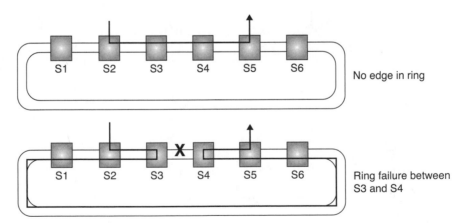

Figure 12.11   Wrap protection

Protection Hierarchy

The MAC supports the protection hierarchy listed in Table 12.2. The protection conditions and the resulting topologies are described in Figure 12.12.

As described in Figure 12.12, only FS and SF conditions can coexist and severe the ring in more than one span. Tie condition of non fatal span failures (e.g., SD, MS) is ignored and no protection operation is performed.

The topology and protection (TP) frames are used to detect that the ringlet0 transmit signal of one station as been wrongly connected to the ringlet1 receive of its neighboring, and vice versa. This defect is known as a miscabling defect. A station declares a miscabling defect if the TP frame from its neighbor indicates that it has been transmitted in a ringlet different from the one it was received.

As already mentioned in the fairness clause, the fairness frames are transmitted regularly at short intervals. These frames are used as a keep alive signal to verify the operation of the RPR layer. An SF is declared upon the detection of a major physical layer outage (e.g., signal loss, loss of frame), if fairness frames are not detected within a period of time (loss of keep alive), or a miscabling defect has been declared. A SD is declared upon the detection of degradation in the signal received by the physical layer (e.g., low bit error ratio in SONET), some physical layers may not be able to generate the SD indication.

Passthrough Mode The optional passthrough mode enables stations to enter or exit the ring without disconnection of fibers (e.g., upon detection of internal failure conditions), and without triggering a signal fail event. Passthrough allows a station to leave the ring while maintaining a closed-ring topology, avoiding a protection switch in the case that the transit path of the station is operating normally, but another part of the station failed.

Periodic transmission of TP frames allows detection of a station entering passthrough. When another station appears to have changed its location, TP frame transmission is triggered to facilitate fast rediscovery of the topology and restoration of strict mode traffic.

Lower Layer Protection A configurable holdoff timeout can suppress spurious responses to expected span status glitches, by extending the time between detection and reporting

TABLE 12.2   Protection Hierarchy

Name	Acronym	Description
Forced Switch	FS	A management directive that forces a span to be deactivated
Signal Fail	SF	A signal failure that deactivates a span
Signal Degrade	SD	A signal degradation that can deactivate a span
Manual Switch	MS	A management directive that can deactivate a scan
Wait to Restore	WTR	A timer that improves stability in the presence of transient failures
Idle	IDLE	None of the above

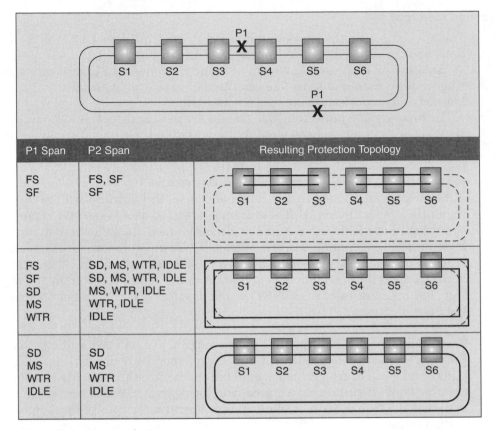

Figure 12.12 Protection topologies

of a physical failure condition. The glitches could be due to protection switching of RPR traffic by underlying SONET infrastructure, as shown in Figure 12.13.

As illustrated in Figure 12.13, if the hold off timeout is omitted, the RPR will protect the services before SONET layer protection is completed. Soon after the SONET layer completes its protection task, the RPR will detect that the failure has been removed, and will restore the original path for the services. An unnecessary protection hit has been performed.

If the hold off timeout is set to allow the SONET layer to complete protection, then no RPR protection is implemented and the additional hit is avoided.

The RPR MAC builds a topology data base that is partitioned into multiple components: ring level information, local station information, and per station information. The information used to configure the values in the topology data base comes from a variety of sources such as: TP frames, ATD frames, LRTT frames, and topology checksum (TC) frames.

Figure 12.14 shows an example of a data base built by an RPR station. The TP frames are used to position the stations in the table, according to their hop count distance

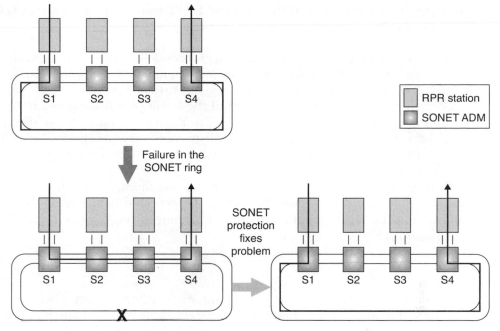

Figure 12.13   RPR over SONET without holdoff

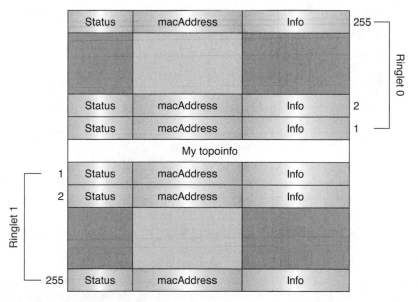

Figure 12.14   Topology data base

from the specific station, and the ATD and LRTT frames are used exclusively to fill in additional information regarding each station.

Context Containment   Context containment assists in preventing duplication and re-ordering of strict mode traffic during topology changes. Context containment is entered on detection of a passthrough, or when a span status changes.

Context containment is not exited until the topology is determined to be stable and valid and the local topology database is determined to match those of its reachable neighbors. Each station calculates a topology checksum, unique to the ring, and uses the Topology Checksum (TC) frames to make its calculated topology checksum available to other stations in the ring.

During context containment all strict frames are discarded. Stations receiving strict frames whose hops count does not match the expected hops counts for a station, as reflected in the topology data base, discard them. In these cases, relaxed frames are not discarded.

OAM

The Operations, Administration, and Maintenance (OAM) entity of RPR provides a set of control functions and indications to support fault management, and performance management.

The services provided by the RPR OAM are

- Determine and validate connectivity between any two stations on the ring
- Determine and validate transit path operation for any service class
- Provide a mechanism to help in misorder prevention
- Provide performance monitoring parameters

Special control frames enable the detection and isolation of failures at the ring layer. These frames can be used either during service provisioning or continuously to minimize the correction time of abnormal operation.

The OAM frame types supported are: Echo request/response, Flush and Organization specific.

Echo Request/Response   The client can request an echo request/response operation to a specified destination in order to check the reachability of that station. An echo operation allows a frame to be inserted at one station in the ring, and an echo response returned by another station through the same or opposite ringlet. Echo request/response frames can be assigned to any CoS.

Flush   The client can request to perform a flush operation. A flush has the effect of clearing the selected ringlet of previously sourced traffic. A flush is expected to be used when changing the ringlet selection by the client, to implement client controlled steer protection, or for traffic engineering reasons. A flush is a special control frame that is sent from a station to itself. Flush operations prevent mis-order during steer protection.

The flush frames can be assigned to any CoS, with distinct flush action results, as follows:

- ClassA. Previously-sourced primary transit queue (PTQ) traffic is flushed.

- ClassB or classC. Previously-sourced PTQ and secondary transit queue (STQ) traffic is flushed.

Organization Specific   A client may use the optional organization specific OAM frame to implement additional OAM functions not specified by the standard.

Stations may accumulate performance parameters related to the RPR layer to enable the detection of developing failures before a total outage is detected.

RPR error monitoring is based on the fairness frame errors. Performance monitoring counters are accumulated for: errored fairness frames, errored seconds, severely errored seconds, and unavailable seconds.

Errored Seconds   An errored second is a second in which any of the following occurs:

- A fairness frame error is detected.

- A miscabling defect was present.

- A keepalive timeout was present.

- A physical layer failure was present.

Severely Errored Second   A severely errored second is a second in which any of the following occurs:

- More than a predefined threshold of fairness frame errors were detected.

- A miscabling defect was present.

- A keepalive timeout was present.

- A physical layer failure was present.

Unavailable Seconds   Once available, the RPR service transitions to unavailable at the onset of 10 contiguous severely errored seconds. Once unavailable, the RPR service transitions to available at the onset of 10 contiguous seconds, none of which are classified as a severely errored second.

Data Path

The MAC supports several paths along which frames move. Frames added by the MAC either directly, or indirectly from the client, are transmitted via the add paths. Frames received from the ring and intended to be re-transmitted, are transmitted via the transit path, which include the transit queues. These paths collectively form the datapaths of the MAC. Figure 12.15 illustrates the single transit queue implementation, and Figure 12.16 the dual transit queue implementation. Each set of datapaths are duplicated per ringlet.

Add Path   The client's labeling of its frames as classA, classB, or classC informs the MAC which shaper to apply to the added frames. The classA client add traffic flows through the subclassA0 shaper or the subclassA1 shaper, as determined by the MAC according to the MAC configuration. Since, as noted earlier, the amount of subclassA1 supported by the MAC is a function of the secondary transit queue (STQ) length, single transit queue implementations of the data path support only subclassA0.

The classB client add traffic flows through the classB shaper or the fairness eligible shaper, as determined by the MAC according to the configured classB-CIR and classB-EIR. The classC client adds traffic flows through the fairness eligible shaper which is controlled by the fairness algorithm.

The add queues are not part of the MAC, they are implemented by the client. The MAC indicates which frames can be forwarded by controlling the send signals. Accepted client traffic is placed into a stage queue, one frame at a time. The stage queue is a logical construct that might or might not correspond to any physical structure.

Frames added by the MAC control sublayer are shaped by the MAC control shaper that limits the amount of control traffic added by the MAC. Control frames are usually labeled

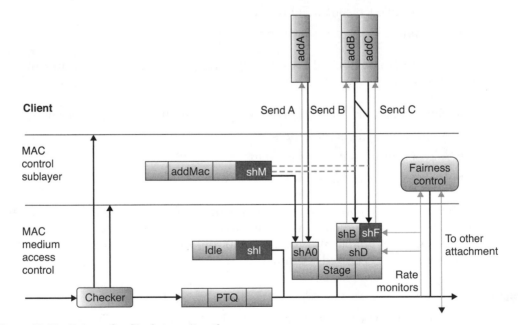

Figure 12.15   Data path—Single transit path

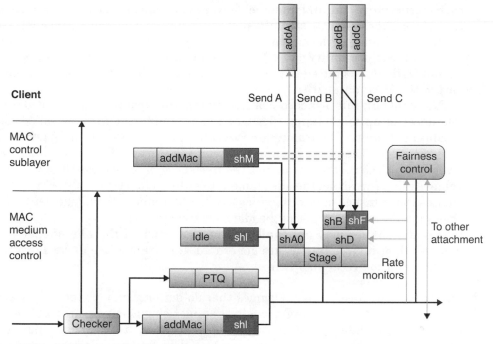

Figure 12.16 MAC data path—Dual transit queue

subclassA0 and also shaped by the subclassA0 shaper, but can be labeled classB or classC (e.g., echo request and response) and directed to the classB shaper or the fairness eligible shaper, respectively, as illustrated by the dotted lines in Figures 12.15 and 12.16. Shaping by the MAC control shaper is applied first and in addition to the other shapers.

All shapers other than the downstream shaper are applied only to add traffic. All unreserved add and transit traffic flows through the downstream shaper. The function of the downstream shaper is to constrain the MAC to sustain the downstream allocated subclassA0 rate.

Optionally, rate synchronization idle frames are added by the MAC and shaped by the idle shaper.

Idle Frames RPR stations and networks can be implemented with either synchronous (e.g., SONET/SDH) or asynchronously-timed PHYs (e.g., Gigabit Ethernet). In a synchronous network, the transmit clock for each station is locked to a common timing source that may be recovered from the received data stream or provided through an external timing interface, and the transmit data rate from each station is exactly identical to the received data rate. However, in an asynchronous network, the transmit data rate at each station is determined by a local clock source, and the transmit data rate from each station varies slightly from the network data rate. In the case of a station transmitting at a slower data rate than the preceding station, this could cause PTQ overflow.

The idle shaper performs an optional transmit rate synchronization function that eliminates the possibility of PTQ overflow by inserting a variable number of small idle frames in the transmitted data stream. The transmit rate synchronization function is part of the MAC datapath.

The transmit rate synchronization function supports PHYs with data rate clock tolerances of up to ±100 ppm. The idle shaper limits the MAC-supplied idle traffic to its allocated limits. Idle frames are inserted into the transmit datapath at a fixed rate equivalent to 0.05% of the line rate. The rate of inserted idle frames is controlled by the level of the PTQ. As the queue fills, the free space becomes less than the *idleThreshold* value. At this threshold, the idle frame rate reduces to 0.025% of the line rate, which increases the transmit data rate, which eventually reduces the queue depth. Figure 12.17 shows a numerical example of the idle shaper operation.

The idle shaper may optionally be implemented. If the idle shaper is not implemented, then no idle frames are generated. Idle frames are always discarded by the neighbor station receiving them.

Transit Path   A MAC transits frames that do not originate or terminate at that MAC. There are two types of MAC transit queuing designs: single transit queue and dual transit queue. The single transit queue design places all transit traffic into a primary transit queue (PTQ). The dual transit queue design places classA transit traffic into a higher-precedence primary transit queue, and classB and classC transit traffic into a lower-precedence secondary transit queue (STQ). Neither path supports preemption of either the transit or ingress frames. Once a frame has begun transmission, its transmission cannot be interrupted by the transmission of another frame. Single and dual transit queue MAC can interoperate in the same ring.

Transmit Operation   The selection of the frame to be transmitted depends on the transit path implementation. For single transit queue implementations the intent is to always

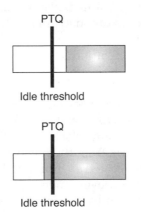

Figure 12.17   Idle shaper operation

empty the PTQ before client frame transmissions. This is achieved by assigning a strict higher priority to the transit traffic (regardless of its class of service) than to any local added traffic.

For dual transit queue implementations the intent is to always empty the PTQ before client frame transmissions, but to allow the STQ to fill somewhat while adding client frame transmissions.

A dual transit queue MAC implementation is more complicated, but it has the advantages of supporting the more efficient subclassA1, and safely delivering higher amounts of ring traffic since the low priority transit traffic can not preempt the local high priority (classA) traffic.

Frame Formats

There are four types of RPR frames:

- Data frames
- Control frames
- Fairness frames
- Idle frames

The minimum data frame size is 24 bytes, and the maximum is 1616 bytes if jumbo frames are not supported and 9216 bytes if jumbo frames are supported. The minimum control frame size is 24 bytes and the maximum is 1616 bytes, no jumbo control frames are defined.

Figure 12.18 illustrates the data frame options and shows the HEC and FCS error coverage. The extended frame option is used for bridging.

Figure 12.19 illustrates the control frame formats and the control type values.

DA and SA are 48-bit fields that specifies the destination and source stations for the frame. These fields contain individual 48-bit MAC address as specified in IEEE.

The flood indication is used to avoid persistent flooding in bridged applications of RPR. Flooded frames are forwarded to the client bridge entity regardless of their destination address.

The passed source bit is used by wrapping systems (along with other fields) to prevent frame misorder and duplication by preventing the frame from being wrapped more than two times by the wrapping network. It is set to 0 when a frame is first transmitted by a station and set to 1 when a wrapped frame (i.e., a frame traveling on the secondary ringlet) passes the source station.

A frame with a bad HEC is discarded since the header information is corrupted and no reliable delivery of the frame can be assured. A data frame with a bad FCS is not discarded on transit, but it is stomped by the first station detecting a bad FCS to avoid multiple counting of the same errored frame in different stations along the transit path.

A station receiving a frame with a corrupted FCS may decide to accept it or discard it, according to a configuration parameter. Accepting a frame with corrupted FCS may be of value for services such as TDM pseudo wire emulation, where some bit errors may be tolerated.

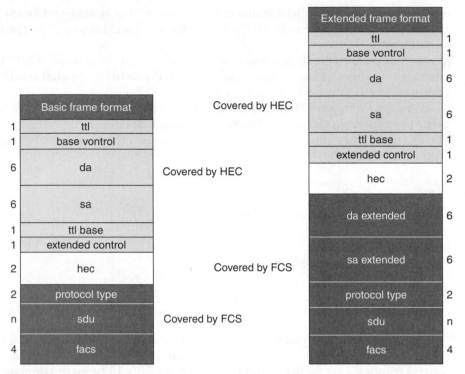

Figure 12.18 Data frame formats

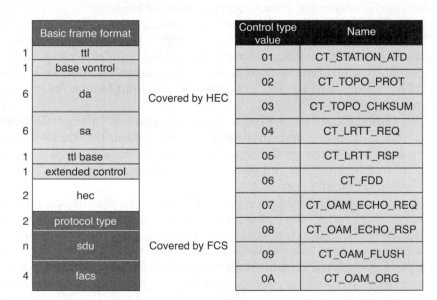

Figure 12.19 Control frames format

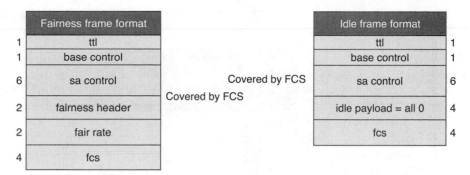

Figure 12.20 Fairness and idle frame formats

Figure 12.20 illustrates the fairness and idle frame formats. For fairness frames, the *saControl* field specifies the station that provided the values contained in the *fairnessHeader* and fairRate fields. This station is not necessarily the station that generated this frame, which is always the upstream neighbor. For idle frames it contains the address of the upstream neighbor station.

Physical Interface

Two families of optional reconciliation sublayers are defined: The Packet PHYs and SONET/SDH PHYs. The reconciliation sublayers map the MAC physical layer service primitives to standard electrical interfaces used by these PHYs. To ensure interoperability, an interface that is compliant to the standard shall implement at least one of the defined PHYs. Packet PHYs are 1 Gb/s and 10 Gb/s PHYs, similar to those defined by IEEE 802.3, but with some deviations.

The SONET/SDH reconciliation sublayers provide interfaces to adaptation sublayers that specify either frame-mapped generic framing procedure (GFP), byte-synchronous high-level data link control (HDLC)-like framing, or link access procedure-SDH (LAPS) framing for SONET/SDH networks and PHYs operating at 155 Mb/s to 10 Gb/s or higher.

Figure 12.21 shows the relationship between the RPR MAC and the other sublayers.

Packet PHYs   The requirements for the 1 Gb/s and 10 Gb/s Packet PHYs are described in IEEE 802.3. The following exceptions and changes apply to the specifications:

- Repeaters are not supported.
- The minimum frame size is 16 bytes.
- The maximum frame size is 9216 bytes.
- Auto-negotiation is not used.
- Flow control is disabled.
- Remote fault is not generated by the transmitter and if present is ignored by the receiver.

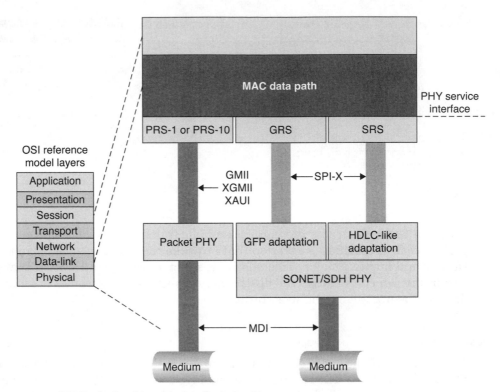

Figure 12.21   MAC relationship with the physical sublayers

SONET/SDH PHYs   RPR can be mapped to SONET/SDH through three types of adaptation sublayers:

- GFP
- HDLC-like
- LAPS

Frame-mapped GFP framing for RPR complies with ITU-T G.7041 using a null extension header as defined by the extension header identifier (EXI), no GFP FCS field, and with a user payload identifier (UPI) corresponding to an RPR payload.

Byte-synchronous HDLC-like framing for RPR complies with IETF RFC 1662 using byte-stuffed framing, with references to PPP frames to be interpreted as RPR frames. Instead of using LCP for link negotiation, byte-synchronous HDLC-like framing for RPR uses the following statically-defined link parameters:

- Address and Control Field compression is always used. The fields are not used.
- The Protocol Field is not used.

- The FCS is neither computed nor appended to the frame.
- The asynchronous control character map (ACCM) is not used.

LAPS framing for RPR complies with ITU-T X.85/Y.1321.

Drivers for This Solution

The Ethernet we use today is significantly different than the Ethernet that was originally created in the IEEE 802.3 group. It is now full duplex and has lost CSMA/CD as an access method. It has new physical interfaces, different data rates, new port aggregation features, VLAN functions and many other modifications that have been introduced over the years to facilitate new applications and uses. In many ways the RPR MAC is another case of an IEEE standard that facilitates the evolution of Ethernet, in this case, to the WAN environment.

Sometime around Calendar Year 2000 packet traffic surpassed circuit traffic on service provider networks worldwide. This fact and the success and proliferation of Ethernet equipment and packets on Corporate networks meant that a great percentage of the packet traffic on service provider networks were Ethernet packets. Much of this traffic originated on TDM circuits with Enterprise customers. However, existing circuit based networks while reliable were economically inefficient for carrying the increasing demands of Ethernet packet traffic. So in 2000 the IEEE recognizing the difficulty of creating metropolitan networks with Ethernet equipment authorized the creation of the IEEE 802.17 working group. It had the charter of creating a Layer 2 protocol, specifically a Media Access Controller (MAC) that would be appropriate for transporting Ethernet and other packet traffic on fiber rings in metro and regional configurations. Between 2000 and 2004 a standard was developed and approved. Some of the characteristics of the Ethernet MAC that RPR was designed to overcome. These have been discussed next.

No Support for Ring Topologies

The Ethernet MAC is specified for mesh and point-to-point topologies. Ring structures are prohibited to prevent endless circulation of errored, rogue, or misdirected packets. There are Ethernet devices that can be connected in a ring configuration, however they do not conform to the IEEE 802.3 protocol in this respect.

Ring topologies have practical benefits and are frequently deployed in carrier networks. They, (1) uses less fiber than mesh or hub and spoke configurations and (2) in most cases are simpler and quicker to restore in the event of failure.

Slow and Non-deterministic Restoration

A key consideration in carrier networks is protection and restoration. Ethernet has protection mechanisms, Spanning Tree and Rapid Spanning Tree, but these hierarchical and mesh restoration schemes do not converge fast enough for networks with strict Service Level Agreements.

Protection and topology discovery protocols are tightly related to each other. Protection information is used to update the topology data base, and a common frame carries information relevant to both functions. Topology discovery provides a reliable and accurate means for all stations on a ring to discover the topology of the stations on the ring, and any changes to that topology. It also provides a mechanism for rapid detection of topology changes, and a mechanism to convey additional node information to the other nodes on the ring.

No Control of Delay and Delay Variation from Switch to Switch

Mechanisms that control delay and delay variation are crucial for networks that deliver IPTV and voice services. In a network of 3 or more switches, connected serially, there is no provision within the 802.3 MAC to ensure packets on the network are delivered. Ethernet LANs require retransmission of dropped or lost packets or induce significant delay due to queuing. However, carrier networks cannot maintain SLAs or quality of user experience for consumers of IPTV or voice services if they encounter significant amount of lost packets or packet delay and variation.

No Fairness Control Mechanism

The 802.3 MAC has no signaling mechanism among devices to communicate the congestion state of other switches on the network. This lack of visibility often leads to unexpected congestion on individual links. In addition, due to head of line blocking customers that are closest to their destination, a Central Office for instance, will receive better service than those that are farther away.

To overcome these issues, fairness algorithms are built into the RPR protocol. These messages are part of the RPR header and tell the MAC how to treat each packet. The various classes and sub classes can be used to create any service profiles appropriate for any application. High priority, guaranteed traffic is never subject to fairness. High priority traffic always gets the bandwidth assigned to it, always receives priority on the ring and is therefore never subject to delay or delay variation. The fairness algorithm ensures weighted dynamic distribution of available link bandwidths to source stations using those links.

This feature enables two real benefits. One, it allows users to burst into any unused network capacity and get high throughput in these instances. Secondly, it ensures that no service is ever starved of bandwidth, since some network managers can always reserve a portion of the ring bandwidth for Best Effort traffic.

RPR is the only standardized packet-based Layer 2 mechanism for ring topologies that provides both the resilience and jitter/delay control necessary for the voice and video services increasingly desired by telecommunications subscribers. Public carriers prefer and often require standards based products to facilitate interoperability and to ensure they are not dependent on a single supplier.

When Does this Solution Fit?

RPR is not normally applied as a service or technology by itself. RPR's primary role comes into play at the first point where customers are aggregated at central facilities owned by the service provider. It makes the access from business and consumers more robust and ensures that subscribers SLAs are enforced and maintained. Aggregation could occur at a DSLAM for DSL subscribers, a CMTS for cable subscribers, an ADM for SONET/SDH access, PON for new fiber builds or a L2/L3 Ethernet switch for Ethernet access. Any of these technologies can be aggregated onto an RPR ring. In addition many private Enterprise networks are built on RPR rings using the technologies mentioned above, however, the facilities are wholly owned by the Enterprise rather than by the service provider. As such they are dedicated to a single company and not shared among many customers.

Terminating these access technologies into an RPR network provides a number of benefits for the customer of TDM and data services. These are discussed next.

Restoration

A key consideration in carrier networks is protection and restoration. Rapid restoration on an Ethernet switches could be done using an additional layer, MPLS. This adds complexity and increases OpEx for any carrier adopting MPLS for protection in the metro network. The approach requires manual configuration of the MPLS protection paths.

These functions are automated at Layer 2 in the RPR protocol. Sub 50 ms restoration and the substantial elimination of jitter, delay, and packet loss are the result of the signaling protocol that is native to the RPR MAC.

The standard defines two protection mechanisms: Steer (mandatory), and Wrap (optional). It is important to have both mechanisms available since they have different uses. They are designed to overcome fundamental issues that arise during a protection event. Packets are either mis-ordered, lost, or delayed. Each of these events has an impact on services. Table 12.3 shows how steering or wrapping affect applications.

In addition, unlike SONET/SDH restoration mechanisms, RPR restoration mechanisms have the ability to partially restore a service. As an example, if a customer is

TABLE 12.3   Wrap and Steer Restoration Characteristics

Application	Steer	Wrap
Speed	Slower (signaling)	Faster (local)
Packet loss	Higher	Lower
Delay	Lower	Higher
Bandwidth efficiency (for BE)	Higher	Lower
Reordering (after recovery)	Lower	Higher
Support multicast traffic	Complex	Simple
Implementation	Client	MAC

receiving a 20 Mbps Ethernet service and desires protection in the event of an outage there are three options available. These are: (a) restore the entire 20 mbps service, (b) do not restore any service and (c) partially restore the service i.e., default to some number of mbps lower than 20 mbps during the protection event.

QoS

Another important aspect of 802.17 for video and voice services is the ability of the RPR MAC to signal to every other node on the ring the state of its links and the available bandwidth on all network segments. As noted above transit queues allow traffic to pass right through a node without queuing or inspection beyond the RPR header. This ensures that there is no delay or delay variation for this high priority traffic. Since the 802.17 MAC can automatically control these variables it is ideally suited to carry video and voice; both of which are subject to interference from latency and jitter.

Fairness

Fairness algorithms are also built into the RPR protocol. These messages are part of the RPR header and tell the MAC how to treat each packet. The various classes and sub classes can be used to create any service profiles appropriate for any application. High priority, guaranteed traffic is never subject to fairness. High priority traffic always gets the bandwidth assigned to it, always receives priority on the ring and is therefore never subject to delay or delay variation. The fairness algorithm ensures weighted dynamic distribution of available link bandwidths to source stations using those links.

This feature enables two real benefits. One it allows users to burst into any unused ring capacity and get high throughput in these instances. Secondly, it ensures that no service is ever starved of bandwidth. Network managers can always reserve some portion of the ring for Best Effort traffic. These two facts mean that network owners with RPR transport equipment can overbook their networks to a much greater extend and enjoy much greater revenue as a result.

The 802.3 Ethernet MAC has no comparable mechanisms. There is no signaling among devices to understand the congestion state of other switches on the network. This lack of visibility often leads to unexpected congestion and makes IPTV and other services delivery potentially unpredictable.

When Does This Solution Not Fit?

Applications Don't Require It

One of the first things to consider when evaluating requirements for RPR is the application. RPR transport equipment delivers strict QoS and guaranteed availability. However, there are applications, like residential internet access where these qualities are less important. Standard Ethernet switching or routing solutions are appropriate solutions when the QoS and restoration requirements are less strict. With applications like file transfer or internet access the key strengths of the RPR protocol are not utilized. When a pure data application is not sensitive to delay and delay variation and when restoration times that can be as high as 30 seconds do not affect application performance, then RPR is not required.

Existing SONET/SDH Transport

Another case where RPR may not be required is where the Ethernet packets are already traveling over traditional or next-generation SONET/SDH networks. Restoration, Fairness, QoS, and OAM benefits of RPR are not required since the operation of SONET/SDH transport already provides these characteristics, albeit by different and less efficient methods. These networks are quite common and indeed most data traffic currently traverses these networks. One of the objectives in creation of the RPR protocol was to provide these characteristics in a pure packet transport network.

Over-provisioning Alternative

There are other cases where the RPR provides no benefit or may be inappropriate or impossible to implement. A primary one is when the physical topology of the fiber does not allow for the creation of a ring. RPR must operate in a ring configuration. If the fiber topology is a mesh or tree configuration than creation of an RPR will be impossible. Another case where IEEE 802.17 is not required is one where the point-to-point link between switches or routers has approximately twice the peak required bandwidth as required by the applications or customers. In this case the QoS is provided by over provisioning the link obviating the need for the rigorous QoS provided by RPR. Likewise, if there are two fiber access routes (dual homing) to buildings that require communication services, the restoration properties of RPR are redundant.

Typical Deployment Scenarios

RPR is deployed by service providers or by large organizations such as Fortune 500 companies, government, and educational institutions. An individual RPR device usually contains other technologies to create a fully functioning system. Interface ports to an RPR switch may be SONET/SDH, TDM, Ethernet or a combination of both. In addition, VCAT and LCAS may be added to more efficiently fill SONET/SDH circuits. MPLS and pseudo-wires can be added for traffic management and service interworking. All of these technologies provide a backbone for high bandwidth service aggregation and connectivity.

Consumers or Enterprise data and voice service customers are often unaware of the existence of RPR in the networks their data traverses. However, it is often a critical component that ensures that they receive the Service Level Agreements they are promised in their contracts.

The RPR portion of the network will sometimes begin at the Broadband Loop Carrier. This is the first aggregation point in the network for many customers. One level up from that is where the aggregation of circuits and packets occurs. In this metro aggregation portion of the network, Multi Service Provisioning Platforms (MSPP) or Packet Transport Switches (PTS) aggregate traffic from DSLAMs, wireless base stations, SONET/SDH and Ethernet ports for transmission in the metro and regional networks. Some companies use RPR between routers to form the data backbone in cable networks. RPR is not usually used in the transcontinental core networks. For that purpose IP Routers connect the packet traffic and SONET/SDH transport devices connect the circuit traffic. All of these technologies could ride on top of Wave Division Multiplexing equipment.

Ongoing Developments

The growth of packet traffic and the necessity of supporting Ethernet and IP is driving changes in all telecommunications equipment from the access (DSLAM) to metro transport (PTS, MSPP, WD) and core (Routing and Optical Transport). Every part of the network is under pressure to deliver, greater bandwidth, more control, better QoS, higher availability, more rapid service delivery, and lower operational expenses. RPR can be implemented in equipment in the access, metro and core portions of the network. As the table at the end of the chapter shows RPR has been implemented in Broadband Loop Carriers, DSLAMs, Packet Transport Switches, and Multiservice Provisioning Platforms and Switch/Routers. Each of these categories of devices is evolving to support the new business cases required by service providers offering the latest in broadband services.

RPR was initially designed to support QoS, Availability, Management, and many of the key characteristics required in this new networking environment. Still there are developments that are being implemented to deliver even greater functionality from the protocol. Some of these are being done within the standards organizations and others are being done by vendors seeking to deliver more functionality within their devices.

Within the IEEE 802.17 there is work being done to improve the spatial reuse capabilities of the RPR ring. 802.17b defines two types of connections: directed and undirected. This has to do with efficient use of bandwidth when a remote address is not known by any of the RPR nodes. If the relationship between a remote address and an RPR station address has not been established the frames will be flooded using undirected transmission. As soon as the location of the remote node is learned directed transmission is used. This way unknown frames travel the minimum hops to reach their destination. Another standard based approach to this issue is to use MPLS Pseudowires to interconnect RPR rings. Both of these approaches bring the ability to maintain both availability and QoS between multiple rings. Since many users do not reside on the same metro or regional ring, the ability to interconnect rings is an important evolution of the solution.

In addition vendors are providing mechanisms for scaling RPR rings beyond 10Gbps. The availability and cost of 40Gbps components and the complexity of switching at those speeds is limiting, for now, the introduction of faster rate connections. However, the vendor community is using bonding technologies to aggregate 10 Gpbs rings so that it is now possible to create N × 10 Gbps RPR rings for high bandwidth applications.

With this capability service providers can now create rings with very high aggregate data rates. This capability will be important in dense urban environments where millions of customers are aggregated and in high bandwidth research applications that are required by business, government, and scientific applications.

Economic Assessment

The models shown below demonstrate how the RPR performs financially compared to alternatives based on different network criteria. These business models are representative of actual network results. Every network is unique and the flexibility of an RPR based ring means that its' actual benefits are best calculated using specific data from real networks. These tools are provided as a template to demonstrate the many ways that the devices incorporating RPR can yield superior ROI.

RPR creates a shared ring with a common signaling and control plane implemented in the standards based IEEE 802.17 MAC. Capital and operating expenses are lower when management and switching functions are automated at lower layers of the OSI model due to reduced manpower required for designing and maintaining network wide QoS.

Point-to-point connections must be individually and manually configured. The common control plane among RPR nodes in a network enables the automation configuration of services between endpoints without configuration of each intermediary point. This means that customers and services can be added to the ring once and their configuration information can be replicated across all the switches without further intervention. This saves significant operational cost for physical or logical point-to-point topologies. Ethernet rings exist but they are proprietary implementations. Likewise, Wave Division Multiplexing is configured in logical point-to-point topologies even when the physical topology is a ring. Indeed SONET/SDH is topologically a ring but the configuration requires creation of individual point-to-point circuits.

The manpower and operational expense required for these activities is difficult to quantify, although from the foregoing discussion it is logical that they should be lower in RPR networks. However, CapEx is more straightforward. The following model demonstrates that equipment expenses as well as OpEx are reduced in the RPR-based ring network.

More Bandwidth

As an illustration let's examine a Pay TV service that offers 100 channels over an RPR ring verses a point-to-point approach. These 100 broadcast channels, in aggregate, will consume approximately 350 Mbps of bandwidth from the servers to the nodes. Each customer receives identical feeds simultaneously.

For this illustration let's compare a 10 Gbps RPR ring with a point-to-point solution. Each of the ten 1 Gbps connections is discreet. Therefore, each connects the head end with only one of the Gig E uplinks from the aggregation equipment either over WDM or SONET/SDH equipment. This means that the 350 Mbps worth of feeds from the 100 Pay TV channels must be sent on each lambda or connection individually. Therefore, the bandwidth consumed by Pay TV is 350 Mbps × 10 connections or 3.5 Gbps out of the total 10 Gbps available. Each 1 Gbps connection feeding the Gig uplinks will receive its' own individual broadcast TV signal even though it is identical to the broadcast TV signals simultaneously going to the remaining 9 connections.

The RPR solution is quite different. Since all signals are aggregated and multiplexed in the RPR device the use of multicasting protocols make more efficient use of the ring bandwidth. Since the Pay TV signals are identical we only need to send them around the ring once. Then each node can replicate them out each 1 Gig port to the aggregation equipment.

With RPR the portion of ring bandwidth used for this service is 350 Mbps or 1/10 of that required for point-to-point solutions. As Table 12.4 shows this frees an additional 3.15 Gbps of ring bandwidth.

Lower Capex

RPR architecture consolidates network elements resulting in significantly lower CapEx. Due to the reduction of network elements OpEx is reduced as well. The use of RPR traffic management and MPLS control plane means fewer network elements in the metro network.

Figure 12.22 below represents a point-to-point design that shows L2/L3 switching devices connected to a transport node. In Figure 12.23 you see a comparable design using an RPR ring. The functions of the ADM and the L2/L3 device have been consolidated into one intelligent transport node. When you compare this design to one using SONET/SDH with L2/L3 switching /routing the savings are significant.

Figure 12.22 shows how a configuration of L2/L3 switches requires (1) twice the amount of fiber and (2) more optical ports to achieve the same connectivity as the ring. This demands twice the investment in fiber and an increase in ports required to build the metro transport network.

Figure 12.23 shows an RPR network that supports the transport functions of the traditional ADM while simultaneously supporting the L2 traffic management and switching functions provided by the Layer 2/3 switching equipment.

Fiber Route Savings

Notice that to connect the nodes to the L2/L3 Network in the diagram above requires twice the amount of fiber to achieve the same connectivity as the ring. This demands twice the investment in fiber to build the metro transport network.

TABLE 12.4   RPR and Multicast Bandwidth Savings

RPR Multicast Efficiency by Technology	RPR	Point-to-Point
Bandwidth Consumed by Pay TV	350Mbps	3.5Gbps
Bandwidth Available after Multicasting	9.6Gbps	6.5Gbps
Bandwidth Advantage of RPR	3.15Gbps	

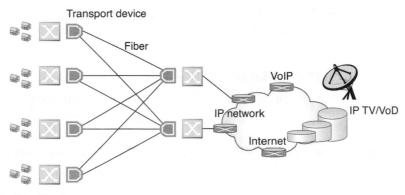

Figure 12.22 Star Topology

Formula A – Point-to-Point Fiber Cost

Cost of Fiber from Hub#1 to Network × 2 = Fiber Cost A
Cost of Fiber from Hub#2 to Network × 2 = Fiber Cost B
Cost of Fiber from Hub#3 to Network × 2 = Fiber Cost C
Cost of Fiber from Hub#4 to Network × 2 = Fiber Cost D

Hub & Spoke Fiber Cost = Formula B – Ring Fiber Cost

Cost of Fiber from Hub #1 to Hub #2 = Fiber Cost E
Cost of Fiber from Hub #2 to Hub #3 = Fiber Cost F
Cost of Fiber from Hub #3 to Hub #4 = Fiber Cost G
Cost of Fiber from Hub #4 to Hub #5 = Fiber Cost H
Cost of Fiber from Hub #5 to Hub #1 = Fiber Cost I

Using published average fiber cost per mile per month from the Wall Street Journal May 12th, 2005 Section B page 10 of $400 we can calculate the relative cost of these

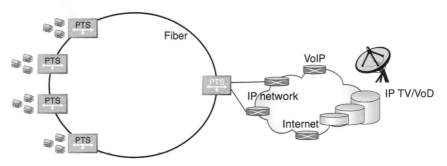

Figure 12.23 Hub and Spoke Topology

two approaches. To make the calculations simple, we will assume that all ADMs and PADMs are an equal 10 miles apart from one another. Using these two figures and the formulas presented above yields the following results.

$$\text{Total Cost for Fiber in Hub and Spoke Configuration} = \$384,000$$
$$\text{Total Cost for Fiber in Ring Configuration} = \$240,000 = 100\%$$
$$\text{Savings with RPR Ring} = \$144,000 = 62.5\%$$

The point-to-point approach represented by the hub and spoke architecture results in 62.5% higher fiber cost for the equivalent connectivity.

Optical Port and Equipment Savings

The Hub and Spoke architecture requires the use of both a transport device, in this case, an ADM and a L2/L3 switch as shown in Figure 12.23. The RPR ring collapses the functions of these two devices into one. This reduces equipment requirements and costs for optical ports and rack space in CO facilities.

Table 12.5 above compares the optical ports required for the two architectures. More equipment involves higher costs for buying, installing, configuring, maintaining, and troubleshooting. The hub and spoke design requires 28 optical ports verses only 14 needed for the RPR ring design.

Separately managing L2/L3 switching and SONET/SDH devices at each location presents more challenges as well. Integrating these functions into an RPR packet ring and managing that one device using existing OSS systems presents additional operational savings.

TABLE 12.5　Optical Port Savings

Optical Port Comparisons	Segment 1 Ports	Segment 2 Ports	Segment 3 Ports	Segment 4 Ports	Segment 5 Ports	Hub A Ports	Hub B Ports	Totals
Hub and Spoke								
L2 / L3 Switch	1	1	1	1	0	0	0	4
ADM	2	2	2	2	0	6	6	20
Router	0	0	0	0	0	2	2	4
Total								28
Ring								
RPR Node	2	2	2	2	2	2	0	12
Router						2	0	2
								14

Vendors Promoting This Solution

Vendor Name	Solution/Product Name	Comment
ADTRAN	Total Access 5000	IP & TDM Broadband Loop Carrier
ALCATEL	1850 TSS	Multiservice Packet Transport Switch (PTS)
CISCO	ONS 15310 Metro Access	Multiservice Provisioning Platform (MSPP)
CORRIGENT	CM-4000	Multiservice Packet Transport Switch (PTS)
FUJITSU	Flashwave 4500	Multiservice Provisioning Platform (MSPP)
HUAWEI	Quidway NetEngine 40	Switch/Router
LUCENT (Alcatel-Lucent)	Metropolis DMX	Multiservice Provisioning Platform (MSPP)
NORTEL	OME 6500	Switch/Router
UTSTARCOM	NetRing10000	Multiservice Provisioning Platform (MSPP)
ZHONE	MALC	IP & TDM Broadband Loop Carrier

Adtran   Adtran's RPR offering is the Total Access(R) 5000 Multi-Service Access and Aggregation Platform. It is designed to deliver IPTV and VOIP along with legacy services across and IP/Ethernet core. Port types include both copper and fiber uplinks for supporting TDM and data applications at many data rates. It has the ability to convert traditional voice and legacy data to IP and provides carriers with a platform capable of integrating with IP Multimedia Subsystems (IMS) standards.

The Total Access 5000 is designed to support IP DSLAM, broadband loop carrier, Fiber to the Node (FTTN), Metro Ethernet services via both fiber and bonded copper access and aggregation. It is available in a 23-inch chassis for US applications as well as a 19-inch chassis for international applications.

Alcatel   Alcatel is an active proponent of RPR with their 1850 Transport Service Switch (TSS). This device integrates Ethernet, TDM, and WDM in a single platform and is promoted as a way for service providers to transition from circuit-based to packet-based transport infrastructures.

The 1850 does not map TDM into Ethernet or data over SONET but rather carries the traffic in a packet format natively on the platform. This contrasts with Multiservice Provisioning Platforms (MSPP) that must map data payloads onto circuits.

The 1850 TSS aggregates, switches, and transports any combination of Ethernet / MPLS / RPR, SONET/SDH, and WDM services.

Carriers can use the 1850 as a universal platform for either TDM or packet with all services on any line card as opposed to having line cards side by side dedicated to each service. This helps with transport network migration issues since any ratio of packet to TDM can be supported in the system. Alcatel claims that the device can provide CapEx savings of more than 30 percent and OpEx savings of more than 40 percent, compared to alternative architectures based on separate platforms.

The 1850 TSS supports a number of sizes to match transport switching capacity requirements. Designed for the metro access market, the Alcatel 1850 TSS-100 supports 60 Gb/s wire-speed data switching capacity and up to 100 Gb/s in mixed packet/TDM/WDM configurations. Other configurations include: 1850 TSS-15, TSS-320, and TSS-640.

Cisco   Cisco got the RPR movement started with their prestandard packet ring protocol known as Dynamic Packet Transport (DPT). It was successfully integrated into routers and sold chiefly into the MSO environment for internet data transport between routers. Over time standard IEEE 802.17 technology has been integrated into specific platforms within the Cisco line. Chief among those is the Cisco ONS 15310 Metro Access (MA) multiservice provisioning platform (MSPP), which delivers Carrier Ethernet services over SONET.

The ONS 15310-MA is a modular access platform that complements the successful Cisco ONS 15454 family of products. It supports existing time division multiplexing (TDM) services with a high-density of DS1/DS3 ports, as well as Ethernet services, over SONET-based networks. It is 1-rack unit (1RU)-high platform designed for use as the last network element in a service provider's network located at the customer premises. It could also be used as an end node in enterprise or campus environment.

Extending the metropolitan edge to customer premises and providing direct high-speed LAN connectivity, the ONS 15310-CL allows service providers to efficiently offer scalable, high-speed data services over their transport networks. The platform supports high optical bandwidth and can drop a DS-1 from an OC-3 or OC-12 stream. In addition, the 15310-CL also provides comprehensive STS- and VT-level bandwidth management and integrated data switching.

Corrigent   The Corrigent CM-4000 line of Packet Transport Switches (PTS) are packet-based multiservice nodes that support the complete range, from 100% circuit traffic, to 100% packet traffic, all on the same device.

The CM-4000 provides efficient packet-based transport for all services including Ethernet, Packet over SDH/SONET (PoS), Frame Relay, ATM and Fiber Channel with full support for all TDM interfaces and SONET/SDH at all data rates. With a 160Gbps or 320 Gbps switching capacity it supports Ring, Linear, and Mesh topologies and scales up to 100Gbps thru link aggregation or ring bonding. It also has Layer 1 and Layer 2 interworking functions. The CM-4000 comes in two sizes, 14 and 6 I/O slot versions; both are 19" ANSI and NEBs compliant.

The Corrigent PTS line was designed for data-centric applications and supports the native transport of Ethernet frames and other data services as packets (without requiring the mapping of Ethernet frames into TDM). When deployed in ring topologies, it relies on RPR to create a lossless shared-media that allows for statistical multiplexing of both data and TDM traffic over the same packet transport infrastructure.

Corrigent incorporates RPR with MPLS, PWE3, Ethernet, and SONET/SDH to deliver a packet-based transport platform for metro and regional applications. Corrigent has been an active advocate of RPR since it's inception as contributors to and editors of the IEEE 802.17 standard. Corrigent provided the Steering and Wrapping portions of the standard.

Fujitsu   Fujitsu's Flashwave 4500 MSSP is a Multiservice switching platform that supports, SONET, Ethernet over SONET (EoS), RPR, Generic Framing Procedure (GFP), Virtual Concatenation (VCAT), and high/low order grooming and switching capabilities. The 4500 allows carriers to offer a wide variety of traditional DS1, DS3, and OC-n private line services, plus carrier-class 10-Mbit to Gigabit Ethernet Private Line (EPL) services, on a single network.

12-port DS3 Transmux interface card enable services across a VT1.5 switch fabric of the 4500 platform to maximize the efficiency of TDM circuits. DS3 Transmux cards can gather hundreds of low capacity VT1.5 circuits from DS1 interface and multiplex them into fully utilized, high capacity STS-1 payloads. Consolidating circuits this way before they enter a digital cross-connect system (DCS) helps carriers postpone or eliminate the capital expense of adding or expanding a DCS.

4-port 10/100Base-T and 2-port Gigabit Ethernet RPR over SONET interface cards operate at Layer 2 on Ethernet circuits. RPR cards create customized partitions between TDM and packet bandwidth. The platform also supports dual port OC-48 units, which double the OC-48 density of the platform from 60 ports to 120 ports in multishelf Flashwave 4500 systems.

Huawei   Huawei offers the Quidway NetEngine 40 as it's entry into the RPR arena. It comes in three configurations the NE40-2, NE40-4, and NE40-8. They have Layer 3 forwarding capabilities and can be used for routing applications and features 2.5G POS interfaces. There are two kinds of modules for the NE40 line: switched and routed. The routed modules support routing features such as wire speed IP/MPLS forwarding, advanced QoS, and MPLS VPN, while the switched modules support Layer 2 VLAN forwarding, VLAN aggregation, VLAN Trunk, L2QoS, RSTP, HGMP (Huawei Group Management Protocol), and VPLS (Virtual Private LAN Service).

Lucent   Lucent's primary RPR platform is the Metropolis DMX Access Multiplexer. It is a SONET/SDH platform that integrates Ethernet/SAN/SONET and is designed to fit between LANs and core backbone networks. It enables Multiservice offerings of both voice and Ethernet/SAN data services. Its contains a scalable switch fabric that can scale from 2.5G to 10G, while its in-service capacity can be upgraded from low to high-density DS1/DS3 circuit, as well as OC-12 to OC-48 and OC-192.

The Metropolis DMX can reduce the requirement for separate routers and data switches by merging SONET and Ethernet functionality onto a single platform. It also supports SAN distance extension with native FC/FICON (1G or 2G) or ESCON interfaces.

Nortel   Nortel was also an early and vigorous proponent of the IEEE 802.17 standard. They were founding members of the RPR Alliance and Editors of the standard. Their primary RPR offering is the OME 6500. It enables service convergence with the availability of integrated, standards-compliant resilient packet ring (RPR) technology on the OME 6500.

RPR capabilities on the OME 6500 include support for multiple Ethernet rings of up to 10Gbps and the ability to provision up to eight classes of service on a per customer and per application basis. Nortel was one of the first vendors to commercially deploy RPR-based technology in 1999. According to the company, since that time they have shipped more than 44,000 RPR ports to customers.

UTStarcom   UTStarcom's NetRing 10000-I is an STM-64 multi-service optical transport system that enables the delivery of SDH services and data services including: ATM, Fast Ethernet, and Gigabit Ethernet. It unifies the functions of a next-generation SDH/SONET ADM, Digital Cross-connect System (DCS), ATM / Ethernet aggregation switch, and Resilient Packet Ring (RPR) in a single shelf device.

It also supports continuous and virtual concatenation at VC-12/3/4 in SDH as well as Generic Framing Procedure (GFP), Link Capacity Adjustment Scheme (LCAS) and provides standards-based Ethernet service functions. The device uses the GFP protocol to map Fast Ethernet and Gigabit Ethernet services into NxVC-12/3/4 circuits. In addition, it provides STM-1/STS-1 and Inverse Multiplexing for ATM (IMA) interfaces.

Zhone   Zhone Technologies, Inc., incorporates RPR technology into their MALC packet loop carrier platforms which are designed to support transport and distribution of voice, data, and video services. MALC facilitates the migration to packet networks by allowing carriers to deploy TDM and ATM technology and provides a path to migrate to IP packet access and transport as needed.

The MALC 319, MALC 719, MALC 723 are Broadband Loop Carrier (BLC) platforms optimized for delivering voice, data, and video services over a pure packet access networks. Designed for use in Central Offices, Remote Terminals, outdoor cabinets, or basements, it supports densities from 24 to 960 ports per shelf with integrated packet ring transport. The MALC integrates line cards, cabling, provisioning and management into one common chassis.

Organizations Adopting RPR Solutions

A number of traditional voice service providers are using RPR based networks to offer high bandwidth services and other high bandwidth applications around the world.

Service Provider Networks in North America   One of the largest service providers in the US, ATT, offers a portfolio of Ethernet services over its' RPR network. Known as Ultravailable and Managed OptEring Services they are designed to provide customers with highly available transport of data, packet video, and voice services. The service creates a virtual LAN and can connect multiple locations in a metro area. It can also be configured as strictly a point-to-point configuration. The service is available in 70 metropolitan locations in 38 states where ATT has local facilities.

According to ATT the OptEring service extends the reach of simplified Layer 2 Ethernet LAN infrastructure across the metro, region or nation. It also supports any mix of TDM and packet traffic. This is a crucial requirement as the mix of circuit and voice traffic evolves and changes over time. It also reduces the need for multi-protocol routers between customer locations simplifying equipment and reducing costs for ATT's customers. In the ATT SLA they offer $24 \times 7 \times 365$ performance monitoring and management. It is recommended for mission-critical applications that require continuous availability and for applications that have unpredictable network demand.

Another large service provider in the US, Verizon, also offers packet services over RPR. The Verizon network, with 11.2 million fiber miles and 6000 SONET rings, is one of the largest in the world. Their RPR offering called EDSR supports Ethernet LAN services. In the US Verizon offers Ethernet (E-LAN services) in 55 metro markets and it also offers the service in 9 European countries. The Verizon service brings simplicity, flexibility, reliability, and total cost of ownership (TCO) advantages that are unmatched by other service types.

EDSR supports private line (DS1-OCn) and Gigabit Ethernet and capacity for scaling from OC-12 to OC-192 are planned for the future. The service is available in bandwidth increments of 50 Mbps, 150 Mbps, 450 Mbps, 600 Mbps, and 1 Gbps.

This RPR based service is designed to address the needs of large enterprise organizations. The following applications and benefits derive from this network offering.

Network Convergence   Currently, most enterprises have a patchwork of technologies within their WAN network. By converging all services onto one packet-based network, significant savings arise from establishing a more uniform network platform.

Multimedia and Application Convergence   Verizon expects packet video and VOIP traffic to increase rapidly. The Yankee Group projects VOIP traffic to double in the next two years. Video is expected to follow the same trajectory. A packet-based RPR network will provide them with the QoS and resilience required of these high-bandwidth applications.

Migration to IP   Enterprise customers are transitioning their multi-office connectivity from private line and Frame Relay to IP so they can build IP-VPNs.

Business Continuity and Disaster Recovery   The requirement to maintain corporate data integrity in times of distress or chaos is driving the need for survivable data networks that insure access to crucial data.

Wiltel Communications, now part of Level 3 is another U. S. provider that has elected to use the IEEE 802.17 standard as a way to construct their next generation converged transport network. Its integrated fiber-optic network provides local-to-global connectivity that links more than 100 cities in the U. S. and reaches five continents. WilTel is also the preferred provider of nationwide long-distance voice and data services for ATT. In addition, it has relationships with more than 40 non-RBOC carriers that add an additional 12,000 off-net locations.

Wiltel built a series of RPR based rings for Multiservice transport platform for the following reasons among others.

■ *Two network elements are consolidated into one.* WDM and ADM network elements were eliminated. In their place the 10 Gbps packet rings provides more bandwidth with ½ the number of devices so they can generate more revenue and reduce costs simultaneously. However, when traffic exceeds the 10 Gbps ring capacity, WDM is still planned as Layer1 transport to scale past 10 Gbps.

■ *Willtel can sell TDM or Data service interchangeably.* The reduction of complexity of equipment and provisioning required to create a new service was important. In addition, services can be changed from circuit to data on the same device and often on the same port. This reduces the time it takes to deliver a new customer service while it increases the probability of competing successfully for new customers.

■ *Only one network is required whatever the mix of services.* Historically, there have been 2 networks required to support both data and voice services. As the proportion of these two services changes, planning for upgrade and support of the services requires educated guesswork about when and where equipment will be needed. The new network supports both services interchangeably, there is never an imbalance between customer demand and carrier infrastructure.

■ *Customers can migrate from TDM to Ethernet with no change to the network.* WilTel expects the mix of services between TDM and Ethernet to fluctuate over time, with Ethernet increasing and TDM decreasing. Because both services are efficiently supported on the same platform, customers can change their service mix over time without a negative impact on the CO equipment requirements.

■ *Statistical multiplexing gains enable higher revenues.* The network was also built because of its efficient use of all bandwidth by best effort services when it is not being used for high priority services.

The cable MSO's in the U. S. have also been actively deploying RPR. Cisco has installations of prestandard RPR (DPT) throughout the U. S. cable industry. More recently ,Cox Communications, Time Warner Cable, Comcast Cable, and Adelphia have installed RPR based rings for their internet access and video requirements. Farther north, Canada also has significant installations of RPR. Bell Canada and Telus both have RPR network installations to provide packet and circuit services in their operating areas.

Service Providers and Utility Networks in Asia   Japan Telecom Co., Ltd. a part of the Softbank Group has built a nationwide network using RPR technology. The Otoku Line services are enabled by the QoS and resilience of RPR. This service has been available since December 2004.

In China utility companies are becoming significant communication service providers both for their own operations and as a service for their customers. One organization that is developing a large regional RPR network is the Central China Power Group. This group is comprised of; Jiangxi Power Company, Jiangxi Province; Hangzhou Power

Company, Zhejiang Province; Baoding Power Company; Tangshan Power Company; and Tangshan Power Plant, Hebei Province. They are using RPR to support mission-critical voice and data traffic for power grid operations.

One of the largest RPR networks in China has been built for another utility the Huazhong Electric Power Group. They use the network to support TDM private line services as well as IP broadband data services on a single converged optical transmission network.

The major incumbent service providers in China are also using RPR for their new network builds. China Unicom recently announced that they have awarded new network contracts to build RPR networks in their service area.

It is not just the fixed-line providers that are deploying RPR. Wireless operator China Mobile, one of the largest mobile operators in the world is also deploying RPR to build a converged network for their customers. They will deliver voice, data, and video services to customers in metropolitan areas throughout their operating area. One of the first deployments Is in Tianjin in northern China where they will add over 200 nodes to their existing network.

Carriers worldwide are adopting RPR as their primary transport method for packet traffic. One is TOKAI inc. a leading LPG company covering the area from Shizuoka prefecture to Fukushima prefecture. This group company, established in 1950, currently engages in many public utility businesses including LP gas, city gas, security, telecommunication, and CATV.

Within the TOKAI group there is a telecommunication business. VicTokai is certified to provide an optical fiber network from Tokyo to Osaka. TOKAI Inc. sells consumer services over ADSL and FTTH and VicTokai sells enterprise services.

Using RPR Tokai and VicTokai offer "partial guaranteed access" which provides maximum bandwidth when it is available and a smaller guaranteed bandwidth when the network is under heavy traffic conditions. This gives the carrier an advantage in pricing. They can offer competitive prices for guaranteed bandwidth and allow their customers to use more bandwidth when it is available. In this case the guaranteed traffic passes through the High Priority transit queues and the Best Effort is allowed on the ring only when space is made available when there is a lack of High Priority traffic.

Japan's largest wireless service provider, KDDI, offers Triple Play and IP TV services to millions of residential customers nationwide over an RPR network. The service includes DVD-grade Video-on-demand, Voice services, Broadband Internet Access, and even KOD (karaoke-on-demand). Moreover, they also offer enhanced-Ethernet services to business customers and backhaul wireless services over the same infrastructure.

Governments and Carrier Networks in the U.S.   Besides being deployed in Japan and China there are many other examples of new IEEE 8021.17 networks being built. Cities and Governments are building private RPR networks for efficient communications among their own buildings and employees.

A number of cities in the U. S. have implemented RPR for their internal networks. The city of Austin, Texas, with a population of 700,000, is implementing resilient packet ring technology for use by its Public Service and Public Communications Departments. The city's telecommunications network is a 350-mile ring architecture that includes all police, emergency medical and fire stations, libraries and administrative offices around the city. There are over 100 nodes covering a total of 170 locations in the city.

The city of Beverly Hills in California and also Philadelphia, Pennsylvania have implemented similar networks to enable communications and conferencing among their various buildings, departments, and offices.

Time Warner Telecom recently announced a large private RPR network for Kettering Medical Center that covers 5 counties in Ohio. 100 Mbps links on the network will be used for patient imaging applications. Other lower speed links will support VOIP and administrative functions like registration, billing, and patient records.

Service Provider Networks in Europe   In Spain, ONO offers telephony, television, and Internet services to customers in 22 regions throughout the country. The company moved to all IP transport network in 2004 for the distribution of 155 TV and five audio channels to enjoy the savings it could realize by dispensing with analogue regional headends. The RPR QoS mechanisms were critical for this video network. Additionally, the ability to (1) simply add and distribute local radio and TV channels and (2) easily create new services were important factors in ONOs selection of RPR for this new network.

Pan-European service provider Vitel recently added RPR to their network in an effort to gain competitive advantage in their service area. Vitel offers Ethernet services in Germany, France, the Netherlands, Belgium, and Switzerland.

In 2004 JSC Ukrtelecom, the national operator in Ukraine also began building a nationwide RPR network. JSC Uketelecom delivers voice and data to 9 million fixed-line subscribers.

FiberNet is a competitive service provider in the UK. In 2004 the Metro Ethernet Forum awarded them the "European Metro Ethernet Service Provider of the Year 2004—Best in Business" for their Ethernet service offering and network implementation. FiberNet also uses RPR as the transport layer for their Ethernet services.

References

1. ANSI T1.105-2001, Synchronous Optical Network (SONET)–Basic Description including Multiplex Structure, Rates, and Formats.

2. ITU-T G.783, Characteristics of Synchronous Digital Hierarchy (SDH) equipment functional blocks.

3. GR-1400-CORE, SONET Dual-Fed Unidirectional Path Switched Ring (UPSR), Generic Criteria.

4. GR-1230-CORE, SONET Bidirectional Line-Switched Ring Equipment, Generic Criteria.

5. GR-253-CORE, SONET Transport Systems, Common Criteria.

6. IEEE 802.17 Resilient Packet Rings.

7. IEEE 802.1d MAC bridges.

8. IEEE 802.1s Multiple Spanning Trees.

9. IEEE 802.1w Rapid Reconfiguration of Spanning Tree.

10. IEEE 802.3ad Link Aggregation.

11. IETF RFC 3469, Framework for Multi-Protocol Label Switching (MPLS)-based Recovery.

12. ITU-T G.783, Characteristics of Synchronous Digital Hierarchy (SDH) equipment functional blocks.

Ethernet Bridging

by Norman Finn

No standards organization owns the term *Ethernet*. But if you had to define *Ethernet*, you would do well to start with the definition of the services offered by a wired or wireless network, including bridges, as defined by the Institute of Electrical and Electronic Engineers Standards Association LAN/MAN Standards Committee, or IEEE 802. This starting point is merited by the ubiquity of IEEE 802-compliant equipment. Practically any protocol or service that can utilize an Ethernet link of any type can also utilize a bridged network of Ethernet devices.

The simplest and most straightforward way to deliver Ethernet services to customers is to use established Ethernet equipment and services, rather than "Ethernet over *xyz*," where *xyz* can be SONET, MPLS, ATM, or any other technology. When looking at how a service provider can implement a metro Ethernet network, try starting with the question, "Can you scale an enterprise network to one supporting millions of subscribers spread over a continent?" This is a problem that a number of bridge vendors have addressed successfully and that the IEEE 802.1 Higher-Layer Interworking Group has been standardizing.

Figure 13.1 shows the architecture. The overall network consists of independent clouds of bridges. There are two kinds of clouds, provider bridged networks (clouds C through H) and provider backbone bridged networks (clouds A and B). Each provider bridged network supplies up to 4094 instances of the MAC service to customers, each with an Ethernet Virtual Connection (EVC).

Provider bridged networks can be linked together, as are clouds F and G. Within each cloud, there are 4094 service instances (EVCs), but only those EVCs that span both clouds require VLANs (each identified by a VLAN ID (VID)). VLANs for EVCs that span only a single cloud can be reused in the attached cloud. For example, you could use 1000 VIDs for VLANs spanning both clouds F and G, leaving 3000 VIDs for local use in each cloud F and G, for a total of 7000 VLANs.

Provider bridged networks can be interconnected via backbone clouds in two different ways. In Figure 13.1, clouds D, E, F, and H are connected in the most typical manner.

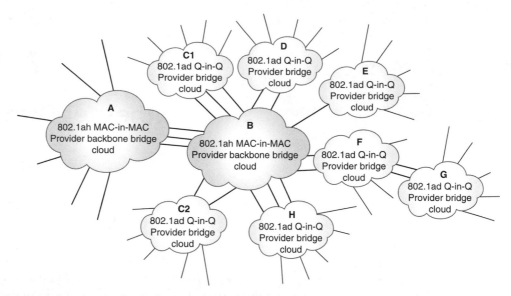

Figure 13.1   Metro Ethernet implemented with IEEE 802.1 bridges

Up to 16 million (2^{24}) individual EVCs can traverse the backbone core. (More, if you are willing to accept the headache caused by spatial reuse of identifiers.) Each of the 4094 EVCs in a given provider bridge network is translated to one of the 16M backbone instances at the edge of the backbone network. Those EVCs are, in turn, tunneled inside an outer encapsulation that enables the backbone network to see only tunnels containing 1 or 1000s of EVCs, instead of seeing individual EVCs. An EVC can be connected in an arbitrary fashion to any number of provider bridge networks, and each provider bridged network's VID is independent of any other cloud's VID.

Alternatively, two provider bridge networks, C1 and C2 in Figure 13.1, can tunnel through the backbone cloud using a single 16M backbone EVC. In this case, clouds C1 and C2 are in the same logical relationship as clouds F and G; they are simply using the backbone cloud, instead of a physical link, for their connectivity.

Technology Description

In order to understand fully how the network shown in Figure 13.1 works, we must start with some basics. In spite of their ubiquity, the knowledge of exactly how bridges work is somewhat scarce, so a semi-historical introduction is in order.

The original DEC/Intel/Xerox Ethernet was standardized by IEEE Std 802.3, Carrier Sense Multiple Access/Collision Detection (CSMA/CD) Ethernet. The original Ethernet provided users with access to a local area network (LAN) consisting of a single large-diameter coaxial trunk cable (usually bright yellow), with "taps" (or medium attachment units) through which stations could connect to the cable. Every data frame transmitted by any station was seen by every other station attached to the trunk cable.

Every station had a globally unique 48-bit Media Access Control (MAC) address. It was up to each station to filter the frames whose destination addresses were of no interest, i.e., those whose destination address fields contained another station's address or a multicast address that the station was not interested in receiving. Thus, since Ethernet's beginnings, both *unicast* (the destination address corresponds to a particular station) and *multicast* (the destination address corresponds to some subset of stations or to all stations) frames have been an essential part of the service offered by a LAN. So has the notion that the service offered by an Ethernet LAN (the "MAC service") is one of getting a message to at least the station(s) to whom it is addressed, not necessarily to just those stations.

The need to concatenate two or more coaxial trunk cables economically into what, to the connected stations, appeared to be a single trunk cable, arose almost instantly. The bridge, standardized by IEEE Std 802.1D, was one result[1]. At first approximation, a bridge between two coaxial trunks is trivial. It appears as a station on each trunk; every frame it receives from trunk 1, it relays to trunk 2, and vice-versa.

One obvious optimization, not relaying every frame, was made in the first bridge standard. For example, suppose stations A and B are both on trunk 1. If A sends a frame with B as its destination address, there is no point in the bridge relaying that frame to trunk 2. But how does the bridge know which trunks A and B are connected to? They could somehow register with the bridge, but one of the goals of IEEE Std 802.1D was to make the bridge invisible to the stations. That is, no station (and as important, no software in a station) needed to be modified when a coaxial trunk was extended with a bridge.

When first initialized, therefore, the bridge does relay every frame between the two trunks; it doesn't know any better. Soon, however, the bridge receives a frame, with A in its source address (the address of the station sending the frame), on trunk 1. The bridge remembers that it received a frame from A on trunk 1 while it relays that frame to the other trunks. If it later receives another frame with A as the destination address (perhaps from station B), also from trunk 1, it knows not to relay that frame to trunk 2. The bridge knows that A will also receive it, because it has learned that station A is on trunk 1. If the bridge receives a frame addressed to station A on trunk 2 (or on trunk 3 or trunk 4) however, it knows to relay that frame to trunk 1, where it has learned that A resides. The bridge stores this information about stations' addresses and trunks in its filtering database.

What if someone disconnects station A from trunk 1 and connects it to trunk 2 instead? If A transmits any frame on trunk 2, the bridge learns its new LAN association

---

[1] The term *switch* has, in recent years, come to be almost synonymous with the term *bridge*. Historically, the difference has not been a technical one: "*Your* company makes those old-fashioned bridges; *my* company makes those cool new switches!" The term *switch* was first applied to bridges in the mid-1990s when the ability to snoop on, and even act on, Layer 3 IP information was added to bridges. Terminology inflation has since ensured that even the most basic standard bridges are marketed as "switches." Now that the common carrier world, whose networks are traditionally composed of switches, is utilizing Ethernet technology, there are standards emerging from the ITU-T that define Ethernet switches. This chapter uses the term *bridge* when referring to an IEEE 802-defined device and *switch* when referring to an ITU-T-defined circuit switching device.

immediately. But, if A remains silent waiting for another station to talk to it, and if that other station is on, say, trunk 1, it might wait forever; the bridge, having learned that A is on trunk 1, will not relay frames addressed to A from trunk 1. Therefore, there is a timeout on every entry in the bridge's filtering database. After five minutes without receiving a frame with A in its source address, the entry for A is removed. The next frame sent to A will be relayed to all trunks because the bridge no longer knows what else to do. As soon as A responds, its location is learned.

Note that in the worst case, A responds on some other medium entirely, so the bridge never learns A's Ethernet MAC address. In that case, the bridged LAN is no worse off than if it were all one coaxial trunk.

Redundancy and Spanning Trees

What if the bridge fails now? All of the stations on any given LAN can speak to each other, but no frames can flow from LAN to LAN. Figure 13.2 shows two bridges, X and Y, both connecting trunk 1 to trunk 2. What happens if station A on trunk 1 transmits a broadcast frame (a frame whose destination MAC address is FF-FF-FF-FF-FF-FF)? Both bridges would receive the frame, and if both behaved as described in the preceding section, both would forward the frame to trunk 2.

It is important, at this point, to note something about basic IEEE 802.1D bridges; they do not alter the forwarded frame. The broadcast frame forwarded by each bridge to trunk 2 is exactly the same, bit-for-bit, as the original frame transmitted by station A.

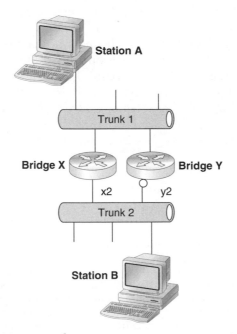

Figure 13.2 Simple spanning tree example

Each bridge sees the frame transmitted by the other bridge. There is nothing in the frame that indicates the frame was transmitted by a bridge and not by station A; the frame still has station A as its source address. Therefore, each of the two bridges learns that station A has moved to trunk 2, based on the frame's source address (!) and forwards the frame back to trunk 1. Each of the two copies of the broadcast frame is relayed back and forth between the two trunks forever, or until a transmission error causes the frame to be lost. In the meantime, each station on both trunks receives thousands of copies of the broadcast, so frames destined for station A are often erroneously forwarded to the wrong trunk 2, where A was mistakenly (though briefly) learned, and the network's bandwidth is quickly saturated. This condition is called a *broadcast storm*.

The solution to this problem is that bridges do not automatically start forwarding frames from one port to another the instant they are turned on. Instead, they run a version of the Spanning Tree Protocol (STP). The two bridges, X and Y in Figure 13.2, detect each others' presence, and one of them (let's suppose bridge Y) disables the forwarding of frames through one of its ports (port Y2 in Figure 13.2, which is marked with a circle). With no data frames passing through this one port, there are no longer any loops in the network and therefore no broadcast storm. If bridge X later fails, bridge Y detects the loss of STP packets and re-enables its port Y2, restoring connectivity between the LANs.

STP and its successors, the Rapid Spanning Tree Protocol (RSTP) and the Multiple Spanning Tree Protocol (MSTP), operate on the same principles:

- One bridge in the network is elected *root bridge* and serves as the anchor for the spanning tree.

- One of the bridges connected to each LAN is elected *designated bridge* for that LAN. This bridge is either the root bridge itself or the bridge closest to the root bridge as measured by the costs described in the next point. The designated bridge's port on a LAN is called a *designated port*, and always forwards data. A bridge advertises its distance (*total path cost*) to the root bridge on each of its designated ports.

- Each bridge that is not the designated bridge for a given LAN assigns a "cost" parameter to that LAN, adds that cost to the cost advertised by the designated bridge, and computes the total cost to reach the root bridge through that port. The port with the lowest total path cost to the root bridge is that bridge's root port. That port forwards data. All the other ports on that bridge that are not designated ports or alternate ports are blocked from forwarding data.

- If two or more ports in a single bridge are connected to the same LAN, and one of those ports is a designated port or a root port, then the others are backup ports and are blocked.

- If the selection of the root bridge, designated bridge, or root port results in a tie, e.g., if two candidates for designated bridge are equidistant from the root bridge, then tiebreakers are used. The first tiebreaker is a priority configured on the bridge or port by the system administrator, followed by the MAC address assigned to the bridge or port. Because MAC addresses are globally unique, all ties can be broken.

■ Whenever a port first appears, the bridge waits a certain amount of time, transmitting Spanning Tree Protocol packets, before it forwards traffic to or from that port. This prevents temporary loops in case the port is connected to another bridge and should be blocked. Other timers are invoked in certain situations to block ports for a short period of time to make it impossible to have even a temporary forwarding loop.

In-band Signaling

In order to pass the control protocols that run the STP and protocols that are particular to single LANs, and in order to provide for future expansion, 16 multicast destination MAC addresses have been reserved. These addresses are of the form, 01-80-C0-00-00-0x (hexadecimal), where the last 4 bits (x) range from 0 through F. A non-VLAN bridge never forwards a frame from one port to another if it has one of these addresses as its destination. Stations should never use these addresses, except when running protocols defined to use these addresses, generally between the station and the nearest bridge.

Bridging versus Routing

Bridging has been presented so far as a natural progression based on the characteristics of the original Ethernet media and the need for plug-and-play interoperability. It is now time to step back and see what the essential differences are between bridges and routers, which are a somewhat more familiar technology to many readers.

The essential characteristics of a bridged LAN and some of the differences between bridged networks and routed networks include the following:

■ Bridges operate on 48-bit Ethernet MAC addresses, not 32- or 128-bit IP addresses. MAC addresses are, in essence, globally unique manufacturers' serial numbers. Unlike IP addresses, MAC addresses convey no information about where a device is located. Because there is no geographical hierarchy to MAC addresses, there are no subnetworks.

■ Routes are established among the bridges, irrespective of the addresses of the stations. These routes are spanning trees. Each spanning tree is "spanning" in the sense that there is a path between every pair of LANs, and it is a "tree" in the sense that there is only one such path. Routes are not computed to stations or to subnetworks.

■ Given that there is only one path between any pair of LANs, A and B, and that the path from A to B is identical to the path from B to A, each bridge is able to learn the direction in which each station lies by observing the flow of traffic. Unlike routing, no station addresses (or subnetwork addresses) are conveyed by the control protocols.

■ The spanning tree protocols are mathematically incapable of forwarding frames in a closed loop, even momentarily. Therefore, except at the entrance to or exit from a service boundary, a bridge does not alter the frames it forwards. Unlike with routers, with bridges, there is no time-to-live (TTL) decremented as a frame is forwarded from bridge to bridge for two reasons: no routing loops are possible, and bridges must be transparent to the stations they serve.

- Because of the spanning trees, bridges almost always deliver frames in the same order in which they were transmitted. Exceptions cannot occur in the older versions of the Spanning Tree Protocols and are extremely rare in the newer versions, even when a link or bridge is lost or regained in the network. Routers attempt to keep packets in order, but make no guarantees. Duplicated or out-of-order packets are common when the network topology changes.

Virtual LANs

Since the completion of IEEE Std 802.1Q-2005, Virtual LANs (VLANs) have been available as a standard feature of bridges. VLANs enable a bridged network to offer up to 4094 separate instances of the MAC service, with each one connecting one or more LANs. Since a VLAN bridge cannot transfer a frame from one VLAN to another, and since the MAC address space of each VLAN can be configured to be independent of every other VLAN, VLANs provide the basic service characteristic that customers of Carrier Ethernet service require—isolation from other customers. A VLAN is perfectly equivalent to an EVC. As a consequence, the IEEE Std 802.1Q VLANs were offered to customers by service providers as soon as they were standardized.

A VLAN bridge associates every received data frame with a VLAN, either implicitly by configuring the port on which it was received or explicitly by a VLAN tag, as shown in Figure 13.3. (Figure 13.3 calls this a *C-VLAN tag*, for reasons that will become apparent in the next section.) Most stations are not VLAN-aware. They transmit and receive untagged Ethernet frames, as shown in Figure 13.3a. Each port of a VLAN bridge is configured with a port VLAN ID (PVID). Untagged frames received by the bridge are assigned to the PVID. The bridge may be configured to discard tagged frames or to discard frames not tagged with the PVID, in order to enforce its configuration upon the stations on the LAN. Similarly, all frames transmitted by the bridge to non-VLAN-aware stations are untagged; otherwise, a non-VLAN-aware station would be unable to decode the frame.

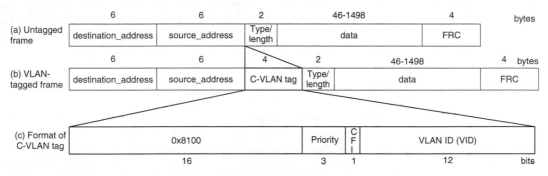

Figure 13.3   C-tag or Q-tag frame format for 802.1Q VLAN bridges

If a station knows about VLAN tags, but does not know what particular VID its LAN has been assigned by the bridge, then it may transmit a tagged frame as in Figure 13.3b, but with a 0 in the VLAN ID. A 0 VLAN ID means, "I don't know"; the bridge assigns the frame to the PVID. This enables a station to indicate a priority in the frame's VLAN tag. The bridge attached to such a station may be configured either to transmit frames VLAN-tagged with the PVID or to transmit untagged frames. Bridges cannot transmit frames with a 0 VID.

On a LAN that connects two (or more) bridges, the bridges typically include the VLAN tag, as in Figure 13.3b and 13.3c. This allows frames on as many as 4094 VLANs to be carried on a single LAN. Typically, the only VLAN-aware stations are routers. (To a bridge, a router is a station, just like a PC or a printer is a station.) In an enterprise network, each VLAN typically corresponds to an IP subnetwork, and the router is required to route packets from one subnetwork (VLAN) to another subnetwork (VLAN).

VLAN and MAC Address Pruning

If a bridge has not learned a particular MAC address, then when a frame destined for that address is received, the bridge floods the frame on all ports on the spanning tree. Similarly, by default, any broadcast or multicast frame is flooded to all ports on the spanning tree. When the loss or recovery of a link or a bridge changes the spanning tree, many MAC addresses are forgotten and the flooding of unknown addresses can saturate a network's physical carrying capacity. Furthermore, ordinary amounts of broadcast and multicast traffic, if flooded everywhere, could waste considerable bandwidth on an ongoing basis.

Bridged networks avoid this problem by pruning both VLANs and multicast MAC addresses. VLANs are pruned using the *Multiple VLAN Registration Protocol* (MVRP, IEEE 802.1ak), recently completed. Multicast MAC addresses are pruned by means of the bridges "snooping" on the same Layer 3 Internet Group Multicast Protocol (IGMP) used to regulate the IP multicasts that carry most high-volume multicast traffic.

In a nutshell, MVRP allows each bridge to register with each of its neighbors which VLANs' frames it needs to have delivered to it. A bridge registers with its neighbors all of the VLANs for which it has ports configured. For example, if a bridge has two untagged ports, A and B, configured to default incoming frames to VLANs 5 and 7, respectively, then it will register VLANs 5 and 7 with its neighbor bridges. In addition, if a bridge receives a registration for an additional VLAN from a neighbor bridge, then it registers that VLAN with all of the other bridges (but not back toward that neighbor bridge, unless some other bridge needs it). Whenever the spanning tree topology changes, MVRP immediately reregisters the VLANs.

Given this VLAN registration information, each bridge creates one-way filters that prevent any traffic for a given VLAN from being transmitted on a port, unless a neighbor attached to that port has registered that it needs to receive that VLAN. Thus, frames on a particular VLAN are never forwarded toward those parts of the network where they are not needed.

Although there was a similar protocol, the Generic Multicast Registration Protocol (GMRP), for registering multicast MAC addresses, it did not gain acceptance in the market. Instead, bridges typically "snoop" on IGMP packets, and may even intercept, summarize, and reissue IGMP packets themselves, as if they were routers. Although this violates the principles of proper layering, it has proven to be a cost-effective solution to the problem of distributing multicast streams, which can take up considerable bandwidth, to parts of the bridged network where they are not needed.

Priority

The 3-bit priority field in the Q-tag provides eight priority levels. This is supported by bridges in one standard way, with each vendor free to add additional capabilities. So the default priority can be 0, but not the lowest possible priority, the order of importance of frames is, from most important to least important, 7, 6, 5, 4, 3, 0, 2, 1.

In all implementations, each output bridge port has some number of output queues from 1 to 8. The 3-bit priority field is used to decide in which queue to place each frame for subsequent output. A bridge may implement any number from 1 to 8 queues, and this may be a configurable parameter. Every bridge must offer the capability of draining those queues in strict priority order. That is, if any frames are in the queue to which priority 7 frames are assigned, then that queue must be selected for output. If that queue is empty, then a frame is transmitted from the queue to which priority 6 frames are assigned, and so on through priorities 5, 4, 3, 0, 2, and finally 1. Which priority values are mapped to which queues if fewer than 8 queues are implemented are defined in IEEE Std. 802.1Q-2005; however, these assignments can be overridden by management.

A bridge may provide other queue-draining algorithms as well. Practically every vendor that supplies bridges with multiple queues offers the capability of limiting the share of bandwidth available to each priority level, so that a long burst of high-priority traffic does not lock out all lower priority traffic. Although the field is called *priority* field, it is really a class-of-service indicator.

Provider Bridges—Q-in-Q

As soon as providers started using VLANs to carry different customers' data, the question arose, "What if customers are already using VLANs?" Several ad hoc solutions were tried by various vendors, and these led eventually to IEEE Std 802.1ad-2005 for provider bridges.

An 802.1ad provider bridge is simply an 802.1Q VLAN bridge with five modifications:

- A provider bridge uses a slightly different format for its VLAN tag (see Figure 13.4.)
- A provider bridge blocks a reduced set of destination multicast MAC addresses. Of the 16 addresses never forwarded by a non-VLAN bridge, a provider bridge still blocks 11 of them, but forwards 5 of them transparently.
- A provider bridge can implement standardized rate policing.

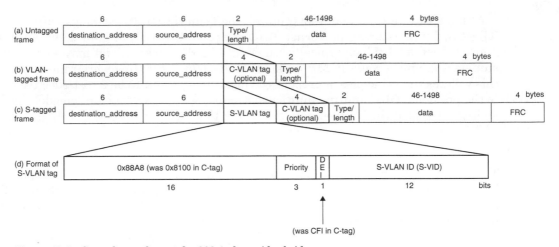

Figure 13.4   S-tag frame format for 802.1ad provider bridges

- A provider bridge has VID translation capability at each port.
- A provider bridge has a "C-tagged interface" that can deal with the customers' Q-tags in interesting ways.

We will examine these modifications one at a time, in the context of the problems they solve.

S-VLAN Tags   The existing 802.1Q tag is now called a *C-tag*, or *customer tag*. Looking back at Figure 13.3c, you can see that tag has an Ethertype (0×8100), a 3-bit priority field, a 1-bit Canonical Format Indicator (CFI) field, and a 12-bit VLAN ID (VID). As mentioned previously, a VID of 0 indicates "unknown VID," so the VID is determined by the bridge's configuration, and that VID 4095 ($0 \times FFF$) is illegal. The priority field has the same meaning as in the C-tag.

The CFI was defined for use in mixed token ring (IEEE 802.5) and Ethernet environments. If this bit is set, it indicates that a variable-length routing information field follows the C-tag and precedes the type/length field. This field has never found widespread use and thus was available for redefinition in the S-tag.

The S-tag is shown in Figure 13.4d. It is identical to the C-tag except for the EtherType ($0 \times 88A8$ instead of 0×8100) and the Drop Eligible Indicator (DEI) bit in place of the CFI bit. The DEI bit and its associated implementation inside the bridge provide two levels of delivery priority on top of the eight priority levels provided by the C-tag. The DEI is explained in "Rate Policing," later in this chapter.

On the typical provider bridge port, the EtherType used to recognize a VLAN tag is the S-tag value $0 \times 88A8$. A frame tagged (by the customers' equipment) with a C-tag (EtherType 0×8100) is, therefore, as far as the provider bridge's receiving port is concerned, untagged. (The exception to this rule is the C-tagged interface, described next.) The received frame is assigned the PVID for that port. You may assume, for the moment, that each customer is assigned to a different VLAN and that VLAN's ID is the PVID for each port connected to that customer. The port is configured to allow only that VID to pass in or out. When frames belonging to different customers pass over the same trunk between provider bridges, those frames may have both a C-tag and an S-tag. This is the "Q-in-Q" format shown in Figure 13.4c. Whether the C-tag is present is the choice of the customer; it makes no difference to the provider. The S-tag is necessary for the provider to keep each customer's traffic separate from the other customers.

Figure 13.5 points out one limitation of the Q-in-Q model. In Figure 13.5, there are three customer VLAN bridges, X, Y, and Z, connected via four provider bridges, P, Q, R, and S. For clarity, no other customers' ports or equipment is shown. The customer is using two C-VLANs, the solid and the dotted lines. The provider is carrying the customer's traffic in a single S-VLAN, shown as a wide gray band in the illustration. Each of the customer's five stations, of which two are routers and three are workstations, are labeled with their MAC addresses, A through D.

Every Ethernet station is built with a globally unique MAC address. A network can, however, be operated by overriding that globally unique MAC address with a locally administered MAC address. These addresses are defined in IEEE Std 802-2006. If the next-to-low-order bit in the first byte of the MAC address (02-00-00-00-00-00) is set, then the network administrator is free to use any value in the remaining 46 bits (the low bit of the first byte is the multicast/unicast indication). This technique is not commonly used today because of the likelihood that a configuration error will result in unintentionally duplicated MAC addresses.

There is, unfortunately for bridges, a far more likely reason for duplicate MAC addresses. IETF RFC 3768 defines the Virtual Router Redundancy Protocol (VRRP). Running this protocol can result in two (or more) routers having the same MAC address, though on different VLANs. In Figure 13.5, two routers are circled. One is on the customer's dotted VLAN and one on the customer's solid VLAN, but both have the same MAC address, A.

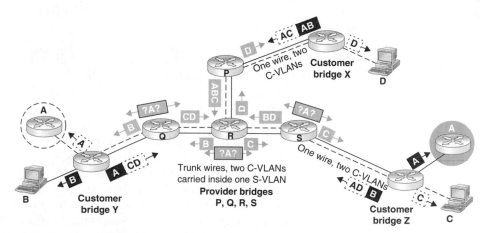

Figure 13.5 Duplicate MAC address problem

This duplicated MAC address is no problem for the three customer bridges, X, Y, and Z. As shown in Figure 13.5, each of the customer bridges is aware of the two VLANs and keeps the MAC addresses in the two VLAN separate in its filtering database. Each learns that dotted A is on one port and solid A is on another port.

Some of the provider bridges, particularly bridge R, have a problem, however. Once the customer's frames enter the provider's network, they have an outer S-tag applied. The provider bridges forward frames based on the S-VID and the MAC addresses in the frame. They do *not* look inside the frame at the C-tags. (See "Proper Layering" next) Bridge R sees a frame with source MAC address A on the gray S-VLAN coming from both directions and cannot tell in which direction to send frames from D bound for (solid) A.

Note that there is no confusion in the provider's network among different customers. MAC addresses in the gray S-VLAN are kept completely separate from any other customers' MAC addresses. The problem is strictly one of duplicated MAC addresses within a single S-VLAN.

Fortunately, this situation is relatively easy for the customer to avoid. One way is for the customer to configure VRRP so the two routers do not share a common MAC address. The other is for the customer to purchase two separate EVCs in two separate S-VLANs and make sure no address is duplicated in either S-VLAN. In this case, the dotted C-VLAN could stay in the same S-VLAN, and the solid C-VLAN could be moved to a new S-VLAN. If the customer is unaware of this possibility, however, it can take some effort to resolve and can involve some avoidable finger pointing.

Although this problem condition is easy for a customer to avoid, it does point out why you cannot easily build a "Q-in-Q-in-Q" bridge (or a "4-Q" or a "5-Q" bridge). One customer can adjust his or her configuration to avoid this problem. But, adding a third VLAN tag means that two or more different customers' EVCs are packed inside a single outermost VLAN tag. A provider cannot expect those customers, perhaps all running VRRP, to cooperate in their network configurations in order to avoid this duplicate address problem. This is especially true since, if one of those customers' network administrators makes a configuration error, all of the customers will suffer from the consequent misdirection of frames.

Proper Layering   Why can't a bridge simply look at two tags and differentiate between the two routers? The answer is *layering*. Protocol layering is the most fundamental principle in networking, and its use is precisely why you do not need to upgrade every piece of network equipment in the world every time one carrier or another adds a new feature to its network. Layering means that a new LAN can be substituted for Ethernet, as long as it looks to the upper layers like Ethernet. VLANs were added to bridges without disrupting the operations of stations because the same service was offered to the stations as was offered before VLANs were introduced.

When protocols are properly layered, protocol "entities" in different systems communicate with each other as peers, utilizing the services provided by lower layers and offering some service to the higher layers. They can be stacked ad infinitum. Although this sounds trivial, it has a direct effect on tags added to frames. If one entity adds a tag (e.g., a C-tag) as a frame leaves a port, then its peer entities, and *only* its peer entities, have any business inspecting the contents of that tag, and if the frame is passed up the stack of entities at the receiving end, the tag is removed. That way, the next-higher layer of entities in each stack can peer with each other.

If one entity tries to "peek" at another entity's tag besides its own, e.g., if a bridge looks at both tags, it violates the layering principle and thus stifles future progress. If it cannot peek at the other tag, however, it cannot do its job. If it does peek at the other tag, then no new layer of entities, and hence no new tag, can ever be inserted between the two. Layer insertion, one of the principle justifications for layering, would be lost. And of course, layer insertion is exactly how VLANs came about! Thus, peeking at two VLAN tags would inhibit the ability of bridges to grow new features in the future.

The astute reader will observe that "IGMP snooping" violates layering principles. If a tag is added to Ethernet frames being carried transparently through a bridged network, one that the bridges do not peer with, then the bridges can no longer snoop on IGMP frames. Introducing a useful layer-crossing feature has thus placed a restriction on future development.

MAC Address Transparency   The provider, of course, runs a Spanning Tree Protocol algorithm to maintain a loop-free active topology in the provider network. The many customers of that provider network, assuming for a moment they are using bridges (as shown in Figure 13.5), are also presumably running STP. This is especially important if a customer has two or more connections from one of his or her networks to the provider's network.

Forwarding loops and the consequent broadcast storms could be avoided if all of these interconnected bridges, both customer and provider bridges, ran a single globally connected instance of the Spanning Tree Protocol. This is not practical, however. One reason is that the STP protocols simply do not scale to encompass all of the provider and all of the customer bridges in the world. Another is that these protocols depend on certain configuration parameters that must be coordinated in the different bridges in a network. The cooperation required among system administrators would be prohibitive, and any error by any administrator could affect the whole world.

A very simple way to keep the providers' spanning trees separate from the customers' spanning trees was adopted by IEEE Std 802.1ad-2005. As mentioned in "In-Band Signaling," a standard customer bridge (C-bridge) transmits and receives frames carrying the Spanning Tree Control protocols (*bridge protocol data units*, or *BPDUs*) using the destination MAC address 01-80-C2-00-00-00 and prevents all frames whose destination MAC address is in the 01-80-C2-00-00-00 through ...-0F range from being relayed from port to port. A provider bridge, however, is different. It uses 01-80-C2-00-00-08 for its BPDUs and forwards frames with destination MAC addresses ...-00, ...-0A, ...-0B, ...-0C, and ...-0F through the provider bridge just like any other ordinary multicast frame. The customers' BPDUs are thus just like any other multicast data to the provider bridge.

Rate Policing   In the carrier environment, it may be convenient for the provider to supply an interface that works at a higher physical rate than the bit rate offered the customer, especially since standard IEEE 802.3 Ethernet link speeds are whole powers of

10–10 Mbps, 100 Mbps, 1 Gbps, and so on. The simple rate policing offered by a provider bridge simply discards all frames in excess of the customer's guarantee. However, more sophisticated control is made possible by the *Drop Eligible Indicator (DEI)* bit in the S-tag.

The need for the DEI bit can be illustrated by a provider/customer service-level agreement (SLA) that specifies that the provider guarantees the customer can transfer 15 Mbps and can transfer up to 50 Mbps on a best-effort basis as the provider's network bandwidth allows. Let's suppose that four customers, all with this same SLA, are being carried over a single 100 Mbps LAN. The 60 Mbps total of guaranteed traffic is perhaps sustainable. Suppose, however, three of the customers are blasting 50 Mbps, and the fourth only the guaranteed 15 Mbps. The offered load is then 165 Mbps on a 100 Mbps LAN. Certainly, the provider does not want the excess traffic from the three customers to cause the remaining customer to lose frames.

If the bridge transmitting to this LAN simply marked, for each customer, all frames in excess of 15 Mbps to a lower priority (say, from 5 to 4), and if those two priority levels went into different queues (so the frames conformant to the SLA could be transmitted in preference to those in the 15–50 Mbps range), there would be a problem. Suppose a customer transmits first frame A and then frame B. Suppose the bridge decides that frame A is in excess of the 15 Mbps limit and marks it with priority 4, but frame B is OK and marks it with priority 5. Then, frame B could be delivered to its destination before frame A. Using this example, this would happen very frequently.

Provider bridges, therefore, have a Drop Eligible Indicator (DEI) in the S-tag and a definition of rate policing that supports the DEI. A bridge port can be configured, for example, to discard all of the above customers' traffic exceeding 50 Mbps, to set the DEI bit for all frames between 15 Mbps and 50 Mbps, and to clear the DEI bit for frames under 15 Mbps. Thus, frames are either "green" (DEI = 0), "yellow" (DEI = 1), or "red" (discarded). In a typical implementation, each queue (selected by the priority, not by the DEI bit) has two thresholds for discarding frames that don't fit when the queue is full—the real size of the queue is used for green frames, and a smaller size is used for yellow frames. So yellow frames can only be queued for transmission if the buffer is, say, less than half full, while green frames can use the whole queue.

With the addition of the DEI, the 15/50 Mbps example works. The traffic from each customer in excess of 15 Mbps is marked yellow. That traffic can compete for queue space only to a point; if the queue starts to fill up, only green traffic can pass. This way, even if alternate frames of a stream are marked yellow, all of the frames not dropped go to the same queue and are delivered in order.

VID Translation   Two different provider networks may need to be connected together so that both can cooperate in serving some number of customers' needs that neither can satisfy alone. The two providers cannot be expected to manage their VLANs in the same manner so the same EVC may use two different VLAN IDs in the two different provider networks. Across the network-network interface (NNI), therefore, some translation of the VLAN IDs is necessary.

IEEE Std 802.1ad-2005 provides for translation from one VLAN ID to another in both the input and output directions on each bridge port. When such translation occurs, if the providers are using any of the bridge control protocols that have internal references to VLAN IDs, those internal references are translated by the bridges in the same manner as the data frames. Any VLAN tags carried inside the outermost VLAN tags, e.g., C-tags inside S-tags, are unaffected by this transformation, as proper layering dictates.

Note that translating in one direction only would be adequate for point-to-point links. However, as soon as three bridges or more are connected to a single medium, e.g., to an EVC offered by another provider, translation in both directions is necessary in the general case. On a shared medium, there must be a "wire" VLAN ID for each EVC, and each bridge must translate in both directions between the "wire" VLAN ID and the ID used in that bridge's network.

Interconnecting Clouds of Bridges An EVC with three ports, as shown in Figure 13.5, looks to the customer's spanning tree algorithm just like the large diameter coax cable in Figure 13.2. There are some things that a customer must be very careful of, however, if he or she sends BPDUs over a provider's network.

First of all, the provider's network components are not, of course, perfectly reliable. When a failure, an addition to the network, or a significant configuration change takes place, the flow of customer data may be interrupted until the provider's spanning tree algorithm can correct the situation. If both the provider's and the customer's spanning tree algorithms are using the same default timers for the transmission and timeout intervals, then there is a very real chance that both networks will detect an error when a provider change occurs. When the provider has restored connectivity, the customer may experience a temporary data loop.

The customer can avoid this problem simply by increasing the value of the port hello time on those ports that face the provider. The default is 2 sec. You can ask the provider what time is appropriate for a customer network that is transmitting BPDUs over the provider network, but a value three times larger than the provider's bridge hello time is appropriate.

An interesting situation for the customer who runs BPDUs over the provider network is shown in Figure 13.6. In this figure, the customer is using the provider network as a four-port E-LAN EVC connecting four ports in the customer's two clouds. The purpose of the EVC is to provide redundant connectivity for each cloud, so the two clouds can have maximum connectivity in the face of failures. Presumably, each of the eight ports shown as small black circles in Figure 13.6 are in eight different bridges in the provider's and the customer's network.

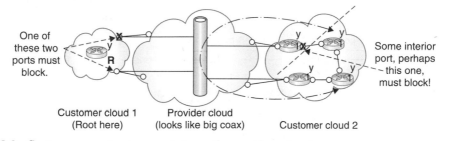

Figure 13.6 Customer spanning tree carried over the provider network

The root bridge of the customer's spanning tree must be somewhere; we assume it is in the left cloud in Figure 13.6. One of the ports from this cloud must be blocked in order to prevent frames from looping through the provider network in and out of the left cloud. What is interesting in Figure 13.6 is that, because both of the customer bridge ports facing the EVC have equal costs to reach the root bridge in the left cloud, neither of those two ports will be blocked. Some other port on one of those bridges will be blocked in order to prevent endless forwarding loops. Therefore, those stations in the right cloud connected directly to the bridge whose port is blocked can only reach the other parts of the right cloud via the provider network!

Again, this problem has solutions. See "Bridge Gateways," later in the chapter.)

C-tagged Interfaces   A number of considerations led to the standardization of C-tagged interfaces in IEEE Std 802.1ad-2005. One was the port blocking problem shown in Figure 13.6. The other was the desire of providers to offer more than just the port-based EVC described so far, wherein everything entering the provider bridge port is assigned to the same S-VLAN in the provider network. With the C-tagged interface, the customer can select from among any number of EVCs (up to 4094) using C-tags.

Figure 13.7 shows a simple example of complex EVCs, with two customers attached to a single provider edge bridge. The provider edge bridge is split into two kinds of components, the S-components and the C-components. Each is, in theory, simply an 802.1Q VLAN bridge. The C-component is exactly the same as the customer's 802.1Q VLAN bridge. The S-component is identical, except that it uses the S-tag instead of the C-tag. As far as the S-component is concerned, C-tags do not exist; should it receive one, it considers it simply an untagged frame with an unknown Ethertype.

The C-components that link to the S-component certainly can be physical, but they are usually virtual. In the example shown in Figure 13.7, the upper C-component is configured to pass C-VIDs 1, 2, and 40 over virtual link 1, and C-VID 18 only on virtual link 2. Also, this C-component is configured so its port on virtual link 2 emits its frames untagged, and when untagged frames are received, they are assigned to C-VLAN 18.

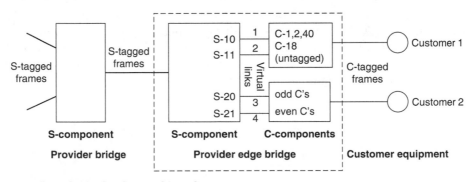

Figure 13.7   Provider bridge C-tagged interface

The lower C-component delivers all of the odd-numbered C-VIDs to virtual link 3 and the even-numbered C-VIDs to virtual link 4.

On the S-component side, frames received on a virtual link are tagged with the S-VID indicated, and each frame is emitted untagged. The net effect of these VID transformations is that

- Customer 1s C-VLANs 1, 2, and 40 are encapsulated (double-tagged) in S-VLAN 10.
- Customer 1s C-VLAN 18 is translated (single-tagged) into S-VLAN 11.
- A frame tagged with any other C-VID received from customer 1 is discarded.
- Customer 2s odd-numbered C-VLANs are encapsulated in S-VLAN 20.
- Customer 2s even-numbered C-VLANs are encapsulated in S-VLAN 21.

It appears that placing a full VLAN bridge on every physical port of a provider edge bridge can be a very complex and expensive task. Fortunately, two key limitations on the way C-components can be used reduce its complexity to a simple VID translation table:

- A C-component can have only one physical link on the customer side, no matter how many virtual links it has.
- No C-VID can be enabled on more than one of the virtual ports to the S-component. Therefore, a C-component never has to bridge from one virtual link to another and never has to replicate multicast frames; every frame passes directly across the C-component between a single virtual link and the single physical link.

These two limitations mean that the C-component never has to learn MAC addresses. Each frame that passes from the S-component to the physical link has its S-tag stripped, or perhaps (e.g., in the case of customer 1s C-VLAN 18) translated to a C-tag. On input, every frame is either discarded, wrapped in an S-tag, or translated to an S-tag.

The C-component also has the ability to translate the C-tags' priority fields into appropriate values for the priority fields in the S-tags and may be able to filter (not output) selected C-VIDs in the direction from the provider to the customer. Thus, it is an exceptionally simple bridge, consisting simply of Q-tag translation tables and not requiring MAC address inspection.

As a VLAN bridge, however, the C-component does participate in the customer's bridge control protocols such as spanning tree, 802.1X port authentication, and/or MVRP. If the provider is willing to accept the configuration requirements to participate fully in the customer's spanning tree, the customer's data can be controlled easily. (Note that these customer BPDUs pass transparently through the S-components.) However, much simpler, and much better, alternatives are presented in "Bridge Gateways," later in the chapter.

Provider Bridge Solutions and Challenges

Some very substantial provider networks have been implemented using the Q-in-Q technology of 802.1ad. However, there are limitations:

- The provider's bridges learn the customers' MAC addresses. If a substantial number of customers are using their EVCs to carry bridged traffic, so that the number of customer MAC addresses is large, the total number of MAC addresses over all customers can exceed the limitations of most bridge implementations.

- A VLAN tag allows for only 4094 EVCs. A large provider needs to offer many more EVCs than this in a single network.

- A network serving all of a provider's customers can have more bridges than the 802.1 spanning tree algorithms can support and still maintain adequate response times to failure conditions.

Some of these limitations have workarounds, and some do not.

Number of Customer MAC Addresses   The problem of Q-in-Q provider bridges having to learn too many customer MAC addresses can be solved in several ways. The most obvious is for the provider to charge for customers who require more than two or three MAC addresses per port. Because many customers' EVCs connect routers to those services, this is not a problem for most customers. If customers who use a provider network to connect their bridges together are charged extra for burdening the provider with a large number of MAC addresses, then the provider can afford more memory for MAC address tables.

A second way to mitigate the problem is provided by IEEE Std 802.1ad-2005. If the provider bridges are running MVRP, they can prune back each S-VLAN so each EVC goes only to those bridges in the network that are required to carry it. If a given EVC is an E-Line, with only two endpoints, then every bridge along its path will have exactly two ports that are not pruned for that VLAN—the two that are necessary to carry that VLAN from endpoint to endpoint. Any bridge that has only two active ports can disable MAC address learning for that VLAN. If many of the EVCs are E-Lines, doing this can greatly reduce the number of customer MAC addresses learned.

Furthermore, because each VLAN follows a spanning tree, on an E-LAN EVC with three customer ports, exactly one bridge in the network will have three ports on that EVC; all other bridges will have, at most, two active ports. Thus, only one bridge in the provider's network will be learning that customer's MAC addresses. Proper alignment of multiple spanning trees can ensure that the learning load is spread properly around the network to reduce the need for MAC address learning.

See "Backbone Bridges—Mac-in-Mac," for a more complete solution to the MAC address problem.

Number of VLANs   The limit of 4094 VLANs is set by the size of the VLAN ID field in the Q-tag. It has 12 bits, allowing 4096 combinations; 0 means "I don't know" and 4095 is illegal, leaving 4094 useful VLANs. This may not be enough.

One big reason for the existence of Carrier Ethernet networks is the connection of Internet service providers (ISPs) to their subscribers. The most obvious way to connect is to dedicate a VLAN for each subscriber and bring the VLANs to the ISP's router. This solution is inadequate for more than 4094 subscribers.

Many ISPs have, for years, used a solution often called *private VLANs* for this problem. Instead of using one VLAN per subscriber, a Carrier Ethernet network can use two VLANs for any number of subscribers, say 500. The two VLANs are the "Up VLAN" and the "Down VLAN," as shown in Figure 13.8. The bridges are configured so that on each subscriber port

- In the bridge's VLAN filtering table, only the Down VLAN is allowed to pass through the port.
- All frames emitted from the port (all are on the Down VLAN) are emitted untagged.
- On ingress, tagged frames are not allowed. (They are discarded.) All incoming frames are assigned to the Up VLAN.
- VLAN filtering is disabled for input frames and enabled only for output frames.

The net result of this configuration is that only the Down VLAN can pass out the port, and all frames coming into the port are accepted and marked with the Up VLAN. Furthermore, the bridge ports connected to the ISP's routers (presumably at least two of them for redundancy) are configured so that

- Both the Up and Down VLANs can pass through the ports.
- Frames in the Up VLAN passing out from the bridge to the router are translated to the Down VLAN.

Looking at Figure 13.8, you can see that data from subscriber A is tagged with the Up VLAN. That VLAN is not permitted to exit the port to subscriber B, but can reach both

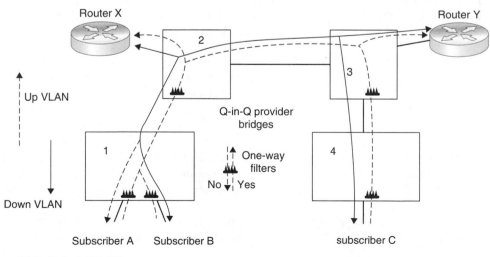

Figure 13.8   Private VLANs

router X and router Y. The two routers can speak to each other on the Down VLAN, and both routers can transmit to both subscribers on the Down VLAN. Note that bridge 3 does not forward data on the Up VLAN down toward bridge 4—even though there are subscribers on that bridge—because of the one-way filters installed on the Up VLAN.

MVRP creates these one-way filters automatically. Each subscriber port, customer port, and bridge trunk registers the Down VLAN. The propagation of these registrations allow all ports and bridges to reach each other on the Down VLAN. The Up VLAN, however, is registered only on the router ports. The propagation of these registrations allows all ports and bridges to reach the router ports on the Up VLAN, but blocks the Up VLAN in the direction toward the subscriber ports, where the Up VLAN is not registered.

As far as the routers are concerned, there is exactly one VLAN, the Down VLAN. The two routers can talk to each other on the Down VLAN. They can send data, whether broadcast, multicast, or unicast, to the subscribers. The VLAN looks to the routers like an ordinary subnet with, in this example, 500 hosts. The subscribers can talk to the routers with broadcasts, multicasts, or unicasts. Their frames, input on the Up VLAN, are delivered to the router(s) as if they were on the Down VLAN. The only catch is that the subscribers cannot talk to each other at all. Any frame from a subscriber is on the Up VLAN and thus cannot be emitted on any other subscriber's port. Any subscriber-to-subscriber traffic must pass through the router. (In IPv4 terms, the routers have the correct IP network mask, and the subscribers are told that the network mask is 255.255.255.255, so they send all IP packets to the router.)

With private VLANs, hundreds of subscribers can be served with one pair of VLANs, and up to 2047 VLAN pairs are available. In this way, a Q-in-Q Carrier Ethernet network can connect a sufficient number of subscribers to satisfy any carrier.

Private VLANs cannot, however, solve the problem of private networks for customers, such as businesses typically expect. In these instances, only one VLAN per customer will work, and the 4094 limit can be a problem. While many bridges are able to break the network into segments and to translate VLAN IDs as frames move from segment to segment, such techniques are prone to misconfiguration and provide only a modest increase in the number of VLANs effectively available. See "Backbone Bridges—MAC-in-MAC," for a more complete solution to the VLAN problem.

Spanning Tree Convergence Time   As network size increases, the time required for the spanning tree algorithms to converge can increase. In particular, a ring topology, which is often the topology imposed on a provider by the available physical links, is slow to converge. The basic problem is the "counting to infinity" problem inherent in any distance vector routing algorithm such as RIP (IETF RFC2453, STD0056) or the Multiple Spanning Tree Protocol. Rings almost invariably invoke the "chatty timer" that suspends the operation of the protocol for 1 sec. This allows the spanning tree protocol to converge more quickly, with less network disruption than otherwise would happen, but the invocation of this timer necessarily results in a 1-sec interruption in connectivity.

Furthermore, topology changes in networks with rings often trigger "sync events," where each bridge must cut off connectivity with each of its neighbors until the two agree that they understand the new network topology. This can, in many bridges, take some time to accomplish. The net effect is that in large networks, especially those with ring topologies, the Spanning Tree Protocols can often take more than 1 sec to converge after a failure or a recovery. This is adequate for most customers, but not for all.

The most serious problem with the spanning tree algorithms as currently standardized and implemented is the potential for the creation of permanent forwarding loops. When loops occur, bridged frames can circulate forever; each multicast frame, in particular, spews out a copy of itself each time it traverses the loop. If the Spanning Tree Protocol is executed correctly, this is an impossible occurrence. However, if a software bug or hardware failure results in a bridge that sinks, but does not source, the bridge protocol data units (BPDUs) that carry the Spanning Tree Protocol, while allowing that bridge to continue forwarding data frames, also create a permanent loop.

These drawbacks to the spanning tree algorithms are well-known in the networking community, and as a result, the spanning tree algorithms have acquired a bad reputation. This is compounded by the lack of good information on these protocols in the available literature (a lack that this chapter is intended to address). All of them, however, have solutions—see "Using Spanning Tree Effectively" and "Spanning Tree Alternatives."

Backbone Bridges—MAC-in-MAC

The simplest way to introduce the concept of backbone bridges is simply to display the format of a frame carried across a network of backbone bridges, as in Figure 13.9. This figure shows the frame format as defined in Draft 3 of IEEE Project 802.1ah, the draft standard for backbone bridges. (It should be emphasized that, as of this writing, this standard has not been approved by IEEE, but this format is likely to be very close to the one in the final version of the standard and is very close to what some vendors have actually implemented.)

What has happened in the transition from the S-tagged frame (Figure 13.9c) to the I-tagged frame (Figure 13.9e) is that

- The S-tag has been removed from the (perhaps tagged) customer frame in Figure 13.9a or b, so that the original customer's frame is restored.
- A pair of MAC addresses, a new S-tag (called the *B-tag* for *Backbone tag*), and an I-tag have been prepended to the customer's frame (Figure 13.9d and e).
- The FRC has been recomputed.

The 24-bit I-SID field in the I-tag carries the EVC identifier information that was in the 12-bit VLAN ID field in the S-tag. Thus, the number of customers has expanded from 4094 to 16,777,216, which should be adequate for most providers. This solves the problem of the number of available EVCs. The priority and DEI bits are the same as in the S-tag, and there are 4 bits for future expansion.

The B-tag is simply an S-tag. Its name has changed, but its function relative to the MAC addresses is the same in a backbone bridge as in a provider bridge.

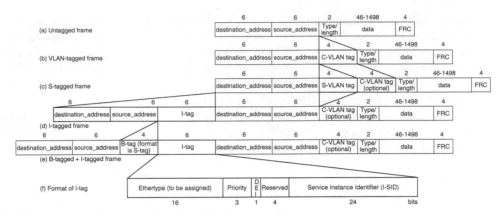

Figure 13.9 I-tag frame format for 802.1ah backbone bridges

The I-Component The MAC addresses in the MAC-in-MAC format identify I-components. An I-component is equivalent to a VLAN bridge with certain additional functionality. It may be implemented as a separate system or, more likely, as an additional chip (or chops) on a line card in a larger bridge. Figure 13.10 shows a simple backbone network serving four 802.1ad provider bridge networks (S-clouds). In Figure 13.10, you can see

- Four S-clouds, 1A, 1B, 2, and 3. Each S-cloud is attached to up to 4094 EVCs.
- Three provider edge bridges (PEBs), P, Q, and R. Each PEB has two I-components. The I-components are lettered A through F.
- Two backbone bridges, X and Y.
- Two customer devices, C-S and C-T.
- Only two connections from the S-clouds to the customer devices are shown, both in black. These connections carry C-tagged frames (Figure 13.9a and b).
- The physical connections between the S-clouds and the I-components are shown with dash-dot lines. They carry frames with S-tags (Figure 13.9c), as do the connections (not shown) among the provider bridges in each S-cloud.
- The (typically) virtual connections between the I-components and the B-component of each provider edge bridge are shown with dashed lines. They carry frames with I-tags, but no B-tags (Figure 13.9d).
- The physical connections between the various B-components in the backbone network are shown with heavy lines. They typically carry both B-tags and I-tags (Figure 13.9e).

You can see in Figure 13.10 that one S-cloud can connect in any fashion to the provider edge bridges—it can have a single connection to one PEB or multiple connections

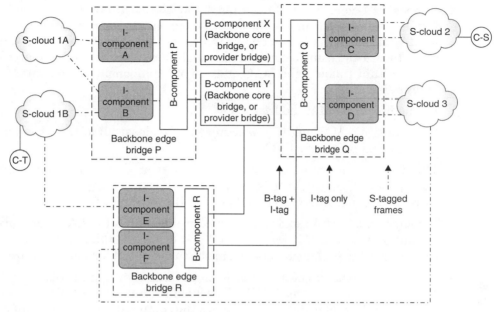

Figure 13.10   802.1ah backbone bridge architecture

to two or more PEBs. Each I-component, however, serves only one S-cloud, meaning one set of 4094 VLANs, each with a distinct VLAN ID. Since the I-component is, for all practical purposes, itself a provider bridge—even playing its part in the S-cloud's Spanning Tree Protocols—its redundant connections can even connect the two halves of an S-cloud that is split, whether intentionally or by failure. This is the case for S-cloud 1, which is split into 1A and 1B. Thus, in Figure 13.10, I-components A, B, and E all serve (split) S-cloud 1.

Each I-component has its own individual MAC address and can recognize certain multicast MAC addresses. These are the outer MAC addresses shown in Figure 13.9e and f.

Interconnecting I-Components   The method used by the I-components to acquire each others' MAC addresses, and to use them once acquired, can best be illustrated by following a "day in the life of a packet":

1. A customer frame (Figure 13.9a) is transmitted by C-S to S-cloud 2 in Figure 13.10.

2. Without worrying about whether the S-cloud knows the destination MAC address or not, the S-cloud delivers the frame, tagged with an S-tag identifying the customer's particular EVC, to I-component C, part of PEB Q.

3. I-component C learns the {source MAC address, S-VLAN} pair in the received frame, along with the port on which it was received, in the standard fashion of VLAN bridges.

4. Supposing I-component C does not know the destination MAC address of the frame, it floods the frame to the other I-components by encapsulating it in a MAC-in-MAC frame in the format shown in Figure 13.9d. It removes the S-tag, translating it to an I-tag using a configured translation table. The outer source address of the resultant frame is the MAC address of I-component C. The outer destination address is either

- The broadcast MAC address.

- A multicast MAC address recognized by at least all of the I-components that carry this particular EVC.

5. This frame is delivered to B-component Q as an I-tagged frame (Figure 13.9d). I-component C may deliver the frame to either (or both) of its virtual ports; each corresponds to a different virtual port on B-component Q.

6. B-component Q associates the received frame with a B-VLAN appropriate to the virtual port on which it was received and distributes the multicast or broadcast throughout the backbone network in the fully tagged format of Figure 13.9f.

7. The frame reaches all of the other I-components shown in the diagram. Only those I-components that serve the EVC specified in the frame's I-SID pay attention to the frame; the others discard it. Ideally, the combination of B-tag and/or multicast MAC address chosen by I-component C results in the frame reaching only those I-components that serve this EVC.

8. I-component E receives the frame. You can assume the Spanning Tree Protocols have resolved the loops inherent in the connections shown and, in particular, that the link between I-component B and S-cloud 1B has been severed by the spanning tree blocking one port or the other of the link.

9. I-component E de-encapsulates the frame. It learns that this particular {customer source MAC address, EVC} pair is associated with the I-component whose MAC address is the outer source MAC address of the frame (I-component C). Thus, I-component E knows how to get back to I-component C when the reply is returned.

10. I-component E does not know the destination MAC address, so it floods the frame to all ports in the EVC. Only the port to S-cloud 1B belongs to the EVC, so it floods it only in that direction. I-component E translates the I-SID into the appropriate S-VLAN value for S-cloud 1. The VLAN ID may be different from the VLAN-ID used in S-cloud 2; their VLAN ID spaces are totally independent.

11. S-cloud 1B delivers the frame to customer device C-T.

12. When C-T replies to C-S, I-component E gets the frame and uses its learned information to encapsulate the frame, as shown in Figure 13.9d. It has learned what unicast outer destination MAC address to use, so the backbone network can deliver the frame straight to I-component C.

13. While delivering the return frame, I-component C learns from this return frame what outer MAC address to use to reach customer device C-T. Now, these two devices can communicate with no flooding involved.

Advantages of Backbone Bridges   From the previous rather complex example, you can see why backbone bridging is attractive. The most important result is that the number of EVCs has been brought up from 4094 to 16 million. The second result is less obvious. Only those I-components that handle a particular EVC need to learn the customers' MAC addresses. No B-component had to learn any customer MAC addresses. Therefore, all learning of customer MAC addresses is isolated. The backbone bridges X and Y in Figure 13.10 know nothing at all of the customer's MAC addresses. Each I-component knows, at most, the MAC addresses of only the 4k EVCs it serves and no others. Of course, the schemes for reducing the MAC addresses learned for provider bridges are available to the I-components, since they are, themselves, provider bridges.

In particular, EVCs known to be E-Lines can be handled specially. For example, if an I-component knows that an EVC is an E-Line, then it does not need to learn any customer MAC addresses; it only needs to learn the MAC address of the one I-component at the other end of the EVC. Even multicasts from the customer are wrapped in a unicast outer destination MAC address because there is only one I-component that needs to receive it.

Backbone bridges have the same ability to prune B-VLANs and multicast MAC addresses that were available to provider bridges. Note, however, that IGMP snooping plays no part in the operation of the B-components. This is because each EVC's multicast needs are independent of every other EVC's needs. Instead, the backbone bridges have available the *Multiple Multicast Registration Protocol (MMRP)*. This protocol is similar to MVRP, but it registers multicast MAC addresses instead of VLANs. This allows the backbone network administrator to assign a multicast MAC address/B-VLAN to each EVC and allows each I-component to register with the B-components those {multicast address, B-VLAN} pairs that it needs to receive. Then, no multicast is delivered across the backbone to any I-component that does not need to receive it. Of course, the administrator is free to reduce the amount of work done by MVRP and MMRP and accept excess deliveries of multicasts in the backbone network. The administrator can trade control plane activity for data plane activity.

For maximum scalability, the B-components know nothing of individual EVCs. The B-components distribute frames only based on the outer MAC addresses and B-tags; they do not forward frames based on the I-tags. The I-tags are used only by the I-components. Hiding per-EVC information allows a network of backbone bridges to support a very large number of EVCs with a minimum of internal state.

Using Spanning Tree Effectively

Although the spanning tree protocols have deficiencies, as addressed in the following section, many of the complaints about spanning tree protocols stem from ignorance of its current development state and/or poor implementations, rather than from its real flaws. Most commonly, the complaint is either, "There is only one path—everything has to go the long way around, through the root of the tree"; "It takes forever to converge after a failure"; or "It floods frames with unknown unicast addresses everywhere in the network." All such problems are solvable by current bridge technology (and/or are, in fact, not problems).

A Single Path for the Customer's Data   Imagine for a moment an EVC connecting eight sites, spread across a continent, providing the equivalent of a single shared medium to the customer. Then assume, further, that this customer's data traffic patterns are highly variable, with high-volume unicast and multicast streams originating and being consumed at different sites at different moments in time, as the customer sees fit. Question: Does the provider actually want to carry that customer's traffic along the most direct path from site to site?

Figure 13.11 shows such a network, simplified to only four customer connections C1–C4. Assuming that the most direct paths between the various customer sites are as shown by the dotted arrows in Figure 13.11, you can see that this one customer's data is scattered all over the network. In fact, there are only three links, T-V, T-W, and V-Y, that never carry data for this customer. And even those links would be used if some sort of equal-cost multipathing were used in the network. While such diffusion is often desirable in an enterprise network, in order to spread the load as much as possible in a carrier network, such advantages can easily be outweighed by the added difficulty of ensuring quality of service guarantees, determining how much bandwidth is required on any given link, and debugging data-dependent customer problems.

In Figure 13.12, this customer's EVC is assumed to be confined to a single spanning tree rooted at bridge W. Only the physical links shown as solid lines are used to carry the EVC. Compared to Figure 13.11, traffic between one pair of customer sites, C1-C3, takes a longer path through the network. However, only this one pair suffers; the other five possible pairings take optimal paths. The amount of bandwidth required by the customer on any given link can reasonably be set by the provider, and debugging problems is simpler. More importantly, if you assume that the network shown is a provider

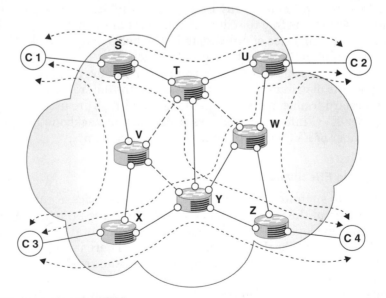

Figure 13.11   Direct routing of an EVC

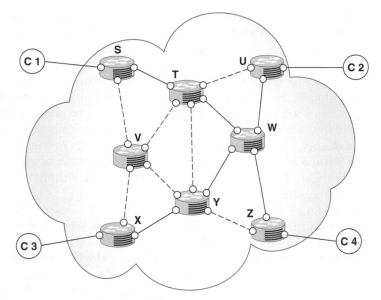

Figure 13.12 Spanning tree routing of an EVC

bridge (802.1ad) network, only bridge W in Figure 13.12 learns this customer's MAC addresses. All the other bridges, S-V and X-Z, have only two ports each that carry this customer's data, and hence they do not need to learn any customer MAC addresses. By contrast, in Figure 13.11, every bridge except bridge V has at least three ports carrying this customer's data, and hence all but that bridge must learn at least some of this customer's MAC addresses. Thus, you can see by this comparison that having a single spanning tree for a given customer can be, on balance, an improvement over the "perfect" routing of data.

Multiple Paths for Customers' Data   Clearly, as shown in Figure 13.12, it is not desirable for a provider network to leave seven links unused. This is one reason why the Multiple Spanning Tree Protocol (MSTP) was developed. While any given VLAN, and therefore any given customer, is confined to a single spanning tree, up to 64 spanning tree instances may be constructed in a single provider network, which, in practice, is far more than are necessary to get excellent usage of all the network's links. In Figure 13.12, for example, adding a second tree rooted at bridge V would ensure that all of the links except T-Y is in use. Even the largest real networks seldom need more than four to six instances of the spanning tree.

   To avoid needless reconfiguration of the bridges each time a new EVC is added to the network, best practice is to create all of the spanning trees at the start and assign each of the 4094 possible VLANs to a spanning tree, even though only a few may initially be used. Whenever a new EVC is added, it can be assigned to a VLAN carried on a spanning tree appropriate for the customer's needs. Only the bridges on which the customer UNI ports reside need be configured; all other ports are automatically activated by MVRP. Unused VLANs not assigned to customers cost absolutely nothing for the network control protocols to maintain.

Reliable Roots   Any properly designed network contains redundant paths so a single failure cannot split the network. (These redundant paths are, of course, the reason that routing protocols and/or spanning tree protocols are required.) The convergence time problem caused by the "chatty timer," which results in convergence times greater than 1 sec, occurs only when a network port is separated from the root of a spanning tree. Thus, the failure of the root bridge of a spanning tree can trigger a network disconnect (for the users of that spanning tree) that is greater than 1 sec. Single link failures should not cause this long outage.

A network can be constructed to avoid this type of slow convergence, in the face of a single failure, by making, at least, those bridges that serve as spanning tree roots extra reliable. A number of bridge vendors offer proprietary features whereby two separate bridges appear to all external devices (including the other bridges in the network) to be a single bridge. Multiple connections between a single bridge and the coupled pair, or between two coupled pairs, can be made using link aggregation. If one bridge of the coupled pair fails, the other takes over, with the disruption confined to the inevitable loss of the bandwidth in the links connected to the failed bridge; the spanning tree topology need not change at all. (The system administrator may elect to allow the topology to change quickly, in this situation, to account for the lost bandwidth.)

Failed Bridges   As mentioned previously in "Spanning Tree Convergence," when the spanning tree software process fails in a bridge, in a manner that does not bring down the whole bridge, a permanent forwarding loop can result that can severely disrupt the network operation. Fortunately, this problem is solvable. The first obvious solution is, of course, to build more reliable software, or at least software that is able to detect its failures and recover from them more readily and thus be more robust. The second is to improve the robustness of the spanning tree protocol, so the other bridges recognize the problem and avoid creating loops.

The problem of protocol robustness is very amenable to a solution in the standard, and in fact, the solution to this problem is one of the tasks in the Project Authorization Request for IEEE Project 802.1aq Shortest Path Bridging. The solution is in three parts:

1. The spanning tree protocols' state machines are modified slightly to transmit BPDUs even from ports that are not designated ports. (This change can be made in any bridge without disrupting its ability to interoperate with bridges that have not been so updated.)
2. Each bridge port in configured as to whether the port is expected to connect to another bridge or not.
3. If a bridge port is configured to expect another bridge, and if that other bridge is not transmitting BPDUs, then the port is disabled.

Currently, in a bridge running spanning tree, if a bridge is not receiving BPDUs on a given port, then it forwards traffic to that port. If a bridge goes "brain dead," it stops sending BPDUs, so all bridges forward traffic toward it, creating loops. With these changes, that brain dead bridge is recognized and avoided by its neighbors. The system administrator can, therefore, quickly find the problem and fix it.

This change has been implemented by some vendors and will become part of IEEE Std 802.1aq. With this change, the chance of permanent forwarding loops is no greater for bridged networks than for routed networks. The cost of this solution is that the required configuration makes the bridges no longer "plug and play." This, of course, is not a problem for Carrier Ethernet provider networks.

Flooded Unicast Frames   When a frame is received by a bridge that has a destination MAC address that is not known to that bridge, the bridge floods the frame on all ports on which that frame's VLAN is enabled. The frame may be eventually flooded on all the ports in the network configured for that VLAN, presumably meaning all the ports belonging to that particular customer. This is often perceived as a flaw in bridged networks.

Let's look at the problem more closely. First, only one customer is affected by this flood—the customer on whose VLAN the frame is being carried. The frame cannot be flooded to any port not associated with that one VLAN and that one customer. Second, this behavior is normal and desirable when a bridge has only two ports for a given VLAN, as is the case for most customers in most bridges, even when the customer's EVC has more than two ports. (In Figure 13.12, for example, only one bridge in the entire network has more than two ports for the customer illustrated.) Third, such behavior on a continued basis is very unusual; it requires that a unicast "conversation" between two customer addresses be purely one-way, or at least that frames in one direction are emitted no more often than once every 5 minutes, the default timeout period for MAC addresses. Over the many years of employing bridges in enterprise networks, network administrators, protocol designers, and users have come to understand the undesirability of one-way bridged traffic and learned to avoid it.

So why is this behavior used by bridges? Consider the alternative:

- If a frame with an unknown destination MAC address is not flooded, the only real alternative is to discard it, until the address can be discovered.

- Discovering which bridge every customer MAC address is attached to is not trivial. Although there are special cases, e.g., when every customer station logs on to a bridge using IEEE Std 802.1X or when all MAC addresses are known, customer MAC addresses cannot, in general, be discovered by a provider.

- Even if the MAC addresses can be reliably learned (this is not impossible, if all of the stations are running the IP, they would have to be passed around in control protocols if not learned. This imposes a significant added burden to the bridge's control plane processing capability.

Put simply, it has proven more economical for bridges to set up a single path for any given VLAN, so MAC addresses can be learned in hardware, from the data in flight, rather than going to the trouble of discovering all MAC addresses, passing them around among the bridges in control protocols, and installing those MAC addresses in the tables through software. Remember that MAC addresses are a flat address space, and that unlike IP host addresses and subnets, no summarization can be performed on MAC addresses to lighten the burden on the control plane. From a practical standpoint, enterprise users have found that the excess bandwidth consumed by flooding is dampened by learning faster than software can update forwarding tables from addresses passed in the control plane.

Spanning Tree Alternatives

If the preceding discussion has not convinced the reader that the use of the spanning tree protocols is a viable option, here are a number of alternatives either available today or in development in standards organizations. They include bridge gateways, both within and among clouds; IEEE Project 802.1aq Shortest Path Bridging and IETF TRILL, both described in "ISP Access Services," later in the chapter; various proprietary ring topology algorithms; and various proprietary paired virtual bridge solutions.

Bridge Gateways   Either at a boundary between two bridged clouds, as between the provider cloud and either of the customer clouds in Figure 13.13, or at the edge of a single cloud, as in Figure 13.14, shown later in this section, a bridge or a cloud of bridges can be separated from another bridge or cloud of bridges at arm's length, without the two bridges' or clouds' spanning trees being concatenated into a single spanning tree. This is important because, as described in "Interconnecting Clouds of Bridges" carrying one cloud's BPDUs over another cloud is undesirable. This technique can be called a *bridge gateway*. The principles of bridge gateways are firmly established and have been implemented by some vendors, though their standardization is still in progress (as part of IEEE P802.1ah).

The bridge gateway is based on the following principles:

- There are two separate spanning tree domains. There may be any number of point-to-point links between the domains. (Shared media connections can be handled, but require some additional effort.)
- One bridge, or a cloud of bridges, makes all of the decisions as to which of the links are used for which VLANs. This is the "client cloud."

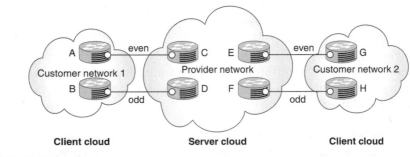

Figure 13.13   Bridge gateways

- The other bridge, or a cloud of bridges, is needed to deliver all of the VLANs on every port connected to the client cloud. This is the "server cloud."
- The client cloud may inform the server cloud about which VLANs are passed on each link in order to minimize wasted bandwidth.

On the server cloud side, the bridge ports connected to a client cloud are configured to not transmit BPDUs and to discard them on receipt. This applies to bridges that otherwise would be exchanging BPDUs, such as provider edge bridge C-components and customer bridges. Bridges such as simple S-components, which pass BPDUs as ordinary data, need not be specially configured. The server-side bridges do, however, respect the Multiple VLAN Registration Protocol (MVRP). They register all VIDs with the client bridge (thus saying, "I'll take anything"). The server-side bridges accept MVRP registrations from the client bridges as well and filter those VIDs that are not registered by the client cloud.

On the client side, the bridge or cloud of bridges simply runs a spanning tree algorithm, presumably MSTP, so that different VLANs can be blocked on different links. The only oddity is, again, that the bridge ports connecting to the server cloud are specially configured. This configuration involves a few changes to the normal MSTP algorithms:

- BPDUs received from the server cloud are discarded and ignored.
- No BPDUs are transmitted toward the server cloud.
- Each of these ports *pretends* to receive a BPDU from the server cloud that claims a path to a root bridge that is superior to any potential claim to being a root bridge for any bridge in the client cloud. This information is propagated through the client network in the normal way.
- If a server-facing port in the client cloud is ever chosen as a designated port, then the port is placed in the blocked state, instead of the forwarding state.

Each server-facing port in the client cloud is configured with different root bridge information. Presumably, with two links available, you would configure one such port with a very high priority root for one spanning tree and a not-quite-so-high priority root for the other VLANs, and the other server-facing port would be configured in an opposite manner. As the spanning tree operates normally in the client cloud, the port that has the best claim becomes a root port and goes into the forwarding state. When that information propagates to any other server-facing port, one that has a second- or third-best claim, that port becomes a designated port and is blocked. Thus, exactly one of the server-facing ports is in the forwarding state for any given spanning tree.

In the event of the failure of either one of the links or bridges, one of the secondary ports becomes the root port. This happens almost instantaneously if the client cloud is a single bridge, and it happens through the normal spanning tree operations if it is a cloud of bridges. Either way, there is no possibility of temporary loops. When the link or bridge recovers, then normal operation resumes.

In the event that the server network becomes split into two parts, connected only through the two links of server cloud, then the network remains divided because the client cloud *never* enables more than one connection to the server cloud. This is a purposeful limitation. The most likely reason for the server cloud to use the client cloud as the principle data highway is a configuration blunder. In the case of a single-edge bridge connected to a core cloud, such errors are most common in the bridges that are most often configured, namely, as the edge bridges.

To see the power of this idea, let's assume that the server cloud in Figure 13.13 consists of 802.1ad provider bridges (802.1ah MAC-in-MAC bridges would work similarly). Let's also suppose that the provider is offering two EVCs. The provider edge bridges' C-components are encapsulating all of the customer's odd-numbered C-VLANs into S-VLAN 20, and the even-numbered C-VLANs into S-VLAN 21, as shown in Figure 13.7.

Suppose customer cloud 1 determines that the odd-numbered VLANs will use the A-C link and that the even-numbered VLANs will use the B-D link. Similarly, customer cloud 2 decides that the odd-numbered VLANs will pass through F-H and the even VLANs will use E-G. Both customer clouds inform the provider's C-components of this decision via MVRP. Each of the C-components, which learn only the odd-numbered VLANs are needed (bridges C and F in Figure 13.13), knows from this that S-VLAN 20 is not needed by that S-component, since none of its constituent VLANs are being delivered through that C-component. The C-component can signal through the provider cloud using the provider's MVRP. Bridges C and F are pruned from the tree for S-VLAN 20, and bridges D and G are pruned from the tree for S-VLAN 21. Thus, these two S-VLANs, 20 and 21, each become point-to-point, instead of four-point, VLANs.

Among the results of using bridge gateways are

- None of the provider bridges in this example need to learn any of the customer's MAC addresses. (Of course, if there were three client clouds sharing a 3-UNI EVC, learning in the provider network would be needed.)

- A failure or restoration in the interior of the server (provider) cloud does not cause any activity in either of the client (customer) clouds' spanning trees.

- A failure or restoration in the interior of a client cloud does not cause any activity in the server cloud's spanning tree or in any other client clouds' spanning trees.

- Changes in the interconnect topology between clouds can result in changes to the one directly affected client cloud's spanning tree and in the server cloud's VLAN pruning, but not in the server cloud's spanning tree and not in any other client clouds' spanning trees.

A cloud X can be both a client cloud, say to server cloud Y, and a server cloud, say to client cloud Z. Clouds can be chained. If clouds are chained together in a circle, then a hard forwarding loop will result because there is no over-arching Spanning Tree Protocol running everywhere in the world. Fortunately, this is not possible as long as the server cloud always adds an encapsulation, as for instance, if the server-client relationship is between an 802.1ad provider bridge network (server) and an 802.1Q client network (client), or between an 802.1ah backbone network (server) and an 802.1ad provider bridge network (client). In such a loop, the ever-increasing mountain of tags being added, as a frame traverses the loop, eventually causes a discard due to excessive frame length (a crude form of TTL).

It appears, at this writing, that this separation of different clouds' spanning trees will be incorporated into the provider backbone bridge standard, IEEE 802.1ah.

Ring Topology Algorithms   As mentioned previously, a ring topology is the worst topology in terms of the time taken by the current spanning tree algorithms to converge after a failure. A number of vendors have created proprietary solutions. These solutions have in common the ability to reconfigure very quickly after the failure of a link in a ring of bridges and to handle two (or more) rings connected to each other at multiple points.

Similarly, they have in common the ability to disrupt the operation of the network completely if the topology of the network is not, in fact, as configured—whether that is due to improper configuration or to miswired connections. In practice, many network operators find the faster convergence time well worth the chances for disruption due to misconfiguration or miswiring. These proprietary algorithms vary in their ability to work well with the spanning tree algorithms, which are necessary in mesh networks. Enquiries of potential vendors in this regard are encouraged.

IEEE 802.1aq Shortest Path Bridging, by replacing the distance vector algorithms with link state algorithms, will fix this problem in a general way. Whether SPB will give convergence times as fast as the proprietary ring algorithms remains to be seen.

Paired Virtual Bridges   Several vendors offer another alternative to spanning tree, or at least to minimizing the size of the network protected by spanning trees—the virtual bridge pair. A network employing virtual bridge pairs is shown in Figure 13.14. This technique allows a provider to build an extremely large network using a minimum of spanning tree techniques.

In Figure 13.14, you have a core network, simplified to only four bridges A–D. This network is likely a mesh network, in order to carry such a massive load of data, but it could be another topology such as a ring if sufficient bandwidth is available. Each bridge in the core is a completely separate entity as far as the control plane is concerned.

At the distribution layer, Figure 13.14 shows a number of paired virtual bridges E through K. Each pair of bridges looks, to the rest of the network, like a single bridge. Presumably, the provider would take the precaution of using separate power sources for each bridge in the pair. They could even be in different rooms or different buildings to maximize the resiliency of the network. The two connections from paired virtual bridge E to bridge A are aggregated by IEEE Std 802.3ad link aggregation into a single virtual link. Similarly, the two links between the paired virtual bridge E to bridge B are aggregated. Bridge A sees one connection to bridge E via an aggregated link, as does bridge B. If either of the bridges fail, or if any of the four links fail, connectivity remains unchanged.

Figure 13.14 shows a second layer of bridges in the access layer—paired virtual bridges, P through Z. Each of these bridges has a single aggregated link, consisting of

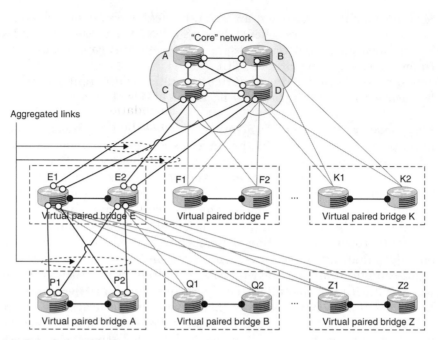

Figure 13.14 Paired virtual bridges

four physical links each, to one of the paired virtual bridges in the distribution layer. Only those access bridges connected to paired virtual bridge E are shown. The number of access bridges, and hence UNI ports, could clearly be quite large.

The important thing to notice about Figure 13.14 is that, as far as the control protocols are concerned, there are no redundant links, and hence no possible loops, present in this network, except in the core cloud (A–D). Between the distribution layer and the core, you can employ a technique such as the one described in "Bridge Gateways" so that the distribution layer bridges can determine which of the links to the core are used for which EVCs. From there on down, there is only a single path from paired virtual bridge to paired virtual bridge available; hence no routing protocol is necessary.

Of course, to get from one distribution layer paired virtual bridge to another, the data must pass through the core. However, this structure is extremely robust, failures and recoveries are handled extremely quickly, and the simplicity of the network enables the operator to configure quality of service or bandwidth guarantees easily.

Ethernet OAM and Connectivity Fault Management

There are three versions of Ethernet OAM, all of which can be very useful in conjunction with any Ethernet-over-*xyz* technology, not just Ethernet bridging. IEEE Std 802.3ah-2004 defines an Ethernet OAM capability for a single point-to-point physical IEEE 802.3 link. It provides for keep-alive pings at one-second intervals; a remotely controlled loopback capability for arbitrary data; and the ability to extract byte, packet, and error statistics from the interface at the other end of the link and to generate error reports when error thresholds are exceeded. However, IEEE 802.3ah OAM applies only to single links, not to networks.

IEEE Project P802.1ag Connectivity Fault Management (CFM) is nearing completion at this writing. IEEE 802.1 has developed this standard in cooperation with the development in ITU-T Q.5/13 of ITU-T recommendation Y.1731, Ethernet OAM. Y.1731 builds upon P802.1ag and defines a superset of the P802.1ag capabilities. Their provisions are useful to providers, customers, and intermediate providers who are both.

IEEE P802.1ag provides three operations in the context of a layered environment of providers and customers. The three operations are

- **Connectivity checking**   Every endpoint of an EVC (two UNIs for an E-Line and two or more for an E-LAN) transmits a periodic multicast connectivity check message (CCM) that contains the identity of the EVC and the transmitting endpoint. Every endpoint listens for the other endpoints' CCMs and issues an error notification if three or more are missed from any other endpoint. This guarantees the detection of loss of connectivity with a minimum of packets sent. Equally important, it also detects excessive connectivity, e.g., the accidental concatenation of two EVCs that are supposed to be separate. This latter capability is an advance over the OAM capabilities of other Carrier Ethernet technologies.

- **Loopback**   An endpoint can transmit a unicast loopback message (LBM) to any other endpoint in the EVC and to intermediate points along the paths among endpoints. The target point returns the LBM as a loopback reply (LBR). This corresponds to many other technologies' similar capabilities, but the loopback capability is not used as the primary means for connectivity checking; it is used for fault isolation after the CCMs detect a connectivity fault.

- **Linktrace**   An endpoint can issue a linktrace message (LTM) that traces the route taken by a given target MAC address. Each intermediate point along the path returns a unicast linktrace reply (LTR) to the endpoint originating the LTM, so that the originator can construct the path to the target address. Linktrace produces similar results to, but operates completely differently than, the IP traceroute capability familiar to the Layer 3 world.

These three functions are specified in great detail in IEEE 802.1ag. Further functions are described in the ITU-T Y.1731 Ethernet OAM recommendation, though the equipment specification (G.8021) is not yet complete. Among the most important of these functions are

- **Alarm indication signal (AIS)**   An endpoint that detects a connectivity failure transmits this message toward the user of the EVC to notify the user of the failure.

- **Frame loss measurement**   Frames can be sent, between the endpoints of an E-Line EVC only, that allow each endpoint to determine separately for each direction exactly how many frames have been lost in transit between the endpoints.

- **Frame delay measurement**   Timestamp information in these messages allow endpoints to determine how long it takes to convey a frame from one endpoint to another.

Just as important as the functions themselves, are the context in which these functions operate. Ethernet CFM/OAM operates in a strictly layered environment (see Figure 13.15). CFM/OAM assumes there may be multiple levels of customer-provider relationships involved in providing Carrier Ethernet services. An operator in a city may run a Q-in-Q network. An end-to-end provider may contract with Q-in-Q networks in several cities and with a MAC-in-MAC backbone provider to create the end-to-end service required by a customer. The customer, in turn, may be offering services to clients internally to an enterprise.

In this kind of layered environment, it is important to hide information. For example, if a customer initiates a linktrace operation, the provider does not want each bridge in his network to be visible as a waypoint to that customer's linktrace. This is especially true if that "customer" is a rival provider that is subcontracting services. The various frame encapsulations (Q-in-Q, MAC-in-MAC) often ensure that a CFM/OAM message at a higher level cannot be detected as such by a lower level device. Where business relationships add additional layers not reflected in the actual data frames themselves, CFM/OAM provides a "Maintenance Domain Level (802.1ag)" or "Maintenance Entity Group Level (Y.1731)" in every CFM/OAM message to differentiate the levels. Thus, in Figure 13.15, the end-to-end provider cannot see either operators' network except at the four points where the end-to-end EVC enters and leaves the operators' networks. Similarly, the customer can see only the entry and exit points of the end-to-end service.

At each level, the visible intermediate points are the endpoints of the lower level. In addition to essential information hiding, this model provides an excellent means for reporting and diagnosing faults. The endpoints of each level can report failures to the enclosing level. If a failure is detected at any given level, it can be isolated to that part of the network between intermediate points, and the appropriate subnetwork can then be inspected to isolate the difficulty further.

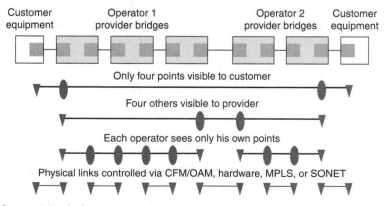

Figure 13.15   Connectivity fault management

As a final note, you may observe that the only thing guaranteed to be transported through a Carrier Ethernet network end to end, no matter what technology (SONET, MPLS, bridges, ATM, or anything else) is used in the network, is an Ethernet frame. IEEE 802.1ag and ITU-T Y.1731 define a means of determining, reporting, and diagnosing the health of a Carrier Ethernet network using only Ethernet frames, with no dependencies on the underlying technologies. Thus, Ethernet CFM/OAM can be very useful to a customer or a provider, even if bridges are not employed at all in providing the Carrier Ethernet service. (For that matter, CFM can be of considerable use in an enterprise network.)

Drivers for This Solution

As implied by the layout of the preceding section, "Technology Description," the development of the Ethernet bridging solution for Carrier Ethernet has been, for the most part, a straightforward process of development from enterprise scale networks. This process has been driven by

- The observation that the VLANs of IEEE Std 802.1Q-1995, widely deployed in the enterprise space, are equivalent to provider services.

- The recognition by IEEE 802.1 of economic considerations—namely, the assumption by 802.1 that the bridge will become obsolete the instant any other packet technology with equivalent functionality can undercut its price.

- The obvious fact (obvious, at least, to the bridging community) that since the behavior of bridges define "Ethernet service," they have a significant role to play in providing such services to customers.

The challenges, of course, have been in scaling up an enterprise network into a provider network. It is the opinion of an increasing number of vendors and providers that these challenges are being met.

When Does This Solution Fit?

As (the author hopes) this chapter has made clear, there are a number of scenarios where an IEEE 802.1 bridge-based solution performs most effectively:

- Bridges are not just useful for constructing multipoint-to-multipoint (E-LAN) or point-to-multipoint EVCs, they define the model for such services. Wherever a provider is offering a significant number of ports connected to such E-LAN EVCs, compared to the number of ports connected to E-Line EVCs, bridges are a viable choice. Keep in mind, when making this determination, that if 10 percent of the EVCs are E-LANs, they may easily constitute 50 percent of the total number of UNIs.

- Where the links used to interconnect the nodes of the provider's network are Ethernet links and where a large portion of the frames on those links is Carrier Ethernet traffic, it is straightforward, economical, and sensible to make those nodes bridges and let them do what they do best. Almost all bridges offered by vendors for Carrier Ethernet applications are capable of functioning both as bridges and as routers and often as MPLS switches as well, so one system can handle a multiplicity of protocols and services.

- When customers are using the provider's network to interconnect their bridges, rather than to interconnect their routers, the use of bridges in the provider's network, at least at the edges, becomes more important. As discussed in this chapter, there are a number of optimizations for traffic delivery, such as those provided by MVRP, that are offered only by 802.1 bridges.

- "Network religion" and/or the ability to clearly differentiate one's offerings from a competitor's can play important roles in a provider's selection of an implementation technology.

When Does This Solution Not Fit?

There are scenarios where bridges are not as suitable for offering Carrier Ethernet solutions:

- When Carrier Ethernet services are only a small portion of the traffic carried by an existing network, for example, an MPLS network, it is not practical to run provider bridges directly on the links between bridges; those links are best left to the MPLS world. IETF solutions work very well for E-Line EVCs or for a modest number of E-LAN EVCs. As the number of E-LANs grows, interconnecting virtual provider bridges via MPLS pseudowires becomes feasible.

- When a provider's physical plant consists primarily of non-Ethernet (technology "*xyz,* perhaps ATM) links, and when much of the traffic on that network is not carried as Ethernet over *xyz,* then it may (or may not) be more practical to use another technology (e.g., Ethernet over MPLS over *xyz*).

- If the provider's physical plant consists primarily of rings of devices, rather than a mesh topology, nonstandard solutions are not acceptable, physical redundancy is required for robustness against failures, and 1 to 2 sec convergence times are not acceptable, a bridge-based solution does not exist. There are nonstandard solutions to the ring problem, however, and the new 802.1aq standard should solve the problem.

- "Network religion" and/or the ability to clearly differentiate one's offerings from a competitor's can play an important role in a provider's rejection of an implementation technology.

Benefits and Shortcomings

When compared to the alternatives, bridged Carrier Ethernet networks have both benefits and shortcomings.

The MPLS world offers an excellent means for providing a point-to-point service that can carry many different kinds of payloads, including Ethernet frames. Not only the data movement parts of the network are available, but the important ancillary and infrastructure components, such as network maintenance, EVC creation, and billing, have been developed around the MPLS architecture.

The Ethernet-over-MPLS story is weaker when it comes to E-LAN EVCs or few-privileged-points-to-many-unprivileged-points EVCs. This is because MPLS does not have multipoint-to-multipoint paths, but only point-to-point paths. Thus, an E-LAN requires a full mesh of point-to-point paths; a 10-UNI EVC requires 45 point-to-point paths. Such a mesh of connections is slow and expensive to create and maintain. It requires that every multicast, broadcast, or flooded unicast must be replicated and transmitted $(n - 1)$ times in an n-UNI network, potentially wasting enormous amounts of bandwidth. To cut the bandwidth requirement, a full mesh of point-to-multipoint paths, on top of the full mesh of point-to-point paths, is required, thus greatly increasing the path creation and maintenance load.

Ethernet over MPLS starts with a connectionless IP network. MPLS creates point-to-point connections over this connectionless network. Ethernet over MPLS then emulates a connectionless network using the MPLS connections. Running two network emulations in order to get back to where you started is inherently inefficient. If Ethernet services are a small part of the services offered by a large MPLS network, this makes sense. If one is starting from scratch to create a network offering primarily Ethernet services, bridges can do a more efficient job.

Similarly, SONET, ATM, and other circuit-switching technologies are reliable, proven ways to carry point-to-point and point-to-multipoint traffic, including Ethernet. If only E-Line or single-point-to-multipoint EVCs are to be offered, these technologies are perfectly adequate. But like MPLS, when using circuit technology to emulate a shared medium technology, you wind up with an inherently inefficient emulation.

Bridges have limits, of course. The power of bridges lies in their ability to provide millions of independent EVCs, each of which can reasonably connect a modest number of endpoints. A network constructed properly along the lines of Figure 13.1 could serve a continent.

It is equally true that as so far developed, a network that offers almost exclusively E-Line EVCs would better be implemented with MPLS or another circuit technology, rather than with bridges. A VLAN is optimized for providing a multipoint-to-multipoint service. If it has only two endpoints, it certainly works, but many of the bridge protocols and much of data plane hardware is then wasted. However, techniques for efficiently supporting point-to-point circuits with bridges are in development and are being offered for standardization.

Finally, when assessing whether or not a large number of E-Line EVCs are needed, it is important to understand that connecting thousands of subscribers to their ISP does not require thousands of E-Line EVCs. As described in "Number of VLANS," one pair of VLANs is sufficient to create an EVC with a few privileged points (the ISP's routers) and thousands of unprivileged points (the subscriber's routers). It can prevent the subscribers from communicating directly with each other, allow them to communicate with the routers, allow the routers to communicate with each other, and efficiently distribute multicasts from the router, using only one EVC comprising two VLANs.

Typical Deployment Scenarios

Typical deployment scenarios for Carrier Ethernet services using bridged networks include, from the most general to the most narrow:

- Ethernet backbone services
- Sparse wide area business services
- Metro area business services
- ISP access services

Given the techniques presented in this chapter, all of these scenarios play together, can be interconnected, and can cooperate with each other, even across provider-to-provider connections.

Ethernet Backbone Services

Ethernet services can be offered at the largest scale using the network depicted in Figure 13.1. One can imagine a national network of such EVCs, with the routers that provide the IP connectivity using these EVCs, instead of being directly connected. This backbone service does not itself provide universal connectivity! Ethernet's flat address space, if nothing else, makes that fundamentally impractical. This backbone service is not equivalent to an enterprise network, where a VLAN can spread anywhere in the network at the whim of the users and lead to gross inefficiencies in packet distribution. It is more like a national-scale patch panel for interconnecting the routers that provide universal connectivity and for providing EVCs to customers.

Such a network will be practical only when bridges acquire the capability of offering a large number of point-to-point connections with very fast (on the order of 10s of milliseconds) failure recovery capabilities. This capability is still in development.

Sparse Wide Area Business Services

Given an underlying network of point-to-point services, whether MPLS, SONET, or ATM, you can create very simple E-Line EVCs such as MPLS pseudowires. Provider bridges can use both physical Ethernet links and these virtual links equally well for connecting to customers and to each other. For example, taking just one of the IEEE 802.1ad provider bridge Q-in-Q clouds from Figure 13.1, up to 4094 E-LAN business EVCs can be created and overlaid upon the MPLS network. MPLS can continue to be used for all E-Line EVCs, including Ethernet-over-MPLS services.

Metro Area Business Services

A single IEEE 802.1ad provider bridge Q-in-Q cloud can offer 4094 business EVCs, enough for many metropolitan networks, without recourse to a MAC-in-MAC backbone. As the network grows and the limitations of this Q-in-Q network are approached, it can be split in two, using VID translation. When that limitation is exceeded, it can be split into multiple Q-in-Q clouds interconnected by a small MAC-in-MAC backbone, and so on, as hinted at in Figure 13.1.

An IEEE 802.1ah MAC-in-MAC backbone network can also connect directly to a customer; an intervening 802.1ad Q-in-Q network is not required. Using a MAC-in-MAC network to connect directly to the UNIs has the obvious advantage of eliminating the Q-in-Q technology from the picture, thus simplifying management and training. It scales better than Q-in-Q alone, because more than 4094 EVCs are available. However, the MAC address of each I-component in the network (see "The I-Component") is carried across the backbone. As the backbone network extends out to the edge, it gets bigger and bigger, and the number of I-components increases. Eventually, the network gets larger than the spanning tree protocols can handle, even after being extended by the various techniques given in this chapter. As these issues approach, Q-in-Q networks can be added to separate the backbone from the customers, and the network grows toward the complete picture shown in Figure 13.1.

ISP Access Services

As shown in Figure 13.8, Q-in-Q provider bridges are an excellent method for connecting ISP subscribers to their routers. In addition, other services besides routers, e.g., IP television sources, can be attached to the Up VLANs as well. Depending on the scaling capabilities of the bridges and routers, their relative numbers may be different from that shown in the figure.

Note that this model does not have a place for PPP over Ethernet. Ethernet is inherently more reliable than the modem lines for which PPP was developed. As long as the network uses Ethernet from the subscriber to the router, and as long as the bridges employed follow the recommendations of IEEE 802.1 with regard to handing the frames' hardware checksums, PPP adds more complexity and expense than it helps.

Ongoing Developments

IEEE Project 802.1ah is, as of this writing, still under development in IEEE 802.1. However, most of the current technical draft of that document is stable, hence its inclusion in the "existing" parts of this chapter. References have also been made in this chapter to other ongoing standards work. The four major items that may affect the provision of Carrier Ethernet services by bridges are IEEE Project P802.1aq Shortest Path Bridging, ITU-T protection switching, provider bridge backbone traffic engineering, and IETF TRILL.

IEEE Project P802.1aq Shortest Path Bridging

This project is in progress. Although nothing can be said for certain until the project has been completed, the scope and purpose of the project are clear, and a consensus is emerging among the participants. For one, you can expect that SPB will include a provision for computing the required spanning trees using a link state protocol such as IS-IS, instead of using the distance vector technology of the current Spanning Tree Protocols. This will eliminate the "counting to infinity" problem.

Second, you can expect SPB to create a spanning tree for each bridge participating in the protocol. Normally, this list does not include edge bridges, only "core" bridges. This technique allows the bridges to forward every frame along a tree that will carry it to its destination along the least-cost path. This will require the use of VLAN IDs to identify bridges, as well as their current use for identifying VLANs. This makes the technique unsuitable for 802.1ad Q-in-Q provider bridge networks, because of the reduction in the number of available VLANs, one of which is required for each customer. However, it could be used profitably in the core of an 802.1ah MAC-in-MAC network.

Optionally, SPB will be used only to construct a few spanning trees, and these will be used exactly as they are used today in MSTP. As described, this is an advantage, not a disadvantage, for provider networks. The use of link state, instead of distance vector, technology by SPB will ensure that the convergence times of the network are more predictable and the worst-case convergence time will be shorter than for the current MSTP algorithm.

It is a major goal of P802.1aq to ensure that the changes to the data forwarding plane and thus the existing bridge hardware are as few and simple as possible. The details will depend on exactly what features of P802.1aq will be employed, on the specifics of each implementation, and of course, on the details of the standard as finally approved. However, you can expect that many of the capabilities of P802.1aq will be available to all existing bridges, and that many existing bridges will be able to take full advantage of P802.1aq with few, if any, hardware updates.

ITU-T Protection Switching

ITU-T Study Group 15, Working Party 3, Question 12, has produced a recommendation G.8031, "Ethernet Protection Switching." So far, only point-to-point protection switching has been approached. The basic idea is to have a network of bridge-like devices. For each E-Line EVC, the network management system creates both a primary and an alternate path through the network. The endpoints of the EVC use ITU-T Y.1731 Ethernet OAM to determine the operational state of each of the two paths, and use the primary path if it is up and the secondary path if the primary path fails.

This means of offering provider services has not, so far, been integrated with the capabilities of standard IEEE 802 bridges, and the details of the data plane supporting these E-Line EVCs have not been fully determined within ITU-T. There are proponents for at least two different approaches for the underlying data plane operation. The reader may track the progress of these standards from the ITU-T websites for these two study groups: www.itu.int/ITU-T/studygroups/com13 and www.itu.int/ITU-T/studygroups/com15.

Provider Backbone Bridge Traffic Engineering

The IEEE Standards Association has authorized the development of Project 802.1Qay Provider Backbone Bridge Traffic Engineering (PBB-TE). It is related to ITU-T protection switching, in that it creates point-to-point links protected by IEEE P802.1ag CFM or ITU-T Y.1731 OAM. It is closely related to IEEE P802.1ah backbone bridges, in that a specific data plane is proposed, using the format of 802.1ah MAC-in-MAC frames.

The point-to-point path between a pair of I-components is not established by learning the I-components' MAC addresses as the data frames traverse the backbone network's spanning tree. Rather, the entries in the filtering database for those MAC addresses are created by management operations, based on knowledge of the topology of the network—much as private connections are created in current telephony networks. Other alternatives have also been discussed: the filtering database entries could be created by dynamic protocols such as IS-IS, carrying MAC addresses, or by a variant of GMPLS, the MPLS signaling protocol.

Typically, two such paths are created between any pair of I-components, a primary and a secondary. IEEE 802.1ag CFM and/or Y.1731 OAM can be used end-to-end to detect the failure of either path, notify management, and switch traffic to the other path if needed.

Extensions of this point-to-point mechanism could be made for multipoint-to-multipoint networks. As the number of endpoints increases, the difficulty of finding two independent paths to all of those endpoints increases, until at some point, you have to run two networks in parallel. Also, two failures in the network, one in each half, can render all services inoperable. Then, only a dynamic bridging protocol such as MSTP or SPB can rescue the network. Fortunately, the changes to MSTP required to allow a division of the VLAN IDs and port bandwidth allocations between PBB-TE circuits and dynamically controlled topologies are trivial; both control techniques could coexist in the same backbone bridged network.

The characteristics of PBB-TE make it attractive to many vendors and providers:

- Its deployment requires no changes to the data plane frame forwarding behavior defined for a P8021.ah backbone bridge, a project for which a number of vendors have been developing equipment. This makes PBB-TE attractive to bridge vendors.

- The similarity of PBB-TE to existing telephony circuit-switching techniques makes it attractive to network operators; the cost of training large numbers of technicians to understand dynamic control protocols such as MSTP is not trivial.

- Since it is the ends (the bridges in which the I-components are embedded) that decide which paths to use, the bridges in between are not involved. The worst case for failure detection and recovery is both fast and predictable.

- The price paid for the speed and predictability of recovery is that multiple failures can bring down both the primary and secondary links. The Spanning Tree Protocols can take longer, but can provide connectivity between nodes as long as a physical path remains. However, this is a situation with which most carriers are both accustomed and comfortable.

IETF TRILL

A project is underway in the Transparent Interconnection of Lots of Links (TRILL) working group of IETF. It is not explicitly tackling the problem of provider networks, but is mentioned here for completeness. Its basic purpose is to employ routing techniques to forward bridged traffic. The TRILL website should be consulted for further information at: www.ietf.org/html.charters/trill-charter.html.

Economic Assessment

The cost of creating a Carrier Ethernet network using bridging technology is dependent on a number of questions that will have very different answers for different carriers:

- Does the access network—those parts of the network that multiplex and demultiplex Ethernet frames, but never switch them (bridge or route them)—exist?

- If the access network exists, does it deliver Ethernet frames to the bridges in a manner that they can digest easily, or does it require complex edge interfaces?

- Is the bridged Carrier Ethernet network a provider bridge (802.1ad) or a backbone bridge (802.1ah) network?

- Does the bridged network provide the foundation for other services, e.g., IP, L3VPN, MPLS, Frame Relay? Does it work in parallel with those services on a separate physical infrastructure, does it work in parallel on the same infrastructure in a "ships in the night" fashion, or does it float on top of those services that it bridges switching MAC addresses over virtual Ethernet links?

- What sort of redundancy and reliability features are required for this configuration? (Does the provider want redundant forwarding engines in every box, multiple boxes without redundancy within the box, or both?)

    And of course, most importantly:

- What sort of deal can the provider strike with the vendor, based on quantity and/or other considerations?

Some representative numbers are shown in Table 13.1 for three classes of provider bridges. These numbers are for high-end equipment with redundancy and routing capabilities. In Table 13.1, "LH" refers to long-haul (fiber) ports and "SH" to short-haul (copper) ports.

A typical provider bridge supporting nine 1 Gbit/sec long-haul links, with essentially all of the features described in this chapter for a provider bridge network, can be obtained for approximately $71,000. Two such devices can reliably provide a redundant interconnection capability for thousands of 1 Mbit/sec services through multiplexing/demultiplexing devices feeding their ports.

TABLE 13.1   Provider Bridge Pricing

Product	Component	Price ($)
Terabit class provider bridge or backbone bridge	Base	130,000
	10 Gbit/s LH port	11,400
	1 Gbit/s LH port	1,900
100 Gbit class provider bridge	Base	51,000
	1 Gbit/s LH port	1,200
10 Gbit class provider bridge	Base, Four 1 Gbit/s LH ports 24 10/100/1000 SH ports	24,000

Vendors Promoting this Solution

Table 13.2 shows a list of vendors currently offering Ethernet bridging solutions and their products that support bridging. Products that only support related technologies, including access multiplexing without directing frames based on MAC address, MPLS-based technologies, or router termination of Q-in-Q frames, are not included in this list. Of course, this list is constantly changing, as new product lines and new features are introduced.

TABLE 13.2   Vendors Offering Carrier Ethernet Bridged Solutions

Vendor	Solution/Product Name	Comments
Alcatel	7450	Provider bridge
Alcatel/Lucent/Riverstone	15800	Provider bridge
Cisco	Catalyst 7600	Provider bridge
	Catalyst 3750	Provider bridge
	ME3400, Catalyst 3750ME	Provider bridge
	ME2400	Provider bridge
	Catalyst 4000, 4500, ME4900	Provider bridge
	ME6500, Catalyst 6500	Provider bridge
Extreme	Summit X450	Provider bridge
	Black Diamond 12804	Backbone edge bridge
	Black Diamond 10808	Provider bridge
Nortel	8600	Provider bridge, backbone edge bridge
Siemens	SURPASS hiD 6610/15	Provider bridge
	SURPASS hiD 6630/50/70	Provider bridge
Tellabs	6315	Provider bridge

References

The best and most current description of the Rapid Spanning Tree Protocol is currently found in IEEE Std. 802.1Q-2005.

1. All IEEE 802 standards can be obtained from the Get 802 website at http://standards .ieee.org/getieee802/. Standards more than six months old are free. Those less than six months old can be obtained for a fee.

2. See the IEEE 802.1 website at www.ieee802.org/1 for additional information about IEEE 802.1 standards.

3. All IETF standards and requests for comments can be obtained from the Internet Engineering Task Force at www.ietf.org.

14

MPLS

by Giles Heron and Luca Martini

Multiprotocol Label Switching, or MPLS, was developed in the late 1990s. It is a packet-switching technology that has both connectionless and connection-orientated characteristics and that sits somewhere between the second and third layers of the OSI model (one of the reasons it is sometimes described as being "Layer 2.5"). Although originally designed to transport IP traffic, MPLS has developed into one of the key technologies in delivering Carrier Ethernet services.

Technology Description

We will now go on to give an overview of MPLS, and of the pseudowire and VPLS technologies that extend MPLS to offer Ethernet services, before examining how Ethernet over MPLS meets the MEF-defined Carrier Ethernet attributes.

Connectionless and Connection-Orientated Forwarding

There are two classes of packet-switched network technologies—connectionless and connection-orientated. Ethernet MAC switching is an example of connectionless forwarding, whereas ATM switching is an example of connection-orientated forwarding.

In a connectionless network, each router (or switch) decides independently how to forward each packet. Of course, in order for packets to be forwarded successfully across the network, routers must make consistent forwarding decisions. A router's forwarding decision is reached by running a forwarding algorithm using two pieces of input data: the packet header and a "forwarding table" held by the router. Thus, for consistency in forwarding decisions, the forwarding algorithms and forwarding tables of the routers must be consistent. The algorithms used to forward packets in IP networks are, for example, documented in RFC 1812 and the various routing protocols that may be used to populate the forwarding tables (such as OSPF and BGP) are documented in other IETF RFCs.

In a connection-orientated network, however, packets are forwarded along predefined connections from the source to the destination. Forwarding is again based on running an algorithm using the packet header and a forwarding database as inputs, but in this case, the information encoded in the packet header is simply a connection identifier (or "label"), which is generally assigned locally by the router and swapped to the identifier assigned by the next hop router (i.e., the next router in the path toward the destination) before forwarding to that router. The forwarding database consists simply of a list of labels—each associated with an egress interface and next hop router and, if labels are locally assigned, the label assigned by that next hop router. Connections (in MPLS these are called *Label Switched Paths* or *LSPs*) may be established either by manual configuration or by using a signaling protocol.

MPLS Forwarding

The MPLS architecture and protocols were developed in the late 1990s in response to concerns about the limitations of connectionless IP forwarding. Specific issues identified in the MPLS architecture and documented in RFC 3031 include

- It is easier to implement label lookup and replacement than the IP forwarding algorithms. This was one of the initial drivers for MPLS (though its importance has often been overstated) since label switching was implemented in hardware (e.g., in ATM switches) at a time when IP forwarding was only implemented in software—and hence label switches could support higher packet forwarding rates than IP routers. Carrier-class IP routers today are able to forward packets at line rate using hardware switching, so this issue is no longer considered important (though it is still true that label switching is simpler than IP forwarding).

- The ingress router may use information not included in the packet header (and which would thus not be available to a subsequent router) when assigning a packet to an LSP. Because subsequent routers (*Label Switching Routers* or *LSRs*) along the LSP need to examine only the label, and not the IP header, this can be generalized to enable non-IP traffic to be forwarded on MPLS LSPs (as with Ethernet over MPLS). This is probably the most important driver for MPLS, and is central to the layer 3 VPN technology that has driven much of the deployment of MPLS up to now.

- Packets may be assigned to LSPs that follow explicit paths rather than the path chosen by the IP routing protocols. This enables traffic engineering (a full description of traffic engineering is beyond the scope of this chapter) and could only be accomplished in a connectionless network by including a "source route" with each packet.

MPLS was designed to carry IP packets (though the *multiprotocol* in its name refers to its ability to work with other network layer protocols). MPLS also uses as much as possible of the existing IP infrastructure in its operation. Thus, MPLS uses IP addressing and IP routing protocols, and encapsulates its signalling traffic in IP. Indeed, MPLS is often known as *IP/MPLS*. MPLS forwarding operates at Layer 2; however, MPLS is often referred to as "Layer 2.5" because it has some Layer 3 characteristics, and because

Layer 2 header	MPLS header	IP packet	L2 FCS

Figure 14.1   Encapsulation of an IP packet in MPLS

the MPLS header (known as the *MPLS label stack*) generally sits between the Layer 2 header and the IP (Layer 3) header (see Figure 14.1).

MPLS supports both connection-orientated and connectionless modes of operation, depending on which signalling protocol is used to establish LSPs. LSPs established using RSVP-TE, which creates a point-to- point path across the network, or using static provisioning behave in a connection-orientated fashion. LSPs established using LDP, which creates a multipoint-to-point path congruent with the shortest path calculated by the *Interior Gateway Protocol*, or *IGP* (the IP routing protocol used within the service provider's network) behave in a connectionless fashion—although forwarding along the LSP is still based on label swapping.

RFC 3031 defines the concept of the *Forwarding Equivalence Class (FEC)*. The FEC (generally pronounced as "feck" rather than as "Eff Eee Cee") is the set of all packets that will follow the same path (or set of equivalent paths) through the network. Packets are classified into FECs at ingress into the network, and the FECs are encoded into labels—enabling packets to be forwarded along LSPs. FECs may be arbitrarily complex—for example, packets from different source interfaces, with different QoS requirements, or destined for different IP addresses may be mapped to the same FEC or to different FECs. Note that although the most commonly used FEC is the Address Prefix, which maps packets to routes in the IP routing table based on their Layer 3 forwarding information, packets may be mapped to FECs based on Layer 1, Layer 2, or Layer 4 forwarding information. The use of Layer 1 or Layer 2 information to map packets to FECs is a key building block in the pseudowire architecture that will be presented in "Pseudowires," later in this chapter.

The MPLS label is a 20-bit value that is included within a 32-bit "label stack entry," as defined in RFC3032 and as shown in Figure 14.2.

The fields in the MPLS label stack entry are used as follows:

- Each LSR along the LSP decrements the TTL (Time to Live) by one when forwarding a packet. If the TTL reaches zero, the packet is discarded. The TTL is used to prevent packets from recirculating when loops are created as a result of inconsistent router forwarding tables, such as during a *routing transient*—the period between a change in network topology and the point where all routers have learned the new topology. The TTL field is also used for traceroute where a sequence of packets is sent with increasing TTL. When sending IP traffic over MPLS, the IP TTL may be copied into the MPLS TTL at ingress to the LSP and then overwritten

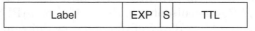

Label	EXP	S	TTL

Figure 14.2   The MPLS label stack entry

with the new MPLS TTL at egress (this is known as the *uniform model* and makes the MPLS LSP visible to IP traceroute), or alternatively the MPLS TTL may be set to an operator defined value—generally 225—at ingress (this is known as the *pipe model* and makes the MPLS LSP appear to be a single hop to IP traceroute). TTL processing for MPLS is documented in RFC 3443.

- MPLS supports label stacking, where multiple label stack entries are prepended to a single packet. This is useful in creating hierarchy to scale networks or to separate administrative domains, and in separating forwarding through the network from service multiplexing at a given endpoint. You will see that in the Ethernet over MPLS case, a packet typically has at least two labels—one used to reach the egress router and one used to identify the specific Ethernet service at the egress router. The S (or "bottom of stack") bit is set to 1 for the entry in the label stack closest to the payload and to 0 for all previous labels.

- There are two basic QoS models in MPLS. The E-LSP model uses the EXP (or "experimental") field to infer QoS. The L-LSP model infers QoS from the label and, optionally, also from the EXP field. Most routers and networks only support the E-LSP model. There have also been other suggestions as to the use of the EXP field (such as for congestion notification) but none has been standardised.

- The outermost label (the "top" label in the stack) is looked up at each LSR along the LSP. The lookup determines the next hop LSR for the packet and also the label operation to be performed on the packet. The supported operations are

  - **Swap** Replace the outermost label with a new label. Intermediate routers along an LSP will always perform a swap operation.

  - **Push** Add one or more label stack entries to the top of the label stack. At the ingress, LSR labels are always pushed. At intermediate LSRs along an LSP, labels may be pushed after first swapping the outermost label.

  - **Pop** The outermost label stack entry is removed. At the end of the LSP, the label stack is popped either by the egress LSR or by the penultimate router (the latter mode is known as *penultimate hop popping* or *PHP* and is permitted in MPLS because it reduces the load on the egress LSR in some cases). A pop operation may also instruct the LSR to process the next label—for example at intermediate LSRs along an LSP, a label may be popped before swapping the next label.

MPLS Signalling

MPLS LSPs may be established using various methods. The most commonly used are covered in this section.

Static Configuration The operator can provision LSPs through the network by statically configuring label mappings at each LSR. This can be labour intensive, of course, and unless OAM flows are sent (see the section on MPLS Protection below), it also creates an unprotected LSP; if any of the nodes or links on the paths fail, the LSP will no longer forward from ingress to egress.

LDP Signalling   The *Label Distribution Protocol (LDP)* is documented in RFC 3036 (though the specification is in the process of being revised). It was also extended to offer Constraint-Based Routing as CR-LDP in RFC 3212 but CR-LDP lost out in the market to RSVP-TE (see the description of RSVP-TE in the next section).

LDP LSRs discover each other by sending multicast "hello" messages to UDP port 646 over their physical links. It is also possible to run LDP between nonadjacent LSRs by using "extended discovery" procedures where each LSR is configured to send unicast "hello" messages to the IP address of the other (again using UDP port 646). This is known as *targeted LDP* and has applications in MPLS scaling and in pseudowire signalling (discussed in the sections on MPLS scaling and establishing pseudowires below). Once two LSRs have discovered each other, they establish an LDP session over which labels can be advertised. The LDP session runs over TCP using port 646 and is typically established between loopback IP addresses on the two LSRs (these are addresses that are internal to the node and are reachable if any of the nodes' physical interfaces are up). Note that two LSRs will generally only establish one LDP session to each other, even if LDP hellos have discovered multiple physical links between them.

As mentioned previously, LDP creates LSPs that follow the IGP shortest path. Where there are multiple equal cost paths (multiple equal-cost links to the same next-hop router and/or multiple next-hop routers with equal cost), packets will generally be load-shared across those paths using an Equal-Cost Multi-Path (ECMP) algorithm. LSRs only advertise labels for FECs when they have matching forwarding entries for those FECs—most commonly IP routes learned using the IGP. LSPs may be established either using independent control (in which case, an LSR may advertise a label for a FEC regardless of whether it has received a label mapping from a downstream LSR) or using ordered control (in which case, all LSRs other than the egress LSR may only advertise a label for a FEC once they have received a mapping from a downstream LSR). Ordered control ensures that LSPs are established end to end, whereas with independent control, partial LSPs may be created; though in a network where all LSRs share a correctly configured IGP, this condition may only occur temporarily during routing transients. Independent control is thought to result in slightly faster network convergence than ordered control.

LDP uses the following label messages to distribute labels:

- **Label Request**   Optionally sent by an upstream LSR to request a label from its downstream neighbour.

- **Label Mapping**   Sent by a downstream LSR to its upstream neighbour to advertise a label for a FEC. It may be sent either in response to a label request, known as downstream-on-demand label distribution, or simply when the LSR is ready to advertise the label, known as downstream-unsolicited label distribution. The label mapping message identifies both the FEC and the label to be advertised for that FEC. Both the FEC and label are encoded using TLV (Type-Length-Value) syntax—as are all LDP objects.

- **Label Withdraw**   Sent by a downstream LSR to its upstream neighbour to invalidate a previously advertised label mapping.

- **Label Release**   Sent by an upstream LSR to its downstream neighbour to indicate that it will no longer retain a label mapping. It may be sent either in response to a Label Withdraw or because the upstream LSR is using *conservative label retention* (i.e., it will only retain a label if it was learned from the next hop for that FEC in the IP routing table) and either the downstream LSR has advertised a FEC when it is not the next hop for that FEC, or the downstream LSR is no longer the next hop for the FEC. It is more common, however, to use liberal label retention, where the LSR retains all label mappings learned for a FEC and simply uses the one corresponding to the current next hop. Liberal label retention results in faster convergence since, when the next hop changes, the LSR already has a label for that next hop, but of course requires the LSR to store more label mappings.

LDP has also been extended to create point-to-multipoint and multipoint -to-multipoint LSPs (as *mLDP*). The point-to-multipoint LSPs created are analogous to the trees created by PIM-SSM in IP multicast, and the multipoint-to-multipoint LSPs to trees created by bidirectional PIM. mLDP may be used to carry IP multicast over MPLS or in multicast VPLS (see section on IP multicast in VPLS below).

RSVP-TE Signalling   As mentioned previously, RSVP-TE (documented in RFC 3209) creates point-to-point LSPs. RSVP-TE is an extension of the RSVP protocol (documented in RFC 2205), which was designed to create bandwidth reservations across IP networks. An RSVP-TE LSP is established using the following steps:

- The ingress LSR computes a path to the egress LSR. In general, this path is computed using a *Constrained Shortest Path First* algorithm (CSPF) that takes as inputs the LSP destination, the bandwidth, and QoS requirements for the LSP, any explicit user-supplied constraints (for example, links or nodes to include or exclude from the path), and the *Traffic Engineering Database (TED)*. The TED is an enhanced version of the IGP link state database that includes information on available bandwidth, link affinities (such as which links are suitable for different traffic types), and traffic engineering metrics, which can be used as an alternative to the IGP metric. The TED is built from information flooded by the IGP using the traffic engineering extensions to OSPF (documented in RFC 3630) or to IS-IS (documented in RFC 3784).

  1. The computed path is encoded into an Explicit Route Object (ERO), which is included in an RSVP-TE Path message sent toward the egress LSR (and forwarded hop by hop to that router using IP—but processed by the IP control plane at each LSR).

  2. Each router along the path creates state for the path and then forwards the message toward the next router in the ERO. The ERO may contain a complete list of the routers on the path to the egress (the usual case when using CSPF) or may be partial or even omitted.

  3. The egress LSR validates the Path message and then creates a Resv message containing a Label Object for the LSP.

4. The Resv message is forwarded back to the ingress LSR along the same path followed by the Path message, using the path state at each LSR to ensure it follows the same path. At each LSR, the label indicated in the received Label Object will be used as the egress label for the LSP, and a new Label Object will be included in the Resv message sent upstream to the previous LSR.

5. When the Resv message reaches the ingress LSR, the LSP setup is complete.

RSVP-TE has also been extended to enable it to create point-to-multipoint LSPs, which may also be traffic engineered. The LSPs created are analogous to the trees created by PIM-SSM in IP multicast. P2MP RSVP-TE is useful for applications such as multipoint video distribution or multicast VPLS (see section on IP Multicast in VPLS below).

BGP Signalling BGP is used by service providers as an exterior gateway protocol (i.e., to distribute routes to other service providers and to carry external routes within each service provider's network). RFC 2858 defines multiprotocol extensions to BGP, and RFC 3107 builds on this by defining how to advertise labelled routes using BGP. In RFC 3107, a label for FEC is piggy-backed on the BGP update message used to advertise the FEC itself.

BGP is used to signal the VPN labels used in the RFC 2547 standard for implementing IP VPNs over MPLS (now updated in RFC 4364), but it may also be used to advertise labelled FECs between different autonomous systems within one service provider's network or between service providers.

MPLS Protection

In looking at the subject of MPLS protection it is important to consider the MPLS OAM mechanisms that may be used for fault detection and diagnosis, as well as the traffic protection mechanisms that may be used to route traffic away from a failed link or node, and the node protection mechanisms that have been developed to enhance node availability in IP/MPLS networks.

MPLS OAM Since MPLS reuses IP addressing and IP routing protocols and transports its signalling over IP, the key tools used in MPLS network operation are the same as those defined for use in IP networks. If LSPs are established dynamically using RSVP-TE or LDP, and if the network elements operate correctly, then IP tools themselves are sufficient for network operation. However, additional tools and protocols have been defined to enable detection of MPLS data plane failures.

LSP ping is defined in RFC 4379. LSP ping may be used to verify connectivity along an MPLS LSP, and if the ping fails, then LSP pings may be sent in traceroute mode to diagnose the location of the fault. The key to LSP ping is to ensure that packets are forwarded along the LSP rather than using hop by hop IP forwarding, and if the LSP is broken, that the LSP ping is dropped. This is achieved by sending LSP ping requests along an LSP but to an IP destination address in network 127/8 (i.e., in the range 127.0.0.1 to 127.255.255.254). Network 127/8 is guaranteed never to be forwarded by an IP router, so if the LSP terminates prematurely, the packet will be dropped. Packets addressed to network 127/8 are also typically discarded by hosts (reducing the risk of LSP ping packets being misdelivered to hosts). Finally, by sending packets to varying destination addresses in 127/8, the sender can exercise all ECMP paths for an LDP-signaled LSP (since routers typically do a hash of the IP destination address, or source and destination address, when performing ECMP).

LSP ping packets are sent to UDP port 3503 (requests) or from UDP port 3503 (replies). The TTL is set to 255 for LSP ping and starts at 1 when being used in traceroute mode (being incremented to probe to subsequent LSRs). Note that a response will only be sent if the destination implements LSP ping—in the traceroute case, this may result in "missing hops" from routers that don't implement the standard. Each packet indicates how its recipient should send its reply; because MPLS LSPs are unidirectional, the reply can't be sent back over the LSP. Most commonly replies are sent as IP packets, but they may be sent as IP packets with the router alert option set (which forces the packet to the control plane of each router in the path, and which may therefore enable a response to reach its target in the presence of forwarding plane bugs on the return path, but does require all routers on the return path to implement LSP ping), or using an associated control channel, such as VCCV (see the section on Pseudowire OAM below). The LSP ping request also carries a copy of the FEC being tested, so the egress LSR may verify that it is an egress for that FEC in both the control and forwarding planes.

If proactive detection of forwarding-plane faults is required, then a lighter-weight protocol than ICMP ping (or LSP ping) is required. The IETF-defined forwarding-plane OAM mechanism for IP (and for MPLS) is Bidirectional Forwarding Detection (BFD). BFD may be used for rapid detection of routing/signalling neighbour failure in cases where the router fails to detect loss of the physical layer, and may also be applied end-to-end on MPLS LSPs to detect LSP failure, as discussed below in the section on OAM-based Fault Detection. BFD has a simple packet format and is designed to be implemented in the router's forwarding engine, rather than in the control plane. However, BFD is unable to support traceroute functionality or to verify the mapping between the control and forwarding planes at egress (hence LSP ping is still a useful tool for problem diagnosis in the event that BFD detects a problem).

When sent over MPLS LSPs, BFD is used in asynchronous mode, where the ingress LSR periodically sends BFD control packets to the egress LSR over the LSP being tested, and the egress LSR periodically sends BFD control packets to the ingress LSR. If the egress LSR fails to receive a BFD packet from the ingress LSR in a negotiated multiple of the period at which the ingress LSR sends them, it sends a BFD packet identifying the fault condition. The ingress LSR sends BFD packets to a destination address in 127/8 and to UDP port 3784, setting the IP TTL to 1. The egress LSR sends BFD packets to the same IP address that the ingress LSR sources its packets from and from UDP port 3784.

When using BFD to detect MPLS LSP failures in conjunction with MPLS fast reroute (see section below on fast reroute), it is essential to tune the frequency with which BFD packets are sent so that fast reroute repairs problems faster than BFD detects them. Given the speed with which fast reroute typically repairs problems (a few milliseconds), this is generally easy to ensure. When using BFD in conjunction with backup LSPs (see section below on backup LSPs), BFD may detect link or node failures faster than the control plane, but since both BFD and the control plane will take the same action on detecting a failure, this isn't a problem. In general, when using BFD, the upper bound on the sending rate is determined by the ability of the LSRs to process BFD control packets.

The ITU-T has also defined an MPLS OAM mechanism in Y.1711. Y.1711 is designed to run end-to-end along an MPLS LSP with a 1-sec frequency. There has also been work on enhanced OAM mechanisms for MPLS which use elements of Y.1711 and of Y.1731 Ethernet OAM.

Traffic Protection   MPLS supports a range of traffic protection mechanisms. Note that there are two stages to traffic protection—the fault must first be detected, and then the traffic must be diverted away from the fault.

LDP-signaled LSPs   Because LDP-signaled LSPs follow the IGP, shortest path protection of these LSPs depends on IGP reconvergence. When a link or node on the shortest path for an LSP fails, the upstream nodes will remove the label mapping for the LSP from their forwarding information base (FIB) until a new shortest path and a matching label for that path is found. Failure of a link or node may be detected using physical layer mechanisms (such as loss of light), layer 2 mechanisms (such as PPP keepalives), or using BFD sessions between adjacent LSRs. The same detection mechanisms may be used for backup LSPs and for fast reroute (both described below).

Backup LSPs   One commonly used protection mechanism is to define a backup path for an RSVP-TE signaled LSP, ideally disjoint from the primary path signaled for the LSP. The backup path (often known as a stand-by LSP or as a secondary LSP) may either be presignaled (so label state is instantiated along all LSR in the backup path) or simply precomputed (so signalling will be required to re-establish the LSP along the backup path). When a link or node along the LSP fails, the upstream node will generate an RSVP-TE PathErr message toward the ingress LSR. The PathErr message needs to traverse all the nodes and links on the path back to the ingress LSR. On receipt of the PathErr message, the ingress LSR will switch to the backup path. If the backup path is presignaled, this can happen within a few milliseconds of the PathErr message reaching the ingress LSR—for an overall protection time in the order of hundreds of milliseconds.

Fast Reroute   SONET/SDH networks achieve protection switching in 50 ms for a ring of up to 1000 km circumference. When running MPLS directly over unprotected infrastructure (fibres and wavelengths), there may be a requirement to achieve similar (or better) protection switching at the MPLS layer—especially when providing circuit-based services over MPLS. MPLS fast reroute addresses this challenge by repairing failures at the point of failure, rather than waiting for the PathErr to propagate to the ingress LSR. When signalling an LSP, the ingress LSR requests fast reroute protection and indicates whether link or node protection is required. There are two fast reroute models: one-to-one backup, where each LSR along the path creates a "detour" LSP for each protected LSP, and facility bypass, where each LSR along the path creates a single "bypass" LSP for all protected LSPs through the link or node being protected—generally to the next hop LSR for link protection or to the next-next hop LSR for node protection. The facility bypass case is, of course, much more scalable than one-to-one backup (since fewer fast reroute LSPs are required), but requires the node that detects the failure (the *Point of Local Repair* or *PLR*) to tunnel traffic for all the affected LSPs by swapping the outermost label to the one expected by the next hop or next-next hop (the *merge point* or MP) and then pushing on a label corresponding to the bypass LSP. This is a good example of MPLS label stacking in operation. In addition to forwarding traffic over a detour or bypass LSP, the PLR sends a PathErr message upstream to the ingress LSR, which may then choose to create a new protected LSP that avoids the failed resource. It is best practice that the new LSP will be created using "make before break" methodology where traffic is forwarded on the old LSP (and thus over the fast reroute detour or bypass) until the new LSP has been fully established. Many fast reroute implementations are capable of protecting 1000s of LSPs within a few milliseconds—far surpassing the protection times required in SONET/SDH.

OAM-based Fault Detection   The three protection mechanisms mentioned above are all based on use of the IP/MPLS control plane to propagate fault status. An alternative is to use OAM messages in the MPLS forwarding plane (e.g., BFD) and to send these along each LSP from the ingress LSR to the egress. This would generally be used for LSPs provisioned either with static configuration or an out-of-band control plane such as GMPLS. In either case, there will be no in-band control plane to propagate fault status. OAM-based fault detection may be used with LSPs provisioned either in a 1:1 mode, where traffic is forwarded over the primary path but is switched to the secondary path when OAM flows detect a break in the primary path, or in a 1+1 mode where traffic is forwarded simultaneously over both paths and the egress LSR selects which traffic to forward, and which to discard, based on receipt of OAM messages. The 1+1 mode is capable of sub-50-ms protection (detection time is a function of the frequency with which OAM packets are sent—typically the LSP is declared down after three packets are missed). However, the 1:1 mode, requires the egress to inform the ingress of the error condition, and the ingress to switch from the working to the protect path, and thus incurs at least one roundtrip time of additional delay when compared to the 1+1 mode.

Node Protection   Although traffic protection techniques may be used to route around failed links or nodes in the core of the network, they are generally unable to protect against failure of the ingress or egress LSRs, since customers attach directly to these. It is also, of course, desirable that core LSRs be as resilient as possible in order to minimise the protection switching required to bypass failed nodes.

Modern routers, and LSRs, are designed to have no single point of failure—power supplies, switching fabrics, and control cards are duplicated and network interfaces are distributed across multiple independent line cards. However, in order to take advantage of this hardware redundancy, additional software support is required. With respect to the routing and signalling protocols used to establish LSPs, there are two basic techniques that may be used:

- **Nonstop routing** In order for routing and signalling protocols to continue to operate when a control card switchover occurs (due to failure of the active control card), it is necessary to replicate all state changes resulting from the operation of those protocols from the active to the backup control card. If the active card fails, the backup is thus able to assume the active role without its neighbours being aware of the switchover. One disadvantage of this approach is that state synchronisation requires significant additional CPU resources to operate.

- **Nonstop forwarding** An alternative to ensuring continued operation of routing and signalling protocols during a control card switchover is to enhance the protocols so that when a switchover occurs, the failed node is given time to recover by its neighbours and is able to ask those neighbours to refresh its state. Graceful Restart extensions have been implemented for OSPF, IS-IS, RSVP, LDP, and BGP to facilitate this. One disadvantage of this approach is that for a router to perform a graceful restart its neighbours must also implement the protocol extensions.

Another area of concern for operators is the need to upgrade node software periodically to take advantage of new features or to fix bugs. If this occurs in the core of the network, it is possible to steer LSPs away from the node being upgraded for the duration of the upgrade. However, as with node switchovers, if an edge node needs to be rebooted to activate a software upgrade, this will impact customers directly connected to that node. Many router vendors are now adding in-service software upgrade support to address this problem. Nonstop routing or forwarding techniques are used to enable upgrade of the active control card; however, the most complex problem is upgrading the line cards, especially where these have programmable forwarding ASICs.

MPLS Scaling

Scaling a connectionless network such as IP is largely an issue of increasing the forwarding performance of the nodes as link speeds increase, and of scaling the routing tables (either by increasing the memory used to store the routing tables or by aggregating routes to reduce the memory required). Scaling a connection-orientated network adds issues of scaling forwarding state. Since MPLS has both connectionless and connection-orientated characteristics both sets of issues must be addressed, as must some specific issues relating to MPLS itself.

Routing State In order to establish an RSVP-TE signalled LSP, each router along the LSP must know how to reach the egress LSR. Thus, routes may be summarized without impacting LSP signalling. However, the traffic engineering extensions to OSPF and IS-IS operate only within a single IGP area (to restrict the scope over which their messages are flooded), and thus when CSPF is used, RSVP-TE LSPs may only be signaled across a single IGP area. Although there have been various efforts to define solutions for inter-area traffic, engineering size limitations for a single IGP area (typically several hundred nodes) are greater than the number of nodes that can be meshed with RSVP-TE LSPs (the "N squared" problem discussed below).

For LDP LSPs, each LSR must have a host route for every other LSR to which it wishes to build an LSP. This prevents these routes from being summarised at area boundaries within the SP's network if LDP is to be used, but does not prevent other routes (for example, those corresponding to the interfaces connecting routers) from being summarised. An IGP can typically scale to several thousand routes, ensuring that LDP LSPs can scale for most networks.

Label State   Each MPLS LSR along the path of an LSP installs state for that LSP. In the case of RSVP-TE, LSPs are point-to-point, and if connectivity is required between a set of N LSR, then $N(N-1)$ LSPs are required. This is known as the "N squared" problem and limits network scaling at the intermediate LSRs. LDP LSPs are generally multipoint-to-point in nature since an LSR forwards all traffic to a given FEC to the same next hop and using the same label. Thus, for connectivity between a set of N LSR, just N LDP LSPs are required.

LSP Hierarchy   One solution to improving network scaling is to use LSP hierarchy, based on adding labels to the MPLS label stack. For example, one popular approach is to run LDP "over" RSVP-TE. In this approach, LDP LSPs are used end to end, but RSVP-TE LSPs are used to cross the backbone area. This enables service providers to use the rapid restoration mechanisms of RSVP-TE and to traffic engineer within the backbone (typically from city to city), but to scale the network to a similar size to that achievable with a pure LDP design. In order for this approach to operate, the Area Border Routers (ABRs) must be configured with targeted LDP sessions to each other, so that the ABRs for each area can advertise labels to the ABRs for all other areas for each edge router (Label Edge Router or LER) in the area. For a network of N LERs and M areas with two ABRs per area, this results in $N + 2M(M-1)$ LSPs for a network where each LER has a single LSP to every other LER.

This "LDP over RSVP-TE" approach may be extended to use an RSVP-TE LSP from the LER to the ABR, from ABR to ABR, and from ABR to LER. To do this, targeted LDP sessions are configured between the ABRs in each area and all their local LERs, and a full mesh of RSVP-TE LSPs is created between all the ABRs and LERs in each area.

Further hierarchical scaling approaches are possible, for example using RSVP-TE to create forwarding adjacencies over which other RSVP-TE LSPs may be signalled.

MPLS QoS

There are two fundamental aspects to Quality of Service (QoS) in packet-switched networks:

- Ensuring the network can meet the QoS requirements before the packet is sent
- Enforcing QoS in the network elements as packets are forwarded

The former requirement is addressed in the control plane, and the latter in the forwarding plane. The forwarding plane mechanisms used for QoS enforcement are generally based on using multiple queues that are scheduled in strict order of priority, using some form of round robin mechanism or a combination of both. Packets that are classified into the same queue will maintain order throughout the network, but order will not be maintained across queues. Packets may also be marked with an indicator of their *drop precedence* to enable the network elements to decide which packets to drop first during congestion, using algorithms such as Weighted Random Early Detection (WRED).

QoS models themselves may be divided into two major classes:

- **Soft QoS (Class of Service or CoS)**   In this model (epitomised by the IETF DiffServ architecture), forwarding plane QoS techniques are used to provide different forwarding treatment to different classes of traffic. This model scales well, since there is no need for per-flow state, and is applicable to connectionless and connection-orientated forwarding, but is unable to provide guaranteed forwarding behavior.

- **Hard QoS**   In this model (epitomised by the IETF IntServ architecture) resources are reserved for the each connection using the control plane, and then forwarding plane techniques are applied to ensure that each connection gets the required level of QoS. This model is less scalable (as per-flow reservations are required), but can be used to enable a firm guarantee that a traffic contract will be met.

Control Plane QoS   When signalling an MPLS LSP with RSVP-TE, an LSR signals the bandwidth required for the LSP. Each LSR in the path checks the bandwidth requested against the bandwidth available on its outbound link and only forwards the Path message if there is sufficient bandwidth available for the LSP on that link. The available bandwidth on each link is also advertised using the TE-enhanced IGP (i.e., OSPF-TE or ISIS-TE) and will be stored in the TED at each LSR. When an LSR runs CSPF, it will only select a path that has sufficient bandwidth to allow the LSP to be established. However, LSP reservations and IGP advertisements run asynchronously to each other, and the LSP setup may still fail due to insufficient bandwidth at one of the LSRs in the path as described above. In that case, the ingress LSR will run CSPF again to find another path. The process of checking whether resources are available before attempting to reserve them is known as *Connection Admission Control (CAC)* and required to provide hard QoS.

LDP does not reserve bandwidth for LSPs, and control plane QoS is not applicable for LDP-signalled LSPs.

Forwarding Plane QoS   As mentioned previously, there are two QoS models for MPLS LSPs:

- **E-LSP model**   In this model, QoS is inferred solely from the value of the EXP bits in the MPLS label shim. Traffic from two LSPs with the same EXP value will receive identical QoS treatment. This is an implementation of the soft QoS model—even if bandwidth is reserved per LSP in the control plane, there is no way to enforce this in the forwarding plane. Because there are only three EXP bits, there are only eight possible combinations of output queue and drop precedence that may be encoded into each packet.

- **L-LSP model**   In this model, QoS is inferred both from the label and the EXP bits in the MPLS label shim. Each LSP has a dedicated queue assigned to it, and then the EXP bits may be used to encode multiple levels of drop precedence within that queue. This is an implementation of the hard QoS model because bandwidth may be both reserved and policed per LSP. Since there are rarely more than three or four levels of drop precedence, one EXP bit is "spare" and may be used for congestion notification. In fact, it is also possible to accommodate congestion notification in the E-LSP model by assigning codepoints to indicate the presence of congestion—but that, of course, further reduces the number of queues and/or drop precedences that can be encoded in the EXP field.

The E-LSP and L-LSP models are defined in RFC 3270 ("MPLS Support of Differentiated Services"), though there has been little or no implementation of the signalling extensions defined in that RFC.

MPLS Applications

Having discussed the MPLS technology it is useful at this point to briefly introduce some of the applications for MPLS.

IP-VPNs   One of the first applications for MPLS was to offer IP-VPNs. As mentioned previously, the MPLS VPN architecture is described in RFC 4364 but is often known as RFC 2547 after the initial RFC published to describe it. Most IP-VPN networks use LDP-signaled LSPs, since a full mesh of tunnels is required between the LERs and these can most easily be created using LDP.

"BGP Free" Core Networks   Some service providers have deployed MPLS as a means of keeping their core networks free from external routes. Edge routers still use BGP to learn external routes; however, they reach each other using LSPs across an MPLS core. Since the core routers now switch packets over LSPs, each core router only needs to know how to reach the edge routers. This also enhances security since external customers are unable to communicate with the core routers. Multiple sets of edge routers (e.g., one for public Internet, one for IP-VPNs, one for Layer 2 VPNs, and one for Voice over IP services) may be independently interconnected over a common MPLS core.

Traffic Engineering   Many service providers have deployed MPLS traffic engineering using RSVP-TE to enable them to optimise the efficiency of their networks and to specify explicit routes for traffic in cases where certain constraints must be met (for example, routing voice traffic over the shortest possible path and best-effort traffic over the cheapest possible path). Traffic engineering may be applied for some, or for all, traffic and may be applied either in an "online" mode where each MPLS LER calculates the optimal path for an LSP using CSPF or in an "offline" mode where the service provider calculates optimal paths for all required LSPs and then configures an explicit route for each LSP at its ingress LER. A third mode where LSRs may request a path from a dedicated server is being standardised and is known as the *Path Computation Element (PCE)*.

Layer 2 VPNs   A fourth application for MPLS is the establishment of Layer 2 VPNs either by using sets of point-to-point connections (known as *pseudowires*) or by emulating a switched Ethernet LAN (using a technology known as VPLS). These are discussed in the next two sections of this chapter. Although service providers offering IP-VPN have generally used LDP-signalled LSPs, providers offering Layer 2 services more commonly use RSVP-TE in order to offer deterministic bandwidth and delay guarantees and rapid service restoration in the event of failures.

Pseudowires

Historically, IP networks have been layered on top of connection-orientated Layer 1 or Layer 2 technologies—for example, SDH/SONET virtual containers or ATM virtual circuits—which have then adapted the traffic onto the underlying transport infrastructure (fibres or wavelengths). As IP (and especially Internet) traffic grew exponentially in the mid-1990s, it became an ever greater consumer of the SDH/SONET or ATM infrastructure, but with routers using general-purpose microprocessors to forward traffic, there was still a speed gap between the fastest IP interface and that of the long-haul transport systems. However, by the late 1990s, routers became available with ASIC-based forwarding able to fill the 2.5 Gbps and 10 Gbps links provided by transport systems, making it possible to bypass the ATM and SDH layers.

New entrant carriers with "all-IP" networks now faced a challenge in offering ATM and Frame Relay services over their networks because IP networks supported connectionless Layer 3 service rather than connection-orientated Layer 2 service. However MPLS, with its mix of connectionless and connection-orientated characteristics, was increasingly being used both to offer IP VPN services and to enable traffic engineering for IP core networks and could easily be extended to offer Layer 2 services.

One early solution to offering Layer 2 services over MPLS was Juniper's Circuit Cross Connect (CCC). With CCC, an LSR associated a pair of RSVP-TE signalled LSPs (one for which it was ingress and one for which it was egress) with an attachment circuit (either a physical interface or a logical interface such as a port and VLAN). Any frame received on the attachment circuit was sent over the outbound LSP, and any frame received from the inbound LSP was sent over the attachment circuit. The problem with such a solution, however, is that if a carrier wished to offer Layer 2 services to its customers, then for each Layer 2 circuit, there was a pair of RSVP-TE LSPs through the core of the IP/MPLS network, resulting in poor scaling properties for the service.

A more scalable approach was invented by a team working at Level(3) Communications, and published in IETF as draft-martini (after its inventor, Luca Martini). In the draft-martini approach, each attachment circuit is associated with a pair of MPLS labels—one for each direction—however these labels are then carried within MPLS LSPs (using MPLS label stacking), so that a single MPLS LSP can carry a large number of customer services (and, in fact, the LSPs may be the same ones that are used to carry IP traffic). The draft-martini approach was eventually standardized in the IETF PWE3 ("Pseudowire Emulation Edge to Edge") Working Group and forms the basis of the pseudowire architecture.

One key to the draft-martini approach was to maximise reuse of existing hardware and software technology. Using MPLS labels as the forwarding plane identifiers for pseudowires and extending LDP signalling to establish pseudowires made it relatively straightforward to implement pseudowires on the IP/MPLS router platforms available at the time. Some minor compromises were, in fact, made to make it easier for existing hardware to implement the technology.

Layer 2 pseudowires have been defined to carry Ethernet, ATM, Frame Relay, HDLC, and PPP traffic. Layer 1 pseudowires have also been defined to enable service providers to transport TDM signals and SONET/SDH frames across IP/MPLS networks. IP pseudowires have been defined to enable interconnection of IP endpoints running different Layer 2 protocols but using Layer 2 forwarding (the IP pseudowire encapsulation removes all Layer 2 framing and carries only the IP payload). In the pseudowire architecture, as in the Layer 2 and Layer 3 VPN architectures, the LER is known as a *provider edge* or *PE* device (core LSRs are known as *provider* or *P* devices), and the device at the far end of the attachment circuit to the LER is known as the *customer edge* or *CE* device.

Pseudowire Forwarding As just discussed, the draft-martini architecture relies on MPLS LSPs to transport Layer 2 (or Layer 1) information across IP/MPLS networks. In order to send a Layer 2 frame across the network, an ingress PE prepends a label stack to the frame and sends the resulting packet into an MPLS LSP.

The bottom label in the stack is known as the *PW label*. This label is used to identify the pseudowire and the corresponding egress port at the egress PE and is assigned by the egress PE. If the payload of the MPLS packet is, for example, an Ethernet frame, the PW label will correspond to an Ethernet port or port and VLAN at the egress PE. So when the egress PE receives the packet, it will remove the PW label and switch the payload to the corresponding port or port and VLAN. This process is unidirectional and will be repeated independently for bidirectional operation.

Any labels above the PW label in the stack are used simply to transport the packet from the ingress PE to the egress PE along the selected MPLS LSP. In general, only one such label is required, and it is known as the *tunnel label*. Note that the tunnel label, if present, must be immediately above the PW label (except for the case where an intermediate label is used for router alert VCCV, as described in the pseudowire OAM section below). The tunnel label may be removed before the packet reaches the egress PE if PHP is used, and if the ingress and egress PE are adjacent, may never be pushed on.

So when the ingress PE wants to send a frame along a pseudowire to the egress PE, it first pushes on the PW label assigned by the egress PE and then (in the general case) adds a tunnel label corresponding to the selected tunnel LSP and possibly additional labels.

Any intermediate LSRs along the LSP need only examine the tunnel label in order to forward the packet along the tunnel LSP—they do not need to be aware of the existence of one or more pseudowires within the tunnel LSP. Intermediate LSRs may also push or pop additional labels, for example, for fast reroute protection or in cases where LSP hierarchy is used. The egress PE uses the PW label to determine which attachment circuit to forward the received Layer 2 frame on. Note that for some Layer 2 protocols, such as Ethernet (see Figure 14.3 below), the frame header is carried across the pseudowire, whereas for others, such as Frame Relay, it is removed and a new header is added by the egress PE.

NOTE   When carrying Layer 2 traffic over MPLS, the MPLS label stack sits between the service provider's Layer 2 header and the service user's Layer 2 frame (which may or may not include a header). When Ethernet is carried over MPLS and there is an Ethernet link between two MPLS LSRs, there will be two MAC headers on each packet, separated by an MPLS label stack.

The Control Word   The Generic PW MPLS Control Word defined in RFC 4385 and shown in Figure 14.4 is required for some pseudowire types, such as Frame Relay, and is optional for others, including Ethernet. When used, it is inserted between the label stack and the payload.

The fields in the control word are used as follows:

- The first four bits of the control word are set to all zeroes. This enables core LSRs, which perform ECMP by inspecting the packet to identify flows, to distinguish pseudowire payloads from IP packets (where the first four bits will be 0100 for IPv4 and 0110 for IPv6).

- In cases where the Layer 2 header is removed, there may be a need to carry header flags such as congestion notification to the egress PE. Four bits are provided for this. These bits are not used for Ethernet pseudowires, as there are no flags in the Ethernet header.

- There may be cases where large frames need to be carried over LSPs with insufficiently large Maximum Transmission Units (MTUs). In such cases, it may be necessary to fragment the frames before transmission and to reassemble the fragments at egress and hence to carry an indication of whether a packet contains a fragment, and if so, whether it contains the final fragment of the frame. Two bits are provided for this. Fragmentation is rarely implemented for Ethernet pseudowires. Service providers generally ensure that the MTU of their LSPs is sufficient to transport the largest frame size supported by their service.

Layer 2 header	Tunnel label	VC label	Ethernet frame (FCS removed)	L2 FCS

Figure 14.3   Ethernet pseudowire encapsulation

0 0 0 0	Flags	Frg	Length	Sequence number

Figure 14.4 The Generic PW MPLS Control Word

- One potential issue in carrying Layer 2 protocols over MPLS is that if the payload plus MPLS headers is smaller than the minimum Ethernet payload length (46 bytes), then padding will be added to the packet when it crosses an Ethernet segment on the LSP path. Because MPLS has no length field, this padding will be retained until the packet reaches the egress PE. When carrying IP over MPLS, the length field in the IP packet header can be used to determine how much padding must be removed; however, most Layer 2 protocols have no length field and instead rely on physical layer framing to detect the end of the frame. The length field is 6 bits and is only valid if the frame length is less than 64 octets. Since this is greater than the minimum Ethernet payload length, this enables transport of small frames over Ethernet links. These bits are, of course, not used for Ethernet pseudowires since a minimum-sized Ethernet frame (the smallest frame the pseudowire will carry) is bigger than the minimum Ethernet payload length!

- The 16-bit sequence number may be useful when carrying Layer 2 protocols such as ATM and Frame Relay, which have strict requirements that frame order be maintained over a network that may reorder packets. It is rarely implemented in the Ethernet pseudowire case because most Ethernet applications do not have strict frame order requirements; IP/MPLS networks do not generally reorder packets, and many routers have forwarding plane implementations that are unable to support sequence number processing.

Given all the above, it is not surprising that the control word is rarely used for Ethernet pseudowires.

Establishing Pseudowires   Pseudowires may be established either using static configuration—where an operator configures the labels to be used to identify the pseudowire on the PEs at either end of the pseudowire and configures each PE to push the label expected by the other onto the payload before adding the tunnel label—or using LDP signalling between the PEs at either end of the pseudowire. Note that the choice of pseudowire establishment mechanism is completely independent from the choice of LSP establishment mechanism.

The procedures used to establish pseudowires using LDP are documented in RFC 4447. Because the pseudowire labels need to be known only to the PEs at either end of the pseudowire, targeted LDP is used between them. Two new FEC types (TLVs) are defined here.

PWid FEC   The *PWid FEC* (also known as "FEC 128") was defined in the original draft-martini and uses a dual-ended model, where the PE at either end of the pseudowire are configured with an identical 32-bit PW ID that enables each to correlate the label mapping sent to its peer with the label received from that peer. FEC 128 also identifies the PW type (e.g., Ethernet VLAN, FR DLCI, etc.) and advertises a Group ID. The Group ID provides a means of identifying a set of pseudowires—for example, all pseudowires corresponding to VLANs on the same physical port or all pseudowires being carried over a specific LSP to the egress PE—and may be used to notify the peer of changes in status of all pseudowires in that set in a single operation. Additional optional interface parameters are also carried in FEC 128 (for example, the maximum frame size that will be transported across the pseudowire). In this model, a pseudowire is uniquely identified by the PW type, PW ID, and the pair of PEs at either end of the pseudowire.

Generalized PWid FEC   The *generalized PWid FEC* (also known as "FEC 129") was added in a later revision of draft-martini and provides for a range of provisioning models. Instead of a unique identifier for each pseudowire, this model creates unique identifiers for the attachment circuits at either end of the pseudowire. These are structured as an Attachment Group Identifier (AGI) that must match between both ends of a circuit and an individual identifier. The FEC consists of the AGI plus Source and Target individual identifiers (SAII and TAII). A sent FEC matches a received FEC if the AGIs match and if the TAII of each matches the SAII of the other. Two additional objects are signalled along with FEC 129, the PW grouping TLV (which is analogous to the Group ID in FEC 128) and the interface parameters TLV (which is analogous to the interface parameters in FEC 128).

Pseudowire OAM   Because pseudowires are carried over MPLS LSPs, the pseudowire architecture assumes that network faults will be corrected at the MPLS layer. However, it is still essential for a PE to be able to inform a remote PE if its local attachment circuit goes down or if it becomes aware that the LSP to or from that remote PE has failed (the remote PE may be unaware of the LSP failure). In the general case, the PE also informs the device connected to the local attachment circuit that there is a fault; however, in the Ethernet VLAN case, there is no mechanism by which a PE may notify a CE of a fault (when doing a port-mode Ethernet pseudowire, the PE may disable the link), though the MEF is currently working on an Ethernet LMI to address this.

The initial versions of draft-martini relied on the PE sending a label withdraw for the pseudowire to the remote PE to notify it of failures. Thus, there were only two states that could be distinguished: pseudowire up and pseudowire down. There was no means of identifying whether a pseudowire was down due to administrative purposes or due to a fault.

The next step in pseudowire OAM was the addition of the status TLV. This object may be sent in an LDP notification message to inform the remote PE of pseudowire status changes, instead of withdrawing the PW label. The notification message includes both the status TLV, which carries a code indicating the reason for the PW fault, and an FEC 128 or 129 TLV to identify the pseudowire, or pseudowires, for which the change in status is being relayed.

Although control plane–based OAM techniques are sufficient in the absence of software or hardware bugs, there may also be a requirement for forwarding plane–based OAM, especially in cases where pseudowires are established manually. The forwarding plane OAM technique for pseudowires is known as Virtual Circuit Connectivity Verification (VCCV) and creates an OAM control channel along which LSP ping or BFD packets can be transported. VCCV supports three control channel types:

- The PW Associated Channel is defined in RFC 4385, and is known as inband VCCV. The PW Associated Channel may only be used on pseudowires that carry a control word and is identified by a 32-bit header starting with the bits "0001" (to distinguish it from the control word).

- Insertion of a router alert label between the tunnel label and the PW label, known as out-of-band VCCV. Because of the change to the label stack, this approach may result in OAM packets taking a different path to data packets when ECMP is used.

- TTL expiry—by setting the TTL in the PW label to 1, the ingress PE can force the egress PE to process the packet in the control plane. Again, in this mode, the control word must be present.

The key in all three control channel cases is that VCCV packets are sent along the same LSP, and using the same PW label, as user data on the pseudowire, but are intercepted by the control plane of the egress PE rather than being forwarded on the egress attachment circuit.

LSP ping over VCCV may be used as a reactive troubleshooting tool to verify that the pseudowire is passing traffic correctly. LSP ping packets identify the FEC (FEC 128 or 129) for the pseudowire. Since pseudowires only have a single-hop LSP, traceroute is not used. In the VCCV case, the PE sending the LSP ping will typically indicate that it wants the reply sent over the reverse path of the pseudowire, but if the ping fails, it may try other response methods to identify whether the problem is on the forward or reverse direction of the pseudowire.

BFD, however, may be used as a proactive tool for pseudowire monitoring—though since routers can generally support only a relatively small number of BFD sessions, VCCV BFD is rarely enabled except for very high value pseudowires or where potential issues have already been identified. VCCV BFD runs in asynchronous mode, with each PE sending BFD packets to the remote PE. If either PE misses a negotiated number of BFD packets from its peer, it will send a BFD packet indicating that it cannot "hear" its packets. Both PEs will (if possible) notify their attached CEs of the fault condition.

Ultimately, even with VCCV, the OAM mechanisms only test the pseudowire itself; they do not test the adaptation function that encapsulates Layer 2 frames into pseudowire packets or the functioning of the attachment circuit itself. For this reason, it may be useful for the PE to perform client-layer OAM tests across the pseudowire and toward the attachment circuit.

Pseudowire Redundancy   A pseudowire connects two PE devices over an MPLS network. However, there are cases where providers want to provide backup for a pseudowire.

One example might be when connecting a DSLAM to two BRAS devices so that the subscriber's broadband service can recover from BRAS failures.

The simplest form of pseudowire redundancy is to configure pseudowire with active and standby remote PE IP addresses. If the pseudowire to the primary remote PE fails (either because the remote PE has failed or because there is no LSP to the remote PE), then the local PE will establish a pseudowire to the standby remote PE instead.

However, establishing a pseudowire takes time (for LDP signalling, etc.), so a better model is to preestablish the pseudowire to the standby PE and then use PW status signalling to switch between active and standby remote PEs. An additional status bit has been defined in the status code signaled by the PW status TLV to enable the PE to signal PW status as "active" or "standby." If one or both PE devices at either end of a pseudowire signal a status of standby, then neither PE will send any data over the pseudowire (though they may send OAM messages).

One very useful model for pseudowire redundancy, as shown in Figure 14.5, is one where the local PE sets up pseudowires to a pair of remote PEs that connect to a single CE device using a multi-chassis Layer 2 redundancy protocol (e.g., multi-chassis 802.3ad link aggregation, using LACP signalling). In this case, the two remote PEs will agree which is active and which is standby and will signal appropriate status to the local PE. Should the active remote PE, or the link from that PE to the protected CE, fail, then the standby remote PE will assume the active role. Note that switchover in the case of PE-CE link failure is triggered by the Layer 2 redundancy protocol.

Ethernet Pseudowires   There are two different types of Ethernet pseudowire, both defined in RFC 4448:

- **Tagged mode**   In this mode, each transported Ethernet frame must contain at least one 802.1Q VLAN tag, and both PEs must agree how to process the tag. This mode exists because many routers available at the time the original draft-martini was written were unable to add and remove VLAN tags. If the VLAN tag is different on the ingress and egress PE, then the tag is rewritten at egress—though it may be rewritten at ingress if the egress PE has signaled the optional requested VLAN ID and if the ingress PE is able to rewrite the tag at ingress.

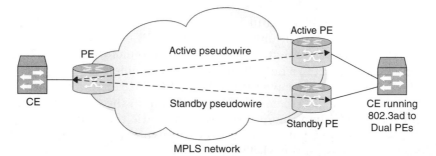

Figure 14.5   Redundant Pseudowires

- **Raw mode** In this mode, the transported Ethernet frame may contain 802.1Q VLAN tags, but if so, the tags will then pass through the egress PE without modification.

In general, the tagged mode is used for VLAN-based services and the raw mode for port-based services, though the raw mode may be used for VLAN-based services if the tag is stripped at ingress and a new tag added at egress.

An Ethernet pseudowire emulates a point-to-point Ethernet LAN with two end-stations. It acts as a nonlearning bridge—all packets received from the attachment circuit at the ingress PE will be forwarded over the pseudowire and transmitted over the attachment circuit at the egress PE. The one exception to this is 802.3x PAUSE frames, which are processed locally by each PE (the 802.3x protocol works over short time windows, and hence it is better to have the local PE buffer frames, if possible, than to send the PAUSE frames over the network).

Multi-Segment Pseudowires One limitation of the pseudowire architecture is that PEs must be connected over MPLS LSPs. This becomes a problem in three cases:

- Very large networks where there are too many PE devices for them to be fully meshed over MPLS LSPs and where RSVP-TE is used for LSP signalling meshes of more than around 100 nodes.

- Networks where different pseudowire signalling and encapsulation techniques are used in different areas of the network (for example, when interoperating between FEC 128 and 129 pseudowire signalling or between RSVP-TE and LDP-signalled LSPs).

- Pseudowires established between different service providers where the two service providers would rather not allow each other to set up LDP sessions and MPLS LSPs directly from PE to PE.

In the segmented pseudowire architecture, a pair of Terminating PEs (T-PEs) may establish a pseudowire to each other via one or more Switching PEs (S-PEs). Each S-PE connects two PW segments—and performs the necessary signalling and encapsulation for each one.

Forwarding along a multi-segment pseudowire (or MS-PW) is the same as forwarding along an LSP, except that the S-PE performs a label swap on the PW label, rather than the tunnel label. When a fault is detected in a segment of an MS-PW, LDP is used to propagate that fault information toward the T-PEs (or, in the case of a fault detected at one T-PE, to propagate that information to the remote T-PE).

Additional LDP TLVs have been defined to enable the path of MS-PWs to be traced in the control plane, as have extensions to VCCV to enable the path to be traced in the forwarding plane (and to enable fault detection in the forwarding plane).

Initial MS-PW implementations rely on static configuration of the S-PEs, though there is work ongoing in the IETF to enable dynamic discovery of switching points (see the section on ongoing developments below).

VPLS

Multipoint Transparent LAN Services were offered by many service providers using native Ethernet switching or using Ethernet over ATM before the advent of MPLS. Following the adoption of Ethernet over MPLS using pseudowires for point-to-point services, various vendors and service providers commenced standards work on multipoint Ethernet over MPLS. These multipoint Ethernet services are an implementation of the MEF E-LAN model.

Of the three groups that commenced work on multipoint Ethernet services in the IETF, two selected LDP as their signalling protocol and the third selected BGP. The two LDP groups merged, and industry consensus emerged for their proposal, which is documented in RFC 4762. Both the LDP and BGP approaches came to be known as Virtual Private LAN Services (VPLS).

There are two applications for VPLS:

- **Router interconnection**   In this application, a VPLS instance interconnects multiple customer routers. This offers simpler configuration than interconnecting the routers over Ethernet pseudowires (where a separate VLAN pseudowire would need to be configured between each pair of routers).

- **Switch interconnection**   In this application, a VPLS instance connects multiple customer Ethernet switches and/or hosts. Although there are advantages in being able to connect switches directly to the SP's network at Layer 2, this ability brings with it potential scalability issues that will be discussed in the VPLS scaling section below.

VPLS Architecture   As with pseudowires, a key requirement in the VPLS architecture was to reuse as much as possible from existing IP/MPLS router capabilities. Since the LDP VPLS effort lagged the pseudowire effort by two years, those existing capabilities were assumed to include both Ethernet pseudowire forwarding and LDP signalling for pseudowires.

The basic VPLS architecture consists of a set of PEs, with a full mesh of MPLS LSPs between them (however established). For each VPLS instance, a full mesh of Ethernet pseudowires is provisioned to interconnect the PEs that are members of the VPLS, and then each PE acts as a multipoint learning Ethernet bridge with one port per pseudowire and one per local attachment circuit.

MAC addresses are learned from the source addresses of frames, whether received from a local attachment circuit or from a pseudowire. Frames are forwarded toward known MAC destinations and are replicated by the ingress PE to all pseudowires and local attachment circuits in cases where the destination address is broadcast, multicast, or unknown. In order to avoid traffic loops a "split horizon" rule is applied to the pseudowire ports. That is, if a packet is received from a pseudowire, it may never be forwarded to another pseudowire. The split horizon rule may only be applied because there is a full mesh of pseudowires between the PEs. If that mesh is broken, then the VPLS instance will fail to operate correctly. As with point-to-point pseudowire services, the assumption is made that the MPLS network will ensure full connectivity and will repair any network faults other than PE failure.

VPLS Forwarding   The selection of the multipoint learning bridge as the basis for the VPLS forwarding architecture constrains its implementation to MAC-learning-capable devices—except in cases where the MAC addresses are statically configured at the PE (an undesirable overhead). It also centralises VPLS functionality in the PE in contrast to some designs where MAC learning has been separated from MPLS signalling or designs such as ATM LANE where dedicated servers have been used for replication. Each PE maintains a separate MAC FIB for each VPLS instance—known as a *Virtual Switching Instance* or *VSI*—where the destination for each MAC address may be either a local attachment circuit or a pseudowire to a remote PE. Since there is only one VSI per VPLS instance, and since MAC addresses are unique per VSI, there is typically only one VLAN mapped to each VPLS. This is known as *qualified learning* and is an implementation of "Independent VLAN Learning" as per 802.1Q. If multiple VLANs are mapped to one VPLS, then the MAC addresses may not overlap between the VLANs. This is known as *unqualified learning* and is an implementation of "Shared VLAN Learning" as per 802.1Q.

One key decision made in the LDP VPLS design was to reuse the Ethernet pseudowire encapsulations without modification. This was not without controversy. The benefit of using the existing encapsulation, of course, is that no changes need to be made to pseudowire forwarding for VPLS. However, the disadvantage of using the existing format is that in order for the PE to know from which pseudowire a packet has been received, it must assign a separate PW label to each peer PE (since there is no information in the pseudowire payload to identify the sender and the tunnel label may be stripped by the penultimate hop or may not uniquely identify the sender, for example, when multipoint-to-point LDP is used to establish the tunnels). Typically, raw mode Ethernet pseudowires are used for VPLS rather than tagged mode pseudowires. This is because the devices that implement VPLS generally have full Ethernet switching functionality, including the ability to add and remove VLAN tags.

When a frame arrives on a VPLS attachment circuit, the PE learns the source address of the incoming Ethernet frame and, if needed, adds it to its VPLS FIB. The PE then looks up the destination MAC addresses in the FIB. If the destination MAC is known in the FIB, then the frame is forwarded to the indicated attachment circuit or pseudowire. If the destination MAC is unknown (or is broadcast or multicast), then the PE replicates the packet and sends one copy to each other local attachment circuit and to each pseudowire. Service-delimiting VLAN tags will be removed before sending to raw mode pseudowires and may be added when sending to tagged mode pseudowires.

When a frame arrives from a VPLS pseudowire, the PE strips the PW label and uses it to identify the VPLS instance and the sending PE. The PE then learns the source address of the Ethernet frame encapsulated in the pseudowire packet and, if needed, adds it to the VPLS FIB. The PE then looks up the destination MAC address in the FIB. If the MAC is known and corresponds to a local attachment circuit, then the PE forwards the frame on that attachment circuit. If the MAC is unknown (or is broadcast or multicast), then the PE replicates the packet and sends a copy to each local attachment circuit. VLAN tags may again be added or removed at this stage on a per-attachment circuit basis.

VPLS Signalling   As already discussed, VPLS signalling is simply an extended version of pseudowire signalling. Each VPLS PE establishes an Ethernet pseudowire to each of the other PEs in the VPLS. A unique PW label is assigned to each peer PE to enable the local PE to identify the source of packets received over a PW. If LDP signalling is used, then the pseudowires are signalled as tagged or raw mode Ethernet pseudowires.

Specific rules for LDP signalling are defined next.

PWid FEC   A single PW ID is assigned for all pseudowires in the VPLS. Because there is only one pseudowire between a pair of PEs, each pseudowire may still be uniquely identified by the PW type, PW ID, and the pair of PEs it interconnects.

Generalized PWid FEC   A single AGI is assigned for all pseudowires in the VPLS. This acts as a VPN identifier and is a unique name for the VPLS. The TAII and SAII are null, as the VPLS terminates on VSI at each PE rather than on an attachment circuit. This is rarely, if ever, implemented; however, the Generalized PWid FEC is used in conjunction with VPLS BGP autodiscovery—albeit with different FEC encodings (see "BGP Autodiscovery" next).

One additional LDP object is defined for VPLS, the MAC list TLV. This may be sent in an LDP address withdrawal message to indicate a list of MAC addresses for a remote PE to "unlearn." If the list is empty, then this is taken to mean "unlearn all MAC addresses except the ones you learned over this pseudowire." This may be used to speed up VPLS convergence when there is an attachment circuit failure that results in MAC addresses moving to another attachment circuit (generally because spanning tree or multi-chassis 802.3ad is operating in a Layer 2 access network between the MAC addresses and the PE devices) or when a dual-homed MTU-s switches over from one serving N-PE to another (see "H-VPLS" section below).

BGP Autodiscovery   One advantage that the BGP VPLS approach had over the LDP approach was the ability to autodiscover VPLS peers through BGP—in other words, for a PE device to learn the IP addresses of the other PE devices in the VPLS using BGP rather than the administrator having to statically configure those addresses. Various approaches to autodiscovery were investigated for LDP VPLS, including LDP itself (operating in hop by hop mode), OSPF-TE, and RADIUS, but none of these were ultimately adopted. More recently, consensus has formed around the use of BGP for autodiscovery while still using LDP for signalling. The BGP attributes used for autodiscovery are modelled closely on those used for IP VPNs and are similar to those used in BGP VPLS.

BGP autodiscovery is used only in conjunction with the FEC 129. A VPLS instance is identified by a BGP Layer 2 VPN Identifier extended community (known hereafter as the VPLS ID). Additionally one or more BGP Route Target (RT) extended communities are used to define connectivity within the VPLS. In the usual case where the VPLS has a full mesh of pseudowires, only one RT is required, which will be advertised by all PEs.

One or more 8-byte Route Distinguishers (RDs) are also assigned to each VPLS. Each VSI is then identified by a combination of the RD and a globally unique 32-bit PE identifier (which may be an IP address belonging to the PE where that VSI is located or be locally configured). The PE identifier is then encoded into a BGP NLRI (Network Layer Reachability Information, i.e., a route advertised by BGP). The RD is used solely to disambiguate BGP NLRIs for different VPLS instances since, in general, all NLRIs advertised by the same PE will have the same IP address portion—usually the loopback address of the PE. Each PE advertises the NLRI for each of its local VSIs using BGP, including the BGP community identifying the VPLS and one or more RTs and setting the BGP next hop for the NLRI to its local loopback IP address. In most provider networks, BGP route reflectors will be used to ensure that advertised NLRIs reach all PEs in the network.

Each PE learns all BGP NLRIs with VPLS IDs matching locally configured VPLS instances and with RTs matching configured RTs for those VPLS instances. For each learned NLRI, the PE then uses FEC 129 signalling to establish a pseudowire to the BGP next-hop for the NLRI (i.e., the loopback address of the PE that advertised the NLRI). The AGI is set to the VPLS ID, the SAII to the PE identifier portion of the local NLRI (i.e., the NLRI with the RD stripped off), and the TAII to the PE identifier of the learned NLRI. This ensures that exactly one pseudowire will be established between any two VSIs with matching VPLS identifiers and RTs.

Configuring separate values for the VPLS ID, the import/export RTs (i.e., the RTs to advertise and the RTs to learn NLRIs from) and the RD are, in most cases, unnecessarily complex. Implementations may choose to simplify configuration by automatically creating RDs and RTs based on the configured VPLS ID.

VPLS Scaling   The goal for VPLS is to provide a scalable Ethernet service. However, it is important to remember that there are intrinsic limits to scaling a single Ethernet LAN, and since VPLS emulates an Ethernet LAN, it is impossible to overcome these. For example, as hosts are added to an Ethernet LAN, the broadcast and multicast traffic load typically increases due to hosts issuing periodic ARP requests or searching for local network resources (this is protocol dependent, of course).

The LANE and MPOA architectures in the 1990s attempted to address Ethernet scaling, but used a very complex design including dedicated servers for forwarding broadcast, multicast, and unknown packets. This experiment was not a great success; hence VPLS adopted a simplified architecture where the PE devices themselves replicate those packets.

One specific issue when connecting Ethernet switches to a VPLS instance is that the VPLS learns all MAC addresses for the switched network. This constrains VPLS scaling as the PE devices have to learn all active MAC addresses in the switched network. For this reason, many service providers offering VPLS service either limit the number of MAC addresses per attachment circuit, effectively restricting customers to attaching routers, or charge customers for blocks of MAC addresses.

H-VPLS   The flat topology of VPLS (where every PE has a pseudowire to every other PE) causes two major scaling challenges:

- The ingress PE has to replicate broadcast, multicast, and unknown frames to all other PEs in the VPLS. As the number of PEs in the VPLS grows, the replication overhead also grows. Because PEs are generally located at the edges of the network, they may have limited bandwidth available for replicating traffic.

- A full mesh of MPLS LSPs, Ethernet pseudowires, and targeted LDP sessions are required between all the PEs in the VPLS. If RSVP-TE LSPs are used, this may severely constrain VPLS scaling (see "MPLS Scaling," earlier in the chapter).

The Hierarchical VPLS (or H-VPLS) model addresses these problems by segmenting the VPLS service into a core of "hub" devices that are fully meshed, as in a standard VPLS, and a number of "spoke" devices that are each connected through a single "hub." The hub devices are generally known as *Network-facing PEs (N-PEs)*, and the spoke devices as *User-facing PEs (U-PEs)*.

In RFC 4762, the N-PEs are referred to as "PE-rs" devices, since they must be PE devices that are capable of routing and switching. The U-PEs are known as "MTU-s" devices since they are often located at Multi-Tenant Units and are capable of switching, but do not need to be capable of routing as they have only a single path into the network.

The H-VPLS model also enables devices that are unable to learn MAC addresses to participate in VPLS as U-PEs (known, in this case, as "PE-r" devices, as they are capable of routing but not of switching). A PE-r has one pseudowire to its serving N-PE for each attachment circuit (since it is unable to bridge between those attachment circuits). Each pseudowire is signalled with a unique PW ID (in the FEC 128 case), to enable the N-PE to distinguish between them.

The split horizon rule is now modified so that an N-PE applies split horizon only on the pseudowires to other N-PEs and not on pseudowires to U-PEs.

When a U-PE sends a broadcast, multicast, or unknown frame, it sends a single copy to its serving N-PE. Unless the N-PE knows the destination MAC address, it will flood the frame on all pseudowires to other N-PEs or served U-PEs and to any local attachment circuits. When a remote N-PE receives the frame, it will flood it (unless it knows the destination MAC address) on all pesudowires to served U-PEs and on any local attachment circuits. Thus, the replication load is distributed across the ingress and egress N-PEs.

One potential issue in the H-VPLS model is that if an N-PE fails, then its served U-PEs will be isolated from the rest of the network. This is addressed by the ability to configure dual-homed U-PEs that have pseudowires to two different N-PEs. Only one pseudowire is active at a time, and if it fails, the U-PE switches over to the other pseudowire.

If the pseudowire has failed because the N-PE has failed, then traffic from other N-PEs will immediately start flowing to the backup N-PE (since those N-PEs will remove FIB entries corresponding to the failed N-PE). If, however, the pseudowire has failed because the LSP from the U-PE to the primary N-PE has failed, then other N-PE devices may still attempt to send traffic through the primary N-PE as they are unaware of the LSP failure. (It may be desirable to let the failure happen if the physical path from the U-PE to the primary N-PE fails, to avoid "tromboning" traffic through the core of the network to the primary N-PE.) To prevent traffic from being blackholed until MAC timers age out, the U-PE may send an LDP address withdraw message, containing an empty MAC list TLV, to the (now active) backup N-PE, which will then send a similar message to all other N-PEs in the VPLS, resulting in them removing all FIB entries for the VPLS except those destined for the backup N-PE.

NOTE   With H-VPLS, there is no requirement for nodes to have fixed roles. Some VPLS instances in a provider's network may be provisioned as "flat" VPLS instances with no hierarchy, whereas others are provisioned as H-VPLS instances where some nodes act as N-PEs and others as U-PEs.

IP Multicast in VPLS   Many service providers have a requirement to carry IP multicast traffic over VPLS, either for corporate services or when backhauling IP TV traffic in residential broadband networks. The standard VPLS design replicates multicast traffic at ingress and floods it to all attachment circuits in the VPLS, making it unsuitable for this application.

Attempts to improve multicast handling in VPLS have tended to focus either on replacing ingress replication with another technique (for example, point-to-multipoint LSPs) or on applying IGMP or PIM snooping to the VPLS to prune IP multicast traffic from PEs and attachment circuits that have no active listeners for a specific multicast group.

When PE devices are deployed in rings, it is possible to improve VPLS multicast efficiency—this is described in "Typical Deployment Scenarios," later in the chapter.

VPLS OAM   Because VPLS instances are built from a mesh of pseudowires interconnecting virtual switching instances, the key tools for VPLS OAM are the pseudowire OAM tools (e.g., VCCV) and Ethernet OAM tools.

Pseudowire OAM enables providers to verify that the pseudowires that interconnect VPLS instances are operating correctly. However, pseudowire OAM tools do not verify that a pseudowire is connected to the correct VPLS instance or that packets destined to a specific MAC address are forwarded correctly in the VPLS instance.

Ethernet OAM is still in its infancy. The IEEE has specified both link-layer OAM (802.3ah) and service-layer OAM (802.1ag Connectivity Fault Management). The ITU-T has also standardised Y.1731—a variant of 802.1ag. The MEF is standardising an Ethernet LMI that enables a PE to inform a CE of the available VLANs on the UNI and to report the status of those VLANs. When troubleshooting a VPLS service, the Ethernet OAM tools may be most useful for troubleshooting the portion outside the service provider's MPLS domain (and, of course, are generally the only tools available for troubleshooting that portion of the service).

Although Ethernet OAM tools are useful for troubleshooting the end-to-end Ethernet service, and especially for troubleshooting the portions of the service outside the service provider's MPLS backbone, specific VPLS OAM tools may also be developed in the future to enable service providers to troubleshoot the VPLS portion of an end-to-end service.

How Ethernet over MPLS Meets the Carrier Ethernet Attributes

As described previously in this book, the Metro Ethernet Forum (MEF) has identified five key attributes of Carrier Ethernet. This section examines the five attributes and how Ethernet over MPLS satisfies these requirements.

Standardised Services By standardising MPLS, pseudowires, and VPLS, the IETF has ensured that vendors can develop interoperable equipment that offers EoMPLS services. Organisations such as Isocore host interoperability testing events at which vendors of EoMPLS equipment are able to verify conformance to IETF standards and interoperability of their equipment. Ethernet pseudowires implement the MEF's E-Line service, whereas VPLS implements the MEF's E-LAN service. Circuit emulation services may also be offered using TDM pseudowires. Service providers are able to offer a range of different bandwidth and QoS options and to converge voice, video, and data services onto a common IP/MPLS core.

Scalability By layering multiple services onto each MPLS LSP, the EoMPLS model supports an immense number of services in each network because the network core maintains no state on a per-service basis. Services may be provisioned across an arbitrary geographic distance since IP/MPLS networks may be global in reach and since one service may be provisioned over multiple service providers' networks. Each service may be provisioned with the bandwidth required by the customer—whether a few megabits per second or several gigabits per second (though, as discussed in the solution fit discussion below, EoMPLS may not be ideal for point-to-point services where the speed of each service approaches that of a single wavelength in the provider's network).

Reliability By layering EoMPLS services over MPLS LSPs, the EoMPLS model protects against network failures at the network layer and propagates fault notification to the service layer only when the fault is unrecoverable. MPLS LSPs protect against any link or node failure between the PEs providing the service, and they offer a range of protection mechanisms with fast reroute able to restore service within a few milliseconds of a fault occurring.

Quality of Service MPLS offers a range of QoS mechanisms that can be applied to the EoMPLS service. The E-LSP model offers a scalable "soft QoS" mechanism suitable for most services, whereas the L-LSP model offers the "hard QoS" required to guarantee performance under all network conditions. The different QoS mechanisms offered by MPLS may be offered simultaneously on the same network in order to offer a variety of

SLAs to different customers. By layering services on MPLS LSPs, the EoMPLS model also offers a means of aggregating QoS reservations through the network core.

Service Management   EoMPLS relies on the well-understood and widely deployed IP and MPLS tools for service management. These tools are already deployed in service providers' IP/MPLS networks and are integrated into operational procedures. Where existing tools have proven insufficient, new tools have been added (for example, VCCV for pseudowire OAM). Because these tools have been standardised through IETF RFCs, they are interoperable across multiple vendors' equipment. Services are provisioned and managed from PE to PE, avoiding provisioning of customer circuits in core network elements—thus greatly simplifying network operations.

Drivers for This Solution

We will now address the key applications for Ethernet over MPLS, looking firstly at how it may be used to add Ethernet services to existing IP/MPLS networks, secondly at where it may be introduced to scale an existing Ethernet deployment, and finally at where it may be one component of a converged network offering.

Ethernet Services over IP WANs

As stated previously, Ethernet over MPLS was originally developed for carriers who wished to offer point-to-point Ethernet services across Layer 3 IP/MPLS backbones. This was fundamentally a wide area application providing PoP to PoP Ethernet private lines. One of the key drivers for carriers in deploying this application was to offer services to customers such as Internet Service Providers or large enterprises that wanted high bandwidth from point-to-point and wanted to keep their routing separate from that of the carrier.

Scaling Metro Ethernet Deployments

The second phase of Ethernet over MPLS deployments came as carriers looked to scale Carrier Ethernet services that had been deployed using Layer 2 Ethernet switches. Layer 2 Ethernet switching suffers from a number of limitations when applied to carrier networks:

- **Protection**   Ethernet-switched networks depend on the Spanning Tree Protocol for protection. This is acceptable in simple topologies, but becomes hard to manage in larger and more complex networks. Spanning tree timers have to be increased as the topology grows, in order to prevent stability problems (the default timers impose a maximum diameter of seven hops). Disabling links may also be unacceptable as a protection mechanism in the network core. Deploying MPLS in the metro core enables carriers to constrain spanning tree to the edge of the network, enabling networks with larger numbers of nodes to be deployed and to make use of all available core links. MPLS also offers protection mechanisms that converge faster than Rapid Spanning Tree Protocol.

- **VLANs**   802.1Q has a 12-bit VLAN space, allowing 4094 VLANs. Since most Ethernet switches are unable to translate VLANs, this creates a fixed limit on the number of VLANs, and hence on the number of services per network. By deploying MPLS in the metro core, using PE devices that have per-port VLAN scopes, carriers can constrain the scope of VLAN uniqueness to much smaller domains—removing the restriction on the number of services supported. Another issue with VLAN switching is that in order to provision a VLAN through the network, multiple switches must be configured, or the provider must run protocols such as GVRP to propagate VLAN knowledge. Many PE devices support 802.1ad provider bridging (or "Q-in-Q") on their access ports, enabling carriers to assign a unique Provider VLAN to each customer-facing Layer 2 switch port and then to support multiple Customer VLANs within each of those ports. Thus, customer VLAN provisioning can be constrained to the PE device.

- **MAC address scaling**   In a Layer 2 switched network, each switch learns the MAC addresses of all active stations on all VLANs that pass through that switch. With Ethernet pseudowires PEs do not have to learn MAC addresses, whereas for VPLS MAC address knowledge is constrained to the PE devices that are members of each VPLS instance (hiding MAC addresses from core LSRs). MPLS PE devices also typically support larger numbers of MAC addresses than Layer 2 Ethernet switches. This scaling is critical in cases where carriers connect customer switches directly to a Layer 2 service. The N-PE devices in H-VPLS will typically learn more MAC addresses than the U-PEs, and for this reason, there has been some investigation of solutions that remove the requirement for the N-PEs to learn customer MAC addresses.

- **Use of facilities**   Layer 2 Ethernet switches are interconnected using Ethernet links. If a provider has access to dark fibre (or wavelengths), then Ethernet interconnection is generally the most cost-effective option; however, in some cases, providers may only be able to obtain SONET/SDH connectivity, which is not suitable for interconnecting Ethernet switches unless additional adaptations such as Ethernet over SONET/SDH are deployed. MPLS enables providers to use the cheapest available transport to interconnect PE devices because MPLS is link-layer agnostic.

Network Convergence

Many network technologies, from ISDN to ATM, have promised to offer convergence of multiple voice and data services over one common infrastructure, but without much success. However, carriers are now increasingly standardising on Ethernet and on IP for future services. Ethernet over MPLS offers a way to provide Ethernet services over an IP core. Some carriers are now deploying multi-service PE devices that enable them to offer Ethernet, IP, and legacy services (e.g., ATM, frame relay, and TDM) over the same network using EoMPLS for Ethernet services, IP VPNs for IP services, and pseudowires for legacy services.

When Does This Solution Fit?

In this section we will look at ideal deployment scenarios for Ethernet over MPLS, describing cases where the technology may be the optimal choice of the different options available (many of which are described in other chapters of this book).

Inter-regional Support of Ethernet Services over Any L2 Transport

EoMPLS enables Ethernet to be transported over any Layer 2 transport and over existing IP/MPLS wide area networks, as discussed previously. Where service providers want to offer inter-regional Ethernet services with statistical gain, EoMPLS is the natural choice. Statistical gain is important when offering Ethernet services as most Ethernet links are very lightly loaded and is even more important in the inter-regional case where transport costs are relatively high. Where service providers have "islands" of Layer 2 Ethernet in major metropolitan areas Ethernet over MPLS may be used to interconnect those islands, enabling the provider to traffic engineer the wide area links and to ensure fast protection against failures of those links. The alternative would be to use Ethernet over SONET/SDH to interconnect the islands. Ethernet over SONET/SDH could be provisioned with a single GFP-encapsulated VCAT group per pair of islands, but this, in fact, will tend to cause increased latency and jitter and lower network utilisation as only a few services would be mapped onto each VCAT group and as each VCAT group would have a much lower speed than the overall bandwidth demand per island (lower speed increases serialisation delay as packets are "clocked" out onto the link and also increases jitter for any given level of link loading). Ethernet over SONET/SDH could alternatively be provisioned with much larger VCAT groups connecting adjacent "islands," but in this case, spanning tree protection would have to be used over the wide area, leading to some links being unused unless multiple spanning trees were constructed, for example, one spanning tree per pair of "islands".

Ethernet Access to MPLS-based Metro Core Network

Ethernet is rapidly becoming the standard interface for handoff from service providers to customers. Where all services are delivered over Ethernet interfaces, the cheapest access technology is generally to deploy Ethernet switches. But in order to scale such a deployment, carriers need to deploy a carrier-class technology into the metro core. Because most service providers wish to offer IP services as well as Ethernet services, they often deploy IP/MPLS routers into the metro edge and core and use them to interconnect the access layer of Ethernet switches, offering both Layer 2 and Layer 3 services. In very large metros, carriers may deploy as many as four layers of equipment (see Figure 14.6):

- MPLS Core Routers provide connectivity between PE devices.
- Large MPLS Edge Routers provide the N-PE layer for L2 VPNs and the PE layer for L3 VPNs.

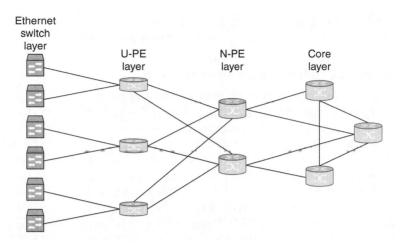

Figure 14.6   Large MPLS metro network

- Smaller MPLS-enabled nodes provide the U-PE layer for L2 VPNs and a pseudowire access layer toward the L3 VPN PEs (this requires "pseudowire into VRF" capability at the L3 VPN PEs).
- Layer 2 Ethernet switches provide access to the MPLS network, acting as 802.1ad Provider Bridges.

Metro Core for Ethernet over Multiple Access Networks

Many service providers use a mixture of on-net and off-net facilities to reach enterprise customers. However, these providers still face the market demand to deliver IP and Ethernet services and to use Ethernet as the standard interface for handoff to their customers. Many such providers are moving to a model where one or two EoMPLS PE devices are deployed into each city (or several into a large city) and are connected to each other over MPLS and to their service platforms (such as IP-VPN PE devices and public Internet routers) over Ethernet NNIs (often provisioned today using VLANs over gigabit Ethernet ports). Customers connect to provider-owned network demarcation devices that have Ethernet ports toward the customer and Ethernet, Ethernet over SONET/SDH, Ethernet over TDM, or Ethernet over DSL interfaces toward the network. Existing aggregation networks belonging to the service provider or to third party carriers (often regional or national incumbents) and comprised of devices such as Ethernet switches, SONET/SDH MSPPs and DXCs, PDH muxes, and DSLAMs are used to aggregate the customer traffic. The connection from the aggregation network to the MPLS PE may be an Ethernet UNI (i.e., one physical connection per customer), an Ethernet NNI (i.e., multiple customers delivered on one physical Ethernet connection), or may be in the native format of the aggregation network (e.g., channelised SONET/SDH with a GFP-encapsulated VCAT group per customer). In this case, the value of MPLS is that it enables the service provider to offer Layer 2 Ethernet services between cities (or within large cities) and also to offer Layer 3 services from Ethernet concentration nodes that aren't connected directly to a local Layer 3 service PE.

Multiple Services on One Network (Not Just Ethernet)

As discussed in the section on network convergence, MPLS is the natural technology choice for offering a range of Layer 1, Layer 2, and Layer 3 services over a common network. Again, the expectation is generally that over time most services will be Ethernet- or IP-based and that most customers will be connected to the service provider over an Ethernet interface, yet carriers will continue to offer legacy Layer 1 and Layer 2 services for many years, and in many cases will wish to retire the platforms currently deployed to offer such services (often those platforms have already reached their end of life) and migrate those services onto the next-generation networks currently being deployed to offer IP and Ethernet services. Since MPLS pseudowires are the technology of choice for legacy service migration and since MPLS-based IP VPNs are the technology of choice for IP services, a carrier wishing to offer all services over a common platform is most likely to select EoMPLS for Ethernet services.

Inter-provider Handoffs Are Required

Ultimately, no service provider is able to offer services in every location, and so providers look to extend their footprint by partnering with others. For providers of Ethernet services, the simplest way to interconnect with other networks is the "back-to-back UNI" method—typically just interconnecting a pair of GigE ports between providers and provisioning a new VLAN for each inter-provider service instance. This is analogous to the inter-provider IP-VPN "option A," as defined in RFC 4364, and although simple and secure, the two providers must agree on VLANs at the inter-connect and provision a new VLAN for each new service. This method also presents a single point of failure at the interconnect, though this can be alleviated somewhat by using pairs of GigE ports running 802.3ad link bundling over redundant fibre paths.

The MEF is working on a standardised Ethernet NNI to address the lack of standards support for inter-provider Ethernet services, but in the interim many providers are looking to use MPLS-derived mechanisms for interconnects. MS-PWs may be used, with the border routers between two providers' networks both acting as S-PEs. The pseudowire segment between the two border routers may be provisioned either statically or using LDP. BGP may be used by the border routers to discover which pseudowires to signal across the interconnect. See Figure 14.7 and the section below on dynamic multi-segment pseudowires for more discussion on the use of BGP for establishing MS-PWs.

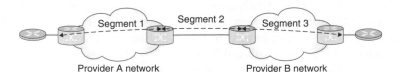

Figure 14.7   Inter-provider Ethernet service using multi-segment pseudowire

For VPLS, the same mechanisms used for BGP autodiscovery may be extended to enable service to be offered across two providers' networks in an analogous fashion to the inter-provider IP-VPN "option B" defined in RFC4364. The benefits of using BGP, or any other routing protocol, for dynamic discovery of the pseudowires to signal at the interconnect are twofold:

- It reduces the manual configuration required per service.
- It facilitates architectures with multiple redundant interconnects.

Large Numbers of Carrier-class Services Need to be Supported

Ethernet over MPLS enables providers to offer an immense number of service instances over one common network and to provide carrier-class Service-Level Agreements (SLAs) for those services. The reason an immense number of services may be offered is because EoMPLS layers services onto MPLS LSPs, isolating the core of the network from any knowledge of the services being carried over the network. Carrier-class SLAs may be offered because EoMPLS typically runs on carrier-class nodes, supporting the node and traffic protection mechanisms discussed in "MPLS Protection," and supporting the QoS mechanisms discussed in "MPLS QoS." The ability of MPLS to offer differentiated QoS enables service providers to offer their customers a range of tiered SLAs.

Carriers Wish to Backhaul Residential Broadband Traffic

Early residential broadband deployments used ATM backhaul; however; as DSLAMs and OLTs now provide Gigabit Ethernet uplinks; providers are migrating to Ethernet backhaul. Carriers offering triple play services over the broadband infrastructure require advanced QoS and redundancy features from the backhaul network that are hard to address with Layer 2 switching. For example, carriers may wish to perform Connection Admission Control (CAC) for video services and may need to have sub-50-ms restoration for both voice and video services. Also, as broadband deployments increase in scale, the ability of EoMPLS to support MAC hiding (for point-to-point services) and VLAN translation becomes more useful. A common architecture is to use Ethernet pseudowires for unicast traffic, with redundant pseudowires toward dual BRAS devices, and H-VPLS for multicast IP TV (as discussed in "Triple-play Aggregation," later in this chapter). Another benefit when using EoMPLS is that legacy ATM DSLAMs may be connected to the same infrastructure using ATM pseudowires. Also, because EoMPLS uses the IP control plane, it may be possible to integrate the backhaul and service control planes into one routing instance, reducing the operational overhead of operating multiple networks.

When Does This Solution Not Fit?

No technology is applicable to all environments. The Ethernet over MPLS technology is reasonably complex, and provides benefits in terms of network scaling and statistical gain which may not be required in all deployments. We will now look at some examples where alternative technologies may be a better choice than Ethernet over MPLS, as well as at an example where the technology is sometimes mis-used.

When Access Speed Is Equal to Trunk Speed

Packet switching technologies obtain statistical gain by multiplexing many traffic demands onto shared facilities that are much larger than any single traffic demand. Where providers wish to offer point-to-point services of similar speed to that of the trunks in their network, it is generally best to dedicate facilities to each service to avoid congestion when multiple services send traffic at full rates simultaneously. For Ethernet services, this generally implies dedicating a fibre or wavelength to each such service, in which case, it is much more cost effective for the provider to connect their customer directly to a transponder than to deploy additional packet switching equipment. For multipoint services, EoMPLS still makes sense, however, as different flows across the access interface need to be switched to different destinations on the provider's network.

Deployment of a Small Number of Ethernet Services Where Alternative Infrastructure Is Available

Where carriers wish to offer a small number of Ethernet services and where they have existing infrastructure (for example, SONET/SDH or ATM), it is generally more cost effective to offer Ethernet services over the existing network platform rather than to deploy a new EoMPLS platform. However, in general, carriers are migrating to IP and Ethernet for all services—and to Ethernet as the common handoff to all services—hence, this is unlikely to be a common scenario in future. In fact, many carriers started deploying Ethernet services by using Ethernet over SONET/SDH or Ethernet over ATM and are now looking to deploy Ethernet over MPLS in order to enable mass deployment of those services.

To Extend LANs Across Regions

As previously discussed, Ethernet services are unable to scale Ethernet beyond the constraints of Ethernet itself. It is generally unwise to attempt to extend an Ethernet segment interconnecting hosts (rather than routers) over the wide area, as Ethernet-based protocols and applications are designed to operate in the local area (for example, they often use broadcasts to discover local resources). When connecting across the wide area, a better model is often to place a routing device at the boundary between the WAN and LAN. Of course, this is also possible with EoMPLS if the customer connects a router to the EoMPLS service (whether that is an E-Line service over pseudowires or an E-LAN service over VPLS).

Benefits and Shortcomings

We will now discuss the benefits of the Ethernet over MPLS technology, as well as some of its shortcomings.

The benefits of any service technology may be looked at in terms of the quality of the service the technology enables (the benefit to the customer of the service), but also in terms of its capital and operational savings (the benefit to the provider of the service). We will now look at some specific benefits of Ethernet over MPLS technology—spanning these two areas.

Benefits of Ethernet over MPLS

Enabling Carrier-Class Ethernet   Layer 2 Ethernet switching doesn't scale (for the reasons discussed previously in "Drivers for This Solution") and doesn't offer carrier-class protection switching or per-flow QoS. Providers offering Ethernet services need to be able to offer large numbers of service instances and generally want to offer Service-Level Agreements that mirror those offered for other services (such as ATM or Frame Relay). In particular, carriers often want to offer guaranteed sub-second protection against network failures and differentiated SLAs (for example, tiered levels of service with different latency and packet loss metrics).

EoMPLS enables providers to offer carrier-class Ethernet services to their customers on a platform that also enables the provider to take advantage of statistical gain to reduce the bandwidth provisioned through their network. Typically, Ethernet links are loaded to less than 20 percent, making statistical gain an essential component of any large Carrier Ethernet deployment.

Fast and Scalable Convergence   The use of the IP/MPLS control plane for failure detection in MPLS enables much faster and more scalable convergence than OAM-based mechanisms because failure of a physical link (whether detected at the physical layer or using BFD) immediately triggers the control plane to propagate failure information through the MPLS network. LSP failures are notified to all LERs, each of which is then able to repair its failed LSPs. Each LSP may carry large numbers of EoMPLS services, each of which is repaired automatically as a result of LSP repair. Isolating service instances from network topology enables the network to scale to an immense number of service instances.

In the OAM-based approach, each circuit has its own end-to-end OAM flow, and failures are only detected when a number of consecutive OAM packets are dropped. In this approach, speed of convergence is always in tension with scalability, since increasing the frequency with which OAM packets are sent on a circuit reduces the total number of circuits that can be supported without overwhelming the edge devices (and the network links) with OAM traffic.

Notwithstanding the above, MPLS also supports OAM-based approaches to fault detection, and these may be used either in conjunction with, or instead of, the IP/MPLS control plane.

Ability to Offer Ethernet Services over Existing IP Networks   MPLS is a cost-effective way to offer multiple services over a packet-switched network. EoMPLS is a small addition to an existing IP/MPLS network and enables carriers to add new revenue streams from Ethernet services. Although some customers are willing to buy Layer 3 services, others prefer to buy Layer 2 services—often because they prefer to manage and maintain their own routing infrastructure. Offering Ethernet services at Layer 2, therefore, enables a service provider to sell to new groups of customers.

Reduction in Operational Expense   Opponents of MPLS often portray it as a complex technology to operate. In fact, MPLS has a range of advanced troubleshooting tools— some inherited from IP (such as ping and tracereoute), some enhanced from their IP equivalents (such as LSP ping/traceroute), and some new (for example VCCV). The control plane, which again is often seen as complex, is the most effective way to ensure that all nodes in the network have the same view of network status. EoMPLS is also a good mechanism for separating customer and provider domains because separate service instances are configured per customer and knowledge of a service instance is constrained to the PE nodes that have local ports that are members of that instance. Ethernet-based approaches to providing Carrier Ethernet have, in fact, copied many of their ideas from EoMPLS (for example, 802.1ah Provider Backbone Bridging uses "MAC in MAC" to separate the customer and provider MAC address spaces—resulting in an encapsulation rather similar to that of Ethernet over MPLS over Ethernet).

Traffic Engineering   By using RSVP-TE, carriers are able to pin the primary and secondary paths for any given service to specific links in their network and to optimise use of physical resources. Although this is possible with some alternative techniques (such as Ethernet over SDH/SONET or over ATM), there are other techniques (such as 802.1ah Provider Backbone Bridging) that are unable to do so. The benefits of traffic engineering are sufficiently clear to operators that technologies which lack the capability are often extended to include it (for example the PBB-TE effort in IEEE).

Shortcomings of Ethernet over MPLS

The shortcomings of Ethernet over MPLS may be divided into two classes: shortcomings of Ethernet itself and shortcomings of the Ethernet over MPLS architecture.

Ethernet Shortcomings   Ethernet over MPLS services are still Ethernet services and don't enhance the Ethernet UNI. Enhancements in the UNI are being standardised by the Metro Ethernet Forum and are required for Ethernet services to offer the same carrier-class features that already exist in protocols such as ATM.

VPLS services emulate Ethernet LANs. As discussed, Ethernet LANs are inherently unscalable. When VPLS services are used to connect routers, the service scales adequately, but when VPLS is used to connect Ethernet switches, the number of MAC addresses the PE device has to learn imposes a severe scaling limitation.

EoMPLS Shortcomings   Ethernet pseudowires provide a simple point-to-point service and have no intrinsic shortcomings, other than the inability of the PE to signal VLAN failures to the CE (as discussed previously in "Pseudowire OAM"). VPLS services, however, have specific shortcomings resulting from the VPLS architecture:

Mesh Failures   The VPLS architecture assumes that all PE devices are fully meshed over Ethernet pseudowires. If any pseudowire breaks (for example, because of LSP failure), then the VPLS service no longer offers full connectivity between all attached devices. This can cause severe issues with IP routing protocols that rely on multicast to transport network reachability information.

Multicast Efficiency   The EoMPLS architecture is designed to hide per-pseudowire state from the core of the network to improve scalability. In multicast networks, there is an inevitable tradeoff between core state and replication efficiency. VPLS today is at one extreme of this tradeoff. Further enhancements to VPLS are being standardised to offer more efficient multicast forwarding at the expense of adding state to the network core (see "Ongoing Developments," later in this chapter).

Forwarding Plane Bugs   VPLS has no means of detecting forwarding plane bugs except for VCCV per-pseudowire or Ethernet OAM mechanisms applied to the service layer. VPLS OAM mechanisms may be required to detect software or hardware failures in nodes that implement VPLS. Efforts are ongoing in the IETF to add this capability to VPLS.

Typical Deployment Scenarios

In this section we will present examples drawn from real-world networks, showing how carriers have deployed Ethernet over MPLS in their networks.

MPLS in the Access

In this architecture, Layer 2 capable Multi-Service Access (MSA) devices are deployed as U-PEs and are aggregated toward Layer 3 capable Multi-Service Edge (MSE) devices acting as N-PEs (see Figure 14.8). The MSA devices groom traffic from attachment circuits

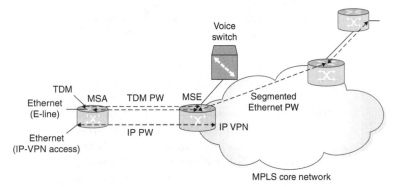

Figure 14.8   MPLS in the access

into pseudowires, and the MSE devices perform a mixture of pseudowire switching for point-to-point services and termination into VPLS or IP-VPN instances for multipoint services. The MSA devices run a limited set of MPLS features, whereas the MSE requires a more complex feature set (including, for example, BGP). Per-flow QoS may either be applied at the MSA, or at the MSE, depending on the feature sets of the two devices.

The benefits of using MPLS and pseudowires in this application are twofold:

- MPLS provides rapid protection in the event of link or node failure.

- Pseudowires provide adaptation of multiple services onto a common set of facilities.

Triple Play Aggregation

The first generation of DSL aggregation networks deployed by carriers were typically based on ATM. This was dictated by the ATM uplinks available on early DSLAMs (DSL Access Multiplexors). ATM switches were typically used to aggregate a number of DSLAMs and then to feed traffic toward higher-layer ATM aggregation switches or directly to ATM interfaces on Broadband Remote Access Servers (BRAS) devices.

A second generation of DSLAMs has emerged with Gigabit Ethernet uplinks and with higher throughputs suitable for video services (these typically support ADSL2+ rather than the ASDL or ADSL2 of earlier DSLAMs and have high-speed backplanes). Multi-Service Access Nodes (MSANs) are also being deployed by some carriers. These are DSLAMs with POTS voice capabilities—able to connect directly to the customer line, rather than in parallel with a class 5 voice switch and with a passive splitter directing POTS voice to the switch and broadband DSL to the DSLAM.

Although, in some cases, carriers have opted to connect the DSLAM or MSAN directly to the BRAS over a point-to-point GigE link, this is typically much more expensive than deploying a layer of Ethernet aggregation between the DSLAM and BRAS—especially if the carrier is able to bypass the BRAS for voice and video traffic (known as a *multiple edge* architecture—see Figure 14.9). In the longer term, many carriers plan to replace dedicated BRAS devices with MPLS-enabled service edge routers that incorporate a subset of BRAS functionality, for example, using DHCP and 802.1x for session management rather than PPPoE.

EoMPLS proves to be an ideal solution for Ethernet aggregation in the "multiple edge" case. Layer 2 U-PE devices are typically deployed in rings to aggregate DSLAMs, whereas Layer 3 capable N-PE devices are located at carrier head-end locations with each ring terminated on two N-PEs (often in different locations). A separate EoMPLS service topology may then be built for each service. For example,

- **POTS voice** may be supported by a VPLS instance for each aggregation ring of U-PEs, with each MSAN appearing as a single MAC address in the VPLS and with the two N-PEs at the head-end acting as routers for the VPLS (using VRRP for router redundancy). MPLS PE devices are typically highly resilient and have fast restoration and advanced QoS support—helping to ensure the voice service is as robust as the TDM voice service it replaces.

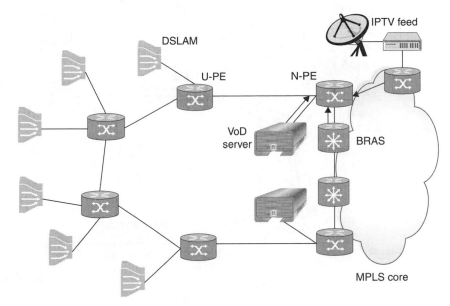

Figure 14.9 Multiple edge architecture for triple play

- **Broadband Internet** may be backhauled using a redundant pseudowire from the U-PE, with a primary path to one N-PE (typically one of the N-PEs at the head-end of the ring) and a backup path to another. Each N-PE is directly connected to a BRAS or integrates BRAS functionality. This design avoids the PEs having to learn customer MAC addresses (which would reduce scalability). If an N-PE or BRAS fails, then the customer devices will reestablish PPPoE sessions to the backup.

- **Video on Demand** may be transported over a VPLS per-aggregation ring, in much the same fashion as POTS voice. Video servers or caches may be connected directly to the N-PEs at the head-end locations.

- **Broadcast TV** may be supported using a modified H-VPLS topology where each U-PE has pseudowires only to the two adjacent PEs on the ring (see Figure 14.10). Each of the two N-PEs at the head-end of the ring has a single pseudowire to its adjacent layer U-PE and acts as a multicast router for the VPLS instance with one N-PE being elected as the IGMP querier for the ring. IP multicast traffic is forwarded hop by hop around the ring (generally with IGMP snooping enabled toward DSLAMs, if not on the pseudowires). Thus, instead of N copies of each multicast packet being sent on a ring of N devices, just one copy is sent. In this topology, it is possible to use MPLS fast reroute to protect against link failure, though IP multicast techniques are used to protect against node failure (if a U-PE fails, then each of the two N-PEs becomes the IGMP querier for the part of the ring between itself and the failed node).

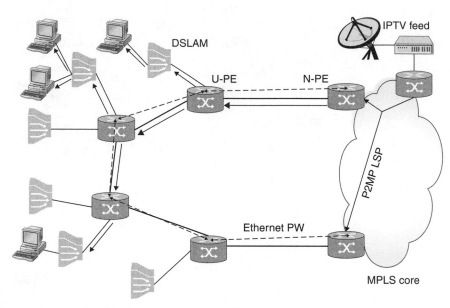

Figure 14.10   Using H-VPLS for broadcast TV forwarding

Scaling Metro Ethernet

Many service providers initially built Metro Ethernet networks in major cities using enterprise-class Layer 2 switches in customer buildings and in PoP locations. As these networks grew, various challenges emerged:

- How to scale the network within each city
- How to improve the availability of the network, which was often far below that of traditional SONET/SDH networks
- How to link Metro Ethernet networks in different cities together
- How to provide access outside the major city centres and in locations that were off-net for fibre
- How to offer differentiated service offerings, especially in the case of services with enhanced SLAs for availability and QoS

Many service providers have opted to address these five challenges by deploying large MPLS PE devices in the core of each Metro Ethernet network (see Figure 14.11). Each network may then be subdivided into smaller Layer 2 domains, improving scaling by segmenting the VLAN space, reducing the number of MAC addresses learned on each Ethernet switch, and reducing the size of spanning tree protection domains. The PE devices themselves are typically larger and more resilient than the core Ethernet switches they replace—both increasing the scale of the network and improving its

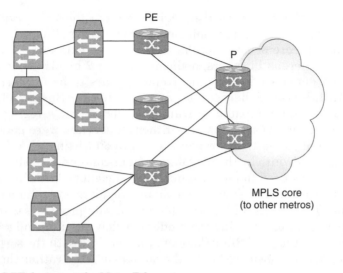

Figure 14.11   MPLS PE devices at the Metro Ethernet core

availability. Since the MPLS PEs are typically deployed in the core PoPs for each metro, they can be easily connected to inter-city transport facilities, enabling the carrier to link different city networks together. Likewise, the core PoPs are generally also con-centration points for metro TDM networks, making these good locations for bringing Ethernet traffic groomed over the TDM network onto the MPLS network. Finally, the MPLS PE devices generally support fine-grained QoS, which may be used to provide differentiated service offerings and give carriers the option of connecting customers di-rectly to the PE device where the highest levels of QoS and availability are required.

Business Ethernet Services

In the few years immediately preceding the bursting of the dot-com bubble in 2001, several startups in the U.S. and in Europe obtained funding to build Metro Ethernet networks to offer business services. While some initially deployed enterprise-class Ethernet switches, others deployed MPLS-enabled Ethernet switches and offered service using Ethernet pseudowires. The service providers that deployed MPLS were generally able to offer better SLAs than those that relied on Layer 2 switching and were also able to make better use of leased facilities—since MPLS enables use of all available paths in contrast to spanning tree, which turns links off to break loops, and gives operators the flexibility to traffic engineer their networks, placing specific traffic demands on specific paths.

Another benefit of using MPLS to offer Ethernet services, as noted above, is the ease with which services can be offered over the wide area. Many providers of business Ethernet services offer a mix of intra-metro and inter-metro services (in addition to using their Ethernet platforms to provide access to the Internet and to IP-VPN platforms).

Most incumbent carriers also offer Business Ethernet services now, using a variety of different networking technologies. In some cases, Business Ethernet services have been offered more or less piecemeal, layered on existing SDH/SONET, ATM, or fibre networks, whereas in others, dedicated Layer 2 or MPLS-based Ethernet platforms have been deployed. The overall trend appears to be for carriers to migrate toward single MPLS-based Ethernet platforms both to offer Business Ethernet services and to backhaul consumer broadband traffic (see "Triple Play Aggregation").

The first generation of business Ethernet services were generally based on offering point-to-point connections (or point-to-multipoint using VLANs at the central site) and on selling bandwidth by the megabit on an uncontended basis (though oversubscription was sometimes used to increase network efficiency). With increasing competition, and increasing customer sophistication, many providers now offer a much wider range of services and QoS options. VPLS provides a means for providers to offer multipoint services, whereas the use of PE devices that offer per-flow queuing and traffic engineering enable them to offer enhanced SLAs (for example, services with the sort of bounded latency and jitter previously considered to be the domain of ATM rather than of Ethernet).

Ongoing Developments

In this section we will address some of the ongoing work addressing limitations in the Ethernet over MPLS architecture. Necessarily this is a snapshot in time, and hopefully the technologies presented here will find their way into network deployments over the next several months from the time of writing.

Dynamic Multi-Segment Pseudowires

As discussed, there are various applications for MS-PWs. However, the MS-PW architecture presents new challenges when compared with the single-segment pseudowire (SS-PW) architecture. In the SS-PW case, the PE devices are able to rely on the MPLS layer to provide connectivity from one PE to the other PE, and thus the pseudowire layer need not concern itself with topology or with service restoration. In the MS-PW case, however, the MPLS layer now only provides connectivity from T-PE to S-PE and from one S-PE to another. This creates two challenges:

- The service provider must define *a-priori* the set of S-PEs through which a pseudowire will flow from T-PE to T-PE and must configure each one to switch the pseudowire.

- Failure of an S-PE now implies failure of the pseudowire.

To address these challenges, work is ongoing in the IETF on "dynamic placement" of MS-PWs. In this model, globally unique FEC 129 Type 2 AIIs are constructed, consisting of a 32-bit global ID, a 32-bit prefix (typically, the IP address of the T-PE where the attachment circuit is located) and a 32-bit Attachment Circuit ID. When setting up a dynamic MS-PW, a source T-PE performs a longest prefix match (similar to the longest prefix match used in IP forwarding) on its local Layer 2 AII PW routing table. Each entry in the table consists of a 96-bit Type 2 AII with a mask; for example, an entry with a /64 mask (i.e., 64 ones and 32 zeroes) would match all Attachment Circuit IDs for a given global ID and prefix, and a matching next hop (i.e., the IP address of the next S-PE toward the destination T-PE, or of the destination T-PE itself if the pseudowire only has one segment). The source T-PE then sets up a pseudowire segment to that next hop using targeted LDP. The next-hop S-PE repeats this process until the final S-PE sets up a pseudowire segment to the target T-PE.

NOTE   Because FEC 129 implements "single-sided signalling," only one T-PE needs to initiate the pseudowire setup. To prevent both T-PEs starting pseudowire setup, the T-PEs compare AIIs, and the one with the higher SAII initiates setup.

Of course, if the Layer 2 AII PW routing table at each T-PE and S-PE was configured manually, the solution would fail to address the two challenges. The solution, therefore, also includes mechanisms for using multiprotocol BGP to advertise NLRIs for the Type 2 AIIs. These NLRIs are advertised as 96-bit prefixes with a mask (in a similar manner to the way in which IPv4 addresses are advertised by routers as 32-bit prefixes with a mask). S-PEs may choose to advertise aggregated reachability—for example, if a Global ID is assigned to a service provider, then that service provider may configure its border routers to advertise that Global ID with /32 mask to neighbouring border routers supporting MS-PWs—indicating that all PW endpoints matching that Global ID can be reached through those border routers.

The dynamic MS-PW model also adds support for signalling the bandwidth required by a pseudowire. In the SS-PW case, this is unnecessary because each PE can select an LSP with the required bandwidth to meet the requirements of the pseudowire and can adjust the available bandwidth of the LSP appropriately. Likewise, in the statically configured MS-PW case, each S-PE can select the appropriate LSP for its attached pseudowire segments. However, in the dynamic MS-PW case, it is useful to have a mechanism by which the source T-PE can indicate the bandwidth required to each S-PE in the path. Consideration has also been given to enabling the source T-PE to select an explicit path to the target T-PE (i.e., a set of S-PEs to traverse).

The dynamic MS-PW architecture represents the final stage in the evolution of pseudowires from being simply an edge-to-edge multiplexing mechanism for carrying circuits over LSPs to being a fully dynamic system capable of scaling to the largest networks and supporting inter-provider operation. This system consists of the set of interconnected T-PEs and S-PEs and uses Type 2 AIIs as its addressing mechanism, MP-BGP as its routing protocol (and, in fact, work has also commenced on using IGPs to flood Layer 2 reachability), and targeted LDP as its signalling protocol.

Solving the VPLS Ingress Replication Problem

One major issue with VPLS is that it uses ingress replication to flood broadcast, multicast, and unknown traffic from the ingress PE to each egress PE. Although this issue is ameliorated somewhat by H-VPLS (in that replication now occurs at the ingress and egress N-PEs, and no replication at all at the ingress U-PE), it still presents a major challenge to providers who wish to support IP multicast traffic over VPLS instances. As noted in "Triple Play Aggregation," there are topology-specific workarounds that may be used to provide efficient support for IP multicast; however, many providers are looking for a generic solution to the problem.

The multicast VPLS solution makes use of mLDP and/or P2MP RSVP-TE to build multipoint LSPs to carry broadcast, multicast, and unknown VPLS traffic (though unknown unicast packets may optionally be replicated at ingress). For each VPLS, there may be one "inclusive tree" that may be used to send traffic to all PEs in the VPLS (in fact, multiple VPLS instances may share one inclusive tree to reduce multicast state in the network core). As a further optimisation, selective trees may be used for IP multicast traffic being carried in a VPLS. Each selective tree only sends traffic to a set of PE devices, each of which has interested receivers for the IP multicast traffic being sent. Again, one selective tree may be shared between multiple VPLS instances.

When mapping a single VPLS onto one point-to-multipoint LSP, a single label is used to identify the VPLS instance. This is in contrast to unicast VPLS traffic where a two-level stack of tunnel label and PW label is used. However, when using one point-to-multipoint or multipoint LSP to carry traffic for multiple VPLS instances, it is necessary to use a two-level label stack so the inner label can identify the VPLS instance. In this case, all egress PEs will see the same inner label since it is not swapped in the network. Thus, upstream label allocation is required for these inner labels—in contrast to the downstream label allocation normally used in MPLS.

Economic Assessment

It is hard to provide generic costs for the EoMPLS solution because network CAPEX (capital expense) and OPEX (operational expense) are functions of many variables. However, this section attempts to provide a simple CAPEX model for EoMPLS. EoMPLS CAPEX is generally high relative to other Carrier Ethernet solutions. This is the result of the increased functionality and complexity of EoMPLS platforms relative to other solutions. As noted previously, many carriers in fact use EoMPLS in the core of their networks to enable the network to scale, but use alternative mechanisms for the access layer. However, over time the cost of MPLS platforms will continue to fall, with the result that the MPLS layer will expand toward the edge of carrier networks.

There are two main costs to consider in an EoMPLS network: the cost of the PE device and the cost of transport across the MPLS backbone (including the cost of the network-facing ports on the PE device). The cost of PE devices is typically dominated by the cost of the MPLS-enabled Ethernet port to which the customer connects either directly or via a carrier-owned non-MPLS aggregation device. Typical end-customer prices for Gigabit Ethernet ports today are in the range of $1000—or $1 per megabit. Transport across an MPLS network is more expensive—and costs are highly dependent on the equipment used, the number of hops in the network, and the cost of the transmission links interconnecting the equipment. Assuming, for example, a cost of $20,000 per 10-Gigabit Ethernet link on a PE or P router and 4 P routers between the 2 PE devices at either end of a pseudowire, it would cost approximately $20 per megabit in 10-Gigabit Ethernet port costs alone. Assuming 1:1 protection through the network, this rises to $40 per megabit—much higher than the $2 per megabit for the Gigabit Ethernet ports at either end of the pseudowire. One factor to remember though is that utilisation levels on customer-facing ports are typically much lower than on network-facing ports. In fact, customers may often connect to providers over a Gigabit Ethernet link, yet only purchase a few tens of megabits across that port. Where utilisations on customer-facing ports are high and where customers buy point-to-point service, Ethernet over fibre or CWDM are generally more cost-effective than Ethernet over MPLS for metro applications and Ethernet over SONET/SDH is often more cost-effective for long-haul applications.

OPEX for Ethernet over MPLS is often considered to be high relative to other solutions. This is because routers are generally considered to have higher OPEX than simpler switches. However, this need not be the case if networks are operated correctly. As discussed already, the EoMPLS architecture constrains service provisioning to the PE devices at the edges of the network, freeing the operator from the burden of having to provision connections through core elements (as is often the case in Layer 2 Ethernet networks or on SDH/SONET networks, though such networks often automate the provisioning process using network management tools). Network management tools may also be added to MPLS to simplify configuration and fault management, and, in fact, it is sometimes observed that the service layer of an EoMPLS network should be operated from a service management platform in a similar fashion to a Frame Relay network, but the network layer should be operated using IP/MPLS tools.

Vendors Promoting This Solution

Because the Ethernet over MPLS solution is based on publicly available IETF standards, any vendor who chooses to implement it may do so. Thus, any list of vendors is necessarily incomplete. However, the table below summarises some of the key vendors and products implementing Ethernet over MPLS.

Vendor	Model/Family	Comments
Alcatel	7450-ESS, 7750-SR	7450 is an EoMPLS-optimised platform 7750 is an MPLS service edge router with additional routing and multi-service capabilities.
Cisco	7600 OSR	Based on the Catalyst 6500 Ethernet switch and supports a mixture of Ethernet switching and enhanced QoS cards
	12000 GSR	Multi-service Edge Router
Extreme	BlackDiamond 10000 and 12000	Carrier Ethernet switches with MPLS
Foundry	NetIron MLX and XMR	Ethernet-centric Edge and Core Routers
Juniper	M120, M320	Multi-service Edge Router
	MX960	Ethernet Services Router—Ethernet-optimised MPLS router
Redback	SmartEdge 400, SmartEdge 800	Multi-service Edge Routers
Tellabs	8800	Multi-service Edge Router

WiMAX

by Prasanna Adhikari

The past century has seen tremendous growth in the need for broadband networks as the demand for broadband access has increased significantly. We have also witnessed the growing need for untethered communications as our dependency on information in our day-to-day life has grown. With the proliferation of portable computing, communication, and entertainment devices, the need for untethered communication is expected to skyrocket.

In the developed parts of the world, the demand for broadband communication has mostly been met by newer technologies making use of existing infrastructure such as copper wires. Demand has also been met by the use of newer infrastructure, such as fiber-optic cables. However, the reach of these infrastructures is not ubiquitous, partly because such ubiquity is not commercially feasible. Additionally, even for those with access to the infrastructure, these technologies are limited in their ability to deliver users' mobile and nomadic communication needs. In parts of the populous world with undeveloped communication infrastructure, growth in bandwidth demand is no less intense. However, delivering bandwidth by deploying wired infrastructure in these parts of the world is equally cost prohibitive.

Broadband Wireless Access (BWA) technology has been seen as the technology that can meet the broadband needs of much of the world. It is expected to meet the broadband needs of nomadic and mobile users always hungry for more bandwidth. It is also expected to serve as a medium to deliver broadband communication to populations without access to wired broadband services. Even for the masses with other means of broadband access, it creates an opportunity for alternate carriers to enter a market even if they do not have access to the wired infrastructure.

WiMAX is a BWA technology that has gained a very wide acceptance among major broadband service providers and equipment manufactures. Because of its technical soundness and its wide acceptance in the industry, it is poised to be the most widely deployed BWA in the world.

This chapter discusses some of the technology of WiMAX and how it fits within the context of delivering carrier-grade Ethernet services. The terms *WiMAX* and *IEEE 802.16* are used interchangeably; even though, the industry standard–accepted meaning of WiMAX may not exactly overlap with that of IEEE 802.16.

Technology Description

WiMAX is a shared medium point-to-multipoint multi-user wireless communication technology where multitudes of devices share a common medium—a band of RF spectrum—to serve their communication needs. WiMAX offers a multiple access protocol that is highly flexible yet highly efficient in its use of limited resources. It allows for a diverse set of physical layer protocols, each of which makes very efficient use of the spectrum. And it was designed from the ground up with the demanding QoS needs of applications in mind. Throughout this section, we discuss some of the salient features of WiMAX, including WiMAX Mesh and how it fares in its ability to deliver carrier-grade Ethernet services.

MAC

Multiple Access Control (MAC) is the protocol that defines the method of access to the shared medium by multiple devices. WiMAX provides a fairly sophisticated MAC protocol that enables efficient utilization of resources, while being independent of the details of the Physical Layer Protocol (PHY). Unlike other popular MAC standards that do not have a central controller (e.g., 802.3, 802.11, etc.), WiMAX uses a central controller, referred to as the *Base Station (BS),* which coordinates access to the wireless medium by all other devices, referred to as *Subscriber Stations (SSs).* In PMP networks, communications from BS to SS, referred to as *downlink (DL),* and communications from SS to BS, referred to as *uplink (UL),* are scheduled by the BS. In Mesh networks, a central controller, referred to as the *Mesh BS,* schedules all communications (Mesh also allows for distributed scheduling).

Each WiMAX device is uniquely identified by a 48-bit MAC address. It is used for the purpose of initial authentication and registration of a SS during its entry into a WiMAX network. However, MAC addresses are not used to identify the destination of data packets.

The MAC performs several key functions such as mapping data from higher layer protocols to WiMAX-specific PDUs, creating and maintaining connections, scheduling of data transmissions, authenticating and encrypting data, and providing all necessary control of the PHY.

Convergence Sublayer (Mapping of Ethernet Packets)   The Convergence Sublayer (CS) is the interface through which WiMAX MAC provides its services to higher-layer networking protocols. The standard currently defines two distinct types of CS, one referred to as *ATM CS*, designed for ATM packets, and another referred to as *Packet CS*, designed for packet-based protocols such as IP, PPP, and Ethernet.

One of the key functions of CS is classification of packets, which is the process of mapping higher PDUs to a particular connection for transmission. The mapping process creates an association between the PDU and a particular connection. The association with a connection enables the lower layer MAC entity to deliver the packet to its destination with the QoS criteria as specified by the service flow characteristic of the connection.

The classification is done on the basis of matching criteria that is applied to each packet from the higher layer protocol. The matching criterion includes matching based on a protocol-specific packet header (e.g., IP header). If the packet matches the specific matching criteria, then it is associated with the specific connection. If the packet fails to match the classification criteria, then it is dropped. The exact rules and parameters for mapping depend on the higher layer protocol.

The classification of Ethernet packet is based on one or more of the following Ethernet header fields: Destination MAC Address, Source MAC Address, Ethertype/SAP, 802.1D-Priority, 802.1Q-VLAN ID. The ability to classify packets based on these fields facilitates delivery of Ethernet services over the WiMAX network.

Another important, though optional, function of CS is payload header suppression by the transmitter and reconstruction by the receiver. This feature, which is inherited from DOCSIS, allows for efficient utilization of the RF bandwidth for traffic with static header information (e.g., Ethernet MAC address, VLAN, etc.). The detail of payload header suppression is negotiated by the two sides of a connection.

Connections   WiMAX is a connection-oriented protocol, where *all* communications between two devices are in the context of a predefined connection. Connections are used for user data, management, and multicast and broadcast traffic. This is unlike many other networking protocols, such as Ethernet and WiFi, which are connectionless and are often contention based.

Each connection is identified by a Connection ID (CID). The 16-bit CID allows for 64K connections in each channel, some of which are reserved for specific purposes such as broadcast traffic and initial ranging. There can be (and there always are) multiple connections between a BS and SS, while a common CID may be used for communication between a BS and multiple SSs (for multicast and broadcast traffic).

Connections (and CIDs) are very central to the operation of WiMAX MAC. All services (and service flows, which are discussed in the following section), including management services, are associated with their unique connection. Services provided to higher layer protocols are mapped to specific connections. Connections are also the entities for which bandwidths are requested and reserved. They are also used for the purpose of classification and scheduling to ensure that service levels and fairness are maintained. CIDs, instead of MAC addresses, are used during transmission of the data over-the-air interface to uniquely identify the source and destination of the packet.

Each SS always has at least two pairs of connections that are established during its initialization. These connections are used exclusively to exchange MAC management information between the BS and SS. A third pair of management connections may also be established for the purpose of transporting standards-based management protocol traffic like DHCP, SNMP, and so on. All other connections are established based on the services that are provisioned.

For pre-provisioned services, connections are set up during the registration of the SS associated with the service. Other connections may be established on an ongoing basis to support new services or to modify existing services. A connection can be terminated when the service associated with it is no longer needed, such as when a customer's service contract expires.

Service Flows   Just like connections, service flows are also central aspects of the WiMAX MAC protocol. Concurrent with the notion of connections, WiMAX uses the notion of service flow, which identifies services. Every data transport service provided by the WiMAX network is associated with a service flow. Each service flow is uniquely identified by a 32-bit SFID number and is associated with a connection through which it provides the transport service. Associated with each service flow are three sets of QoS parameters that define the QoS characteristic and the corresponding state of the service flow.

- **Provisioned QoS parameter set**   This parameter set defines the QoS parameters of the service flow as provisioned to provide the service. The provisioned parameters may be based on a SLA between a customer and a service provider. However, it only defines what has been agreed upon for the service and does not mean that such a service has been admitted or corresponding resources have been reserved. For example, a network may be provisioned for a voice service, but the resources are not reserved until the call has been set up. A service flow that has this parameter defined but the other two QoS parameters set to null is called a *provisioned* service flow.

- **Admitted QoS Parameter Set**   This set defines the parameter sets for which resources have been allocated and reserved. This also means that the service has been admitted and can make use of the resources allocated to it at any time. It does not necessarily mean that the resources are actually being used to serve the service flow. If a flow is not using all the resources reserved for it, the network may temporarily reallocate the excess resources to other flows whose resource utilization may be exceeding what is reserved for them. However, as long as a service flow is using all its reserved resources, a network would not reallocate those resources to serve the excess needs of other service flows. A service flow that has this parameter defined but has its *Active QoS Parameter* set to null is called an *admitted* service flow.

- **Active QoS Parameter Set**   This parameter set defines the parameter set for which resources are reserved and actually being used. Only flows that have active QoS parameters defined can request and be granted bandwidth for transmission. A service flow for which this parameter is defined is called an *active* service flow.

The two types of service flows, *admitted* and *active*, facilitate two-phase service activation models widely used in telephony applications. For example, when an end-to-end call is being set up, a flow may get admitted but the actual data may not flow until the service flow has been admitted by all the entities involved. Once the end-to-end call setup is complete, the flow is activated. The notion of admitted flow and active flow serves the purpose of conserving network resources until a complete end-to-end connection has been set.

Types and parameters of service flows can be very dynamic, but their dynamic behavior is dictated by a logical entity called an *Authorization Module*. This entity defines an outer bound "envelope," referred to as an *AuthorizedQoSParameterSet*, within which all the QoS parameter sets have to remain as service flows change. It ensures that the *Admitted QoS Parameters Set* is subset of the *Provisioned QoS Parameter Set* and the *Active QoS Parameter Set* is a subset of the *Admitted QoS Parameter Set*. In other words, the Authorization Module ensures that active service flows do not require more resources than admitted service flows, which in turn do not require more resources than provisioned service flows.

QoS   As discussed in the previous section, service flows associate a set of QoS parameters with each connection, which in turn are used to provide transport service to the higher layer protocol. The discussion of some of these parameters in this section will shed some light on the type of QoS that developers of the standard intended WiMAX networks to deliver. The standard however does not mandate the implementation of a specific QoS algorithm and leaves it up to vendors.

- **Traffic Priority**   Traffic Priority, with values ranging from 0 to 7 for low to high priority, respectively, specifies the priority assigned to a specific service flow. However, unlike many other networking protocols (e.g., Ethernet) where priority alone defines the QoS parameters, priority in WiMAX is meaningful only when all other QoS parameters are identical.

- **Maximum Sustained Traffic Rate**   This parameter, expressed in bits per second, defines the peak data rate of the service flow. This defines the maximum data rate that a service flow can achieve in absence of congestion. The parameter is meaningful only when there is an excess bandwidth above the total needed to serve the minimum needs of all flows. For uplink traffic (from BS to SS), some form of policing needs to be done by the SS to ensure that the uplink traffic pattern, on average, does not exceed this parameter. For downlink traffic, the policing is expected to be done at the ingress point of the network.

- **Maximum Traffic Burst**   The maximum burst of data traffic, given in bytes, specifies the maximum burst of ingress traffic that the system can accommodate. This parameter, which is mostly dictated by the characteristic of the ingress port, is meant to ensure sufficient system resources such as buffer space, CPU cycles, and so on, to handle the burst.

- **Minimum Reserved Traffic Rate**   This is one of the key QoS parameters that specify, in bits per second, the minimum data rate reserved for the service that is statistically guaranteed over time. Systems are designed such that no service is denied its minimum reserved traffic rate because of another service getting more than its minimum reserved traffic rate. There are two key points about this parameter that should be noted. First, resource reservation does not necessarily mean that the resources are not to be used for any other purpose. For example, if a service flow is transmitting less than its minimum reserved traffic rate, its excess reserve bandwidth may be reallocated to serve other flows. Second, the sum total of the minimum reserved traffic rate of all service flows over a channel *can* be more than the overall available bandwidth of the channel provided that the statistical multiplexing of service utilization would guarantee that the minimum traffic rate is satisfied over time for all services. This allows for over subscription and efficient use of resources.

- **Minimum Tolerable Traffic Rate**   As the name implies, this specifies the minimum traffic rate below which the user (customer or application) would not tolerate the service. For example, for VoIP or IPTV applications, traffic rates below a certain threshold may not be useful. A WiMAX network can make use of the knowledge of such minimum tolerable thresholds in two ways. When resources are busy and the network cannot deliver the minimum reserved traffic rate, it can make sure that the service is maintained by delivering at least the minimum tolerable traffic rate. However, when it cannot even maintain the minimum tolerable traffic rate, it can make better use of the bandwidth by not attempting to deliver the less than the minimum tolerable rate traffic and allocating the bandwidth to another flow.

- **Tolerated Jitter**   This parameter defines the maximum jitter, specified in milliseconds, tolerated by the user of the service. Although this parameter is defined by the standard, the detail of its meaning, scope, and implication is not very clearly stated. Nonetheless, the standard allows for the definition of this parameter as part of the QoS of a service flow.

- **Maximum Latency**   Maximum Latency specifies the latency between time when a packet is received by a device at its network interface and the transmission of the packet over the air interface. For all service flows within their minimum reserved rate, this parameter represents a service commitment and guarantee by a BS or SS. It is specified in milliseconds.

- **Vendor-specific QoS parameter**   The standard allows for vendor-specific QoS parameters that may be used to develop proprietary QoS algorithms. However, all devices are still required to maintain interoperability with other devices by honoring the QoS parameters as specified in the standard.

- **Service Flow Schedule Type**   This parameter defines the type/class of the service, which in turn defines the type of scheduling enabled for the service flow. The standard defines four types of services: Unsolicited Grant Service (UGS), real-time Polling Service (rtPS), non-real-time Polling Service (nrtPS), and Best-effort Service (BE). The details of these services and their scheduling are discussed later in section "Scheduling of Services."

Bandwidth Requests and Allocation   The success of the very centralized WiMAX MAC protocol in serving the QoS needs of the service flows depends on its effectiveness in serving the bandwidth demands of the flows. Specifically, it depends on having an effective mechanism for the SS to request for uplink bandwidth and for BS to timely allocate the requested bandwidth on a dynamic basis.

The requests are made by SSs to the BS on per-connection basis. Bandwidth grants are made by the BS scheduler based on multitude of parameters such as QoS parameters, bandwidth usage and other pending requests. However, bandwidth grants are made to the requesting SS without being specific about the CID for which the bandwidth grant is made. This allows for SS to use the allocated bandwidth for whatever fits its need. For example, if an SS has an urgent need to send a MAC management message to the BS, it could use its allocated bandwidth for this purpose.

Ability to allocate bandwidth as requested by an SS in itself is not sufficient to serve the QoS in a shared medium. Equally important is the mechanism and opportunities for SSs to request bandwidth in a timely manner to serve the QoS needs of its service flows. The MAC defines bandwidth request mechanisms that provide such opportunities for SSs to request uplink bandwidth:

- **Unicast polling**   Unicast polling is a mechanism by which an SS is granted (by the BS) bandwidth (meaning a TDMA slot) solely for the SS to make bandwidth requests. The rate of such unsolicited polling depends on the QoS requirement of the service associated with the SS. SS can use each instance of the periodically available bandwidth for any purpose that fits its need. It may use the bandwidth to send data traffic piggy-backed with requests for more bandwidth or it may send just its bandwidth requests to the BS. Unicast polling also serves the purpose that with each SS transmitting some data to the BS periodically, it allows the BS to monitor the quality of the physical channel. The frequency of unicast polling of an SS is determined by the type QoS requirement of the services being associated with the SS, as well as by the need to monitor the physical channel.

- **Broadcast/multicast polling**   Instead of periodically granting all SSs dedicated bandwidth for the purpose of bandwidth requests (as done with unicast polling), it may be more efficient to give such bandwidth to a set of SSs and allow them to use this bandwidth on a contention basis. This may be desirable when the set of SSs are only serving best-effort traffic or the SSs are sitting idle. The broadcast/multicast polling mechanism allows a BS to do just that by making transmission opportunities (e.g., a transmission timeslot) available to all SSs (broadcast polling) or a group of SSs (multicast polling) on a periodic basis. If a node belonging to the group has a bandwidth need, it sends a request for bandwidth using the transmission opportunity. Once the BS receives the request, it subsequently makes bandwidth available to the requesting SS. The bandwidth request mechanism is contention based, and the MAC provides several mechanisms to minimize the impact of such contentions.

Scheduling of Services   As was discussed in an earlier section, one of the QoS parameters of a service flow is Service Flow Schedule Type. Four types of scheduling services are defined by the standard and dictate how the services are scheduled:

- **Unsolicited Grant Service (UGS)**   This is equivalent to CBR in ATM and is intended for applications that have real-time data streams consisting of fixed-size data packets generated at periodic intervals. Examples include T1/E1 services. For this type of service, BS grants fixed-size bandwidths periodically to SSs associated with the service flows without being solicited for the bandwidth by the SSs. The size of the bandwidth grants at periodic intervals is sufficient to transport the fixed-size data needed by the service flow.

- **Real-time Polling Service (rtPS)**   rtPS is designed for real-time traffic with variable size packets generated at *periodic* intervals. Examples of such traffic are MPEG video stream, VoIP with silence compression, and so on. For this type of service, SSs are given opportunities to specify their bandwidth needs by means of periodic unicast polling. If the bandwidth requests are within the realm of what can be granted, the bandwidth is granted to the SS.

- **Non-real-time Polling Service (nrtPS)**   nrtPS is designed to support delay-tolerant data traffic for which a minimum data rate is required. Examples of such traffic include various forms for Internet data transfer protocols. In order for SSs to provide this type of service, the BS provides bandwidth request opportunities to the SS by means of unicast polling on a regular basis—at an interval comparable to 1 sec. Additionally, contention-based broadcast/multicast polling may be used by the SS to request bandwidth allocations dynamically as needs arise.

- **Best-effort Service (BE)**   BE, as the name suggests, is designed to transport data traffic on a best-effort basis with no minimum service level specified. In order to provide this type of service, SSs use broadcast/multicast polling mechanisms to request necessary bandwidth. SSs providing this kind of services may also be given transmission opportunities to request bandwidth using unicast polling.

Multicast Services   Being able to provide multicast services so that bandwidth is not wasted on transmitting identical packets to each and every recipient, is very important for wireless networks as they have limited transmission resources. Such networks are routinely expected to use multicast services for applications such as video surveillance, TV broadcast, online games, or point-to-multipoint virtual LAN services. Shared medium networks such as PMP RF-wireless networks also provide an ideal ground for providing multicasting services, and WiMAX is no exception.

WiMAX supports multicast connections that can be used for multicast services on the downlink (transmission from BS to SS). The BS does so by associating a connection (and a CID) with the multicast service and associating all the SSs in the multicast group with the connection. The CID used for the multicast service is the same for all the SSs in the same channel that are in the multicast group. The standard does not specify a separate group of CIDs for multicast services, and the CIDs do not need to be distinguished in any way from the CID used for unicast traffic. In fact, each SS does not need to be aware of the fact that it is receiving multicast traffic in the connection. The BS "broadcasts" the multicast data, with the multicast CID, and is received by all the SSs sharing the same channel. However, only those associated with the CID would accept it.

The WiMAX standard allows for per-service encryption techniques (to be discussed in the next section). which enable effective encryption of multicast services such that SSs that are not in the multicast group are not able to decrypt the multicast packet even if they are able to receive it.

Security

The security mechanism provided by WiMAX MAC has two objectives: the first to provide the subscriber of the network services privacy across the wireless network and the second to provide the network operator with protection from unauthorized use of its services. In order to serve the first objective, a set of industry-standard cryptographic suites are supported. Additionally, key management protocol is also defined for the secure distribution of an encryption key from the BS to a select set of SSs. The key management protocol also serves the purpose of meeting the second objective.

Authentication and Authorization   SSs use the PKM protocol to obtain their authorization and keys from the BS and to refresh those keys periodically. The PKM uses an established shared secret, i.e., an Authorization Key (AK), between the SS and the BS. The AK is used to secure subsequent exchanges of traffic keys.

The authorization process also involves initial authentication of the identity of SS by means of a unique X.509 digital certificate of the SS. Once authenticated, the BS authorizes the SS by issuing an AK that is used to derive a Key Encryption Key (KEK) and a message encryption key. Each AK has an expiration time before which SS is reauthenticated and reauthorized. Along with the authorization, the SS is also issued the identities and properties of the Security Associations that the SS is authorized to obtain.

Security Association   IEEE 802.16 standard uses the notion of a Security Association (SA) which defines a set of security information shared between a BS and one or more SSs in order to support secure transfers of data between these devices. Each SA defines a Cryptographic Suite used for the SA. The SA may also contain the encryption key and other parameters associated with the Cryptographic Suite.

There are three types of SA defined by the standard. *Primary SA* is an SA established by a SS during its initialization into the network. The Primary SA established by an SS is shared between the SS and the BA only. *Static SAs* are created by the BS based on provisioning. *Dynamic SAs* are established and torn down as service flows are created and eliminated. Dynamic and Static SAs can be shared among multiple SSs (e.g., for multicast traffic). The cryptographic suite and keys associated with each service flow is used to secure the service flow data.

Cryptographic Suite   A Cryptographic Suite is a set of methods for data authentication, data encryption, and key exchange. The standard allows for five different Cryptographic Suites as shown in Table 15.1.

Among the two data encryption methods supported, CBS-mode DES is not considered a very strong encryption method. The only benefit it offers over the AES method is that the data size is not expanded by the encryption process. The AES method, on the other hand, has been widely accepted as a very strong encryption technique.

PHY

The Physical Layer Protocol (PHY) defines the technical details of the use of the physical layer medium for communication and dictates the spectral efficiency of the protocol. The MAC layer protocol of WiMAX was designed to be mostly independent of the details of the Physical (PHY) Layer Protocol in general, allowing for the development of a diverse set of PHY standards, each optimized for a different type of application. As a consequence of this principle, several PHY standards have been developed as the acceptance of WiMAX has grown for a wider set of applications since its origin.

During the early stages of the standard's development, the primary application of the technology was for fixed–wireless extensions of fiber as well as PMP backhaul of cell sites. For these applications, availability of a large spectrum to deliver higher capacity was certainly more important than the need for non-line-of-sight (NLOS) operation or spectrum licensing. A large spectrum was (and still is) potentially available between 10–66 GHz. Therefore, the early PHY standard, targeted for LOS applications, was developed for spectrum between 10–66 GHz without locking it to a specific band of spectrum. The 10+ GHz frequencies allowed for implementation of broadband channels delivering high bandwidth and the creation of narrow beams using highly directional antennas. This standard was based on a single-carrier modulation scheme.

The single-carrier standard operating at frequencies between 10 GHz and 66 GHz is not practical for two other applications of WiMAX that gained momentum during the later stages of the standard's development: NLOS in general and mobility specifically. Higher data rate single carrier schemes are susceptible to the adverse effects of multipath signal propagation in NLOS applications. Additionally, RF signals in the

TABLE 15.1   Supported Cryptographic Suites

Cryptographic Suite	Encryption Method	Authentication Method	Key Exchange Method
1	No encryption	No authentication	3-DES, 128
2	CBC-mode 56-bit DES	No authentication	3-DES, 128
3	No nncryption	No authentication	RSA, 1024
4	CBC-mode 56-bit DEC	No authentication	RSA, 1024
5	CCM-mode AES	No authentication	AES,128

higher frequency range have much poorer penetrating properties than lower frequency RF signals. Finally, Doppler shift encountered due to mobility complicates the design of higher frequency systems. In order to address the NLOS applications, and subsequently to support mobility, PHY protocols operating below 11 GHz using multi-carrier modulation were subsequently developed.

Single-Carrier Modulation The single-carrier PHY standard (SC-PHY) was the first PHY standard developed by IEEE 802.16, which referred to it as *WirelessMAN-SC*. It was designed to operate at frequencies between 10 GHz and 66 GHz. (Another single-carrier PHY standard, referred to as *WirelessMAC-SCa*, was subsequently developed to operate below 11 GHz but does not appear to have found much support in the industry.)

SC-PHY supports both Time-Division Duplexing (TDD) and Frequency-Division Duplexing (FDD) operations in order to accommodate a diverse set of worldwide spectrum regulation. In FDD, DL and UL communications use two different non-overlapping bands of spectrum, enabling them to take place simultaneously. In TDD, both DL and UL communications use the same band of spectrum and the transmission time is divided into timeframes, one for uplink and another for downlink. Both TDD and FDD framing structures are very similar to allow for support for both without incurring significant system complexity. In either case, the frame used for the purpose of uplink traffic is referred to as the *uplink channel* and the frame used for the purpose of downlink traffic is referred to as the *downlink channel*.

Multiple Access For DL communication, the PHY uses the Time-Division Multiplexing (TDM) scheme whereby data is transmitted by the BS as a single stream with data for each SS multiplexed onto the stream and received by all SSs within the sector. All the SSs using the same channel attempt to receive all portions of the DL, but retain only the portion of the data they are meant to retain (identified by the CID for unicast, multicast, and broadcast. Encryption also ensures that an unintended SS cannot make meaningful use of the data). Though transmitted as a single stream of data, the transmission may change its transmission characteristics (burst profile) multiple times within the DL frame to tradeoff between channel robustness and throughput. The properties and the boundary of each burst profile within the DL frame are indicated at the beginning of the DL frame (called *DL-MAP*) for all the SSs to understand.

For UL communication, the PHY uses TDMA and Demand Assigned Multiple Access (DAMA) to allow communication from multiple SSs to a BS. The UL transmission frame is further divided into a number of timeslots, each of which is assigned by the BS for various purposes, including transmission of data by an SS to the BS. Two slots are reserved for contention-based communication; a large number of the timeslots are reserved for communication from SSs to the BS on an assignment basis. The assignment information is provided as part of the DL frame (referred to as *UL-MAP*). The SS that is assigned a timeslot transmits its data during the slot using the burst profile specified as part of the UL-MAP. The burst profile for one timeslot may be different from the burst profile for another timeslot.

This ability to adjust transmission properties, such as modulation scheme and FEC code types during transmission, allows for varying degrees of transmission robustness and throughput based on the channel condition experienced by each SS and the quality of service needed by each service.

Forward Error Correction   Forward Error Correction (FEC) techniques are used to correct for or detect errors in received data, which allows for additional robustness to the channel at the cost of information overhead and/or processing complexity.

The PHY supports four different types of FEC techniques, each providing performance suitable for different applications. The parameter of each type of FEC can be further adjusted for additional optimization.

Modulation   To make an efficient use of the bandwidth, the PHY makes use of a multilevel modulation scheme, which includes QPSK, 16-QAM, and 64-QAM. For the same average transmit power and channel bandwidth, the different modulation schemes provide a tradeoff between channel throughput and robustness. For example, 64-QAM can transmit three times as much data as QPSK can, however, at the cost of immunity from noise.

The modulation scheme can be selected on per-subscriber basis based on the quality of the RF channel. For example, for a distant SS that would require more link margin, it may be desirable to use QPSK. However, for a nearby SS with plenty of link margin, it may be desirable to use 64-QAM to maximize the utilization of the spectrum. The modulation scheme can thus be adjusted both for UL and DL channels for each burst profile.

Channel Bandwidth   The PHY also defined default RF channel bandwidths in order to ensure the products' interoperability over the RF interface. The channel bandwidth and the achievable throughput are listed in Table 15.2.

Multi-Carrier Modulation (OFDM and OFDMA)   One of the significant limitations of the original PHY development, which would have ruled out ubiquitous deployment of WiMAX, was its LOS limitation. Subsequent to the development of the original PHY, a new PHY standard was developed that was targeted for NLOS operation.

Due to the propagation characteristic of waveforms below 11 GHz, use of a single-carrier system gets severely affected by multipath, where the multipath duration could be larger than the short symbol duration needed to transmit high-bandwidth data using

TABLE 15.2   Channel Bandwidth and Throughput *(Source: IEEE 802.16-2004)*

Channel Size (MHz)	Symbol Rate (MBd)	Bit rate (Mb/s) QPSK	Bit rate (Mb/s) 16-QAM	Bit rate (Mb/s) 64-QAM
20	16	32	64	96
25	20	40	80	120
28	22.4	44.8	89.6	134.4

a single carrier. One of the techniques that has gained significant ground combating the effects of multipath is Orthogonal Frequency Division Multiplexing (OFDM). In this technique, the physical channel is split into large numbers of subchannels and the data transmission is multiplexed among the multiple channels. With each channel transmitting data at a much slower rate, the ISI due to multipath is minimized, allowing for recovery of transmitted data.

Multiple Access   One of the key differences between OFDM and OFDMA is the multiple access methods used by the two schemes. In the case of OFDM, all the subcarriers are addressed to a single receiver at any given time and multiple access is provided by means of TDMA. However, in the case of OFDMA, a subset of subcarrier can be addressed to any one of the SSs at any given time. In OFDMA, multiple access is provided by a combination of time and subcarriers. This combination raises the complexity of OFDMA significantly.

As in the case of OFDMA, OFDM also uses a group of subcarriers (known as a subchannel) to address a specific receiver, a technique referred to as *subchannelization*. However, a key difference is that, in the case of OFDM, each subchannel can be thought of as a separate independent channel, and the mapping of data to the channel is solely based on TDMA, very similar to the TDMA scheme in the case of SC-PHY discussed in the previous section. The channel is divided into frames, which is divided further into DL subframes and UL subframes. The DL frame is further divided into smaller slots, each with its own burst profile. The first two frames are transmitted with frame management information that includes both UL-MAP and DL-MAP. In a similar fashion as SC-PHY, the UL subframe is divided into several slots with their own burst profile, some of which are used for contention-based UL communication, while most of which are assigned to a specific SS for UL communication by UL-MAP.

The multiple access method in OFDMA is significantly more complex. OFDMA supports both TDD and FDD, whereby the downlink and uplink are divided into different timeframes or frequencies, respectively. The mapping for both UL and DL happens in two steps. First, the data gets mapped to one or more timeslots on one or more logical channels. Second,, data in logical subchannels in each timeslot gets mapped to one more physical subchannel. The end result is a complex mapping of data transmission into a complex framework of timeslot and channel. Within this complexity, OFDMA also allows for various burst profiles accommodating adaptive transmission techniques.

Forward Error Correction   The OFDM PHY specified three different forward error correction schemes, including block turbo codes and convolution turbo codes, which provide 2–3 dB of additional gain. However, due to their implementation complexity, they have been left as an option. In addition to these three, OFDMA specifies two more optional FEC methods.

Modulation   Both OFDM and OFDMA PHYs support four different types of modulations: BPSK, QPSK, 16-QAM, and 64-QAM. Adaptive modulation both for uplink and downlink are supported.

Smart Antenna Technology

Advanced antenna technologies take advantage of spatial diversity that can be provided by multiple antennas to improve the performance of an RF channel. Some of the well-developed advanced antenna technologies are Smart Antenna Systems (SASs), Space-Time Coding (STC), and Multiple-In-Multiple-Out (MIMO). WiMAX provides support of technologies for frequencies below 11 GHz. Among these technologies, perhaps the most interesting is the smart antenna technology.

Smart Antenna Systems, referred to as *Adaptive Antenna Systems (AASs)* in the standard, allow for beam forming of the RF signal by using multiple antenna elements spatially separated from each other. Beam forming by means of smart antennas creates a narrower beam of signals bringing with it several benefits. Narrow beam means higher gain, which in turn means longer range or higher capacity links. It also means higher network capacity and spectral use efficiency, as the same frequency can be used to communicate with multiple SSs simultaneously with nonoverlapping breams. Unlike the narrower beam created by directional single-element antennas, beams created by AAS can be steered very dynamically without having to steer the antenna system physically. For example, a BS with AAS can steer its beam on a per-SS or per-burst profile basis.

The use of AAS capability is valuable usually only in the context of BS, as it has to communicate with SSs located at diverse locations. Therefore, in WiMAX networks, AAS operation is defined only in the context of BS, with SS requiring only basis supporting functions. SSs are not expected to use AAS, but they are not precluded from using an AAS. SSs are unlikely to use AAS because SSs communicate with only one BS, the location of which is usually fixed. (An exception may be in Mesh networks where SSs communicate with other SSs. However, in this case, the small number of neighbors, their diverse locations, and their relatively close proximity may not make use of AAS very meaningful.) Mostly, the benefits of AAS at SS do not outweigh the complexity and cost associated with it.

WiMAX MAC and OFDM/OFDMA PHY provide support for AAS use at the BS. The hardware and algorithm support for AAS, however, is considered an implementation detail and left to be vendor specific.

WiMAX Mesh

Much of our discussion of WiMAX in this chapter has been centered on PMP operations, whose underlying restriction is that SSs have to communicate with only a central BS. This restriction poses several limitations on a BWA network. For example, range of a BS is limited to a certain geographic region, extension of the network beyond which would require deployment of another BS which is significantly more complex and perhaps significantly more expensive than an SS.

In Mesh networks, if physical conditions allow for it, any two devices (called *nodes*), including a pair of SSs, can directly communicate with each other. If channel conditions are such that more than two pairs of nodes can communicate with each other, they are allowed to communicate with each other simultaneously. Finally, each node is capable of relaying data packets from one node to another. IEEE 802.16 protocol allows for creation of such wireless Mesh networks, as illustrated in Figure 15.1. With these capabilities, Mesh networks offer several benefits that cannot be easily realized by PMP networks.

- **Cost-effective network expansion** With each SS capable of communicating with and relaying the traffic of other SSs, expansion of a network beyond the range of a BS could be done by just deploying more SSs beyond the range. As long as such an SS can communicate directly or indirectly (through other SSs) with another SS within the range of the BS, the network can be expanded without having to deploy additional costly BSs.

- **Increased network capacity/spectral efficiency** Two or more pairs of nodes not sharing the same channel are allowed to communicate with each other simultaneously. This results in an increased network capacity. Additionally, increased spectral efficiency can be achieved when traffic between a BS and distant SS is routed through an intermediate SS instead of by means of direct communication.

- **Redundancy and resiliency** Mesh networks allow for multiple redundant paths to route traffic between two nodes, which in turn provide resiliency against failures. Redundancy in the backhaul connection can be achieved by providing direct backhaul connections to two or more nodes.

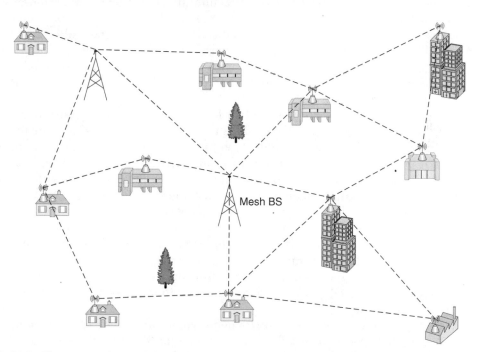

Figure 15.1 Illustration of a wireless Mesh network

■ **Peer-to-peer communication**   Mesh networks allow for communication, direct or indirect, between two SSs, without having to send the traffic through the BS. This results in efficient use of the spectrum.

There are several downsides to Mesh networks. Routing data traffic through multiple hops can degrade the cumulative latency and jitter experienced by the data traffic. Additionally, Mesh networks may not be very scalable as the complexity of the control mechanism and the mesh management traffic may grow significantly as the size of the network grows. Finally, the controllers of Mesh networks are also significantly more complex and costly than that of PMP networks.

There are, in general, two categories of Mesh networks: physical and logical mesh. Physical mesh consists of nodes using highly directional antenna such that physical links are created between any two nodes. At all times, a physical link connects only two nodes and a node would use such a physical link to communicate with its neighbor. On the contrary, a logical mesh consists of nodes using wide beams to create multiple logical links with its neighbors. IEEE 802.16 MAC operation is completely defined for logical mesh using OFDM-PHY, whereas physical mesh operation may still require some more work. Despite the mesh MAC protocol sharing substantial similarity with the PMP MAC protocol, they are not interoperable.

One of the most important differences between a PMP and Mesh network is that, unlike in PMP networks where all communications are connection-oriented, Mesh network communications are connectionless. All *direct* communications between two nodes are in the context of a link, specified by an 8-bit number called a *Link ID* (in place of CID), unique only in the local neighborhood. QoS parameters are not associated with Link IDs but instead are associated with each packet and are specified by parameters in the packet header. The destination of a packet is also identified by a 16-bit Node ID specified in the packet header.

A key prerequisite for a Mesh network is the ability of more than two pairs of nodes to communicate directly. In a logical Mesh network, this means all transmissions among different nodes have to be coordinated and scheduled such that a communication between one pair of nodes will not interfere with a communication between another pair of nodes. 802.16 mesh standard allows for two different types of such coordinated scheduling: centralized scheduling and distributed scheduling.

In centralized scheduling, resources (and not the transmission schedules) are granted in a more centralized manner by a specially designated node referred to as the *Mesh BS*. The Mesh BS gathers resource requirements from all the Mesh SSs within a certain hop range. It then computes the amount of resources for each link in the network, both in downlink and uplink, and communicates these grants to the Mesh SSs within the hop range. Based on the resources granted to its links, the node computes its transmission schedule.

In distributed scheduling, all the nodes coordinate their transmission in their two-hop neighborhood and broadcast their schedule to all their neighbors. The schedule may also be established by direct requests and grants between two nodes. With all the nodes knowing the schedule of all other nodes in the two-hop neighborhood, they can ensure that the resulting transmissions do not cause collisions with the data and control traffic scheduled by any other node in the neighborhood.

Carrier Ethernet Services over WiMAX

As stated previously, the early development of the IEEE 802.16 standard was driven by the objective to serve the needs of carriers. Therefore, much of the effort was on developing the technology to satisfy the needs of the carriers. In this section, we discuss how it fares in some of the carrier-centric attributes.

Failure Resiliency   One of the key necessities for failure resiliency of a communication protocol is the robustness of its PHY protocol. WiMAX defines very resilient PHY protocols. All PHY protocols define an adaptive modulation scheme that allows for transmission methods to be changed as the channel characteristics of the physical medium changes. PHYs also allow for adaptive FEC algorithms, which provide an added level of data transmission resiliency. In addition to the robustness provided by the PHY, WiMAX also adds to the resiliency by allowing for retransmission (ARQ and H-ARQ) on a per-connection basis.

Scalability   It is often the case that limitation of a shared medium is its scalability. Examples are some variants of Ethernet and WiFi, which are not very scalable because of their contention-based MAC protocol. However, both WiMAX PHY and MAC are designed such that the network can be scaled significantly without compromising the efficiency of the network. Due to the coordination performed by the BS, almost all the transmissions are scheduled on a predefined basis. Only a small part of the bandwidth is used for contention-based communications. Such efficient allocation of bandwidth ensures that the efficiency with which the available bandwidth can be used is almost independent of the number of SSs in the network.

WiMAX does not require the use of a specific RF band and can be used over a large number of RF spectrums. This allows for scaling of the network beyond what can be served by a single band of RF spectrum. In addition, it allows for techniques such as adaptive antenna and beam-forming, allowing for efficient use of the RF spectrum and, in turn, allowing for the network to be scaled.

In addition to the scalability of the network in terms of the number of subscribers and total network capacity, WiMAX also enables deployment of services that are very scalable. The bandwidth allocated to a service flow can scale from a few Kbps to the entire bandwidth of the channel. Such allocated bandwidth can also be scaled on a dynamic basis as the need arises and bandwidth becomes available.

Quality of Service   QoS framework is one of the key aspects of WiMAX that distinguishes it from most other wireless networking standards. As discussed earlier, all services offered by WiMAX are in the context of service flows that have a fairly large set of QoS parameters associated with them. WiMAX also provides scheduling and bandwidth request techniques that facilitate serving the flow as demanded by their QoS parameters.

Support for TDM Services   Both the MAC and PHY aspects of the WiMAX standard are inherently based on a TDM-like protocol, which facilitates implementation of TDM services. WiMAX also allows for service scheduling and polling (e.g., UGS), which supports implementation of real-time TDM services like T1/E1. Additionally, it allows for clock synchronization between BS and SS to prevent bit slip, facilitating delivery of robust TDM services.

Service Management   WiMAX uses the notion of service flows and the mapping of higher layer services to these service flows. The notion of service flow provides a handle through which the services are managed. The standard also defines a protocol-agnostic management framework and a set of MIBs to manage these services.

Drivers for This Solution

In the opening paragraphs of this chapter, we attempted to make a compelling case for BWA technologies. It would not be too much of a simplification to say that this was the genesis, in one way or the other, of all BWA technologies including WiMAX.

The technology, IEEE802.16 in particular, was originally developed to serve the high bandwidth needs of enterprise networks with the evolutionary path to serve the needs of access networks such as cellular backhaul. The technology was later amended to use lower frequency bands, targeting its application in NLOS environments. Over time, the interest in its use as a BWA technology grew, evolving toward becoming an access technology with the ability to support nomadic and mobile applications.

When Does This Solution Fit?

WiMAX has a wide set of applications, both in urban and rural environments where other technologies have limitations of their own. In this section, we discuss these applications. In none of these application is carrier-grade Ethernet service precluded.

Fiber Extension: Commercial Broadband Service

In many of the urban commercial environments of developed countries such as the U.S., several office towers are connected to broadband infrastructure like fiber-optics networks. Tenants of such buildings can enjoy access to broadband services such as multi-T1/E1 or Ethernet services. However, even in such urban commercial environments, less than only 10 percent of the buildings fall under this category. Tenants of the remaining 90 percent of the buildings are left without access to fiber and are limited to traditional services such as T1/E1.

WiMAX network can be used to extend the reach of fiber beyond where the fiber terminates, extending the plethora of services that can be made available to tenants of other buildings. This can be accomplished in at least three different ways. In all these method, a BS would be installed on the rooftop of the building or tower with access to the fiber infrastructure. In the first case, the single carrier SC-PHY technology could be used to extend services from the BS to the building in Line-of-Sight (LOS) of the BS, from where it would be distributed to the tenants of the building, using the building's internal networking infrastructure, as illustrated in Figure 15.2. In the second case, the OFDM-PHY technology could be used to extend service from the BS to the building or directly to its tenants that are directly reachable from the BS, though not necessarily in line-of-sight of the BS. In the third case, the WiMAX Mesh technology could be used to extend the service from the BS to the building or tenants that are reachable from the Mesh network. Regardless of which method is employed, the wireless network can be used to extend the services offered on the fiber-optics network, such as Carrier Ethernet services, to the users of the wireless network.

Even though any of the PHY standards could be used, SC-PHY technology is usually more desirable for this type of application. Extensions of fiber services demand high bandwidth from the network. The SC solution can offer higher bandwidth per channel than the OFDM solution (96 Mbps vs. 75 Mbps with 20 MHz band) can a large pool of suitable spectrum in the 10–66 GHz region is already available for this type of applications, both on a license-exempt basis or for low-cost licensing fees. Because of their propagation properties, which do not allow efficient NLOS operation or long range operations, these spectrums are not sought after as much as the lower frequency spectrums are. Most locations with access to fiber-optics networks are tall buildings, the rooftops of which are ideal locations to provide LOS services to the rooftops of surrounding commercial buildings. Additionally, high-gain and highly directional antennas can be made use of very effectively in these higher frequencies, allowing for better reuse of the spectrum and delivery of higher bandwidth.

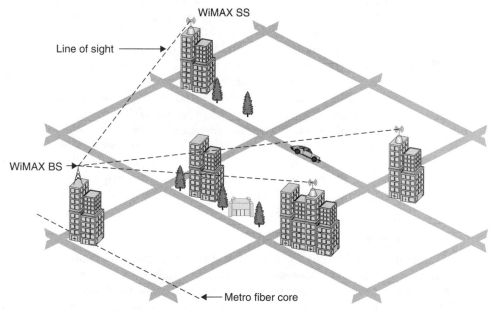

Figure 15.2   Fiber extension with WiMAX

Backhaul for Cellular/WiFi Hotspot and Muni-Networks

In the U.S., wireless operators had until recently enjoyed the benefit of the FCC mandate requiring wired infrastructure providers to lease lines to third-party service providers. With that mandate no longer in existence, the case for alternate means to backhaul cellular traffic looks more attractive. Additionally, the cost-effective wired backhaul infrastructure may not be available at all cell sites. This is particularly true as cellular operators persuade their customers to subscribe to their lucrative broadband services and need to increase their spectral efficiency by deploying more cell sites.

It should be remembered that the early development of the standard was also driven partly by the need to provide a standardized technology to backhaul cellular traffic. As was stated earlier, the SC-PHY standard was developed primarily for backhaul applications, and it is still the most suitable standard to be used for backhauling cellular traffic. This is primarily because the majority of cellular sites are either on top of large buildings and towers that are likely to be in line-of-sight of another building or tower with access to a wired infrastructure. In addition, all the reasons presented in favor of SC-PHY for fiber-extension applications apply equally well to this application also. The backhaul of cell towers could be provided by installing a BS on the rooftop of a building with access to a wired backhaul facility and installing SSs on the rooftops of cell-sites buildings or on top of cell towers.

The cost of deploying WiFi has come down considerably in the past few years, allowing for large ubiquitous use of the technology and a widespread deployment of WiFi hotspots. However, the cost of backhauling a hotspot remains the single biggest cost for hotspot operators. Unlike cellular operators that enjoy a single backhaul connection covering a larger footprint per cell tower, WiFi hotspots have smaller coverage, requiring more hotspots to cover a comparable area. For Muni-WiFi networks, the problem is even more acute as the number of hotspot access points per square mile is significantly more than in the case of cellular networks. Lately, the problem of backhauling WiFi traffic has been addressed to some extent by WiFi mesh technologies. However, it has its own limitations, the least of which is the lack of a common standard.

WiMAX poses as a very strong candidate for providing connections to WiFI hotspots. In particular, OFDM-PHY is much better suited to this application, primarily because, unlike relatively conspicuously located cell towers, WiFi hotspots usually do not have easy LOS to a central location. For example, a café providing a WiFi hotspot is unlikely to be in line-of-sight of a building with WiMAX BS. The lower bandwidth of OFDM-PHY is not likely to be a limitation because WiFi hotspots do not usually serve real-time high bandwidth traffic. In addition, because of a larger coverage area of the OFDM-PHY standard, a larger number of WiFi hotspots can be covered per BS (see Figure 15.3).

Rural Broadband Services

Even though broadband access has become almost a daily necessity in developed nations, the means of fulfilling these necessities have their own limitations. The technologies commonly used to fulfill these needs are DSL and cable modems. Cable TV networks are neither ubiquitous nor have been upgraded in all areas to enable broadband services.

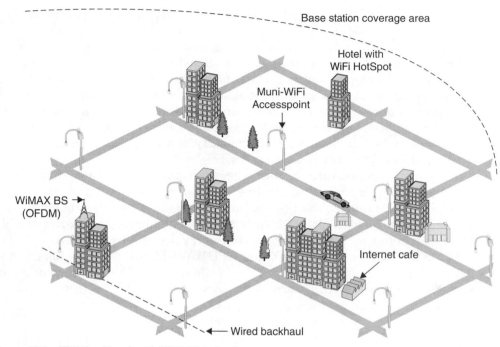

Figure 15.3 WiFi backhaul with WiMAX technology

Telephone networks, which are ubiquitous in developed nations, do not necessarily have the sufficient reach to enable broadband services ubiquitously. The cost of upgrading the cable and copper infrastructure to enable delivery of broadband services in rural areas where the population density is very is low is not economically feasible. Therefore, even though the broadband services are readily available in many of the urban and suburban areas of developed nations, many rural areas are underserved. WiMAX is very well suited to provide broadband services in such rural environments.

In rural applications of WiMAX, where subscriber density is low and spread out, a BS has to cover a larger area in order to make any economic sense. This necessitates the use of frequencies below 10 GHz, which have favorable propagation characteristics over longer distances. In this kind of environment, subscribers are usually in LoS of a central tower. Therefore, for this kind of application, networks using the SC-PHY standard, which uses spectrum below 11 GHz but is based on a single-carrier technique, would be ideally suited. Alternately, an SC-PHY-based solution (when the BS coverage area is small and LOS is viable) or an OFDM-PHY-based solution (when the BS coverage area is large or LOS is not viable) are both suitable for this application.

Urban Fixed and Mobile Broadband Services

In the previous section, we discussed the limitations of wired broadband services such as DSL and cable modems in urban environments. However, their limitations are not confined to rural environments alone. Cable TV networks are neither ubiquitous nor have been upgraded in all areas to enable broadband services. Telephone networks, which are ubiquitous in developed nations, neither have the sufficient reach nor have been upgraded everywhere to enable broadband services ubiquitously. In urban environments of developing nations, even though sufficient economic conditions exist to demand broadband services, the cost of building wired infrastructure is prohibitive.

In urban areas of the world where wired infrastructure can provide broadband services, the choice of service providers is limited to one or two at the most. Such infrastructures are also limited in their ability to provide the type of services that are demanded by sophisticated urban users.

The wired infrastructures have another fundamental limitation: they cannot provide nomadic or mobile broadband services. As small devices like cameras, PDAs, and laptops become ubiquitous, the need to provide mobile or seamless nomadic services becomes more important. Although such mobile broadband services are already provided by some wireless operators, the bandwidth provided is fairly limited.

WiMAX based on OFDM-PHY and OFDMA-PHY are well positioned to serve the needs of urban stationary as well as mobile users. In a dense urban environment, such as the one shown in Figure 15.4, where LOS operation is impractical, the NLOS

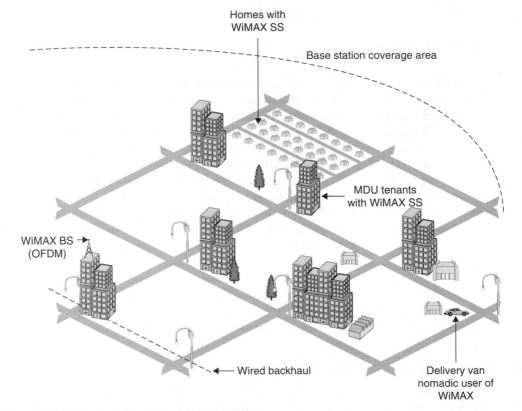

Figure 15.4   Urban broadband services with WiMAX

capability of OFDM is highly desirable. The IEEE 802.16e standard defines a mobile broadband service that can compete well with other alternate standards.

When Does This Solution Not Fit?

WiMAX is a very versatile and flexible technology that finds applications in wide variety of scenario. However, there are scenarios where, as compared to an alternate technology, WiMAX may not be the best solution. Provided below is a list of examples scenarios where WiMAX does not fit at all or is not the best fit as compared to alternate solutions.

- **When ultra-high bandwidth is needed**   As compared to other competing wireless technologies, WiMAX can offer fairly high bandwidth. However, for applications that demand ultra-high bandwidths, such as core of a network, alternate solution such as fiber-optics technology is usually a better fit that WiMAX.

- **When ultra-high reliability is needed**   WiMAX provides a very robust transport medium. However, generally speaking, a wireless medium is less reliable than a wired medium. Although WiMAX based solution can be engineered to rival the reliability of a wired medium, such a solution may not be the best fit when ultra-high reliability is needed and a wired solution is readily available.

- **Long-haul application**   RF signals have limited range of propagation, especially in dense urban environment. WiMAX is no exception to this rule. Therefore, it does not fit in scenarios demanding long-haul data transmission.

- **Indoor applications**   WiMAX was designed for outdoor applications and is not well suited for indoor applications, either due to regulatory or technical limitations.

Benefits and Shortcomings

Throughout this chapter, much of the material have been focused on key features of WiMAX, which no doubt form the basis of some of the key benefits of the technology, In this section, we revisit those benefits, both technical and non-technical, as well discuss what may be considered some of the shortcomings of the technology.

Technical Benefits

As has been discussed throughout this chapter, WiMAX provides several technical features that are highly desirable.

- **Adaptive channel robustness versus throughput**   In all communications systems with a given bandwidth, there is always a tradeoff between robustness and throughput. One of the key benefits of the WiMAX standard is its use of adaptive encoding and modulation techniques that allow it to dynamically increase robustness at the expense of throughput or increase throughput at the expense of robustness. Not only can a system do this on a per-endstation basis but also on a per-service basis. For example, a BS can use higher throughput coding and modulation to communicate with an SS located at 1 km but use higher robustness (but lower throughput) modulation to communicate with an SS located at 10 km. Alternately, even for an SS located at 1 km, it may use higher robustness modulation for services that require more protection than throughput, like MAC management traffic.

- **Flexible use of the RF medium**   The MAC protocol of WiMAX is independent of the PHY protocol. The higher layer MAC protocol does not make much assumption about the nature of the PHY protocols. This allows for development of newer PHY protocol to fit new applications as well as to take advantage of newer technologies. We have already seen the benefit of this with the development of OFDM and OFDMA standards. In addition, the MAC also allows support for TDD, FDD, and half-duplex operation. This facilitates flexible use of the PHY standard without any restriction from the higher layer protocol. The outcome of this flexibility is wider adaptation of the technology for larger sets of applications.

- **Flexible use of RF bandwidth**   All the PHY protocol standards developed by IEEE 802.16 are not locked to a specific frequency and bandwidth. This allows for use of the technology in whatever spectrum a usable bandwidth is available. It may be used by certain operators using licensed spectrum and others using license-free spectrum. This also allows for flexible deployment in various regulatory regions of the world, as the allocation of spectrum in different regulatory regions is different.

- **Efficient use of spectrum**   WiMAX MAC was designed to be highly centralized with the BS controlling all the accesses to the medium as well as dictating how efficiently the spectrum is used. The use of RF spectrum is controlled at all times by the BS such that a large majority of the channel utilization is scheduled by the BS based on the need of various SSs and their services. This allows for an extremely efficient use of RF spectrum as virtually no channel capacity is wasted. It is not only the scheduling part but also the adaptive coding technique that makes it very efficient in terms of use of the spectrum. In addition, the notion of various stages of service flow, which allows a WiMAX system to reserve a resource for a service flow but allocate the resource to other services if the owner of the resource has no immediate use for it, allows efficient use of the spectrum.

- **Advanced QoS**   The QoS feature of WiMAX has already been extensively discussed in this chapter. It should be apparent from those discussions that the QoS capability of WiMAX is one of its key benefits. It was designed to provide support for a wide spectrum of applications, ranging from TDM-like applications with constant bit rates to bursty applications. WiMAX MAC allows for scheduling that can look at a large set of parameters such as latency and jitter requirements of services and make scheduling decisions. Such capabilities make WiMAX highly capable of serving the needs of many services with diverse sets of QoS requirements.

- **Mobility**   One of the key benefits of WiMAX compared to other technologies of broadband services is its ability to serve mobile broadband services.

- **Scalability**   As discussed in earlier sections, WiMAX is a highly scalable technology. It is highly scalable in terms of the number of users of the network as well as the services offered.

Nontechnical Benefits

Technical benefits of a technology alone are not sufficient for it to be widely accepted. A well-developed standard and its wide acceptance in the industry is also very important. A technology based on a widely adapted standard allows for a large number of alternative solutions, not locking a network operator to a one-vendor solution. It also means interoperability among different vendor solutions, allowing providers to use products from different vendors based on where they fit best. The wider acceptance of the technology also has the benefit of the economics of scale, bringing the cost down.

The key nontechnical benefits of WiMAX are the well-developed standard developed by a professional organization (IEEE), a large number of vendors offering WiMAX products, and an industry alliance (WiMAX Forum) with large industry participation to ensure compatibility and interoperability among these products.

Shortcomings

- **Limitations of a wireless technology:** As compared to other wired technologies, WiMAX has limitations that come with being a wireless technology. For example, limited bandwidth, limited range, need for spectrum license and susceptibility to interference are all limitations of wireless technologies and WiMAX is no exception. WiMAX stacks up better than may other wireless technologies in many of these limitations. Nonetheless, these are the inherent shortcoming of WiMAX as a wireless technology.

- **Risks a new technology:** Although WiMAX seems to have taken a strong foothold as a promising solution, it is an emerging new technology and its future is far from certain. Its wide market acceptance has yet to be established and competing technologies can still be threats to its long term survival, Therefore, although, WiMAX has garnered very strong support from some the key forces in the industry, the risk associated with being an emerging technology at this time is one of its shortcomings.

Typical Deployment Scenarios

The most widely anticipated deployment of WiMAX is in wireless access networks as an access technology. However, in terms of topology, the typical deployment scenarios for the other applications discussed previously would not differ significantly from the simple deployment scenario described here.

A typical deployment consists of a set of wireless base stations, each covering a specific region referred to as the footprint of the base station. In urban environments, the base station is most likely to be located on a centrally located tall building. In rural environments, it is likely to be located on a communication tower. Each base station is connected by means of a backhaul connection to a wired infrastructure. Each base station may also consist of additional networking equipment connecting the base station to the wired network. The base stations also consist of WiMAX base-station equipment including base-station antennas. In a typical deployment scenario, the antennas consist of multiple elements (or multi-sectored antennas), with each element covering a geographical region. For example, it may consist of six sectors, each sector covering 60 degrees of angle.

Each subscriber is assigned a subscriber station (SS). The SS may be a simple device with an omnidirectional antenna located inside the building of the subscriber. It may also be a device with a directional antenna installed on the roof of the subscriber building in the line-of-sight of the base station. In either case, the SS would be connected to the WAN interface of the subscriber's network.

This deployment scenario most likely represents most of the applications of WiMAX discussed previously. However, the complexity and configuration of base stations and subscriber stations are dictated by the type of services being supported. For example, for delivery of carrier-grade Ethernet services, bases stations and subscriber stations capable of meeting the demanding needs of carrier-grade Ethernet services would typically be deployed. On the contrary, for the delivery of broadband Internet access with SLA comparable to DSL, much simpler base stations and subscriber stations with limited QoS capabilities may be deployed.

The number of subscribers served by each base station also varies based on the Service-Level Agreement profiles of the services being offered. It also depends on the traffic pattern of each subscriber and the oversubscription model that may be used. For example, a service provider may feel comfortable oversubscribing a network by five times while delivering 10 Mbps carrier-grade Ethernet to 35 customers in each sector. However, another service provider with full-featured QoS capability may be willing to serve 100 customers per sector, oversubscribing by a factor of 14. Therefore, the actual deployment scenario, though may have the same topological look as what is described here, would vary significantly from application to application.

Ongoing Development

IEEE 802.16 has been an active standardization body, working on the standardization since 1999, and it continues to do so. Standardization is an ongoing process that is constantly either adjusting the standard or adding additional features. As it continues to standardize the protocol, there are also industry consortiums that are working together to facilitate growth in this field.

At the time of this writing, there are several ongoing or recent task groups within IEEE 802.16 enhancing the standard. These task group and their activities include

- Network Management Task Group developing amendments to the standard on
  - Management Plane Procedures & Services
  - Mobile Management Information Base
  - Amendment to IEEE Std 802.1D on 802.16 Bridging
- License-Excempt Task Group developing amendments on License-Exempt Coexistence
- Relay Task Group developing amendments on Mobile Multihop Relay
- Maintenance Task Group working on
  - Developing IEEE Std 802.16-2004/Cor2-2006: Corrigendum to IEEE Std 802.16-2004
  - Overseeing the Working Group Maintenance Process

In addition to the IEEE 802.16 organization, perhaps the organization with the most activity is the WiMAX Forum. It is an industry alliance of component and equipment vendors, service providers, and system integrators ensuring interoperability of WiMAX equipment from different vendors. Like IEEE 802.16, it has various working groups, each focusing of specific aspects of WiMAX, such as applications, certification, global roaming, higher-layer networking specifications, and regulatory issues.

In addition to standards bodies and industry alliances dedicated to furthering the development of WiMAX, there are also several working groups within other standards bodies, such as Internet Engineering Task Force (IETF), working toward harmonization of different standards and also influencing the further development of the WiMAX standard to achieve such harmonization.

European TSI (ETSI) is also involved in ongoing efforts on Broadband Radio Access Networks, called HiperMAN, which are based on the IEEE 802.16 standard.

Economic Assessment

In earlier sections, we discussed various applications where WiMAX can provide economically competitive broadband access solutions. In this section, we do a rough economic assessment of building a WiMAX network to deliver Carrier Ethernet services to business customers in an urban commercial environment.

In an earlier discussion, it was argued that LOS technology using SC-PHY is a more suitable candidate for this kind of application. However, because of the lack of sufficient numbers of vendors offering PHY-SC solutions at this time, it is difficult to provide a meaningful economic assessment of that technology. Additionally, given the conservative bias of the estimate provided here, it is believed that the cost per customer of PHY-SC-based WiMAX would be no more than what is discussed here for comparable services due to the amortization of the cost of single Subscriber Stations (SS) over multiple customers in one building that can be realized using PHY-SC technology. Therefore, for the sake of this economic assessment, we assume that NLOS technology using OFDM-PHY is used.

Let us assume that Ethernet services are provided from a WiMAX Base Station (BS) located on the roof of a high-rise building with access to a metro fiber core. Let us also assume that the service area is divided into three sectors with only one channel per sector, with each channel using a 20 MHz bandwidth spectrum to deliver 75 Mbps of shared bandwidth per sector.

Based on the current state of the industry, the cost of a BS as described in this scenario can be conservatively estimated to be about $30K. The cost of additional networking equipment required at the site of the base station can be estimated to be about $10K. Additional $10K (a very rough estimate) may be required for additional installation expenses such as cabling and mounting. Therefore, based on this rough but very conservative estimate, the cost of deploying a WiMAX base station is about $50K. In addition to the base station, a CPE device (a WiMAX subscriber station) would be required at each customer site; the cost of each is estimated to be about $1.5K.

The WiMAX network thus deployed can deliver a total of 225 Mbps of bandwidth shared among the users of the network, as much as 75 Mbps of which could be delivered to each customer. In a typical scenario, customers are provided various types of services distinguished from each other by the bandwidths they offer. The network operators also oversubscribe their network to various degrees to achieve better cost amortization. Given such a diverse set of scenarios, Table 15.3 provides the cost per customer for deploying WiMAX services for various types of broadband services and under various oversubscription scenarios.

It should be noted that the model only provides an estimates of upfront capital expenditure and does not provide the operational expenses. Such expenses may include roof leasing and spectrum licensing cost (if licensed spectrum is used). However, such expenses are not expected to be significant when amortized over several subscribers.

TABLE 15.3   Estimated Cost per Customer of a 75 Mbps WiMAX Network for Various Services and Subscription Models

Oversubscription Rate	1.5 Mbps Service	5 Mbps Service	10 Mbps Service
No oversubscription	$1.8K	$2.6K	$3.7K
Two times	$1.7K	$2.1K	$2.6K
Five times	$1.6K	$1.7K	$1.9K
Ten times	$1.5K	$1.6K	$1.7K

Vendors Promoting This Solution

Vendors	Model/Family	Comments
Adaptix	BX-3000	WiMAX Base Station, OFDMA, MIMO option
	SX-500, SX-300	WiMAX SS, OFDMA
Airspan	AS.MAX	OFDM, PMP, PtP, licensed and unlicensed
Aperto Networks	PacketMAX	OFDM
Axxcelera	ExcelMAX BS	3.3–3.8 GHz OFDM, FDD, NLOS, licensed
	AB MAX	Unlicensed
Azonic Systems	MAXGear	5.725–5.850 GHz NLOS, LOS, OFDM
Huawei		Trial announced but not available yet
Motorola		Product announced but not available yet
Navini Networks	Ripwave MX	Beam-forming, OFDMA, software upgradeable to WiMAX compatible
Nokia	Flexi WiMAX	WiMAX BS announced but not available yet
Nortel		Teamed with LG to announce product plan
Polonix (ENTE)	e!max	3.5 GHz, 5.15–5.85 GHz, OFDM, 35 Mbps
Proxim Wireless	Tsunami	3.4–3.6 GHz, OFDM, 25.4 Mbps
Redline Communications	RedMAX	3.4–3.6/3.3–3.5 GHz, OFDM, 23 Mbps
Telsima	StartMAX	3.3–3.8 GHz, 2.4–1.7 GHz, OFDM/OFDMA
WiNetworks	WinMAX	3.5 GHz, 5.8 GHz, NLOS

A Look into the Future

16

Evolution of Carrier Ethernet Solutions

by Abdul Kasim
(with support from Nan Chen)

This chapter has two distinct sections; the first summarizes the various commercial solutions for delivering Carrier Ethernet services. Specifically, it considers the solutions described in Part II of the book and attempts to provide a perspective of the entire landscape with respect to where and when each of them fits best. A direct one-on-one comparison is, in most cases, a less meaningful exercise (it would be akin to comparing apples to oranges). This is critically important to understand since all the solutions are not equal in the sense that some of them are more applicable in one situation versus another; further more—and importantly, there are inherently distinct functional differences between the solutions. Understanding where they fit is, therefore, essential for both Service Providers and enterprise end users alike and equips them to choose the right solution or solutions (in fact, as the few real-life examples described illustrate, it is not uncommon for several Carrier Ethernet solutions to be employed in complementary roles by a single Service Provider[1]). This task is often considerably more complex given the plethora of options that they (appear to)[2] typically have.

The second section of this chapter *attempts*[3] to deduce the possible evolution of Carrier Ethernet and its underlying delivery mechanisms over a span of the next few years. Emerging activities in the standards bodies, technological advancements, applications, demand, competition, and substitutes are some of the considerations that are extrapolated to get a reasonable picture of the future.

---

[1] As usual, this Service Provider may use several Network Operators' networks to deliver the service.
[2] Even though it may appear that there are numerous options available, there are usually fewer that are actually optimally suited for a particular Service Provider's (or an Enterprise's) circumstance. Nonetheless, it is still a challenge to discern the best fit.
[3] It would be presumptuous to assert anything more definitive in this very dynamic realm.

Delivering Carrier Ethernet: A Summary of the Solutions

Part II of the book discussed almost the entire gamut of solutions for delivering Carrier Ethernet services; these spanned a wide range of physical media, transport technologies, design focus, applications support, and economics. Some of them are better suited than others in a particular circumstance; nonetheless, they are all commercially viable, revenue generating solutions that are currently being deployed to varying degrees by Service Providers. Chapter 3 gives an idea about the extent of this deployment and Figure 16.1 illustrates the landscape of these solutions used in the delivery of Carrier Ethernet services to business enterprises.

Deciding on the optimal solution that a Service Provider should employ is typically a function of numerous variables. These commonly encompass the provider's current and future (or strategic) focus, the existing technology infrastructure and its footprint, (perceived) competitive threats and advantages, economic profitability targets, customer demand and growth opportunities, the availability of substitutes to Carrier Ethernet, and so on.

It is enormously useful, therefore, to understand the relative applicability of these solutions as well; after all, it should be evident from the previous chapters that

- There is no single solution that fits every Service Provider's (or, for that matter, every enterprise's) needs
- Each of these solutions is particularly well suited in certain contexts and less so—or not at all—in others.

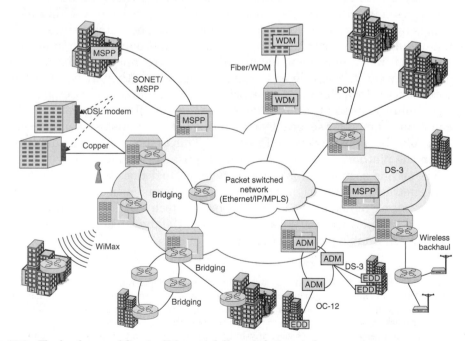

Figure 16.1   The landscape of Carrier Ethernet delivery solutions today

The rest of the section attempts to evaluate factually—and based largely on the material from Part II—each of these solutions in a holistic manner.

An Assessment of Carrier Ethernet Delivery Solutions

A relatively straightforward approach is used to review the different solutions. Specifically, the various carrier-class attributes that define and differentiate Carrier Ethernet are used as the basis for the assessment; these underlying attributes also provide a fairly holistic framework. The review is supplemented by another very important dimension— economics—to offer a more practically meaningful assessment.

It is important to reinforce that this assessment considers only currently available and *mainstream* commercial solutions presented previously. But first, some general observations are in order.

Diverse Origins The various solutions that are currently employed for delivering Carrier Ethernet each originated for a different purpose; for example, SONET/SDH was devised to deliver mission-critical voice services efficiently over a fiber infrastructure while also providing an unprecedented level of network resiliency, whereas WiMax was developed primarily to enable wireless broadband access over a reasonably large metro area. As noted in Part II, each solution has its own history, and in many cases, was only recently enhanced to support Carrier Ethernet. Naturally, some are more optimal than others, but a combination of factors such as the types of services supported (both Ethernet and non-Ethernet), depreciation of the solution infrastructure, and competitive issues, makes each of them commercially tenable.

It needs to be reiterated that most of these solutions were conceived for delivering commercial services other than Ethernet and, in fact, primarily continue to serve that purpose. Thus, while assessing any of these "Ethernet" solutions, one must consider its primary functionality and its relevance in this broader context.

Different (OSI Layer) Functions The Carrier Ethernet solutions discussed provide functionality that can be categorized across Layer 1, 2, and/or 3 of the OSI model (the physical, link, and/or network layer, respectively). As such, they either merely serve as a transport mechanism for delivering Carrier Ethernet services (basically enabling point-to-point E-Line services) or also, provide switching and routing functionality that will allow them to provide multipoint E-LAN services. Figure 16.2 illustrates the OSI defined functionality that is provided by the different solutions.

Carrier Ethernet attributes may inherently be present in the "base" solutions, either partially or fully; for example, reliability is an attribute that is inevitably present in all SONET/MSPP solutions (even pre-Carrier Ethernet). Likewise, an MPLS solution inherently offers QoS and can scale as required of Carrier Ethernet solutions. Most of these solutions are, in fact, feasible because they possess some of the attributes dictated by Carrier Ethernet and can carry Ethernet frames, albeit some more efficiently than others. Some of these solutions, in their attempt to be relevant in the long-term, are also being actively augmented with additional (Carrier Ethernet) attributes for optimizing Ethernet delivery.

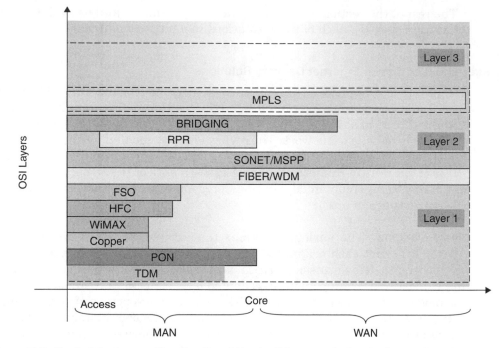

Figure 16.2 Typical deployment/functionality of Carrier Ethernet solutions in Service Provider networks

NOTE   These delivery solutions usually provide the Carrier Ethernet attributes in the TRAN layer, not necessarily in the ETH layer. Because these attributes are only being defined in the ETH layer by the MEF[4] and, in most cases, are far from being standardized (refer to Chapter 2 for more information), these TRAN-layer capabilities are often the only realistic—and obviously acceptable—recourse.

Different Parts of the Network   Each of these solutions is usually deployed in different parts of the network, based on their technical and economic feasibility. Some, such as copper and WiMax are typically used only in the access portion of the network—between the customer premise and Service Provider's Point Of Presence (POP)—whereas others such as SONET and WDM are often used in the Service Provider's MANs and WANs (these can also be employed in the access MAN as well and in fact are when the economics work out). Figure 16.2 also identifies the portion of the Service Provider network where each of the solutions is usually deployed.

---

[4] After all, defining these capabilities in the ETH layer fundamentally enables Carrier Ethernet to extend, quite literally, everywhere and become a globally viable solution.

NOTE   Some solutions, like Bridging, are able to go into the Access and deeper in the network (especially for E-LINE services, with emerging technologies such as Provider Bridge Bridging/Transport) but are usually not likely to be deployed in the WAN (at least exclusively).

Not Necessarily Mutually Exclusive   Some of the commercial solutions in Part II are not mutually exclusive from the standpoint of functionality. For example, a Bridging/ Switching solution (Chapter 13) may employ WDM (Chapter 8) or SONET (Chapter 11) to extend the reach of the particular solution. Similarly, an FSO/Wirless Mesh solution may employ Bridging to offer E-LAN services.

It is important to note that there are no rigorous boundaries as such for each of the solutions discussed, and solution vendors may, and often do, combine previously distinct solutions to offer new differentiated solutions.

An Assessment Using Carrier Ethernet Attributes

Tables 16.1 through 16.8 illustrate the compliance of the various *commercial* delivery solutions in the market currently, with respect to the Carrier Ethernet attributes. A fairly broad, but reasonably distinct scale attempts to capture the actual level of support by signifying whether a commercial solution (category) supports a specific underlying attribute fully, substantially, partially, marginally, or not at all.[5]

Standardized Services Support   This attribute determines the breadth of the revenue-driven portfolio that a Service Provider can conceive; specifically, it will define the infrastructure constraints, types of both Ethernet and non-Ethernet services at the optimal bandwidth, and any QoS assurances that it can deliver (and charge for).

Solutions such as Bridging, MPLS, and also traditional voice-oriented solutions such as SONET and TDM provide for a fairly robust offering across the board (which, to some extent, may explain why Service Providers are not migrating from the latter quickly). Most of the solutions can support voice, data, and video applications (although high-speed video over copper is not optimal). Layer 1–based solutions can naturally support E-LINE services only, and one has to look at solutions such as Bridging, MPLS, and Wireless mesh (FSO) for delivering E-LAN services. This point is notable and practically necessitates Layer 1 solutions to coexist with other solutions, if the gamut of Ethernet services are to be provided. Circuit emulation over Ethernet is yet another area that is still being developed for most of the packet-based solutions (in case of TDM-based solutions, of course, this consideration is often moot). Tables 16.1 and 16.2 summarize the solutions with respect to supporting standardized services.

Scalability   The Scalability attribute basically identifies whether a Service Provider can minimize its delivery cost structure by leveraging its available bandwidth over a large

---

[5] There is a degree of subjectivity involved here; however, the same level of subjectivity is enforced across the gamut of solutions thereby "normalizing" the assessment. Note also, this exercise assumes mainstream commercial solutions in each of the solution categories.

TABLE 16.1   Support of Carrier Ethernet Attribute—Standardized Service Support

Commercial Solution	Ubiquity	Ethernet Services	Circuit Emulation
Copper	Partially supported Limited to dry copper facilities within a km or so	Partially supported E-Line only	Not supported
HFC	Partially supported Limited to HFC facilities only	Partially supported E-Line only	Not supported
PON	Partially supported Limited to fiber facilities only	Partially supported E-Line only	Not supported (in IEEE 802.3ah; proprietary solutions exist)
WDM	Partially supported Limited to fiber facilities only	Partially supported E-Line only	Fully supported
FSO	Substantially supported Limited under certain weather conditions	Fully supported	Not supported
TDM	Fully supported	Fully supported	Fully supported
SONET	Partially supported Limited to fiber facilities only	Substantially supported Fully supports E-Line and marginally supports E-LAN	Fully supported Generally not required
RPR	Partially supported Limited to fiber infrastructures in ring topology	Fully supported	Fully supported
Bridging	Substantially supported Some standards not yet ratified	Fully supported	Marginally supported Standards lacking
MPLS	Fully supported IETF-defined standards enable multi-vendor interoperability	Fully supported E-Line using pseudowires, E-LAN using VPLS	Fully supported
WiMax	Partially supported Limited by distance	Fully supported	Not supported

customer base spread across a wide geographic area. The extent of scalability required is obviously a function of the Service Provider's (real/virtual)[6] footprint. Table 16.3 summarizes the solutions with respect to this attribute.

Packet-oriented solutions such as MPLS, WiMax, and Bridging were expressly designed to scale and consequently can scale better than solutions such as Copper, which is inherently limited in its geographic reach. Pure transport solutions such as WDM are also extremely well suited to scale (again, this was the primary reason for WDM's popularity outside of Ethernet) whereas wireless-based solutions (such as FSO and WiMax) are also limited by their underlying technology to serving meaningfully in metro access networks.

---

[6] Service Providers commonly use their own or leased infrastructure to deliver services.

TABLE 16.2   Support of Carrier Ethernet Attribute—Standardized Service Support

Commercial Solution	Granularity of Bandwidth & Quality of Service	Converged Transport
Copper	Partially supported Up to 10 M (Mid-Band Ethernet) in Metro Access networks	Substantially supported Limited to voice and data
HFC	Partially supported Up to 100 M; inherently shared bandwidth impacts QoS	Partially supported Voice functionality limited
PON	Substantially supported (using MPCP and DBA mechanisms)	Fully supported
WDM	Substantially supported	Fully supported
FSO	Fully supported	Fully supported
TDM	Substantially supported Three levels of CoS and hard QoS	Fully supported
SONET	Marginally supported	Fully supported
RPR	Fully supported	Fully supported
Bridging	Substantially supported Eight levels of CoS	Fully supported
MPLS	Fully supported	Fully supported
WiMax	Partially supported	Fully supported

Reliability   If Carrier Ethernet is to be widely employed as the convergent (access) platform to deliver mission-critical applications enterprises need to be assured of its robustness before they migrate from legacy services such as ATM and Frame Relay. The attributes encompassing reliability are, therefore, necessary to provide this assurance.

Most of the solutions provide some degree of service resiliency, except for PON (usually used for best-effort services). This is not surprising given that this is typically a prerequisite to be even considered by Service Providers. Some level of path protection is also generally available in almost all of the solutions discussed.

Restoration meeting or bettering the sub-50 ms benchmark is also available in most of the solutions, albeit in a few the restoration times are longer. Table 16.4 summarizes the solutions with respect to this attribute.

Quality of Service (QoS)   The QoS attribute enables Carrier Ethernet solutions to be meaningfully employed in a carrier-context; specifically, it allows Service Providers to offer Ethernet services that can support applications that mandate a stringent level of performance. The absence of this capability in some of the Carrier Ethernet solutions, in fact, usually serves as a big detriment for enterprises to move to Carrier Ethernet.

Packet-based solutions such as MPLS have incorporated QoS capabilities by design, whereas traditional transport solutions have long supported it, albeit not always as fully. The need for this QoS capability becomes more acute as services traverse beyond the access part of the network and into the core, where they are often aggregated over

TABLE 16.3   Support of Carrier Ethernet Attribute—Scalability

Commercial Solution	Millions of End Users/Points	Geographic Reach	Bandwidth Granularity
Copper	Marginally supported	Marginally supported Access only	Marginally supported Up to 10 M only
HFC	Partially supported Hundreds are common	Partially supported	Partially supported Up to 100 M
PON	Fully supported	Marginally supported Up to 20 km for broadband access	Fully supported
WDM	Fully supported	Fully supported Up to 10,000 Km	Substantially supported
FSO	Partially supported	Partially supported Access only	Fully supported
TDM	Fully supported	Fully supported Over both copper and fiber	Fully supported
SONET	Marginally supported	Substantially supported Using installed base, offering Carrier meet point	Marginally supported
RPR	Fully supported Up to 255 nodes and millions of end users	Fully supported Up to 2000 km	Fully supported
Bridging	Fully supported Backbone bridging required	Fully supported	Fully supported
MPLS	Fully supported	Fully supported On a global scale	Substantially supported
WiMax	Partially supported Hundreds	Partially supported In the access only	Fully supported

a common (and shared) infrastructure. Solutions that are employed in this context—notably MPLS, RPR, and WDM—have better developed capabilities, whereas Bridging is beginning to incorporate new standards-based capabilities for this purpose as well.

Some transport-oriented solutions such as PON are poorly equipped to deliver carrier-class QoS, and so tend to be used for best-effort services and not mission-critical latency-sensitive applications.

Provisioning new Ethernet services is one area where substantial development is still required. Table 16.5 summarizes the solutions in respect to this attribute.

Standardized Management   This is one area where the existing Carrier Ethernet solutions probably are most lacking. It is also the area that will have a big impact on transforming Carrier Ethernet into a mass-market service.

OAM is usually offered at the transport/network layer and not at the service layer (i.e., end to end), but several Bridging solutions on the market are integrating the ITU/

TABLE 16.4   Support of Carrier Ethernet Attribute—Reliability

Commercial Solution	Service Resiliency	Protection	Restoration
Copper	Marginally supported	Partially supported Access link only	Fully supported
HFC	Marginally supported Impacts bandwidth	Partially supported	Partially supported
PON	Not supported Only proprietary solutions exist currently	Not supported Only proprietary solutions exist currently	Not supported Only proprietary solutions exist currently
WDM	Fully supported	Fully supported	Fully supported Rerouting capabilities
FSO	Marginally supported	Partially supported Path only	Fully supported
TDM	Fully supported	Substantially supported Diverse routing	Fully supported
SONET	Fully supported	Fully supported	Fully supported
RPR	Fully supported	Substantially supported Wrap or steer or both	Fully supported
Bridging	Fully supported	Substantially supported end-to-end protection switching not standardized	Substantially supported
MPLS	Fully supported	Substantially supported At the network layer	Fully supported
WiMax	Marginally supported	Partially supported	Fully supported

IEEE standards' work in this area and delivering OAM capability. Some like the PON, FSO, and Copper solutions discussed in this book are restricted to providing OAM on a link-level only (which by itself is insufficient), often based on standards such as EFM OAM. Established solutions such as SONET, RPR, and WDM do, however, offer a fairly robust OAM capability (albeit in some cases not at the service level).

Widely deployed transport solutions such as SONET and WDM are also well positioned to support a unified management capability since Service Providers typically deploy these solutions in a multi-vendor context (i.e., with other SONET, switching, and routing vendors whose management systems often have to interwork to deliver a service).

Rapid provisioning, which translates to speed to market, is generally quite poor across the entire solution set save for MPLS and RPR. As Ethernet becomes more prevalent, this capability will become a differentiator to Service Providers. Table 16.6 summaries the solutions with respect to this attribute.

A snapshot of how the different commercial solutions fare with respect to complying with Carrier Ethernet attributes is provided in Table 16.7.

TABLE 16.5   Support of Carrier Ethernet Attribute—QoS

Commercial Solution	Granular QoS	End-to-End SLA	Provisioning
Copper	Marginally supported Up to 10 M	Partially supported In the access network only	Marginally supported
HFC	Marginally supported Up to 10 M	Not supported	Marginally supported
PON	Not supported	Substantially supported	Not supported
WDM	Fully supported	Substantially supported	Substantially supported Semi automatic and on-demand paths
FSO	Marginally supported Up to 10 M	Partially supported	Marginally supported
TDM	Fully supported	Fully supported	Fully supported
SONET	Marginally supported	Fully supported	Marginally supported
RPR	Fully supported	Fully supported Guaranteed control of delay and jitter	Fully supported
Bridging	Substantially supported Not yet standardized	Fully supported	Substantially supported
MPLS	Fully supported	Fully supported	Substantially supported using L-LSP model
WiMax	Partially supported	Not supported	Marginally supported

Economics   Ultimately, economics is one of the key considerations driving a decision on which solution to use. While this typically encompasses several direct factors such as revenues, costs, profitability, and indirectly, factors such as the speed to market, strategic opportunity, opportunity costs, and so on, the high-level assessment in Table 16.8 is restricted to the total relative cost of delivering Carrier Ethernet services (captured as Total Cost of Ownership or TCO).

The initial cost (typically, the CAPital EXpenditure or CAPEX) and ongoing costs (typically, the OPerational EXpenditure or OPEX) are the two major components associated with the TCO. In several of the commercial solutions (SONET, TDM, HFC, Copper, et al.), these costs are typically overstated from the standpoint of delivering Carrier Ethernet services because they usually encompass the cost of delivering non-Ethernet services as well (i.e., the costs incurred by Carrier Ethernet and non-Carrier Ethernet services are shared). From the standpoint of CAPEX, the same platform solution is usually employed (albeit with minor additions like interfacing cards, etc.) for both Ethernet and non-Ethernet services. Usually, many of the same Service Provider resources (personnel, systems, common equipment, methods, and procedures) are used

TABLE 16.6 Support of Carrier Ethernet Attribute—Standardized Management

Commercial Solution	Unified Management	Carrier-Class OAM	Rapid Provisioning
Copper	Partially supported	Partially supported EFM only	Marginally supported
HFC	Marginally supported	Marginally supported	Marginally supported
PON	Marginally supported	Marginally supported	Marginally supported
WDM	Fully supported TL-1 OSS, GMPLS	Substantially supported	Substantially supported
FSO	Marginally supported	Marginally supported	Marginally supported
TDM	Not supported	Not supported	Not supported
SONET	Substantially supported Typically deployed in multi-vendor environments	Substantially supported	Marginally supported
RPR	Fully supported	Fully supported	Fully supported
Bridging	Substantially supported Only SNMP MIBs standardized	Fully supported	Substantially supported
MPLS	Fully supported Uses IETF standardized tools and across multi-vendor environments	Fully supported	Fully supported
WiMax	Marginally supported	Marginally supported	Substantially supported

to provide lifecycle support (installation, provisioning, management, upgrades, etc.) for both Ethernet and non-Ethernet services, so it is usually difficult to quantify the OPEX associated exclusively with Carrier Ethernet; the integrated nature of the platform functionality, and often the support infrastructure, make it impractical.

In addition to the CAPEX and OPEX associated with the solution itself (which is usually comprised of hardware, software, documentation, etc.), one must be mindful of the infrastructure costs associated with a solution; for instance, a fiber infrastructure is mandatory for SONET, PON, and Bridging solutions, and the costs associated with this must be considered to understand the true costs of deploying a particular solution. Often though, such an infrastructure usually exists, and the question may be moot.

While the respective chapters in Part II provide a more detailed cost analysis for each of the solutions, Table 16.8 attempts to gauge the relative costs as low, reasonably attractive, or high to provide a general "feel." Most of the costs of the access-only solutions such as Copper, HFC, and so on, are relatively low and account for their fairly wide (re)use as an Ethernet delivery solution (notwithstanding their limitations due to scale, management, functionality, etc). Fiber-based solutions such as SONET and WDM, on the other hand, are relatively expensive because their key benefits (notably resiliency and scalability) incur a higher cost to implement and manage. Wireless solutions are

TABLE 16.7   Snapshot of Carrier Ethernet Compliance

Carrier Ethernet Attribute/Delivery Solution	Copper	HFC	PON	WDM	FSO	TDM	SONET	RPR	Bridging	MPLS	WiMax
Standardized Service Support											
Ubiquity	P	P	P	P	S	F	P	P	S	F	P
Ethernet Services	P	P	P	P	F	F	S	F	F	F	F
Circuit Emulation	N	N	N	F	N	F	F	F	M	F	N
Granularity of B/W and QoS	P	P	S	S	F	S	M	F	S	F	P
Converged Transport	S	P	F	F	F	F	F	F	F	F	F
Scalability											
Millions of End Users	M	P	F	F	P	F	M	F	F	F	P
Geographic Reach	M	P	M	F	P	F	S	F	F	F	P
Bandwidth Granularity	M	P	F	S	F	F	M	F	F	S	F
Reliability											
Service Resiliency	M	M	N	F	M	F	F	F	F	F	M
Protection	P	P	N	F	P	S	F	S	S	S	P
Restoration	F	P	N	F	F	F	F	F	S	F	F
Quality of Service (QoS)											
Granular QoS	M	M	N	F	M	F	M	F	S	F	P
End-to-End SLA	P	N	S	S	P	F	F	F	F	F	N
Provisioning	M	M	N	S	M	F	M	F	S	S	M
Standardized Management											
Unified Management	P	M	M	F	M	N	S	F	S	F	M
Carrier-Class OAM	P	M	M	S	M	N	S	F	F	F	M
Rapid Provisioning	M	M	M	S	M	N	M	F	S	F	S

Legend: F, Fully supported; S, Substantially supported; P, Partially supported; M, Marginally supported; N, Not supported

attractive economically since they speed up deployment and preclude the need for costly infrastructure.

Ultimately, of course, as noted before, economics is just one factor to consider, and several other pertinent factors are usually taken into account before a Service Provider can meaningfully settle on an optimal solution.

TABLE 16.8   Economic Comparison of the Different Carrier Ethernet Solutions

Commercial Solution	Total Cost of Ownership
Copper	Relatively low. Supports other services as well. Speed to market a plus.
HFC	Relatively low and carries other (video/broadcast) services as well.
PON	Relatively low but requires expensive fiber infrastructure. OPEX high due to relatively limited management capabilities.
WDM	Relatively high. Also requires expensive fiber infrastructure but transports other services as well.
FSO	Relatively attractive, but when fiber is the only alternative. Speed to market is a plus.
TDM	Relatively high, but supports other services as well. OPEX mitigated.
SONET	Relatively high cost per user, but also supports other services.
RPR	Relatively high, but with attendant benefits for mission-critical applications deployed over fiber rings.
Bridging	Relatively attractive. OPEX fairly high due to complexity.
MPLS	Relatively high in the access, but relatively attractive in core. Higher OPEX.
WiMax	Relatively high primarily due to infancy. High OPEX due to newness of technology. Speed to market definite plus.

How Service Providers Are Employing Carrier Ethernet Solutions Today

As mentioned earlier, while there are multiple solutions for delivering Carrier Ethernet, the specific set of solutions that are optimal for a Service Provider to consider is largely a function of several variables such as its strategy, existing infrastructure, types of services being offered, competitive positioning, and other prevailing conditions that are relevant. Some real-life scenarios illustrate common deployments and highlight the complex reality of how Carrier Ethernet solutions are offered today.

Scenario 1

A Service Provider wants to provide Internet access service with an Ethernet handoff that could vary between 1M and 10M. The Service Provider owns a TDM infrastructure (T1/E1) between the target customer locations and its own Point Of Presence (POP), where it connects to a router that serves as a gateway to the Internet.

Assuming the Service Provider would likely use its existing TDM access infrastructure, it would like employ an Ethernet over TDM solution (Chapter 7) and may use one or more T1s bonded together to provide Ethernet access (since a bandwidth of 10M would require 7 to 8 T1s). This simple solution could be employed in a book-ended fashion, as depicted in Figure 16.3, and handoff an Ethernet connection to the router at the POP.

NOTES   If the target customers are served through (physically) different POPs and the single gateway router/switch (Chapter 13) resides at another POP (i.e., it is not the serving POP), as shown in Figure 16.3 for customers of POP 2, then a switching/routing solution may be necessary to interconnect the different POPs. Furthermore, these switches/routers can be interconnected over a SONET and/or WDM infrastructure as well (Chapters 11 and 8, respectively), or alternatively, employ a wireless meshed FSO solution (Chapter 9).

If the Service Provider is a Cable/MSO with an HFC infrastructure, then it could use this as an access to a central (head-end) location where the gateway router/switch would usually be located. If it has a fiber infrastructure, it could also use a PON (Chapter 7) solution. If the Service Provider has a Copper access infrastructure, it could also employ Ethernet over First Mile (EFM) Copper (Chapter 5) solution in the access.

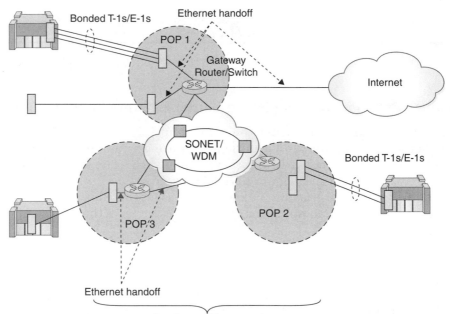

Figure 16.3 A typical scenario offering Carrier Ethernet services

Scenario 2

A Service Provider wishes to offer an any-to-any connectivity between 10 and 100M to its business customers; typically, these customers each have multiple locations in a metro area and want their LANs to be interconnected at these locations, creating in essence a larger LAN across the metro. The Service Provider infrastructure is comprised of fiber connectivity to most but not all of the potential customer buildings.

A Service Provider can simply offer this transparent LAN connectivity between multiple locations using an Ethernet over Bridging/Switching solution (Chapter 13) in the metro, basically deployed in its POPs, as shown in Figure 16.3. It may also use an Ethernet over WDM solution (Chapter 8) to optimize some of its fiber infrastructure, especially in densely served, high-growth areas.

NOTES   The Ethernet over WDM may, alternatively, be integrated into the switching solution (i.e., the switches themselves may have WDM blades or modules). The wavelength solution would also work well[7] when the Service Provider can only lease a wavelength from another Service Provider (rather than dark fiber) to reach an off-net customer (i.e., a customer not physically connected to its network).

An FSO (Chapter 9) solution may also be employed to connect the off-net customers as well.

Scenario 3

A Service Provider targets offering a nationwide Ethernet WAN service, basically an Ethernet pipe between any two locations in the country. Customer access is Ethernet, ranging from 10M to 10G over fiber. Customer locations are usually densely clustered. The Service Provider owns fiber to most customer locations (but not all) and also the WAN infrastructure, which is largely comprised of SONET rings.

Here, a Service Provider may consider an Ethernet over WDM (Chapter 8) in the access, basically to extend and aggregate customers over the same fiber infrastructure, and then employ Ethernet over SONET (Chapter 11) rings in the MAN/WAN to handoff the Ethernet stream to the Ethernet over WDM solution on the far end to ultimately deliver the service. A Service Provider has, of course, other options and may (or may not) use WDM in the access, but rather use some form of switching and then handoff to a WDM -based core (instead of SONET). Naturally, these decisions are influenced by other competitive and economic factors.

If Scenario 3 was augmented to provide an any-to-any connection (i.e., the Ethernet streams could be sent to different destinations at different times), then an MPLS solution (Chapter 14) would be very feasible.

---

[7] Assuming that the wavelength scheme is common, i.e., ITU-compliant.

Scenario 4

In this case, a Service Provider with a different access infrastructure (SONET, TDM, fiber, copper) at different locations within its footprint is serving a medium-sized enterprise with offices at each of these locations and a couple outside.

Requiring a standardized (and consistent) Ethernet service across these customer locations (albeit with the bandwidth varying between 10 and 100M) is an increasingly common scenario. The Service Provider may consider introducing a simple Ethernet Demarcation Device (EDD)—based solution (see Chapter 2 for some details on EDD) with the corresponding network links (OC-n, T1, Ethernet-over fiber/copper). This is shown in Figure 16.4 and provides a cost-effective solution that enables offering a standardized Ethernet handoff rapidly, irrespective of the last/first mile infrastructure and without disrupting this infrastructure. By employing an EDD, it can also extend this standardized offering over the leased facility (from another operator) to support out-of-region customer locations.

These fairly straightforward scenarios depict that often more than a single solution is feasible in a particular environment and also that multiple solutions frequently coexist in the same Service Provider network. Obviously, more complex offerings would make the underpinning delivery solutions more involved. It bears repitition that the solutions described in each of the above scenarios are not necessarily the only feasible options.

Competitiveness in Delivering Carrier Ethernet

In a recently released survey by Heavy Reading, over 150 Ethernet Service Providers identified the main areas that need to be addressed effectively in order to gain a

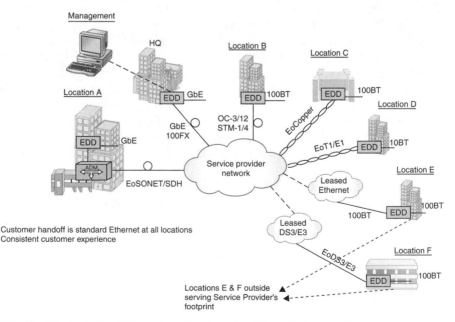

Figure 16.4   Rapidly deploying Ethernet services by using Ethernet demarcation

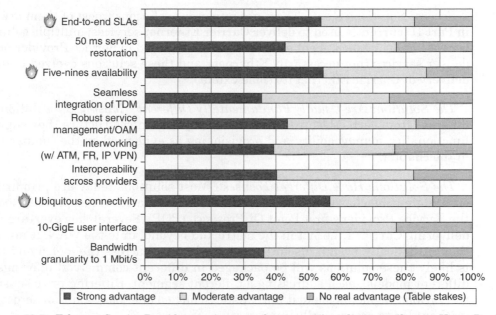

Figure 16.5 Ethernet Service Provider requirements for competitive advantage *(Source: Heavy Reading, 2006)*

competitive advantage.[8] These are shown in Figure 16.5 and note the key features that were deemed important. As should be evident, they align very closely with the feature attributes of Carrier Ethernet. The three most important ones were identified to be Ubiquitous Connectivity, Five-Nines availability, and End-to-End SLAs. However, all the capabilities identified collectively in the figure inexorably allow Service Providers to offer the entire gamut of carrier-class services, with the attendant QoS assurances for mission-critical applications.

It is fair to assume, of course, that these feature capabilities, especially the ones deemed most important (i.e., ubiquity, five-nines, SLAs) are not widely present/ available in the Service Providers' Carrier Ethernet offerings todays. In the next year or so, the focus will invariably be on incorporating this set of features as completely as possible in Carrier Ethernet (delivery) solutions.

Key Conclusions on the Current State of Carrier Ethernet Solutions

The current state of Carrier Ethernet delivery solutions is summarized next and characterizes the transition underway from essentially delivering marginally carrier-oriented Ethernet services to the Carrier Ethernet services as defined in Chapter 2.

---

[8] It is fair to assume, of course, that these requirements are being driven by the (enterprise) end users.

Several Solutions Exist There are numerous solutions (most of them are described in Part II) currently used to deliver Carrier Ethernet services; multiple solutions exist because multiple incumbent solutions were being used in Service Provider networks to deliver services (not necessarily Ethernet), and these solutions evolved to incorporate delivery of Carrier Ethernet (to some extent).

The Solutions Are Usually Fundamentally Different Most of the solutions are very different from each other, from the type of physical infrastructure they support to the functionality, manageability, and provisioning as evidenced by the comparison earlier in the chapter.

The Solutions Have Different Focuses Most solutions today are primarily focused on bridging the chasm in metro access—between the customer premise location and the Service Provider's first Point Of Presence (POP). Several, however, are focused on delivering Carrier Ethernet in the metro and beyond, in to the WAN. It must be noted that realistically, even if a solution can be deployed across the metro and the core, it is likely these solutions will be packaged in different commercial offerings (i.e., two different models), each addressing a different segment. Differing price sensitivities in the various segments make it unrealistic to have a one "box" solution across segments (without being economically unattractive).

Carrier Ethernet Is Still Evolving and So Are the Solutions A fundamental challenge to Carrier Ethernet solutions is that Carrier Ethernet is still very much in its infancy and in the process of standardizing and evolving to support the next generation of applications. Within such a dynamic context, the solutions are also invariably evolving to align with these developments; albeit it must be noted that solution vendors, in an attempt to competitively differentiate, often offer new features that may still not be ratified by standards bodies.

However, as shown in Figure 16.5, there appears to be a long way to go—even with regards to making available most of the fairly well-defined Carrier Ethernet attributes.

There Is No One All Encompassing Solution There is no one solution that is both economical and has adequate features to support the delivery of Carrier Ethernet—from simple point-to-point E-Line connectivity in the access to a multipoint solution in the core of the Service Provider network.

Therefore, it is not uncommon for Service Providers to employ multiple solutions in their networks, perhaps one in the access and another, deeper in the metro.

A Look into the Future of Delivering Carrier Ethernet

The future of Carrier Ethernet (services) and its delivery in Service Provider networks are intimately intertwined. If the demand for Carrier Ethernet itself wanes, then it is more than likely that the delivery solutions will correspondingly stagnate (at least from the standpoint of Carrier Ethernet services[9]); on the other hand, if Carrier Ethernet thrives,

---

[9] Note that most of the solutions also support other non-Carrier Ethernet services.

it will spur an aggressive effort in further optimizing (more features, lower cost, etc.) its delivery solutions, which in turn will accelerate the demand for Carrier Ethernet. This "reinforcing" cycle could result in exponential growth, very much like that forecasted in Chapter 3, and perhaps, even mirror the Ethernet growth story in the LAN.

While the recent rate of growth for Carrier Ethernet (past couple of quarters) appears to support—in fact, even significantly improves upon the rosy projections made by industry analysts, it would be disingenuous to assert that this trend can be linearly extrapolated over the next few years with a great deal of certainty. Carrier Ethernet is after all still very much in its infancy and as it becomes more widespread, attendant challenges and issues would inevitably emerge, and effect subsequent deployment (by either hastening or slowing it) in a non-linear—and very difficult-to-predict manner.

It would be a more meaningful exercise to take a closer look at the underlying dynamics of the Carrier Ethernet market. This will provide insights into how the demand for Carrier Ethernet might grow and the current set of solutions evolve in the course of the next three to five years. And although this will not likely yield a definitive answer either[10], it will help Service Providers and others better understand the relevant variables, their respective influence and risk, and ultimately enable them to craft more effective strategic plans with respect to offering, delivering and using Carrier Ethernet services.

Understanding the Future Demand for Carrier Ethernet

While Carrier Ethernet is very well positioned as the platform for delivering the next-generation of applications, it is important to understand that this automatically does not assure its growth, much less its dominance, especially in the future. There are several independent variables[11] that will determine the outcome. Figure 16.6 shows a fairly comprehensive (though by no means exhaustive) set of eight variables[12] that will, either directly or indirectly, influence the demand for Carrier Ethernet services; a straightforward diagrammatic technique derived from the field of Systems Dynamics[13][1] is used for this purpose. A brief explanation is in order to illustrate this simple but powerful approach.

Arrows are employed to indicate the relationship/influence that a variable has on other variables and/or directly on the demand itself. So arrows originating at each of the eight variables and terminating at one or more of the other variables indicate a direct relationship between the variables (and an indirect influence on the demand); arrows from each of the eight variables directly terminating in "Carrier Ethernet Demand" indicate the direct influence that the respective variable has on the demand.

---

[10] It would presumptuous to assert with any certainty the non-linear impact of the many primary and secondary variables on Carrier Ethernet

[11] The terms *variables, factors,* and *influencers* are all used interchangeably.

[12] These are fairly 'coarse' variables; each of these variables in turn are driven by other variables.

[13] The relatively new field of Systems Dynamics, pioneered at MIT, uses the principles of feedback control systems to model complex dependencies and to understand their collective impact; it can be applied in a vast variety of scenarios and is used here to understand the drivers that can impact the growth of Carrier Ethernet.

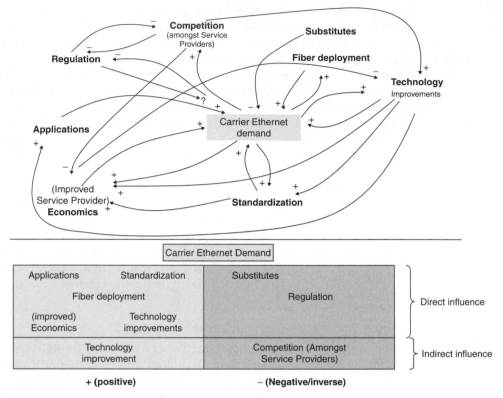

Figure 16.6 Factors influencing the demand for Carrier Ethernet

Note that an arrow originating at "Carrier Ethernet Demand" and terminating at one or more of the eight variables indicates a causal relationship between the demand and that variable.

A '+' or '−' is adjacent to the head of an arrow and should be interpreted as described in the following example. Consider an arrow originating from the variable "(Improved Service Provider) Economics" and terminating at "(Carrier Ethernet) Demand." The + sign with this arrow indicates that an increase (or decrease) in improvement in Service Provider economics will have a correspondingly positive (or negative) impact on the demand; a negative sign instead indicates an inverse relationship, i.e., a negative impact (demand will decrease) if economics improve or a positive impact (demand will increase) if economics decreases.

The arrow pointed in the other direction (i.e., from "...Demand" to "...Economics") indicates that an increase in demand would mean improvement in economics (perhaps due to the effects of scale). These arrows, in both directions, form a loop; if they both have the same sign they are called *reinforcing loops* and result in exponential growth/reduction.

Figure 16.6 shows a fairly complex set of (positive and negative) factors influencing the demand for Carrier Ethernet, both directly and indirectly, and largely from the standpoint of the Service Provider.[14] Some key points can be observed:

- There are eight key influencers identified here: Applications (supported), (Improvement in Service Provider) Economics, Regulation, Substitutes (to Carrier Ethernet), Technology (improvements), Competition (amongst Service Providers), Fiber Deployment, and Standardization (of Carrier Ethernet).

- Each of these influencing factors is itself influenced by a set of secondary factors: for instance, the (Improvement in Service Provider) Economics is invariably a function of the market/end user price of Carrier Ethernet, the cost to Service Providers, and so on. Such factors are assumed in the analysis but not explicitly noted to keep it simple.

- Almost all the factors can be considered as direct influencers of Carrier Ethernet demand (with the exception of Competition and Technology, which are indirect). Note that Technology is both a direct and indirect influence, i.e., it influences demand for Carrier Ethernet via Economics, Standardization, and Applications, as shown in the figure.

- (Carrier Ethernet) Demand itself also directly influences Economics, Standardization, Technology, Fiber Deployment, and Competition in a positive manner, and Regulation in an inverse fashion. This is depicted in the lower part of Figure 16.6. In fact, with the exception of Competition, it forms a reinforcing loop with each of the other influencers. *These are the most important and significant influencers for Carrier Ethernet Demand* (and are present in the top-left quadrant of the figure). This means that an increase (or decrease) of each influencer will lead to a corresponding increase (or decrease) in demand for Carrier Ethernet, which in turn will lead to a corresponding increase (or decrease) in that influencer, and on it goes.

- With the exception of Substitutes, Regulation, and Competition, all the other factors influence in a positive fashion; these three impact in a negative or inverse manner, i.e., an increase (or decrease) in Substitutes/Regulation/Competition will likely lead to a decrease (or increase) in the demand for Carrier Ethernet. This is clarified in Figure 16.6, which highlights, to some degree, the extent and direction of this influence.

- There are several influencing relationships between the factors themselves; in these cases, they only indirectly influence the demand for Carrier Ethernet.[15] (Increased) Competition for instance, can lead to an increased focus on technology (feature) development (which, of course, in turn can stimulate demand).

---

[14] Note that these are the first level of variables; including the second and tertiary levels (i.e., variables which influence the first level) would make this a more realistic but also much more complicated analysis for the purpose of this discussion. What is missing is the level of relative influence of the variables (i.e., compared to each other) but realistically this analysis framework should give a fair idea when modeled with some data points.

[15] Of course, as noted earlier, a variable can both directly and indirectly influence demand.

Having identified the main factors that will likely influence the demand for Carrier Ethernet and also the nature of this influence (direct/indirect, positively/inversely), a brief assessment of the developments in their respective areas helps gauge the extent of their impact over the course of the next few years. These are captured in Table 16.9.

Applications driving Carrier Ethernet   Commercial applications will be the primary—and direct, drivers for Carrier Ethernet services; some of the key existing and emerging applications that are expected to drive Carrier Ethernet are shown in Figure 16.7 and briefly discussed below. Individual (category of) applications could of course be delivered by other means (than over a Carrier Ethernet service, perhaps even more optimally) but as should be evident from the figure, Carrier Ethernet is expected to be the optimal solution

TABLE 16.9   How Demand for Carrier Ethernet Will be Influenced in the Future

Variable	Expected Influence on Carrier Ethernet demand	Key Developments in the Next 3–5 years	Conclusion
Applications (driving Carrier Ethernet)	Direct, +	VOIP extending widely, video and other bandwidth intensive multimedia applications becoming the norm	Significant growth in demand
Technology	Direct, +, Reinforcing	100G standards being developed. Distance extending over several thousand km. Carrier Ethernet attributes increasingly incorporated in commercial solutions	Huge growth in demand
Substitutes (to Carrier Ethernet)	Direct, –	ATM and Frame Relay are increasingly weak options. Fear of the unknown remains but Carrier Ethernet has advantage of incumbency	Marginal negative impact on demand (depends on how fast Carrier Ethernet is embraced)
(Service Provider) Economics	Direct, +, Reinforcing	Urgent need for improvement to make services profitable	Huge potential to stimulate demand for Carrier Ethernet which in turn will improve economics (due to scope and scale)
Fiber Deployment	Direct, +, Reinforcing	Rapid deployment, offset in some areas by wireless substitutes	Fairly significant growth in demand
(Service Provider) Competition	Indirect, both – and +	Intensifying across the board in the U.S. and worldwide	Fairly significant growth in demand
Standardization	Direct, +, Reinforcing	MEF and other bodies accelerating development of standards	Significant growth in demand
Regulation	Direct, Unknown	Expected to be low	Largely unknown

Emerging Applications

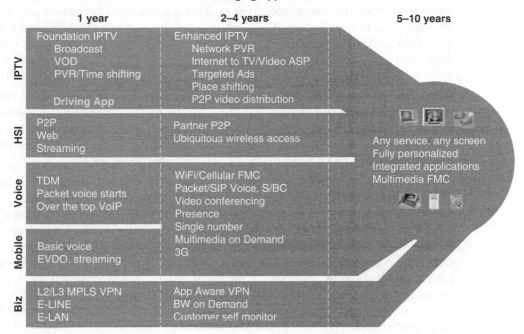

Figure 16.7   Emerging applications and their evolution (source: MEF)

for the *entire* set of wired/mobile applications; hence these applications will drive the demand for Carrier Ethernet.

- **Voice/VoIP**   Even though VoIP has been already established as a viable alternative to traditional voice delivery (over a TDM infrastructure), it is likely to make even more significant inroads into the voice services market, which still accounts for a very large portion of the telecom services market. TheInfoPro (TIP) predicts over 2/3rds of enterprises will eventually originate and terminate their voice traffic on VOIP equipment (as opposed to only 15% in 2007).

- **IPTV/Video**   Newer video-based applications will proliferate to a much larger extent over the next few years. All the traditional telephony providers in North America have announced that they already are or will shortly deliver IPTV, to counter the Cable/MSOs and make in roads in to the latter's traditional market. In addition, the phenomenal success of commercial video streaming applications like You Tube (recently purchased by Google) will invariably spur significant innovation in this specific area.

- **Business Applications/Enterprise Storage**   Given the enormous amount of mission critical and sensitive data that is being generated at enterprises, as well as concurrent developments in the area of server consolidation due to virtualization, back-up storage (to remote locations or data centers) will become much more common place than ever before. And with most of the servers in an enterprise coming with Ethernet interfaces, and Ethernet becoming a viable candidate for high-speed data transfers, Carrier Ethernet services will inevitably be used increasingly (as opposed to traditional storage specific solutions such as Fibre Channel etc.).

- **High Speed Internet (HSI)/Internet Access** The number of shared, bandwidth intensive and business enabling applications (accessible) on/through the public Internet (or the 'web') will inevitably increase; this, along with the increasing importance of the end user experience (which is becoming less tolerant to delays etc) will drive the need for higher speed Internet access.

- **Mobile/Wireless backhaul** As mobile/wireless applications will continue to explode, and new bandwidth intensive applications proliferate (increasingly personalized, streaming and web enabled), wireless Service Providers will have to focus on reducing the cost of the transport between the cellular base stations and their POPs/COs (where they aggregate traffic from base stations and transport on their backbones) since this is/will be a significant component (estimated variously at nearly 25%) of the overall cost. Whether it will employ existing T-1/Copper infrastructure to back haul this traffic from the base stations to the CO or fiber or even other wireless solutions (such as WiMAX), it is clear that Carrier Ethernet will play an important role. The newer (4G) base stations designed to support mobile broadband have Ethernet interfaces and will cost effectively transport Ethernet natively, while older base stations may still employ T-1 interfaces but will be carried using Ethernet back haul (aggregating multiple T-1s and using circuit emulation).

Ultimately, these and other new applications will increasingly have at least some or all of the following characteristics: they will consume higher (and possibly symmetrical) bandwidth to offer a tolerable end user experience, they will have (near) real-time component (i.e., they may be increasingly interactive in real time), be delivered over longer distances (i.e., widely available and to multiple sites) and will involve voice, data, video streaming (especially video, since it will be the most effective communication in widely distributed enterprise organizations).

To be able to deliver this broad range of applications optimally over a Service Provider infrastructure is what would likely make Carrier Ethernet a very appealing choice (these reasons are discussed in some detail in Chapter 1).

Technology Improvements in technology are expected across multiple dimensions and are briefly described next. These improvements are primarily driven to support the commercial applications discussed previously and, more broadly, to optimize Service Provider networks.

- **Bandwidth** The next step in Ethernet bandwidth—in line with its increments of 10x historically—is 100 Gbps. Numerous demonstrations by Bell Labs, NTT, and so on in late 2006 have already proven its feasibility. And, in November 2006, the IEEE 802.3 High Speed Study Group (HSSG) agreed to target 100G as the next version of the Ethernet standard, albeit at short distances (10 km) and employing the standard frame size and full duplex operation. It is not likely that a (full fledged) standard will emerge for the next year or so, but some high bandwidth applications in supercomputing and storage may consider using pre-standard versions to accommodate the demand.

- **Distance**   The distance of transmission over fiber will continue to increase, and there are already ultra-long WDM systems that can carry several thousand kilometers at 10G and more recently over 3000 km at 40 Gbps. It is expected that this distance will only increase over the next few years enabling delivery of Carrier Ethernet services over much longer distances.

- **Wireless developments**   Wireless transmission using technologies such as FSO and WiMax will only improve in terms of bandwidth and distance, while becoming more attractive economically. With wireless deployment poised to explode globally, 4G and newer technologies will only proliferate to meet the demand for mobile broadband applications.

- **Carrier Ethernet Feature improvements**   Competitive features for Carrier Ethernet solutions such as ubiquity, SLAs, OAM and so on are continually being incorporated in commercial solutions (as should be evident in Part II of this book) and this trend will only continue. Numerous standards will be ratified shortly or in the near term (discussed at some length in Chapter 2) and further the acceptability of—and demand for Carrier Ethernet.

As noted in Chapter 2, Security will inevitably be addressed either in commercial solutions itself or as an adjunct to the Carrier Ethernet delivery solutions. The MEF has already begun discussing this aspect.

Substitutes   While existing substitutes such as Frame Relay, Private Line, and ATM are decelerating in a growth market, hitherto unknown technologies may conceivably undermine Carrier Ethernet in the future. However, there have not been any notably visible substitutes to Carrier Ethernet emerging. And given that incumbency, familiarity and maturity are much valued factors in the Service Provider realm, Carrier Ethernet, appears to be in a fairly safe position (though one can never rule out the threats from a potent mix of some disruptive emerging technologies and a healthy dose of competition/politics!).

As long as Carrier Ethernet—like its LAN parent, continues to mature, adapt, and self-optimize, it will likely neutralize any challenges.

One other substitute to potentially watch out for is cost-optimized MPLS; it may extend from a fairly dominant position in the Service Provider Core and make in roads in to the Access networks. Again, the economics, complexity, and familiarity may dictate which way the Service Provider community may sway.

The net conclusion is that while substitutes can slow the penetration of Carrier Ethernet, it is unlikely that this will happen any time soon based on the data available thus far; and with time, unless new requirements make Carrier Ethernet unadaptable, it will in fact become more difficult to dislodge in any significant manner.

(Service Provider) Economics   The economics of Service Providers with respect to offering new/emerging applications (discussed above) will be a key driver or impediment to the demand for Carrier Ethernet services. Service Providers, in order to be competitive, will invariably have to optimize their delivery (i.e., network) infrastructures especially given the intense competition (discussed below) and the inherently lower revenue/bit to be expected in future applications (at least as compared to traditional telephony applications). To remain profitable (their primary reason to exist), they must reduce their fundamental cost structure to deliver these applications. Carrier Ethernet for reasons discussed in Chapter 1, provides a very compelling solution, and thus will likely be the candidate of choice. While the exact specifics of a Service Provider's underlying delivery infrastructure depends on a complex set of variables (discussed later in this chapter), the Service Providers will nonetheless likely introduce an independent Carrier Ethernet layer that can support a broad range of applications delivery in a cost efficient manner.

Thus, Service Providers' economic models, over the next few years, will gravitate toward aggressively reducing their cost structures, while being able to deliver the next generation of packet-based applications. Competition and strategic positioning will likely make Carrier Ethernet the most attractive choice, especially as the latter matures, and incorporates and standardizes new features commercially.

As the quest for improved economics will drive Service Providers towards Carrier Ethernet, this resulting demand will further improve the economics (of Carrier Ethernet, due to both the scope and scale of increased deployment). Service Provider economics and demand for Carrier Ethernet services therefore form a powerful, reinforcing loop.

Fiber Deployment   According to a recent study by AMI partners, Small and Medium Businesses despite moving relatively slow, will spend over $30 Billion in 2007 in the U.S. alone for (converged and unified) IP communications and other managed services, and this is expected to grow at a CAGR of over 15% until 2010. Given this substantial opportunity, Service Providers, especially the Cable MSOs (for whom this is a relatively new market opportunity while for traditional Service Providers this remains a profitable segment) are sure to pursue this vigorously.

This will inevitably translate in to accelerated fiber deployment since Service Providers will have to offer a host of new value-added services (and consequently, new streams of revenues) while optimizing their delivery costs. Carrier Ethernet delivered natively over fiber provides for an optimal converged solution which can also scale (and hence ensure that the Service Provider is well positioned to retain the customers).

Fiber deployment, at least in the U.S., though reasonably widespread, still has a long way to go. Only about 11 percent or so of the buildings in the U.S. are connected via fiber, but there is a considerable effort underway to extend this coverage quite rapidly. Verizon's FIOS (albeit mostly focused on residential communities) and almost all cable companies in the U.S. are aggressively deploying fiber in all metropolitan areas. This situation is also consistent with other countries, although wireless options such as FSO and WiMax are being considered actively especially in developing countries.

Competition   There is widespread competition amongst Service Providers to deliver a new generation of packet applications (discussed above); with blurring of the boundaries between the traditional Telephony providers, Cable providers and the type of services they deliver, competition will especially intensify to capture the customers. Of course, profitability (economics, see above) is another factor. Thus, to deliver the new set of packet optimized applications profitably will force the Service Providers to embrace a platform that will do both; hence Carrier Ethernet demand will increase.

In the U.S. alone over 200 or so Service Providers are offering applications over Ethernet services currently. With Carrier Ethernet demand growth exceeding even optimistic projections, and the addressable market growing substantially (estimated to be well over $20B by 2009), these and new Service Providers will invariably pursue such services even more aggressively, leading to intense competition. Furthermore, the retarding market for substitutes such as ATM and Frame Relay, even though relatively huge compared to Carrier Ethernet, will make them a less compelling part of a Service Provider's portfolio.

Standardization   Several standardization activities are underway that will further solidify the standing of Carrier Ethernet. They are briefly noted here and are designed to enable Carrier Ethernet to make further inroads in to the Service Provider network—especially deeper in the MAN/WAN.

- **Ethernet OAM**   Technically, the Ethernet OAM (notably IEEE 802.1ag) is not yet ratified; once this is finalized, OAM functionality will be more widely incorporated in products.

- **Ethernet in WAN**   The MEF has begun work on ensuring Ethernet is viable "deeper in the Service Provider" networks. This will greatly guide the deployment of Ethernet beyond the MAN/access where it is largely concentrated.

- **Provider Backbone Bridge (PBB)**   This is the IEEE 802.1ah standard (currently underway) that enables a MAC-in-MAC encapsulation. Basically, this creates separate customer and Service Provider domains by encapsulating customer/ end user MAC addresses with Service Provider—based MAC addresses. This approach will remove the scaling limitations traditionally posed by Ethernet, and extend the number of service instances from over 4K to several million.

- **Provider Backbone Bridging—Transport Engineering (PBB-TE)**   The IEEE 802.1Qay standard is addressing PBB-TE, which is focused on providing Point-to-Point Ethernet tunnels across a metro and beyond. These connections will ensure a solid QoS and effectively simulate a circuit switched path, and are targeted to support mission-critical and latency sensitive applications. It must be noted, however, that they will invariably face opposition from the more established MPLS, at least deeper in the Service Provider networks.

Regulation Regulation is limited and expected to remain as such as long as there is competition in the (Carrier Ethernet) market, which appears to be the case, at least in the U.S. However, this variable is difficult—and vastly outside the scope and capability of this book, to assess in the context of various countries. As Carrier Ethernet begins to reach a critical mass in its march to supplant traditional TDM access technologies (T-1/E-1), however, the regulatory agencies may review it carefully given that it would increasingly become a choke point for broadband access (akin to a telephone line a few decades ago), and may introduce measures to regulate it.

Conclusions on Carrier Ethernet Demand

The overall conclusions that can be drawn from reviewing the key developments expected in each of the areas are

- Basically, there are promising developments in the areas of Applications, Technology, Fiber Deployment, and Standards. Given that most of these are also mutually reinforcing, they will cause aggressive growth in demand for Carrier Ethernet services.

- Existing Substitutes do not appear to pose a major threat; the bigger fear is that of hitherto unknown solutions emerging to address an ostensibly very attractive market in the longer term. Regulation, while unknown in its impact (hence, the question mark in Figure 16.6 and in Table 16.9), is not likely to be a significant influencer especially when competition is expected to be fierce (benefiting the end user and hence precluding the need for regulatory oversight).

- Given the intense competition amongst Service Providers, it will likely make the (Service Provider) economics less attractive (since more competition usually means a reduction in end-user pricing, which in turn reduces the profitability for Service Providers). Because profitability is a key performance criterion for Service Providers, it is to be expected that Service Providers will try and *reduce the cost structure associated with delivering Carrier Ethernet, while incorporating as many of the underlying feature attributes of Carrier Ethernet* as possible. This will certainly lead to a corresponding evolution in the existing solutions delivering Carrier Ethernet.

Evolution of Solutions Delivering Carrier Ethernet

Over the longer run, especially as the market matures, it is reasonable to assume that the solutions will evolve in the manner illustrated in Figure 16.8. The key points of this evolution are

- Multiple solutions for Carrier Ethernet will continue to be actively deployed over the next several years, but it is likely that the number of such solutions will be reduced.

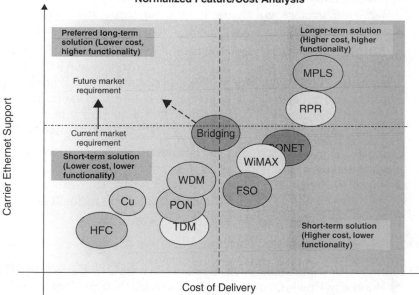

Figure 16.8 Possible evolution of Carrier Ethernet Delivery Solutions

- As the overall trend to packet-based applications continues to accelerate and voice applications (the mainstay of the many legacy solutions) are also migrating to packet infrastructure, Service Providers will increasingly find the prospect of maintaining legacy networks less attractive.

- As competition intensifies and price pressure correspondingly increases, Service Providers will have to move to more economically efficient infrastructures to protect profitability.

- The solutions that will coexist will do so for a variety of reasons, most notably because there is no silver bullet, i.e., no single solution that addresses the multitude of real-life deployment scenarios economically.

- Carrier Ethernet solutions, however, will converge toward a Bridging/Switching solution especially in the Access/MANs. This class of solutions will likely also integrate other technologies such as WDM, FSO, and so on. The situation in the WAN is less clear.

  - Bridging/Switching Layer 2 solutions form the most efficient approach to deploying Carrier Ethernet, as noted earlier. Specifically, they are perhaps the most optimized, native Carrier Ethernet solutions that will support the host of E-Line and E-LAN services.

  - With fiber deployment accelerating rapidly in the U.S. and elsewhere, such solutions will become the natural choice for broadband applications.

- The intensity of competition in delivering Carrier Ethernet will also mean that Service Providers will choose the most optimal solution for delivery and hence will invariably move toward a native Ethernet solution with minimal overhead.

- With MPLS already fairly well established in Service Provider networks (in the Metro core), there is not a significant incentive to move to a Bridging solution in their core/WAN. However, where it is not present, a Bridging solution will be a viable and an economically attractive candidate, especially as new standards such as PBT and PBB are ratified. It is also very much a likely scenario that Bridging and MPLS will co-exist in Service Provider networks.

- The path from the status quo to an optimal Bridging solution will likely take several years, perhaps over a decade, and will traverse through numerous intermediate steps, as shown in Figure 16.8. It must be noted again, that this solution will likely also incorporate scalable (in both distance and capacity) technologies such as WDM.

References

1. Managerial Applications of System Dynamics, Edited by Edward Roberts, Productivity Press, Cambridge, MA, 1978 ISBN 0-915299-59-3.

Final Thoughts

by Abdul Kasim

Carrier Ethernet Is Here to Stay...

Carrier Ethernet is here to stay. It has long reached an inflection point and demonstrates continued—and exponential—growth fueled by a widespread acceptance both by the Service Provider and the enterprise community. Equipment manufacturers have, of course, also recognized this opportunity and, in fact, are providing numerous carrier-class solutions to deliver Carrier Ethernet. (Chapters 1 and 2 provide some insight into the evolution of Carrier Ethernet from its LAN origins to a formidable Service Provider solution while Chapter 3 presents its market proliferation). Carrier Ethernet services are incorporating new feature capabilities required to support the next-generation of applications and are quickly being standardized (also noted in Chapter 2).

...But It's a Long Way to Domination

Notwithstanding Carrier Ethernet's very impressive growth, it is still, in relative terms, addressing only a minor portion of the total addressable opportunity. At the current time, it is largely supplanting existing substitutes such as ATM but still has a long way to go to overtake solutions such as Frame Relay and Private Line. And while it is capable of enabling sophisticated, real-time multimedia applications on a large scale, it is currently being used to mostly offer simple applications (such as Internet access, LAN interconnection, Ethernet Private Line, and to a much lesser extent Layer 2 VPNs).

However, it is increasingly becoming the de facto solution when higher bandwidth is required (even on legacy solutions) and for all new service offerings; this, along with the development of a highly competitive landscape, continual technical improvements and standardization, make the prospect of Carrier Ethernet dominating the future of carrier services, a very distinct possibility—it appears to be more a question of *when* this will likely happen and not if it will happen. Market trends confirm this conclusion as well. Chapter 3 and this chapter (16) highlight Carrier Ethernet's growth prospects while Chapters 2 and 16 identify the challenges that it would face in this quest.

Multiple Delivery Solutions Exist Today...

There is no one commercial solution that provides the entire gamut of Carrier Ethernet capabilities today, at least economically; realistically though, there is still not an immediate need for all these features in any substantial measure, and consequently, the numerous (partial) solutions for Carrier Ethernet that have emerged are perfectly acceptable. In fact, multiple commercial solutions exist because the different legacy (pre-Carrier Ethernet) solutions, be it SONET or TDM or Copper, have also been augmented with features to address the customer requirements for Carrier Ethernet (although perhaps not optimally), and are eminently viable from an economic standpoint. (Part II, Chapters 5 through 15, describe most of the solutions in use today.)

...But Will Slowly Converge to Fewer, Optimized Solutions

The demand for Carrier Ethernet, which is projected to grow exponentially, will intensify the competition amongst Service Providers, who in turn will have to invariably respond with differentiation and/or lowering prices. They, in turn, will have to seek out ways to lower their Total Cost of Ownership (TCO) and optimize the delivery of Carrier Ethernet services and raise profitability. As a result, they will seek out solutions that will offer both a higher probability of differentiation, and aligned with new revenue generating opportunities (supporting new applications), as well as the lowering of their cost structure. This will mean that it will no longer be possible to employ legacy delivery solutions that entail more overhead, limited in terms of new Carrier Ethernet capabilities and not positioned to scale. With time, and additional fiber deployment, the preferred solutions will minimize overhead (i.e., transport natively) and provide a higher level of functionality (switching, etc.). These solutions will necessary represent a subset of the current (category of) solutions in the market. (This chapter has provided a plausible evolution of the solution landscape)

It is difficult to gauge the time it will take to evolve toward fewer, more optimized Carrier Ethernet solutions. The existing solutions, largely depreciated, imposing a low operational overhead, and offering sufficient carrier-class features (as well as developing new ones), will continue to provide a compelling rationale for quite some time. And so it would be very useful to understand these solutions in some depth —*which is what this book strives to provide.*

Index

3m